M000168935

Honda CRF1000L Africa Twin
Service and Repair Manual

by Matthew Coombs

(6434-368)

Models covered
CRF1000A. 998cc. 2016 to 2019
CRF1000D (DCT). 998cc. 2016 to 2019
CRF1000A2 Adventure Sport. 998cc. 2018 to 2019
CRF1000D2 (DCT) Adventure Sport. 998cc. 2018 to 2019

© Haynes Publishing 2019

A book in the Haynes Service and Repair Manual Series

ABCDE
FGHIJ
KLMNO
PQRST

ISBN: **978 1 78521 434 9**

British Library Cataloguing in Publication Data
A catalogue record for this book is available from the British Library

Library of Congress Control Number 2018954565

Printed in Malaysia

Haynes Publishing
Sparkford, Yeovil, Somerset BA22 7JJ, England

Haynes North America, Inc
859 Lawrence Drive, Newbury Park, California 91320, USA

Printed using NORBRITE BOOK 48.8gsm (CODE: 40N6533) from NORPAC; procurement system certified under Sustainable Forestry Initiative standard. Paper produced is certified to the SFI Certified Fiber Sourcing Standard (CERT - 0094271)

Contents

LIVING WITH YOUR HONDA CRF1000L AFRICA TWIN

Introduction

The Birth of a Dream	Page	0•4
Acknowledgements	Page	0•8
About this manual	Page	0•8
Safety first!	Page	0•9
Model development	Page	0•10
Bike spec	Page	0•11
Identification numbers	Page	0•12
Buying spare parts	Page	0•12

Pre-ride checks

Engine oil level	Page	0•13
Suspension, steering and drive chain	Page	0•13
Coolant level	Page	0•14
Brake fluid levels	Page	0•14
Legal and safety checks	Page	0•15
Tyres	Page	0•16

MAINTENANCE

Routine maintenance and servicing

Maintenance schedule	Page	1•2
Component locations	Page	1•4
Specifications	Page	1•8
Lubricants and fluids	Page	1•8
Maintenance procedures	Page	1•9

Contents

REPAIRS AND OVERHAUL

Engine, transmission and associated systems

Engine, clutch and transmission — Page 2•1

Cooling system — Page 3•1

Engine management system — Page 4•1

Chassis components

Frame and suspension — Page 5•1

Brakes, wheels and final drive — Page 6•1

Bodywork — Page 7•1

Electrical system

Page 8•1

Wiring diagrams

Page 8•30

REFERENCE

Tools and Workshop Tips — Page REF•2

Security — Page REF•20

Lubricants and fluids — Page REF•23

MOT Test Checks — Page REF•26

Storage — Page REF•31

Conversion factors — Page REF•34

Fault Finding — Page REF•35

Index

Page REF•46

The Birth of a Dream

by Julian Ryder

There is no better example of the Japanese post-War industrial miracle than Honda. Like other companies which have become household names, it started with one man's vision. In this case the man was the 40-year old Soichiro Honda who had sold his piston-ring manufacturing business to Toyota in 1945 and was happily spending the proceeds on prolonged parties for his friends. However, the difficulties of getting around in the chaos of post-War Japan irked Honda, so when he came across a job lot of generator engines he realised that here was a way of getting people mobile again at low cost.

A 12 by 18-foot shack in Hamamatsu became his first bike factory, fitting the generator motors into pushbikes. Before long he'd used up all 500 generator motors and started manufacturing his own engine, known as the 'chimney', either because of the elongated cylinder head or the smoky exhaust or perhaps both. The chimney made all of half a horsepower from its 50 cc engine but it was a major success and became the Honda A-type.

Less than two years after he'd set up in Hamamatsu, Soichiro Honda founded the Honda Motor Company in September 1948. By then, the A-type had been developed into the 90 cc B-type engine, which Mr Honda decided deserved its own chassis not a bicycle frame. Honda was about to become Japan's first post-War manufacturer of complete motorcycles. In August 1949 the first prototype was ready. With an output of three horsepower, the 98 cc D-type was still a simple two-stroke but it had a two-speed transmission and most importantly a pressed steel frame with telescopic forks and hard tail rear end. The frame was almost triangular in profile with the top rail going in a straight line from the massively braced steering head to the rear axle. Legend has it that after the D-type's first tests the entire workforce went for a drink to celebrate and try and think of a name for the bike. One man broke one of those silences you get when people are thinking, exclaiming 'This is like a dream!' 'That's it!' shouted Honda, and so the Honda Dream was christened.

Mr Honda was a brilliant, intuitive engineer and designer but he did not bother himself with the marketing side of his business. With hindsight, it is possible to see that employing Takeo Fujisawa who would both sort out the home market and plan the eventual expansion into overseas markets was a masterstroke. He arrived in October 1949 and in 1950 was made Sales Director. Another vital new name was Kiyoshi Kawashima, who along with Honda himself, designed the company's first four-stroke after Kawashima had told them that the four-stroke opposition to Honda's two-strokes sounded

> ## 'This is like a dream!' 'That's it' shouted Honda

nicer and therefore sold better. The result of that statement was the overhead-valve 148 cc E-type which first ran in July 1951 just two months after the first drawings were made. Kawashima was made a director of the Honda Company at 34 years old.

The E-type was a massive success, over 32,000 were made in 1953 alone, a feat of mass-production that was astounding by the standards of the day given the relative complexity of the machine. But Honda's lifelong pursuit of technical innovation sometimes distracted him from commercial reality. Fujisawa pointed out that they were in danger of ignoring their core business, the motorised bicycles that still formed Japan's main means of transport. In May 1952 the F-type Cub appeared, another two-stroke despite the top men's reservations. You could buy a complete machine or just the motor to attach to your own bicycle. The result was certainly distinctive, a white fuel tank with a circular profile went just below and behind the

Honda C70 and C90 OHV-engined models

The CB250N Super Dream became a favorite with UK learner riders of the late seventies and early eighties

saddle on the left of the bike, and the motor with its horizontal cylinder and bright red cover just below the rear axle on the same side of the bike. This was the machine that turned Honda into the biggest bike maker in Japan with 70% of the market for bolt-on bicycle motors, the F-type was also the first Honda to be exported. Next came the machine that would turn Honda into the biggest motorcycle manufacturer in the world.

The C100 Super Cub was a typically audacious piece of Honda engineering and marketing. For the first time, but not the last, Honda invented a completely new type of motorcycle, although the term 'scooterette' was coined to describe the new bike which had many of the characteristics of a scooter but the large wheels, and therefore stability, of a motorcycle. The first one was sold in August 1958, fifteen years later over nine-million of them were on the roads of the world. If ever a machine can be said to have brought mobility to the masses it is the Super Cub. If you add in the electric starter that was added for the C102 model of 1961, the design of the Super Cub has remained substantially unchanged ever since, testament to how right Honda got it first time. The Super Cub made Honda the world's biggest manufacturer after just two years of production.

Honda's export drive started in earnest in 1957 when Britain and Holland got their first bikes, America got just two bikes the next year. By 1962 Honda had half the American market with 65,000 sales. But Soichiro Honda had already travelled abroad to Europe and the USA, making a special point of going to the Isle of Man TT, then the most important race in the GP calendar. He realised that no matter how advanced his products were, only racing success would convince overseas markets for whom 'Made in Japan' still meant cheap and nasty. It took five years from Soichiro Honda's first visit to the Island before his bikes were ready for the TT. In 1959 the factory entered five riders in

The GL1000 introduced in 1975, was the first in Honda's line of Goldwings

Carl Fogarty in action at the Suzuka 8 hour on the RC45

the 125. They did not have a massive impact on the event being benevolently regarded as a curiosity, but sixth, seventh and eighth were good enough for the team prize. The bikes were off the pace but they were well engineered and very reliable.

The TT was the only time the West saw the Hondas in '59, but they came back for more the following year with the first of a generation of bikes which shaped the future of

motorcycling - the double-overhead-cam four-cylinder 250. It was fast and reliable - it revved to 14,000 rpm - but didn't handle anywhere near as well as the opposition. However, Honda had now signed up non-Japanese riders to lead their challenge. The first win didn't come until 1962 (Aussie Tom Phillis in the Spanish 125 GP) and was followed up with a world-shaking performance at the TT. Twenty-one year old Mike

Hailwood won both 125 and 250 cc TTs and Hondas filled the top five positions in both races. Soichiro Honda's master plan was starting to come to fruition, Hailwood and Honda won the 1961 250 cc World Championship. Next year Honda won three titles. The other Japanese factories fought back and inspired Honda to produce some of the most fascinating racers ever seen: the awesome six-cylinder 250, the five-cylinder 125, and the 500 four with which the immortal Hailwood battled Agostini and the MV Agusta.

When Honda pulled out of racing in '67 they had won sixteen rider's titles, eighteen manufacturer's titles, and 137 GPs, including 18 TTs, and introduced the concept of the modern works team to motorcycle racing. Sales success followed racing victory as Soichiro Honda had predicted, but only because the products advanced as rapidly as the racing machinery. The Hondas that came to Britain in the early '60s were incredibly sophisticated. They had overhead cams where the British bikes had pushrods, they had electric starters when the Brits relied on the kickstart, they had 12V electrics when even the biggest British bike used a 6V system. There seemed no end to the technical wizardry. It wasn't that the technology itself was so amazing but just like that first E-Type, it was the fact that Honda could mass-produce it more reliably than the lower-tech competition that was so astonishing.

When in 1968 the first four-cylinder CB750 road bike arrived the world of motorcycling changed for ever, they even had to invent a new word for it, 'Superbike'. Honda raced again with the CB750 at Daytona and won the World Endurance title with a prototype DOHC version that became the CB900 roadster. There was the six-cylinder CBX, the CX500T – the world's first turbocharged production bike, they invented the full-dress tourer with the GoldWing, and came back to GPs with the revolutionary oval-pistoned NR500 four-stroke, a much-misunderstood bike that was more a rolling experimental laboratory than a racer. Just to show their versatility Honda also came up with the weird CX500 shaft-drive V-twin, a rugged workhorse that powered a new industry, the courier companies that oiled the wheels of commerce in London and other big cities.

It was true, though, that Mr Honda was not keen on two-strokes – early motocross engines had to be explained away to him as lawnmower motors! However, in 1982 Honda raced the NS500, an agile three-cylinder lightweight against the big four-cylinder opposition in 500 GPs. The bike won in its first year and in '83 took the world title for Freddie Spencer. In four-stroke racing the V4 layout took over from the straight four, dominating TT, F1 and Endurance championships with the RVF750, the nearest thing ever built to a Formula 1 car on wheels. And when Superbike arrived Honda were ready with the

An early CB750 Four

RC30. On the roads the VFR V4 became an instant classic while the CBR600 invented another new class of bike on its way to becoming a best-seller. The V4 road bikes had problems to start with but the VFR750 sold world-wide over its lifetime while the VFR400 became a massive commercial success and cult bike in Japan. The original RC30 won the first two World Superbike Championships is 1988 and '89, but Honda had to wait until 1997 to win it again with the RC45, the last of the V4 roadsters. In Grands Prix, the NSR500 V4 two-stroke superseded the NS triple and became the benchmark racing machine of the '90s. Mick Doohan secured his place in history by winning five World Championships in consecutive years on it.

In yet another example of Honda inventing a new class of motorcycle, they came up with the astounding CBR900RR FireBlade, a bike with the punch of a 1000 cc motor in a package the size and weight of a 750. It became a cult bike as well as a best seller, and with judicious redesigns continues to give much more recent designs a run for their money.

When it became apparent that the high-tech V4 motor of the RC45 was too expensive to produce, Honda looked to a V-twin engine to power its flagship for the first time. Typically, the VTR1000 FireStorm was a much more rideable machine than its opposition and once accepted by the market formed the basis of the next generation of Superbike racer, the VTR-SP-1.

One of Mr Honda's mottos was that technology would solve the customers' problems, and no company has embraced cutting-edge technology more firmly than Honda. In fact Honda often developed new technology, especially in the fields of materials science and metallurgy. The embodiment of that was the NR750, a bike that was misunderstood nearly as much as the original NR500 racer. This limited-edition technological tour-de-force embodied many

The CX500 – Honda's first V-Twin and a favorite choice of dispatch riders

of Soichiro Honda's ideals. It used the latest techniques and materials in every component, from the oval piston, 32-valve V4 motor to the titanium coating on the windscreen, it was – as Mr Honda would have wanted – the best it could possibly be. A fitting memorial to the man who has shaped the motorcycle industry and motorcyles as we know them today.

Desert song

To understand the Africa Twin, and indeed the whole adventure bike market, you need to go back to 1979 and the first Paris-Dakar Rally. The first two events were won by modified Yamaha XT500s, entered by the French importer, Sonauto. The event, a stupendously difficult traversing of a large chunk of the Sahara desert, ending in the capital of Senegal on the coast of West Africa,

immediately captured the public imagination. In an incredibly short time the Rally was as important in France as the le Mans 24 Hours, F1 or MotoGP. BMW, who'd launched the first GS in 1980, entered a factory team with cigarette company sponsorship in 1981 and won. Honda entered their first factory bike the same year, a modified 500cc motocrosser. The same bike won the following year, when the BMWs hit problems. From then on the Paris-Dakar became a battleground for factory teams from Yamaha, BMW, Honda and Ducati (using the Cagiva brand). The Japanese teams even carried the same big-budget tobacco sponsors as their road-race GP teams.

In 1984 Honda decided they had to attack the event properly, with the objective of winning in '86. As is Honda's way, the objective was achieved. HRC, Honda's

The 2016 CRF1000L

The 2018 CRF1000D

The 2018 CRF1000D2 Adventure Sport

Tank emblem marks the 30th anniversary of the Africa Twin

racing arm, realized a single-cylinder motor was no longer up to the job and produced the NXR750V, which promptly won four Dakars in a row. It is important to realize the background to this achievement. European bike buyers, and the TV-viewing public, had gone Paris-Dakar mad. Yamaha sold over 60,000 XT600s between 1975 and '85. You saw more XT600Z Teneres in the bike park at the Bol d'Or than sports bikes. All the other manufacturers tried to emulate Yamaha's sales, without success. Honda's first go was the 1983 XLV750R, which was horrible in just about every respect. The TransAlp, launched in 1987, was much more successful and, if I recall correctly, was the first bike to which the Adventure Sports label was affixed. It was, however, an understated roadster built around an engine from a factory custom. It didn't have the desert racer DNA in any shape or form.

The first bike to bear the name Africa Twin appeared in 1988 as a limited-edition machine for privateers to race in the Marathon class

of the Paris-Dakar. Bikes had to be standard and not have any of the massive support organization that the factory teams enjoyed. Produced by HRC, the new bike was based around an overbored Transalp motor and was a knobbly-tyred equivalent of the RC30 known as the RD03, it was a proper NXR replica, a homologation special built to race and not down to a price. These original Africa Twins are now seriously rare and collectable.

The true production Africa Twin, with 750cc motor, appeared in 1990. This bike was produced by Honda Motor Co on the usual production line, not hand-built by HRC, and therefore lacked the pure racing edge of the RD03. It was a true production machine and had to compete on the market, so no trick quick-release fairing fasteners, no stone guard for the lights, no suede seat, and obviously lower-spec suspension etc. None of which means it was anything other than a great motorcycle. It was superb roadster and as competent off-road as any bike that size

has a right to be. It stayed in the Honda range until 2003.

The new-generation Africa Twin, the CRF1000L, is very much a descendant of the original bike, despite being a totally new design around a parallel-twin motor. Indeed, the design team used an original 750 as their reference and achieved the very clever trick of imbuing the new bike with the same character. Both are superb on the highway and, with unashamedly high seat, more than competent off road. This is exactly what Honda wanted, a true go-anywhere bike. The only major difference between then and now, apart from the level of technology in things like the dual-clutch option, which is effectively an automatic gearbox, and associated electronics, is the level of competition. The CRF has to deal not just with BMW's GS but serious opposition from KTM, Yamaha and Triumph plus slightly less obvious competition from Ducati's Multistrada. It's really is difficult to think of a market sector as crowded with truly excellent motorcycles as adventure sport.

Acknowledgements

Our thanks are due to Bransons Motorcycles of Yeovil who supplied the machines featured in the illustrations throughout this manual. We would also like to thank NGK Spark Plugs (UK) Ltd for supplying the colour spark plug condition photographs, the Avon Rubber Company for supplying information on tyre fitting and Draper Tools Ltd for some of the workshop tools shown.

Thanks are also due to Julian Ryder who wrote the introduction 'The Birth of a Dream' and to Honda (UK) Ltd. who supplied model photographs.

About this Manual

The aim of this manual is to help you get the best value from your motorcycle. It can do so in several ways. It can help you decide what work must be done, even if you choose to have

it done by a dealer; it provides information and procedures for routine maintenance and servicing; and it offers diagnostic and repair procedures to follow when trouble occurs.

We hope you use the manual to tackle the work yourself. For many simpler jobs, doing it yourself may be quicker than arranging an appointment to get the motorcycle into a dealer and making the trips to leave it and pick it up. More importantly, a lot of money can be saved by avoiding the expense the shop must pass on to you to cover its labour and overhead costs. An added benefit is the sense of satisfaction and accomplishment that you feel after doing the job yourself.

References to the left or right side of the motorcycle assume you are sitting on the seat, facing forward.

We take great pride in the accuracy of information given in this manual, but motorcycle manufacturers make alterations

and design changes during the production run of a particular motorcycle of which they do not inform us. No liability can be accepted by the authors or publishers for loss, damage or injury caused by any errors in, or omissions from, the information given.

Professional mechanics are trained in safe working procedures. However enthusiastic you may be about getting on with the job at hand, take the time to ensure that your safety is not put at risk. A moment's lack of attention can result in an accident, as can failure to observe simple precautions.

There will always be new ways of having accidents, and the following is not a comprehensive list of all dangers; it is intended rather to make you aware of the risks and to encourage a safe approach to all work you carry out on your bike.

Asbestos

● Certain friction, insulating, sealing and other products - such as brake pads, clutch linings, gaskets, etc. - contain asbestos. Extreme care must be taken to avoid inhalation of dust from such products since it is hazardous to health. If in doubt, assume that they do contain asbestos.

Fire

● Remember at all times that petrol is highly flammable. Never smoke or have any kind of naked flame around, when working on the vehicle. But the risk does not end there - a spark caused by an electrical short-circuit, by two metal surfaces contacting each other, by careless use of tools, or even by static electricity built up in your body under certain conditions, can ignite petrol vapour, which in a confined space is highly explosive. Never use petrol as a cleaning solvent. Use an approved safety solvent.

● Always disconnect the battery earth terminal before working on any part of the fuel or electrical system, and never risk spilling fuel on to a hot engine or exhaust.

● It is recommended that a fire extinguisher of a type suitable for fuel and electrical fires is kept handy in the garage or workplace at all times. Never try to extinguish a fuel or electrical fire with water.

Fumes

● Certain fumes are highly toxic and can quickly cause unconsciousness and even death if inhaled to any extent. Petrol vapour comes into this category, as do the vapours from certain solvents such as trichloroethylene. Any draining or pouring of such volatile fluids should be done in a well ventilated area.

● When using cleaning fluids and solvents, read the instructions carefully. Never use materials from unmarked containers - they may give off poisonous vapours.

● Never run the engine of a motor vehicle in an enclosed space such as a garage. Exhaust fumes contain carbon monoxide which is extremely poisonous; if you need to run the engine, always do so in the open air or at least have the rear of the vehicle outside the workplace.

The battery

● Never cause a spark, or allow a naked light near the vehicle's battery. It will normally be giving off a certain amount of hydrogen gas, which is highly explosive.

● Always disconnect the battery ground (earth) terminal before working on the fuel or electrical systems (except where noted).

● If possible, loosen the filler plugs or cover when charging the battery from an external source. Do not charge at an excessive rate or the battery may burst.

● Take care when topping up, cleaning or carrying the battery. The acid electrolyte, evenwhen diluted, is very corrosive and should not be allowed to contact the eyes or skin. Always wear rubber gloves and goggles or a face shield. If you ever need to prepare electrolyte yourself, always add the acid slowly to the water; never add the water to the acid.

Electricity

● When using an electric power tool, inspection light etc., always ensure that the appliance is correctly connected to its plug and that, where necessary, it is properly grounded (earthed). Do not use such appliances in damp conditions and, again, beware of creating a spark or applying excessive heat in the vicinity of fuel or fuel vapour. Also ensure that the appliances meet national safety standards.

● A severe electric shock can result from touching certain parts of the electrical system, such as the spark plug wires (HT leads), when the engine is running or being cranked, particularly if components are damp or the insulation is defective. Where an electronic ignition system is used, the secondary (HT) voltage is much higher and could prove fatal.

Remember...

✗ **Don't** start the engine without first ascertaining that the transmission is in neutral.

✗ **Don't** suddenly remove the pressure cap from a hot cooling system - cover it with a cloth and release the pressure gradually first, or you may get scalded by escaping coolant.

✗ **Don't** attempt to drain oil until you are sure it has cooled sufficiently to avoid scalding you.

✗ **Don't** grasp any part of the engine or exhaust system without first ascertaining that it is cool enough not to burn you.

✗ **Don't** allow brake fluid or antifreeze to contact the machine's paintwork or plastic components.

✗ **Don't** siphon toxic liquids such as fuel, hydraulic fluid or antifreeze by mouth, or allow them to remain on your skin.

✗ **Don't** inhale dust - it may be injurious to health (see Asbestos heading).

✗ **Don't** allow any spilled oil or grease to remain on the floor - wipe it up right away, before someone slips on it.

✗ **Don't** use ill-fitting spanners or other tools which may slip and cause injury.

✗ **Don't** lift a heavy component which may be beyond your capability - get assistance.

✗ **Don't** rush to finish a job or take unverified short cuts.

✗ **Don't** allow children or animals in or around an unattended vehicle.

✗ **Don't** inflate a tyre above the recommended pressure. Apart from overstressing the carcass, in extreme cases the tyre may blow off forcibly.

✔ **Do** ensure that the machine is supported securely at all times. This is especially important when the machine is blocked up to aid wheel or fork removal.

✔ **Do** take care when attempting to loosen a stubborn nut or bolt. It is generally better to pull on a spanner, rather than push, so that if you slip, you fall away from the machine rather than onto it.

✔ **Do** wear eye protection when using power tools such as drill, sander, bench grinder etc.

✔ **Do** use a barrier cream on your hands prior to undertaking dirty jobs - it will protect your skin from infection as well as making the dirt easier to remove afterwards; but make sure your hands aren't left slippery. Note that long-term contact with used engine oil can be a health hazard.

✔ **Do** keep loose clothing (cuffs, ties etc. and long hair) well out of the way of moving mechanical parts.

✔ **Do** remove rings, wristwatch etc., before working on the vehicle - especially the electrical system.

✔ **Do** keep your work area tidy - it is only too easy to fall over articles left lying around.

✔ **Do** exercise caution when compressing springs for removal or installation. Ensure that the tension is applied and released in a controlled manner, using suitable tools which preclude the possibility of the spring escaping violently.

✔ **Do** ensure that any lifting tackle used has a safe working load rating adequate for the job.

✔ **Do** get someone to check periodically that all is well, when working alone on the vehicle.

✔ **Do** carry out work in a logical sequence and check that everything is correctly assembled and tightened afterwards.

✔ **Do** remember that your vehicle's safety affects that of yourself and others. If in doubt on any point, get professional advice.

● If in spite of following these precautions, you are unfortunate enough to injure yourself, seek medical attention as soon as possible.

Model development

The CRF1000L Africa Twin was launched in 2016.

The engine is an all-new 998cc parallel twin with a 270° crank. The single overhead camshaft is chain driven off the right-hand end of the crankshaft. The camshaft opens the two intake valves per cylinder, and actuates rocker arms that open the two exhaust valves per cylinder.

On models with the standard transmission the clutch is a conventional wet multi-plate unit actuated by cable, and the gearbox is 6-speed. Drive to the rear wheel is by chain and sprockets.

On models with dual clutch transmission (DCT) there are two clutches that are electro-hydraulically actuated, with the options of either manually controlling gear selection via buttons on the left handlebar switch, or by allowing fully automatic control using the systems electronics. One clutch is used for 1st, 3rd and 5th gears and the other for 2nd, 4th and 6th.

Honda's PGM-FI fuel injection system supplies fuel and air to the engine via 44 mm throttle bodies and two intake valves per cylinder, with exhaust gases exiting via another two valves per cylinder into a two-into-one under-slung exhaust system with closed-loop catalytic converter. An electronic engine management system controls both the injection system and the ignition system. All Europe models feature Honda's immobiliser system (HISS).

The engine sits in a steel semi-double cradle frame.

Front suspension is by Showa upside-down oil-damped 45 mm forks with adjustable damping and spring pre-load. Rear suspension is by a monoblock cast aluminium swingarm and a single shock absorber via a rising rate linkage, with adjustable damping and spring pre-load.

The hydraulic braking system on all models has two four-piston calipers acting on 310 mm discs at the front, and a single piston

sliding caliper acting on a 256 mm disc at the rear. For the Europe market ABS was available as an option on 2016 models with standard transmission, and is fitted as standard on all 2017 and 2018 models. For the US market ABS is fitted as standard on all models.

All models have LED headlights and tail light, and many models have LED turn signals.

A number of updates were introduced in 2018, the most significant of which was new throttle bodies with full fly-by-wire operation. Other updates include the use of a lithium-ion battery, new instruments, stainless steel spokes, and twin catalytic converters in the exhaust system.

2018 also saw the launch of the Adventure Sports version, with a higher seat, raised suspension with longer travel, a larger fuel tank for greater range, a larger fairing and screen, crashbars and a larger sump guard, heated grips and accessory socket as standard, and different rear bodywork.

There were no changes to 2019 models.

Dimensions and weights

Overall length
    2016/17 models . . . . 2335 mm
    2018-on standard model . . . . 2330 mm
    Adventure Sports model. . . . . 2340 mm
Overall width. . . . . 930 mm
Overall height
    Standard model . . . . 1475 mm
    Adventure Sports model. . . . . 1570 mm
Wheelbase
    Standard model . . . . 1575 mm
    Adventure Sport model . . . . 1580 mm
Seat height (standard/low)
    Standard model . . . . 870/850 mm
    Adventure Sport model . . . . 920/900 mm
Footrest height
    2016/2017 models . . . . 351 mm
    2018-on standard model . . . . 352 mm
    Adventure Sports model. . . . . 372 mm
Ground clearance
    Standard model . . . . 250 mm
    Adventure Sports model. . . . . 270 mm
Kerb weight
    2016/17 models without ABS. . . . . 228 kg
    2016/17 models with ABS . . . . 232 kg
    2016/17 models with DCT . . . . 242 kg
    2018-on standard model with standard transmission . . . . 230 kg
    2018-on standard model with DCT . . . . 240 kg
    Adventure Sports model with standard transmission . . . . 243 kg
    Adventure Sports model with DCT. . . . . 253 kg

OVERALL WIDTH

Engine – all models

Type . . . . Four-stroke parallel twin
Capacity . . . . 998 cc
Bore . . . . 92.0 mm
Stroke . . . . 75.1 mm
Compression ratio . . . . 10.0 to 1
Cooling system. . . . . Liquid cooled
Clutch . . . . Wet multi-plate
Transmission. . . . . Six-speed constant mesh
Final drive. . . . . Chain and sprockets
Camshaft . . . . Uni-cam SOHC, chain-driven
Fuel system . . . . PGM-FI fuel injection, 44 mm throttle bodies
Ignition system . . . . Computer-controlled digital transistorised with electronic advance

Chassis – all models

Frame type. . . . . Steel semi-double cradle
Rake and trail. . . . . 27.5°, 113 mm
Fuel tank
    Capacity (including reserve)
        Standard model . . . . 18.8 litres
        Adventure Sports model. . . . . 24.2 litres
    Reserve volume . . . . approx. 3.4 litres
Front suspension
    Type . . . . Showa 45 mm upside-down oil-damped telescopic forks
    Travel
        Standard model . . . . 204 mm
        Adventure Sports model. . . . . 224 mm
    Adjustment . . . . Spring pre-load, rebound damping, compression damping
Rear suspension. . . . .
    Type . . . . Single shock absorber, rising rate linkage, aluminium swingarm
    Travel (at axle)
        Standard model . . . . 220 mm
        Adventure Sport model. . . . . 240 mm
    Adjustment . . . . Spring pre-load, rebound damping, compression damping
Wheels . . . . Aluminium rim with steel spokes 21 inch front, 18 inch rear
Tyres
    Front 90/90-21M/C 54H
    Rear 150/70-R18M/C 70H
Front brake. . . . . Twin 310 mm floating discs with four piston calipers
Rear brake . . . . Single 256 mm disc with single piston sliding caliper

Frame and engine numbers

The frame serial number is stamped into the right-hand side of the steering head. The engine number is stamped into the top of the crankcase on the right-hand side. Both of these numbers should be recorded and kept in a safe place so they can be given to law enforcement officials in the event of a theft. There is a colour code label under the seat which also states the model suffix letter. The throttle bodies also have an ID number stamped into them.

The frame serial number, engine serial number, and colour code should also be kept in a handy place (such as with your driver's licence) so they are always available when purchasing or ordering parts for your machine.

The model name CRF1000L applies to all models in all countries. In the UK and Europe a suffix letter is used to identify the year of production (see table below). Suffix letters indicate that a model has ABS (anti-lock braking system) in which case the letter A is used, or DCT (dual clutch transmission), in which case the the letter D is used (note that all models with DCT have ABS so the letter A is not used together with the letter D). The number 2 after any suffix letter(s) indicates the Adventure Sports model. For example a CRF1000LA2J is a UK/Europe 2018 Adventure Sport model with ABS. Differences in procedure within the manual are identified in different ways: by stating whether a model has the standard brake system or ABS, whether a model has the standard transmission or DCT, whether it is the standard model or the Adventure Sport model, or by using the years or year of production, i.e 2016/17 models or 2018/19 models.

UK and Europe model suffix letter	Year
G	2016
H	2017
J	2018
K	2019

Buying spare parts

Once you have found all the identification numbers, record them for reference when buying parts. Since the manufacturers change specifications, parts and vendors (companies that manufacture various components on the machine), providing the ID numbers is the only way to be reasonably sure that you are buying the correct parts for your model.

Whenever possible, take the worn part to the dealer so direct comparison with the new component can be made. Along the trail from the manufacturer to the parts shelf, there are numerous places that the part can end up with the wrong number or be listed incorrectly.

The two places to purchase new parts for your motorcycle – the franchised or main dealer and the parts/accessories store – differ in the type of parts they carry. While dealers can obtain every single genuine part for your motorcycle, the accessory store is usually limited to normal high wear items such as chains and sprockets, brake pads, spark plugs and cables, and to tune-up parts and various engine gaskets, etc. Rarely will an accessory outlet have major suspension components, camshafts, transmission gears, or engine cases.

Used parts can be obtained from breakers for roughly half the price of new ones, but you can't always be sure of what you're getting. Once again, take your worn part to the breaker for direct comparison, or when ordering by mail order make sure that you can return it if you are not happy.

Whether buying new, used or rebuilt parts, the best course is to deal directly with someone who specialises in your particular make.

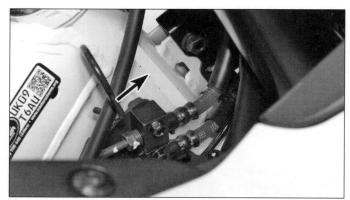

The frame number is stamped into the right-hand side of the steering head...

...and also appears on the VIN plate

The engine number is stamped into the right-hand side of the crankcase

The colour code label is under the seat

Note: *These checks are outlined in your owner's manual and should be performed every time you ride the machine.*

Engine oil level

Before you start:

✔ Oil level is checked using the dipstick, which is screwed into the front of the alternator cover on the left-hand side of the engine. The oil filler cap screws into the rear of the alternator cover.
✔ Make sure the motorcycle is on level ground.
✔ Start the engine and let it idle for 3 to 5 minutes.
Caution: Do not run the engine in an enclosed space such as a garage or workshop.
✔ Stop the engine and allow the oil level to stabilise for 2 to 3 minutes. Support the motorcycle upright by having an assistant hold it.

Bike care:

● If you have to add oil frequently, check whether you have any oil leaks from the engine joints, oil seals and gaskets. If not, the engine could be burning oil, in which case there will be white smoke coming out of the exhaust (see *Fault Finding in the Reference section*).

The correct oil:

● Modern, high-revving engines place great demands on their oil. It is very important that the correct oil for your bike is used.
● Always top up with a good quality motorcycle oil of the specified type and viscosity and do not overfill the engine. Do not use oils designed for use in car engines.
Caution: Do not use chemical additives or oils labelled "ENERGY CONSERVING". Such additives or oils could cause clutch slip.

Oil type	API grade: SG or higher; JASO T 903 grade: MA
Oil viscosity	SAE 10W30

1 Unscrew and remove the dipstick and wipe it clean

2 With the bike held upright insert the dipstick so that the cap threads rest on the engine, but do not screw it in.

3 Remove the dipstick and check the oil mark – it should lie between the upper and lower level lines (arrowed)

4 If the level is on or below the lower line, unscrew the filler cap

5 Top up with the recommended grade and type of oil to bring the level almost up to the upper line. Do not overfill.

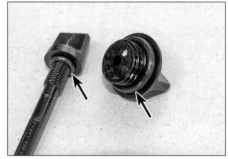

6 Make sure the O-rings (arrowed) on the underside of the dipstick and filler cap are in good condition and properly seated before screwing them in. Run the engine for a few minutes, then turn it off and wait a few minutes before re-checking the level.

Suspension, steering and drive chain

Suspension and Steering:

● Check that the front and rear suspension operates smoothly without binding (see Chapter 1).
● Check that the forks and shock absorber are adjusted as required, and that when any adjustment is made to the forks the settings on each fork are the same (see Chapter 5).

● Check that the steering moves smoothly from lock-to-lock.

Drive chain:

● Check that the chain isn't too loose or too tight, and adjust it if necessary (see Chapter 1).
● If the chain looks dry, lubricate it (see Chapter 1).

Coolant level

Before you start:

✔ The coolant reservoir is located at the back of the engine on the right-hand side, behind the brake pedal.

✔ Support the motorcycle upright by having an assistant hold it, making sure it is on level ground.

Bike care:

● Use only the specified coolant mixture of 50% distilled water and 50% ethylene glycol anti-freeze with corrosion inhibitors – ready-mixed coolant is available in one litre containers, and Pro Honda HP Coolant is recommended. It is important that the correct proportion of anti-freeze is used in the system all year round, and not just in the winter. Do not top the system up using only water, as the system will become too diluted. Note that there are different ready-mixed coolant types available, IAT (inorganic additive technology) and OAT (organic additive technology), and these should not be mixed – if in doubt about which product to buy ask a Honda dealer.

● Do not overfill the reservoir. If the coolant is significantly above the UPPER level line at any time, the surplus should be siphoned or drained off to prevent the possibility of it being expelled out of the overflow hose.

> **Warning: DO NOT remove the pressure cap from the filler neck to add coolant. Topping up is done via the coolant reservoir tank filler. DO NOT leave open containers of coolant about, as it is poisonous.**

● If the coolant level falls steadily check the system for leaks (see Chapter 1). If no leaks are found and the level continues to fall, fit a new pressure cap to the radiator filler neck (see Chapter 1). If that fails to solve the problem take the bike to a Honda dealer for a pressure test.

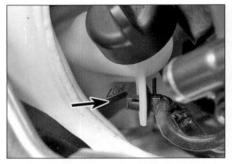

1 The coolant level should lie between the upper and lower level lines (arrowed) that are marked on the reservoir.

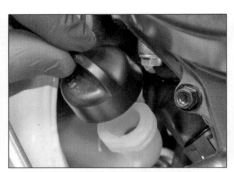

2 If the coolant level is on or below the LOWER line, unscrew the reservoir filler cap.

3 Top up the reservoir with the recommended coolant mixture to the UPPER level line, using a suitable funnel if required. Fit the cap.

Brake fluid levels

Before you start:

✔ The front brake fluid reservoir is on the handlebar. The rear brake fluid reservoir is on the right-hand side of the bike.

✔ Make sure you have the correct hydraulic fluid – DOT 4.

✔ Wrap a rag around the reservoir being worked on so that any spillage does not come into contact with painted surfaces.

✔ When checking the fluid in the front reservoir turn the handlebars so the reservoir is level.

✔ When checking the fluid in the rear reservoir support the motorcycle upright.

Bike care:

● The fluid in the front and rear brake master cylinder reservoirs will drop as the brake pads wear down. If the fluid level is low check the brake pads for wear (see Chapter 1), and replace them with new ones if necessary (see Chapter 6), then check the level again – the fluid displaced by the extra thickness of the new pads should bring the level back up to the maximum level, but if not, top it up.

● If either fluid reservoir requires repeated topping-up there is a leak somewhere in the system. Check for signs of fluid leakage from the hydraulic hoses and/or brake system components – if found, rectify immediately (see Chapter 6).

● Check the operation of both brakes before taking the machine on the road; if there is evidence of air in the system (spongy feel to lever or pedal), it must be bled (see Chapter 6).

> **Warning: Brake hydraulic fluid can harm your eyes and damage painted surfaces, so use extreme caution when handling and pouring it and cover surrounding surfaces with rag. Do not use fluid that has been standing open for some time, as it is hygroscopic (absorbs moisture from the air), which can cause a dangerous loss of braking efficiency.**

FRONT BRAKE

1 The front brake fluid level is visible through the window in the reservoir body – it must be above the LOWER level line (arrowed).

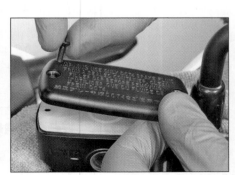

2 If the level is on or below the LOWER line, undo the reservoir cover screws and remove the cover, diaphragm plate and diaphragm.

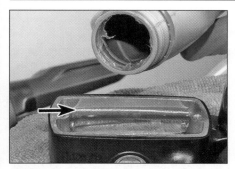

3 Top up with new clean DOT 4 hydraulic fluid, until the level is up to the upper level line (arrowed) cast inside the reservoir. Do not overfill and take care to avoid spills (see **Warning**).

4 Wipe any moisture off the diaphragm with a tissue.

5 Fit the diaphragm, making sure it is correctly seated, then fit the plate and cover. Secure the cover with its screws.

REAR BRAKE

1 The rear brake fluid level is visible through the reservoir body – it must be between the UPPER and LOWER level lines (arrowed).

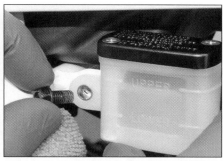

2 Unscrew the reservoir bolt and displace the reservoir so the cover is clear.

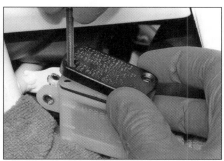

3 Undo the reservoir cover screws and remove the cover, diaphragm plate and diaphragm.

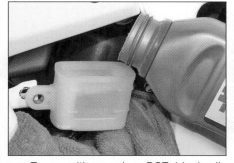

4 Top up with new clean DOT 4 hydraulic fluid, until the level is up to the UPPER line. Do not overfill and take care to avoid spills (see **Warning**).

5 Wipe any moisture off the diaphragm with a tissue.

6 Fit the diaphragm, making sure it is correctly seated, then fit the plate and cap. Fit the reservoir, making sure it is level and correctly located against the bracket, and tighten the bolt.

Legal and safety

Lighting and signalling:

● Take a minute to check that the headlights, tail and brake lights, licence plate light, instrument lights and turn signals all work correctly.
● Check that the horn sounds when the button is pressed.
● A working speedometer, graduated in mph, is a statutory requirement in the UK.

Safety:

● Check that the throttle grip rotates smoothly when opened and snaps shut when released, in all steering positions. On 2016/17 models also check for the correct amount of throttle cable freeplay (see Chapter 1).
● Check that the brake lever and pedal, clutch lever and gearchange lever (where fitted) operate smoothly. Lubricate them at the specified intervals or when necessary (see Chapter 1).
● Check that the engine shuts off when the kill switch is operated. Check the starter interlock circuit (see Chapter 1).
● Check that the sidestand return springs hold the stand up securely when retracted.

Fuel:

● This may seem obvious, but check that you have enough fuel to complete your journey. If you smell petrol (gasoline) or notice signs of fuel leakage, rectify the cause immediately.
● Ensure you use the correct grade fuel – see Chapter 4.

Tyres

Tyre care:

● Check the tyres carefully for cuts, tears, embedded nails or other sharp objects and excessive wear. Operation of the motorcycle with excessively worn tyres is extremely hazardous, as traction and handling are directly affected.

● Pick out any stones or nails that may have become embedded in the tyre tread. If left, they will eventually penetrate through the casing and cause a puncture.

● Make sure a dust cap is fitted. If air escapes when the cap is removed the valve core could be loose – a simple tool that is cheaply available and sometimes incorporated in the cap is needed to tighten the valve. Check the condition of the valve.

● If tyre damage is apparent, or unexplained loss of pressure is experienced, seek the advice of a tyre fitting specialist without delay.

Tyre tread depth:

● At the time of writing UK law requires that tread depth must be at least 1 mm over 3/4 of the tread breadth all the way around the tyre, with no bald patches. Many riders, however, consider 2 mm tread depth minimum to be a safer limit. Honda recommends a minimum of 1.5 mm on the front and 2 mm on the rear, but note that German law requires a minimum of 1.6 mm for each tyre.

● Most tyres incorporate wear indicators in the tread. Identify the location marking on the tyre sidewall to locate the indicator bar and replace the tyre if the tread has worn down to the bar.

The correct pressure:

● The tyres must be checked when cold, not immediately after riding. The pressure inside

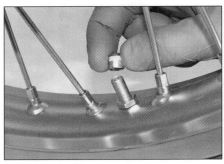

1 Remove the dust cap from the valve. Do not forget to fit the cap after checking the pressure.

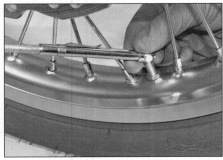

2 Check the tyre pressures when cold.

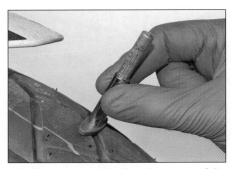

3 Measure tread depth at the centre of the tyre using a depth gauge.

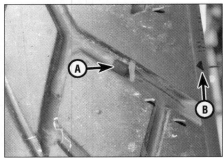

4 Tyre tread wear indicators (A) and its location marking (B) on the edge or sidewall (according to manufacturer).

the tyre will increase when the tyre is hot. Note that tyre pressure will also change from one day to the next as air temperature changes.

● Correct tyre pressure will increase tyre life and provide maximum stability and

ride comfort. Incorrect pressure will cause abnormal tread wear and unsafe handling. Low tyre pressures may cause the tyre to slip on the rim or come off.

● Use an accurate pressure gauge.

2016/17 models	Front	Rear
Up to 90 kg load (i.e. rider only or rider plus normal luggage)	29 psi (2.0 Bar)	36 psi (2.5 Bar)
Over 90 kg load (i.e. rider plus heavy luggage, rider and passenger, rider and passenger plus luggage)	29 psi (2.0 Bar)	41 psi (2.8 Bar)

2018-on standard models	Front	Rear
Up to 90 kg load (i.e. rider only or rider plus normal luggage)	29 psi (2.0 Bar)	36 psi (2.5 Bar)
Over 90 kg load (i.e. rider plus heavy luggage, rider and passenger, rider and passenger plus luggage)	33 psi (2.25 Bar)	41 psi (2.8 Bar)

Adventure Sports models	Front	Rear
Up to 90 kg load (i.e. rider only or rider plus normal luggage)	33 psi (2.25 Bar)	41 psi (2.8 Bar)
Over 90 kg load (i.e. rider plus heavy luggage, rider and passenger, rider and passenger plus luggage)	33 psi (2.25 Bar)	41 psi (2.8 Bar)

Chapter 1
Routine maintenance and servicing

Contents

Section number

Air filters	23
Battery	24
Brake system	6
Clutch (standard transmission)	7
Cooling system	12
Crankcase breather	5
Drive chain and sprockets	4
Emission control systems	13
Engine oil and filter(s)	11
Fuel system	8
General information	3
General lubrication	19
Headlight aim	14

Section number

Idle speed	9
Maintenance schedule – UK/Europe	1
Maintenance schedule – US	2
Nuts, bolts and screws	20
Sidestand and starter interlock circuit	15
Spark arresters (US models)	25
Spark plugs	22
Steering head bearings	17
Suspension	16
Throttle system	10
Valve clearances	21
Wheels, tyres and wheel bearings	18

Degrees of difficulty

Easy, suitable for novice with little experience	Fairly easy, suitable for beginner with some experience	Fairly difficult, suitable for competent DIY mechanic	Difficult, suitable for experienced DIY mechanic	Very difficult, suitable for expert DIY or professional

1 Maintenance schedule – UK/Europe

Pre-ride
☐ See *Pre-ride checks* at the beginning of this manual

After the initial 600 miles (1000 km)
Note: *This check is performed by a Honda dealer after the first 600 miles (1000 km) from new. Thereafter, maintenance is carried out according to the following intervals of the schedule.*

Every 600 miles (1000 km)
☐ Check, adjust, clean and lubricate the drive chain (Section 4)

Every 4000 miles (6000 km) or 12 months
☐ Check the condition of the wheels, tyres and wheel bearings (Section 18)

Every 8000 miles (12,000 km) or 12 months
Note: *Carry out the 4000 mile (6000 km) checks, plus the following:*
☐ Clean the crankcase breather (Section 5)
☐ Check the brake pads for wear (Section 6)
☐ Check the brake system and brake light switch operation (Section 6)
☐ Check the clutch (standard transmission models) (Section 7)
☐ Check the fuel system and hoses (Section 8)
☐ Check engine idle speed (Section 9)
☐ Check the throttle system (Section 10)
☐ Change the engine oil (Section 11)
☐ Check the cooling system (Section 12)
☐ Check the headlight beam aim (Section 14)
☐ Check the sidestand and starter interlock circuit (Section 15)
☐ Check the front and rear suspension (Section 16)
☐ Check the steering head bearings and adjust if necessary (Section 17)

Every 8000 miles (12,000 km) or 12 months (continued)
☐ Lubricate the clutch lever, front brake lever, parking brake lever, brake pedal, gearchange lever and stand pivot as required according to model (Section 19)
☐ Check the tightness of all nuts, bolts and fasteners (Section 20)

Every 16,000 miles (24,000 km)
Note: *Carry out the 4000 mile (6000 km) and 8000 mile (12,000 km) checks, plus the following:*
☐ Fit a new oil filter, and a new clutch oil filter on models with DCT (Section 11)
☐ Check the valve clearances and adjust if necessary (Section 21)
☐ Check the spark plugs (Section 22)
☐ Fit a new air filter (Section 23)
☐ Check the PAIR (pulse secondary air) system (Section 13)
☐ Check the EVAP system hoses (where fitted) (Section 13)

Every 32,000 miles (48,000 km)
Note: *Carry out the 4000 mile (6000 km), 8000 mile (12,000 km) and 16,000 mile (24,000 km) checks, plus the following:*
☐ Fit new spark plugs (Section 22)

Every two years
☐ Change the brake fluid (Section 6)

Every three years
☐ Change the coolant (Section 12)

Non-scheduled maintenance
☐ Check the battery (Section 24)
☐ Change the front fork oil (Section 16)
☐ Re-grease the swingarm pivot, linkage and shock absorber bearings (Section 16)
☐ Re-grease the steering head bearings (Section 17)

2 Maintenance schedule – US

Pre-ride
☐ See *Pre-ride checks* at the beginning of this manual

After the initial 600 miles
Note: *This check is performed by a Honda dealer after the first 600 miles from new. Thereafter, maintenance is carried out according to the following intervals of the schedule.*

Every 600 miles
☐ Check, adjust, clean and lubricate the drive chain (Section 4)

Every 4000 miles
☐ Clean the crankcase breather (Section 5)
☐ Check the brake pads for wear (Section 6)
☐ Check the parking brake lock (DCT models) (Section 6)
☐ Check the clutch (standard transmission models) (Section 7)
☐ Check the condition of the wheels, tyres and wheel bearings (Section 18)
☐ Clean the spark arrester (Section 25)

Every 8000 miles or 12 months
☐ Change the engine oil (Section 11)

Every 8000 miles
Note: *Carry out the 4000 mile checks, plus the following:*
☐ Check the brake system and brake light switch operation (Section 6)
☐ Check the fuel system and hoses (Section 8)
☐ Check engine idle speed (Section 9)
☐ Check the throttle system (Section 10)
☐ Check the cooling system (Section 12)
☐ Check the headlight beam aim (Section 14)
☐ Check the sidestand and starter interlock circuit (Section 15)
☐ Check the front and rear suspension (Section 16)
☐ Check the steering head bearings and adjust if necessary (Section 17)
☐ Lubricate the clutch lever, front brake lever, parking brake lever, brake pedal, gearchange lever and stand pivot as required according to model (Section 19)
☐ Check the tightness of all nuts, bolts and fasteners (Section 20)

Every 12,000 miles
Note: *Carry out the 4000 mile checks, plus the following:*
☐ Fit a new air filter (Section 23)

Every 16,000 miles
Note: *Carry out the 4000 mile and 8000 mile checks, plus the following:*
☐ Fit a new oil filter, and a new clutch oil filter on models with DCT (Section 11)
☐ Check the valve clearances and adjust if necessary (Section 21)
☐ Check the spark plugs (Section 22)
☐ Check the PAIR (pulse secondary air) system (Section 13)
☐ Check the EVAP system hoses (Section 13)

Every 32,000 miles (48,000 km)
Note: *Carry out the 4000 mile, 8000 mile, 12,000 mile and 16,000 mile checks, plus the following:*
☐ Fit new spark plugs (Section 22)

Every two years
☐ Change the brake fluid (Section 6)

Every three years
☐ Change the coolant (Section 12)

Non-scheduled maintenance
☐ Check the battery (Section 24)
☐ Change the front fork oil (Section 16)
☐ Re-grease the swingarm pivot, linkage and shock absorber bearings (Section 16)
☐ Re-grease the steering head bearings (Section 17)

Component locations on the right-hand side – models with standard transmission

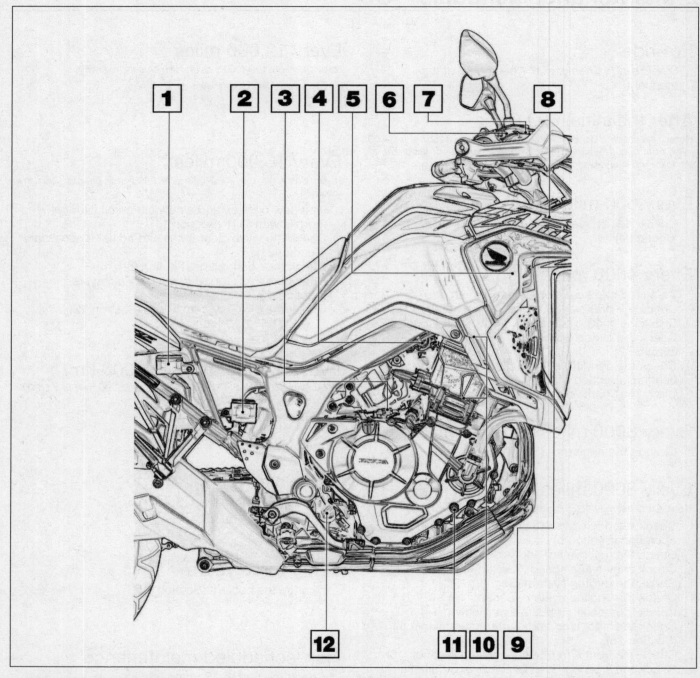

1 Rear brake fluid reservoir (2016/17)
2 Rear brake fluid reservoir (2018-on)
3 Clutch cable adjuster at lower end
4 Throttle cable adjusters at lower end (2016/17 only)
5 Air filter
6 Throttle cable adjuster at upper end (2016/17 only)
7 Front brake fluid reservoir
8 Steering head bearing adjuster
9 Cooling system pressure cap
10 Spark plugs
11 Coolant drain screw
12 Coolant reservoir filler cap

Component locations on the left-hand side – models with standard transmission

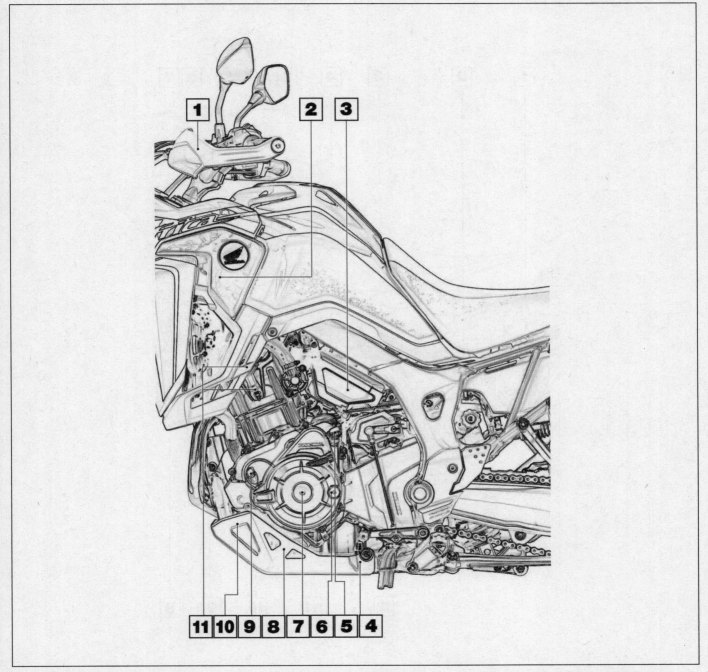

1 Clutch cable adjuster at the upper end
2 Air filter
3 Battery
4 Engine oil drain plug (rear)
5 Engine oil filler cap
6 Timing mark plug
7 End cap for engine turning
8 Engine oil drain plug (front)
9 Engine oil level dipstick
10 Engine oil filter
11 Spark plugs

Component locations on the right-hand side – models with DCT

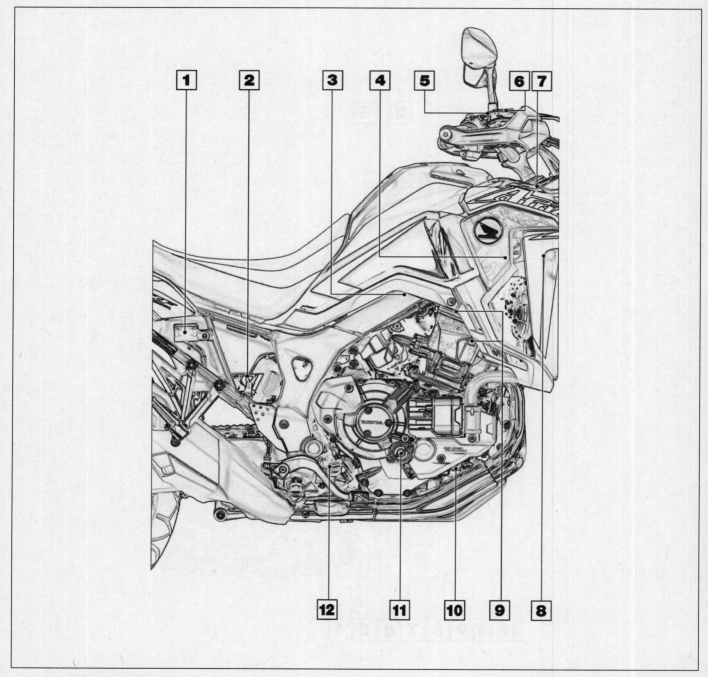

1 Rear brake fluid reservoir (2016/17)
2 Rear brake fluid reservoir (2018-on)
3 Throttle cable adjusters at lower end (2016/17 only)
4 Air filter
5 Throttle cable adjuster at upper end (2016/17 only)
6 Front brake fluid reservoir
7 Steering head bearing adjuster
8 Cooling system pressure cap
9 Spark plugs
10 Coolant drain screw
11 Clutch oil filter cover
12 Coolant reservoir filler cap

Component locations on the left-hand side – models with DCT

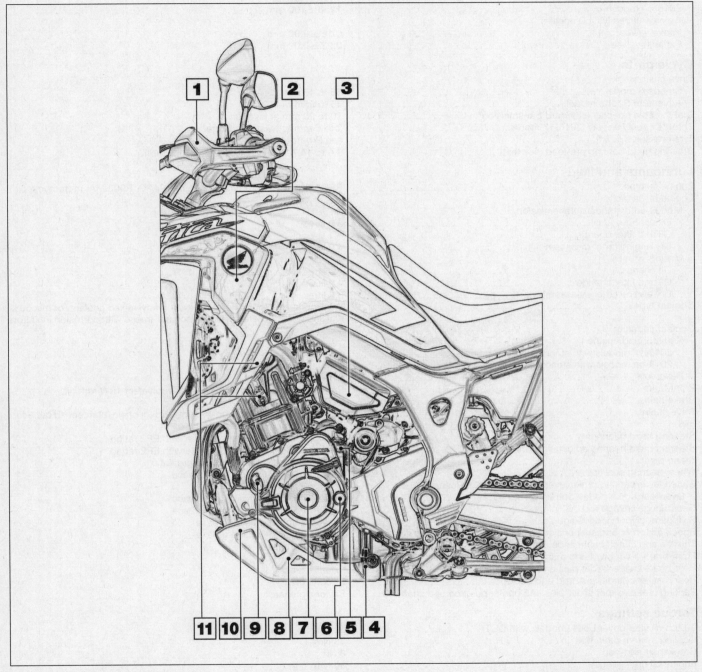

1 Parking brake cable adjuster	5 Engine oil filler cap	9 Engine oil level dipstick
2 Air filter	6 Timing mark plug	10 Engine oil filter
3 Battery	7 End cap for engine turning	11 Spark plugs
4 Engine oil drain plug (rear)	8 Engine oil drain plug (front)	

Engine

Cylinder numbering	1 – left, 2 – right
Spark plug type	NGK SILMAR8A9S
Spark plug electrode gap	0.8 to 0.9 mm
Engine idle speed	
2016/17 models	1200 ± 100 rpm
2018-on models	1250 ± 100 rpm
Valve clearances (COLD engine)	
Intake valves	0.16 ± 0.03 mm
Exhaust valves	0.23 ± 0.02 mm

Cycle parts

Drive chain slack	
Standard model	35 to 45 mm
Adventure Sports model	45 to 55 mm
Clutch cable freeplay (standard transmission)	10 to 20 mm at lever end
Throttle cable freeplay (2016/17 models)	2 to 6 mm at twistgrip flange
Tyre pressures (cold)	see Pre-ride checks
Steering head bearing pre-load (see text)	9.8 to 14.7 N (1.0 to 1.5 kgf; 2.2 to 3.3 lbf)

Lubricants and fluids

Engine oil type	SAE 10W30, API grade SG or higher, JASO T 903 MA, motorcycle oil
Engine oil capacity	
Models with standard transmission	
Oil change	3.9 litres
Oil and filter change	4.1 litres
Dry engine (after disassembly)	4.9 litres
Models with DCT	
Oil change	4.0 litres
Oil and filter change	4.2 litres
Dry engine (after disassembly)	5.2 litres
Coolant type	Pro Honda HP Coolant or equivalent ready-mixed coolant, or mix 50% distilled water/50% ethylene glycol anti-freeze with corrosion inhibitors
Coolant capacity	
Radiator and engine	
2016/17 models with standard transmission	1.63 litres
2018-on models with standard transmission, all models with DCT	1.65 litres
Reservoir	0.33 litre
Front forks	Pro-Honda suspension fluid SS8 or equivalent 10W fork oil
Brake fluid	DOT 4
Drive chain	Honda HP chain lube or equivalent aerosol chain lubricant suitable for O-ring chains, or SAE 80/90 gear oil
Steering head bearings	Urea based multi-purpose grease with EP2 rating
Steering head bearing adjuster nut threads	Urea based multi-purpose grease with EP2 rating
Stand pivot	Molybdenum disulphide grease grease
Wheel bearing seal lips	Lithium-based multi-purpose grease
Clutch lever/parking brake lever and locking plate/gearchange lever/rear brake pedal/footrest pivots	Lithium-based multi-purpose grease
Gearchange linkage rod ball joints	Lithium-based multi-purpose grease
Swingarm pivot bearings and seals	Molybdenum disulphide grease
Shock absorber and suspension linkage pivot bearings and seals	Molybdenum disulphide grease
Throttle and clutch cable ends	Multi-purpose grease
Front brake lever pivot and master cylinder pushrod end	Silicone grease
Rear brake caliper slider pins and boots	Silicone grease
Rear master cylinder pushrod and boot	Silicone grease
Parking brake caliper slider pins and boots, pushrod and shaft	Silicone grease

Torque settings

Clutch oil filter cover bolts (models with DCT)	12 Nm
Cooling system drain bolt	13 Nm
Crankshaft end-cap	8 Nm
Engine oil drain plugs	30 Nm
Engine oil filter	26 Nm
Fork clamp bolts (top yoke)	22 Nm
Rear axle nut	100 Nm
Silencer exit pipe (spark arrester) bolts (US models)	9 Nm
Spark plugs	22 Nm
Steering head bearing adjuster nut	15 Nm
Steering stem nut	100 Nm
Timing inspection cap	6 Nm

4.3a Push up on the chain and zero the ruler at a selected point against it...

4.3b ...then release the chain and measure the slack

3   General information

1 This Chapter is designed to help the home mechanic maintain his/her motorcycle for safety, economy, long life and peak performance.
2 Deciding where to start or plug into the routine maintenance schedule depends on several factors. If your motorcycle has been maintained according to the warranty standards and has just come out of warranty, start routine maintenance as it coincides with the next mileage interval. If you have owned the machine for some time but have never performed any maintenance on it, start at the nearest interval and include some additional procedures to ensure that nothing important is overlooked. If you have just had a major engine overhaul, then start the maintenance routine from the beginning. If you have a used machine and have no knowledge of its history or maintenance record, combine all the checks into one large service initially and then settle into the specified maintenance schedule.
3 Before beginning any maintenance or repair, clean the machine thoroughly, especially around the oil filter, oil drain plugs, drive chain, suspension, wheels, etc. Cleaning will help ensure that dirt does not get into components or where they fit, and will allow you to detect wear and damage that could otherwise easily go unnoticed. If you use a pressure washer make sure you do not direct the jet at wheel bearing and suspension seals and at the steering head, or at any electrical/ignition components and connectors.
4 Certain maintenance information is sometimes printed on labels attached to the motorcycle. If the information on the labels

differs from that included here, use the information on the label.

4   Drive chain and sprockets

Check

1 A neglected drive chain won't last long and will quickly damage the sprockets. Routine chain adjustment and lubrication isn't difficult and will ensure maximum chain and sprocket life.
2 To check the chain, place the bike on its sidestand and shift the transmission into neutral. Make sure the ignition switch is OFF. On models with DCT, make sure the parking brake is off.
3 Push the lower run of the chain up midway between the sprockets and place a ruler against it with the zero mark at a selected point (such as the upper or lower edge or one of the link pins as shown), hold the ruler steady, then release the chain and note the reading on the ruler where the same part of the chain now rests **(see illustrations)**. Compare your measurement to that listed in the Specifications at the beginning of the Chapter. As the chain stretches with wear, adjustment will periodically be necessary (see below). Since the chain will rarely wear evenly, roll the bike forward so that another section of chain can be checked (having an assistant to do this makes the task a lot easier); do this several times to check the entire length of chain, and mark the tightest spot.
Caution: Riding the bike with a chain that is too tight or too loose could lead to damage.
4 In some cases where lubrication has been neglected, corrosion and dirt may cause the links to bind and kink, which effectively

shortens the chain's length and makes it tight **(see illustration)**. Thoroughly clean and work free any such links, then highlight them with a marker pen or paint. Take the bike for a ride.
5 After the bike has been ridden, repeat the measurement for slack in the highlighted area. If the chain has kinked again and is still tight, replace it with a new one (see Chapter 6). A rusty, kinked or worn chain will damage the sprockets and a tight chain can damage transmission bearings. If in any doubt as to the condition of a chain, it is far better to fit a new one than risk damage to other components and possibly yourself.
6 Check the entire length of the chain for damaged rollers, loose links and pins, and missing O-rings and replace it with a new one if necessary (see Chapter 6).
Note: *Never fit a new chain onto old sprockets, and never use the old chain if you fit new sprockets – replace the chain and sprockets as a set.*

Adjustment

7 Move the bike so that the tightest point of the chain is at the centre of its bottom run, then put it on the sidestand.

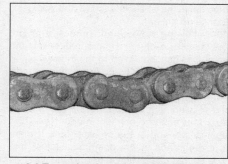

4.4 Example of a tight and kinked link

4.8 Slacken the axle nut

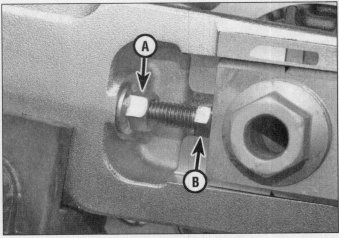

4.9 Slacken the locknut (A) on each side, then turn each adjuster bolt (B) as required

4.10 Make sure the adjustment markers are in the same position each side relative to the index lines

4.11 When the index notch (arrowed) aligns with the red zone, fit a new chain

8 Slacken the rear axle nut **(see illustration)**.
9 Slacken the locknut on the adjuster bolt on each side of the swingarm **(see illustration)**. Turn each adjuster bolt equally until the amount of chain slack is as specified – if the chain was slack turn the bolts anti-clockwise; if the chain was tight turn them clockwise, then move the wheel forwards in the swingarm to take up the gap.
10 Following adjustment, check that the rear edge of each adjustment marker is in the same position in relation to the index lines on each end of the swingarm **(see illustration)**. It is important the position is the same on each side otherwise the rear wheel will be out of alignment with the front. Always make sure that each adjustment marker is butted against the end of the adjuster bolt. If there is a difference in the positions, adjust one side so that its position is exactly the same as the other. Check the chain freeplay again and readjust if necessary.

11 Also check the alignment of the index notch on the top of the left-hand adjustment marker with the wear decal on the swingarm **(see illustration)**. When the arrow meets the red zone, the drive chain has stretched excessively and must be replaced with a new one (see Chapter 6).
12 When adjustment is complete, counter-hold the adjuster bolts and tighten the locknuts **(see illustration 4.9)**. Make sure the adjustment markers are butted against the bolts then counter-hold the head of the axle and tighten the nut to 100 Nm **(see illustration 4.8)**. Recheck the adjustment as above.

Cleaning and lubrication

13 If required, wash the chain using a dedicated aerosol cleaner, or paraffin (kerosene) or a suitable non-flammable or high flash-point solvent that will not damage the O-rings, using a soft brush to work any dirt out if necessary **(see illustration)**. Wipe

4.13 Using a chain cleaning brush

4.14 Apply the lubricant to the overlapping sections of the sideplates

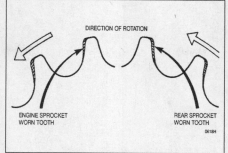

4.15 Check the sprocket teeth in the areas indicated for the sprocket being checked

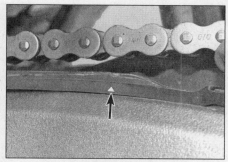

4.16 Chain slider wear limit marker (arrowed)

the cleaner off the chain and allow it to dry. If the chain is excessively dirty remove it from the bike and allow it to soak in the paraffin or solvent (see Chapter 6).

Caution: Don't use petrol (gasoline), an unsuitable solvent or other cleaning fluids which might damage the internal sealing properties of the chain. Don't use high-pressure water to clean the chain. The entire process shouldn't take longer than ten minutes, otherwise the O-rings could be damaged.

14 The best time to lubricate the chain is after the motorcycle has been ridden. When the chain is warm, the lubricant will penetrate the joints between the side plates better than when cold. Honda specifies Honda HP chain lube or an equivalent aerosol chain lube that it is suitable for O-ring chains, or SAE 80 to SAE 90 gear oil. Do not use any other chain lubricants – the solvents could damage the O-rings. Apply the lubricant to the area where the sideplates overlap – not the middle of the rollers **(see illustration)**.

⚠️ *Warning: Take care not to get any lubricant on the tyre or brake system components. If any of the lubricant inadvertently contacts*

them, clean it off thoroughly using a suitable solvent or dedicated brake cleaner before riding the machine.

Sprocket check

15 Remove the front sprocket cover (see Chapter 6). Check the teeth on the front and rear sprockets for wear **(see illustration)**. If the teeth are worn excessively, replace the chain and both sprockets with a new set.

16 Every so often check the amount of wear on the chain slider **(see illustration)**. If the rubbing surfaces of the slider have worn to the marker remove the swingarm and replace the slider with a new one (see Chapter 5). Note that you'll need to clean all old chain grease and road dirt off the slider in order to see the marker clearly.

5 Crankcase breather

Note: *The crankcase breather system should be checked more frequently if the bike is constantly ridden in wet conditions or at full throttle, or if it has fallen over, or whenever deposits are seen in the drain collectors.*

1 The air filter housing has three drain tubes that collect deposits from the crankcase breather system, one on the right and two on the left **(see illustrations)**. Check for any deposits – if there are any they should be drained. To drain the deposits from the front hoses first remove the fairing side panel(s) (see Chapter 7). Place some absorbent rag under each one in turn, then release the clamp, remove the plug and allow any deposits to drain **(see illustration)**. Fit the plug and secure it with the clamp.

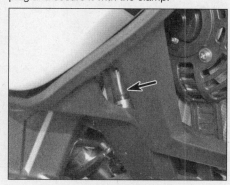

5.1a There is a drain hose (arrowed) on the inner side of each fairing side panel...

5.1b ...and one at the back of the left-hand side of the cylinder head

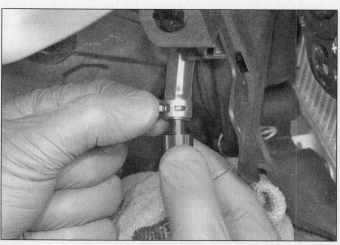

5.1c Release the clamp and remove the plug

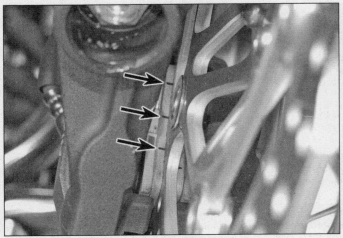

6.1a Front brake pad wear indicator grooves (arrowed)

6.1b Rear brake pad wear indicator cutout (arrowed)

6.10a Check all hoses and their banjo unions...

6.10b ...and the hose/pipe joints and unions for cracks and leaks

6 Brake system

Brake pad wear check

1 Each brake pad has wear indicators in the form of grooves in the face or edge of the material. The wear indicators should be visible by looking at the underside of each front caliper, and at the back of the rear caliper, but note that an accumulation of road dirt and brake dust could make them difficult to see **(see illustrations)**. If necessary, particularly for the front calipers, displace the caliper for best visual access (see Chapter 6).

2 If the front pads are worn to the bottom of the grooves or the rear pads are worn to the beginning of the cutout, they must be replaced with new ones (see Chapter 6). Note

that some after-market pads may use different indicators to those on the original equipment.

3 If the indicators are difficult to see, the amount of friction material remaining is easily visible, and it will be obvious when the pads need replacing. Honda do not specify a minimum thickness for the friction material, but anything less than 1 mm should be considered excessively worn.

4 On the front calipers also check for different amounts of wear in each pad and for uneven wear across each pad, which is indicative of a sticking or seized piston or pistons. On the rear caliper check for different amount of wear in each pad, which means that the caliper may not be sliding on its bracket. If found, the caliper must be checked, cleaned and if necessary overhauled (see Chapter 6).

5 If the pads are dirty or if you are in doubt as to the amount of friction material remaining, remove them for inspection (see Chapter 6). If

the pads are excessively worn, also check the brake discs (see Chapter 6).

6 On models with DCT also check the pads in the parking brake on the rear caliper, but note that unless you have been riding with the brake on these pads should not wear down.

Brake system check

7 A routine general check of the brake system will ensure that any problems are discovered and remedied before the rider's safety is jeopardised.

8 Check the brake pads for wear (see above) and make sure the fluid level in each reservoir is correct (see Pre-ride checks).

9 Check the brake lever and pedal pivots for sloppy or rough action, excessive play, bends, and other damage. Replace any damaged parts with new ones (see Chapter 5). Clean and lubricate the lever and pedal pivots if their action is stiff or rough (Section 19). If the

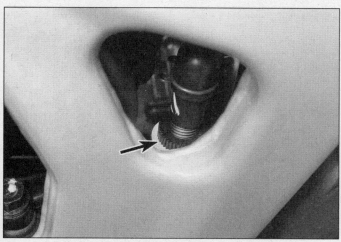

6.12 Rear brake light switch adjuster ring (arrowed)

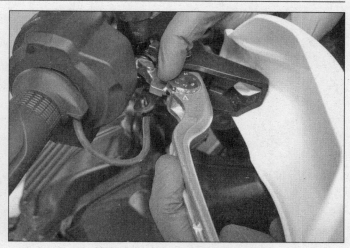

6.13a Adjusting brake lever span

6.13b Align the required setting number with the triangular index mark

6.14 Slacken the locknut (A) and turn the pushrod using the hex (B) to adjust pedal height

lever or pedal is spongy, bleed the brakes (see Chapter 6).

10 Look for leaks at the hose and pipe connections and check for cracks in the hoses, pipes and unions **(see illustrations)**. If leakage or cracked or damaged hoses are found, replace the hoses with new ones (see Chapter 6). Make sure all brake hose and pipe fasteners are tight. Similarly check for any signs of fluid leakage from the calipers and master cylinders – overhaul will be necessary if found (see Chapter 6).

11 Make sure the brake light operates when the front brake lever is pulled in. The front brake light switch, mounted on the underside of the master cylinder, is not adjustable. If it fails to operate properly, check it (see Chapter 8).

12 Make sure the brake light is activated just before the rear brake takes effect. The rear brake light switch is mounted on the inner

side of the frame above the brake pedal. If adjustment is necessary, hold the switch body and turn the adjuster ring until the brake light is activated when required – do not turn the switch itself **(see illustration)**. If the brake light comes on too late or not at all, turn the ring clockwise so the switch is drawn up out of its bracket. If the brake light comes on too soon or is permanently on, turn the ring anti-clockwise so the switch is drawn down into the bracket. If the switch doesn't operate the brake light, check it (see Chapter 8).

13 The front brake lever has a span adjuster that adjusts the distance of the lever from the handlebar to suit different hand sizes. To adjust the span push the lever away from the handlebar and turn the adjuster to the required setting **(see illustration)**. Make sure the setting number is exactly aligned with the index triangle on the lever **(see illustration)**.

14 The height of the rear brake pedal can be

adjusted slightly to suit the rider's preference if required. Slacken the locknut securing the clevis on the master cylinder pushrod, then turn the pushrod using a spanner on the hex at the top of the rod until the pedal is at the desired height **(see illustration)**. On completion tighten the locknut. Note that the bottom of the pushrod must always be visible under the top of the clevis – Honda specify an adjustment range of 83.0 to 85.0 mm as measured from the centre of the master cylinder's bottom mounting bolt hole to the centre of the clevis pin hole (where the clevis pin joins the pedal to the pushrod), measured parallel to the centreline of the master cylinder. Adjust the rear brake light switch after adjusting the pedal height (see Step 12).

Parking brake check and adjustment – models with DCT

15 Apply the parking brake and check that it

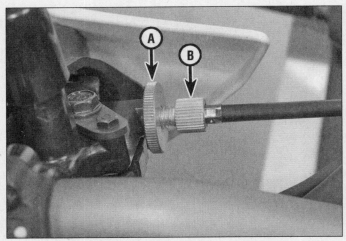

6.16 Slacken the lockring (A) and turn the adjuster (B) as required

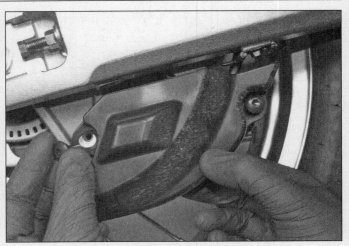

6.18 Undo the screws and remove the cover

locks the wheel so the bike cannot be pushed forwards. If the brake does not stop the bike from moving, it can be adjusted. Periodic adjustment is necessary to compensate for wear in the pads and stretch of the cable.

16 If adjustment is required, this can be done first at the lever. Place the bike on a rear paddock stand so the rear wheel is off the ground. Set the parking brake lock onto its first notch. Slacken the adjuster lockring and turn the adjuster out until there is a slight drag when the rear wheel is turned, then hold the adjuster and tighten the lockring **(see illustration)**. Make sure the adjuster is not threaded too far out of the bracket so that it is only held by a few threads – this will leave it unstable and the threads could be damaged.

17 If all the adjustment has been taken up at the lever, release the parking brake, then thread the adjuster all the way into the bracket to give the maximum amount of freeplay, then

back it out one turn – this resets the adjuster to its start point.

18 Now set the correct amount of freeplay using the adjuster on the caliper. Remove the caliper cover **(see illustration)**.

19 Set the parking brake lock onto its first notch. Slacken the caliper pushrod locknut **(see illustration)**. Turn the rear wheel slowly by hand and turn the pushrod using a hex key until there is a slight drag on the wheel. Hold the pushrod and tighten the locknut. Fit the cover. Subsequent adjustments can now be made using the lever adjuster.

Brake fluid change

20 The brake fluid should be changed every two years (see Chapter 6). Make sure that all the old fluid is pumped from the hydraulic system and that the level in the fluid reservoir is checked and the brakes tested before riding the motorcycle.

7 Clutch (standard transmission)

1 Check that the clutch lever operates smoothly and easily.

2 If the clutch lever operation is heavy or stiff, lubricate it (Section 19). If the action is still stiff, replace the cable with a new one (see Chapter 2).

3 With the cable operating smoothly, check that it is correctly adjusted. Periodic adjustment is necessary to compensate for wear in the clutch plates and stretch of the cable. Check that the amount of freeplay at the clutch lever end is within the range given in the Specifications at the beginning of the Chapter **(see illustration)**.

4 If adjustment is required, this can be done

6.19 Slacken the nut (A) and adjust the pushrod (B) as described

7.3 Freeplay measured from the centre of the ball end of the lever when at rest to the point freeplay is taken up

first at the lever end of the cable. Loosen the adjuster lockring, then turn the adjuster in or out until the required amount of freeplay is obtained **(see illustration)**. To increase freeplay, thread the adjuster into the lever bracket. To reduce freeplay, thread the adjuster out of the bracket.

5 Make sure that the slots in the adjuster, the lockring and the lever bracket are not aligned – these slots are to allow removal of the cable, and if they are all aligned while the bike is in use the cable could jump out. Also make sure the adjuster is not threaded too far out of the bracket so that it is only held by a few threads – this will leave it unstable and the threads could be damaged. Tighten the lockring on completion.

6 If all the adjustment has been taken up at the lever, thread the adjuster all the way into the bracket to give the maximum amount of freeplay, then back it out one turn – this resets the adjuster to its start point.

7 Now set the correct amount of freeplay using the adjuster on the clutch end of cable. The

adjuster is set in a bracket on the top of the crankcase on the right-hand side of the engine.

8 Slacken the nuts on each side of the bracket **(see illustration)**. To increase freeplay, thread the nuts up the cable, and to reduce freeplay thread them down the cable, until the freeplay is as specified, then tighten the nuts against the bracket. Subsequent adjustments can now be made using the lever adjuster.

8 Fuel system

⚠ **Warning: Petrol (gasoline) is extremely flammable, so take extra precautions when you work on any part of the fuel system. Don't smoke or allow open flames or bare light bulbs near the work area, and don't work in a garage where a natural gas-type appliance is present. If you spill any fuel on your skin, rinse it off immediately with soap and water. When you perform any kind of work on the fuel system, wear safety glasses and have a fire extinguisher suitable for a Class B type fire (flammable liquids) on hand.**

1 Raise and support the fuel tank (see Chapter 4).

2 Check the fuel tank, the fuel supply hose and the tank drain and breather hoses for signs of leaks, cracks, deterioration or damage **(see illustration)**. In particular check that there are no leaks from the fuel hose or hose unions. Replace hoses with new ones as required, referring to the relevant section in Chapter 4.

3 Check the joint between the fuel pump mounting plate and the tank. If there is evidence of fuel leakage, check the nuts are tight (see Chapter 4 for the torque setting). If the leak persists, remove the pump and fit a new seal (see Chapter 4).

4 Inspect the joints between the fuel rail, the injectors and the throttle bodies **(see illustration)**. If there are any leaks, remove

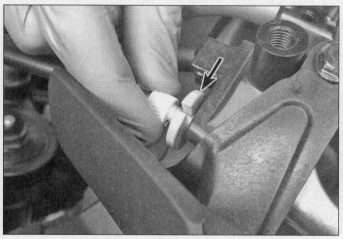

7.4 Slacken the lockring (arrowed) and turn the adjuster as required

7.8 Slacken and adjust the nuts (arrowed) as described

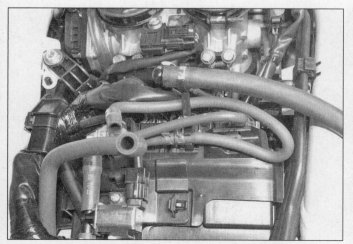

8.2 Check the tank and hoses – tank removed for clarity

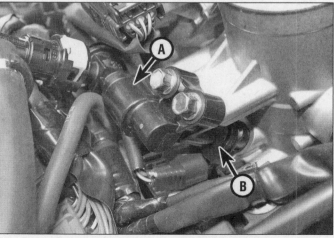

8.4 Check the fuel rail (A) and injectors (B)

the fuel rail and injectors and fit new seals and O-rings as required (see Chapter 4).

5 Fitting a new fuel filter is not a service item. If fuel starvation is experienced, and all other possibilities have been checked, a blocked fuel pick-up strainer or filter could be the cause, in which case remove and disassemble the pump, clean the pick-up strainer, and fit a new filter (see Chapter 4) – the strainer is not available as a spare part.

9 Idle speed

1 With the engine at normal working temperature check the engine idle speed is within the range given in the Specifications at the beginning of the Chapter.

2 Idle speed is controlled automatically. On 2016/17 models it is controlled by the idle air control valve (IACV), which adjusts a flow of air that by-passes the throttle valves in the throttle bodies. The valve is actuated by the ECM and adjusts according to information received from sensors on engine and air temperature and throttle position. When the ignition is switched ON the valve self-checks

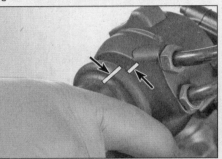

10.2 Check freeplay at grip flange

by turning through its range of movement, which you should be able to hear. On 2018-on models it is controlled through the engine management and throttle-by-wire (TBS) systems.

3 If there is a fault, a code should be indicated by the engine management system warning light (engine symbol) in the instrument display (see Chapter 4).

4 If the idle speed is not as specified, and there is no fault indicated, check the throttle cable freeplay (2016/17 models), spark plugs, air filter and the valve clearances, referring to the relevant Sections in this Chapter.

5 Next raise and support the fuel tank (see Chapter 4). Inspect the intake rubbers between the throttle bodies and the cylinder head for loose clamps or splits that could cause an air leak, causing a weak mixture. On 2016/17 models the IACV has an O-ring and the valve housing a rubber seal between it and the throttle bodies, which if deteriorated could cause an air leak – if necessary remove the valve and/or the valve housing and replace the O-ring and seal with a new one (see Chapter 4).

6 If all is good have the system checked by a Honda dealer.

10.3a Slide the rubber boot back to access the adjuster

10 Throttle system

1 Make sure the throttle grip rotates smoothly and freely from fully closed to fully open with the front wheel turned at various angles. The grip should return automatically from fully open to fully closed when released. If the throttle sticks, check and lubricate the system as described below for your model.

2016/17 models

Cable freeplay check and adjustment

2 Check for a small amount of freeplay in the cables, measured in terms of the amount of twistgrip rotation before the throttle opens, and compare the amount to that listed in the Specifications **(see illustration)**. If it's incorrect, adjust the throttle opening cable as follows.

3 Initially adjust freeplay using the adjuster at the upper end of the cable where it leaves the throttle pulley housing on the handlebar. Slide the rubber boot off the adjuster, then loosen the locknut and turn the adjuster in or out as required until the specified amount of freeplay is obtained, then retighten the locknut **(see illustrations)**.

4 If the adjuster has reached its limit of adjustment, reset it to its start point by turning it fully in, so that freeplay is at a maximum, then raise and support the fuel tank (see Chapter 4) to access the throttle body end of the cable.

5 The opening cable is the front cable in the bracket **(see illustration)**. Slacken the cable locknut on the underside of the bracket, then turn the adjuster nut up or down as required until the specified amount of freeplay is obtained, then tighten the locknut. Subsequent adjustments can be made at the throttle twistgrip end when required. If the cable cannot be adjusted as specified, replace both cables

10.3b Slacken the thin locknut and turn the adjuster as required

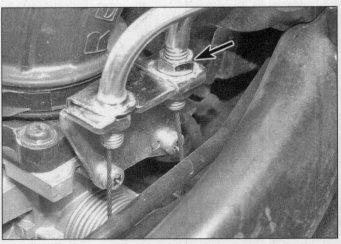

10.5 The opening cable adjuster (arrowed) at the cable lower end

11.2 After-market tool for holding the front brake lever on

11.3 Engine oil drain plugs (arrowed)

with new ones (see Chapter 4). Check that the throttle twistgrip operates smoothly and snaps shut quickly when released.

 Warning: With the engine idling turn the handlebars all the way through their travel – the idle speed should not change. If it does, the cables may be routed incorrectly. Correct this condition before riding the bike.

Cable check and twistgrip lubrication

6 If the throttle sticks, disconnect the cables (see Chapter 4 – there is no need to remove them) and check that the inner cables slide freely and easily in the outer cables. If not, remove the cables and fit new ones.

7 With the cables disconnected, make sure the throttle twistgrip rotates freely on the handlebar – dirt combined with a lack of lubrication can cause the action to be stiff. If necessary, undo the handlebar end-weight screw and remove the rubber washer, move the handguard aside and remove the the end-weight, then slide the twistgrip off the handlebar. Clean any old grease from the bar and the inside of the tube. Smear some multi-purpose grease onto the bar, then refit the twistgrip. On installation clean the threads of the screw, and apply a suitable non-permanent thread locking compound.

8 Also check the action of the throttle pulley and linkage on the throttle bodies by manually turning the pulley by hand. If the action is rough or stiff (taking into account the return spring), remove the throttle bodies and clean and check the linkage and the throttle butterflies (see Chapter 4).

9 Connect the cables (see Chapter 4).

2018-on models

10 Refer to Chapter 4 to remove the throttle twistgrip/APS (accelerator position sensor) and to check and lubricate it as described.

11 Engine oil and filter(s)

Special tool: *A filter removing tool is necessary for the engine oil filter. You can purchase one as a Honda spare part (as a kit along with the oil filter, or separately) or alternatively there are several after-market options (see Step 6).*

 Warning: Be careful when draining the oil, as the exhaust, the engine, and the oil itself can cause severe burns.

1 Consistent routine oil and filter changes are the single most important maintenance procedure you can perform. The oil not only lubricates the internal parts of the engine, transmission and clutch, but it also acts as a coolant, a cleaner, a sealant, and a protector. Because of these demands, the oil takes a terrific amount of abuse and should be replaced often with new oil of the recommended grade and type. The oil filter(s) should be changed with every other oil change.

 HAYNES HINT *Saving a little money on the difference in cost between a good oil and a cheap oil won't pay off if the engine is damaged.*

2 The bike should be upright and on level ground. Support the bike on a rear paddock stand, and tie or clamp the front brake on **(see illustration)**. Remove the sump guard (see Chapter 7).

3 Before changing the oil, warm up the engine so the oil will drain easily. There are two oil drain plugs in the sump on the underside of the engine, one at the front and one at the back on the left-hand side **(see illustration)**. The engine oil filter is on the front of the engine. On models with DCT the clutch oil filter is on the right-hand side of the engine, and should be changed along with the engine oil filter at every second oil change. The oil and filter change can be carried out with the bike on the sidestand.

4 Position a large drain tray under the engine so it will catch the oil from both drain plugs, and from the filter(s) if being changed. Unscrew the dipstick and oil filler cap from the alternator cover to vent the crankcase **(see illustrations)**.

5 Unscrew the oil drain plugs and

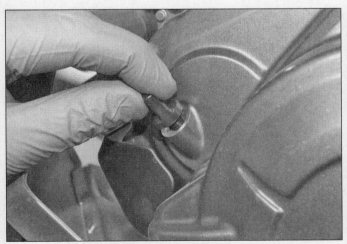

11.4a Remove the dipstick...

11.4b ...and the oil filler cap to act as a vent

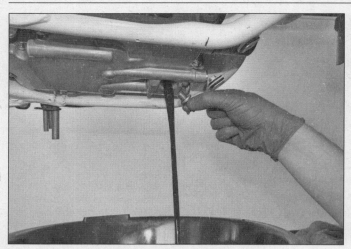

11.5a Unscrew each oil drain plug...

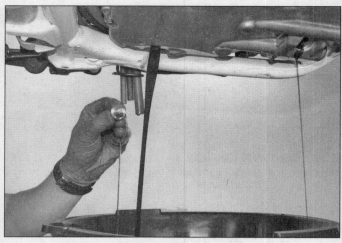

11.5b ...and allow the oil to completely drain

11.6a Unscrew the filter using a filter removing socket or strap...

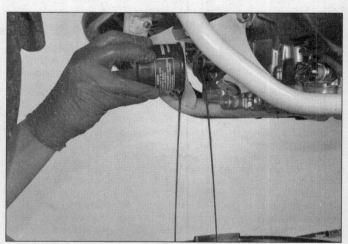

11.6b ... and allow the oil to drain

11.7a Unscrew the bolts...

11.7b..and remove the cover...

11.7c ...the spring...

11.7d ...and the filter

allow the oil to flow into the tray (see illustrations). Remove the sealing washer from each drain plug – you may have to cut them off. New washers must be used.

6 Unscrew the engine oil filter using a filter socket (one can be obtained with the new filter from Honda dealers under part No. 07HAA-PJ70101 (Europe) or 07AAA-PLCA100 (US), or otherwise there are commercially available equivalents available), filter pliers, or a filter removing strap or a chain-wrench, and tip any residual oil into the drain tray (see illustrations). The filter socket is preferable because it provides a means of tightening the new filter to the correct torque.

7 On models with DCT unscrew the clutch oil filter cover bolts and remove the cover

and the spring, then withdraw the filter (see illustrations). Remove the cover O-ring – a new one must be used.

8 When the oil has completely drained, fit the new sealing washers onto the plugs, then fit the plugs into the sump and tighten them to 30 Nm (see illustrations). Do not overtighten them as the threads in the sump are easily damaged.

9 Before fitting the engine oil filter measure the length of exposed thread on the oil filter boss to check that it didn't unscrew when removing the filter – there should be 15.5 to 16.5 mm of thread exposed (see illustration). Clean the filter mating surface on the crankcase.

10 Smear clean engine oil onto the threads and rubber seal on the new filter (see

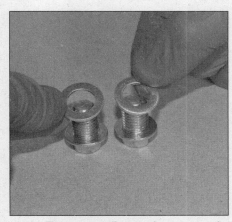

11.8a Fit a new sealing washer onto each drain plug...

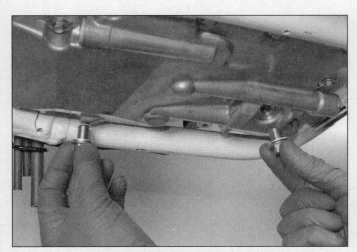

11.8b ...and fit them into the sump

11.9 Check the amount of exposed thread on the filter boss

11.10a Smear clean oil onto the seal...

11.10b ... then fit the filter and tighten it as described

11.11a Make sure the filter is the correct way round as described and shown on the filter itself

11.11b Fit the spring into the end of the filter, then fit the cover using a new O-ring (arrowed) smeared with oil

11.12a Add the specified oil...

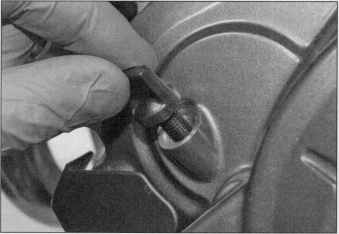

11.12b ...checking the level with the dipstick resting on the threads...

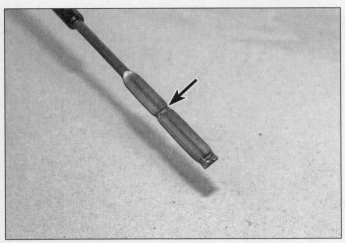

11.12c ...until the level is almost up to the upper level line (arrowed)

11.12d Make sure the O-rings are in good condition and correctly seated

illustration). Thread the filter onto the engine and tighten it to 26 Nm using the filter socket if available, or tighten the filter as tight as possible by hand, or by the number of turns specified on the filter itself or its packaging **(see illustration)**. Do not use a strap or chain-type filter removing tool to tighten the filter as you will damage it.

11 On models with DCT fit a new O-ring smeared with oil onto the clutch oil filter cover. Fit the new clutch oil filter with the rubbered end facing in and the OUTSIDE mark facing out – fitting it the wrong way round will cause severe damage because the oil will not flow as it should **(see illustration)**. Fit the spring and the cover and tighten the bolts to 12 Nm **(see illustrations)**.

12 Refill the engine via the filler hole (not the dipstick hole) using the recommended type and amount of oil (see Specifications) **(see illustration)**. Before you have added all the oil, and with the motorcycle held upright, insert the dipstick so that the cap threads rest on the engine (do not screw it in), then remove it and check the oil mark, and continue to add oil and check the dipstick until the oil is up to the upper level line on the disptick **(see illustrations)**. Check the condition of the O-rings on the dipstick and filler cap and fit new ones if necessary, then thread them into the cover **(see illustration)**.

13 Start the engine and let it run for two or three minutes, checking that the oil pressure light extinguishes after a few seconds. Turn the engine off, wait a few minutes, then check the oil level again. As the oil is distributed around the engine and into the filter(s) you may need to add more to bring the level back between the upper and lower level lines.

14 Check around the drain plugs and the engine oil filter, and on DCT models the clutch oil filter cover, for leaks. If leaks are evident, check that the plugs and filter/filter cover are correctly tightened using new washers and a lubricated seal and O-ring.

HAYNES HiNT *Check the old oil carefully – if it is very metallic coloured, then the engine is experiencing wear from break-in (new engine) or from insufficient lubrication. If there are flakes or chips of metal in the oil, then something is drastically wrong internally and the engine will have to be disassembled for inspection and repair. If there are pieces of fibre-like material in the oil, the clutch is experiencing excessive wear and should be checked.*

15 Install the sump guard (see Chapter 7).
16 The old oil drained from the engine cannot be re-used and should be disposed of properly. Check with your local refuse disposal company, disposal facility or environmental agency to see whether they will accept the used oil for recycling. Don't pour used oil into drains or onto the ground.

Note: It is illegal and anti-social to dump oil down the drain. To find the location of your local oil recycling bankin the UK, call 03708 506 506 or visit www.oilbankline.org.uk

OIL CARE FOLLOW THE CODE

12 Cooling system

Check

⚠ *Warning: The engine must be cool before beginning this procedure.*

1 Check the coolant level in the reservoir (see *Pre-ride checks*).

2 Remove the fairing side panels (see Chapter 7).
3 Examine each rubber coolant hose along its entire length. Look for cracks, abrasions and other damage. Squeeze each hose at various points to see whether they are dried out or hard **(see illustration)**. They should feel firm, yet pliable, and return to their original shape when released. If necessary, replace them with new ones (see Chapter 3).
4 Check for evidence of leaks at each cooling system hose connection, and around the outlet union on the back of the engine, the pipe into the top of the clutch cover, and the thermostat housing on the left-hand end of the cylinder head. If a leak is found tighten the hose clamp(s), union, pipe or thermostat bolts as required carefully to prevent future leaks. If necessary remove the union, pipe or thermostat cover and replace the O-ring or seal with a new one (see Chapter 3).
5 To prevent leakage of coolant from the cooling system to the lubrication system and vice versa, two seals are fitted on the pump shaft. The coolant seal on the water pump side is of the mechanical type and bears on the rear face of the impeller. The oil seal, which is mounted behind the mechanical seal, is of the normal feathered lip type. On the

12.3 Check all the coolant hoses as described

12.5 Check the pump drain hole (arrowed) for signs of leakage

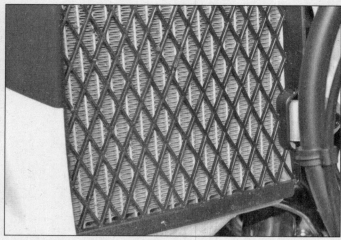

12.7 Check the radiator fins for blockages and straighten bent fins using a small screwdriver

underside of the pump housing in the clutch cover there is a drain hole **(see illustration)**. If either seal fails, the drain allows the coolant or oil to escape. If on inspection the drain shows signs of continuous leakage, particularly with the engine running, remove the pump and replace it with a new one (see Chapter 3) – it comes as an assembly and the seals are not available separately. Honda states that a small amount of coolant weeping is normal, so you may have to decide for yourself the difference between that and continuous leakage – if in doubt seek the advice of a Honda dealer.

6 Check the radiators for leaks and other damage. Leaks in the radiator leave tell-tale scale deposits or coolant stains on the outside of the core below the leak. If leaks are in noted in either radiator remove it (see Chapter 3) and have it repaired, or fit a new one – do not use a liquid leak-stop compound to try to repair leaks.

7 Check the radiator fins for mud, dirt and insects, which may impede the flow of air through it **(see illustration)**. If the fins are blocked, remove the radiator (see Chapter 3) and clean it using water or low pressure compressed air directed through the fins from the inner side of the radiator. If the fins are bent or distorted, straighten them carefully

12.8 Remove the pressure cap as described

with a small flat-bladed screwdriver. If the airflow is restricted by bent or damaged fins over more than 20% of the radiator's surface area, replace the radiator with a new one.

⚠ *Warning: Do not remove the pressure cap from the radiator when the engine is hot. It is good practice to cover the cap with a heavy cloth and turn the cap slowly anti-clockwise. If you hear a hissing sound (indicating that there is still pressure in the system), wait until it stops, then continue turning the cap as described until it can be removed.*

8 Refer to the **Warning,** then remove the pressure cap from the filler neck by turning it anti-clockwise to the first stop, then pressing it down and turning it further to release it **(see illustration)**.

9 Check the condition of the coolant in the system. If it is rust-coloured or if accumulations of scale are visible, drain, flush and refill the system with new coolant (see below). Check the antifreeze content of the coolant with an antifreeze hydrometer – a 50% content should give a reading of 1.084 at 5°C to 1.074 at 25°C, varying accordingly in between. The system must have the correct coolant mixture (see Specifications) – if the coolant is weak (too little anti-freeze) there will not be adequate protection against freezing and corrosion, and if it is too strong the ability to cool the engine is reduced. If the hydrometer indicates an incorrect mixture, drain, flush and refill the system (see below).

10 The function of the pressure cap is crucial to the correct running of the cooling system. Check the cap seal for cracks and other damage. If the coolant level consistently drops and/or the bike overheats, and no evidence of leaks can be found, have the cap pressure checked by a Honda dealer. If a new cap does not cure the problem have the entire system pressure checked by a dealer.

11 Fit the cap by turning it clockwise until

it reaches the first stop then push down on it and continue turning until it can turn no further. Start the engine and let it reach normal operating temperature, then check for leaks again. As the coolant temperature increases, the electric fans (one is mounted on the back of each radiator) should come on automatically and the temperature should begin to drop. If not, refer to Chapter 3 and check the fans and fan circuit.

12 Install the fairing side panels (see Chapter 7).

Coolant change

⚠ *Warning: Allow the engine to cool completely before changing the coolant. Don't allow anti-freeze to come into contact with your skin or the painted surfaces of the motorcycle. Rinse off spills immediately with plenty of water. Anti-freeze is highly toxic if ingested. Never leave anti-freeze lying around in an open container or in puddles on the floor; children and pets are attracted by its sweet smell and may drink it. Check with local authorities (councils) about disposing anti-freeze – many have collection centres that dispose it safely. Anti-freeze is also combustible, so don't store it near open flames.*

13 To drain and fill the cooling system the bike should be upright and on level ground. Support the bike on a rear paddock stand, and tie or clamp the front brake on **(see illustration 11.2)**.

Draining

14 Remove the right-hand fairing side panel (see Chapter 7).

15 On models with DCT remove the clutch EOP sensor cover **(see illustration)**.

16 Remove the pressure cap from the radiator filler neck by turning it anti-clockwise until it reaches a stop **(see illustration 12.8)**. If you hear a hissing sound (indicating there is still pressure in the system), wait until it stops.

12.15 Undo the screws and remove the cover

12.17a Unscrew the bolt (arrowed)...

12.17b ...and allow the coolant to drain

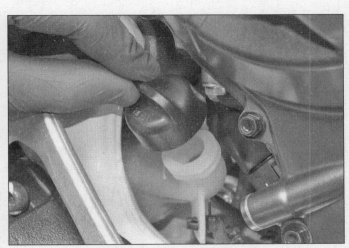

12.18a Open the reservoir cap

12.18b Draw the contents out of the reservoir

Now press down on the cap and continue turning the cap until it can be removed. Also remove the coolant reservoir cap.

17 Position a suitable container beneath the water pump on the right-hand side of the engine. Unscrew the drain bolt and allow the coolant to completely drain **(see illustrations)**. A new sealing washer must be fitted.

18 Open the reservoir cap **(see illustration)**. Draw the coolant out of the reservoir using a syphon pump or syringe **(see illustration)**. Mop up any spilt coolant.

Flushing

19 Flush the system with clean tap water by inserting a hose in the filler neck. Allow the water to run through the system until it is clear and flows out cleanly. If the radiators are extremely corroded, remove them (see Chapter 3) and have them cleaned by a specialist. Also flush the reservoir, then draw the water out.

12.20 Use a new sealing washer

12.21a Fill the system as described

12.21b Fill the reservoir to the UPPER level line

12.26 Make sure the collars are fitted

Refilling

20 Fit the drain bolt using a new sealing washer and tighten it to 13 Nm **(see illustration)**.

21 Fill the system to the base of the radiator filler neck with the specified coolant mixture **(see illustration)**. Pour the coolant in slowly to minimise the amount of air entering the system. Fill the reservoir to the UPPER level line, then fit the cap **(see illustration)**.

22 Start the engine and allow it to idle for 2 to 3 minutes. Flick the throttle twistgrip part open 3 or 4 times, so that the engine speed rises to approximately 4000 rpm, then stop the engine. Any air trapped in the system should bleed back to the radiator filler neck.

23 If necessary, top up the coolant level to the base of the radiator filler neck, then fit the pressure cap. If necessary top up the reservoir to the UPPER level line, then fit the cap.

24 Start the engine and allow it to reach normal operating temperature, then shut it off. Let the engine cool then remove the pressure cap as described above. Check that the coolant level is still up to the base of the radiator filler neck. If it's low, add the specified mixture until it reaches the base of the filler neck. Refit the cap.

25 Check the coolant level in the reservoir and top up if necessary. Check the system for leaks.

26 On models with DCT check the collars are in place in the EOP sensor cover **(see illustration)**. Fit the cover **(see illustration 12.15)**.

27 Install the fairing side panel (see Chapter 7).

28 Do not dispose of the old coolant by pouring it down the drain. Instead pour it into a heavy plastic container, cap it tightly and take it into an authorised disposal site or service station.

13 Emission control systems

PAIR (Pulse secondary air supply) system

1 To reduce the amount of unburned hydrocarbons released in the exhaust gases, a pulse secondary air supply (PAIR) system is fitted. The system consists of the control valve (mounted above the valve cover on the top of the engine), the reed valves (fitted in the valve cover) and the hoses between the air filter housing, the control valve and the reed valves. The control valve is actuated electronically by the ECM/PCM.

2 Under normal operating conditions, the valve allows filtered air to be drawn through the reed valves and cylinder head passages and into the exhaust ports. The air mixes with the exhaust gases, causing any unburned particles of the fuel in the mixture to be burnt in the exhaust port/pipes. This process changes a considerable amount of hydrocarbons and carbon monoxide into relatively harmless carbon dioxide and water. The reed valves in the valve cover are fitted to prevent the flow of exhaust gases back up the cylinder head passages and into the air filter housing.

3 The system is not adjustable and requires little maintenance. For full visual access of all the components remove the air filter housing (see Chapter 4).

4 Check that the PAIR system hoses are not kinked or pinched, are in good condition and are securely connected at each end **(see illustration)**. Fit new hoses if they are cracked or split or have deteriorated.

5 Refer to Chapter 4 for further information on the system and for checks if it is believed to be faulty.

EVAP system

6 On models fitted with an EVAP system check all the breather hoses between the fuel tank, the EVAP system canister, the purge valve and the throttle body for loose connections, cracks and deterioration, and fit new ones if necessary. Refer to Chapter 4 for access to the components and more information on the EVAP system.

14 Headlight aim

Note: *An improperly adjusted headlight may cause problems for oncoming traffic or provide poor, unsafe illumination of the road ahead. Before adjusting the headlight aim, be sure to consult with local traffic laws and regulations – for UK models refer to MOT Test Checks in the Reference section.*

1 The headlight beam can adjusted vertically.

Before making any adjustment, check that the tyre pressures are correct and the suspension is adjusted as required. Make any adjustments to the headlight aim with the machine off its stand and on level ground, with the fuel tank half full and with an assistant sitting on the seat. If the bike is usually ridden with a passenger on the back, have a second assistant to do this.

2 The adjuster knob is positioned centrally on the back of the headlight unit **(see illustration)**. To move the beam up turn the knob anti-clockwise. To move the beam down turn the knob clockwise **(see illustration)**.

15 Sidestand and starter interlock circuit

1 Check the stand springs for damage and distortion **(see illustration)**. The springs must be capable of retracting the stand fully and

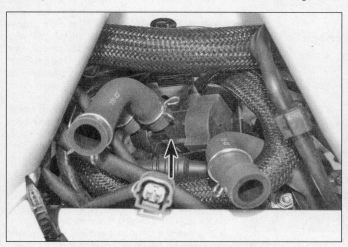

13.4 PAIR control valve (arrowed) and hoses

14.2a Headlight beam height adjuster (arrowed)

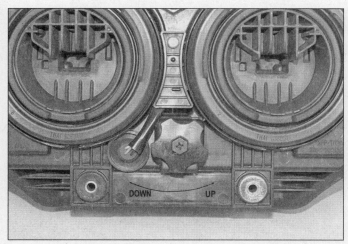

14.2b View of adjuster showing directional arrows

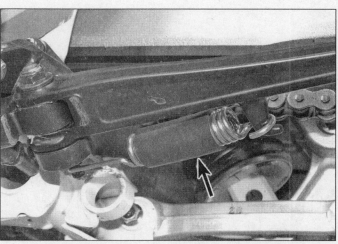

15.1 Check the sidestand springs (arrowed)

holding it retracted when the motorcycle is in use – if the springs do not hold the stand fully retracted fit a new pair.

2 Lubricate the stand pivot regularly (Section 19).

3 Check the stand and its mount for bends and cracks. Stands can often be repaired by welding.

4 Check the operation of the starter interlock circuit on standard transmission models as follows:
● Turn the ignition on. Make sure the engine stop switch is in the RUN position and the transmission is in neutral, then retract the stand and start the engine. Pull in the clutch lever and select a gear. Keeping the clutch lever pulled in, extend the sidestand. The engine should stop as the sidestand is extended.
● Make sure the engine is in neutral and the sidestand is down, then start the engine. Pull the clutch lever in and select a gear. The engine should cut out.
● Check that when the sidestand is down the engine can only be started if the transmission is in neutral, and when the sidestand is up and the transmission is in gear the engine can only be started if the clutch lever is pulled in.

5 Check the operation of the starter interlock circuit on DCT models as follows:
● Turn the ignition on and make sure the engine stop switch is in the RUN position. The N neutral light in the instruments should be on. With the sidestand down it shouldn't be possible to select gear.
● With the sidestand up, engine running and N neutral light on, select gear. Now lower the sidestand – the engine should cut out.

6 If the circuit does not operate as described, check the sidestand switch, gear position/ neutral switch, clutch switch and diode block, and the circuit between them (see Chapter 8).

16 Suspension

1 The suspension components must be maintained in top operating condition to ensure rider safety. Loose, worn or damaged suspension parts decrease the motorcycle's stability and control.

Front suspension check

2 While standing alongside the motorcycle, apply the front brake and push on the handlebars to compress the forks several times (see illustration). See if they move up-and-down smoothly without binding. If binding is felt, the forks should be disassembled and inspected (see Chapter 5).

3 Inspect each fork inner tube for scratches, corrosion and pitting in the area of travel through the seals, which will cause seal failure, and for oil leakage, which means the seal has failed. If the corrosion damage is excessive, new inner tubes should be fitted (see Chapter 5), or the originals re-chromed using hard chrome. If leakage is evident, new seals must be fitted (see Chapter 5).

4 Check the tightness of all suspension nuts and bolts to be sure none have worked loose, referring to the torque settings specified at the beginning of Chapter 5.

Rear suspension check

5 Inspect the rear shock absorber for fluid leakage. If leakage is found, fit a new shock (see Chapter 5).

6 With the aid of an assistant to support the bike, compress the rear suspension several times (see illustration). It should move up-and-down freely without binding. If any binding is felt, the worn or faulty component must be identified and checked. The problem could be due to either the shock absorber or its bush, the suspension linkage bearings, or the swingarm bearings.

7 Support the bike using an auxiliary stand that does not take the weight of the bike through any part of the rear suspension. Grab the swingarm and rock it from side-to-side (see illustration) – there should be no discernible movement at the rear.

8 Next, grasp the top of the rear wheel and pull it upwards (see illustration) – there should be no discernible freeplay before the shock absorber begins to compress.

9 If there's a little movement or a slight clicking can be heard, check the swingarm pivot bolt nut is tight, referring to the torque

16.2 Check the feel of the forks by pumping them

16.6 Check the feel of the rear suspension by pushing down on the back of the bike

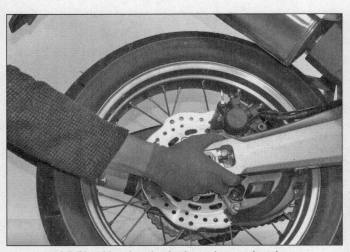

16.7 Checking for play in the swingarm bearings

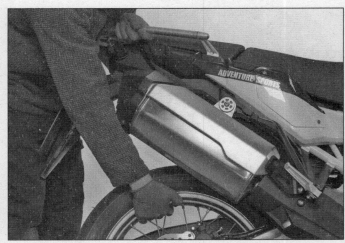

16.8 Checking for play in the swingarm and suspension linkage bearings and the shock mounts

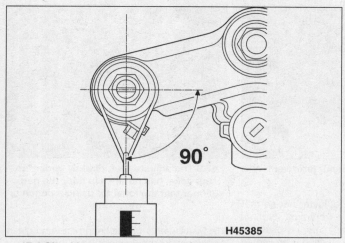

17.4 Checking steering head bearing pre-load using a spring balance

17.5 Feeling for play in the steering head bearings

setting in Chapter 5, and re-check for movement. Also check the shock absorber and suspension linkage mounting bolts/nuts. If there is still some noise or freeplay after everything has been correctly tightened then there is either a worn bush or bearing in the shock absorber or suspension linkage mountings, or worn swingarm bearings. The worn components must be identified and new ones fitted (see Chapter 5).

10 To make an accurate assessment of the suspension bearings, remove the rear wheel (see Chapter 6) and the bolt securing the suspension linkage to the swingarm (see Chapter 5). Grasp the rear of the swingarm with one hand and place your other hand at the junction of the swingarm and the frame. Try to move the rear of the swingarm from side-to-side. Any wear (play) in the bushes should be felt as movement between the swingarm and the frame at the front. If there is any play the swingarm will be felt to move forward and backward at the front (not from side-to-side). If there is any play in the swingarm, remove it for inspection (see Chapter 5). Also check for movement between the suspenion linkage components, the shock absorber, and the frame.

11 If necessary remove the suspension components and check for corrosion and wear and failure of the seals, referring to Chapter 5 for details, and clean and re-grease or fit new components as required.

Front fork oil change

12 Although there is no set interval for changing the fork oil, the oil will degrade over a period of time and lose its damping qualities. Refer to Chapter 5 for details of front fork removal, oil draining and refilling. The forks do not need to be completely disassembled to change the oil.

Rear suspension bearing lubrication

13 Although there is no set interval for

re-greasing the suspension bearings, over a considerable mileage, and if the bike is often ridden in wet conditions (or through incorrect use of jet washers) the seals may fail and allow dirt and water to get in, in which case the grease in the bearings will be washed out or will harden.

14 Remove the suspension linkage and swingarm and clean and re-grease the bearings as necessary (see Chapter 5).

17 Steering head bearings

Freeplay check and adjustment

1 Steering head bearings can become dented, rough or loose during normal use of the machine. In extreme cases, worn or loose steering head bearings can cause steering wobble – a condition that is potentially dangerous.

Check

2 Support the bike on a rear paddock stand then raise the front wheel off the ground using a jack under the sump guard, with a piece of wood between them to spread the load. Always make sure that the bike is properly supported and secure.

3 Point the front wheel straight-ahead and slowly move the handlebars from lock to lock. Any dents, tightness or roughness in the bearing races will be felt – if the bearings are too tight the bars will not move smoothly and freely. Again point the wheel straight-ahead, and tap the front of the wheel to one side. The wheel should 'fall' under its own weight to the limit of its lock, indicating that the bearings are not too tight (take into account the restriction that cables, hoses and wiring may have). Check for similar movement to the other side.

4 If a spring balance (graduated zero to 30N) is available, attach one end around the

fork tube and hold it straight out to the front **(see illustration)**. With the steering straight-ahead, pull on the balance and check the reading at which the handlebars start to turn. If the reading is below the minimum value specified in the pre-load range given in the Specifications at the beginning of the Chapter, the steering head is too loose, if the reading is above the maximum value specified the steering head is too tight. If the steering doesn't perform as described, and it's not due to the resistance of cables or hoses, then the bearings should be adjusted as described below.

5 Next, grasp the bottom of the forks and gently pull and push them forward and backward **(see illustration)**. Any looseness or freeplay in the steering head bearings will be felt as front-to-rear movement of the forks. If play is felt, adjust the bearings as described below.

HAYNES HiNT *Make sure you are not mistaking any movement between the bike and stand/jack, or between the stand/jack and the ground, for freeplay in the bearings. Do not pull and push the forks too hard – a gentle movement is all that is needed. Freeplay between the fork tubes due to worn bushes can also be misinterpreted as steering head bearing play – do not confuse the two.*

Adjustment

Special tool: *Either the Honda special tool (part No. 07916-KA50100), equivalent peg spanner, or a punch or other drift that will locate in the notches in the adjuster nut is necessary for this procedure – see Step 9. The advantage of the Honda tool or a peg spanner is that you can apply the specified torque setting to the adjuster nut, but it is not*

17.7 Top yoke fork clamp bolts (arrowed)

17.8 Steering stem nut (arrowed)

17.9 The adjuster nut, directly under the top yoke, has notches in it for the peg spanner that are ideal for using a punch or other drift

essential, especially if you have the spring balance mentioned in Step 4. The advantage of just using a drift is that there is no need to displace the top yoke. Note that access for using a C-spanner is restricted.

6 Remove the right-hand inner panel cover (see Chapter 7). Cover the fuel tank in plenty of rag.

7 Slacken the fork clamp bolts in the top yoke, and if you are using the Honda tool or alternative peg spanner fully unscrew the right-hand clamp bolts to free the wiring bracket from the yoke **(see illustration)**.

8 Slacken the steering stem nut **(see illustration)**. If you are using the Honda tool or alternative peg spanner remove the nut and gently ease the top yoke/handlebar assembly up and off the forks and support it on some rag.

9 Slacken the adjuster nut slightly until pressure is just released **(see illustration)**. If the Honda tool or a peg spanner is available, tighten the adjuster nut to 15 Nm, then turn the steering from lock-to-lock five times, then reapply the same torque setting to the nut. If the tool is not available, tighten the adjuster nut using a drift until all freeplay is just taken up, yet the steering is able to move freely (as described in the checks in Steps 3 and 5).

The object is to set the adjuster nut so that the bearings are under a very light loading, just enough to remove any freeplay (Step 5), but not so much that the steering is prevented from moving freely from side-to-side (Step 3). If the torque setting is applied check the physical feel as described as well. If you have the spring balance (see Step 4), set the adjuster nut so that the steering starts to move at around the mid-point of the pre-load range given in the Specifications at the beginning of the Chapter.

Caution: Take great care not to apply excessive pressure because this will cause premature failure of the bearings.

10 If the bearings cannot be correctly adjusted, disassemble the steering head and check the bearings and races (see Chapter 5).

11 If displaced slide the top yoke down the forks. Fit the steering stem nut and tighten it to 100 Nm. Tighten the fork clamp bolts to 22 Nm.

12 Check the bearing adjustment as described above and re-adjust if necessary.

13 Install the inner panel cover (Chapter 7).

Lubrication

14 Over a considerable time the grease in the bearings will be dispersed or will harden allowing the ingress of dirt and water.

15 Disassemble the steering head and clean and re-grease the bearings (see Chapter 5).

18 Wheels, tyres and wheel bearings

Wheels

1 Visually check the spokes for damage and corrosion **(see illustration)**. Early models have steel spokes; from 2018-on stainless steel spokes are fitted. A broken or bent spoke must be replaced with a new one immediately because the load taken by it will be transferred to adjacent spokes which may in turn fail. Check the tension in each spoke by tapping each one lightly with a screwdriver and noting the sound produced – each should make the same sound of the correct pitch – properly tensioned spokes will make a sharp pinging sound, loose ones will produce a lower pitch dull sound, and tight ones will be higher pitched. If a spoke needs adjustment turn the adjuster nut at the rim using a spoke adjustment tool or open-ended spanner **(see illustration)** – Honda specify a torque setting

18.1a Check the spokes for corrosion

18.1b Adjusting the tension of a spoke

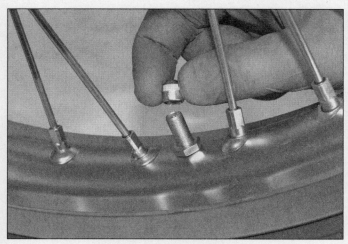

18.3 Make sure a cap is fitted

18.6 Checking the wheel bearings

of 3.7 Nm for the spoke nuts, but without special tools and a low range torque wrench you will have to do it by feel and sound.

2 Unevenly tensioned spokes will promote rim/hub misalignment and excessive runout – refer to information on wheel runout in Chapter 6 and seek the advice of a dealer or wheel building specialist if the wheel needs realigning, which it may well do if many spokes are unevenly tensioned. Check that any wheel balance weights are fixed firmly to the wheel rim. If you suspect that a weight has fallen off, have the wheel rebalanced by a motorcycle tyre specialist.

Tyres

3 Check the tyre pressures, condition and tread depth – see *Pre-ride checks*. Make sure the valve stem cap is in place and tight **(see illustration)**.

Wheel bearings

4 Wheel bearings will wear over a considerable mileage and should be checked periodically to avoid handling problems.

5 Support the motorcycle upright using a paddock stand or similar so that the wheel being checked is off the ground.

6 Check for any play in the bearings by pushing and pulling the wheel against the hub **(see illustration)**. When checking the front wheel turn the handlebars to full lock on one side and hold the wheel against the lock. Also spin the wheel and check that it turns smoothly and without any grating noises (bearing in mind that the brakes and final drive chain make some noise – do not confuse them).

7 If any play is detected in the hub, or if the wheel does not rotate smoothly (and this is not due to brake or transmission drag), remove the wheel and check the bearings for wear or damage (see Chapter 6).

Rear wheel cush drive rubbers

8 Have an assistant apply the rear brake and check for any rotational play between the sprocket coupling and the wheel, which indicates worn cush drive rubbers. Remove the wheel and fit new rubbers if necessary (see Chapter 6).

19 General lubrication

1 Since the controls and various other components of a motorcycle are exposed to the elements, they should be checked and lubricated periodically to ensure safe and trouble-free operation.

2 The footrest pivots, clutch and brake lever pivots, brake pedal and gearchange lever pivots and linkage, and sidestand pivot should be lubricated frequently. In order for the lubricant to be applied where it will do the most good, the component should be disassembled and cleaned (see Chapter 5). The lubricant recommended by Honda for each application is listed at the beginning of this Chapter. If an aerosol lubricant is being used, it can be applied to the pivot joint gaps and will usually work its way into the areas where friction occurs, so less disassembly of the component is needed (however it is always better to do so and clean off all corrosion, dirt and old lubricant first). If motor oil or light grease is being used, apply it sparingly as it may attract dirt (which could cause the controls to bind or wear at an accelerated rate).

20 Nuts, bolts and screws

1 Since vibration of the machine tends to loosen fasteners, all nuts, bolts, screws, etc. should be periodically checked for tightness.

2 Pay particular attention to the following:

- Brake caliper and master cylinder mounting bolts
- Brake hose banjo bolts and caliper bleed valves
- Brake disc bolts and ABS wheel speed sensor pulse ring bolts
- Exhaust system bolts/nuts
- Engine oil drain plugs and oil filter, and clutch oil filter cover bolts on models with DCT
- Engine mounting bolts/nuts
- Brake and clutch lever pivot bolt and nut
- Handlebar clamp bolts and handlebar holder nuts
- Footrest bracket bolts
- Sidestand bolt/nut
- Shock absorber and suspension linkage mounting bolts/nuts
- Swingarm pivot bolt nut
- Front fork clamp bolts
- Steering stem nut
- Front axle nut
- Rear axle nut
- Front sprocket bolt and rear sprocket nuts
- Chain adjuster locknuts

3 If a torque wrench is available, use it along with the torque settings given in the Specifications at the beginning of this and other Chapters.

21 Valve clearances

Special tool: *A set of feeler gauges is necessary for this job* **(see illustration 21.7).**
Note: *After checking the valve clearances service the primary spark plugs (Section 22) before installing the ignition coil assembly, as access is easier with them removed.*

Check

1 The engine must be completely cool for this maintenance procedure.

2 Remove the valve cover (see Chapter 2).

21.3a No. 1 cylinder intake valves (A) and exhaust valve rocker arms (B)

21.3b No. 2 cylinder intake valves (A) and exhaust valve rocker arms (B)

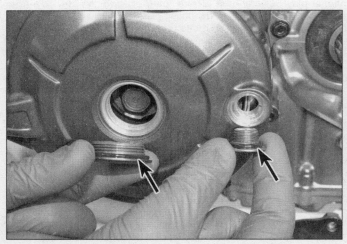

21.4 Unscrew the crankshaft end and timing inspection caps – check the O-rings (arrowed)

21.6a Turn the engine anti-clockwise using the bolt...

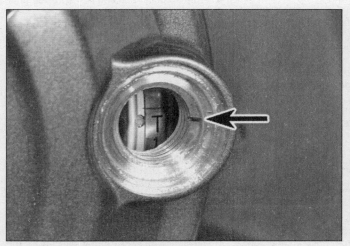

21.6b ...until the line next to the T1 mark aligns with the notch (arrowed)...

21.6c ...and the camshaft sprocket marks are as shown

21.7 Checking the No. 1 intake valves – insert the feeler gauge between the cam and the follower as shown

21.8a Turn the engine 270° until the line next to the T2 mark aligns with the notch...

21.8b ...and the camshaft sprocket marks are as shown

Remove the secondary spark plugs (Section 22).

3 Make a chart or sketch of all valve positions so that a note of each clearance can be made against the relevant valve. The left-hand cylinder is No. 1 and the right-hand No. 2. The intake valves are on the back of the cylinder head and the exhaust valves are on the front **(see illustrations)**.

4 Unscrew the crankshaft end-cap and timing inspection cap from the alternator cover **(see illustration)**. Check the condition of the O-rings and get new ones if necessary.

5 To check the valve clearances the engine must be turned so that the valve being checked is closed. The engine can be turned using a socket on the alternator rotor bolt, turning it in an anti-clockwise direction only **(see illustration 21.6a)**.

6 Turn the engine anti-clockwise until the line next to the T1 mark on the rotor aligns with the static timing mark, which is a notch in the inspection hole rim, and the lines on the

camshaft sprocket are flush with the cylinder head top surface, and the punch mark on the sprocket is visible in the position shown **(see illustrations)**. If the punch mark is not visible (i.e. is opposite its required position), rotate the engine anti-clockwise one full turn (360°) until the line next to the T1 mark again aligns with the static timing mark. The sprocket marks will now be positioned correctly.

7 With the engine in this position, check the clearances on the No. 1 (left) cylinder intake valves (there are two valves per cylinder) **(see illustration 21.3a)**. Insert a feeler gauge of the same thickness as the correct valve clearance (see Specifications) between the cam lobe and the follower of each valve and check that it is a firm sliding fit – you should feel a slight drag when the you pull the gauge out **(see illustration)**. If not, use the feeler gauges to obtain the exact clearance. Record the measured clearances on the chart.

8 Now turn the engine 270° anti-clockwise until the line next to the T2 mark on the

rotor aligns with the static timing mark and the punch mark on the camshaft sprocket is facing forward and in line with the cylinder head top surface **(see illustrations)**.

9 With the engine in this position, check the clearances on the No. 2 (right) cylinder intake valves **(see illustration 21.3b)** using the method described in Step 7 **(see illustration)**. Also check the clearances on the No. 2 (right) cylinder exhaust valves by inserting a gauge of the same thickness as the correct valve clearance (see Specifications) between the cam lobe and the rocker arm roller of each valve and check that it is a firm sliding fit – you should feel a slight drag when the you pull the gauge out **(see illustration)**. If not, use the feeler gauges to obtain the exact clearance. Record the measured clearances on the chart.

10 Now turn the engine 252.5° anti-clockwise until the line next to the E1 mark on the rotor aligns with the static timing mark and the triangular mark on the camshaft sprocket is

21.9a Checking the No. 2 intake valves – insert the feeler gauge between the cam and the follower as shown

21.9b Checking the No. 2 exhaust valves – insert the feeler gauge between the cam and the roller as shown

21.10a Turn the engine 252.5° until the line next to the E1 mark aligns with the notch...

21.10b ...and the camshaft sprocket marks are as shown

facing forward and in line with the cylinder head top surface **(see illustrations)**.

11 With the engine in this position, check the clearances on the No. 1 (left) cylinder exhaust valves using the method described in Step 9 for the No. 2 exhaust valves **(see illustration)**.

12 When all clearances have been measured and charted, identify whether the clearance on any valve falls outside the specified range, in which case it must be adjusted as follows.

Intake valve clearance adjustment

13 If any intake valve clearance requires adjustment the shim that sits between the follower and the valve must be replaced with one of a thickness that will restore the correct clearance. To replace a shim the remove the camshaft (see Chapter 2). Place rags over the spark plug holes and the cam chain tunnel to prevent a shim from dropping into the engine on removal.

14 Using a magnet if available, remove the cam follower of the valve in question, then remove the shim from inside the follower **(see illustrations)**. If it is not in the follower, pick it out of the top of the valve using either a magnet, a small screwdriver with a dab of grease on it (the shim will stick to the grease), or a screwdriver and a pair of pliers **(see**

illustration 21.17). Do not allow the shim to fall into the engine.

15 Measure the thickness of the shim using a micrometer. Its size should be marked on the upper face of the shim (though it could have rubbed off) – a shim marked 175 is 1.75 mm thick, but the shim should measured anyway to allow for wear **(see illustration)**.

16 Calculate the required replacement shim by using the formula $a = (b - c) + d$, where a is the required replacement shim size, b is the measured valve clearance, c is the specified valve clearance, and d is the existing shim thickness. For example:

The measured clearance of an exhaust valve is 0.35 mm, so $b = 0.35$

The specified clearance range for an exhaust valve is 0.22 to 0.24 mm, the mid-point being 0.23 mm, so $c = 0.23$

The thickness of the existing shim is (say) 2.0 mm, so $d = 2$

Therefore, the required replacement shim $a = 0.35 - 0.23 + 2.0$ ($a = 2.12$ mm). The nearest available size to this is 2.125 mm (Step 17).

Note: *If the required replacement shim is greater than 2.450 mm (the largest available), the valve is probably not seating correctly due to a build-up of carbon deposits, and the valve*

and its seat should be checked and cleaned (see Chapter 2).

17 Shims are available in 0.025 mm increments from 1.200 mm to 2.450 mm. A size mark should be stamped on one face of the shim – a shim marked 175 is 1.75 mm thick. Obtain the replacement shim, then fit it into the recess in the top of the valve spring retainer with the size mark facing up **(see illustration)**.

18 Check that the shim is correctly seated, then lubricate the follower with engine oil, and fit it onto the valve **(see illustration)**. Repeat the process for any other intake valves until the clearances are correct, then install the camshaft (see Chapter 2).

19 Rotate the crankshaft (anti-clockwise as viewed from the left-hand side **(see illustration 21.6a)**) several turns to seat the new shim(s), then check the clearances again.

Exhaust valve clearance adjustment

20 If any exhaust valve clearance requires adjustment, slacken the locknut on the adjuster in the rocker arm and turn the adjuster as required using long-nose pliers until the feeler gauge is a sliding fit between the cam lobe and the rocker arm roller **(see illustrations)**. Hold the adjuster and tighten

21.11 Checking the No. 1 exhaust valves – insert the feeler gauge between the cam and the roller as shown

21.14a Lift the follower off using a magnet...

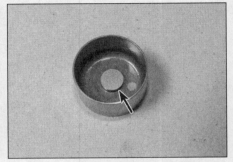

21.14b ...and remove the shim (arrowed) from inside the follower

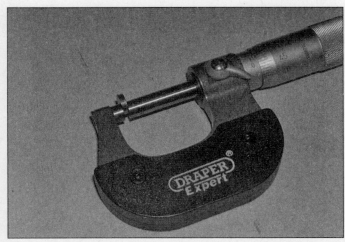

21.15 Check the thickness of the shim using a micrometer

21.17 Seat the shim in its recess...

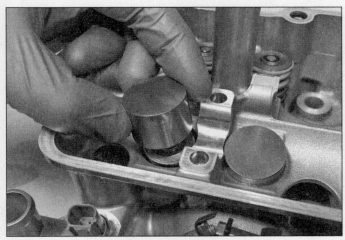

21.18 ...then fit the follower

21.20a Exhaust valve clearance adjuster locknut (A) and adjuster screw (B)

21.20b Slacken the locknut...

21.20c ...and turn the adjuster as required

22.1a No. 1 cylinder primary spark plug (A) and secondary spark plug (B)

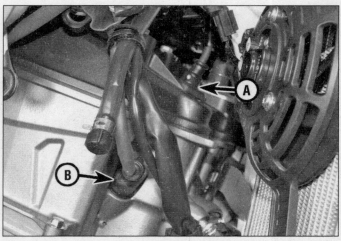

22.1b No. 2 cylinder primary spark plug (A) and secondary spark plug (B)

22.2a Release everything from the shroud...

22.2b ...then remove the shroud

the locknut, then check the clearance hasn't changed.

Installation

21 Install the spark plugs (Section 22). Install the valve cover (see Chapter 2).
22 Fit the crankshaft end and timing inspection caps, using new O-rings if required, and smear the O-rings with oil and the cap threads with grease **(see illustration 21.4)**. Tighten the end cap to 8 Nm and the inspection cap to 6 Nm.

22 Spark plugs

Special tool: *A wire type spark plug gauge is necessary for measuring the spark plug gap – do not use a blade type feeler gauge* **(see illustration 22.8b).**
Note: *All models are equipped with plugs that have an iridium coated centre electrode.*

The plugs must be treated differently to conventional plugs. Do not substitute them with conventional plugs.
Note: *Access to the primary spark plugs is restricted and difficult – if you are only servicing the spark plugs follow the procedure below and access the primary plugs by displacing the radiators. If however you are doing a complete service you will also be doing the valve clearances, in which case accessing the primary plugs is a lot easier from the top after removing the ignition coil assembly for access to the valve cover – see Section 21.*
1 Each cylinder has two spark plugs, a primary (main) plug in the top of the cylinder head and a secondary (sub) plug in the side **(see illustrations)**. In the wiring diagrams at the end of this manual the coils and spark plugs are identified as No. 1 cyl 1 (primary/main) and No. 1 cyl 2 (secondary/sub).
2 Refer to Chapter 3 and displace the radiators – there is no need to drain the

coolant or disconnect the hoses or fan wiring. Release all the wiring and the hose from the shroud on the back of the radiator, noting its routing, then release and remove the shroud, noting how it locates **(see illustrations)**.
3 Pull the caps off the spark plugs **(see illustration)**.

22.3 The primary caps are deep set and must be lifted out

22.5a To remove the primary plugs fit the socket onto the plug...

22.5b ...then fit the extension into the socket...

22.5c ...then fit the ratchet onto the extension and unscrew the plug...

22.5d ... and lift it out with the tool – the rubber insert will grip around the plug top

4 Clean around the base of each plug so that no dirt can enter the combustion chambers when the plugs are removed.

5 Using a deep 14 mm spark plug socket and extension (rather than the tools provided in the bike's toolkit, which, especially for the primary spark plugs, are not very suitable due to the restricted access), unscrew and remove the plugs from each cylinder **(see illustrations)** – lay the plugs out so you know which cylinder each comes from.

6 Check the condition of the electrodes, comparing their firing ends with the generic plug photos on the inside rear cover. If they are contaminated in any way discard them and fit new ones – Iridium spark plugs should not be cleaned.

7 At the specified service interval you should replace the spark plugs with new ones – skip to Step 9.

8 Examine the pointed iridium-tipped centre electrode – if the tip has rounded off, the plug is worn **(see illustration)**. Measure the gap

between the two electrodes with a 1 mm wire type gauge only **(see illustration)** – do not use blade type feeler gauges because the iridium tip might be damaged. If the gauge can fit between the electrodes they have worn and the gap is wider than it should be. Do not bend the outer electrode to adjust the gap. If

you accidentally drop a plug and it lands on the end and the side electrode bends, fit a new plug.

9 Thread the plugs as far as possible into the head turning the tool or plug itself by hand, making sure they do not cross-thread. Once the plugs are finger-tight, tighten them using

22.8a Check the tip for wear

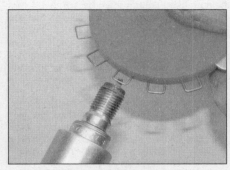

22.8b Only use a wire gauge to check the gap

23.2a Undo the screws (arrowed)...

23.2b ...release the duct from the clip...

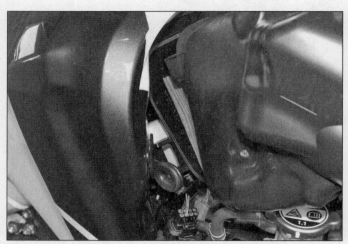

23.2c ...then draw the cover forwards off the housing

23.3a Undo the two screws...

the tool supplied or a socket drive. If a torque wrench can be applied, tighten the spark plugs to 22 Nm. Otherwise, if new plugs are being used tighten them by 1/2 a turn after the washer has seated, and if the old plugs are being reused tighten them by 1/8 to 1/4 turn after they have seated, according to feel. Do not over-tighten them.

10 Fit the caps onto the plugs, pushing them all the way on and checking they are secure.

11 Fit the radiator shrouds and secure the wiring and hose, then fit the radiators (see Chapter 3).

 HAYNES HINT *Stripped plug threads in the cylinder head can be repaired with a thread insert – see 'Tools and WorkshopTips' in the Reference section.*

23 Air filters

Caution: If the machine is continually ridden in wet or dusty conditions, the filter should be replaced more frequently, or at least cleaned between replacement intervals (see Step 4).

1 There are two filters, one in each side of the filter housing. Remove the fairing side panels (see Chapter 7).

2 Undo the cover screws then release the air duct and remove the cover (see illustrations).

3 Undo the filter screws and remove it from the housing (see illustrations).

4 To clean the filter in between replace-

23.3b ...and remove the filter from the housing

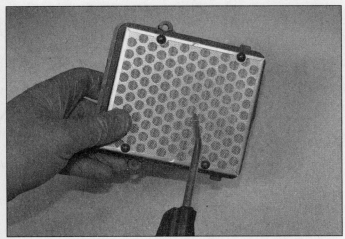

23.4 Clean the filter as described between service intervals, but always fit a new filter at the specified interval

23.6 Check the seal (arrowed)

ment intervals tap it on a hard surface to dislodge dirt and dust and check for flies or other debris lodged between the folds, then blow through it using compressed air directed from the inner side **(see illustration)**. Do not attempt to clean the filter using cleaning products as it is coated with a dust adhesive that will be rendered useless.

5 Fit the new filter onto the housing, making sure it seats properly, and secure it with the screws **(see illustrations 23.3b and a)**.

6 Make sure the cover seal is in good condition and seated in its groove **(see illustration)** – fit a new one if necessary. Fit the cover and tighten the screws **(see illustrations 23.2c, b and a)**.

7 Install the fairing side panels (see Chapter 7).

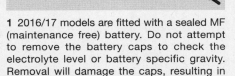

24 Battery

1 2016/17 models are fitted with a sealed MF (maintenance free) battery. Do not attempt to remove the battery caps to check the electrolyte level or battery specific gravity. Removal will damage the caps, resulting in electrolyte leakage and battery damage.

2 2018-on models are fitted with a lithium-ion battery.

3 The only maintenance required is to check that the terminals are clean and tight.

4 On 2016/17 models only, if the machine is not in regular use, disconnect the battery and give it a refresher charge every month to six weeks (see Chapter 8).

25 Spark arresters (US models)

1 Each exit pipe in the silencer contains a spark arrester that should be cleaned at the specified interval.

2 Remove the silencer tail cap and cover, noting the arrangement of the washers, collars and grommets.

3 Undo the exit pipe bolts and draw the pipes out of the silencer, taking care not to scrape the arrester screen mesh. Remove the gaskets – new ones must be fitted.

4 Clean the mesh using a soft brush and check it for splits and holes. If any are found fit a new pipe.

5 Fit the exit pipes using new gaskets and tighten the bolts to 9 Nm.

Chapter 2
Engine, clutch and transmission

Contents

Section number

Balancer shafts. 18
Cam chain and sprockets, tensioner blade and guide blade. 9
Cam chain tensioner 7
Clutch and clutch cable – models with standard transmission 13
Component access 2
Connecting rod and main bearing information. 23
Connecting rods and bearings. 25
Crankcase separation and reassembly 21
Crankcases and cylinder bores 22
Crankshaft and main bearings. 24
Cylinder head 10
Cylinder head and valve overhaul 11
Dual-clutch and linear solenoid valve – models with DCT 14
Engine disassembly and reassembly general information 5
Engine removal and installation 4
Engine wear assessment 3

Section number

Gearchange mechanism – models with DCT. 16
Gearchange mechanism – models with standard transmission. 15
General Information 1
Oil pump and pressure relief valve(s) 20
Oil sump and oil strainer 19
Pistons and rings 26
Primary drive gear 17
Rocker arms and camshaft 8
Running-in procedure. 31
Selector drum and forks. 30
Starter clutch and gears. 12
Transmission shaft overhaul – models with DCT 29
Transmission shaft overhaul – models with standard transmission. . 28
Transmission shaft removal and installation. 27
Valve cover 6

Degrees of difficulty

Easy, suitable for novice with little experience	Fairly easy, suitable for beginner with some experience	Fairly difficult, suitable for competent DIY mechanic	Difficult, suitable for experienced DIY mechanic	Very difficult, suitable for expert DIY or professional

Specifications

General

Type	Four-stroke parallel twin
Capacity	998 cc
Bore	92.0 mm
Stroke	75.1 mm
Compression ratio	10.0 to 1
Cylinder numbering	1 – left, 2 – right
Cooling system	Liquid cooled
Lubrication	Wet sump, trochoid pump
Clutch	
standard transmission	Wet multi-plate, cable operated
DCT	2 wet multi-plate clutches, electro-hydraulically operated
Transmission	Six-speed constant mesh
Final drive	Chain

Camshaft and rocker arms

Intake cam lobe height
- Standard . . . . 41.240 to 41.480 mm
- Service limit (min) . . . . 41.21 mm

Exhaust cam lobe height
- Standard . . . . 41.531 to 41.771 mm
- Service limit (min) . . . . 41.50 mm

Oil clearance
- Standard . . . . 0.020 to 0.062 mm
- Service limit (max) . . . . 0.10 mm

Runout (max) . . . . 0.04 mm

Rocker arm shaft diameter . . . . 11.977 to 11.990 mm

Rocker arm bore diameter
- Standard . . . . 12.000 to 10.018 mm
- Service limit (max) . . . . 12.05 mm

Cam follower diameter
- Standard . . . . 28.978 to 28.993 mm
- Service limit (min) . . . . 28.97 mm

Cam follower bore diameter
- Standard . . . . 29.010 to 29.026 mm
- Service limit (max) . . . . 29.04 mm

Cylinder head

Warpage (max) . . . . 0.10 mm

Valves, guides and springs

Valve clearances . . . . see Chapter 1

Stem diameter
Intake valve
- Standard . . . . 5.475 to 5.490 mm
- Service limit (min) . . . . 5.465 mm

Exhaust valve
- Standard . . . . 5.465 to 5.480 mm
- Service limit (min) . . . . 5.455 mm

Guide bore diameter – intake and exhaust valves
- Standard . . . . 5.500 to 5.512 mm
- Service limit (max) . . . . 5.552 mm

Seat width
Intake valve
- Standard . . . . 1.10 to 1.30 mm
- Service limit (max) . . . . 1.50 mm

Exhaust valve
- Standard . . . . 1.3 to 1.5 mm
- Service limit (max) . . . . 1.9 mm

Valve guide height above cylinder head
- Intake valve . . . . 17.7 to 18.0 mm
- Exhaust valve . . . . 17.8 to 18.1 mm

Valve spring free length
- Standard . . . . 43.20 mm
- Service limit (min) . . . . 42.2 mm

Starter clutch

Starter driven gear hub OD . . . . 57.749 to 57.768 mm
Starter driven gear hub ID . . . . 44.000 to 44.016 mm

Clutch – models with standard transmission

Friction plates 8
Plain plates 7

Friction plate thickness
- Standard . . . . 3.22 to 3.38 mm
- Service limit (min) . . . . 3.0 mm

Plain plate warpage (max) . . . . 0.2 mm

Spring free length
- Standard . . . . 52.48 mm
- Service limit (min) . . . . 51.48 mm

Clutch guide OD . . . . 34.975 to 34.991 mm
Clutch guide ID . . . . 28.000 to 28.021 mm
Input shaft OD at clutch guide . . . . 27.967 to 27.980 mm
Primary driven gear ID . . . . 41.958 to 41.983 mm

Clutch – models with DCT

Clutch initial clearance (measured between set plate and snap ring)
  Standard . . . .   0.70 to 0.90 mm
  Service limit (max) . . . .   1.30 mm
EOT sensor resistance . . . .   2.5 to 2.8 ohms

Oil pump

Oil pressure (at oil filter, with engine warm) . . . .   89 psi (6.3 Bar) @ 5000 rpm, oil @ 80°C
Inner rotor tip-to-outer rotor clearance
  Standard . . . .   0.15 mm
  Service limit (max) . . . .   0.20 mm

Cylinder bores

Bore
  Standard . . . .   92.000 to 92.015 mm
  Service limit (max) . . . .   92.100 mm
Cylinder compression . . . .   181 psi (12.7 Bar) @ 500 rpm

Crankshaft and bearings

Main bearing oil clearance
  Standard . . . .   0.019 to 0.038 mm
  Service limit (max) . . . .   0.05 mm
Runout (max) . . . .   0.04 mm

Connecting rods

Small-end internal diameter
  Standard . . . .   22.030 to 22.044 mm
  Service limit (max) . . . .   22.054 mm
Big-end side clearance
  Standard . . . .   0.10 to 0.20 mm
  Service limit (max) . . . .   0.35 mm
Big-end oil clearance
  Standard . . . .   0.027 to 0.045 mm
  Service limit (max) . . . .   0.065 mm

Pistons

Piston diameter (measured 12 mm up from skirt, at 90° to piston pin axis)
  Standard . . . .   91.981 to 91.996 mm
  Service limit (min) . . . .   91.89 mm
Piston-to-bore clearance
  Standard . . . .   0.004 to 0.034 mm
  Service limit (max) . . . .   0.21 mm*
Piston pin diameter
  Standard . . . .   21.994 to 22.000 mm
  Service limit (min) . . . .   21.98 mm
Piston pin bore diameter in piston
  Standard . . . .   22.002 to 22.008 mm
  Service limit (max) . . . .   22.02 mm

* If the piston-to-bore clearance exceeds the service limit, the cylinders can be rebored – Honda supply +0.25 oversize pistons and rings. Following rebore, the piston-to-bore clearance must be as standard for normal pistons

Piston rings

Ring end gap (installed)
  Top ring
    Standard . . . .   0.15 to 0.30 mm
    Service limit (max) . . . .   0.40 mm
  Second ring
    Standard . . . .   0.45 to 0.60 mm
    Service limit (max) . . . .   0.70 mm
  Oil ring side-rail
    Standard . . . .   0.20 to 0.70 mm
    Service limit (max) . . . .   0.90 mm
Ring-to-groove clearance (top and second rings) . . . .   0.03 to 0.06 mm

Transmission

	Standard	DCT
Gear ratios (no. of teeth)		
Primary reduction	1.733 to 1 (78/45)	1.883 to 1 (81/43)
Final reduction	2.625 to 1 (42/16)	2.625 to 1 (42/16)
1st gear	2.866 to 1 (43/15)	2.562 to 1 (41/16)
2nd gear	1.888 to 1 (34/18)	1.761 to 1 (37/21)
3rd gear	1.480 to 1 (37/25)	1.375 to 1 (33/24)
4th gear	1.230 to 1 (32/26)	1.133 to 1 (34/30)
5th gear	1.100 to 1 (33/30)	0.972 to 1 (36/37)
6th gear	0.968 to 1 (31/32)	0.882 to 1 (30/34)

Selector drum and forks

Selector fork end thickness	
Standard	5.93 to 6.00 mm
Service limit (min)	5.83 mm
Selector fork bore ID	12.000 to 12.018 mm
Selector fork shaft OD	11.957 to 11.968 mm

Torque settings

Cam chain tensioner blade pivot bolt	23 Nm
Camshaft holder bolts	12 Nm
Camshaft sprocket bolts	20 Nm
Clutch cover bolts	12 Nm
Clutch nut (standard transmission models)	128 Nm
Clutch oil feed pipe cover bolts (DCT models)	12 Nm
Clutch oil feed pipe guide plate bolts (DCT models)	5 Nm
Clutch spring plate bolts (standard transmission models)	12 Nm
Connecting rod bolts	
Initial setting	22 Nm
Final setting using new bolts for installation	+120°
Final setting using old bolts for oil clearance check only	+ 90°
Coolant pipe bolts to clutch cover (DCT models)	12 Nm
Crankcase bolts	
10mm crankshaft journal bolts	43 Nm
Crankcase 10mm bolt	39 Nm
Crankcase 8mm bolts	24 Nm
Crankcase 6mm bolts	12 Nm
Crankshaft end-cap	8 Nm
Cylinder head 9mm bolts	83 Nm
Engine mountings	see Section 4
Front balancer shaft bearing retainer plate bolts	12 Nm
Front balancer shaft driven gear bolt	103 Nm
Gearchange control motor bolts (DCT models)	14 Nm
Gearchange control motor cover bolts (DCT models)	12 Nm
Gearchange mechanism retainer plate bolt (standard transmission models)	12 Nm
Gearchange reduction gear cover bolts (DCT models)	14 Nm
Gearchange shaft angle sensor bolt (DCT models)	12 Nm
Linear solenoid valve cover bolts (DCT models)	12 Nm
Linear solenoid valve mounting bolts (DCT models)	12 Nm
Linear solenoid valve retainer plate bolt (DCT models)	12 Nm
Oil pressure relief valve cap	30 Nm
Oil pump assembly bolts	12 Nm
Oil pump driven gear retainer bolt	12 Nm
Oil pump mounting bolts	16 Nm
Primary drive gear bolt (standard transmission models)	103 Nm
Primary drive gear nut (DCT models)	118 Nm
Rear balancer shaft holder bolts	29 Nm
Rocker arm shaft alignment bolts	12 Nm
Rocker arm shaft plug	18 Nm
Selector drum bearing/fork shaft retainer bolts	12 Nm
Selector drum cam bolt (DCT models)	31 Nm
Selector drum cam bolt (standard transmission models)	23 Nm
Selector drum shifter guide plate bolts (DCT models)	12 Nm
Starter clutch bolts	29 Nm
Stopper arm bolt (standard transmission models)	12 Nm
Timing inspection cap	6 Nm
Transmission input shaft bearing retainer plate bolts	12 Nm
Valve cover bolts	10 Nm

1 General Information

1 The engine/transmission unit is a liquid-cooled parallel twin cylinder. The single overhead camshaft is chain driven off the right-hand end of the crankshaft. The camshaft opens the two intake valves per cylinder, and actuates rocker arms that open the two exhaust valves per cylinder. The engine/transmission is a unit assembly constructed from aluminium alloy. The crankcase divides horizontally.

2 The crankcase incorporates a wet sump, pressure-fed lubrication system that uses a dual rotor (standard transmission) or triple rotor (DCT) trochoidal oil pump that is driven off the rear balancer shaft. The system has an oil strainer in the pick-up, a pressure relief valve in the feed from the pump to the filter, an oil filter, and an oil pressure switch in the main gallery.

3 The water pump is on the right-hand side of the engine, and is driven off the front balancer shaft.

4 The alternator is on the left-hand end of the crankshaft, and the starter clutch is mounted on the back of it. The ignition timing triggers are on the outside of the alternator rotor, and the crankshaft position sensor is mounted in the alternator cover.

3.6a Select the correct adapter...

5 There are two balancer shafts, with the front one driven off the left-hand end of the crankshaft and the rear driven off the right-hand end.

6 Power from the crankshaft is routed to the transmission via the primary drive gear on the right-hand end of the crankshaft and the primary driven gear on the clutch assembly, then through the clutch(es). The clutch(es) is/are of the wet, multi-plate type, and is cable operated on models with standard transmission and electro-hydraulically operated on models with DCT. The transmission is a six-speed constant-mesh unit. Final drive to the rear wheel is by chain and sprockets.

2 Component access

Operations possible with the engine in the frame

1 The components and assemblies listed below can be removed without having to remove the engine/transmission assembly from the frame. If however, a number of areas require attention at the same time, removal of the engine is recommended.

● Valve cover
● Cam chain tensioner
● Camshaft and rocker arms
● Cam chain, tensioner blade and guide blade
● Cylinder head
● Clutch(es)
● Oil pump
● Primary drive gear
● Gearchange mechanism
● Alternator and starter clutch
● Balancer shafts
● Oil sump, oil strainer and oil pressure relief valve
● Starter motor
● Water pump
● Operations requiring engine removal

2 It is necessary to remove the engine/transmission assembly from the frame to gain access to the following components.

● Crankshaft and bearings
● Connecting rods and bearings
● Pistons, piston rings and cylinder bores
● Transmission shafts
● Selector drum and forks

3 Engine wear assessment

Cylinder compression check

Special tool: *A compression gauge with a threaded adaptor to fit the spark plug holes is needed. Depending on the outcome of the initial test, a squirt-type oil can may also be needed.*

1 Poor engine performance can be caused by leaking valves, incorrect valve clearances, a leaking head gasket, or worn pistons, piston rings or cylinder walls. A cylinder compression check will highlight these conditions and can also indicate the presence of excessive carbon deposits in the cylinder head, and a leakdown test (for which special equipment is needed – consult a Honda dealer) will pinpoint the actual cause(s) of the problem.

2 Start by making sure the valve clearances are correctly set (see Chapter 1). Also make sure the battery is fully charged.

3 Run the engine until it is at normal operating temperature.

4 Remove the secondary (sub) spark plug from each cylinder (see Chapter 1).

5 Raise the fuel tank and disconnect the fuel pump wiring connector (see Chapter 4).

6 Make sure the gauge hose/adapter threads are the same as the spark plug **(see illustrations)**. Fit the gauge into the secondary spark plug hole of the cylinder being checked **(see illustration)**.

7 With the ignition switch ON, the kill switch set to RUN, N (neutral) displayed in the instruments and the throttle held fully open,

3.6b ...and fit it onto the gauge hose...

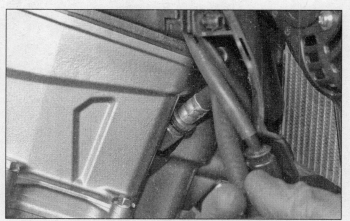

3.6c ...then thread it into the plug hole

turn the engine over on the starter motor until the gauge reading has built up and stabilised (see illustration).

8 Compare the reading on the gauge to the cylinder compression figure given in the Specifications at the beginning of the Chapter. Repeat for the other cylinder.

9 If a reading is low, it could be due to a worn cylinder bore, piston or rings, failure of the head gasket, or worn valve seats. To determine which is the cause, pour a small quantity of engine oil into the spark plug hole to seal the rings, then repeat the compression test. If the figures are noticeably higher the cause is a worn cylinder, piston or rings. If there is no change the cause is a leaking head gasket or worn valve seats.

10 If the reading is high there could be a build-up of carbon deposits in the combustion chamber and on the pistons. Remove the cylinder head and scrape all deposits off.

Leak-down (cylinder leakage) test

11 A leak down or 'cylinder leakage' test is similar to a compression test in that it tells you how well a cylinder is sealing, but it does so by testing how much pressure is lost through leakage, as opposed to how much pressure is created through compression. Many professionals prefer a leak test to a compression test as it more accurately pin-points the cause of the problem before any disassembly is done. However the required equipment is more expensive than for a compression test and a source of compressed air is essential. If you think a test is needed take the bike to a suitably equipped dealer or workshop. If you decide to purchase your own equipment follow the manufacturer's instructions.

12 A leakage test can also be used in conjunction with a compression test to diagnose other kinds of problems, such as a faulty valve train component, incorrect valve timing, faulty ignition or fuel delivery problems.

Engine oil pressure check

Special tool: *An oil pressure gauge adaptor* *that fits between the oil filter and the crankcase, available from Honda (part No. 070MJ-0010101 or 07AMJ-001A100 in Europe and 07APJ-004A160 in the US) is required to perform this test. Also required are a gauge and hose adapter, available from Honda (part Nos. 07506-3000001 and 07406-0030000) or from good tool suppliers.*

13 An oil pressure check can provide useful information about the condition of the engine's lubrication system, and can also be used as an indicator of excessive wear in the engine if no specific faults with the lubrication or pressure warning system are found.

14 The oil pressure warning light should come on when the ignition switch is turned ON and extinguish a few seconds after the engine is started. If the light stays on, or comes on whilst the engine is running, low oil pressure is indicated – stop the engine immediately and carry out an oil level check (see *Pre-ride checks*). If the oil level is correct, remove the sump and check the oil screen and the oil pick-up strainer for a blockage (Section 19). Also check the drained oil for sludge that reduces its ability to flow. Note that it is possible that the cause of the light staying on or coming on while the engine is running is an electrical fault, so make sure the oil pressure switch, warning light and circuit are all functioning correctly (see Chapter 8). If all appears good, do an oil pressure check.

15 To check the oil pressure, you need the adaptor that fits behind the oil filter, a suitable gauge and hose adapter (see Note above).

16 Drain the engine oil and remove the oil filter (see Chapter 1). Fit the gauge adapter, hose adapter and gauge, then refit the oil filter and fill the engine to the correct level (see Chapter 1).

17 Warm the engine up to normal operating temperature, then raise the speed to 5000 rpm whilst watching the gauge reading. The oil pressure should be similar to that given in the Specifications at the start of this Chapter.

18 If the pressure is significantly lower than the standard, the oil screen or pick-up strainer could be blocked, the wrong grade of oil is being used, or there could be other engine damage. Begin diagnosis by checking the oil strainer (Section 19), then check the oil pump and pressure relief valve (Section 20). If those items check out okay, chances are the bearing oil clearances are excessive and the engine needs to be overhauled.

19 If the pressure is too high, either the oil filter is clogged, the relief valve is stuck closed or the wrong grade of oil is being used.

20 If the pressure is as it should be, and if not already done, then check the oil pressure switch, warning light and circuit (see Chapter 8).

21 Stop the engine and let it cool, then drain the engine oil and remove the oil filter, gauge and adapter, then refit the filter and fill the engine to the correct level with oil (see Chapter 1).

> ⚠ *Warning: Be careful when removing the pressure gauge adapter as the exhaust pipes, the engine and the oil itself can cause severe burns.*

22 Check the oil level.

4 Engine removal and installation

Caution: The complete engine is heavy, and the help of at least one assistant is required to remove and fit the mounting bolts when manoeuvring it out of and into the frame. To make removal and installation easier it is advisable to remove as many components and assemblies as possible while the engine is in the frame (see Section 2), then what is left is obviously much lighter and easier to manoeuvre.

Note: *As each mounting bolt is removed store it along with any related washer, bracket, nut or spacer to avoid parts getting mixed up, making installation easier.*

Removal

1 Support the bike upright using an auxiliary stand or stands that will not interfere with engine removal, but note that you cannot use

3.7 Checking cylinder compression

4.1a Axle stands under the footrest brackets are a good way of supporting the bike – note the blocks of wood to prevent metal-to-metal contact

4.1b After-market tool for holding the front brake lever on

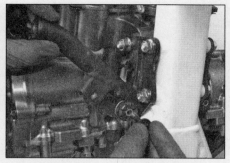

4.10a Unscrew the bolt on each side and remove the bracket…

4.10b …then remove the collar from each grommet

a rear paddock stand as the swingarm must be removed **(see illustration)**. Make sure the bike is on level ground, and tie or clamp the front brake on **(see illustration)**. Work can be made easier by raising the machine to a suitable working height on an hydraulic ramp or a suitable platform. Make sure the motorcycle is secure and will not topple over.

2 Refer to Chapter 7 and remove the rider's seat, the fairing side panels and the sump guard.

3 Remove the exhaust system (see Chapter 4).

4 If the engine is dirty, particularly around its mountings, wash it thoroughly. This will make work much easier and rule out the possibility of caked on lumps of dirt falling into some vital component.

5 Drain the engine oil and the coolant, and if required remove the oil filter (see Chapter 1).

6 Remove the fuel tank, the air filter housing and throttle body assembly (see Chapter 4). Plug the engine intake manifolds with clean rag.

7 Remove the battery and the battery box (see Chapter 8).

8 Remove the ignition coil assembly, and the PAIR system control valve along with its hoses (see Chapter 4).

9 Remove the radiators along with their hoses, noting their routing (see Chapter 3).

10 On the Adventure Sports model remove the protection bar bottom mounting bracket **(see illustrations)**.

11 Remove the rear brake pedal (see Chapter 5).

12 On models with standard transmission remove the gearchange lever and linkage (see Chapter 5). Remove the gearchange shaft cover **(see illustrations 15.2b, c and d)**.

13 Remove the swingarm and the shock absorber (see Chapter 5).

14 Unscrew the coolant reservoir bolt, then displace and support the reservoir, noting how it locates **(see illustrations)**.

15 Remove the rubber connector cover from the back of the engine, noting how it locates **(see illustration)**.

16 On all models with standard transmission release and disconnect the rear brake light switch wiring connector (2-pin grey), the sidestand switch wiring connector (2-pin black), and the alternator assembly 6-pin black wiring connector **(see illustration 4.17a)**. On 2016/17 models disconnect the gear position switch wiring connector (8-pin black). On 2018-on models disconnect the gear position sensor wiring connector (3-pin black), then disconnect the wire from the neutral switch **(see illustration 4.17c)** and

the gearchange shaft switch. Release the oxygen sensor wire clip from the bracket, then remove the bracket **(see illustration 4.17d)**. Disconnect the speed sensor wiring connector (3-pin black) **(see illustration 4.17f)**.

17 On models with DCT release and disconnect the rear brake light switch wiring connector (2-pin grey), the sidestand switch wiring connector (2-pin black), and the alternator assembly 6-pin black wiring connector, the gearchange shaft angle sensor wiring connector (3-pin blue), the inner input shaft sensor wiring connector (3-pin black),

4.14a Unscrew the bolt (arrowed)…

4.14b …and displace the reservoir

4.15 Release and remove the rubber cover – 2018 model with DCT shown

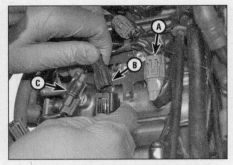

4.17a Brake light switch connector (A), sidestand switch connector (B), alternator assembly connector (C)

4.17b Gearchange shaft angle sensor connector (A), input shaft sensor connector (B), TR sensor connector (C)

4.17c Pull the boot back, unscrew the nut (arrowed) and detach the lead

4.17d Release the connector from the bottom of the bracket, then unscrew the bolt (arrowed), displace the bracket...

4.17e ...and release the wiring

4.17f Speed sensor connector (A), outer input shaft sensor connector (B)

4.18 Release the wiring, then unscrew the bolts and remove the bracket

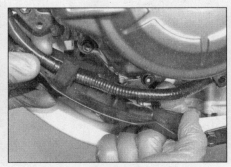

4.19 Disconnect the grey connector

and the TR sensor wiring connector (3-pin black) **(see illustrations)**. Disconnect the wire from the neutral switch **(see illustration)**. Release the oxygen sensor connector clip

from the bracket, then remove the bracket and release the EOT sensor wiring clip **(see illustrations)**. Disconnect the speed sensor wiring connector (3-pin black) and the

outer input shaft sensor wiring connector (3-pin black) **(see illustration)**. Remove the gearchange control motor cover, noting the routing of the wiring, and disconnect the motor wiring connector (2-pin black) **(see illustrations 16.1 and 16.2a)**.

18 Remove the wiring connector bracket **(see illustration)**.

19 Disconnect the alternator 3-pin grey wiring connector from the regulator/rectifier **(see illustration)**. Release the wiring from the frame so it is free to be removed with the engine.

20 Remove the alternator wiring cover **(see illustrations)**.

21 Disconnect the ECT sensor wiring connector **(see illustration)**.

22 On models with standard transmission free the clutch cable end from the release arm

4.20a Undo the screws and displace the cover...

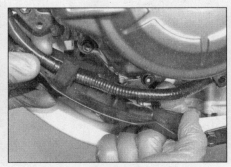

4.20b ...and release the wiring

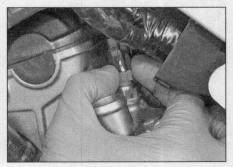

4.21 ECT sensor connector

4.25a Unscrew the nut and withdraw the bolt

4.25b Unscrew the nuts...

4.25c ...and withdraw the bolts, noting the different lengths

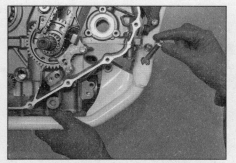

4.25d Unscrew the front bolts, noting the different lengths, and remove the cradle

4.27a Unscrew the upper front mounting bolts...

4.27b ...then remove the upper front bracket

and the cable holder (Section 13) and secure the cable clear of the engine.

23 On models with DCT remove the clutch EOP sensor cover **(see illustration 14.4a and b)**. Disconnect the linear solenoid wiring connector (4-pin black) and release the wiring ties **(see illustration 14.5a)**. Disconnect the clutch oil hose EOP sensor wiring connector (3-pin grey), the No. 1 clutch EOP sensor wiring connector (3-pin grey), and the No. 2 clutch EOP sensor wiring connector (3-pin black) **(see illustrations 14.5b)**. Unscrew the sensor wiring clip bracket bolt **(see illustration 14.5c)**. Remove the EOT sensor (see Chapter 4). Remove the engine oil pressure sensor (see Chapter 8).

24 Remove the front sprocket (see Chapter 6).

25 Unscrew the nut from the right-hand end of the lower front engine mounting bolt, then withdraw the bolt **(see illustration)**. Unscrew the nuts and withdraw the bolts securing the rear of the right-hand frame cradle, noting the washers where fitted **(see illustrations)**. Unscrew the bolts securing the front of the cradle, noting the washers where fitted, and remove the cradle **(see illustration)**.

26 At this point, position an hydraulic or mechanical jack under the engine with a block of wood or similar (we had a rubber block) between the jack head and sump **(see illustration 4.1a)**. Make sure the jack is centrally positioned so the engine will not

topple in any direction when the last mounting bolt is removed. Raise the jack to take the weight of the engine, but make sure it is not lifting the bike and taking the weight of that as well. The idea is to support the engine so that there is no pressure on any of the mounting bolts once they have been slackened, so they can be easily withdrawn.

27 Unscrew the upper front mounting bolts and the upper front bracket bolt and remove the bracket **(see illustrations)**.

28 Unscrew the nut from the right-hand end of the middle front engine mounting bolt and remove the right-hand spacer, then withdraw the bolt and remove the left-hand spacer, noting which spacer fits where **(see illustrations)**. Unscrew the nuts, withdraw the

4.28a Unscrew the nut...

4.28b ...and remove the spacer...

4.28c ...then withdraw the bolt and remove the spacer

4.28d Unscrew the nuts…

4.28e …and remove the bracket(s)…

4.28f …then withdraw the bolts and remove the bracket(s) – Adventure Sports model shown

4.29 Prevent damage using rag as shown

4.30a Unscrew the nut

4.30b Unscrew the bracket bolts and remove the bracket and its spacers…

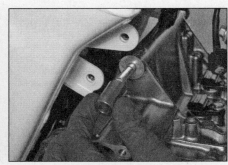

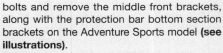

4.30c …and the engine spacer

bolts and remove the middle front brackets, along with the protection bar bottom section brackets on the Adventure Sports model **(see illustrations)**.

29 To protect vulnerable parts wrap some rags around the front section of the frame and around the left-hand side of the engine valve cover and secure it with tape **(see illustration)**.

30 Unscrew the nut from the right-hand end of the upper rear engine mounting bolt **(see illustration)**. Unscrew the upper rear bracket bolts and remove the spacers **(see illustrations)**.

31 Unscrew the nut from the right-hand end of the lower rear engine mounting bolt, then push the bolt in and remove the right-hand (black) spacer **(see illustrations)**. Withdraw

4.31a Unscrew the nut…

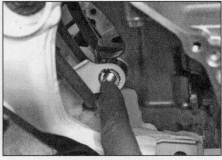

4.31b …push the bolt in…

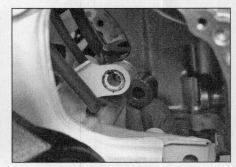

4.31c …and remove the spacer

the bolt and remove the left-hand spacer (marked L) **(see illustration)**.

32 Check that all wiring, cables and hoses are free and clear of the engine and/or frame as required. Make sure the engine is properly supported on the jack and held by an assistant, and read the **Caution** at the beginning of the Section.

33 Withdraw the upper rear mounting bolt and remove the spacer, then carefully manoeuvre the engine out from the right-hand side **(see illustration)**.

Installation

Note: *To prevent corrosion which could lead to bolts being seized, smear copper grease onto the bolt shafts, not the threads, to prevent the possibility of them seizing in the spacers or the engine or frame.*

34 Refit the protective rag to the engine and frame if it has been removed **(see illustration and 4.29)**. Manoeuvre the engine into position in the frame and use the jack to align all the mounting bolt holes, making sure that all cables and wiring are correctly routed and do not get trapped. Note that it may be necessary to adjust the jack as some of the bolts are installed and tightened to realign the other bolt holes.

35 Fit all the mounting bolts/nuts/washers (where fitted) along with the spacers, brackets and frame cradle, tightening the nuts and bolts finger-tight only, in reverse order of the removal sequence (see Steps 33 back to 25), noting the following:

● The upper rear mounting bolt is 217 mm long. The lower rear mounting bolt is 153 mm long. The middle front mounting bolt is 100 mm long. The lower front mounting bolt is 138 mm long.

● For the upper rear mounting the medium spacer fits between the engine and frame on the left-hand side, and the longer spacer fits between the engine and bracket on the right-hand side, and the short spacers fit between the bracket and the frame **(see illustrations 4.33 and 4.30c, b and a)**.

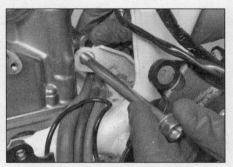

4.31d Withdraw the bolt and remove the spacer

● For the lower rear mounting bolt the spacer marked L fits between the engine and frame on the left-hand side, and the black spacer fits between the engine and frame on the right-hand side **(see illustrations 4.31d and c)**.

● For the middle front mounting bolt the longer spacer fits between the engine and bracket on the left-hand side, and the shorter spacer fits between the engine and bracket on the right-hand side **(see illustrations 4.28c and b)**.

● For the front of the frame cradle the short bolt goes at the top, the long at the bottom **(see illustration 4.25d)**. For the back of the frame cradle the short bolt goes at the front, the long at the rear **(see illustration 4.25c)**.

36 Temporarily insert the swingarm pivot bolt **(see illustration)**.

37 Now tighten the nuts/bolts in the following sequence to the torque settings given:

● Tighten the right-hand frame cradle rear bolts/nuts to 44 Nm on 2016/17 models, and to 30 Nm on 2018-on models.

● Tighten the right-hand frame cradle front bolts to 44 Nm on 2016/17 models, and to 30 Nm on 2018-on models.

● Remove the jack from under the engine.

● Tighten the nut on the lower rear mounting bolt to 44 Nm.

4.33 Withdraw the bolt and remove the spacer

● Tighten the nut on the lower front mounting bolt to 44 Nm.

● Tighten the nuts securing the middle front engine brackets to the frame to 32 Nm, then tighten the nut on the middle front mounting bolt to 44 Nm.

● Tighten the bolt securing the upper front mounting bracket to the frame to 32 Nm, then tighten the bolts securing the bracket to the engine to 32 Nm.

● Tighten the bolts securing the upper rear engine brackets to the frame to 32 Nm, then tighten the nut on the upper rear mounting bolt to 32 Nm.

38 The remainder of the installation procedure is the reverse of removal, noting the following points:

● Refer to the relevant Chapters where directed.

● Make sure all wires, cables and hoses are correctly routed and connected, and secured by any clips or ties.

● Use new gaskets on the exhaust pipe connections.

● Refill the engine with the correct type and quantity of oil and coolant (see Chapter 1).

● Adjust the throttle and clutch cable freeplay (according to model) (see Chapter 1).

● Adjust the drive chain (see Chapter 1).

● Start the engine and check that there are no oil or coolant leaks.

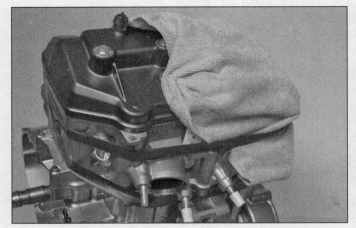

4.34 Protect the engine as shown to prevent possible damage

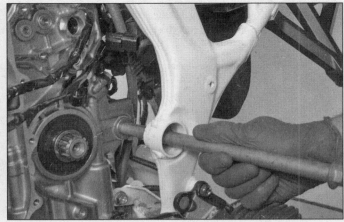

4.36 Fit the swingarm pivot bolt through to ensure correct alignment

5 Engine disassembly and reassembly general information

1 Before beginning the engine overhaul, read through the related procedures to familiarise yourself with the scope and requirements of the job. Overhauling an engine is not all that difficult, but it is time consuming. Check on the availability of parts and make sure that any necessary special tools are obtained in advance.

2 Most work can be done with a decent set of typical workshop hand tools, although a number of precision measuring tools are required for inspecting parts to determine if they are worn.

3 To ensure maximum life and minimum trouble from a rebuilt engine, everything must be assembled with care in a spotlessly clean environment.

Disassembly

4 Before disassembling the engine, thoroughly clean and degrease its external surfaces. This will prevent contamination of the engine internals, and will also make the job a lot easier and cleaner. A high flash-point solvent, such as paraffin (kerosene) can be used, or better still, a proprietary engine degreaser such as Gunk. Use old paintbrushes and toothbrushes to work the solvent into the various recesses of the casings. Take care to exclude solvent or water from the electrical components and intake and exhaust ports.

6.2 Release the clamps and pull the hoses (arrowed) off

6.3b ...and remove the valve cover

 Warning: The use of petrol (gasoline) as a cleaning agent should be avoided because of the risk of fire.

5 When clean and dry, position the engine on the workbench, leaving suitable clear area for working. Gather a selection of small containers, plastic bags and some labels so that parts can be grouped together in an easily identifiable manner. Also get some paper and a pen so that notes can be taken. You will also need a supply of clean rag, which should be as absorbent as possible.

6 Before commencing work, read through the appropriate section so that some idea of the necessary procedure can be gained. When removing components note that great force is seldom required, unless specified (checking the specified torque setting of the particular bolt being removed will indicate how tight it is, and therefore how much force should be needed). In many cases, a component's reluctance to be removed is indicative of an incorrect approach or removal method – if in any doubt, re-check with the text.

7 When disassembling the engine, keep 'mated' parts that have been in contact with each other during engine operation together (i.e. pistons with their piston rings and connecting rods, valves with their shims and other components, etc). These 'mated' parts must be reinstalled together and in their original location.

8 A complete engine/transmission disassembly should be done in the following

6.3a Unscrew the three bolts...

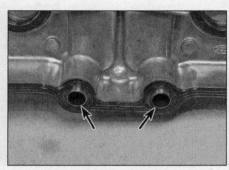

6.8 PAIR system dowels (arrowed)

general order with reference to the appropriate Sections.

● Remove the oil sump and strainer and oil pump – doing this first allows the engine to sit flat and steady
● Remove the valve cover
● Remove the cylinder head
● Remove the clutch(s) and primary drive gear
● Remove the cam chain and blades
● Remove the gearchange mechanism
● Remove the alternator/starter clutch (see Chapter 8)
● Remove the balancer shafts
● Separate the crankcase halves
● Remove the crankshaft
● Remove the transmission shafts and the selector drum and forks
● Remove the connecting rods and pistons

Reassembly

9 Reassembly is accomplished by reversing the general disassembly sequence.

6 Valve cover

Removal

1 Remove the ignition coil assembly (see Chapter 4).

2 If required detach the crankcase breather hose and the PAIR system hose from the cover **(see illustration)**.

3 Unscrew the valve cover bolts, lift the cover off the cylinder head, and remove it from the right-hand side of the frame **(see illustrations)**. If it is stuck, do not try to lever it off with a screwdriver – tap it gently around the sides with a rubber hammer or block of wood to dislodge it. Note the sealing washers for the bolts and the spark plug cap seals and remove them if they are loose **(see illustrations 6.10b and a)**.

4 The rubber gasket seats in the groove in the cover, and is best left there if it is reusable. If the gasket is in any way damaged, deformed or deteriorated, remove it **(see illustration 6.9)**.

5 Note the two dowels that link the PAIR system air passages between the valve cover and cylinder head and remove them for safekeeping if they are loose (which is unlikely), taking care not to drop them if they are not in the valve cover **(see illustration 6.8)**.

6 If required, remove the PAIR system reed valves (see Chapter 4).

Installation

7 If removed, install the PAIR system reed valves (see Chapter 4).

8 If removed, fit the PAIR system dowels into the valve cover **(see illustration)**.

9 Examine the valve cover gasket for signs

6.9 Make sure the gasket locates in the groove and over the dowels

6.10a Make sure the plug cap seals...

6.10b ...and the sealing washers are the correct way up

of damage or deterioration and fit a new one if necessary. If a new one is used, clean the groove in the cover and the cylinder head mating surface with solvent. Fit the new gasket into the perimeter groove, using some dabs of grease to hold it in place if necessary, and making sure it locates correctly **(see illustration)**.

10 If removed, fit the plug cap seals with the OUTSIDE mark facing out, and the bolt sealing washers with the UP mark facing up, using new ones if required **(see illustrations)**.

11 Apply a smear of sealant to the base of each gasket half-circle **(see illustration)**. Position the valve cover on the head, making sure the gasket stays in place and the half-circle locates correctly in the cut-out, and the dowels locate correctly **(see illustration)**. Fit the cover bolts and tighten them to 10 Nm **(see illustration 6.3a)**.

12 Connect the crankcase breather hose and the PAIR system hose if removed **(see illustration 6.2)**.

13 Install the ignition coil assembly (see Chapter 4).

7 Cam chain tensioner

Removal

1 Unscrew the tensioner cap bolt and remove

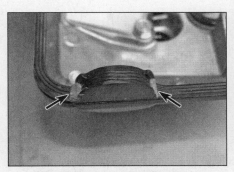

6.11a Place dabs of sealant to the half-circle base as shown (arrows)

6.11b Make sure half-circle locates in the cut-out in the head

the sealing washer, then slacken the tensioner mounting bolts **(see illustration)**.

2 Insert a small flat-bladed screwdriver in the end of the tensioner so that it engages the slotted plunger **(see illustration)**. Turn the screwdriver clockwise until the plunger is fully retracted and hold it in this position while unscrewing the tensioner mounting bolts **(see illustration 7.6c)**. Withdraw the tensioner from the engine and release the plunger – the plunger will spring back out once the screwdriver is removed, but can be easily reset on installation.

3 Remove the gasket. A new gasket and new cap bolt sealing washers must be used on installation. Do not attempt to dismantle the tensioner.

Check

4 Check that the plunger cannot be pushed into the body **(see illustration)** – if it can, fit a new tensioner. Check that the plunger moves smoothly when wound into the tensioner and springs back out freely when released **(see illustration 7.6a)**.

Installation

5 Make sure the tensioner and cylinder head mating surfaces are clean and dry.

6 Insert a small flat-bladed screwdriver in the end of the tensioner so that it engages the slotted plunger and turn it clockwise until the plunger is fully retracted, and hold

7.1 Remove the cap bolt (A) and washer, then slacken the bolts (B)

7.2 Insert the screwdriver and turn it clockwise to retract the plunger

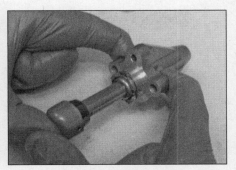

7.4 The plunger must not move in when pushed

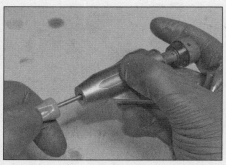

7.6a Insert the screwdriver and retract the plunger...

7.6b ... then fit a new gasket, install the tensioner...

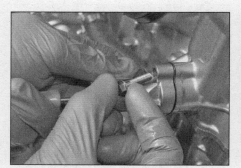

7.6c ...and fit the mounting bolts

7.6d Use a new sealing washer

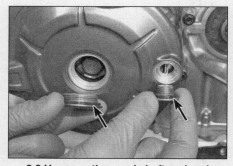

8.2 Unscrew the crankshaft end and timing inspection caps – check the O-rings (arrowed)

8.3a Turn the engine anti-clockwise using the bolt...

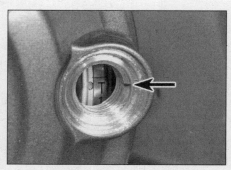

8.3b ... until the line next to the T1 mark aligns with the notch (arrowed)...

8.3c ... and the camshaft sprocket marks are as shown

8.4 Note the identity mark on each arm

it in this position **(see illustration)**. Fit a new gasket onto the tensioner, fit the tensioner and tighten the bolts **(see illustrations)**. Release and remove the screwdriver – you should hear the plunger extend to take up the slack in the chain. Fit the tensioner cap bolt with a new sealing washer and tighten it **(see illustration)**.

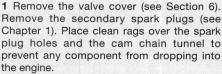

8 Rocker arms and camshaft

Removal

Rocker arms

1 Remove the valve cover (see Section 6). Remove the secondary spark plugs (see Chapter 1). Place clean rags over the spark plug holes and the cam chain tunnel to prevent any component from dropping into the engine.

2 Unscrew the crankshaft end-cap and timing inspection cap from the alternator cover **(see illustration)**. Check the condition of the O-rings and get new ones if necessary.

3 The engine must be turned so that the No. 1 piston is at TDC (top dead centre) on its compression stroke. Turn the engine using a socket on the alternator rotor bolt, turning it in an anti-clockwise direction only, until the line next to the T1 mark on the rotor aligns with the static timing mark, which is a notch in the inspection hole rim, and the lines on the camshaft sprocket are flush with the cylinder head top surface, and the punch mark on the sprocket is visible in the position shown **(see illustrations)**. If the punch mark is not visible (i.e. is opposite its required position), rotate the engine anti-clockwise one full turn (360°) until the line next to the T1 mark again aligns with the static timing mark. The sprocket marks will now be positioned correctly.

4 Each rocker arm is marked A or B, according to type (straight arm – A, angled arm – B), but to ensure they are returned to the same valves they have been actuating also mark them 1 and 2 or L and R according to cylinder **(see illustration)**.

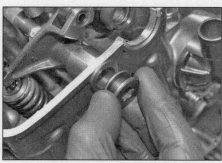

8.5a Unscrew the bore plug...

8.5b ... and the two alignment bolts

8.5c Thread a 6 mm bolt in...

8.5d ...pull the shaft out and remove the rocker arms

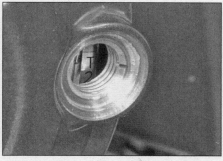

8.7a Turn the engine anti-clockwise until the line next to the T2 mark aligns with the notch...

8.7b ...and the camshaft sprocket marks are as shown

5 Unscrew the rocker arm shaft bore plug **(see illustration)** – a new sealing washer must be used. Unscrew the shaft alignment bolts **(see illustration)**. Thread a 6 mm bolt into the end of the shaft and use it as a handle to draw the shaft out, removing the arms as you do and laying them out in order **(see illustrations)**. Slide the arms back onto the shaft in the correct order and way round.

Camshaft

6 Remove the rocker arms (see above).
7 Turn the engine 270° anti-clockwise **(see**

illustration 8.3a) until the line next to the T2 mark on the rotor aligns with the static timing mark and the punch mark on the camshaft sprocket is facing forward and in line with the cylinder head top surface **(see illustrations)**.
8 Remove the cam chain tensioner (Section 7).
9 There are three camshaft holders, and for identification the left-hand one is marked A and the middle one is marked B **(see illustration)**.
10 Unscrew the camshaft holder bolts,

slackening them evenly and a little at a time in a criss-cross sequence **(see illustration)**. Remove the bolts and lift off the holders, noting how they fit **(see illustrations 8.32c and b)**. Do not remove the dowels unless they are loose and liable to drop out **(see illustration 8.32a)**.
11 Carefully lift the camshaft off the head and disengage the sprocket from the chain **(see illustration 8.31)**.
12 Secure the chain using a piece of wire or cable-tie to prevent it from dropping.

8.9 The left-hand and middle holders are marked A and B respectively, and the right-hand holder is wider

8.10 Unscrew the bolts (arrowed) as described and remove the holders

8.15a Lift the follower off using a magnet...

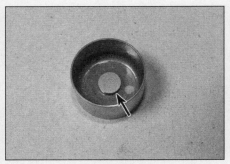

8.15b ...and remove the shim (arrowed) from inside the follower

8.16 Check all related bearing surfaces

13 While the camshaft is out do not rotate the crankshaft – the chain may drop down and bind between the crankshaft and case, which could damage these components. Place rags over the spark plug holes and the cam chain tunnel to prevent anything from dropping into the engine.

14 If you are removing the followers and shims, get a container that is divided into eight compartments, and label each compartment with the location of a valve, i.e. cylinder number, left or right valve. If a container is not available, use labelled plastic bags (egg cartons also do very well!).

8.17a Check the camshaft lobes and the followers and rocker rollers

15 Using a magnet if available, remove the cam follower of the valve in question, then remove the shim from inside the follower **(see illustrations)**. If it is not in the follower, pick it out of the top of the valve using either a magnet, a small screwdriver with a dab of grease on it (the shim will stick to the grease), or a screwdriver and a pair of pliers **(see illustration 8.28a)**. Do not allow the shim to fall into the engine.

Inspection

16 Inspect the bearing surfaces of the camshaft holders and cylinder head and the corresponding journals on the camshafts **(see illustration)**. Look for score marks, deep scratches and evidence of spalling (a pitted appearance). Check the oil passages for clogging.

17 Check the camshaft lobes, followers, and the rollers on the rocker arms for heat discoloration (blue appearance), score marks, chipped areas, flat spots and spalling **(see illustration)**. Measure the height of each lobe with a micrometer and compare the results to the minimum height given in the Specifications at the beginning of the Chapter **(see illustration)**. If damage is noted or wear is excessive, fit new parts as required.

> **HAYNES HiNT** *Refer to Tools and WorkshopTips in the Reference section for details of how to read a micrometer and dial gauge.*

18 Next, check the camshaft journal oil clearances. Clean the camshafts and the bearing surfaces in the cylinder head and camshaft holder with a clean lint-free cloth, then lay the camshaft in the cylinder head with the punch mark on the sprocket facing forward and aligned with the top surface of the cylinder head **(see illustration 8.7b)** – in this position no valves will be compressed by the camshaft lobes as the holders are tightened down, minimising the risk that the camshaft will rotate and disturb the Plastigauge **(see illustration)**.

19 Cut some strips of Plastigauge and lay one piece on each journal, parallel with the camshaft centreline **(see illustration 24.15)**. Make sure the camshaft holder dowels are installed **(see illustration 8.32a)**. Fit the holders and tighten the bolts as described in Step 32. While doing this, don't let the camshaft rotate, or the Plastigauge will be disturbed and you will have to start again.

8.17b Checking camshaft lobe height

8.18 All the camshaft lobes face forwards and back so will not press on a follower

20 Now unscrew the camshaft holder bolts, slackening them evenly and a little at a time in a criss-cross sequence **(see illustration 8.10)** and remove the holders.

21 To determine the oil clearance, compare the crushed Plastigauge (at its widest point) on each journal to the scale printed on the Plastigauge container **(see illustration 24.18)**. Compare the results to the Specifications. If the oil clearance is greater than specified, replace the camshaft with a new one and recheck the clearance. If the clearance is still too great, also replace the cylinder head and holders with new ones.

8.26a Check the fit of each arm on its section of shaft

8.26b Check the bottom of the adjuster screw and top of the valve stem

HAYNES HINT

Before replacing the camshaft, cylinder head or holders because of damage, check with motorcycle cylinder head specialists to see whether worn components can be renewed. Due to the cost of new components it is recommended that all options are explored!

22 Inspect the outer surface of each cam follower for evidence of scoring or other damage. If a follower is in poor condition, it is probable that the bore in the cylinder head in which it works is also damaged. Check for clearance between each follower and its bore. Measure the outer diameter of each follower and the inner diameter of its bore and compare the results to the Specifications. If any follower is worn beyond its service limit replace it with a new one. If any bore is worn beyond its limit, is seriously out-of-round or tapered, replace the cylinder head with a new one.

23 Except in cases of oil starvation, the cam chain should wear very little. If the chain has stretched excessively, which makes it difficult

to maintain proper tension, or if it is stiff or the links are binding or kinking, replace it with a new one (Section 9).

24 Check the sprockets on the crankshaft and camshaft for wear, cracks and other damage, and replace them with new ones if necessary. Refer to Section 9 to remove the drive sprocket on the crankshaft. To remove the driven sprocket on the camshaft, mark its alignment then unscrew the two bolts **(see illustration 8.27)**. If the sprockets are worn, the cam chain is also worn. If severe wear is apparent, the entire engine should be disassembled for inspection.

25 Inspect the cam chain guides and tensioner blade (Section 9).

26 Inspect the working surface of each rocker arm bore and the section of the shaft it runs on. Check for freeplay between each arm and the section of shaft it runs on **(see illustration)**. If freeplay is felt check the clearance between them by measuring the outer diameter of the shaft and the inner diameter of its bore and compare the results to the Specifications. If the shaft or any arm is worn beyond its service limit replace fit new ones. Also check the bottom of the adjuster

screw on each arm and the corresponding valve stem end it actuates for wear and damage, and fit new components as required **(see illustration)** – the adjusters are available separately and can be removed by unscrewing the locknut and threading the adjuster out of the arm.

Installation

Camshaft

27 If the sprocket has been removed from the camshaft, clean the threads of the bolts and apply fresh threadlock. Align the sprocket with the camshaft so the punch mark is on the opposite side to the No. 2 cylinder lobes and the notch in the left-hand end of the shaft **(see illustration)**. Tighten the bolts to 20 Nm.

28 If removed, fit each shim into its recess in the top of the valve spring retainer with the size mark facing up, making sure it is correctly seated **(see illustration)**. It is most important that the shims and followers are returned to their original valves otherwise the valve clearances will be inaccurate. Lubricate each follower with engine oil, and fit it onto

8.27 Correct alignment of the sprocket marks in relation to the camshaft lobes

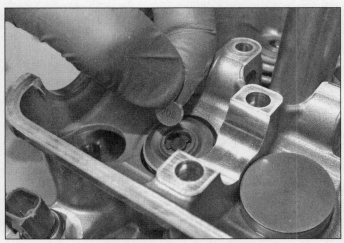

8.28a Seat the shim in its recess...

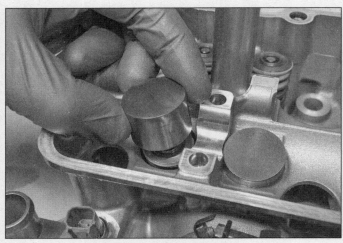

8.28b …then fit the follower

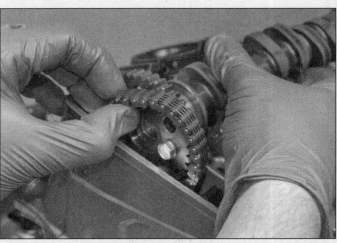

8.31 Check the camshaft is correctly aligned then fit the chain round the sprocket

its valve, making sure it slides smoothly in its bore **(see illustration)**.

29 Make sure the bearing surfaces on the camshafts and in the cylinder head are clean, then apply molybdenum disulphide oil (a 50/50 mixture of molybdenum disulphide grease and engine oil) to each of them. Also apply it to the camshaft journals and lobes.

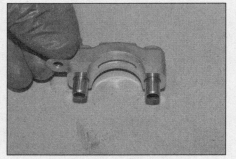

8.32a Each holder has two dowels

Make sure that none gets on the mating surfaces between the holder and the head, or in the bolt holes.

30 Check that the line next to the T2 mark on the alternator rotor aligns with the notch in the inspection hole rim **(see illustration 8.7a)**.

31 Lay the camshaft onto the head with the punch mark on the sprocket facing forward and level with the cylinder head top surface, and fit the cam chain around the sprocket, pulling up on the chain to remove all slack in the front run between the crankshaft and the camshaft **(see illustration and 8.7b)**. Any slack in the chain must lie in the rear run between the intake camshaft and the crankshaft, to be taken up later by the tensioner.

32 Make sure the bearing surfaces in the camshaft holders are clean, then apply molybdenum disulphide oil (a 50/50 mixture of molybdenum disulphide grease and engine oil) to each of them. Make sure the camshaft holder dowels are installed (two per holder) **(see illustration)**. Fit the holders onto the

camshaft and head with the holder marked A on the left-hand end and the holder marked B in the middle, and seating the groove in the right-hand holder over the rib on the camshaft, and with the offset threaded holes for the valve cover bolts towards the middle of the head **(see illustrations)**. Apply clean engine oil to the threads and under the heads of all the camshaft holder bolts. Fit the bolts and tighten them finger-tight, then tighten them evenly and a little at a time in a criss-cross sequence to 12 Nm, making sure they are seated squarely on the head and do not bind on the dowels.

33 Use a piece of wooden dowel to press on the back of the cam chain tensioner blade via the tensioner bore in the cylinder block to ensure that any slack in the cam chain is taken up and transferred to the rear run of the chain (where it will later be taken up by the tensioner). At this point check that all the timing marks are still in **exact** alignment as described in Step 7 **(see illustrations 8.7a and b)**. Note that it is easy to be slightly out

8.32b Make sure the left and middle holders are the correct way round according to the letters…

8.32c …and the right-hand holder sits over the rib on the camshaft

(one tooth on the sprocket) without the marks appearing drastically out of alignment. If the marks are out, remove and reposition the camshaft, and check the marks again.

Caution: If the marks are not aligned exactly as described, the valve timing will be incorrect and the valves may strike the pistons, causing extensive damage to the engine.

34 Install the cam chain tensioner (Section 7).

35 Turn the engine anti-clockwise through two full turns and check everything moves as it should and that the timing marks still align (see Step 7) **(see illustrations 8.7a and b)**.

36 Install the rocker arms (see below).

Rocker arms

37 If removed install the camshaft (see above).

38 Turn the engine so the crankshaft and camshaft are positioned as described in Step 3.

39 Set out each rocker arm according to the marks (see Step 4). Lubricate the rocker arm bores, rollers and thrust surfaces and the shaft with molybdenum disulphide oil (a 50/50 mixture of molybdenum disulphide grease and engine oil). Slide the shaft in and through the arms, aligning the cut-outs for the alignment bolts with the bolt holes **(see illustrations)**. Apply clean engine oil to the threads and under the heads of the alignment bolts and tighten them to 12 Nm **(see illustration 8.5b)**.

40 Remove the 6 mm bolt from the end of the shaft **(see illustration 8.5c)**. Fit a new sealing washer onto the shaft plug and lubricate the plug threads with clean engine oil. Fit the plug and tighten to 18 Nm **(see illustration 8.5a)**.

41 Turn the engine clockwise through two full turns and check again that all the timing marks still align (see Step 3) **(see illustrations 8.3a, b and c)**. Check the valve clearances and adjust them if necessary (see Chapter 1).

42 Fit the crankshaft end and timing inspection caps, using new O-rings if required, and smear the O-rings with oil and the cap threads with grease **(see illustration 8.2)**. Tighten the end cap to 8 Nm and the inspection cap to 6 Nm.

8.39a Insert the arm and fit the No. 1 A rocker...

8.39b ...the No. 1 B rocker...

8.39c ...the No. 2 A rocker...

8.39d ...and the No. 2 B rocker

43 Install the spark plugs (see Chapter 1). Install the valve cover (Section 6).

9 Cam chain and sprockets, tensioner blade and guide blade

Removal

Cam chain and sprockets

1 Refer to Section 8 and follow Steps 1 to 3 to set the No. 1 cylinder at TDC.

2 Remove the cam chain tensioner (Section 7).

3 Remove the clutch cover (Section 13 or Section 14).

4 On models with DCT remove the primary drive gear (Section 17).

5 On models with standard transmission refer to Section 17 and unscrew the primary drive gear bolt and remove the washer.

6 Turn the engine clockwise slightly using the socket on the rotor bolt until the front bolt on the camshaft sprocket is exposed, and unscrew it **(see illustration)**. Now turn the engine back to its No. 1 TDC position and unscrew the rear bolt **(see illustration)**. Displace the sprocket from the camshaft and disengage it from the chain, and allow the chain to drop down the tunnel **(see illustration)**.

7 Slide the sprocket off the end of the

9.6a Expose and unscrew the front bolt...

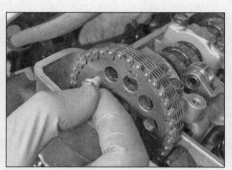

9.6b ...then the rear bolt

9.6c Slip the sprocket off the end of the shaft and out of the chain

9.7 Remove the sprocket and cam chain

9.10a Unscrew the bolt and remove the blade...

9.10b ...noting the washer

9.12 Unscrew the bolts (arrowed) and remove the guide plate

9.15a Align the wide splines (arrowed) to fit the sprocket

9.15b Engage the chain around the wide teeth in the middle of the sprocket

crankshaft, noting the wide splines that mean it can only be installed in one position, and remove the chain **(see illustration)**.

Tensioner blade

8 Remove the clutch cover (Section 13 or Section 14).
9 Remove the cam chain tensioner (Section 7).
10 Unscrew the tensioner blade pivot bolt and draw the blade out of the engine, collecting the washer from behind the blade **(see illustrations)**.

Guide blade and plate

11 To remove the guide blade you must remove the cylinder head – refer to the procedure in Section 10.
12 If required remove the guide plate **(see illustration)**.

Inspection

Cam chain

13 Check the chain for binding, kinks and any obvious damage and replace it with a new one if necessary. Check the sprocket teeth for wear and replace the cam chain and sprockets with a new set if necessary.

Tensioner and guide blades

14 Check the sliding surface and edges of the blades for excessive wear, deep grooves, cracking and other obvious damage, and replace them with new ones if necessary.

Installation

15 Installation of the chain, sprockets and

blades is the reverse of removal, noting the following:
● If removed, clean the guide plate bolts threads and apply fresh threadlock.
● Refer to Section 10 to install the cylinder head.
● Do not omit the washer that fits between the crankcase and the tensioner blade pivot **(see illustration 9.10b)**. Clean the threads of the pivot bolt and apply a suitable non-permanent thread locking compound, and tighten it to 23 Nm.
● Fit the cam chain drive sprocket with the punch mark facing out and aligning the wide splines **(see illustration 9.15a)**. Make sure you engage the chain with the wide teeth in the middle of the sprocket **(see illustration 9.15b)**. When fitting the cam chain driven sprocket onto the camshaft, clean the threads of the bolts and apply fresh threadlock. Make sure the timing marks are correctly set so the No. 1 cylinder is at TDC as described in Section 8, Step 3, fit the rear bolt first with the sprocket marks as shown and tighten to 20 Nm, then turn the engine as on removal to fit and tighten the front sprocket bolt **(see illustrations 9.6b and a)**. Reposition the engine to No. 1 TDC and double-check all the timing marks are in exact alignment. Follow the last three Steps in Section 8 (there is no need to check the valve clearances unless the camshaft has been removed).
● Refer to the relevant Sections as given in the removal procedure to install all other components.

10 Cylinder head

Note: *This procedure describes the cylinder head being removed with the engine in the frame. If the engine has been removed, ignore the initial steps that do not apply and note that you do not have to remove the cam chain tensioner blade or guide blade.*

Removal

1 Drain the engine oil and the coolant (see Chapter 1).
2 Remove the radiators (see Chapter 3) – disconnect the hose from the thermostat cover when removing the left-hand radiator **(see illustration)**. Disconnect the ECT sensor wiring connector **(see illustration 4.21)**.
3 Remove the exhaust system (see Chapter 4).

10.2 Slacken the clamp then disconnect the hose from the thermostat cover

10.8a Unscrew the 6 mm bolts first

10.8b Cylinder head 9 mm bolts (arrowed)

4 Remove the rocker arms and the camshaft (Section 8) – you can let the cam chain drop down the tunnel after removing the camshaft.
5 If required remove the thermostat (see Chapter 3).
6 Remove the cam chain tensioner blade(Section 9).
7 Remove the upper front engine mounting bracket **(see illustrations 4.27a and b)**.
8 The cylinder head is secured by two 6 mm bolts and six 9 mm bolts with fitted washers (i.e. they can't be separated from the bolts). First unscrew and remove the 6 mm bolts **(see illustration)**. Soak up any oil from around the 9 mm bolt heads, then unscrew and remove the bolts, slackening them evenly and a little at a time in a criss-cross pattern working from the outside to the middle until they are all loose **(see illustration)**.
9 Lift the cylinder head up off the block and support it so there is some clearance between them, then push the cam chain guide blade up out of its seat, noting how the pins locate in the cut-outs in the top of the block, twist it anti-clockwise through 90° and draw it out from the top of the head **(see illustrations)**. If the head is stuck, tap around the joint faces with a soft-faced mallet. Do not attempt to free the head by inserting a screwdriver between the head and block mating surfaces – you'll damage them. After removing the guide blade remove the cylinder head from the right-hand side of the frame **(see illustration)**.
10 Remove the cylinder head gasket – a new one must be used. If they are loose, remove the dowels from the crankcase or the underside of the cylinder head **(see illustration 10.16)**.
11 Clean all traces of old gasket material from the cylinder head and crankcase. If a scraper is used, take care not to scratch or gouge the soft aluminium. Be careful not to let any of the gasket material fall into the crankcase, the cylinder bore or the oil and coolant passages.
12 Check the cylinder head gasket and the mating surfaces on the cylinder head and crankcase for signs of leakage, which could

indicate warpage. Refer to Section 11 and check the cylinder head gasket surface for warpage.
13 If required slacken the intake duct clamp screws, noting the alignment of the clamps, and remove the ducts **(see illustration)**.

Installation

14 Make sure both cylinder head and crankcase mating surfaces are clean, and that the cam chain front guide blade is fitted.
15 Fit the intake ducts if removed, with the marked side facing out and seating the tabs on the bottom on each side of the rib on the head **(see illustration)**. Make sure the clamps are correclty aligned and seated with the correct hole over the pin **(see illustration 10.13)**.

10.9a Carefully lift the head up off the block, push the guide blade up and turn it as described…

10.9b …and lift it out the top…

10.9c …then draw the head out to the right

10.13 Note the alignment of the ducts and clamps before removing them

10.15 Make sure the ducts and clamps are correctly aligned and located as shown

10.16 Fit the dowels (arrowed). Always use a new gasket

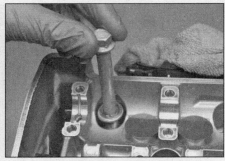

10.18 Lubricate the bolts and tighten them as described to the specified torque setting

16 Fit the dowels if removed, then lay the new head gasket onto the cylinder block, making sure all the holes are correctly aligned (see illustration). Never reuse the old gasket.
17 Carefully fit the cylinder head over the block and support it, then lower the cam chain guide blade into the tunnel with the chain running surface facing out, and when the pins are just above the block twist it 90° clockwise and seat the pins in the cut-outs and the bottom of the blade in its seat in the guide plate, then seat the head making sure it locates correctly onto the dowels (see illustrations 10.9c, b and a). Hook the cam chain up the tunnel using a piece of wire or a magnet and secure it with a piece of wire or cable-tie.
18 Apply some molybdenum disulphide oil (a

50/50 mixture of molybdenum disulphide grease and engine oil) to the threads and the underside of the heads and washers of the 9 mm bolts (see illustration). Fit the bolts and tighten them all finger-tight. Now tighten them evenly and a little at a time in a criss-cross pattern working from the middle to the outside to 83 Nm.
19 Fit the 6 mm bolts and tighten them (see illustration 10.8a).
20 Install the remaining components in reverse order of removal (Steps 7 to 2). Tighten the upper front engine mounting bracket bolts to 32 Nm, tightening the bracket to the frame before tightening it to the engine. Refill the engine and cooling system with the correct type and quantity of oil and coolant (see Chapter 1).

11 Cylinder head and valve overhaul

1 Because of the complex nature of this job and the special tools and equipment required, most owners leave servicing of the valves, valve seats and valve guides to a professional. However, you can make an initial assessment of whether the valves are seating correctly, and therefore sealing, by pouring a small amount of solvent into each of the valve ports. If the solvent leaks past any valve into the combustion chamber area the valve is not seating correctly and sealing.
2 With the correct tools (a valve spring compressor is essential – make sure it is suitable for motorcycle work), you can also remove the valves and associated components from the cylinder head, clean them and check them for wear to assess the extent of the work needed.
3 A dealer service department or specialist can replace the guides and re-cut the valve seats.
4 After the valve service has been performed, be sure to clean the head thoroughly to remove any metal particles or abrasive grit that may still be present from the valve service operations. Use compressed air, if available, to blow out all the holes and passages.

Disassembly

5 Before proceeding, arrange to label and store the valves along with their related components in such a way that they can be returned to their original locations without getting mixed up (see illustration). Either use the same container as the shims are stored in, or obtain a separate container and label each compartment accordingly. Alternatively, labelled plastic bags will do just as well.
6 Compress the spring on the first valve with a spring compressor, making sure it is correctly located onto each end of the valve assembly (see illustration). On the top of the valve the adaptor needs to be about the same size as the spring retainer – if it is too big it will slip over the retainer, and if it is too small it will be difficult to remove and install the collets (see illustration). On the underside of the head make sure the point of the compressor contacts the centre of the valve head (see illustration). Do not

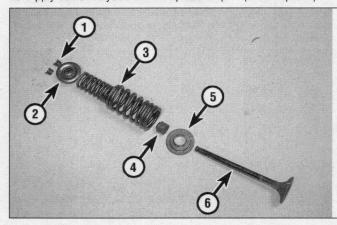

11.5 Valve components

1 Collets
2 Spring retainer
3 Spring
4 Spring seat
5 Valve stem oil seal
6 Valve

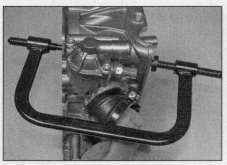

11.6a Compressing the valve spring using a valve spring compressor

11.6b Make sure the compressor locates correctly both on the top of the spring retainer...

11.6c ... and on the bottom of the valve

11.7a Remove the collets...

11.7b ... the spring retainer...

11.7c ...the spring...

compress the spring any more than is necessary to release the collets.

7 Remove the collets, using a magnet or a screwdriver with a dab of grease on it **(see illustration)**. Carefully release the valve spring compressor and remove the spring retainer, noting which way up it fits, the spring, and the valve **(see illustrations)**. If the valve binds in the guide and won't pull through, push it back into the head and deburr the area around the collet groove with a very fine file or whetstone **(see illustration)**.

8 Pull the valve stem seal off the top of the valve guide with pliers and discard it (the old seals should never be reused), then remove the spring seat noting which way up, it fits – using a magnet is the easiest way to remove the seat from the head **(see illustrations)**.

9 Repeat the procedure for the remaining valves. Remember to keep the parts for each valve together so they can be reinstalled in the same location.

10 Clean the cylinder head with solvent and dry it thoroughly. Compressed air will speed the drying process and ensure that all holes and recessed areas are clean. Do not use a wire brush mounted in a drill motor to clean the combustion chambers as the head material is soft and may be scratched or eroded away by the wire brush.

11 Clean the valve components with solvent and dry them thoroughly – do the parts from one valve at a time so that no mixing of parts between valves occurs.

12 Scrape off any deposits that may have formed on the valve, then use a wire brush to remove deposits from the valve heads and stems. Again, make sure the valves do not get mixed up.

Inspection

13 Inspect the head very carefully for cracks and other damage. If cracks are found, a new head is required. Check the camshaft bearing surfaces for wear and evidence of seizure, and check the camshafts and holders for wear as well (Section 8).

14 Using a precision straight-edge and a feeler gauge set to the warpage limit given in the Specifications at the beginning of the Chapter, check the head gasket mating surface for warpage. Refer to *Tools and Workshop Tips* in the Reference section for

11.7d ...and the valve

details of how to use the straight-edge. If the head is warped beyond the specified limit, consult a Honda dealer or take it to a specialist repair shop for an opinion, though be prepared to have to buy a new one.

15 Examine the valve seats in the combustion chamber and the seating surface on each valve **(see illustration)**. If they are pitted,

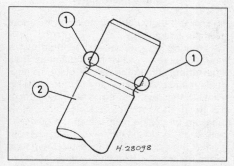

11.7e If the valve stem (2) won't pull through the guide, deburr the area above the collet groove (1)

cracked or burned, or are uneven around the circle, the head will require work beyond the scope of the home mechanic. Measure the valve seat width and compare it to the Specifications at the beginning of the Chapter **(see illustration)**. If it exceeds the service

11.8a Pull the seal off the valve stem...

11.8b ...then remove the spring seat

11.15a Check the valve seat and seating surface

11.15b Measure the valve seat width

11.16a Measure the valve stem diameter with a micrometer

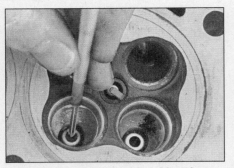

11.16b Measure the valve guide using a bore gauge

11.19 Check the free length of each spring

limit, or if it varies around its circumference, overhaul is required.

16 Working on one valve and guide at a time, measure the valve stem diameter **(see illustration)**. Clean the valve's guide using a guide reamer to remove any carbon build-up – insert the reamer from the underside of the head and turn it clockwise only. Now measure the inside diameter of the guide (at both ends and in the centre of the guide) with a small bore gauge, then measure the gauge with a micrometer **(see illustration)**. Measure the guide at the ends and at the centre to determine if they are worn in a bell-mouth pattern (more wear at the ends). Replace any component that is beyond its limit with a new one. If the valve guide is within specifications, but is worn unevenly, it should be replaced with a new one. Repeat for the other valves.

17 Carefully inspect each valve face, stem and collet groove area for cracks, pits and burned spots.

18 Rotate the valve and check for any obvious indication that it is bent, in which case it must be replaced with a new one. Check the end of the stem for pitting and excessive wear. The presence of any of the above conditions indicates the need for valve servicing.

19 Check the end of each valve spring for wear and pitting. Measure the spring free length and compare it to the Specifications **(see illustration)**. Also place the spring upright on a flat surface and check it for bend by placing a ruler against it, or alternatively lay it against a set-square. If the sag or bend in any spring is excessive, fit a new set of springs.

20 Check the spring seats, retainers and collets for obvious wear and cracks. Any questionable parts should not be reused, as extensive damage will occur in the event of failure during engine operation.

21 If the inspection indicates that no overhaul work is required, the valve components can be reinstalled in the head.

Reassembly

22 Note that the valves should only be ground in (lapped) if the seats have been recut (a specialist task), and this will be done by that person.

23 Working on one valve at a time, lay the spring seat in place in the cylinder head with its shouldered side facing up **(see illustration)**. As it is easy to cock the seat on the top of the valve guide, and then tricky to get it to sit properly, fit it using a rod (such as a screwdriver) as a guide for it to slide down.

24 Lubricate the inside of the new valve stem seal with oil and fit it onto the guide, using finger pressure, a stem seal fitting tool, an appropriate size deep socket, or a small screwdriver (the shaft acts as a guide and the handle is used to push the seal on) to push the seal squarely onto the end of the valve guide until it is felt to clip into place **(see illustrations)**. Make sure the seal does not get cocked sideways as it could be damaged.

25 Coat the valve stem with molybdenum disulphide oil (a 50/50 mixture of molybdenum disulphide grease and engine oil), then slide it into its guide, rotating it slowly to avoid damaging the seal **(see illustration 11.7d)**. Check that the valve moves up-and-down freely in the guide.

26 Fit the spring with the closer-wound coils facing down into the cylinder head **(see illustration 11.7c)**. Fit the spring retainer, with its shouldered side facing down so that it fits into the top of the spring **(see illustration 11.7b)**.

27 Apply a small amount of grease to the collets to help hold them in place. Compress the valve spring with a spring compressor, making sure it is correctly located onto each end of the valve assembly (see Step 6) **(see illustrations 11.6a, b and c)**. Do not compress the spring any more than is necessary to slip the collets into place. Locate each collet in turn into the groove in the valve stem using a screwdriver with a dab of

11.23 Fit the spring seat

11.24a Use the shaft of the screwdriver to guide the seal down...

11.24b ...and the handle to press it squarely into place

11.27 Check the collets are fully seated

12.3 Check the operation of the clutch as described

12.4 Withdraw the driven gear

12.5 Hold the rotor while unscrewing the bolts

grease on it **(see illustration 11.7a)**. Carefully release the compressor, making sure the collets seat and lock in the retaining groove **(see illustration)**.

28 Repeat the procedure for the remaining valves. Remember to keep the parts for each valve together and separate from the other valves so they can be reinstalled in the same location.

29 Support the cylinder head on blocks so the valves can't contact the work surface, then tap the end of each valve stem lightly to fully seat the collets in their grooves.

30 After the cylinder head and camshafts have been installed, check the valve clearances and adjust as required (see Chapter 1).

12 Starter clutch and gears

Check

1 The operation of the starter clutch can be checked while it is in situ. Remove the alternator cover and idle/reduction gears (see Chapter 8). Check that the starter driven gear on the back of the alternator rotor is able to rotate freely clockwise as you look at it, but locks when rotated anti-clockwise. If not, the starter clutch is faulty and should be removed for inspection.

Removal

2 Remove the alternator rotor (see Chapter 8) – the starter clutch is bolted to the back of it. Remove the needle bearing from the starter driven gear hub, or from the crankshaft if it stayed there **(see illustration 12.7b)**.

3 With the alternator rotor face down on a workbench, check that the starter driven gear rotates freely in an anti-clockwise direction and locks against the rotor in a clockwise direction **(see illustration)**. If it doesn't, remove and inspect it as follows.

4 Withdraw the starter driven gear from the starter clutch **(see illustration)** – if it appears stuck, rotate it anti-clockwise as you withdraw it to free it from the starter clutch.

5 To remove the starter clutch, hold the rotor using a holding strap or a large adjustable spanner on the boss flats and unscrew the bolts inside it **(see illustration)**. Lift the clutch off, then remove the sprag assembly from the housing.

Inspection

6 Check the condition of the sprags inside the clutch body and the corresponding surface on the driven gear hub **(see illustration)**. If they are damaged, marked or flattened at any point, they should be replaced with new ones. Measure the outside diameter of the hub and check that it has not worn beyond the service limit given in the Specifications at the beginning of the Chapter.

7 Check the needle bearing and its corresponding surfaces in the starter driven gear hub and on the crankshaft **(see illustrations)**. Measure the inside diameter of the hub and check that it has not worn beyond the service limit given in the Specifications at the beginning of the Chapter. If the bearing or the surface in the hub shows signs of excessive wear fit new ones.

8 Check the teeth of the starter motor drive shaft, idle/reduction gears and starter driven gear. Replace the gears and/or starter motor if worn or chipped teeth are discovered on related gears. Also check the idle/reduction gear shafts for damage, and check that the gears are not a loose fit on the shafts. Replace the shafts and/or gears with new ones if necessary.

Installation

9 Fit the sprag assembly into the housing then seat the housing on the rotor. Clean the bolts and apply a suitable non-permanent thread locking compound, and tighten them to 29 Nm.

10 Lubricate the outside of the starter driven gear hub with clean engine oil, then fit the gear into the clutch, rotating it anti-clockwise as you do so to spread the sprags and allow the hub to enter **(see illustration 12.4)**. Fit the needle bearing into the hub **(see illustration 12.7a)**.

11 Install the alternator rotor (see Chapter 8).

12.6 Check the related surfaces for damage and wear

12.7a Check the bearing and its bearing surfaces in the hub...

12.7b ...and on the crankshaft

13 Clutch and clutch cable
– models with standard transmission

Clutch

Special tool: *A clutch centre holding tool is required – see Step 11.*

Removal

1 Drain the engine oil and the coolant (see Chapter 1).
2 Remove the trim piece from the clutch cover **(see illustrations)**.
3 Slacken the front nut securing the clutch cable in the bracket on the crankcase and thread it up the cable as far as it will go **(see illustration 13.44a)**. Slide the cable into the bracket to get some freeplay and free the cable end from the release lever, noting how it fits **(see illustration 13.44b)**.
4 Disconnect the coolant hoses **(see illustration)**.
5 Working evenly in a criss-cross pattern, unscrew the clutch cover bolts, on the Adventure Sports model noting the bracket for the sump guard **(see illustration)**. Turn

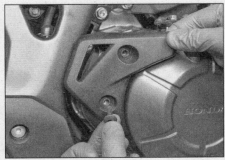

13.2a Undo the screws and remove the trim…

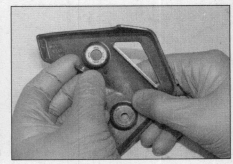

13.2b …noting the collars

the clutch release arm anti-clockwise as far as it will go. Remove the cover, being prepared to catch any residual oil. Remove the gasket. Remove the two dowels from either the cover or the crankcase if they are loose **(see illustration 13.37a)**. Remove the O-ring from the water pump outlet **(see illustration 14.25)**. A new gasket and O-ring will be needed.
6 Plug the coolant passage and hoses with clean rag to prevent residual coolant coming out as it could find its way into the sump.

7 Working in a criss-cross pattern, and holding the clutch to prevent it turning (cover it in rag and hold it by hand, the bolts are not tight), gradually slacken the clutch spring plate bolts until spring pressure is released, then unscrew the bolts and remove the plate and the springs **(see illustrations)**.
8 Remove the pressure plate, bringing the outermost friction and plain plates with it, noting how the tabs of the outer friction plate locate in the shallow slots in the housing,

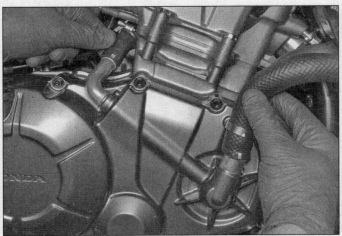

13.4 Slacken the clamps and ease the hoses off

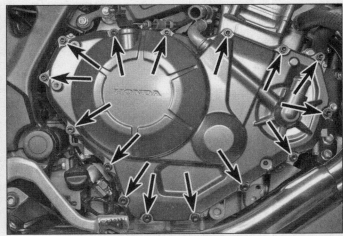

13.5 Clutch cover bolts (arrowed)

13.7a Clutch spring plate bolts (arrowed)

13.7b Unscrew the bolts and remove the plate…

13.7c …and the springs

13.8a Remove the pressure plate...

13.8b ... and the lifter rod

offset from the rest **(see illustration)**. Remove the lifter-rod from the pressure plate bearing or from the transmission shaft **(see illustration)**.
9 Remove the friction and plain plates, keeping them in order, then remove the anti-judder spring and spring seat **(see illustrations)** – unless new plates are being fitted, keep them in their original order as there are different types. If you are just fitting new plates and no further disassembly is required go to Step 15.
10 Use a small pointed tool to unstake the rim of the clutch nut from the indent in the end of the shaft **(see illustration)**.
11 To unscrew the clutch nut, the clutch centre must be held to prevent it turning. To do this you need the Honda service tool (07724-0050002) or an after-market alternative to hold

13.9a You can slide most of the plates out as a pack...

13.9b ...then use a hooked tool to get the rest...

13.9c ...followed by the anti-judder spring and its seat

13.10 Unstake the rim of the nut

13.11a This is the EBC tool specific for this bike…

13.11b …with extension on its handle

13.11c Fit the tool between the clutch centre and housing as shown…

13.11d …hold the tool and slacken the nut

13.14 Hold the sprung gear teeth aligned against the pressure of the spring and slide the clutch housing off

the clutch centre while the nut is loosened. We used the EBC tool CT009 with adapted handle extension to hold the clutch against the turning force required to loosen the nut **(see illustrations)**. With the clutch held, unscrew the nut and remove the washers **(see illustrations)**. A new nut will be needed.

12 Pull the clutch centre off the input shaft **(see illustration 13.28b)**. Remove the thrust washer from the shaft **(see illustration 13.28a)**.

13 If you are removing the primary drive gear as well as the clutch refer to Section 17 and slacken the gear bolt now.

14 Take the tension off the sprung outer gear on the primary drive gear using a screwdriver or punch in the hole as a lever and slide the

clutch housing off **(see illustration)**. Remove the clutch guide and washer from the back of the clutch housing, or slide it off the shaft if it did not come away with the housing **(see illustration 13.26)**.

Inspection

15 After an extended period of service the clutch friction plates will wear and promote clutch slip. Measure the thickness of each friction plate using a Vernier caliper **(see illustration)**. If any plate has worn to or beyond the service limit given in the Specifications at the beginning of the Chapter, or if any of the plates smell burnt or are glazed, the plates must be replaced with a new set.

16 The plain plates should not show any signs of excess heating (bluing). Check for warpage using a flat surface and feeler gauges **(see illustration)**. If any plate exceeds the maximum permissible amount of warpage, or shows signs of bluing, the plates must be replaced with a new set.

17 Measure the free length of each clutch spring using a Vernier caliper **(see illustration)**. Place each spring upright on a flat surface and check it for bend by placing a ruler against it, or alternatively lay it against a set square. If any spring is below the minimum free length specified or if the bend in any spring is excessive, replace all the springs with a new set.

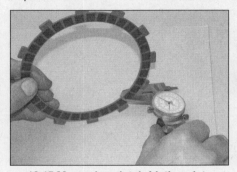

13.15 Measuring clutch friction plate thickness

13.16 Check the plain plates for warpage

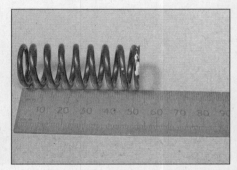

13.17 Measure the free length of the clutch springs and check them for bend

13.18 Check each spring seat (arrowed)

13.19a Check the friction plate tabs and housing slots…

13.19b … and the plain plate teeth and centre slots as described

18 Check the spring plate for cracks and the spring seats in the pressure plate for distortion – you can remove the seats by squeezing their sides until their open ends are clear of the groove **(see illustration)**.
19 Inspect the friction plates and the clutch housing for burrs and indentations on the edges of the protruding tabs on the plates and/or the slots in the housing **(see illustration)**. Similarly check for wear between the inner teeth of the plain plates and the slots in the clutch centre **(see illustration)**. Wear of this nature will cause clutch drag and slow disengagement during gear changes as the plates will snag when the pressure plate is lifted. With care a small amount of wear can be corrected by dressing with a fine file, but if this is excessive the worn components should be replaced with new ones.
20 Inspect the inner and outer bearing surfaces on the clutch guide and the bearing surface on the input shaft **(see illustration)**. Measure the external and internal diameters of the guide and the external diameter of the input shaft where the guide sits, and compare the results to the Specifications at the beginning of the Chapter. If there are any signs of wear, pitting or other damage the affected parts must be replaced with new ones. Also check the needle bearing in the clutch housing for wear and damage and

replace it with a new one if necessary – the old bearing must be pressed out and the new one pressed in using a hydraulic press, so you may need to get a suitably equipped workshop to do this for you. Do not drive the bearing out or in. Fit the new bearing with its marked side facing up into the housing, and so it is set centrally in the bore.
21 Check the pressure plate and its bearing and the lifter rod for signs of wear or damage and roughness **(see illustration)**. Check that the bearing outer race is a good fit in the centre of the plate, and that the inner race rotates freely without any rough spots. Check

the lifter rod head and the corresponding section on the release mechanism shaft that engages it for signs of wear or damage **(see illustration)**. Replace any parts necessary with new ones. If a new bearing is required drive the old one out using a socket or bearing driver applied from the outer side of the plate and seated on the inner race, and drive the new one in using a socket or driver applied from the inner side of the plate and seated on the outer race until it seats.
22 Check the slipper mechanism cams on the pressure plate and clutch centre for wear and damage **(see illustration)**.

13.20 Check the bearing surfaces on the guide and the shaft and the bearing in the housing

13.21a Check the lifter plate and its bearing

13.21b Check the lifter rod head and its cut-out in the shaft for wear

13.22 Check the cam sliding surfaces

13.23a Withdraw the shaft from the cover...

13.23b ...and free the spring

13.23c Lever the seal out

13.23d Check the bearings

13.23e Push the new seal in square

13.23f Correct fitting of return spring ends

23 Check the clutch release mechanism shaft turns smoothly in its housing in the cover. If it is rough, draw the shaft out of the cover and remove the return spring, noting how the spring ends locate **(see illustrations)**. Remove the oil seal (a new one will be required), and clean and check the bearings **(see illustrations)**. Replace the bearings with new ones if necessary, referring to *Tools and Workshop Tips* – make sure the upper bearing is fitted to a depth of 6.5 to 7.5 mm so the recess for the oil seal is fully exposed. On reassembly lubricate the bearings with engine oil. Fit a new oil seal with its marked side facing out, pushing it in until it seats, and lubricate its lip with grease

(see illustration). Slide the shaft in and fit the spring, making sure the ends locate correctly **(see illustration)**.

24 Check the teeth of the primary driven gear on the back of the clutch housing and the corresponding teeth of the primary drive gear on the crankshaft. Replace the clutch housing and/or primary drive gear with a new one if worn or chipped teeth are discovered – refer to Section 17 for the primary drive gear.

Installation

25 Remove all traces of old gasket from the crankcase and clutch cover surfaces.

26 Lubricate the clutch housing needle

bearing and the inside and outside of the clutch guide with molybdenum disulphide oil (a 50/50 mix of molybdenum disulphide grease and engine oil), then fit the washer onto the guide and slide the guide into the housing **(see illustration)**.

27 Align the primary drive gear teeth using a screwdriver or punch and slide the clutch housing onto the shaft **(see illustration 13.14)**. Remove the alignment tool from the gear, and check that the housing is all the way on, in which case the drive and driven gear faces sit flush **(see illustration)**. If the primary drive gear was removed refer to Section 17 and tighten its bolt now.

28 Slide the thrust washer onto the sha

13.26 Fit the washer and slide the guide into the back of the housing

13.27 Check the gear faces are flush where the teeth mesh

13.28a Fit the thrust washer

13.28b Engage the splines and slide the clutch centre on

13.29a Fit the plain washer…

13.29b …the spring washer…

and up against the housing, then slide the clutch centre onto the shaft splines **(see illustrations)**.

29 Fit the plain washer then the spring washer with the OUT mark facing out **(see illustrations)**. Lubricate the new clutch nut threads and seating surface with oil and fit the nut with the thin rim facing out **(see illustration)**. Hold the clutch as before (see Step 11) and tighten the nut to 128 Nm **(see illustration)**. Check that the clutch centre rotates freely after tightening the nut. Stake

13.29c …and a new clutch nut

13.29d Tighten the nut to the specified torque…

13.29e …then use a punch…

13.29f …to stake the rim

13.30a Fit the seat…

13.30b …and the spring…

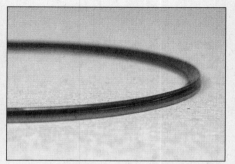

13.30c …so the outer rim of the spring is raised off the seat

the rim of the nut into the indent in the end of the shaft (see illustrations).

30 Fit the anti-judder spring seat, then fit the spring so its outer rim is raised off the seat (see illustrations).

31 There are eight friction plates and seven plain plates. Of the eight friction plates there are three different types, A, B and C. First identify the single type A plate, which has a wider internal diameter and has darker friction faces and is the outermost plate that fits onto the pressure plate, and the two type B plates, which have a wider internal diameter and fit first and last into the clutch housing (see illustration). All other type C friction plates have a narrower internal diameter. Of the seven plain plates there are three different types, A, B and C. First identify the single type A plate, which has a smooth finish and a wider internal diameter and is the outermost plate and fits onto the pressure plate, and the single type B plate, which has a dull and dimpled finish and is the innermost plain plate in the clutch housing (see illustration). All other type C plain plates are shiny and dimpled.

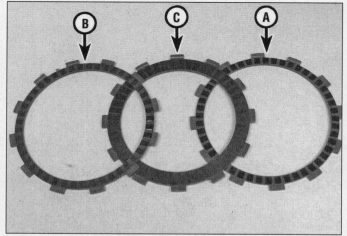

13.31a Type A, B and C friction plates

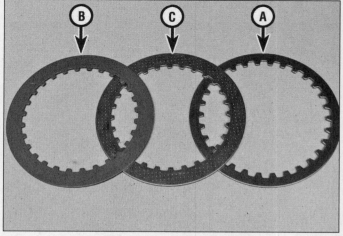

13.31b Type A, B and C plain plates

13.32a Fit a Type B friction plate...

13.32b ...then the Type B plain plate...

13.32c ... then a Type C friction plate...

13.32d ...and a Type C plain plate, and so on as described until all Type C plates are fitted...

13.32e ...then fit the second Type B friction plate

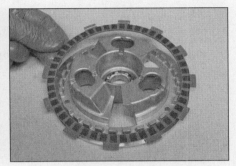

13.32f Fit the Type A friction plate...

32 Lay the clutch plates out in order as described in Step 31. Coat each plate with clean engine oil prior to installation. Build up the plates, starting with a type B friction plate, aligning its tabs with the deep slots, and seating it around the anti-judder spring and seat, then fit the type B plain plate with the different surface, then alternate type C friction plates and type C plain plates until all are fitted, then fit the second type B friction plate **(see illustrations)**. Fit the outermost type A friction plate and the type A plain plate onto the pressure plate **(see illustrations)**.

33 Make sure the bearing and spring seats are correctly seated in the pressure plate and lubricate the bearing with clean engine oil **(see illustration 13.18)**. Fit the lifter-rod into the shaft **(see illustration 13.8b)**. Align and fit the pressure plate, seating the outermost friction plate tabs in the shallow slots in the housing so they are offset from the rest **(see illustration 13.8a)**.

34 Fit the clutch springs, the spring plate, and the bolts, then hold the clutch housing and tighten the bolts evenly and a little at a time in a criss-cross sequence to 12 Nm **(see illustration 13.7c and b)**.

35 To fit the clutch cover you need to align the slot in the end of the water pump shaft with the drive tab on the end of the front balancer shaft, which can be done by removing the secondary (sub) spark plugs (see Chapter 1), and turning the engine clockwise using a socket on the primary drive gear bolt until the line on the primary drive gear aligns with the triangle on the crankcase, at which point the drive tab should be in the position shown **(see illustration)**, and by turning the water pump shaft so the slot aligns with the marks on the pump housing **(see illustration 14.23b)**.

13.32g ...and the Type A plain plate onto the back of the pressure plate

13.35 Align the index line (A) on the gear with the triangle (B) on the crankcase. Drive tab (C)

13.37a Locate the new gasket over the dowels (arrowed)...

13.37b ...then fit the cover

Alternatively you can set the pump shaft slot to align with the drive tab by eye and make small adjustments by turning the pump shaft as you fit the cover.

36 Fit a new O-ring smeared with oil into the groove on the water pump outlet **(see illustration 14.25)**.

37 Apply a smear of silicone sealant (Threebond 1207B or equivalent) 10 to 15 mm long onto each side of the crankcase joints on the cover mating surface **(see illustration 14.26a)**. Fit the two dowels into the crankcase if removed, then fit a new gasket, locating it over the dowels **(see illustration)**. Turn the release arm to the position shown, then fit the cover onto the dowels, and

turn the release arm clockwise so it engages the head of the lifter rod **(see illustration)**. Fit all the bolts finger-tight, not forgetting the sump guard bracket on the Adventure Sports model, and tighten them evenly and a little at a time in a criss-cross pattern to 12 Nm **(see illustration 13.5)**.

38 Connect the coolant hoses, pushing them fully on, and tighten the clamps **(see illustration 13.4)**.

39 Engage the clutch cable end in the release lever arm **(see illustration 13.44b)**. Adjust clutch lever freeplay (see Chapter 1).

40 Fit the cover trim piece **(see illustrations 13.2b and a)**.

41 Fill the engine with the correct amount and type of oil (see Chapter 1). Fill the cooling system (see Chapter 1).

Clutch cable

42 Remove the fuel tank, and for best access the air filter housing (see Chapter 4). For best access at the lever remove the hand guard (see Chapter 7).

43 Fully slacken the lockring on the adjuster at the handlebar end of the cable, then thread the adjuster fully in **(see illustration)**. This provides freeplay in the cable and resets the adjuster to the beginning of its span.

44 Slacken the front nut securing the clutch cable in the bracket on the crankcase and thread it up the cable as far as it will go **(see illustration)**. Slide the cable into the bracket to get some freeplay and free the cable end from the release lever, noting how it fits **(see illustration)**. Slide the rubber boot off then thread the rear nut off and slip the cable out of the bracket **(see illustrations)**.

45 Draw the cable out to the front, noting its routing.

46 Align the slots in the adjuster and lockring at the handlebar end of the cable with that in the lever bracket, then pull the outer cable end from the socket in the adjuster and release

13.43 Slacken the lockring (arrowed) and turn the adjuster in

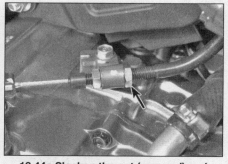

13.44a Slacken the nut (arrowed) and thread it up...

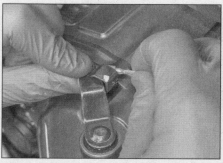

13.44b ...and free the end from the release lever

13.44c Displace the boot and thread the rear nut off, then draw the threaded section out...

13.44d ...so you can slip the inner cable out to the side

13.46a Align the slots and free the cable from the adjuster…

13.46b …and from the lever

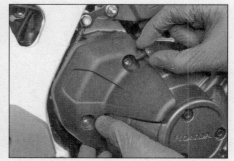

14.2a Undo the screws and remove the trim…

the inner cable from the lever **(see illustrations)**.

47 Installation is the reverse of removal. Apply grease to the cable ends. Make sure the cable is correctly routed. Adjust the amount of clutch lever freeplay (see Chapter 1).

14 Dual-clutch and linear solenoid valve – models with DCT

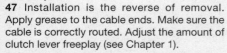

Note: *The DCT management system is covered in Chapter 4.*

Dual clutch

Removal

1 Drain the engine oil and the coolant (see Chapter 1).

2 Remove the trim piece from the clutch cover **(see illustrations)**.

3 Displace the gearchange shaft angle sensor **(see illustration)**. A new O-ring will be needed.

4 Remove the clutch EOP sensor cover **(see illustrations)**.

5 Disconnect the linear solenoid valve wiring connector (4-pin black) and release the wiring ties, then feed the connector down, noting its routing **(see illustration)**. Disconnect the clutch line EOP sensor wiring connector (3-pin grey), the No. 1 clutch EOP sensor wiring connector (3-pin grey), and the No. 2 clutch EOP sensor wiring connector (3-pin black) **(see illustration)**.

14.2b …noting the collars

14.3 Unscrew the bolt and pull the sensor off the cover

14.4a Undo the screws and remove the cover…

14.4b …noting the collars

14.5a Linear solenoid valve wiring connector (arrowed)

14.5b Clutch line EOP sensor connector (A), No. 1 clutch EOP sensor connector (B), No. 2 clutch EOP sensor connector (C)

14.5c Unscrew the bolt and displace the bracket

14.6a Slacken the clamp and disconnect the hose

14.6b Unscrew the pipe bolts...

14.6c ...disconnect the hose...

14.6d ...and remove the pipe, noting the O-ring (arrowed)

Unscrew the sensor wiring clip bracket bolt (see illustration).

6 Disconnect the coolant inlet hose and remove the coolant pipe (see illustrations). A new O-ring will be needed for the pipe.

7 Remove the oil feed pipe cover from the clutch cover (see illustration) – new sealing rings will be needed for the bolts and a new O-ring for the cover. Remove the inner oil feed pipe, the feed pipe guide plate, and the outer oil feed pipe (see illustrations). New O-rings will be needed for the outer feed pipe and the plate (see illustration).

14.7a Remove the cover...

14.7b ...the inner feed pipe...

14.7c ...the guide plate...

14.7d ...and the outer feed pipe

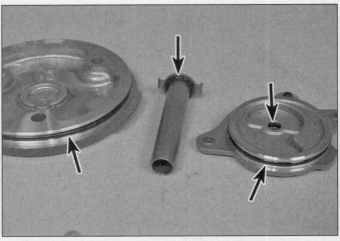

14.7e Replace the cover, outer feed pipe and guide plate O-rings (arrowed) with new ones

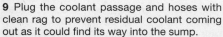

14.8 Clutch cover bolts (arrowed)

14.10a Align and lock the sprung gear teeth as shown

8 Working evenly in a criss-cross pattern, unscrew the clutch cover bolts, on the Adventure Sports model noting the bracket for the sump guard **(see illustration)**. Remove the cover, being prepared to catch any residual oil. Remove the gasket. Remove the two dowels from either the cover or the crankcase if they are loose **(see illustration 14.26b)**. Remove the O-ring from the water pump outlet **(see illustration 14.25)**. Remove the oil joint pipe **(see illustration 14.24)**. A new gasket, a new O-ring for the coolant passage, and new O-rings and back-up rings for the oil joint pipe will be needed.

9 Plug the coolant passage and hoses with clean rag to prevent residual coolant coming out as it could find its way into the sump.

10 Take the tension off the sprung outer gear on the primary drive gear using a screwdriver or punch in the hole as a lever and fit a 6 mm bolt in the other hole to keep the gear teeth aligned **(see illustration)**. Slide the complete dual clutch/primary driven gear assembly off the shaft **(see illustration)**. Remove the four split sealing rings from shaft **(see illustration)** – new ones will be needed.

11 The primary driven gear has an index line on its outer face and there are curved cut-outs **(see illustration 14.18)**. The two clutch plate assemblies are identical, but the clutch centres that fit in them differ. The No. 1 (outer) clutch centre has a narrow splined bore and it engages the inner input shaft. The No. 2 (inner) clutch centre has a wide splined bore and it engages the outer input shaft.

12 Remove the clutch centre and washer from each clutch plate assembly **(see illustrations)**.

13 If you need to remove the clutch plate assemblies from the primary driven gear, mark each one so it can fit on the same side of the gear and therefore be mated with its original clutch centre. Do not attempt to disassemble

14.10b Slide the dual clutch assembly off the shaft

14.10c Remove the sealing rings (arrowed), noting how they locate

14.12a Remove the No. 1 clutch centre...

14.12b ...and its washer...

14.12c ...then remove the No. 2 clutch centre...

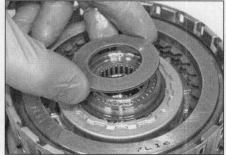

14.12d ...and its washer

14.14a Set the dial gauge up as shown...

14.14b ...then use a screwdriver under the clutch plate teeth to lift the set plate up against the snap-ring

14.15 Check the bearings and all bearing surfaces on the shafts

the clutch plate assemblies. Ease each clutch assembly off the primary driven gear shaft, noting that you must initially overcome the grip of the O-rings. Remove the O-rings – new ones will be needed.

Inspection

14 After an extended period of service the clutch friction plates will wear and promote clutch slip. As wear increases the clearance between the set plate and the snap ring increases. To determine the amount of wear mount a dial gauge on the top of the set plate, then lift the plate up against the snap ring and record the clearance **(see illustrations)**. Repeat at two other points equidistant around the plate so three readings are taken. If the clearance is up to or beyond the service limit given in the Specifications at the beginning of the Chapter fit a new clutch plate assembly – the plates themselves cannot be replaced separately.

15 Check the bearing surfaces on the primary driven gear shaft, the clutch assembly and clutch centre and on the inner and outer input shafts for wear and damage. Affected parts must be replaced with new ones. Also check the needle bearings in the primary driven gear shaft for wear and damage and fit a new primary driven gear if necessary **(see illustration)** – the bearings are not available separately.

16 Check the teeth of the primary driven gear and the corresponding teeth of the primary drive gear on the crankshaft. Replace the drive and/or driven gear with a new one if worn or chipped teeth are discovered – refer to Section 17 for the primary drive gear.

17 Check the bearings in the clutch cover and fit new ones if necessary, referring to *Tools and Workshop Tips* in the Reference Section **(see illustration)**.

Installation

18 Fit new O-rings smeared with oil into the grooves in each side of the primary driven gear shaft. Smear molybdenum disulphide oil (a 50/50 mixture of molybdenum disulphide grease and engine oil) onto the shaft splines. Slide the No. 1 clutch assembly onto the shaft on the side that the primary driven gear face has the index line and curved cut-outs, then slide the No. 2 assembly onto the other side **(see illustration)**.

19 Fit the washer onto the No. 1 (outer) clutch plate assembly, then fit the clutch centre with the narrow splined bore **(see illustrations 14.12b and a)**. Repeat for the No. 2 (inner) clutch plate assembly and the clutch centre with the wide splined bore **(see illustrations 14.12d and c)**.

20 Fit new sealing rings smeared with oil into the grooves in the inner input shaft, making sure their split ends seat together correctly

(see illustration). Apply engine oil to the needle bearings in the primary driven gear shaft. Smear molybdenum disulphide oil (a 50/50 mixture of molybdenum disulphide grease and engine oil) onto the inner and outer shaft splines.

21 Check the bolt holding the primary drive gear teeth aligned is still in place, and if not align the teeth using a screwdriver or punch and refit the bolt **(see illustration 14.10a)**.

22 Slide the dual clutch/primary driven gear assembly onto the shaft with the index line and cut-outs **(see illustration 14.18)** on the primary driven gear facing out, and engage the No. 2 clutch centre splines with those on the outer shaft and the No. 1 clutch centre splines with those on the end of the inner shaft, and engage the primary drive and driven gear teeth using a screwdriver or punch to adjust the alignment of the sprung gear teeth if engagement is difficult **(see illustration 14.10b)**. Remove the alignment bolt from the primary drive gear **(see illustration 14.10a)**.

23 To fit the clutch cover you need to align the slot in the end of the water pump shaft with the drive tab on the end of the front balancer shaft, which can be done by removing the secondary (sub) spark plugs (see Chapter 1), and turning the engine clockwise using a socket on the primary drive gear bolt until the line on the primary drive gear aligns with the triangle on the crankcase, at which

14.17 Check the bearings (arrowed)

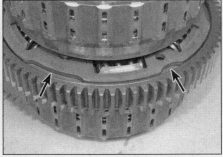

14.18 The outer face of the primary driven gear has cut-outs (arrowed) – fit the No. 1 (outer) clutch onto this side

14.20 Make sure the the ends of the rings seat and align correctly

14.23a Align the index line (A) on the gear with the triangle (B) on the crankcase. Drive tab (C)

14.23b Align the slot in the end of the shaft with the index marks (arrowed)

point the drive tab should be in the position shown **(see illustration)**, and by turning the water pump shaft so the slot aligns with the marks on the pump housing **(see illustration)**. Alternatively you can set the pump shaft slot to align with the drive tab by eye and make small adjustments by turning the pump shaft as you fit the cover.

24 Fit new O-rings and back-up rings

smeared with oil into the grooves in the oil joint pipe, then ease the pipe into the crankcase **(see illustration)**.

25 Fit a new O-ring smeared with oil into the groove on the water pump outlet **(see illustration)**.

26 Apply a smear of silicone sealant (Threebond 1207B or equivalent) 10 to 15 mm long onto each side of the crankcase joints on

the cover mating surface **(see illustration)**. Fit the two dowels into the crankcase if removed, then fit a new gasket, locating it over the dowels **(see illustration)**. Fit the cover onto the dowels **(see illustration)**. Fit all the bolts finger-tight, not forgetting the sump guard bracket on the Adventure Sports model, and tighten them evenly and a little at a time in a criss-cross pattern to 12 Nm **(see illustration 14.8)**.

14.24 Fit the oil joint pipe using a new O-ring (A) and back-up ring (B) on each end

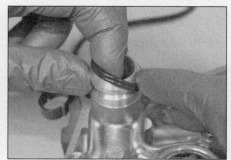

14.25 Fit a new O-ring into the groove

14.26a Apply sealant across the two crankcase joints

14.26b Locate the new gasket over the dowels (arrowed)...

14.26c ...then fit the cover

14.27a Seat the tabs on the outer feed pipe horizontally as shown

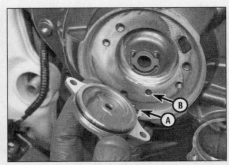

14.27b Fit the pin (A) into the hole (B)

14.27c Seat the tabs on the inner feed pipe vertically as shown

14.27d Use new sealing washers

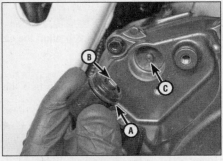

14.30 Fit a new O-ring (A), and align the flat on the sensor (B) with that on the gearchange shaft end (C)

perform the clutch initialise learning procedure (see Chapter 4, Section 10).

Linear solenoid valves

Caution: It is essential that no dirt enters the valve housing or any of the passages from it into the crankcase.

Removal

34 Drain the engine oil (see Chapter 1).

35 Remove the right-hand fairing side panel (see Chapter 7).

36 Remove the clutch EOP sensor cover **(see illustrations 14.4a and b)**. Disconnect the linear solenoid valve wiring connector (4-pin black) and release the wiring ties **(see illustration 14.5a)**.

37 Unscrew the valve housing mounting bolts and remove the housing **(see illustrations)**. Remove the housing seal and the spool valve filter from the clutch cover, then remove the seal from filter **(see illustrations 14.46c, b and a)** – new seals must be fitted.

38 Remove the separator plate and seal from the valve housing, and the dowels if required **(see illustrations 14.45b and a)** – a new seal must be fitted.

Disassembly

39 Unscrew the valve cover bolts and remove the cover **(see illustration)**. Remove the gasket – a new one must be fitted.

27 Fit new O-rings smeared with oil onto the outer oil feed pipe, the guide plate and the feed pipe cover **(see illustration 14.7e)**. Fit the outer feed pipe, seating the tabs horizontally between the ribs **(see illustration)**. Fit the feed pipe guide plate, seating the pin in the hole, and tighten the bolts to 5 Nm **(see illustration)**. Fit the inner oil feed pipe, seating the tabs vertically between the ribs **(see illustration)**. Fit the oil feed pipe cover using new sealing washers on the bolts, and tighten the bolts to 12 Nm **(see illustration)**.

28 Fit the coolant pipe using a new O-ring smeared with oil and tighten the bolts to 12 Nm **(see illustrations 14.6d, c and b)**. Connect the coolant inlet hose, pushing it fully

on **(see illustration 14.6a)**. Tighten the hose clamps.

29 Refer to Steps 5 and 4 and connect and secure the sensor and solenoid wiring and fit the sensor cover.

30 Fit the gearchange shaft angle sensor using a new O-ring smeared with oil and aligning the flats on the sensor and the gearchange shaft end, and tighten the bolt to 12 Nm **(see illustration)**.

31 Fit the cover trim piece **(see illustrations 14.2b and a)**.

32 Fill the engine with the correct amount and type of oil (see Chapter 1). Fill the cooling system (see Chapter 1).

33 If a new dual clutch has been fitted

14.37a Unscrew the bolts...

14.37b ...and remove the valve housing

14.39 Unscrew the bolts and remove the cover

14.40 Valve retainer plate bolt (arrowed)

14.43a Seat the retainer plate around the valves…

14.43b …fit the assembly into the housing…

14.43c …and fit the threadlocked bolt

14.43d Seat the grommet in the cut-out

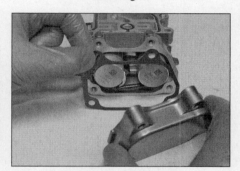

14.44 Use a new gasket

40 Unscrew the valve retainer plate bolt and remove the valve assembly from the housing, noting how the wiring grommet and plate locate **(see illustration)**.

41 Remove all traces of old gasket from the cover and housing mating surfaces, and old

sealant from the wiring grommet. Clean all parts using compressed air.

Reassembly

42 Make sure all components are clean.

43 Clean the threads of the valve retainer

plate bolt threads and apply fresh threadlock. Fit the retainer plate around the valves then fit the assembly into the housing and tighten the bolt to 12 Nm **(see illustrations)**. Smear some sealant onto the wiring grommet and press it into its cut-out in the housing **(see illustration)**.

44 Fit the cover using a new gasket and tighten the bolts to 12 Nm **(see illustration)**.

Installation

45 Fit the dowels if removed, then smear the new separator plate seal with oil and fit the seal onto the housing and fit the plate over the dowels, making sure they are all correctly seated **(see illustrations)**.

46 Smear the new spool valve seal and new housing seal with oil. Fit the seal onto the filter, then fit the filter onto the clutch cover **(see illustrations)**. Fit the housing seal onto the clutch cover **(see illustration)**. Make sure they are all correctly seated.

14.45a Housing dowels (arrowed). Use a new seal and smear it with oil

14.45b Seat the plate over the dowels and onto the housing

14.46a Fit the seal around the rim of the filter…

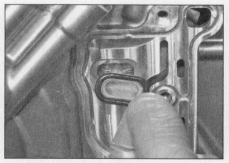

14.46b …then fit the filter with the dished side facing in

14.46c Fit the seal into the groove

15.2a Note the alignment, then unscrew the bolt and slide the arm off

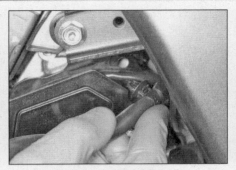

15.2b Release the wiring clip…

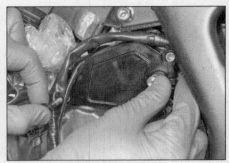

15.2c …then unscrew the bolts and remove the cover

47 Fit the valve housing and tighten the bolts to 12 Nm **(see illustrations 14.37b and a)**.
48 Connect the wiring connector and secure the wiring in its ties, making sure it is correctly routed **(see illustration 14.5a)**. Fit the EOP sensor cover **(see illustration 14.4b and a)**.
49 Fill the engine with the correct amount and type of oil (see Chapter 1).

15 Gearchange mechanism – models with standard transmission

Removal

1 Make sure the transmission is in neutral. Remove the clutch (Section 13). Block the

15.4 Note how the spring ends locate, and how the roller sits in the neutral detent, then unscrew the bolt (arrowed) and remove the arm

15.3a Unscrew the bolt (arrowed) and remove the plate

holes into the sump with clean rag to prevent anything falling in.
2 Unscrew the gearchange linkage arm pinch bolt and slide the arm off the shaft, noting how the slit in the arm aligns with the punch mark on the shaft **(see illustration)**. Remove the gearchange shaft cover **(see illustrations)**. Clean the end of the shaft.
3 Remove the gearchange mechanism retainer plate **(see illustration)**. Note how the gearchange shaft centralising spring ends fit on each side of the locating pin in the casing, and how the pawls on the selector arm locate onto the pins on the end of the selector drum cam. Grasp the end of the shaft and withdraw the shaft/arm assembly **(see illustration)**. Retrieve the washer from the crankcase if it didn't come with the shaft.
4 If required, note how the stopper arm spring ends locate and how the roller on the arm

15.3b Withdraw the shaft/arm assembly, noting the washer (arrowed)

locates in the neutral detent on the selector drum cam, then unscrew the stopper arm bolt and remove the arm, the washer and the spring, noting how they fit **(see illustration)**.
5 Lever out the shaft oil seal with a seal hook or screwdriver **(see illustration 16.22)**. A new seal is needed.

Inspection

6 Check the selector arm for cracks, distortion and wear of its pawls, and check for any corresponding wear on the pins on the selector drum cam **(see illustration)**. Check the arm moves up smoothly and freely and returns under pressure of its spring **(see illustration)**. Also check the stopper arm roller and the detents in the selector drum cam for any wear or damage, and make sure the roller turns freely **(see illustration)**. Replace any

15.6a Check the selector arm pawls and the pins…

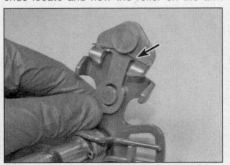

15.6b … and check the action of the arm and its spring (arrowed)

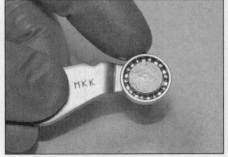

15.6c Check the stopper arm roller and cam as described

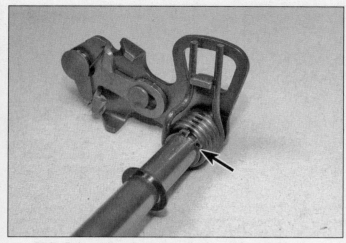

15.7a Release the circlip (arrowed) to remove the spring

15.7b Check the locating pin (arrowed) is tight

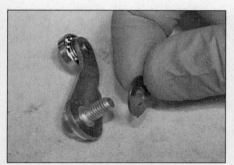

15.10a Seat the arm onto the bolt shoulder as shown then fit the washer…

15.10b …and the spring

15.10c Thread the bolt in then push the arm up against the spring and locate the roller in the neutral detent, and fully tighten the bolt

components that are worn or damaged with new ones. If required, remove the selector drum cam by unscrewing the bolt in its centre. Note the locating pin in the end of the drum and remove it for safekeeping if required. On installation, locate the pin in the bigger cut-out in the back of the cam. Clean the threads of the cam bolt and apply a suitable non-permanent thread locking compound, and tighten it to 23 Nm.

7 Inspect the shaft centralising spring and the stopper arm return spring for fatigue, wear or damage. If any is found, the components must be replaced with new ones. To replace the shaft spring, slide the washer off the shaft, then remove the circlip and slide the spring off the shaft, noting how its ends locate (see illustration). Fit the new spring, locating the ends on each side of the tab, and secure it with the circlip, making sure it locates in its groove. Slide the washer against the circlip. Also check that the centralising spring locating pin in the crankcase is securely tightened. If it is loose, remove it, clean the threads and apply a non-permanent thread locking compound, then tighten it.

8 Check the gearchange shaft is straight and look for damage to the splines. If the shaft is bent you can attempt to straighten it, but if the splines are damaged the shaft must be replaced with a new one.

Installation

9 Press or drive the new shaft oil seal squarely into place with its marked side facing out using your fingers, a seal driver or suitable socket, so it sits flush with its housing rim (see illustration 16.26b).

10 If removed, clean the threads of the stopper arm bolt and apply a suitable non-permanent thread locking compound. Fit the bolt through the stopper arm, then fit the washer and the stopper arm return spring onto the bolt (see illustrations). Fit the arm, locating the roller onto the neutral detent on the selector drum and making sure the spring ends are positioned correctly (see illustration). Tighten the bolt to 12 Nm. Check that the arm and spring ends are correctly positioned (see illustration 15.4).

11 Check that the shaft centralising spring is properly positioned and slide the washer onto the shaft if removed (see illus-

tration 15.7). Apply some grease to the lips of the gearchange shaft oil seal in the left-hand side of the crankcase, and wrap a single layer of thin insulating tape around the shaft splines. Slide the shaft into place and push it all the way through the case until the splined end comes out the other side (see illustration 15.3b). Locate the selector arm pawls onto the pins on the selector drum cam and the centralising spring ends onto each side of the locating pin in the crankcase (see illustration 15.3a). Clean the threads of the retainer plate bolt and apply a suitable non-permanent thread locking compound, then fit the plate and tighten the bolt to 12 Nm (see illustration 15.3a).

12 Remove the rag that was blocking the sump, then install the clutch (Section 13).

13 Remove the insulating tape from around the gearchange shaft splines. Fit the cover and secure the wiring (see illustrations 15.2c and b). Slide the gearchange linkage arm onto the shaft, aligning its slit with the punch mark on the shaft (see illustration 15.2a). Fit the pinch bolt and tighten it.

16.1 Unscrew the bolts and remove the cover

16.2a Disconnect the wiring…

16.2b …unscrew the bolts…

16 Gearchange mechanism – models with DCT

Gearchange control motor and reduction gears

Removal

1 Remove the control motor cover (see illustration).

2 Disconnect the control motor wiring connector and remove the motor (see illustrations). A new O-ring will be needed (see illustration 16.14).

3 Remove the reduction gear cover (see illustrations). Remove the gasket – a new one will be needed (see illustration 16.13). Remove the cover locating dowels if loose.

4 Remove the reduction gears, noting their alignment, how they engage, and how they locate (see illustrations 16.12, 16.11 and 16.10).

Inspection

5 Connect a fully charged 12V battery to the control motor terminals using auxiliary wires and check the motor turns in one direction, then reverse the wires and check it turns in the other direction. If not, fit a new motor.

6 Check the teeth of the control motor drive shaft and reduction gears. Replace the gears and/or control motor if worn or chipped teeth are discovered on related gears.

7 Check the three bearings in the cover and the two in the crankcase and fit new ones if necessary, referring to *Tools and Workshop Tips* in the Reference Section (see illustration) – the bearings should come out

easily if you heat the around the housings to around 80°C using a hot air gun. Fit the new bearings with the marked side facing out, smear them with oil and tap them in using a socket or driver on the outer race until they seat.

Installation

8 Clean all traces of old gasket off the cover and crankcase mating surfaces.

9 Apply Unirex N3 grease or its equivalent to the reduction gear teeth, shaft ends and bearings.

10 Fit the middle reduction gear first, with the larger half-gear on the inside and facing forwards (see illustration).

11 Align the ends of the half gear with the crankcase ribs and fit the front reduction gear with the smaller gear on the inside engaging the half-gear (see illustration).

16.2c …and remove the motor

16.3a Unscrew the bolts, noting the washers…

16.3b …and remove the cover

16.7 Check the bearings (arrowed)

16.10 Fit the middle gear into its bearing

16.11 Align the half-gear as shown and fit the front reduction gear

16.12 Fit the rear reduction gear as shown, aligning the punch marks and the wide splines

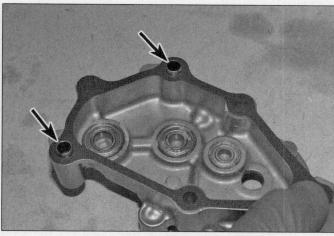

16.13 Fit the gasket onto the dowels (arrowed)

12 Fit the rear gear onto the shaft with the punch mark facing out and aligning the wide splines, making sure the gear teeth engage centrally and the punch mark aligns with that on the middle reduction gear **(see illustration)**.
13 Fit the cover dowels if removed, then seat the new gasket onto the dowels **(see illustration)**. Fit the cover and tighten the bolts to 14 Nm **(see illustrations 16.3b and a)**.
14 Fit a new O-ring smeared with oil onto the control motor **(see illustration)**. Fit the motor and tighten the bolts to 14 Nm **(see illustrations 16.2c and b)**. Connect the wiring **(see illustration 16.2a)**.

15 Fit the control motor cover, making sure the wiring is correctly routed, and tighten the bolts to 12 Nm **(see illustration)**.

Gearchange shaft

Removal

16 Make sure the transmission is in neutral. Remove the gearchange control motor and reduction gears (see above). Remove the dual-clutch/primary driven gear assembly (Section 14). Block the holes into the sump with clean rag to prevent anything falling in.
17 Note how the gearchange shaft

centralising spring ends fit on each side of the locating pin in the casing, and how the hole in the selector arm locates over the roller on the drum shifter. Grasp the end of the shaft and withdraw the shaft/arm assembly **(see illustration)**. Retrieve the washer from the crankcase if it didn't come with the shaft. Remove the roller from the drum shifter pin **(see illustration)**.
18 Unscrew the selector drum shifter guide plate bolts and remove the plate **(see illustrations)**. Remove the guide plate spacer, the dowel if loose, and the washer from the stopper arm **(see illustrations 16.30c, b and a)**.

16.14 Fit the O-ring (arrowed) into the groove

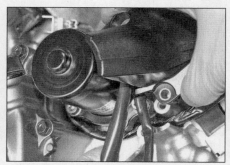

16.15 Make sure the wiring is correctly routed when fitting the cover

16.17a Withdraw the shaft/arm assembly, noting the washer (arrowed)

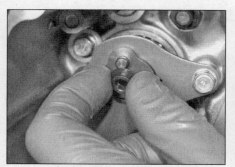

16.17b Remove the roller

16.18a Unscrew the bolts...

16.18b ...and remove the plate

16.19 Remove the shifter assembly and remove the pawls, plungers and springs from it

16.20a Unscrew the bolt...

16.20b ...and remove the cam...

16.20c ...and its locating pin

16.21 Remove the stopper arm

19 Hold the pawls and remove the shifter assembly from the selector drum cam, noting how it locates, then release and remove the pawls, plungers and springs **(see illustration)**.
20 Unscrew the selector drum cam bolt, then hold the stopper arm away from the cam and remove the cam, then move the stopper arm across to relax the spring **(see illustrations)**. Note the locating pin in the end of the drum and remove it for safekeeping if required **(see illustration)**.
21 Note how the stopper arm spring ends locate, then remove the arm assembly **(see illustration)**.
22 Lever out the shaft oil seal with a seal hook or screwdriver **(see illustration)**. A new seal is needed.

Inspection

23 Check the selector arm and its roller, and the drum cam teeth and pawls for wear and damage **(see illustrations)**. Also check the stopper arm roller and the detents in the selector drum cam, and make sure the roller turns freely **(see illustration)**. Replace any components that are worn or damaged with new ones.
24 Inspect the shaft centralising spring and the stopper arm return spring for fatigue, wear or damage. If any is found, the components must be replaced with new ones. To replace the shaft spring, slide the washer off the shaft, then remove the circlip and slide the spring off the shaft, noting how its ends locate **(see illustration)**. Fit the new spring, locating the

16.22 Remove the oil seal

16.23a Check the selector arm and the roller...

16.23b ...the ends of the pawls and where they seat against the drum cam and shifter

16.23c Check the stopper arm roller and cam as described

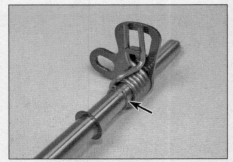

16.24a Release the circlip (arrowed) to remove the spring

16.24b Check the locating pin (arrowed) is tight

16.25 Check the bearing (arrowed)

16.26a Fit the seal with the marked side facing out...

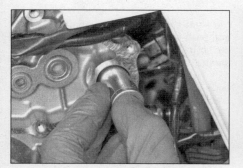

16.26b ...and push it in until it seats

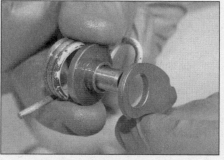

16.27a Assemble the stopper arm components as shown...

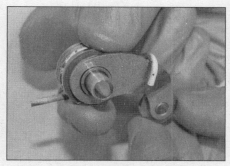

16.27b ...and locate the spring against the arm

ends on each side of the tab, and secure it with the circlip, making sure it locates in its groove. Slide the washer against the circlip. Also check that the centralising spring locating pin in the crankcase is securely tightened (see illustration). If it is loose, remove it, clean the threads and apply a non-permanent thread locking compound, then tighten it.

25 Check the gearchange shaft is straight and look for damage to the splines. If the shaft is bent you can attempt to straighten it, but if the splines are damaged the shaft must be replaced with a new one. Check the shaft bearing in the crankcase, referring to *Tools and Workshop Tips* in the Reference

Section, and fit a new one if necessary (see illustration).

Installation

26 Fit the new shaft oil seal squarely into place with its marked side facing out using a seal driver or suitable socket to push it in until it seats, so it sits recessed by 11.9 to 12.4 mm from its housing rim (see illustrations).

27 If disassembled, fit the stopper arm dowel through the collar, then position the spring and fit the arm against the collar, and locate the spring against the arm as shown (see illustrations). Fit the assembly onto the crankcase, making sure the spring ends are

positioned correctly (see illustration 16.21). 28 Fit the cam locating pin into the end of the selector drum if removed (see illustration 16.20c). Push the stopper arm across against the tension of the spring and hold it clear of the end of the drum, then fit the cam, locating the pin in the cut-out in the back of the cam (see illustration). Allow the stopper arm to rest against the cam. Clean the threads of the cam bolt and apply a suitable non-permanent thread locking compound, and tighten it to 31 Nm (see illustration 16.20a). Check the punch mark on the outer rim of the cam aligns with the stopper arm roller, and turn the cam to align them if necessary (see illustration).

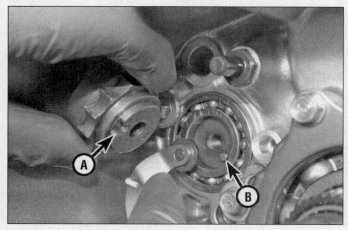

16.28a Push the arm across, then seat the cut-out (A) in the back of the cam over the locating pin (B)

16.28b Align the punch mark with the centre of the roller

16.29a Fit the springs into the holes…

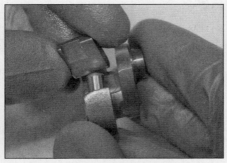

16.29b …then seat the flats on the pawls against the plungers and the rounded ends against the shifter…

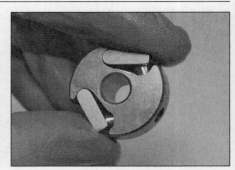

16.29c …as shown, then check the pawls move in and out smoothly

29 Assemble the springs, plungers and pawls onto the selector drum shifter **(see illustrations)**. Compress the pawls and fit the shifter assembly into the selector drum cam with the pin at the top and facing out, and when in place let the pawls seat in the cut-outs in the cam **(see illustration 16.19)**.
30 Fit the washer around the end of the stopper arm collar and against the arm **(see illustration)**. Fit the guide plate dowel if removed **(see illustration)**. Fit the spacer over the dowel **(see illustration)**. Fit the guide plate **(see illustration 16.18b)**, making sure

it locates correctly over the shifter and pawls and onto the dowels **(see illustration)**. Clean the threads of the guide plate bolts and apply fresh threadlock, and tighten the bolts to 12 Nm **(see illustration 16.18a)**.
31 Fit the roller onto the drum shifter pin **(see illustration 16.17b)**. Check that the shaft centralising spring is properly positioned and slide the washer onto the shaft if removed **(see illustration 16.24a)**. Apply some grease to the lips of the gearchange shaft oil seal in the left-hand side of the crankcase, and wrap a single layer of thin insulating tape around

the shaft splines. Slide the shaft into place and push it all the way through the case until the splined end comes out the other side **(see illustration 16.17a)**, and locate the selector arm over the roller and the centralising spring ends onto each side of the locating pin in the crankcase **(see illustration)**.
32 Remove the rag that was blocking the sump, then install the dual clutch/primary driven gear assembly (Section 13).
33 Remove the insulating tape from around the gearchange shaft splines. Fit the reduction gears and control motor (see above).

16.30a Fit the washer…

16.30b …the dowel…

16.30c …and the spacer

16.30d Check the guide plate is correctly located around the pawls and the dowels

16.31 Make sure everything is correctly positioned

17.2 Primary drive gear bolt (arrowed)

17.16a Using a piece of aluminium to jam the gears...

17.16b ...while slackening the nut

17 Primary drive gear

Models with standard transmission

Removal

1 Remove the guide plate, cam chain and tensioner blade, leaving the guide blade loose and the sprocket on the shaft (Section 9).

2 To prevent the crankshaft from turning while unscrewing the primary drive gear bolt, wedge a thick piece of rag material or a piece of aluminium or copper (DO NOT use steel) between the primary drive and driven gears at the top as shown (see illustration 17.23a). Unscrew the bolt and remove the washer (see illustration). Remove the wedge.

3 Remove the clutch (Section 13).

4 Remove the rear balancer (Section 18).

5 Slide the cam chain drive sprocket off the shaft, then hold the bottom of the guide blade just clear – do not bend it more than necessary (see illustration 17.2) – and slide the primary drive gear off.

Inspection

6 Check the teeth of the sprung and main primary drive gears and the corresponding teeth of the primary driven gear on the back of the clutch housing. Fit new primary drive gear(s) as required and/or clutch housing if worn or chipped teeth are found.

7 If there is damage to one of the drive gears and not the other, or if the springs have sagged or broken, the gear can be disassembled and individual components replaced with new ones as required. Lift the sprung gear off the main gear, noting how the tabs on the inner face butt against the ends of the springs (see illustration 17.21b). Remove the springs from their slots (see illustration 17.21a).

8 Fit the springs into their slots (see illustration 17.21a). Apply some molybdenum disulphide oil (a 50/50 mix of molybdenum

disulphide grease and engine oil) to the sliding surfaces on the gears. Align the index line on the face of the sprung gear with the wide spline on the main gear, then butt the tabs against the spring ends and seat the gear (see illustration 17.21b).

Installation

9 Align the wide spline on the main gear with that on the crankshaft, hold the guide blade aside and slide the gear on with the main gear on the inside (see illustration 17.2).

10 Fit the cam chain sprocket with the punch mark facing out and aligning the wide splines (see illustration 9.15a).

11 Install the rear balancer (Section 18).

12 Install the clutch (Section 13).

13 Apply clean oil to the threads and under the head of the primary drive gear bolt. Wedge the rag or piece of aluminium or copper to prevent crankshaft rotation between the primary drive and driven gears at the bottom as shown (see illustration 17.16a). Fit the bolt with its washer and tighten it to 103 Nm. Remove the wedge.

14 Install the tensioner blade, cam chain and guide plate (Section 9).

Models with DCT

Removal

15 Remove the clutch cover (Section 14).

16 To prevent the crankshaft from turning while slackening the primary drive gear nut,

17.18a Remove the nut and its washer...

wedge a thick piece of rag material or a piece of aluminium or copper (DO NOT use steel) between the primary drive and driven gears at the bottom as shown (see illustration). Slacken the nut, turning it clockwise as it has left-hand threads (see illustration). Remove the wedge.

17 Take the tension off the sprung outer gear on the primary drive gear using a screwdriver in the hole as a lever and fit a 6 mm bolt in the other hole to keep the gear teeth aligned (see illustration 14.10a).

18 Unscrew the nut and remove the washer, then slide the primary drive gear off (see illustrations).

Inspection

19 Check the teeth of the sprung and main primary drive gears and the corresponding teeth of the primary driven gear on the back of the clutch housing. Fit new primary drive gear(s) as required and/or clutch housing if worn or chipped teeth are found.

20 If there is damage to one of the drive gears and not the other, or if the springs have sagged or broken, the gear can be disassembled and individual components replaced with new ones as required. Remove the bolt from the hole, then lift the sprung gear off the main gear, noting how the tabs on the inner face butt against the ends of the springs (see illustrations 17.21c and b). Remove the springs from their slots (see illustration 17.21a).

21 Fit the springs into their slots (see

17.18b ...then slide the gear off

17.21a Seat the springs

17.21b Align the index line with the wide spline

17.21c Fit the bolt in to keep the gears together

17.22 Make sure the gear slides fully on so the teeth are engaged correctly and the outer faces are flush

17.23a Fit the wedge between the gears at the top...

17.23b ...and tighten the nut

illustration). Apply some molybdenum disulphide oil (a 50/50 mix of molybdenum disulphide grease and engine oil) to the sliding surfaces on the gears. Align the index line on the face of the sprung gear with the wide spline on the main gear, then butt the tabs against the spring ends, seat the gear and fit the 6 mm bolt loosely into the hole (see illustrations).

Installation

22 Align the wide spline on the main gear with that on the crankshaft and slide the gear on with the main gear on the inside (see illustration 17.18b) – if the teeth on the sprung outer gear do not quite align use the screwdriver or punch to align them as you slide the gear on (see illustration). Apply clean oil to the threads and under the head of the primary drive gear nut, fit the washer and thread the nut on (see illustration 17.18a).

Remove the bolt (see illustration 14.10a).
23 Wedge the rag or piece of aluminium or copper to prevent crankshaft rotation between the primary drive and driven gears at the top as shown (see illustration). Tighten the nut to 118 Nm, turning it anti-clockwise (see illustration). Remove the wedge.
24 Install the clutch cover (Section 14).

18 Balancer shafts

1 There are two balancer shafts. The front one is driven by a gear on the left hand end of the crankshaft. The rear one is driven by the primary drive gear on models with standard transmission, and by a separate gear on the right-hand end of the crankshaft on models with DCT.

Removal

Front balancer shaft

2 Remove the alternator rotor (see Chapter 8). Remove the clutch cover (Section 13 or Section 14). Remove the secondary (sub) spark plugs (see Chapter 1).
3 Make sure the transmission is in neutral. Turn the front balancer shaft clockwise using a socket on the bolt to align the index line on the gear between the two index lines on the drive gear (see illustration 18.22b).
4 To prevent the balancer shaft from turning while unscrewing the bolt, wedge a thick piece of rag material or a piece of aluminium or copper (DO NOT use steel) between the balancer drive and driven gears at the bottom as shown (see illustration). Unscrew the bolt and remove the washer (see illustration). Remove the wedge.

18.4a Using a piece of aluminium to lock the gears...

18.4b ...while slackening the bolt

18.5 Align the teeth and slide the gear off

18.7a Unscrew the bolts…

18.7b …and withdraw the shaft

18.8 Pull the bearing out

18.10a Turn the gear clockwise…

18.10b …and align the index lines as shown

18.11 Unscrew the bolts and remove the holder

5 Take the tension off the sprung outer gear on the balancer driven gear using a screwdriver or punch in the hole as a lever to align the gear teeth and slide the driven gear off the shaft **(see illustration)**.

6 Slide the balancer weight off the shaft **(see illustration 18.21)**.

7 On the right-hand end unscrew the balancer shaft bearing retainer plate bolts **(see illustration)**. Withdraw the shaft with the bearing and plate from the crankcase **(see illustration)**. Remove the plate, aligning it as shown **(see illustration 18.19)**.

8 Remove the bearing from the left-hand side of the crankcase **(see illustration)**.

Rear balancer shaft

9 Remove the clutch cover (Section 13 or Section 14). Remove the secondary (sub) spark plugs (see Chapter 1).

10 Make sure the transmission is in neutral. Turn the primary drive gear clockwise using a socket on the bolt or nut to align the index line on the balancer driven gear between the two index lines on the drive gear **(see illustrations)**.

11 Remove the rear balancer shaft holder **(see illustration)**. Remove the holder dowels if loose **(see illustration 18.29)**.

12 Remove the collar, spring washer, washer, thrust bearing and washer from the outer end of the shaft as an assembly, then remove the components from the collar **(see illustration)**.

13 Slide the balancer driven gear off the shaft **(see illustration)** – if it is difficult to slide off take the tension off the sprung gear using a screwdriver in the hole as a lever to align the gear teeth, and on models with standard transmission note that you may well need to

take the tension off the sprung gear on the primary/balancer drive gear as well.

14 Slide the inner washer off the shaft, then withdraw the shaft **(see illustrations)**.

18.12 Slide the collar assembly off the shaft

18.13 Slide the gear off the shaft

18.14a Remove the washer…

18.14b …and the shaft

18.15 Oil pump drive gear (arrowed)

18.17 Select a new bearing according to the code (arrowed) on the weight

18.19 Align the cut-outs with the weight as shown when fitting the plate

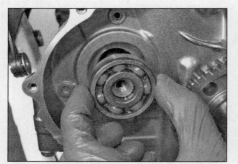

18.20a Fit the bearing with the marked side facing out...

18.20b ...and push it in until it seats and is flush

Inspection

15 Check the teeth on the drive and driven gears for wear and damage. On the rear balancer also check the oil pump drive gear on the back of the balancer **(see illustration)** and the driven gear on the crankcase **(see illustration 20.3a)** – refer to Section 20 to remove the driven gear if required.

16 Check the bearings run smoothly and freely. Fit new bearings if necessary. Refer below to select the correct size bearing for the rear balancer.

Rear balancer bearing selection

17 A replacement bearing for the rear balancer is supplied on a selected fit basis according to the internal diameter (ID) of the balancer bore. A code letter, either a, b or c, stamped on the weight web is used to

identify the correct replacement bearing **(see illustration)**.

18 Measure the internal diameter of the balancer and check it according to its letter against the specifications given in the table below to check the weight bearing surface has not worn. If it has worn beyond its coded specification select a new bearing according to the current size of the bore, or fit a new balancer and select the new bearing according to the letter on it. If the balancer has not worn select the new bearing according to the letter.

Balancer gear/ weight ID codes	Bearing part No.
A – 27.000 to 27.005 mm	91015-MJP-G51
B – 26.996 to 27.000 mm	91016-MJP-G51
C – 26.992 to 26.996 mm	91017-MJP-G51

Installation

Front balancer shaft

19 Lubricate the shaft bearings with oil. Fit the right-hand bearing retainer plate over the weight with the OUTSIDE mark facing out as shown and up against the bearing **(see illustration)**.

20 Slide the shaft into the crankcase and seat the right-hand bearing **(see illustration 18.7b)**, then fit the left-hand bearing **(see illustrations)**. Clean the threads of the right-hand bearing retainer plate bolts and apply fresh threadlock and tighten them to 12 Nm **(see illustration 18.7a)**.

21 Slide the weight onto the left-hand end of the shaft, aligning the wide spline in the weight with the flattened spline on the shaft **(see illustration)**.

22 Slide the driven gear onto the shaft, aligning the wide spline in the gear with the flattened spline on the shaft, and turning the shafts as required so the gear tooth with the index line on the driven gear is between the teeth with the index lines on the drive gear **(see illustration)**, then align the sprung gear teeth on the driven gear with the main teeth using a screwdriver or punch **(see illustration 18.5)** and slide the gear fully on so the teeth are fully engaged and the outer faces are flush **(see illustration)**.

23 Apply clean oil to the threads and under the head of the bolt and fit it with its washer

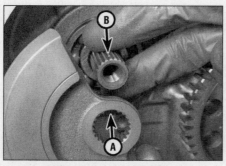

18.21 Align the wide spline (A) with the flattened spline (B)

18.22a Align the splines and the index lines (arrowed) as shown

18.22b Check the teeth are flush and correctly aligned according to the index lines

18.23a Fit the bolt and washer…

18.23b …lock the gears as shown…

18.23c …and tighten the bolt

(see illustration). Wedge the rag or piece of aluminium or copper to prevent rotation between the drive and driven gears at the top as shown **(see illustration)**. Tighten the bolt to 103 Nm **(see illustration)**. Remove the wedge.

24 Install the alternator rotor and clutch cover.

Rear balancer shaft

25 Check that the crankshaft is positioned so the index line on the primary/rear balancer drive gear (models with standard transmission) or the punch mark on the balancer drive gear (models with DCT) aligns with the triangular mark on the crankcase **(see illustration)**. If you removed the oil pump driven gear fit it now (Section 20).

26 Lubricate the bearings and shaft with oil. Fit the needle bearing into the gear **(see illustration 18.17)**. Insert the shaft, then fit the inner washer **(see illustrations 18.14b and a)**.

27 Fit the balancer gear onto the shaft with the weight facing out, aligning it so the gear tooth with the index line on the driven gear is between the teeth with the index lines on the drive gear, and engage the inner sprung gear teeth with the drive gear, then turn the outer gear anti-clockwise against the spring to align the gear teeth and slide the gear fully on so it fully engages the driven gear teeth and the oil pump driven gear **(see illustrations)**.

28 Fit the spring washer onto the collar so its

18.25 Align the line or punch mark with the triangle on the crankcase

18.27a Slide the gear on, aligning the index lines as shown…

18.27b …then turn the weight anti-clockwise to align the sprung gear teeth…

18.27c …and slide the gear fully in so the marks are as shown and the faces are flush

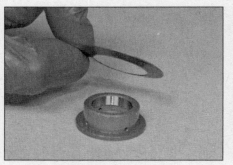

18.28a Fit the spring washer...

18.28b ...so the outer rim is raised off the collar...

18.28c ...then fit the washer...

18.28d ...the bearing...

18.28e ...and the washer

18.29 Make sure the dowels (arrowed) are fitted

outer rim is raised away from it, then fit the washer, the thrust bearing and the washer **(see illustrations)**. Slide the assembly onto the shaft with the collar facing out **(see illustration 18.12)**.

29 Fit the holder dowels if removed, then fit the holder **(see illustration)**. Clean the threads of the holder bolts and apply fresh threadlock. Fit the bolts and tighten them to 29 Nm **(see illustration 18.11)**.

30 Install the clutch cover.

19 Oil sump and oil strainer

Removal

1 Drain the engine oil (see Chapter 1).

2 Slacken the sump bolts evenly in a criss-cross sequence to prevent distortion, then hold the sump (if the engine is in the

frame), remove the bolts and remove the sump **(see illustration)**.

3 Remove the gasket **(see illustration 19.12a)**. Remove the O-rings from the sump oil passages **(see illustration 19.11)**. Remove the oil joint pipes **(see illustration 19.10)**. A new gasket, new O-rings for the oil passages, and new O-rings and back-up rings for the oil joint pipes will be needed.

4 Pull the strainer out of the pump, noting how it locates **(see illustration)**. Remove the

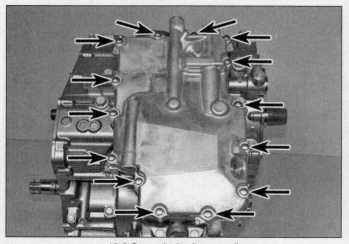

19.2 Sump bolts (arrowed)

19.4a Remove the strainer, noting how the tab locates in the groove

19.4b Remove the seal – if it isn't on the strainer it will be in the pump orifice

19.5 Lift the screen out of its slot

19.7 Clean the mesh

rubber seal **(see illustration)** – a new one must be used.

5 Remove the oil screen from the sump **(see illustration)**.

Inspection

6 Remove all traces of old gasket from the sump and crankcase mating surfaces, and clean the inside of the sump and all passages, and the joint pipes, with solvent. Blow the sump, passages and pipes dry with compressed air if available.

7 Clean the oil strainer and screen in solvent and remove any debris caught in the mesh **(see illustration)**. If the mesh is damaged, replace the strainer or screen with a new one.

Installation

8 Fit the oil screen into the sump with the wider edge facing up **(see illustration)**.

9 Fit a new rubber seal smeared with clean oil

into the orifice in the pump **(see illustration)**. Do not fit it onto the strainer as it will distort when the strainer is fitted. Fit the strainer, locating the tab between the ribs on the crankcase **(see illustration)**.

10 Fit new O-rings and back-up rings smeared with oil into the grooves in the oil joint pipes, then ease the pipes into the sump **(see illustration)**.

11 Fit new O-rings smeared with oil onto the oil passages **(see illustration)**.

12 Clean the mating surfaces of the sump and crankcase with solvent. Lay the new gasket onto the sump if the engine is in the frame, or onto the crankcase if the engine has been removed **(see illustration)**. Position the sump onto the crankcase, making sure the gasket stays aligned, and fit the bolts finger-tight **(see illustration)**. Tighten the bolts evenly and a little at a time in a criss-cross pattern.

19.8 Make sure the strainer is the correct way up or it will not seat all the way in its slot

13 Fill the engine with the correct type and quantity of oil as described in Chapter 1. Start the engine and check that there are no leaks around the sump.

19.9a Lubricate the rubber seal and fit it into the crankcase

19.9b Locate the tab in the slot

19.10 The two oil joint pipes each have two black O-rings and two white back-up rings

19.11 Oil passage O-rings (arrowed)

19.12a Fit the gasket...

19.12b ... then install the sump

20.2 Unscrew the three bolts and remove the pump

20.3a Unscrew the bolt (arrowed) and remove the retainer…

20.3b …and slide the gear shaft out

20 Oil pump and pressure relief valve(s)

Removal

1 Remove the sump and the oil strainer (Section 19).

2 Unscrew the pump mounting bolts and remove the pump, noting how the driveshaft tab locates in the cut-out in the driven gear shaft **(see illustration)**.

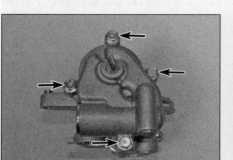

20.6a Unscrew the bolts (arrowed)…

3 To remove the driven gear remove the rear balancer shaft (Section 18). Remove the retainer then withdraw the gear **(see illustrations)**.

Disassembly, inspection and reassembly

4 As you disassemble the pump note any punch marks on the rotors and which way they face.

5 On models with standard transmission the pump has two chambers and pairs of rotors, the right-hand chamber to feed the oil and

20.6b …and remove the DCT chamber…

the left-hand chamber to scavenge the oil. Unscrew the four bolts on the right-hand end, noting which fits where as there are three different lengths, and the two bolts on the left-hand end, again noting which fits where **(see illustrations 20.6a and 20.6f)**. Remove the feed chamber and rotors, and withdraw the inner rotor drive pin. Remove the scavenge chamber and rotors, and withdraw the inner rotor drive pin. Withdraw the shaft.

6 On models with DCT transmission the pump has three chambers and pairs of rotors, the right-hand chamber to feed the DCT, the middle chamber to feed the rest of the engine, and the left-hand chamber to scavenge the oil. Unscrew the four bolts on the right-hand end, noting which fits where as there are three different lengths, and remove the DCT chamber and rotors, and withdraw the inner rotor drive pin **(see illustrations)**. Unscrew the short bolt on the left-hand end and remove the scavenge chamber and rotors, and withdraw the inner rotor drive pin **(see illustrations)**. Unscrew the remaining bolt and remove the pump body from the feed chamber, then withdraw the shaft, remove the drive pin, and remove the rotors from the feed chamber **(see illustrations)**.

7 Clean all components in solvent.

20.6c …the outer rotor…

20.6d …the inner rotor…

20.6e ...and the drive pin

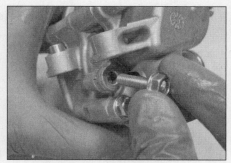

20.6f Unscrew the bolt...

20.6g ...and remove the scavenge chamber...

20.6h ...the outer rotor...

20.6i ...the inner rotor...

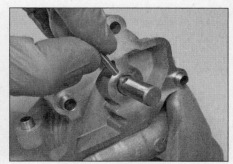

20.6j ...and the drive pin

20.6k Unscrew the bolt...

20.6l ...and remove the pump body...

20.6m ...then withdraw the shaft...

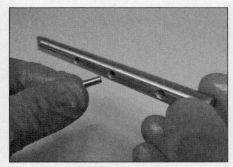

20.6n ...and remove the drive pin...

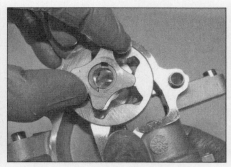

20.6o ...and remove the inner rotor...

20.6p ...and the outer rotor

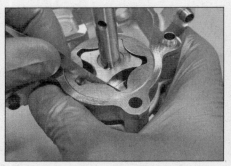

20.9 Measure the inner rotor tip-to-outer rotor clearance

20.13a Fit the two medium length bolts as shown…

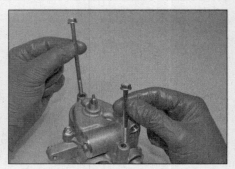

20.13b …and the longest and shortest bolts as shown

8 Inspect the chambers and rotors for scoring and wear. If any damage, scoring or uneven or excessive wear is evident, replace the pump with a new one (individual components are not available).

9 Fit each pair of rotors in turn into their chamber and insert the shaft to align them, then measure the clearance between the inner rotor tip and the outer rotor with a feeler gauge and compare it to the service limit given in the Specifications at the beginning of the Chapter **(see illustration)**. If the clearance measured is greater than the maximum listed, replace the pump with a new one.

10 Check the pump driven gear teeth for wear or damage, and also check the drive gear teeth on the back of the rear balancer (Section 18).

11 If the pump is good, make sure all the components are clean, and lubricate them with new engine oil.

12 On models with standard transmission fit the feed pump outer rotor into the feed chamber with the punch mark facing in, then fit the inner rotor into the outer rotor with the drive pin cut-outs facing out **(see illustrations 20.6p and o)**. Fit the drive pin into the centre hole in the shaft, then insert the shaft, tabbed end first, and seat the drive pin in the cut-outs **(see illustrations 20.6n and m)**. Check the dowels are in place then fit the pump body over the rotors **(see illustration 20.6l)**. Fit the drive pin into the left-hand end of the shaft, then fit the scavenge pump inner rotor, seating the cut-outs over the drive pin **(see illustrations 20.6j and i)**. Fit the outer rotor with the punch mark facing out **(see illustration 20.6h)**. Check the dowels are in place then fit the scavenge chamber and tighten the two left-hand bolts finger-tight **(see illustration 20.6g and f)**. Fit and tighten the four right-hand bolts finger-tight, making

sure each is in its correct location **(see illustrations 20.13a and b)**. Now tighten the the six bolts evenly and a little at a time to 12 Nm.

13 On models with DCT fit the feed pump outer rotor into the feed chamber with the punch mark facing in, then fit the inner rotor into the outer rotor with the drive pin cut-outs facing out **(see illustrations 20.6p and o)**. Fit the drive pin into the centre hole in the shaft, then insert the shaft, tabbed end first, and seat the drive pin in the cut-outs **(see illustrations 20.6n and m)**. Check the dowels are in place then fit the pump body over the rotors, fit the bolt and tighten finger-tight **(see illustrations 20.6l and k)**. Fit the drive pin into the left-hand end of the shaft, then fit the scavenge pump inner rotor, seating the cut-outs over the drive pin **(see illustrations 20.6j and i)**. Fit the outer rotor with the punch mark facing out **(see illustration 20.6h)**. Check the dowels are in place then fit the scavenge chamber and tighten the bolt finger-tight **(see illustrations 20.6g and f)**. Fit the drive pin into the right-hand end of the shaft, then fit the DCT pump inner rotor, seating the cut-outs over the drive pin **(see illustrations 20.6e and d)**. Fit the outer rotor **(see illustration 20.6c)**. Check the dowels are in place then fit the DCT chamber **(see illustration 20.6b)**. Fit and tighten the four bolts finger-tight, making sure each is in its correct location **(see illustrations)**. Now tighten the six bolts evenly and a little at a time to 12 Nm.

14 Rotate the pump shaft by hand and check it turns the rotors smoothly and freely.

15 On models with standard transmission there is one pressure relief valve for the oil feed. On models with DCT there is one pressure relief valve for the engine oil feed, and one for the DCT oil feed. To remove the valve(s) unscrew the cap then push the valve out **(see illustrations)**. Push the relief valve plunger into the valve body and check that it moves smoothly and freely against spring pressure **(see illustration)**. If not, fit a new pump. Fit a new O-ring smeared with oil onto the valve and insert the valve, pushing it fully in. Clean the threads of the cap and apply fresh threadlock, and tighten the cap to 30 Nm.

20.15a Unscrew the cap…

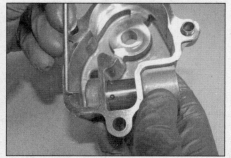

20.15b …and use a hooked tool to push up on the bottom of the valve to displace it

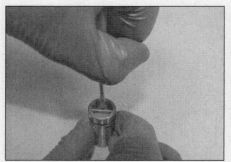

20.15c Push the plunger into the body and check that it moves smoothly

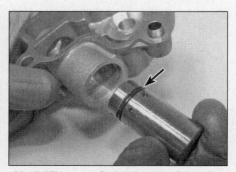

20.15d Fit a new O-ring (arrowed) into the groove

20.16 Insert the shaft, aligning the slot with the tab if the pump is fitted

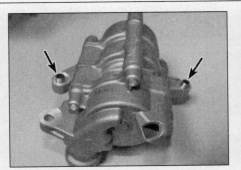

20.17 Pump locating dowels (arrowed)

21.3 Remove the coolant hose and union as required

Installation

16 If removed, apply molybdenum disulphide oil (a 50/50 mixture of molybdenum disulphide grease and engine oil) to the driven gear shaft and fit it into the crankcase, aligning the slot in the end of the shaft with the tabs on the pump shaft if the pump is in place (see illustration). Clean the threads of the retainer bolt and apply fresh threadlock. Fit the washer onto the bolt then fit the retainer, seating the tab between the pins, and tighten the bolt to 12 Nm (see illustration 20.3a).

17 Pour some clean engine oil into the pump and rotate the shaft to prime it. Check the pump dowels are in place (see illustration).

18 Rotate the oil pump drive shaft to align the tab on its end with the slot in the shaft, then fit the pump and tighten the bolts to 16 Nm (see illustration 20.2).

21 Crankcase separation and reassembly

Separation

1 To access the pistons, connecting rods, crankshaft, transmission shafts, selector drum and forks and all related bearings, the crankcase must be split into its two halves.

2 Before the crankcases can be separated the following components must be removed:
● Valve cover (Section 6)
● Camshaft (Section 8) – see Note*
● Cylinder head (Section 10) – see Note*
● Alternator (Chapter 8)
● Cam chain and blades (Section 9) – see Note*
● Clutch or dual clutch (according to transmission type) (Section 13 or Section 14)
● Balancer shafts (Section 18)
● Oil pump (Section 20)
● Gearchange mechanism (Section 15) – see Note*
● Any or all switches and sensors as required according to model (Chapter 8 and Chapter 4)

Note:* To remove the crankshaft without removing the connecting rods and pistons, the cam chain must be removed but the cylinder head can stay. However, if removal of the connecting rod assemblies is intended, full disassembly of the top-end is necessary. To inspect or remove the transmission shafts and selector drum and forks, the camshaft and cylinder head can remain in situ. The gearchange mechanism can remain in situ unless the transmission and selector drum and forks are being removed.

3 If and as required, either disconnect the coolant hose from its union on the back of the cylinder block, or unscrew the bolts and remove the union with the hose attached, or do both (see illustration). A new O-ring will be needed for the union.

4 Turn the engine upside down and support it as required using wooden blocks.

5 The crankcases are joined by many different sizes and lengths of bolt, some with sealing washers. As it is easy to get the bolts mixed up it is best to make a cardboard template of the lower crankcase with holes made in it to store all the bolts, with their washers where fitted, in their correct positions to make it easier to refit them when joining the crankcases. Note that new sealing washers should be used on assembly where fitted.

6 Unscrew the eight 6 mm bolts, the nine 8 mm bolts and the one 10 mm bolt evenly, a little at a time and in a criss-cross sequence until they are finger-tight, then remove them, noting the bolts fitted with sealing washers, and store them in the cardboard template of the crankcase (see illustrations).

7 Now unscrew the six 10 mm crankshaft

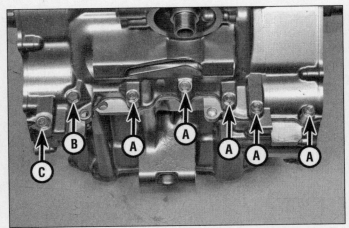

21.6a M6 x 35 mm bolts (A), M6 x 40 mm bolt with blue paint (B), M8 x 40 mm bolt (C)

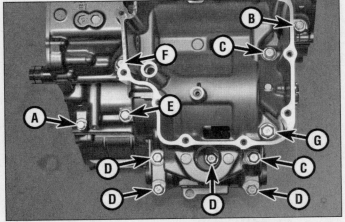

21.6b M6 x 35 mm bolt with sealing washer (A), M6 x 60 mm bolt with sealing washer (B), M8 x 55 mm bolts (C), M8 x 40 mm bolts (D), M8 x 55 mm bolt with sealing washer (E), M8 x 95 mm bolt with sealing washer (F), M10 x 75 mm bolt (G)

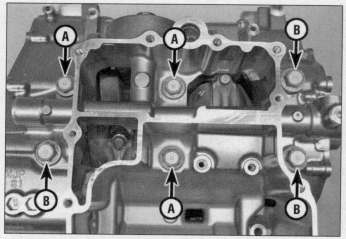

21.7 Crankshaft journal M10 x 110 mm bolts (A) and
M10 x 145 mm bolts (B)

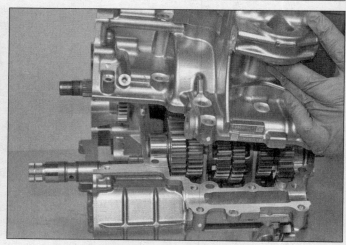

21.8 Carefully separate the crankcase halves

21.9 Remove the dowels (A) if they are loose, and the oil jets (B)

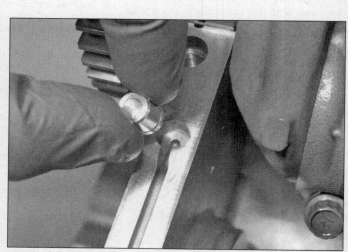

21.14 The jet in the right-hand side of the crankcase fits with the
narrow hole facing into the upper crankcase

21.15a Apply the sealant...

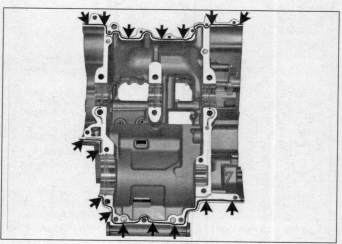

21.15b ...as shown

journal bolts evenly, a little at a time in a criss-cross sequence starting from the outside and working to the centre, until they are finger-tight, then remove them, noting which length fits where and storing them in the template **(see illustration)**.

8 Carefully lift the lower crankcase half off the upper half, using a soft-faced hammer to tap around the joint to initially separate the halves if necessary **(see illustration)**. If the halves do not separate easily, make sure all bolts have been removed. Do not try and separate the halves by levering against the crankcase mating surfaces as they are easily scored and will leak oil in the future if damaged. The lower crankcase half will come away leaving the crankshaft, transmission shafts and selector drum and forks in the upper crankcase half.

9 Remove the three locating dowels from the crankcase if they are loose (they could be in either crankcase half), and the two oil jets, noting how they fit **(see illustration)**.

10 Remove the components housed within the crankcases as required, referring to the relevant Sections.

11 Remove all traces of sealant from the crankcase mating surfaces. Clean the crankcases and oil jets (Section 22).

Reassembly

12 Check that all components and their bearings are in place in the upper and lower crankcase halves. If the transmission shafts have not been removed, fit a new oil seal onto the left-hand end of the output shaft **(see illustration 27.13)**.

13 Generously lubricate the crankshaft and transmission shafts, particularly around the bearings, with clean engine oil, then use a rag soaked in high flash-point solvent to wipe over the mating surfaces of both crankcase halves to remove all traces of oil.

14 If removed, fit the three locating dowels and the two oil jets in the upper crankcase half **(see illustration 21.9)** – fit the right-hand jet with its smaller hole facing into the crankcase **(see illustration)**.

15 Apply a small amount of suitable sealant (Three-Bond 1207B or equivalent RTV sealant – ask your dealer) to the outer mating surfaces of the lower crankcase half as shown **(see illustrations)**.

Caution: Do not apply an excessive amount of sealant as it will ooze out when the case halves are assembled and may obstruct oil passages. Do not apply the sealant close to any of the bearing shells or surfaces, or oil jets.

16 Check again that all components are in position, particularly that the bearing shells are still correctly located in the lower crankcase half. Carefully fit the lower crankcase half down onto the upper crankcase half, making sure the dowels locate correctly **(see illustration 21.8)**.

17 Check that the lower crankcase half is correctly seated all round.

Caution: The crankcase halves should fit together without being forced. If the casings are not correctly seated, remove the lower crankcase half and investigate the problem. Do not attempt to pull them together using the crankcase bolts as the casing will crack and be ruined.

18 Apply molybdenum disulphide oil (a 50/50 mixture of molybdenum disulphide grease and engine oil) to the threads and under the heads of the six 10 mm crankshaft journal bolts. Fit the bolts, making sure they are in their correct positions according to length **(see illustration 21.7)**. Tighten them finger-tight at first, then tighten them in a criss-cross sequence starting in the middle and working outwards first to 15 Nm, then to 30 Nm, and finally to 43 Nm.

19 Clean the threads of the eight 6 mm bolts, the nine 8 mm bolts and the one 10 mm bolt and insert them in their original locations **(see illustrations 21.6a and b)** – do not forget to fit new sealing washers with the two 6 mm and two 8 mm bolts as shown.Secure all bolts finger-tight at first, then tighten them evenly and a little at a time in a criss-cross sequence, tightening the 10 mm bolt to 39 Nm, the 8 mm bolts to 24 Nm, and the 6 mm bolts to 12 Nm – make sure you apply the correct torque to each bolt.

20 With all crankcase fasteners tightened, check that the crankshaft and transmission shafts rotate smoothly and easily. Check that the transmission shafts rotate freely and independently in neutral, then rotate the selector drum by hand and select each gear in turn whilst rotating the input shaft. Check that all gears can be selected and that the shafts rotate freely in every gear. If there are any signs of undue stiffness, tight or rough spots, or of any other problem, the fault must be rectified before proceeding further.

21 If removed fit the coolant union using a new O-ring smeared with oil, and connect the hose, making sure it is correctly aligned **(see illustration 21.3)**.

22 Install all other removed assemblies in a reverse of the sequence given in Step 2.

---

22 Crankcases and cylinder bores

Crankcases

1 After the crankcases have been separated, remove the crankshaft and main bearings, the connecting rods and pistons, the transmission shafts and selector drum and forks, the bearings that are fitted in the crankcase as required, and any switches and sensors not already removed. If there are any other components or assemblies that have not been removed as part of your stripdown procedure, remove these as well, referring to the relevant Chapter.

2 Push each piston oil jet out and remove its O-ring **(see illustration)** – new O-rings must be used.

3 Clean the crankcases and all oil passages and oil jets with new solvent and dry them with compressed air, blowing it through the passages and jets.

4 Remove all traces of old gasket sealant from the mating surfaces. Clean up minor damage to the surfaces with a fine sharpening stone or grindstone.

Caution: Be very careful not to nick or gouge the crankcase mating surfaces or oil leaks will result. Check both crankcase halves very carefully for cracks and other damage.

5 Small cracks or holes in aluminium castings can be repaired with an epoxy resin adhesive as a temporary measure. Permanent repairs can only be done by argon-arc welding, and only a specialist in this process is in a position to advise on the economy or practical aspect of such a repair. If any damage is found that can't be repaired, replace the crankcase halves as a set.

6 Damaged threads can be economically reclaimed using a diamond section wire insert, for example of the Heli-Coil type (though there are other makes), which are easily fitted after drilling and re-tapping the affected thread.

7 Studs or screws that have sheared on or below the surface can sometimes be removed with extractors, which consist of a tapered, left-hand thread screw of very hard, but brittle, steel. These are threaded anti-clockwise into a pre-drilled hole in the stud, and once they bite should unscrew it. Otherwise the stud has to be drilled out and the hole re-threaded, though in some cases a process known as spark erosion, than requires specialist equipment, may be required. If a stud has sheared above the surface, it can be removed using a conventional stud extractor, which avoids the need for drilling.

HAYNES HINT *Refer to Tools and WorkshopTips for details of fitting a thread insert and using stud extractors.*

22.2 Push the oil jets out

22.8a Fit a new O-ring (arrowed) into the groove

22.8b Align the projection with the groove

8 Fit a new O-ring onto each piston oil jet, then align the projection on each jet with the groove in the passage and push them all the way in until they seat **(see illustrations)**.

9 Install all other components and assemblies, referring to the relevant Sections of this and the other Chapters, before reassembling the crankcase halves.

Cylinder bores

10 Check the cylinder walls carefully for scratches and score marks.

11 Using telescoping gauges and a micrometer (see *Tools and Workshop Tips* in the Reference section), check the dimensions of each cylinder to assess the amount of wear. Measure near the top (but below the level of the top piston ring at TDC), centre and bottom (but above the level of the oil ring at BDC) of the bore, both parallel to and across the crankshaft axis **(see illustrations)**. Compare the results to the specifications at the beginning of the Chapter. If the cylinders are worn beyond the service limit they can be re-bored – an oversize (+ 0.25) set of pistons and rings is available. Note that the person carrying out the re-bore must be aware of the piston and bore specifications to maintain the correct clearance for the oversize pistons and rings.

12 If the precision measuring tools are not available, take the upper crankcase to a Honda dealer or specialist motorcycle repair shop for assessment and advice.

23 Connecting rod and main bearing information

1 Even though new main and connecting rod bearings are generally fitted during engine overhaul, the old bearings should be retained for close examination as they may reveal valuable information about the condition of the engine.

2 Bearing failure occurs mainly because of lack of lubrication, the presence of dirt or other foreign particles, overloading the engine and/or corrosion. Regardless of the cause of bearing failure, it must be corrected before the engine is reassembled to prevent it from happening again.

3 When examining the bearings, lay them out on a clean surface in the same general position as their location on the crankshaft journals. This will enable you to match any noted bearing problems with the corresponding crankshaft journal.

4 Dirt and other foreign particles get into the engine in a variety of ways. They may be left in the engine during assembly or they may pass through filters or breathers, then get into the oil and from there into the bearings. Metal chips from machining operations and normal engine wear are often present. Abrasives are sometimes left in engine components after reconditioning operations, especially when parts are not thoroughly cleaned using

the proper cleaning methods. Whatever the source, foreign objects often end up imbedded in the soft bearing material and are easily recognised. Large particles will not imbed in the bearing and will score or gouge the bearing and journal. The best prevention for this cause of bearing failure is to clean all parts thoroughly and keep everything spotlessly clean during engine reassembly. Regular oil and filter changes are also recommended.

5 Lack of lubrication or lubrication breakdown has a number of interrelated causes. Excessive heat (which thins the oil), overloading (which squeezes the oil from the bearing face) and oil leakage or throw off (from excessive bearing clearances, worn oil pump or high engine speeds) all contribute to lubrication breakdown. Blocked oil passages will starve a bearing of lubrication and destroy it. When lack of lubrication is the cause of bearing failure, the bearing material is wiped or extruded from the steel backing of the bearing. Temperatures may increase to the point where the steel backing and the journal turn blue from overheating.

> **HAYNES HiNT** *Refer to Tools and WorkshopTips for bearing fault finding.*

6 Riding habits can have a definite effect on bearing life. Full throttle low, speed operation, or labouring the engine, puts very high loads on bearings, which tend to squeeze out the oil film. These loads cause the bearings to flex, which produces fine cracks in the bearing face (fatigue failure). Eventually the bearing material will loosen in pieces and tear away from the steel backing. Short trip riding leads to corrosion of bearings, as insufficient engine heat is produced to drive off the condensed water and corrosive gases produced. These products collect in the engine oil, forming acid and sludge. As the oil is carried to the engine bearings, the acid attacks and corrodes the bearing material.

7 Incorrect bearing installation during engine assembly will lead to bearing failure as well. Tight fitting bearings which leave insufficient bearing oil clearances result in oil starvation. Dirt or foreign particles trapped behind a bearing shell result in high spots on the bearing which lead to failure.

8 To avoid bearing problems, clean all parts thoroughly before reassembly, double check all bearing clearance measurements and lubricate the new bearings with clean engine oil during installation.

24 Crankshaft and main bearings

Note: *The connecting rod cap bolts are stretch bolts and can only be used once, so new bolts must be fitted when installing the crankshaft. However the bolts can be re-used for the oil*

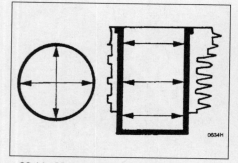

22.11a Measure the cylinder bore in the directions shown…

22.11b … using a telescoping gauge, then measure the gauge with a micrometer

24.4a Unscrew the bolts (arrowed) and remove the connecting rod caps…

24.4b …then push the rods off the crankpin

24.5 Lift the crankshaft out of the crankcase

clearance check if being done, noting that the tightening angle is reduced (see text).

Removal

1 Remove the engine from the frame (Section 4) and separate the crankcase halves (Section 21).

2 Using paint or a felt marker pen, mark the relevant cylinder identity across the front face of each connecting rod and cap to ensure that the caps are fitted the correct way around and onto the correct rod on reassembly. Note that the number already across the rod and cap is the rod size code letter for bearing shell selection **(see illustration 25.19b)**.

3 Before removing the rods from the crankshaft, measure the side clearance (the gap between the connecting rod big-end and the crankshaft web) with a feeler gauge. If the clearance is greater than the service limit given in the Specifications at the beginning of the Chapter, replace the rods with new ones. If the clearance is still excessive, replace the crankshaft with a new one.

4 Unscrew the connecting rod cap bolts **(see illustration)**. Remove the cap from each rod. Push both rods and pistons up to the top of their bores so that the bottom ends are clear of the crankshaft, taking care to keep the rods clear of the cylinder wall **(see illustration)**–

it is best to protect the wall with some rag. If no work is to be carried out on the piston/ connecting rod assemblies there is no need to remove them from the bores. If you do remove them, refer to Section 25. New connecting rod cap bolts are needed (see Note above).

5 Lift the crankshaft out of the upper crankcase half, bringing the cam chain with it if it hasn't been removed, and taking care not to dislodge the main bearing shells **(see illustration)**. Wrap some rag around each connecting rod to protect the cylinder walls.

6 Remove the main bearing shells from the crankcase halves **(see illustration)**. Keep the shells in order.

Inspection

7 Clean the crankshaft with solvent, squirting it under pressure through all the oil passages. If available, blow the crank dry with compressed air, and also blow through the oil passages. Check the balancer drive gear(s) for wear or damage. If any of the gear teeth are excessively worn, chipped or broken, the crankshaft must be replaced with a new one. If wear or damage is found, also inspect the driven gear(s) on the balancer shaft(s).

8 Refer to Section 23 and examine the main bearing shells. If they are scored, badly scuffed or appear to have been seized, new

bearings must be installed. Always replace the main bearings as a set. If they are badly damaged, check the corresponding crankshaft journals. Evidence of extreme heat, such as discoloration, indicates that lubrication failure has occurred. Be sure to thoroughly check the oil pump and pressure relief valve as well as all oil holes and passages before reassembling the engine.

9 Give the crankshaft journals a close visual examination, paying particular attention where damaged bearings have been discovered **(see illustration)**. If the journals are scored or pitted in any way a new crankshaft will be required. Note that undersizes are not available, precluding the option of regrinding the crankshaft.

10 Place the crankshaft outer main journals on V-blocks and check the runout at the right-hand end of the crankshaft using a dial gauge. Compare the reading to the maximum given in the Specifications at the beginning of the Chapter. If the runout exceeds the limit, the crankshaft must be replaced with a new one.

Oil clearance check

11 Whether new bearing shells are being fitted or the original ones are being reused, the main bearing oil clearance should be checked before the engine is reassembled.

24.6 Remove the shells from their housings

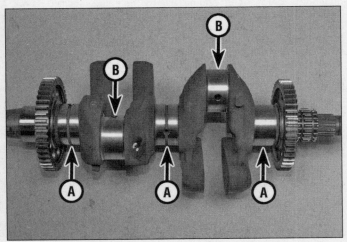

24.9 Main bearing journals (A), crankpin (big-end) journals (B)

24.15 Place a strip of Plastigauge carefully on the journal

24.18 Measure the crushed Plastigauge to establish the oil clearance

Main bearing oil clearance is measured with a product known as Plastigauge.

12 Clean both sides of the bearing shells and the bearing housings in both crankcase halves.

13 Press the bearing shells into their housings, making sure the tab on each shell engages in the notch in the crankcase **(see illustration 24.25)**. Check the bearings are fitted in the correct locations and take care not to touch any shell's bearing surface with your fingers.

14 Make sure the shells and crankshaft are clean and dry. Lay the crankshaft in position in the upper crankcase **(see illustration 24.5)**. Fit the three crankcase dowels if removed **(see illustration 21.9)**.

15 Cut three lengths of the appropriate size Plastigauge (they should be slightly shorter than the width of the crankshaft journals). Place a strand of Plastigauge on each (cleaned) journal, avoiding the oil hole **(see illustration)**. Make sure the crankshaft does not turn.

16 Carefully fit the lower crankcase half onto the upper half **(see illustration 21.8)**. Check that the lower half is correctly seated. Do not tighten the crankcase bolts if the casing is not correctly seated. Apply molybdenum disulphide oil (a 50/50 mixture of molybdenum disulphide grease and engine oil) to the threads and under the heads of the six 10 mm crankshaft journal bolts **(see illustration 21.7)**. Fit the bolts, making sure they are in their correct positions according to length, and tighten them finger-tight at first, then

tighten them in a criss-cross sequence starting in the middle and working outwards first to 15 Nm, then to 30 Nm, and finally to 43 Nm.

17 Slacken each bolt evenly and a little at a time in a reverse of the tightening sequence, i.e. starting from the outside and working to the centre, until they are all finger-tight, then remove the bolts. Carefully lift off the lower crankcase half, making sure the Plastigauge is not disturbed.

18 Compare the width of the crushed Plastigauge on each crankshaft journal to the scale printed on the Plastigauge envelope to obtain the main bearing oil clearance **(see illustration)**. Compare the reading to the specifications at the beginning of the Chapter.

19 On completion carefully scrape away all traces of the Plastigauge material from the crankshaft journal and bearing shells; use a fingernail or other object which is unlikely to score them.

20 If the clearance is within the range given in the Specifications and the bearings are in perfect condition, they can be reused. If the clearance is beyond the service limit, replace the bearing shells with new ones (see Steps 22 and 23). Fit the new shells and check the oil clearance again (the new shells should be thick enough to bring bearing clearance within the specified range). Always replace all of the shells at the same time.

21 If the clearance is greater than the service limit with new shells fitted, measure the crankshaft journals to see if they are worn beyond the size specific to the code (see table

below), and then either select different shells according to the measured size, or replace the crankshaft with a new one and select new shells according to the codes on that.

Main bearing shell selection

22 Replacement bearing shells for the main bearings are supplied on a selected fit basis. Code numbers and letters stamped on the crankshaft and crankcase respectively are used to identify the correct replacement bearings. The crankshaft main bearing journal size numbers are stamped on the outside of the left-hand crankshaft web and will be either 1, 2 or 3 **(see illustration)**. The first number, after the L, is for the left-hand journal, and the numbers correspond consecutively for each journal. The corresponding main bearing housing size letters are stamped into the left-hand side of the upper crankcase half and will be either A, B or C **(see illustration)**. The left-hand letter corresponds to the left-hand journal, and the letters correspond consecutively from left to right.

23 A range of bearing shells is available. To select the correct bearing for a particular journal, use the table below and cross-refer the main bearing journal number (stamped on the crank web) or size (if measured) with the main bearing housing size letter (stamped on the crankcase) to determine the colour code of the bearing required. For example, if the journal code is 3, and the housing code is A, then the bearing required is brown. The colour is marked on the side of the shell **(see illustration)**.

Main bearing journal code on crankshaft web	Main bearing housing code on crankcase		
	A	B	C
1 (44.004 to 44.010 mm)	Yellow	Green	Brown
2 (43.998 to 44.004 mm)	Green	Brown	Black
3 (43.992 to 43.998 mm)	Brown	Black	Blue

Installation

24 Clean both sides of the bearing shells and the bearing housings in both crankcase halves.

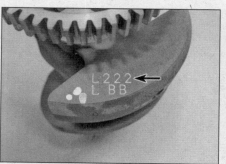

24.22a Main bearing journal size numbers (arrowed)

24.22b Main bearing housing size letters

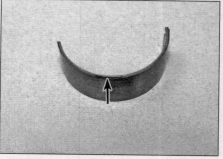

24.23 Bearing shell colour code (arrowed)

24.25 Make sure each shell is correctly aligned and seated

24.27a Pull the connecting rods onto the crankpins…

24.27b …and fit the caps

If new shells are being fitted, make sure all traces of any protective grease are cleaned off using paraffin (kerosene). Wipe the shells and housings dry with a lint-free cloth. Make sure all the oil passages and holes are clear, and blow them through with compressed air if available and not already done.

25 Press the bearing shells into their housings. Make sure the tab on each shell engages in the notch in the casing (see illustration). Make sure the bearings are fitted in the correct locations and take care not to touch any shell's bearing surface with your fingers. Lubricate the bearing surface of each shell with molybdenum disulphide oil (a 50/50 mixture of molybdenum disulphide grease and clean engine oil).

26 Remove the rag from around the connecting rods. Lower the crankshaft into position in the upper crankcase (see illustration 24.5).

27 Lubricate the crankpins with molybdenum disulphide oil (a 50/50 mixture of molybdenum disulphide grease and clean engine oil). Carefully pull the connecting rods onto the crankpins, taking care not to mark the cylinder walls (see illustration). Fit the caps onto the rods (see illustration) – make sure each cap is fitted onto the correct rod and the correct way around so the previously made markings align.

28 Apply some clean oil to the threads and under the heads of the **new** connecting rod bolts, then fit them and tighten them finger-tight (see illustration). Next tighten them evenly and alternately in two or three stages to 22 Nm. Finally tighten them each

in one go through 120° using a degree disc (see illustration). It is highly advisable to have an assistant to hold the crankshaft down in the crankcase while tightening the bolts as it could jump out.

29 Carefully turn the crankshaft – if there are any signs of roughness or tightness, try tapping the bottom of the connecting rod caps as this may relieve tightness, but if in doubt remove the caps and check the bearing clearance (Section 25).

30 Check again to make sure that all components have been returned to their original locations using the marks made on disassembly.

31 Reassemble the crankcase halves (Section 21).

25 Connecting rods and bearings

Note: *To remove the connecting rods the engine must be removed from the frame and the crankcases separated.*

Removal

1 Remove the engine from the frame (Section 4) and separate the crankcase halves (Section 21). Remove the transmission input shaft (Section 27).

2 Before removing the piston and connecting rod assembly from the crankcase, use a sharp scriber or felt marker pen to write the cylinder identity on the crown of each piston (see illustration 25.4). Each piston crown should

already be marked IN, though the mark may be invisible until the piston is cleaned, and this mark faces the intake side of the cylinder.

3 Remove the crankshaft (Section 24). Wrap some rag around each connecting rod to protect the cylinder walls. If you are going to do an oil clearance check do it now (see below), before removing the piston/connecting rod assemblies from the bores.

4 Raise the crankcase onto wooden blocks, or turn it onto its side, to provide room for the connecting rod/piston assemblies to be removed from the tops of the bores. Push each piston/connecting rod assembly up its bore and remove it from the top, making sure the rod does not mark the cylinder wall (see illustration).

HAYNES HINT *To ease removal of the pistons, carefully remove any ridge of carbon built upon the top of each cylinder bore using a scraper, Stanley blade or scouring cloth. If there is a pronounced wear ridge, remove it using a ridge reamer.*

Caution: Do not try to remove the piston/ connecting rod from the bottom of the cylinder bore. The piston will not pass the crankcase main bearing webs. If the piston is pulled right to the bottom of the bore the oil control ring will expand and lock the piston in position. If this happens it is likely the ring will break.

24.28a Use new bolts lubricated as described

24.28b Use a degree disc to tighten the bolts through the specified angle

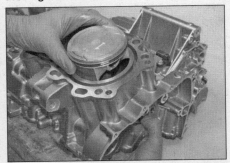

25.4 Push the piston and connecting rod assembly up and withdraw it from the top of the cylinder

25.8 Check for freeplay between the rod and pin

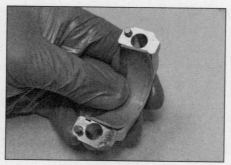

25.9 Remove the shells

5 Keep each rod and its cap, bolts and bearing shells (if they are to be reused) together in their correct positions to ensure correct installation – fit the caps back onto the rods and finger-tighten the bolts to make sure. The bolts can be re-used for an oil clearance check (if being done), but new bolts are need when fitting the crankshaft for final assembly.

6 Remove the pistons from the connecting rods if required (Section 26), but note that if you are doing a big-end oil clearance check they must be on the rods to prevent them rotating on the crankpin and upsetting the Plastigauge.

Inspection

7 Check the connecting rods for cracks and other obvious damage.

8 Apply clean engine oil to the piston pin, slide it into the connecting rod small-end and check for any freeplay between the two **(see illustration)**. If freeplay is felt measure the pin external diameter in its centre and the small-end bore diameter. Compare the results to the measurements given in the Specifications at the beginning of the Chapter and replace the components that are worn beyond their specified limits with new ones.

9 Refer to Section 23 and examine the connecting rod bearing shells. If they are scored, badly scuffed, corroded, or appear to have seized, new shells must be fitted. Remove them from the rod and cap **(see illustration)**. Always replace the shells in the connecting rods as a set. If they are badly damaged, check the corresponding crankpin **(see illustration 24.9)**. Evidence of extreme

heat, such as discoloration, indicates that lubrication failure has occurred. Be sure to thoroughly check the oil pump and pressure relief valve as well as all oil holes and passages before reassembling the engine.

10 Have the rods checked for twist and bend by a Honda dealer if you are in doubt about their straightness.

Oil clearance check

11 Whether new bearing shells are being fitted or the original ones are being reused, the connecting rod bearing oil clearance should be checked prior to reassembly.

12 Clean both sides of the bearing shells and the bearing housings in both the connecting rod and cap.

13 Press the bearing shells into their housings, making sure the tab on each shell engages the notch in the connecting rod/cap **(see illustration 25.22)**. Make sure the bearings are fitted in the correct location and take care not to touch any shell's bearing surface with your fingers. If removed refer to Step 23 and fit the rod and piston into its correct cylinder, making sure it is the correct way round. Lay the crankshaft in the upper crankcase half, then pull the connecting rod onto the crankpin **(see illustration 24.27a)**.

14 Cut a length of the appropriate size Plastigauge (it should be slightly shorter than the width of the crankpin). Place a strand of Plastigauge on the crankpin journal, making sure it is not over the oil hole **(see illustration 24.15)**. Fit the cap onto the rod **(see illustrations 24.27b)**. Make sure the cap is fitted the correct way around so the previously

made markings align. Apply some clean oil to the threads and under the heads of the connecting rod bolts, then fit them and tighten them finger-tight **(see illustration 24.28a)**. Next tighten them evenly and alternately in two or three stages to 22 Nm. Finally tighten them each in one go through 90° using a degree disc, making sure the crankshaft does not turn. It is highly advisable to have an assistant to hold the crankshaft down in the crankcase while tightening the bolts as it could jump out.

15 Unscrew the bolts and remove the connecting rod cap. Compare the width of the crushed Plastigauge on the crankpin to the scale printed on the Plastigauge envelope to obtain the connecting rod bearing oil clearance **(see illustration 24.18)**. Compare the reading to the specifications at the beginning of the Chapter.

16 On completion carefully scrape away all traces of the Plastigauge material from the crankpin and bearing shells using a fingernail or other soft object that is unlikely to score the shells.

17 If the clearance is within the range given in the Specifications and the bearings are in perfect condition, they can be reused. If the clearance is beyond the service limit, replace the bearing shells with new ones (see Steps 19 and 20). Fit the new shells and check the oil clearance again (the new shells should be thick enough to bring bearing clearance within the specified range). Always replace all of the shells at the same time.

18 If the clearance is greater than the service limit with new shells fitted, measure the crankpin journals to see if they are worn beyond the size specific to the code (see table below), and then either select different shells according to the measured size, or replace the crankshaft with a new one and select new shells according to the codes on that.

Bearing shell selection

19 Replacement bearing shells for the big-end bearings are supplied on a selected fit basis. Code letters and numbers stamped on the crankshaft and connecting rod respectively are used to identify the correct replacement bearings. The crankpin journal size letters are stamped on the outside of the left-hand crankshaft web, and will be either A, B or C **(see illustration)**. The first letter after the L is for the No. 1 cylinder connecting rod (left-hand crankpin), and the second letter is the No. 2 cylinder rod (right-hand crankpin). The connecting rod size code number is marked across the flat face of the connecting rod and cap and will be either 1, 2 or 3 **(see illustration)**.

20 A range of bearing shells is available. To select the correct bearing shell colour code for a particular big-end, use the table below and cross-refer the crankpin journal size letter (stamped on the web) with the connecting rod size number (stamped on the rod). For example, if the crankpin size is B, and the connecting rod size is 1, then the bearing required is green. The colour is marked on the side of the shell **(see illustration 24.23)**.

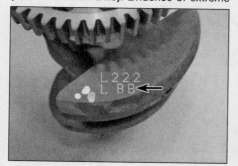

25.19a Crankpin journal size letters

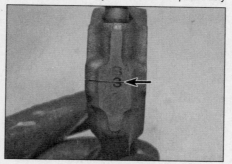

25.19b Connecting rod size number

Crankpin journal code	Connecting rod code		
	1	2	3
A (43.992 to 43.998 mm)	Yellow	Green	Brown
B (43.986 to 43.992 mm)	Green	Brown	Black
C (43.980 to 43.986 mm)	Brown	Black	Blue

Installation

21 If removed fit the pistons onto the connecting rods (Section 26).
22 Clean both sides of the bearing shells and the bearing housings in both cap and rod. If new shells are being fitted, make sure all traces of any protective grease are cleaned off using paraffin (kerosene). Wipe the shells, cap and rod dry with a clean lint free cloth. Fit the bearing shells in the connecting rods and caps, making sure the tab on each shell engages the notch **(see illustration)**. Lubricate the shells with molybdenum disulphide oil (a 50/50 mixture of molybdenum disulphide grease and clean engine oil). Make sure the bolt heads are all correctly seated.
23 Lubricate the piston and rings and the

25.22 Make sure each shell is correctly aligned and seated

cylinder bore with clean engine oil. Check the MJP marks on the side of the piston and rod are on the same side **(see illustration 26.25a)**. Wrap some rag round the bottom of the connecting rod. Insert the piston/connecting rod assembly into the top of its bore with the IN mark on the piston on the intake side of the engine, taking care not to allow the connecting rod to mark the wall **(see illustration 25.4)**. Carefully compress and feed each piston ring into the bore until the piston crown is flush with the top of the bore **(see illustration)**. If

available, a good piston ring compressor of the correct size makes installation a lot easier (though a poor fitting one makes it more difficult, and if it is too big it goes out-of-round when fully tightened, allowing the rings to stick out) – fit the compressor around the piston and over the rings and tighten it to compress the rings, then locate the assembly on the top of the bore and tap the top of the piston using a wooden or plastic tool (such as the handle end of a hammer) until the piston is completely in the bore **(see illustrations)**.
24 Install the crankshaft (Section 24) and the transmission input shaft (Section 27).
25 Reassemble the crankcase halves (Section 21).

26 Pistons and rings

Note: *To remove the pistons the engine must be removed from the frame and the crankcase halves separated.*

Removal

1 Remove the piston/connecting rod assemblies from the crankcase (Section 25).

25.23a Carefully compress and feed each ring in

25.23b Fit the compressor over the piston and rings...

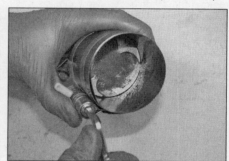

25.23c ...then compress the rings by tightening the bands on the compressor using an Allen key

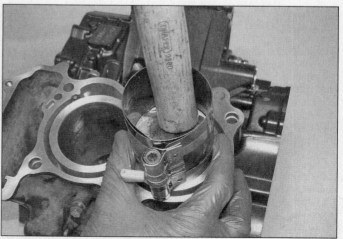

25.23d Fit the rod into the bore and rest the compressor on the crankcase...

25.23e ...then tap the top of the piston with a soft tool so that it enters

26.3a Prise out the circlip using a suitable tool in the notch…

26.3b …then push out the pin and separate the piston from the rod

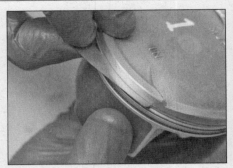

26.10 Measure the piston ring-to-groove clearance with a feeler gauge

2 Before removing the piston from the connecting rod, use a sharp scriber or felt marker pen to write the cylinder identity on the inside of the piston skirt – do this even if you have already marked the crown as the crown should be cleaned and the mark may be erased.

3 Carefully prise out the circlip on one side of the piston using needle-nose pliers or a small flat-bladed screwdriver inserted into the notch **(see illustration)**. Push the piston pin out from the other side to free the piston from the connecting rod **(see illustration)**. If required remove the other circlip. New circlips must be used. When the piston has been removed, slide its pin back into its bore so that related parts do not get mixed up.

 HAYNES HiNT *If a piston pin is a tight fit in the piston bosses, use a heat gun to heat the area around the piston pin – this will expand the alloy piston sufficiently to release its grip on the pin. If the piston pin is particularly stubborn, extract it using a drawbolt tool (see Tools and Workshop Tips in the Reference Section), but be careful to protect the piston's working surfaces.*

4 Using your thumbs or a piston ring removal and installation tool, carefully remove the rings from the pistons **(see illustrations 26.21, 26.20b, 26.18c, b and a)**. Do not nick or gouge the pistons in the process. Carefully note which way up each ring fits and in which groove as they must be installed in their original positions if being reused. The upper surface of the top ring should be marked R at one end, and the second (middle) ring marked RN **(see illustration 26.20a)**. The top and middle rings can also be identified by the fact that the top ring is not as wide as the second (middle) ring, and their cross-section profiles are different.

5 Scrape all traces of carbon from the tops of the pistons. A hand-held wire brush or a piece of fine emery cloth can be used once most of the deposits have been scraped away. Do not use a wire brush mounted in a drill motor to remove deposits from the pistons – the piston

material is soft and will be eroded away by the wire brush.

6 Use a piston ring groove cleaning tool to remove any carbon deposits from the ring grooves. If a tool is not available, a piece broken off an old ring will do the job. Be very careful to remove only the carbon deposits. Do not remove any metal and do not nick or gouge the sides of the ring grooves.

7 Once the deposits have been removed, clean the pistons with solvent and dry them thoroughly. If the identification mark previously made on the piston is cleaned off, be sure to re-mark it with the correct identity. Make sure the oil return holes below the oil ring groove are clear.

Inspection

Piston

8 Carefully inspect each piston for cracks around the skirt, at the pin bosses and at the ring lands. Normal piston wear appears as even, vertical wear on the thrust surfaces of the piston. If the skirt is scored or scuffed, the engine may have been suffering from overheating and/or abnormal combustion, which caused excessively high operating temperatures. Also check that the circlip grooves are not damaged.

9 A hole in the top of the piston, in one extreme, or burned areas around the edge of the piston crown, indicate that pre-ignition or knocking under load have occurred. If you find evidence of any problems the cause must be corrected or the damage will occur again.

10 Measure the piston ring-to-groove clearance by laying each piston ring in its groove and slipping a feeler gauge in beside it **(see illustration)**. Make sure you have the correct ring for the groove (see Step 4). Check the clearance at three or four locations around the groove. If the clearance is greater than that given in the Specifications at the beginning of the Chapter, replace both the piston and rings as a set. If new rings are being used, measure the clearance using the new rings. If the clearance is greater than that specified, the piston is worn and must be replaced with a new one.

11 Check the piston-to-bore clearance by measuring the bore (Section 22), then measure the piston 12 mm up from the bottom of the skirt and at 90° to the piston pin axis **(see illustration)**. Make sure each piston is matched to its correct cylinder. If the piston has worn to the service limit given in the Specifications at the beginning of the Chapter fit a new one.

12 Apply clean engine oil to the piston pin, insert it into the piston and check for any freeplay between the two **(see illustration)**. If freeplay is felt measure the pin external diameter near each end, and the pin bore in each side of the piston. Compare the measurements to those given in the Specifications at the beginning of the Chapter and replace worn components with new ones. If not already done, repeat the measurements between the pin and the connecting rod small-end (Section 25).

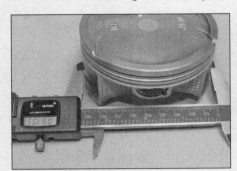

26.11 Measure the piston diameter with a micrometer at the specified distance from the bottom of the skirt

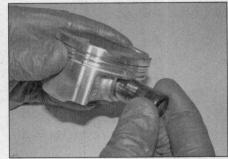

26.12 Check for freeplay between the piston and pin

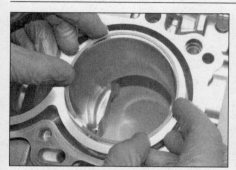

26.14a Fit the ring into its bore...

26.14b ...and measure the end gap using a feeler gauge

26.18a Fit the oil ring expander in its groove...

Piston rings

13 Whether re-using the old rings or fitting new ones, check the installed end gaps with the rings installed in the bore, as follows. Lay out each piston with its ring set and keep them together so the rings will be matched with the same piston and bore during the measurement procedure and engine assembly.

14 Insert the top ring into the top of the bore and square it up with the bore walls by pushing it in with the top of the piston **(see illustration)**. The ring should be at least 20 mm below the top edge of the bore, so it is within its area of travel in the bore. Slip a feeler gauge between the ends of the ring and compare the measurement to the specifications at the beginning of the Chapter **(see illustration)**.

15 If the gap is larger or smaller than specified, double check to make sure that you have the correct rings before proceeding; excess end gap is not critical unless it exceeds the service limit.

16 If the service limit is exceeded with new rings, check the bore for wear (Section 22). If the gap is too small, the ring ends may come in contact with each other during engine operation, which can cause serious damage.

17 Repeat the procedure for the middle ring and the oil control ring side-rails, but not the expander ring. Remember to keep the rings, pistons and bores matched up.

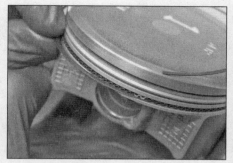

26.18b ...then fit the lower side rail...

Installation

18 Fit the oil control ring (lowest on the piston) first. It is composed of three separate components, namely the expander and the upper and lower side-rails. Slip the expander into the groove, making sure the ends don't overlap **(see illustration)**. Next fit the lower side-rail **(see illustration)**. Do not use a piston ring installation tool on the side-rails as they may be damaged. Instead, place one end of the side-rail into the groove between the expander and the ring land. Hold it firmly in place and slide a finger around the piston while pushing the rail into the groove. Next, fit the upper side-rail in the same manner **(see illustration)**. Check that the ends of the expander have not overlapped.

26.18c ...and the upper side rail on each side of it

19 After the three oil ring components have been installed, check to make sure that both the upper and lower side-rails can be turned smoothly in the ring groove.

20 Fit the second (middle) ring next – it should be marked RN at one end, while the top ring is marked R **(see illustration)**. Make sure that the ring is installed with the identification letters facing up. Fit the ring into the middle groove in the piston **(see illustration)** – do not expand the ring any more than is necessary to slide it into place, and if available use a piston ring installation tool, or a feeler gauge blade.

21 Finally, fit the top ring, marked R, in the same manner into the top groove in the piston **(see illustration)**. Make sure the identification letter near the end gap is facing up.

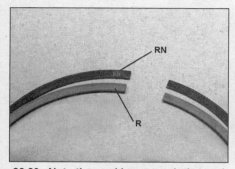

26.20a Note the marking on each ring and make sure it faces up

26.20b Fit the second (middle ring)...

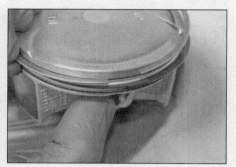

26.21 ...and the top ring as described

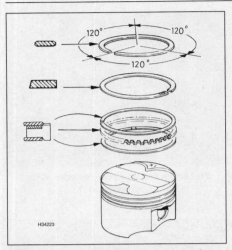

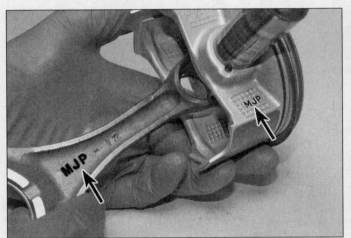

26.22 Piston ring profiles and ring end gap positions

Stagger the end gaps as shown. Note that the oil ring rail end gaps must be 20 mm or more from each other

22 Once the rings are correctly installed, check they move freely without snagging and stagger their end gaps as shown **(see illustration)**.

23 If both circlips were removed fit one **new** circlip into one side of the piston (do not reuse old circlips). When fitting the circlips, compress them only just enough to fit them in the piston, and make sure they are properly seated in their grooves with the open end away from the removal notch.

24 Lubricate the piston pin, the piston pin bore and the connecting rod small-end bore with molybdenum disulphide oil (a 50/50 mixture of molybdenum disulphide grease and clean engine oil).

25 Line up the piston on its correct connecting rod, making sure the previously made cylinder number marks match, and the MJP marks on the the side of the piston and rod face the same way, and insert the piston pin from the opposite side to the fitted circlip **(see illustration)**. Secure the pin with another **new** circlip **(see illustration)**.

26 Install the connecting rods (Section 25).

27 Transmission shaft removal and installation

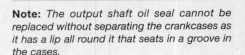

Note: *The output shaft oil seal cannot be replaced without separating the crankcases as it has a lip all round it that seats in a groove in the cases.*

Removal

1 Remove the engine from the frame (Section 4) and separate the crankcase halves (Section 21).

2 Lift the output shaft out of the casing, noting how it engages with the input shaft and its selector forks, and how the hole in the needle bearing housing locates onto the pin **(see illustration)**. If the shaft is stuck, use a soft-faced hammer and gently tap on the ends. Remove the bearing pin – if it is not in its hole in the crankcase, remove it from the bearing on the shaft **(see illustration)**. Slide the oil seal off – a new one must be used **(see illustration 27.13)**.

26.25a Make sure the MJP marks (arrowed) are on the same side

26.25b Use new circlips and make sure they locate correctly

27.2a Remove the output shaft

27.2b Remove the bearing pin from its hole

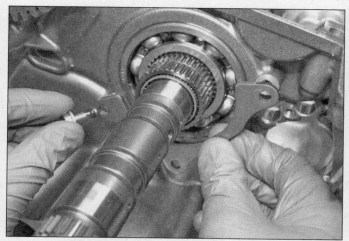

27.4 Unscrew the bolts and remove the plate

27.6a Draw the shaft and bearing out...

27.6b ...then slide the bearing off...

27.6c ...and remove the shaft

3 Remove the selector forks (Section 30) – the drum can stay in place, but remove it as well if required.

4 Unscrew the transmission input shaft bearing retainer plate bolts and remove the plate (see illustration).

5 Turn the crankshaft so the webs are clear of the input shaft.

6 Draw the input shaft a little way out of the crankcase until the right-hand bearing is clear, then slide the bearing off the end of the shaft and lift the shaft out of the crankcase (see illustrations). Check that the thrust washer is on the left-hand end of the shaft – if not it is either stuck to the bearing in the crankcase or has dropped off.

7 If necessary, the transmission shafts can be disassembled and inspected for wear or damage, and individual components replaced with new ones as required (Section 28).

8 Referring to Tools and Workshop Tips in the Reference section, check the bearings on the shafts and in the crankcase. Replace the bearings with new ones if necessary (Section 28),

noting that the left-hand bearing on the output shaft is not available separately from the shaft.

Installation

9 Make sure the crankshaft is positioned so the webs will not be in the way when fitting the input shaft.

10 Lubricate the input shaft bearings with oil. On models with standard transmission check that the thrust washer is on the left-hand end of the shaft. Position the shaft in the crankcase (see illustration 27.6c) (do not yet locate the inner end in its bearing), on models with DCT checking to make sure the tabs on the shaped washer are still seated in the spaces with the shortened splines (see illustration) (it is easy for the outer shaft assembly and the washer to slide along the shaft and turn, and if it does the right-hand bearing will not seat correctly in the crankcase), then fit the right-hand bearing onto the outer end of the shaft with its marked side facing out and slide it along so it is in its correct fitted position on the shaft (see illustration 27.6b). Now slide the

shaft in, locating the inner end in its bearing, and pushing the right-hand bearing into the crankcase (see illustration 27.6a).

11 Clean the threads of the bearing retainer plate bolts and apply fresh threadlock. Fit the plate and tighten the bolts to 12 Nm (see illustration 27.4).

27.10 Make sure the outer shaft assembly is against the washer so its tabs are all seated fully in the cut-outs

12 Install the selector drum (if removed) and the selector forks (Section 30).

13 Lubricate the lips of the new oil seal with grease and slide the oil seal on **(see illustration)**.

14 Fit the output shaft needle bearing pin into its hole in the crankcase **(see illustration 27.2b)**.

15 Lower the output shaft into position in the upper crankcase **(see illustration 27.2a)**, making sure the selector forks locate in their pinion grooves, the hole in the needle bearing engages correctly with the pin, the retaining ring in the ball bearing engages correctly with the inner groove and the oil seal lip locates in the outer groove **(see illustrations)**.

Caution: If the ring retainer or dowel do not locate correctly, the crankcase halves will not seat properly.

16 Position the gears in the neutral position and check the shafts are free to rotate easily and independently (i.e. the input shaft can turn whilst the output shaft is held stationary) before proceeding further. Also check that each gear can be selected by turning the input shaft with one hand and the selector drum with the other.

17 Reassemble the crankcase halves (Section 21).

28 Transmission shaft overhaul – models with standard transmission

1 Remove the transmission shafts from the crankcase (Section 27). Always disassemble the transmission shafts separately to avoid mixing up the components.

> **HAYNES HiNT**
> *When disassembling the transmission shafts, place the parts on a long rod or thread a wire through them to keep them in order and facing the proper direction.*

Input shaft

Disassembly

2 Slide the thrust washer off the left-hand end of the shaft **(see illustrations 28.20c and b)**. Slide the 2nd gear pinion off the shaft **(see illustration 28.20a)**.

3 Slide the tabbed lockwasher off the shaft, then turn the slotted splined washer to offset the splines and slide it off the shaft **(see illustrations 28.19c and a)**. Slide the 6th gear pinion and its splined bush off the shaft, followed by the splined washer **(see illustrations 28.18c, b and a)**.

4 Remove the circlip, then slide the combined 3rd/4th pinion off the shaft **(see illustrations 28.17b and a)**.

5 Remove the circlip, then slide the splined washer, the 5th gear pinion and its bush, and the thrust washer off the shaft **(see illustrations 28.16e, d, c, b and a)**. The 1st

27.13 Lubricate the end of the shaft and fit the oil seal

27.15b ...so the marks on the bearing align with the mating surface

gear pinion is integral with the shaft **(see illustration)**.

6 To remove the left-hand bearing from the crankcase heat around the bearing housing using a hot air gun and see if the bearing will drop out or can be eased out using a hooked tool located behind the inner race **(see illustration 29.6)**. If not you will need an expanding puller to lock behind the inner race and a slide-hammer attachment to jar the bearing out. Heat around the bearing housing first using a hot air gun to make removal easier. Note that if the bearing is removed a new one must be fitted.

Inspection

7 Wash all of the components in clean solvent and dry them off.

8 Check the gear teeth for cracking, chipping, pitting and other obvious wear or damage. Any pinion that is damaged as such must be replaced with a new one.

9 Inspect the dogs and the dog holes in the gears for cracks, chips, and excessive wear especially in the form of rounded edges. Make sure mating gears engage properly. Replace the paired gears as a set if necessary.

10 Check for signs of scoring or bluing on the pinions, bushes and shaft. This could be caused by overheating due to inadequate lubrication. Check that all the oil holes and passages are clear. Replace any damaged pinions or bushes.

11 Check that each pinion moves freely on the shaft or its bush but without undue freeplay. Check that each bush moves freely on the shaft but without undue freeplay.

27.15a Seat the hole onto the pin...

27.15c Make sure the retaining ring and oil seal rim locate correctly

12 The shaft is unlikely to sustain damage unless the engine has seized, placing an unusually high loading on the transmission, or the machine has covered a very high mileage. Check the surface of the shaft for wear and damage, and look for wear in the splines and on the corresponding splines on the pinions or bushes. Damage of any kind can only be cured by replacement.

13 Check the washers and circlips and replace any that are bent or appear weakened or worn. Use new ones if in any doubt. Note that it is good practice to replace all circlips with new ones when overhauling gearshafts.

Reassembly

14 During reassembly, apply molybdenum disulphide oil (a 50/50 mixture of molybdenum disulphide grease and clean engine oil) to the mating surfaces of the shaft, pinions and bushes. When fitting the circlips, do

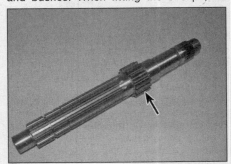

28.5 1st gear pinion (arrowed) is part of the shaft

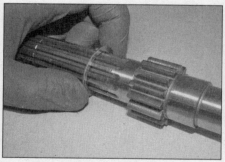

28.16a Slide the thrust washer...

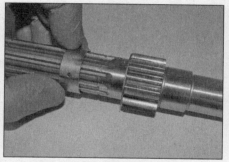

28.16b ...the 5th gear pinion bush...

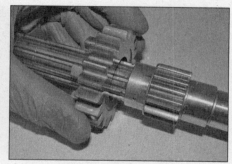

28.16c ...the 5th gear pinion...

28.16d ...and the splined washer onto the shaft...

28.16e ...and secure them with the circlip...

28.16f ...making sure it locates properly in its groove

not expand their ends any further than is necessary. Fit the circlips and washers so that their chamfered side faces away from the thrust side (see *Tools and Workshop Tips* in the Reference section).

15 If removed put the new bearing in the freezer for a while, and when it is cold heat the bearing housing with a hot air gun. Fit the bearing with the marked side facing the inside of the crankcase and tap it squarely in using a socket or bearing driver that bears on the outer race until it seats (see illustration 29.6).

16 Slide the thrust washer onto the left-hand end of the shaft, followed by the 5th gear

pinion bush (see illustrations). Fit the 5th gear pinion onto the bush with its dogs facing away from the integral 1st gear (see illustration). Slide the splined washer onto the shaft, then fit the circlip, making sure that it locates correctly in the groove in the shaft (see illustrations).

17 Slide the combined 3rd/4th gear pinion onto the shaft with the smaller pinion facing the 5th gear pinion (see illustration). Fit the circlip, making sure it is locates correctly in its groove in the shaft (see illustrations).

18 Slide the splined washer onto the shaft, followed by the 6th gear pinion splined

28.17a Slide the combined 3rd/4th gear pinion onto the shaft...

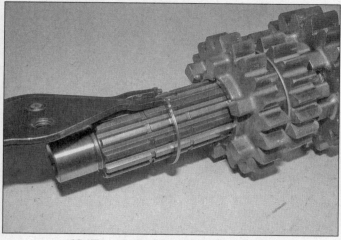

28.17b ...and secure it with the circlip...

28.17c ...making sure it locates properly in its groove

28.18a Slide the splined washer...

28.18b ...the 6th gear pinion splined bush...

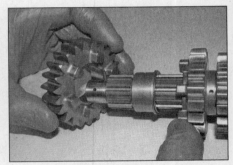

28.18c ...and the 6th gear pinion onto the shaft

28.19a Slide on the slotted splined washer...

28.19b ...and locate it as shown...

28.19c ...then slide on the tabbed lockwasher and locate its tabs in the slots

bush **(see illustrations)**. Slide the 6th gear pinion onto the bush, with its dogs facing the 3rd/4th gear pinion **(see illustration)**.

19 Slide the slotted splined washer onto the shaft and locate it in its groove, then turn it in the groove so that the splines on the washer align with the splines on the shaft and secure the washer in the groove **(see illustrations)**. Slide the tabbed lockwasher onto the shaft, locating the tabs in the slots in the outer rim of the splined washer **(see illustration)**.

20 Slide the 2nd gear pinion onto the end of the shaft with the chamfered side facing out **(see illustration)**. Fit the thrust washer **(see illustration)**.

21 Check that all components have been correctly installed.

Output shaft

Disassembly

22 Slide the outer race and needle bearing off the right-hand end of the shaft **(see illustration 28.37c)**.

23 Slide the thrust washer off the shaft, followed by the 1st gear pinion and its bush, the thrust washer and the 5th gear pinion **(see illustrations 28.37b and a, and 28.36b and a)**.

24 Remove the circlip, then slide the splined washer, the 3rd gear pinion and its

splined bush and the collar off the shaft **(see illustrations 28.35c, b and a)**.

25 Slide the tabbed lockwasher off the shaft, then turn the slotted splined washer to offset the splines and slide it off the shaft **(see illustrations 28.34c and a)**.

26 Slide the 4th gear pinion and its splined bush, followed by the splined washer, off the shaft **(see illustrations 28.33c, b and a)**.

27 Remove the circlip, then slide the 6th gear pinion off the shaft **(see illustrations 28.32b and a)**.

28 Remove the circlip, then slide the splined washer, the 2nd gear pinion and its bush off the shaft **(see illustrations 28.31d, c, b and a)**.

28.20a Slide the 2nd gear pinion...

28.20b ...and the thrust washer onto the shaft

28.31a Slide the 2nd gear pinion bush...

28.31b ...the 2nd gear pinion...

28.31c ...and the splined washer onto the shaft...

28.31d ...and secure them with the circlip...

28.31e ...making sure it locates in the groove

28.32a Slide the 6th gear pinion onto the shaft...

Inspection

29 Refer to Steps 7 to 13 above.

Reassembly

30 During reassembly, apply engine oil to the mating surfaces of the shaft, pinions and bushes. When installing the circlips, do not expand the ends any further than is necessary. Fit the stamped circlips and washers so that their chamfered side faces away from the thrust side (see *Tools and Workshop Tips* in the Reference section).

31 Slide the 2nd gear pinion bush onto the shaft, then slide the 2nd gear pinion onto the bush with its recessed side facing away from the bearing, followed by the splined washer **(see illustrations)**. Fit the circlip, making sure it locates correctly in its groove in the shaft **(see illustrations)**.

28.32b ...and secure it with the circlip...

28.32c ...making sure it locates in the groove

32 Slide the 6th gear pinion on with its selector fork groove facing away from the 2nd gear pinion, then fit the circlip, making sure it is locates correctly in its groove in the shaft **(see illustrations)**.

33 Slide the splined washer and the 4th gear pinion splined bush onto the shaft, then slide the 4th gear pinion onto its bush with its dog holes facing the 6th gear pinion **(see illustrations)**.

28.33a Slide the splined washer...

28.33b ...the 4th gear pinion splined bush...

28.33c ...and the 4th gear pinion onto the shaft

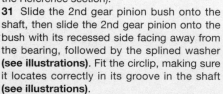

28.34a Slide the slotted splined washer onto the shaft…

28.34b …and locate it as shown

28.34c Slide the lockwasher onto the shaft and engage it with the slotted washer

34 Slide the slotted splined washer onto the shaft and locate it in its groove, then turn it in the groove so that the splines on the washer align with the splines on the shaft and secure the washer in the groove (see illustrations). Slide the lockwasher onto the shaft, locating the tabs on the lockwasher in the slots in the outer rim of the splined washer (see illustration).

35 Slide the collar and the 3rd gear pinion splined bush onto the shaft. Slide the 3rd gear pinion onto the bush with its dog holes facing away from the 4th gear pinion (see illustration). Slide the splined washer on, then fit the circlip, making sure it is locates correctly in its groove in the shaft (see illustrations).

36 Slide the 5th gear pinion onto the shaft

28.35a Slide the collar and bush onto the shaft then slide the 3rd gear pinion onto the bush…

28.35b …then slide the splined washer onto the shaft…

28.35c …and secure them with the circlip…

28.35d …making sure it locates in the groove

28.36a Slide the 5th gear pinion…

28.36b …and the thrust washer onto the shaft

28.37a Slide the bush onto the shaft then slide the 1st gear pinion onto the bush…

with its selector fork groove facing the 3rd gear pinion, followed by the thrust washer **(see illustrations)**.

37 Slide the 1st gear pinion bush onto the shaft, then slide the 1st gear pinion onto the bush with its deep recessed side facing the 5th gear pinion **(see illustration)**. Fit the thrust washer, then fit the needle roller bearing and its outer race over the end of the shaft **(see illustrations)**.

38 Check that all components have been correctly installed.

28.37b …then slide the thrust washer onto the shaft…

28.37c …and fit the bearing and its outer race

29 Transmission shaft overhaul – models with DCT

1 Remove the transmission shafts from the crankcase (Section 27). Always disassemble the transmission shafts separately to avoid mixing up the components.

> **HAYNES HINT** *When disassembling the transmission shafts, place the parts on a long rod or thread a wire through them to keep them in order and facing the proper direction.*

Input shaft

Disassembly

2 Slide the outer shaft assembly off the inner shaft, then slide the needle bearings out **(see illustrations 29.20b and a)**.

3 Slide the 4th gear pinion off the outer shaft **(see illustration 29.19g)**. Remove the circlip, then slide the splined washer, the 6th gear pinion and its bush off the shaft, followed by the thrust washer **(see illustrations 29.19e, d, c, b and a)**. The 2nd gear pinion is integral with the shaft **(see illustration)**.

4 Remove the shaped washer, then slide the 3rd pinion off the inner shaft **(see illustrations 29.18b and a)**.

5 Remove the circlip, then slide the splined washer, the 5th gear pinion and its bush, and the thrust washer off the inner shaft **(see illustrations 29.17e, d, c, b and a)**. The 1st gear pinion is integral with the shaft **(see illustration)**.

6 To remove the left-hand bearing from the crankcase heat around the bearing housing using a hot air gun and see if the bearing will drop out or can be eased out using a hooked

tool located behind the inner race **(see illustration)**. If not you will need an expanding puller to lock behind the inner race and a slide-hammer attachment to jar the bearing out. Heat around the bearing housing first using a hot air gun to make removal easier. Note that if the bearing is removed a new one must be fitted.

Inspection

7 Wash all of the components in clean solvent and dry them off.

8 Check the gear teeth for cracking, chipping, pitting and other obvious wear or damage. Any pinion that is damaged as such must be replaced with a new one.

9 Inspect the dogs and the dog holes in the gears for cracks, chips, and excessive wear especially in the form of rounded edges. Make sure mating gears engage properly. Replace the paired gears as a set if necessary.

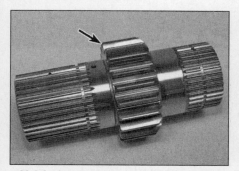

29.3 2nd gear pinion (arrowed) is part of the shaft

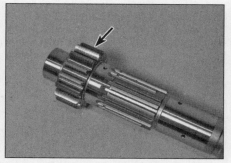

29.5 1st gear pinion (arrowed) is part of the shaft

29.6 Input shaft left-hand bearing

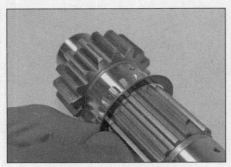

29.17a Slide the thrust washer...

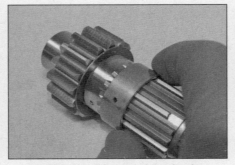

29.17b ...the 5th gear pinion bush...

29.17c ...the 5th gear pinion...

29.17d ...and the splined washer onto the shaft...

29.17e ...and secure them with the circlip...

29.17f ...making sure it locates properly in its groove

10 Check for signs of scoring or bluing on the pinions, bushes and shaft. This could be caused by overheating due to inadequate lubrication. Check that all the oil holes and passages are clear. Replace any damaged pinions or bushes.

11 Check that each pinion moves freely on the shaft or its bush but without undue freeplay. Check that each bush moves freely on the shaft but without undue freeplay.

12 The shaft is unlikely to sustain damage unless the engine has seized, placing an unusually high loading on the transmission, or the machine has covered a very high mileage. Check the surface of the shaft for wear and damage, and look for wear in the splines and on the corresponding splines on the pinions or bushes. Damage of any kind can only be cured by replacement.

13 Check the needle bearings for the outer shaft and fit new ones if necessary.

14 Check the washers and circlips and replace any that are bent or appear weakened or worn. Use new ones if in any doubt. Note that it is good practice to replace all circlips with new ones when overhauling gearshafts.

Reassembly

15 During reassembly, apply molybdenum disulphide oil (a 50/50 mixture of molybdenum disulphide grease and clean engine oil) to the mating surfaces of the shaft, pinions and bushes. When fitting the circlips, do not expand their ends any further than is necessary. Fit the circlips and washers so that their chamfered side faces away from the thrust side (see *Tools and Workshop Tips* in the Reference section).

16 If removed put the new bearing in the freezer for a while, and when it is cold heat the bearing housing with a hot air gun. Fit the bearing with the marked side facing the inside of the crankcase and tap it squarely in using a socket or bearing driver that bears on the outer race until it seats **(see illustration 29.6)**.

17 Slide the thrust washer onto the right-hand end of the inner shaft and up against the integral 1st gear pinion, followed by the 5th gear pinion bush **(see illustrations)**. Fit the 5th gear pinion onto the bush with its dog holes facing away from the 1st gear **(see illustration)**. Slide the splined washer onto the shaft, then fit the circlip, making sure that it locates correctly in the groove **(see illustrations)**.

18 Slide the 3rd gear pinion onto the shaft with the selector fork groove facing the 5th gear pinion **(see illustration)**. Slide the shaped washer onto the shaft with the tabs facing in, making sure it is correctly aligned so the three tabs locate in the spaces where the splines are shorter (the tabs are offset rather than symmetrical so turn the washer as required until all three align) **(see illustrations)**.

29.18a Slide the 3rd gear pinion onto the shaft...

29.18b ...then slide the shaped washer on...

29.18c ...making sure the tabs locate properly in the cut-outs

29.19a Slide the thrust washer…

29.19b …the 6th gear pinion bush…

29.19c …the 6th gear pinion…

19 Slide the thrust washer onto the inner (longer) end of the outer shaft **(see illustration)**. Slide the 6th gear pinion bush onto the shaft, then fit the 6th gear pinion onto the bush with its dog holes facing away from the integral 2nd gear pinion **(see illustrations)**. Slide the splined washer onto the shaft, then fit the circlip, making sure that it locates correctly in the groove **(see illustrations)**. Slide the 4th gear pinion onto the shaft with its selector fork groove facing the 6th gear pinion **(see illustration)**.

20 Slide the needle bearings into the outer shaft, then slide the outer shaft assembly onto the inner shaft and up against the shaped washer **(see illustrations)**.

29.19d …and the splined washer onto the shaft…

29.19e …then fit the circlip…

29.19f …making sure it locates in the groove

29.19g Slide the 4th gear pinion on

29.20a Fit the needle bearings into the shaft

29.20b Slide the outer shaft onto the inner shaft…

29.20c …and all the way along until it butts the shaped washer

29.21 The complete input shaft should be as shown

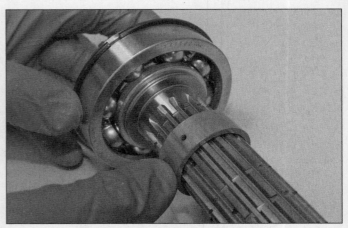

29.31a Slide the 1st gear pinion bush...

21 Check that all components have been correctly installed **(see illustration)**.

Output shaft

Disassembly

22 Slide the outer race and needle bearing off the right-hand end of the shaft **(see illustration 29.37d)**.

23 Slide the thrust washer off the shaft, followed by the 2nd gear pinion and its bush, the thrust washer and the 6th gear pinion **(see**

illustrations 29.37c, b and a, and 29.36b and a)**.

24 Remove the circlip, then slide the splined washer, the 4th gear pinion and its splined bush off the shaft **(see illustrations 29.35d, c, b and a)**.

25 Slide the tabbed lockwasher off the shaft, then turn the slotted splined washer to offset the splines and slide it off the shaft **(see illustrations 29.34c and a)**.

26 Slide the 3rd gear pinion and its splined

bush, followed by the splined washer, off the shaft **(see illustrations 29.33c, b and a)**.

27 Remove the circlip, then slide the 5th gear pinion off the shaft **(see illustrations 29.32b and a)**.

28 Remove the circlip, then slide the splined washer, the 1st gear pinion and its bush off the shaft **(see illustrations 29.31d, c, b and a)**.

Inspection

29 Refer to Steps 7 to 14 above.

Reassembly

30 During reassembly, apply engine oil to the mating surfaces of the shaft, pinions and bushes. When installing the circlips, do not expand the ends any further than is necessary. Fit the stamped circlips and washers so that their chamfered side faces away from the thrust side (see *Tools and Workshop Tips* in the Reference section).

31 Slide the 1st gear pinion bush onto the shaft, then slide the 1st gear pinion onto the bush with its ridged/machined spokes facing away from the bearing, followed by the splined washer **(see illustrations)**. Fit the circlip, making sure it locates correctly in its groove in the shaft **(see illustrations)**.

29.31b ...the 1st gear pinion...

29.31c ...and the splined washer onto the shaft...

29.31d ...and secure them with the circlip...

29.31e ...making sure it locates in the groove

29.32a Slide the 5th gear pinion onto the shaft...

29.32b ...and secure it with the circlip...

29.32c ...making sure it locates in the groove

29.33a Slide the splined washer...

29.33b ...the 3rd gear pinion splined bush...

29.33c ...and the 3rd gear pinion onto the shaft

32 Slide the 5th gear pinion on with its selector fork groove facing away from the 1st gear pinion, then fit the circlip, making sure it is locates correctly in its groove in the shaft **(see illustrations)**.

33 Slide the splined washer and the 3rd gear pinion splined bush onto the shaft, then slide the 3rd gear pinion onto its bush with the flat sides of the spokes facing the 5th gear pinion, so the shaped sides face away **(see illustrations)**.

34 Slide the slotted splined washer onto the shaft and locate it in its groove, then turn it in the groove so that the splines on the washer align with the splines on the shaft and secure the washer in the groove **(see illustrations)**. Slide the lockwasher onto the shaft, locating the tabs on the lockwasher in the slots in the outer rim of the splined washer **(see illustration)**.

29.34a Slide the slotted splined washer onto the shaft...

29.34b ...and locate it as shown

35 Slide the 4th gear pinion splined bush onto the shaft **(see illustration)**. Slide the 4th gear pinion onto its bush with its deeper recessed

side facing away from the 3rd gear pinion **(see illustration)**. Slide the splined washer on, then fit the circlip, making sure it

29.34c Slide the lockwasher onto the shaft and engage it with the slotted washer

29.35a Slide the 4th gear pinion splined bush...

29.35b ...the 4th gear pinion...

29.35c ...and the splined washer onto the shaft...

29.35d ...and secure them with the circlip...

29.35e ...making sure it locates in the groove

29.36a Slide the 6th gear pinion...

29.36b ...and the thrust washer onto the shaft

29.37a Slide the bush...

29.37b ...the 2nd gear pinion...

29.37c ...and the thrust washer onto the shaft...

locates correctly in its groove (see illustrations).

36 Slide the 6th gear pinion onto the shaft with its selector fork groove facing the 4th gear pinion, followed by the thrust washer (see illustrations).

37 Slide the 2nd gear pinion bush onto the shaft, then slide the 2nd gear pinion onto the bush with its dog holes facing the 6th gear pinion (see illustrations). Fit the thrust washer, then fit the needle roller bearing and race over the end of the shaft (see illustrations).

38 Check that all components have been correctly installed (see illustration).

29.37d ...then fit the bearing and its outer race onto the end of the shaft

29.38 The assembled output shaft should be as shown

30 Selector drum and forks

Note: *To remove the selector drum and forks the engine must be removed from the frame and the crankcases separated.*

Removal

1 The selector drum and forks are located in the upper crankcase half. Remove the engine (Section 4) and separate the crankcase halves (Section 21).
2 Remove the transmission output shaft (Section 27). If not already done, remove the gearchange mechanism (Section 15). On models with standard transmission remove the gear position switch or sensor (see Chapter 8). On models with DCT remove the TR (transmission range) sensor (see Chapter 4).

3 Before removing the selector forks, note that each fork has identification letters that face a particular side of the engine, but as two of the forks are identical it is still possible to get them mixed up, so mark each fork with letters or numbers as preferred so you can be sure to return them to their original position on installation.
4 Unscrew and remove the selector drum bearing/fork shaft retainer bolts and washers **(see illustration)**.
5 On models with standard transmission support the selector forks, then withdraw the shaft from the casing and remove the forks as they come free **(see illustration 30.6a)**. Slide the forks back onto the shaft to keep them in the correct order and way round. Withdraw the selector drum from the right-hand side of the engine **(see illustration 30.6b)**.
6 On models with DCT support the output shaft selector forks, then withdraw the fork

shaft from the casing and remove the forks as they come free **(see illustration)**. Slide the forks back onto the shaft to keep them in the correct order and way round. Now do the same for the input shaft selector forks and shaft. Withdraw the selector drum from the right-hand side of the engine **(see illustration)**.

Inspection

7 Inspect the selector forks for any signs of wear or damage, especially around the fork ends where they engage with the groove in their pinion. Check that each fork fits correctly in its pinion groove **(see illustration)**. Check closely to see if the forks are bent. If the forks are in any way damaged they must be replaced with new ones.
8 Measure the thickness of the fork ends and compare the readings to that given in the

30.4 Unscrew the bolts (arrowed)

30.6a Withdraw the shaft and remove the forks

30.6b Withdraw the selector drum

30.7 Check the fit of each fork in its groove

30.8 Measure the fork end thickness

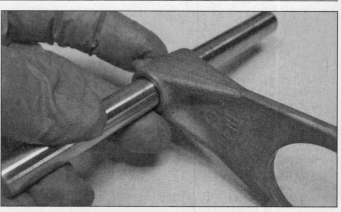

30.9 Check the fit of each fork on the shaft

Specifications **(see illustration)**. Replace the forks with new ones if they are worn beyond their specifications.

9 Check that the forks fit correctly on their shaft **(see illustration)**. They should move freely with a light fit but no appreciable freeplay. If freeplay is felt measure the internal diameter of the fork bores and the corresponding diameter of the fork shaft. Replace the forks and/or shaft with new ones if they are worn. Check that the fork shaft holes in the casing are neither worn nor damaged.

10 Check the selector fork shaft(s) is/are straight by rolling it/them along a flat surface. A bent shaft will cause difficulty in selecting gears and make the gearchange action heavy. Fit a new shaft if it is bent.

11 Inspect the selector drum grooves and selector fork guide pins for signs of wear or damage **(see illustration)**. If either component shows signs of wear or damage the fork(s) and drum must be replaced with new ones.

12 Check that the selector drum bearing rotates freely and has no sign of freeplay between it and the casing. To fit a new bearing, on models with standard transmission refer to Section 15, Step 6, and remove the selector drum cam by unscrewing the bolt in its centre – pass a rod through the drum to counter-hold it. Remove the bearing **(see illustration)**. Fit the new bearing with its marked side facing out. On models with DCT also check the needle bearing in the crankcase and fit a new one if necessary, referring to *Tools and Workshop Tips* in the Reference Section **(see illustration)**.

Installation

13 Lubricate the bearing(s) and left-hand end of the drum with oil. Slide the selector drum into position in the crankcase **(see illustration 30.6b)**. Make sure the drum end locates into its bore or bearing in the crankcase **(see illustration)**.

14 On models with standard transmission lubricate the selector fork shaft with molybdenum disulphide oil (a 50/50 mixture of molybdenum disulphide grease and engine oil) and slide it into the crankcase, locating each fork in the correct order and way round according to the marks made on removal, fitting each fork's guide pin in its groove in the selector drum, and fitting the centre fork ends in its pinion groove in the input shaft.

15 On models with DCT lubricate the input shaft selector fork shaft with molybdenum disulphide oil (a 50/50 mixture of molybdenum disulphide grease and engine oil) and slide it into the crankcase, locating each fork in the correct order and way round according to the marks made on removal, fitting the fork end in its pinion groove in the input shaft and seating the fork's guide pin in its groove in the selector drum **(see illustrations)**. Lubricate the output shaft selector fork shaft with molybdenum disulphide oil (a 50/50 mixture of molybdenum disulphide grease and engine oil) and slide it into the crankcase, locating each fork in the correct order and way round, fitting each fork's guide pin in its groove in the selector drum **(see illustrations)**.

30.11 Check the guide pins and their grooves in the drum

30.12a Slide the bearing off the end of the drum

30.12b Selector drum needle bearing (arrowed) – models with DCT

30.13 Slide the drum end shaft into its bore/bearing

30.15a Insert the shaft into the front hole...

30.15b ...and fit the right-hand fork with the R facing the right-hand side of the engine...

30.15c ...and the left-hand fork with the L facing the right-hand side of the engine...

30.15d ...and seating the guide pins in the drum tracks

30.15e Insert the shaft into the rear hole...

30.15f ...and fit each fork in turn...

30.15g ...with the C facing the left-hand side of the engine

16 Clean the threads of the selector drum/ fork shaft retainer bolts, then apply a suitable non-permanent thread locking compound. Fit the bolts and tighten them to 12 Nm **(see illustration 30.4)**.

17 Install the transmission output shaft, then reassemble the crankcase halves and the rest of the engine – fit the gear position switch or sensor or the transmission range sensor (according to model) before fitting the gearchange mechanism components to prevent the selector drum sliding into the crankcase, making it difficult to fit the drum cam plate.

31 Running-in procedure

1 Make sure the engine oil and coolant levels are correct (see *Pre-ride checks*). Make sure there is fuel in the tank.

2 Turn the engine kill switch to the ON position and make sure the transmission is in neutral. Turn the ignition ON.

3 Start the engine and allow it to run with no throttle applied until it reaches operating temperature.

4 If the oil pressure warning light does not go out, stop the engine immediately and try to find the cause. If an engine is run without oil pressure, even for a short period of time, severe damage will occur.

5 Check carefully for oil and coolant leaks and make sure the transmission and controls, especially the brakes, function properly before road testing the machine.

6 Treat the machine gently for the first few miles to make sure oil has circulated throughout the engine and any new parts installed have started to seat.

7 Even greater care is necessary if new pistons/rings or a new crankcase/bores have been fitted, and the bike will have to be run in as when new. This means greater use of the transmission and a restraining hand on the throttle until at least 300 miles (500 km) have been covered. There's no point in keeping to any set speed limit – the main idea is to keep from labouring the engine and to gradually increase performance up to the 300 miles (500 km) mark. Experience is the best guide, since it's easy to tell when an engine is running freely.

8 Upon completion of the road test, and after the engine has cooled down completely, recheck the valve clearances (see Chapter 1) and check the engine oil and coolant levels (see *Pre-ride checks*).

Chapter 3
Cooling system

Contents

	Section number		Section number
Coolant hoses and union	8	Radiators	5
Coolant reservoir	7	Temperature warning light and ECT sensor	3
Cooling fans and fan relay	2	Thermostat	4
General Information	1	Water pump	6

Degrees of difficulty

Easy, suitable for novice with little experience	Fairly easy, suitable for beginner with some experience	Fairly difficult, suitable for competent DIY mechanic 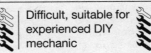	Difficult, suitable for experienced DIY mechanic	Very difficult, suitable for expert DIY or professional

Specifications

Coolant
Mixture type and capacity .... see Chapter 1

ECT sensor
Resistance @ 40°C... 1.0 to 1.3 K-ohms
Resistance @ 100°C.. 140 to 180 ohms

Thermostat
Opening temperature... 80 to 84°C
Fully open.. 95°C
Valve lift .... 8 mm (min)

Radiator
Cap valve opening pressure.................................... 16 to 20 psi (1.1 to 1.4 Bar)

Torque settings
Coolant pipe bolts (models with DCT) .... 12 Nm
Cooling fan assembly
    Fan blade nut .... 1.1 Nm
    Fan shroud bolts...................................... 8.5 Nm
    Fan motor screws..................................... 2.7 Nm
ECT sensor.. 12 Nm
Thermostat cover bolts .... 12 Nm
Water pump mounting bolts..................................... 13 Nm

1 General Information

1 The system uses a water/anti-freeze coolant mixture to carry away excess heat from the engine and maintain its temperature as constant as possible. The cylinders are surrounded by a water jacket around which the heated coolant is circulated by thermo-syphonic action in conjunction with a water pump, which is driven by the front balancer shaft. The hot coolant passes upwards to the thermostat and through to the left-hand radiator, and the across to the right-hand radiator, then to the water pump and back to the engine.

2 A thermostat is fitted in the system to prevent the coolant flowing through the radiators when the engine is cold, therefore accelerating the speed at which the engine reaches normal operating temperature. An engine coolant temperature (ECT) sensor

fitted in the cylinder head provides information to the engine management system ECM (engine control module), and to the high temperature warning light on the instrument panel. A cooling fan fitted to the back of each radiator aids cooling in extreme conditions by drawing extra air through. The fan motors are controlled by a relay, which receives a signal from the ECM, which in turn receives information from the ECT sensor.

3 The complete cooling system is partially sealed and pressurised, the pressure being controlled by a valve contained in the spring-loaded radiator cap on the right-hand raidiator. By pressurising the coolant the boiling point is raised, preventing premature boiling in adverse conditions. The overflow pipe from the system is connected to a reservoir into which excess coolant is expelled under pressure. The discharged coolant automatically returns to the radiator by the vacuum created when the engine cools.

⚠️ *Warning: Do not remove the pressure cap from the radiator when the engine is hot. Scalding hot coolant and steam may be blown out under pressure, which could cause serious injury. When the engine has cooled, place a thick rag, like a towel,*

over the pressure cap; slowly rotate the cap anti-clockwise to the first stop. This procedure allows any residual pressure to escape. When the steam has stopped escaping, press down on the cap while turning it anti-clockwise and remove it.
Caution: Do not allow anti-freeze to come in contact with your skin or painted surfaces of the motorcycle. Rinse off any spills immediately with plenty of water. Anti-freeze is highly toxic if ingested. Never leave anti-freeze lying around in an open container or in puddles on the floor; children and pets are attracted by its sweet smell and may drink it. Check with the local authorities about disposing of used anti-freeze. Many communities will have collection centres which will see that anti-freeze is disposed of safely.
Caution: The cooling system must be filled with either a pre-mix coolant, or anti-freeze and distilled water mixed in the correct proportion. The anti-freeze contains corrosion inhibitors which are essential to avoid damage to the cooling system. A lack of these inhibitors could lead to a build-up of corrosion which would block the coolant passages, resulting in overheating and severe engine damage. Distilled water

must be used as opposed to tap water to avoid a build-up of scale which would also block the passages.

2 Cooling fans and fan relay

Cooling fans
Check

1 There is a cooling fan on the back of each radiator. If the engine is overheating and the cooling fans do not come on, check the cooling fan fuse (see Chapter 8). If the fuse is good, or if the fan is on the whole time, check the relay (see below).
2 If the fans work but are suspected of cutting in at the wrong temperature, check the ECT sensor (Section 3).
3 To test the fan motor displace the relevant radiator and release the wiring and hose from the shroud (see Step 5).
4 Disconnect the fan wiring connector **(see illustrations)**. Using a 12 volt battery and two jumper wires with suitable connectors, connect the battery positive (+) lead to the black/white wire terminal on the fan side of the wiring connector, and the battery negative (–) lead to the black wire terminal on the connector. Once connected the fan should operate. If it does not, and the connector and wiring between it and the motor is good, then the fan motor is faulty.

Removal and installation

5 Refer to Section 5 and displace the radiators – there is no need to drain the coolant or disconnect the hoses or fan wiring. Release all the wiring and the hose from the shroud on the back of the radiator, noting its routing, then release and remove the shroud, noting how it locates **(see illustrations)**.

2.4a Left-hand radiator wiring connector

2.4b Right-hand radiator wiring connector

2.5a Release everything from the shroud…

2.5b …then remove the shroud

2.6 Fan bolts (arrowed)

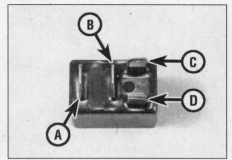

2.11 Fan relay terminal identification

2.13 Cooling fan relay (arrowed)

6 Unscrew the fan mounting bolts and remove the fan assembly **(see illustration)**.

7 If required unscrew the fan blade nut and remove the blade. Free the wiring guide. Undo the fan motor screws and remove the motor.

8 Installation is the reverse of removal. Tighten the fan motor screws to 2.7 Nm. Clean the threads of the motor shaft. Align the flats on the shaft with those in the bore in the fan blade. Apply a suitable non-permanent thread locking compound to the fan blade nut and tighten it to 1.1 Nm. Tighten the shroud bolts to 8.5 Nm.

9 Install the radiator (Section 5).

Cooling fan relay

Check

10 Remove the relay (see Steps 12 and 13).

11 Set a multimeter to the ohms x 1 scale and connect it across the relay's A and B terminals **(see illustration)**. There should be no continuity (infinite resistance). Using a fully-charged 12 volt battery and two insulated jumper wires, connect the positive (+) terminal of the battery to the D terminal on the relay, and the negative (–) terminal to the C terminal on the relay. At this point the relay should be heard to click and the multimeter read 0 ohms (continuity). If this is the case the relay is proved good. If the relay indicates continuity when the battery is not connected, or does not click when battery voltage is applied and still indicates no continuity (infinite resistance) across its terminals, it is faulty.

Removal and installation

12 Remove the seats (see Chapter 7).

13 Displace the relay and remove the cover, then pull the relay off its socket **(see illustration)**.

14 Installation is the reverse of removal.

3 Temperature warning light and ECT sensor

Warning light

1 The circuit consists of the ECT sensor in the cylinder head and the warning light in the instrument cluster.

2 If the temperature warning light does not come on, and all other functions of the instrument cluster are working correctly (if not see Chapter 8), and there is no fault code indicated by the engine management system warning light (if there is see Chapter 4), refer to Chapter 8, Section 2 and check the wiring in the circuit.

3 If the light is on the whole time, disconnect the ECT sensor wiring connector **(see illustration)**. Turn the ignition ON – if the light is off the sensor is faulty.

ECT sensor

Check

4 The resistance of the sensor changes with changes in temperature – see the Specifications at the beginning of the chapter. While in theory it is possible to bench-test the

sensor at those temperatures, in practice the test is difficult to set up and perform.

5 However you can test the resistance of the sensor in the bike with the engine cold, warm and hot. Disconnect the ECT sensor wiring connector **(see illustration 3.3)**. Connect the probes of a multimeter set to read resistance to the terminals on the switch and take several readings as the engine warms up. Resistance should decrease as temperature increases – if the sensor fails it is most likely to give a zero, constant, or infinite resistance reading at all temperatures.

Removal and installation

⚠ *Warning: The engine must be completely cool before carrying out this procedure.*

6 The sensor is in the back of the cylinder head on the left-hand side **(see illustration 3.3)**. Drain the cooling system (see Chapter 1).

7 Disconnect the ECT sensor wiring connector **(see illustration 3.3)**.

8 Unscrew and remove the sensor. Honda specify to fit a new O-ring, but do not list it as a spare part – consult a dealer, or take the old one to an O-ring supplier and get them to match it up.

9 Fit a new O-ring onto the sensor. Fit the sensor and tighten it to 12 Nm. Connect the wiring.

10 Refill the cooling system (see Chapter 1).

4 Thermostat

1 The thermostat is automatic in operation and should give many years service without requiring attention. In the event of a failure, if the valve jams open the engine will take much longer than normal to warm up, and if the valve jams shut, the coolant will be unable to circulate and the engine will overheat.

Removal

⚠ *Warning: The engine must be completely cool before carrying out this procedure.*

2 Drain the cooling system (see Chapter 1).

3 If required release the hose clamp and pull the hose off the thermostat outlet **(see illustration)**.

3.3 ECT sensor wiring connector (arrowed)

4.3 Disconnect the hose if you want to completely remove the thermostat cover

4.4a Unscrew the bolts and detach the cover…

4.4b … then withdraw the thermostat from the housing. Note bleed hole position (arrowed)

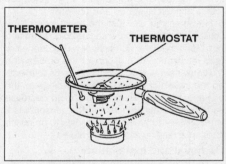

4.6 Thermostat testing set-up

THERMOMETER

THERMOSTAT

4.7 Fit a new seal if necessary

from those given, the thermostat is faulty and must be replaced with a new one.

Installation

7 Check the thermostat seal for signs of damage or deterioration and fit a new one if necessary **(see illustration)**. Fit the thermostat into the housing with the bleed hole at the top, and aligning the ribs with the grooves **(see illustration 4.4b)**.

8 Fit the cover and tighten the bolts to 12 Nm **(see illustration 4.4a)**.

9 If the hose was disconnected push it onto the thermostat cover outlet and secure it with the clamp **(see illustration 4.3)**.

10 Fill the cooling system (see Chapter 1).

5 Radiators

Note: *If the radiator is being removed as part of the engine removal procedure, detach the hoses from their unions on the engine rather than on the radiator and remove the radiator complete with its hoses. Note the routing of the hoses.*

Removal

⚠ **Warning: The engine must be completely cool before carrying out this procedure.**

1 Drain the cooling system (see Chapter 1).

Right-hand radiator

2 Remove the right inner panel (see Chapter 7).

3 Release the wiring and hoses from the radiator shroud as required according to model **(see illustration 2.5a)**.

4 Release the hose clamps and detach the hoses from the radiator **(see illustrations)**.

4 Unscrew the thermostat cover bolts and detach it from the cylinder head **(see illustration)**. Withdraw the thermostat, noting how it fits **(see illustration)**.

Thermostat check

5 Examine the thermostat visually before carrying out the test. If it remains in the open position at room temperature, it should be replaced with a new one. Also check the condition of the seal.

6 Suspend the thermostat by a piece of wire in a container of cold water. Place a thermometer capable of reading temperatures up to 110°C in the water so that the bulb is close to the thermostat **(see illustration)**. Heat the water, noting the temperature when the thermostat opens, and compare the result with the specifications given at the beginning of the Chapter. Also check the amount the valve opens after it has been heated for a few minutes and compare the measurement to the specifications. If the readings obtained differ

5.4a Disconnect the overflow hose from the filler neck…

5.4b …and the three large bore hoses from the radiator

5 Unscrew the radiator mounting bolts, noting the washers **(see illustration)**. Move the radiator out and disconnect the fan wiring connector **(see illustration 2.4b)**, then remove the radiator, taking care not to catch the exposed fins on anything.

6 Note the collars in the rubber grommets **(see illustration 5.13)**. Fit new grommets if they are damaged, deformed or deteriorated.

7 Check the radiator for signs of damage and clear any dirt or debris that might obstruct air flow and inhibit cooling. If the radiator fins are badly damaged or broken the radiator must be replaced with a new one. To enable full examination and cleaning, remove the front grille **(see illustration 5.14)**, the shroud and the cooling fan (Section 2).

Left-hand radiator

8 Remove the left inner panel (see Chapter 7).
9 Remove the horn (see Chapter 8).

5.5 Radiator bolts (arrowed)

5.10a Release the wiring...

10 Release the wiring and hose from the radiator shroud **(see illustrations)**.
11 Release the hose clamps and detach the hoses from the radiator **(see illustration)**.
12 Unscrew the radiator mounting bolts, noting the washers, and the wiring clamp

with the top bolt **(see illustration)**. Move the radiator out and disconnect the fan wiring connector **(see illustration 2.4a)**, then remove the radiator, taking care not to catch the exposed fins on anything.
13 Note the collars in the rubber grommets

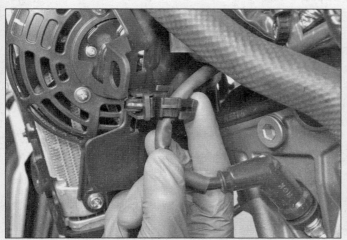

5.10b ...the connectors...

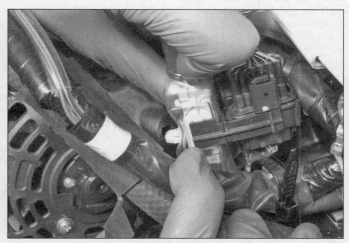

5.10c ...and the connector bracket clip

5.11 Slacken the clamps (arrowed) and disconnect the hoses

5.12 Radiator bolts (arrowed)

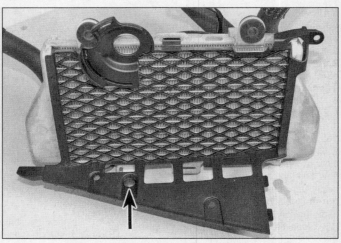

5.13 Note the collars and check the condition of the grommets

5.14 The grille is secured by a screw (arrowed)

(see illustration). Fit new grommets if they are damaged, deformed or deteriorated.

14 Check the radiator for signs of damage and clear any dirt or debris that might obstruct air flow and inhibit cooling. If the radiator fins are badly damaged or broken the radiator must be replaced with a new one. To enable full examination and cleaning, remove the front grille **(see illustration)**, the shroud and the cooling fan (Section 2).

Installation

15 Installation is the reverse of removal, noting the following.

● Check the coolant hoses are in good condition, and are securely retained by their clamps, using new ones if necessary.

● Make sure the rubber grommets are in place and the collars are fitted in them from the back **(see illustration 5.13)**.
● Make sure that the fan wiring is securely connected.
● On completion refill the cooling system as described in Chapter 1.

Pressure cap check

16 If problems such as overheating or loss of coolant occur, check the entire system as described in Chapter 1. If there are no obvious problems and leaks the pressure cap opening pressure should be checked by a Honda dealer with the special tester required to do the job. If the cap is defective, replace it with a new one.

Check

1 Refer to Chapter 1, Section 12.

Removal

2 Drain the engine oil and coolant (see Chapter 1).
3 Remove the clutch cover (see Chapter 2).
4 Unscrew the pump mounting bolts and remove the pump from the cover **(see illustrations)**. Remove the seal ring – a new one must be used **(see illustration 6.7b)**. Remove the locating dowels if loose **(see illustration 6.7a)**.
5 Do not attempt to remove the impeller and seals – the pump comes as an assembly and no internal components are available.
6 Turn and wiggle the water pump impeller and check for rough movement or excessive freeplay **(see illustration)**. Also check for corrosion or a build-up of scale in the pump body and clean or fit a new pump as necessary.

Installation

7 Fit the locating dowels if removed **(see illustration)**. Fit the new O-ring into the groove **(see illustration)**. Clean the threads of

6.4a Unscrew the bolts...

6.4b ...and remove the pump

6.6 Check the impeller as described

6.7a Pump locating dowels (arrowed)

6.7b Fit a new seal into the groove

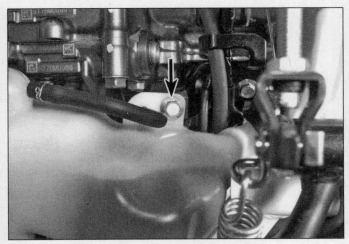

7.2a Unscrew the bolt (arrowed)…

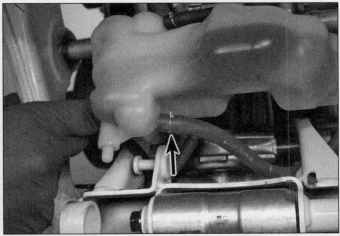

7.2b …displace the reservoir and disconnect the hose (arrowed)

the mounting bolts and apply fresh threadlock, and tighten them to 13 Nm **(see illustration 6.4a)**.

8 Install the clutch cover (see Chapter 2).

9 Add engine oil and coolant (see Chapter 1).

7 Coolant reservoir

Removal

1 The coolant reservoir is located between the back of the engine and the shock absorber. Remove the shock absorber (see Chapter 5). Get a suitable container to drain the coolant into.

2 Unscrew the bolt and displace the reservoir, noting how the peg locates in the hole, then detach the radiator overflow hose from the

8.4 Coolant union

bottom of the reservoir and drain the coolant into the container **(see illustrations)**.

Installation

3 Installation is the reverse of removal. Refill the reservoir to the UPPER level line with the specified coolant mixture (see *Pre-ride checks*).

8 Coolant hoses and union

Removal

1 Before removing a hose, drain the coolant (see Chapter 1).

2 Release the main (large-bore) hose clamps by slackening the clamp screw, then slide them back along the hose and clear of the union **(see illustration 4.3)**. The reservoir hoses are secured by spring clamps which can be expanded by squeezing their ears together with pliers **(see illustration 5.4a)**.
Caution: The radiator unions are fragile. Do not use excessive force when attempting to remove the hoses.

3 If a hose proves stubborn, release it by rotating it on its union before working it off. If all else fails, cut the hose with a sharp knife. Whilst this means replacing the hose with a new one, it is preferable to buying a new radiator.

4 The union on the cylinder block can

be removed by unscrewing its bolts **(see illustration)**. If the union is removed the O-ring must be replaced with a new one.

5 On models with DCT the coolant pipe on the clutch cover can be removed after disconnecting the hose from the cover, then unscrewing the pipe bolts and easing it out of the cover and hose (see Chapter 2, Section 14). A new O-ring must be used.

Installation

6 On models with DCT fit the coolant pipe onto the clutch cover using a new O-ring smeared with oil, and tighten the bolts to 12 Nm (see Chapter 2, Section 14).

7 If the inlet union to the cylinder block has been removed, fit a new O-ring into the groove.

8 Slide the clamps onto the hose and then work the hose on to its unions as far as the spigot, where present. Make sure the hose is correctly aligned so its preformed shape does not distort when connected at both ends.

> **HAYNES HiNT**
> *If the hose is difficult to push on its union, soften it by soaking it in very hot water, or alternatively a little soapy water on the union can be used as a lubricant.*

9 Rotate the hose on its unions to settle it in position before sliding the clamps into place.

10 Refill the cooling system (see Chapter 1).

Chapter 4
Engine management system

Contents

Section number

Air filter housing	3
Catalytic converter	19
DCT system fault diagnosis	8
Engine control module/Powertrain control module (ECM/PCM)	10
Engine management system (PGM-FI and DCT) sensors	9
Engine management system description	6
Engine management system relays	11
Evaporative Emission Control (EVAP) system	20
Exhaust system	17
Fuel level sensor and fuel reserve sensor	15
Fuel pressure check	13
Fuel pump	14

Section number

Fuel rail and injectors	5
Fuel tank	2
General information and precautions	1
Idle air control valve (2016/17 models)	12
Ignition coils	22
Ignition system check	21
Ignition timing	23
Immobiliser system	24
PGM-FI system fault diagnosis	7
Pulse secondary air (PAIR) system	18
Throttle body	4
Throttle cables (2016/17 models)	16

Degrees of difficulty

Easy, suitable for novice with little experience	Fairly easy, suitable for beginner with some experience	Fairly difficult, suitable for competent DIY mechanic	Difficult, suitable for experienced DIY mechanic	Very difficult, suitable for expert DIY or professional

Specifications

General information
Cylinder numbering	1 – left, 2 – right
Spark plugs	see Chapter 1

Fuel
Grade	Unleaded. Minimum 91 RON (Research Octane Number) for Europe
Fuel tank capacity (including reserve of approx. 3.4 litres)	
Standard models	18.8 litres
Adventure Sports models	24.2 litres

Fuel injection system
Idle speed	
2016/17 models	1200 ± 100 rpm
2018-on models	1250 ± 100 rpm
Fuel pressure at specified idle speed	47 to 53 psi (3.3 to 3.7 Bar)
Minimum fuel flow rate	319 cc every 10 seconds

Fuel injection system test data
Engine coolant temperature (ECT) sensor resistance	1.0 to 1.3 K-ohms at 40°C (104°F)
Idle air control valve (IACV) resistance	99 to 121 ohms at 25°C (77°F)
Fuel injector resistance	11 to 13 ohms at 20°C (68°F)
Intake air temperature (IAT) sensor resistance	1 to 1.3 K-ohms at 40°C (104°F)
Oxygen sensor heater resistance	6.7 to 10.5 ohms at 20°C (68°F)
Crankshaft position (CKP) sensor minimum peak voltage (see text)	0.7 volt

Fuel level sensor
Resistance	
Full position	6.4 to 10.4 ohms
Empty position	204.8 to 210.8 ohms

Emission control systems
PAIR control valve solenoid resistance	24 to 28 ohms at 20°C (68°F)
EVAP purge control valve solenoid resistance	30 to 34 ohms at 20°C (68°F)

Ignition coils

Note: *All values given are only accurate at 20°C (68°F)*

Primary winding resistance	approximately 2.6 ohms
Secondary winding resistance	
With plug cap	approximately 17.8 K-ohms
Without plug cap	approximately 13 K-ohms
Plug cap resistance	approximately 4.8 K-ohms
Initial voltage (see text)	Battery voltage (approximately 12 volts)
Minimum peak voltage (see text)	100 volts

Ignition timing

At idle (F mark)	10° BTDC

Torque settings

Clutch EOP sensors	20 Nm
Crankshaft end cap	8 Nm
EOT sensor.	15 Nm
Exhaust system	
Downpipe flange nuts.	20 Nm
Silencer clamp bolts.	17 Nm
Fuel pump mounting plate nuts	12 Nm
Injector holder/fuel rail bolts.	5.1 Nm
Oxygen sensor	24.5 Nm
PAIR system reed valve cover bolts.	12 Nm
Timing inspection cap	6 Nm
TR sensor bolt	12 Nm

---

1   General information and precautions

General information

1 All models are equipped with Honda's programmed fuel injection (PGM-FI) system. It is controlled by a management system, with an engine control module (ECM) on models with standard transmission, and a combined ECM/PCM (powertrain control module) on models with DCT.

Fuel system

2 The fuel supply system consists of the fuel tank with internal fuel pump assembly (incorporating the pressure regulator, filter and strainer) and fuel level sensor, the fuel hose, the fuel rail, the fuel injectors, the throttle body assembly, and on 2016/17 models the throttle cables. The fuel pump is switched on and off via a relay. Fuel and air are supplied to the engine via 44 mm throttle bodies. The injectors are operated by the engine control module or powertrain control module (ECM/PCM) using the information obtained from the various sensors it monitors (refer to Section 6 for more information on the operation of the fuel injection system).

3 All models have a fuel gauge incorporated in the instrument cluster, actuated by the level sensor inside the fuel tank.

Ignition system

4 The transistorised electronic ignition system is combined with the fuel injection system, both being controlled by the ECM/PCM. The ignition system comprises a set of timing triggers, the crankshaft position (CKP) sensor, the ECM/PCM, the ignition coils and the two spark plugs per cylinder. There are four conventional coils, one for each spark plug.

5 The timing triggers are on the alternator rotor on the left-hand end of the crankshaft, and generate a signal in the CKP sensor in the alternator cover as the crankshaft rotates. The CKP sensor sends that signal to the ECM/PCM, which calculates the required ignition timing and supplies the ignition coils with the power necessary to produce a spark at the plugs. There is no provision for adjusting the ignition timing.

6 The system incorporates a safety interlock circuit that will cut the ignition if the sidestand is extended whilst the engine is running and in gear, or if a gear is selected whilst the engine is running and the sidestand is down. It also prevents the engine from being started if the sidestand is down and the engine is in gear. The engine can be started with the sidestand up when it is in gear as long as the clutch lever is pulled in.

7 All UK models are fitted with an immobiliser system (HISS – Honda Ignition Security System) as standard. The system will not allow the engine to be started unless the correct key is used. The immobiliser system has its own fault diagnosis function.

Note: *Individual engine management system components can be checked but not repaired. If system troubles occur, and the faulty component can be isolated, the only cure for the problem in most cases is to replace the part with a new one. Keep in mind that most electronic parts, once purchased, cannot be returned. To avoid unnecessary expense, make very sure the faulty component has been positively identified before buying a new part.*

Precautions

 Warning: Petrol (gasoline) is extremely flammable, so take extra precautions when you work on any part of the fuel system. Always remove the battery (see Chapter 8). Don't smoke or allow open flames or bare light bulbs near the work area, and don't work in a garage where a natural gas-type appliance is present. If you spill any fuel on your skin, rinse it off immediately with soap and water. When you perform any kind of work on the fuel system, wear safety glasses and have a fire extinguisher suitable for a class B type fire (flammable liquids) on hand.

8 With the fuel injection system, some residual pressure will remain in the fuel hose and fuel rail after the motorcycle has been used. Before disconnecting the fuel hose, release fuel system pressure as described in Section 2. It is vital that no dirt or debris is allowed to enter the fuel tank or the fuel rail assembly whilst the fuel hoses are disconnected. Any foreign matter in the fuel system components could result in injector damage or malfunction. Make sure the ignition is switched OFF before disconnecting or reconnecting any fuel injection system wiring connector. If a connector is disconnected or reconnected with the ignition switched ON, the ECM/PCM may be damaged.

9 Always perform service procedures in a well-ventilated area to prevent a build-up of fumes.

10 Never work in a building containing a gas appliance with a pilot light, or any other form of naked flame. Ensure that there are no naked light bulbs or any sources of flame or sparks nearby.

11 Do not smoke (or allow anyone else to smoke) while in the vicinity of petrol (gasoline) or of components containing it. Remember the possible presence of vapour from these sources and move well clear before smoking.

12 Check all electrical equipment belonging to the house, garage or workshop where work is being undertaken (see Safety First!). Remember that certain electrical appliances such as drills, cutters etc, create sparks in the normal course of operation and must not be used near petrol (gasoline) or any component containing it. Again, remember the possible

presence of fumes before using electrical equipment.

13 Always mop up any spilt fuel and safely dispose of the rag used.

14 Any stored fuel that is drained off during servicing work must be kept in sealed containers that are suitable for holding petrol (gasoline), and clearly marked as such; the containers themselves should be kept in a safe place. Note that this last point applies equally to the fuel tank if it is removed from the machine; also remember to keep its filler cap closed at all times.

15 Read the 'Safety First!' Section at the beginning of this manual before starting work.

2 Fuel tank

⚠️ **Warning: Refer to the precautions given in Section 1 before starting work.**

1 Remove the rider's seat, the fairing side panels, the fuel tank covers, and the seat bracket (see Chapter 7).

Raise

2 Make sure the fuel cap is secure.
3 Unscrew the tank mounting bolt and

remove the washer **(see illustration)**.

4 Prepare a suitable piece of wood (about 8 inches of 4 x 2) to fit between the front of the tank and the frame. Carefully draw the tank back until its support hooks are clear of the support rubbers on the frame, then reposition the tank so the hooks seat on top of the rubbers, and relocate the rear mounting grommet back on the lug **(see illustration)**. Loosely fit the rear mounting bolt. Raise the front of the tank and locate the support between the tank and the frame **(see illustration)** – make sure it is secure.

Removal

Note: *Removing the tank involves a small amount of unavoidable fuel spillage, which is obviously dangerous. Refer to the precautions given in Section 1 before starting work, and have some rag to hand. Once the tank has been removed, rest it on some soft rag to prevent damaging the paintwork or hose unions. Try to time the removal procedure with a near empty tank, which makes it much easier to lift. Alternatively transfer as much fuel as possible into a fuel container using a suction pump.*

5 Raise the tank as described above.
6 Disconnect the fuel pump wiring connector **(see illustration)**.
7 Disconnect the fuel level sensor wiring connector **(see illustration)**.

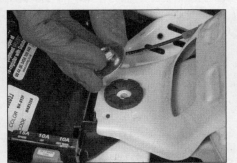

2.3 Remove the bolt and washer

2.4a Position the tank support hooks on top of the rubbers…

2.4b …then lift the front and support it using a piece of wood as shown

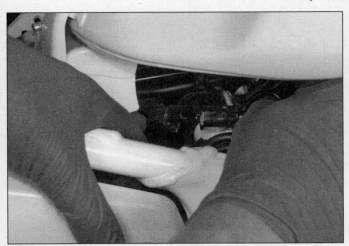

2.6 Disconnect the pump wiring connector…

2.7 …and the level sensor wiring connector

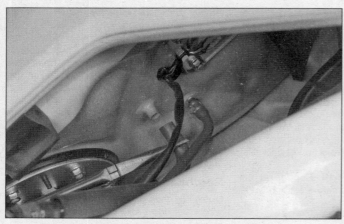

2.10 Pull the hoses off their unions

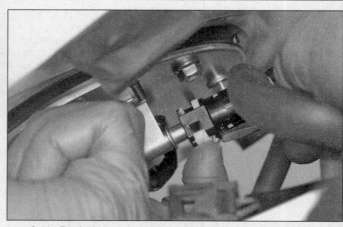

2.11a Push the retainer tab in then push the retainer up...

8 To release any residual pressure in the fuel system start the engine and let it idle until it stops, then turn the ignition off.

9 Disconnect the battery negative (-) lead (see Chapter 8).

10 Disconnect the fuel tank drain and breather hoses **(see illustration)**.

11 Clean any dirt from the quick-release connector on the fuel hose. Place a wad of rag for catching any residual fuel in the hose under the connector. Push the retainer locking tab in, then push the retainer up and pull the connector off the pipe union **(see illustrations)**. Seal the union and the connector with a piece from a plastic bag or the finger from a latex glove, secured with an elastic band, to prevent dirt getting in.

12 Remove the support from under the tank and lower the tank – make sure you don't trap the hoses or wiring.

13 Unscrew the rear mounting bolt **(see illustration 2.3)**. Carefully lift the tank off the frame and remove it.

14 Check all the tank rubbers and hoses for signs of damage or deterioration and replace them with new ones if necessary.

Installation

15 Depending on how the tank has been stood and how full it is there is the possibility of fuel having made its way into the breather pipe which could spurt out of the hose union on the base when it is moved – be prepared with some rag for this. Once the tank is upright the pipe will fill itself with air.

16 Position the tank with the support hooks resting on the rubbers and loosely fit the rear bolt **(see illustration 2.4a and 2.3)**. Raise and support the tank as before **(see illustration 2.4b)**.

17 Fit the fuel hose connector onto the pipe and push it until the retainer tab clicks into place, then try to pull the connector off to make sure it has locked **(see illustration 2.11b)**.

18 Connect the fuel pump and level sensor wiring connectors **(see illustrations 2.6 and 2.7)**.

19 Connect the drain and breather hoses **(see illustration 2.10)** – make sure there is a gap of 9 mm between the end of the breather hose and the base of the union, where it joins the tank.

20 Connect the battery (see Chapter 8). Make sure the kill switch is set to RUN, then

turn the ignition ON to allow the fuel pump to pressurise the system, then turn it off – do not start the engine. Repeat a couple of times and each time check there are no leaks at the hose connector.

21 Remove the support from under the tank and lower it onto the rubbers. Remove the rear mounting bolt and reposition the tank so the supports seat around the rubbers **(see illustration)**. Fit the rear mounting bolt with its washer and tighten it.

22 Fit the seat bracket. Install the bodywork (see Chapter 7).

Repair

23 Repairs to the fuel tank should be carried out by a professional who has experience in this critical and potentially dangerous work. Even after cleaning and flushing of the fuel system, explosive fumes can remain and ignite during repair of the tank.

24 If the fuel tank is removed from the bike, it should not be placed in an area where sparks or open flames could ignite the fumes coming out of the tank. Be especially careful inside garages where a natural gas-type appliance is located, because the pilot light could cause an explosion.

2.11b ...and pull the hose connector off

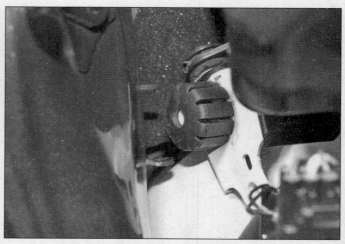

2.21 Locate the supports around the rubbers

3 Air filter housing

⚠️ **Warning: Refer to the precautions given in before starting work.**

Removal

1 Remove the fuel tank (Section 2).
2 Release each air duct from the inner cover **(see illustration)**.
3 Release the front sub-loom wiring connectors (12-pin black and 12-pin grey) from the left-hand side of the housing **(see illustration)**.
4 Release each air filter housing drain hose from its tie and clip(s).
5 Slacken the air intake duct clamp screws **(see illustration)**.
6 Unscrew the front mounting bolt and remove the washer, then unscrew the rear bolts and remove the collars **(see illustration)**.

3.2 Release the ducts

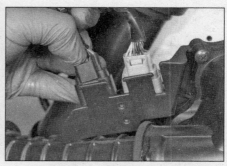

3.3 Displace the two connectors

7 Ease the housing up and disconnect the IAT sensor wiring connector, the crankcase breather hose and the PAIR system hose from the housing **(see illustration)**.
8 Remove the housing, noting the routing of the drain hoses **(see illustration)**. Cover or plug the intake ducts on the cylinder head.

Installation

9 Installation is the reverse of removal, noting the following:
● Check the condition of all hoses and replace them with new ones if they are in any way damaged or deteriorated.
● Do not forget to remove the covers or

3.5 Intake duct clamp screws (arrowed)

3.6 Unscrew the bolts, noting the washer and collars

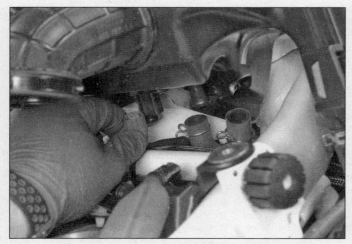

3.7 Disconnect the hoses and the wiring connector

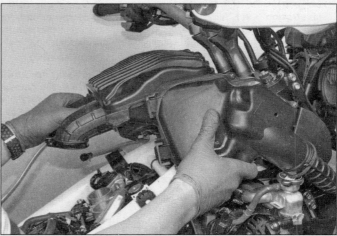

3.8 Note the routing of the hoses as you remove the housing

3.9a Route the drain hoses down…

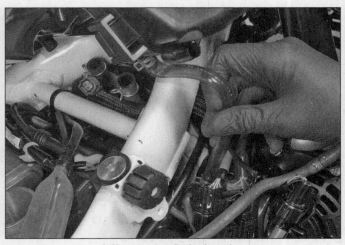

3.9b …as you fit the housing

3.9c Check the ducts are seated over the throttle body all round

plugs from the intake ducts on the cylinder head.

● Make sure the drain hoses are correctly routed (see illustrations 3.9a and b).
● Make sure the IAT sensor connector and the hoses are securely connected (see illustration 3.7).
● Make sure the air intake ducts seat correctly onto the throttle body (see illustration 3.9c). Align the duct clamps correctly (see illustration 3.5).
● Make sure all hoses and wiring are correctly routed and secured – check the drain tube on each side of the housing is not trapped or kinked.

4 Throttle body

 Warning: Refer to the precautions given in Section 1 before starting work.

2016/17 models

Removal

1 Remove the air filter housing (Section 3).
2 Slide the rubber boot off the throttle cable adjuster at the handlebar end, then fully slacken the locknut and thread the adjuster fully in to get maximum freeplay in the cable.
3 Disconnect the MAP sensor and IACV wiring connectors.
4 Where fitted disconnect the EVAP system hose from the 3-way joint.
5 Fully slacken the throttle body clamps and ease the throttle body out of the intake ducts (see illustration 4.24).
6 Disconnect the TP (throttle position) sensor and fuel injector wiring connectors.
7 Disconnect the throttle cables (see Section 16) and remove the throttle body.
8 If required remove the intake ducts from the cylinder head (see Chapter 2, Section 10). Check the condition of the rubbers, especially looking for cracks and splits, and replace them with new ones if necessary.

Caution: Tape over or stuff clean rag into each intake duct or into the cylinder head intakes if the ducts have been removed to prevent anything getting in.

Caution: Do not snap the throttle cam/valves from fully open to fully closed once the cables have been disconnected because this can lead to engine idle speed problems.

Disassembly

Caution: The throttle body assembly must be treated as a sealed unit. NEVER loosen any of the white-painted nuts/bolts/screws on the assembly as these are pre-set at the factory to ensure correct synchronisation of the throttle valves.

9 Before disassembling the throttle body give it a good clean to prevent dirt getting in as components are removed. If you are fitting a new throttle body remove all the components below, otherwise only remove them as required.
10 If you want to detach the fuel hose clean any dirt from the quick-release connector. Place a wad of rag for catching any residual fuel in the hose under the connector. Push the retainer locking tab in, then push the retainer and pull the connector off the pipe union (see illustrations 2.11a and b). Seal the union and the connector with a piece from a plastic bag or the finger from a latex glove, secured with an elastic band, to prevent dirt getting in.
11 Remove the MAP sensor and its hoses (Section 9). DO NOT remove the TP sensor.
12 Remove the fuel rail and injectors (Section 5).
13 Remove the idle air control valve and its housing (Section 12).
14 Remove the throttle cable bracket.
15 Where fitted remove the EVAP system hoses.

Caution: NEVER use a solvent-based cleaner to clean the throttle body components. The throttle bores are covered with a molybdenum coating which could be removed by the cleaner.

16 Remove the plate for the air intake ducts from the top of the throttle body by undoing the screws. Remove the seal from the groove – a new one must be used.

Reassembly and installation

17 Reassembly and installation is the reverse of removal, referring to the relevant Sections where directed, and noting the following:
● Check the condition of all hoses and replace them with new ones if they are in any way damaged or deteriorated.
● Fit the intake ducts onto the cylinder head if removed (see Chapter 2, Section 10).
● Fit the plate for the air intake ducts using a new seal smeared with oil, and make sure it is seated in its groove.
● Fit the fuel hose connector onto the pipe and push it until the retainer tab clicks into place, then try to pull the connector off to make sure it has locked.
● Do not forget to remove the covers or plugs from the intakes.
● Make sure the throttle body clamps are correctly aligned and seated with the hole over the pin. Lubricate the inside of each duct with a smear of engine oil to help the

4.20 Release the hose

4.21 Disconnect the MAP sensor wiring connector…

4.22 …and the TBW wiring connector

throttle body slide in. Seat the ribs on the throttle body between the tabs on the duct.
● Make sure all wiring connectors are securely connected.
● Make sure all cables, hoses and wiring are correctly routed.
● Check and adjust throttle cable freeplay (see Chapter 1, Section 10).

2018-on models

Removal

18 Remove the air filter housing (Section 3).
19 Remove the tool box (see Chapter 7).
20 Release the fuel hose from its clip **(see illustration)**.
21 Disconnect the MAP sensor wiring connector **(see illustration)**.
22 Disconnect the TBW (throttle-by-wire) unit wiring connector **(see illustration)**.
23 Where fitted disconnect the EVAP system hose from the 3-way joint **(see illustration)**.
24 Fully slacken the clamps securing the throttle body in the intake ducts **(see illustration)**.
25 Ease the throttle body out of the ducts and disconnect the fuel injector wiring connectors **(see illustration)**.
26 If required remove the intake ducts from the cylinder head (see Chapter 2, Section 10). Check the condition of the rubbers, especially

4.23 Disconnect the EVAP hose

4.24 Slacken the clamp screw on each side…

looking for cracks and splits, and replace them with new ones if necessary.
Caution: Tape over or stuff clean rag into each intake duct or into the cylinder head intakes if the ducts have been removed to prevent anything getting in.

Disassembly

Caution: The throttle body assembly must be treated as a sealed unit. NEVER loosen any of the white-painted nuts/bolts/screws on the assembly as these are pre-set at the factory to ensure correct synchronisation of the throttle valves.
27 If you want to detach the fuel hose clean

any dirt from the quick-release connector. Place a wad of rag for catching any residual fuel in the hose under the connector. Push the retainer locking tab in, then push the retainer and pull the connector off the pipe union **(see illustrations 2.11a and b)**. Seal the union and the connector with a piece from a plastic bag or the finger from a latex glove, secured with an elastic band, to prevent dirt getting in.
28 If required remove the MAP sensor and its hoses (Section 9). DO NOT remove the TBW unit **(see illustration)**.
29 If required remove the fuel rail and injectors (Section 5).

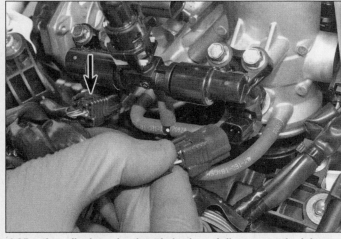

4.25 …then displace the throttle body and disconnect the injector connectors

4.28 The TBW unit is an integral part of the throttle body and must not be removed

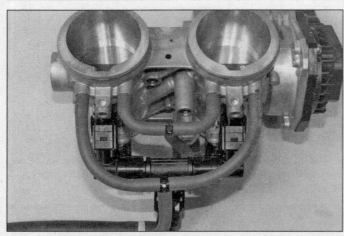

4.30 EVAP and MAP sensor hose arrangement

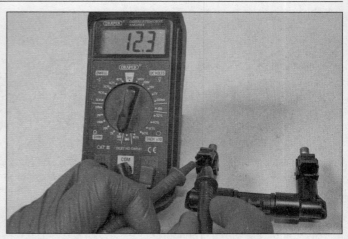

5.4 Check the resistance of each injector

30 Where fitted and if required remove the EVAP system hoses **(see illustration)**.
Caution: NEVER use a solvent-based cleaner to clean the throttle body components. The throttle bores are covered with a molybdenum coating which could be removed by the cleaner.

Reassembly and installation

31 Reassembly and installation is the reverse of removal, referring to the relevant Sections where directed, and noting the following:

● Check the condition of all hoses and replace them with new ones if they are in any way damaged or deteriorated.
● Fit the intake ducts onto the cylinder head if removed (see Chapter 2, Section 10).
● Fit the fuel hose connector onto the pipe and push it until the retainer tab clicks into place, then try to pull the connector off to make sure it has locked.
● Do not forget to remove the covers or plugs from the intakes.
● Make sure the throttle body clamps are correctly aligned and seated with the hole over the pin. Lubricate the inside of each

duct with a smear of engine oil to help the throttle body slide in. Seat the ribs on the throttle body between the tabs on the duct.
● Make sure all wiring connectors are securely connected.
● Make sure all hoses and wiring are correctly routed.

5 Fuel rail and injectors

> ⚠️ *Warning: Refer to the precautions given in Section 1 before starting work.*

Check

1 Raise and support the fuel tank (Section 2).
2 If the engine runs, start it and allow it to idle. Check the operation of each injector using a sounding rod held against it; an injector will emit a 'clicking' noise when functioning. If an injector is silent, either the injector or its wiring harness is faulty.
3 If the engine does not run, remove the fuel

tank (Section 2), then remove the ECM/PCM (Section 10). Disconnect the wiring connectors from the injectors **(see illustration 4.25)**.
4 Connect an ohmmeter between the injector terminals and measure the resistance **(see illustration)**. Compare the reading to that given in the Specifications at the beginning of the Chapter. If the resistance differs greatly remove the fuel rail and injectors (see below) and replace the injector with a new one.
5 To check the wiring and connectors in the injector circuit refer to Chapter 8, Section 2 and to the wiring diagram for your model.

Removal

6 Remove the fuel tank (Section 2).
7 Release the fuel hose from its clip **(see illustration 4.20)**.
8 Disconnect the MAP sensor wiring connector **(see illustration 4.21)**.
9 Clean around the base of each injector using compressed air.
10 Unscrew the injector holder/fuel rail bolts **(see illustration)**. Carefully lift off the fuel rail and injectors as an assembly, then disconnect the injector wiring connectors **(see illustration)**.

5.10a Unscrew the bolts (arrowed)...

5.10b ...lift the fuel rail and injector assembly off and disconnect the injector connectors

5.12 Pull each injector out

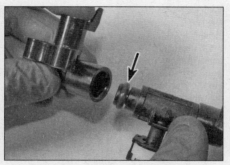

5.13 Separate each injector holder from the fuel rail if required, and remove the O-ring (arrowed)

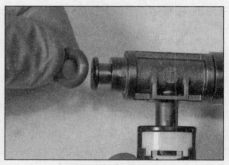

5.14 Use a new O-ring

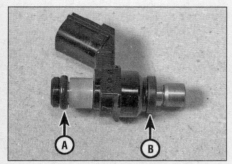

5.15 Injector O-ring (A) and seal (B)

5.17a Align the injectors with their seats and ease them in…

5.17b …then fit and tighten the bolts

11 Remove the seals from the injector seats in the throttle body, or from the injector nozzles if they came away on them **(see illustration 5.15)**. Discard them as new ones must be used.

12 If required pull the injectors out of their holders **(see illustration)**. Remove the O-rings and discard them **(see illustration 5.15)** – new ones must be used.

13 If required pull the injector holders off the fuel rail **(see illustration)**. Remove the O-rings and discard them – new ones must be used.

Installation

14 If the injector holders have been separated from the fuel rail, fit a new O-ring lubricated with clean engine oil into the groove in each end of the rail **(see illustration)**. Push each holder onto the rail, making sure the O-ring stays in place **(see illustration 5.13)**.

15 If the injectors have been removed from their holders, fit a new O-ring lubricated with clean engine oil into the groove in the top of each injector **(see illustration)**. Align the injector socket with the cut-out section in the holder and ease the injector into place, taking care not to dislodge the O-ring **(see illustration 5.12)**.

16 Fit a new seal lubricated with clean engine oil onto each injector **(see illustration 5.15)**.

17 Connect the injector wiring connectors **(see illustration 5.10b)** and fit the fuel rail

assembly, making sure each injector enters its seat and the seals stay in place and locate correctly **(see illustration)**. Fit the injector holder/fuel rail bolts and tighten them to 5.1 Nm **(see illustration)**.

18 Connect the MAP sensor wiring connector and secure the fuel hose in its clip **(see illustrations 4.21 and 4.20)**.

19 Install the fuel tank (Section 2).

20 Run the engine and check that the fuel system is working correctly before taking the bike out on the road.

6 Engine management system description

1 All models are equipped with Honda's programmed fuel injection (PGM-FI) system. It is controlled by a management system with an engine control module (ECM) that operates both the injection and ignition systems on models with standard transmission, and a combined ECM/PCM (powertrain control module) that also operates the gearchange system on models with DCT.

Models with standard transmission

2 The engine control module (ECM) monitors signals from the following sensors:

- Throttle position (TP) sensor.
- Manifold absolute pressure (MAP) sensor.
- Intake air temperature (IAT) sensor.
- Engine coolant temperature (ECT) sensor.
- Crankshaft position (CKP) sensor.
- Speed sensor.
- Oxygen sensor.
- Lean angle sensor.

3 All the information from the sensors is analysed by the ECM, and from that it determines the appropriate ignition and fuelling requirements of the engine. The ECM controls each fuel injector by varying its pulse width – the length of time the injector is held open – to provide more or less fuel, as appropriate for cold starting, warm up, idle, cruising, and acceleration. The injection system is fully sequential, with each injector receiving its own signal from the ECM. The injectors are mounted in the throttle body on the engine side of the throttle valve.

4 On 2016/17 models, cold starting, warm up and idle speed are controlled by the idle air control valve (IACV). The control valve, mounted in a housing on the back of the throttle body and actuated by the ECM, allows additional air to bypass the throttle valves when the throttle is closed, and this increases the engine idle speed. On 2018-on models cold starting, warm up and idle speed are controlled by the TBW (throttle by wire) unit.

Models with DCT

5 The ECM/PCM monitors signals from the following sensors.

- Throttle position (TP) sensor.
- Manifold absolute pressure (MAP) sensor.
- Intake air temperature (IAT) sensor.
- Engine coolant temperature (ECT) sensor.
- Crankshaft position (CKP) sensor.
- Speed sensor.
- Oxygen sensor.
- Lean angle sensor.
- Clutch line oil pressure sensor.
- No. 1 clutch oil pressure sensor.
- No. 2 clutch oil pressure sensor.
- Gearchange shaft angle sensor.
- Transmission range (TR) sensor.

6 All the information from the sensors is analysed by the ECM/PCM, and from that it determines the appropriate ignition and fuelling requirements of the engine. It controls each fuel injector by varying its pulse width – the length of time the injector is held open – to provide more or less fuel, as appropriate for cold starting, warm up, idle, cruising, and acceleration. The injection system is fully sequential, with each injector receiving its own signal from the ECM/PCM. The injectors are mounted in the throttle body on the engine side of the throttle valve.

7 Cold starting, warm up and idle speed are controlled by the TBW (throttle by wire) unit.

All models

8 If there is an abnormality in any of the readings obtained from any sensor related to the PGM-FI system (except the CKP sensor), the ECM/PCM enters its back-up mode. In this event, the ECM/PCM ignores the abnormal sensor signal, and assumes a pre-programmed value that will allow the engine to continue running (albeit at reduced efficiency). If the ECM/PCM enters this back-up mode, or when any faults occur, the engine management system warning light (engine symbol) in the instrument cluster will come on or flash (depending on circumstances), and the relevant fault code will be stored in the ECM/PCM memory. The fault can be identified using the fault codes that can be accessed using the self-diagnosis function (Section 7). However if there are certain faults detected in the injectors or the crankshaft position sensor, the back-up mode becomes ineffective and the ECM will not allow the engine to run at all.

9 On models with DCT, if there is an abnormality in any of the readings obtained from any sensor related to the DCT system, the PCM enters its back-up mode. Depending on the nature of the problem the PCM decides whether gearchanges can still be made, and if not holds the system in the gear selelcted when the fault occurred, or in some circumstances will prevent any gear being selected or the engine from running. If the PCM enters this back-up mode, or when any faults occur, the gear indicator in the instrument cluster will flash, and the relevant fault code will be stored in the PCM memory. The fault can be identified using the fault codes that can be accessed using the self-diagnosis function (Section 7).

10 All UK models have an immobiliser system (HISS – Honda Ignition Security System) that will not allow the engine to be started unless the correct key is used. A fault in this system should not be confused with a fuel injection system fault. The immobiliser system has its own warning light and fault diagnosis function (Section 24).

7 PGM-FI system fault diagnosis

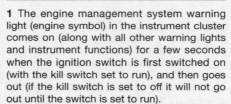

1 The engine management system warning light (engine symbol) in the instrument cluster comes on (along with all other warning lights and instrument functions) for a few seconds when the ignition switch is first switched on (with the kill switch set to run), and then goes out (if the kill switch is set to off it will not go out until the switch is set to run).

2 On 2016 models if the warning light (engine symbol) stays on, or comes on when the motorcycle is running, a fault has occurred in the fuel injection/ignition system. If a fault occurs while the engine is running above 2100 rpm and the motorcycle is being ridden, the light will come on and stay on. If a fault occurs when the motorcycle is on its sidestand and the ignition is on with the kill switch set to run, or when the engine is idling, the light will flash, the pattern of the flashes indicating the code for the fault the ECM has identified. The fault code is recorded and stored in the ECM memory and can be retrieved later if the ignition is switched off before the code has been read.

3 On 2017-on models if the warning light (engine symbol) stays on, or comes on when the motorcycle is running, a fault has occurred in the fuel injection/ignition system. The fault code is recorded and stored in the ECM memory.

4 To read any current or stored fault codes, remove the rider's seat (see Chapter 7). Locate the engine management system data link connector (DLC), which is a red blanked single-sided 4-pin connector under the front of the passenger seat **(see illustration)**. Remove the blanking cap from the connector **(see illustration)**. Either fit the Honda SCS service connector (Part No. 070PZ-ZY30100, available from your dealer), or its after-market equivalent, or bridge the grey/blue and green/blue wire terminals of the connector with a piece of electrical wire **(see illustration)**. With the terminals connected, make sure the kill switch is in the RUN position then turn the ignition ON and observe the engine management warning light. If there are stored fault codes, the light will flash. If there are no stored fault codes the light will come on and stay on.

5 The FI warning light emits long (1.3 second) and short (0.3 second) flashes to give out the fault code. A long flash is used to indicate the first digit of a double digit fault code (i.e. 10 and above). If a single digit fault code is being displayed (i.e. 0 – 9), there will be a number of short flashes equivalent to the code being displayed. For example, seven short (0.3 sec) flashes indicates the fault code 7, two long (1.3 sec) flashes followed by three short (0.3 sec) flashes indicates the fault code number 23. If there is more than one fault code, there will be a gap before the other codes are revealed (the codes will be revealed in order, starting with the lowest and finishing with the highest). Once all codes have been revealed, the ECM/PCM will continuously run through the code(s) stored in its memory, revealing each one in turn with a short gap between them. The fault codes are shown in the table.

7.4a Data link connector (arrowed)

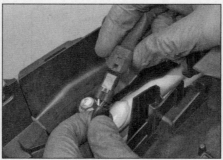

7.4b Displace the connector and remove the cap

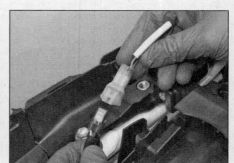

7.4c The Honda SCS service connector

Fault code (no. of flashes)	Symptoms	Possible causes
No code; warning light off	Engine cranks but does not start.	Blown fuse
	Fuel pump does not pressurise when ignition turned on.	Faulty power supply to or from engine control module (ECM)
		Faulty engine stop relay or wiring
		Faulty engine stop switch or wiring
		Faulty ignition switch
		Faulty lean angle sensor or wiring
		Faulty engine/powertrain control module (ECM/PCM)
No code; warning light off	Engine cranks but does not start, or is hard to start, stalls, or has rough idle	Fuel supply contaminated or restricted
		Fuel tank breather/EVAP hose blocked (creating vacuum in tank)
		Intake air leak (loose clamp, split intake rubber)
		Faulty idle air control valve (2016/17)
		Faulty ignition system
No code; warning light off	Engine backfires when throttling off	Faulty PAIR system
No code; warning light off	Engine backfires when accelerating	Faulty ignition system
No code; warning light off	Poor performance and economy	Fuel supply problem (pump, pressure regulator, filter, hose)
		Faulty MAP sensor
		Faulty injector
		Faulty ignition system
No code; warning light off	Low idle and fast idle speeds	Faulty idle air control valve – valve stuck closed (2016/17)
		Fuel supply problem (pump, pressure regulator, filter, hose)
		Faulty ignition system
No code; warning light off	High idle and fast idle speeds	Faulty idle air control valve – valve stuck open (2016/17)
		Intake air leak (loose clamp, split intake rubber)
		Throttle sticking, cable freeplay adjustment incorrect
		Faulty ignition system
No code; warning light never comes on or is permanently on	Engine runs normally	Faulty warning light circuit
		Faulty ECM/PCM
1	Engine runs normally	Faulty manifold absolute pressure (MAP) sensor or wiring
2	Engine runs normally	Faulty manifold absolute pressure (MAP) sensor or disconnected sensor hose
7	Engine difficult to start at low temperatures	Faulty engine coolant temperature (ECT) sensor or wiring
8 (2016/17 models)	Poor throttle response	Faulty throttle position (TP) sensor or wiring
9	Engine runs normally	Faulty intake air temperature (IAT) sensor or wiring
11	Engine operates normally	Faulty speed sensor or wiring
12	Engine does not start	Faulty No. 1 injector or wiring
13	Engine does not start	Faulty No. 2 injector or wiring
21	Engine operates normally	Faulty oxygen sensor or wiring
23	Engine operates normally	Faulty oxygen sensor heating element
29 (2016/17 models)	Engine stalls, hard to start, rough idle	Faulty idle air control valve
33	Engine runs normally	Faulty ECM/PCM EEPROM
41	Engine runs normally, HSTC inoperative	Faulty gear position sensor or wiring, ECM/PCM fault
54	Engine runs normally	Faulty lean angle sensor or wiring
66	Engine runs normally	Faulty rear wheel sensor or wiring
67	Engine runs normally	Faulty front wheel sensor or wiring
71 (2018-on models)	Road speed limited to 75 mph (120 km/h), HSTC inoperative	Faulty No. 1 TP sensor or wiring
72 (2018-on models)	Road speed limited to 75 mph (120 km/h), HSTC inoperative	Faulty No. 2 TP sensor or wiring
73 (2018-on models)	Engine runs at idle speed, HSTC inoperative	Faulty Nos. 1 and 2 TP sensors or wiring
74 (2018-on models)	Engine runs at idle speed, HSTC inoperative	Faulty APS sensor (APS-1) or wiring
75 (2018-on models)	Engine runs at idle speed, HSTC inoperative	Faulty APS sensor (APS-2) or wiring
76 (2018-on models)	Engine runs at idle speed, HSTC inoperative	Faulty APS sensor or wiring

Fault code (no. of flashes)	Symptoms	Possible causes
77 (2018-on models)	Road speed limited to 75 mph (120 km/h), HSTC inoperative	Faulty TBW return spring
78 (2018-on models)	Engine runs at idle speed, HSTC inoperative	Faulty TBW motor or wiring
79 (2018-on models)	Engine runs normally	Faulty TBW system or wiring
83	Engine runs normally	Faulty engine oil pressure (EOP) sensor or wiring
84	Engine runs normally	Faulty ECM/PCM CPU
85 (2018-on models)	Engine runs at idle speed or road speed limited to 75 mph (120 km/h), HSTC inoperative	Faulty TBW relay or wiring
88	Engine runs normally	Faulty EVAP purge control valve or wiring
89	Engine runs normally	Faulty PAIR control valve or wiring
91	Engine runs on No. 2 cylinder	Faulty No. 1 cylinder primary (main) ignition coil or wiring
92	Engine runs on No. 1 cylinder	Faulty No. 2 cylinder primary (main) ignition coil or wiring
93	Engine runs on No. 2 cylinder	Faulty No. 1 cylinder secondary (sub) ignition coil or wiring
94	Engine runs on No. 1 cylinder	Faulty No. 2 cylinder secondary (sub) ignition coil or wiring
103	Engine runs normally, HSTC inoperative	CAN communication failure, faulty instruments or ECM/PCM
107	Engine runs normally, quickshifter inoperative	Faulty quickshifter or wiring
108	Engine runs normally, quickshifter inoperative	Faulty shift spindle switch or wiring
113	Engine runs normally, quickshifter inoperative	Faulty clutch switch or wiring

6 Once all the codes have been revealed, switch off the ignition and (where necessary) remove the auxiliary wire or SCS connector from the data link connector. Identify the faulty component or circuit using the table above, then refer to the following check procedures.

7 First make sure that the relevant system wiring connector(s) is/are securely connected and free of corrosion – poor connections are the cause of the majority of problems. Also check the wiring itself for any obvious faults or breaks, and use a continuity tester to check the wiring between the component, its connectors and the ECM/PCM, and where present the green wire for continuity to earth, referring to the wiring diagram for your model at the end of Chapter 8. Next refer to Section 9 to see if there are any other specific checks that can be made on that particular component using home equipment.

8 Also make sure that any fault is not due to poor maintenance – i.e. check that the air filter element is clean, that the spark plugs are in good condition (see Chapter 1, Section 22), that the valve clearances are correctly adjusted (see Chapter 1, Section 21), the cylinder compression pressures are correct (see Chapter 2, Section 3), and the ignition timing is correct (Section 23). It is also worth removing the sensor(s) in question (Section 9) and checking that the sensing tip or head is clean and not obstructed by anything.

9 If this fails to reveal the cause of the problem, the motorcycle should be taken to a Honda dealer for testing. They will have the special tools that should locate the fault quickly and simply. If a system component or its circuit are not at fault the ECM/PCM could be the problem.

10 Once the fault has been identified and corrected, reset the system by removing the fault code from the ECM/PCM memory. To do this, check the ignition is switched OFF, then bridge the grey/blue and green/blue wire terminals of the data link connector (DLC) (see Step 4). Make sure the kill switch is in the RUN position, then turn the ignition switch ON. Disconnect the auxiliary wire or tool from the DLC. When the wire is disconnected the warning light should come on for about five seconds, during which time the auxiliary wire must be reconnected. The light should start to flash when it is reconnected, indicating that all fault codes have been erased. Turn off the ignition then remove the auxiliary wire. Turn the ignition on again and check the warning light (in some cases it may be necessary to repeat the erasing procedure more than once). On 2017-on models with DCT, note that any stored DCT fault codes will be erased at the same time as the PGM-FI fault codes.

8 DCT system fault diagnosis

1 The gear indicator in the instrument cluster comes on along with all other warning lights and instrument functions for a few seconds when the ignition switch is first switched on and the kill switch is set to run, and then goes out.

2 If a fault occurs the gear indicator blinks "-". The current fault code can be displayed as a series of timed flashes (see Step 4) if the sidestand is put down before the ignition is turned off. Otherwise the fault code is stored and can be read as described in Step 3.

3 To read any stored fault codes, remove the rider's seat (see Chapter 7). Locate the engine management system data link connector (DLC), which is a red blanked single-sided 4-pin connector under the front of the passenger seat **(see illustration 7.4a)**. Remove the blanking cap from the connector **(see illustration 7.4b)**. Either fit the Honda SCS service connector (Part No. 070PZ-ZY30100, available from your dealer), or its after-market equivalent, or bridge the brown and green wire terminals of the connector with a piece of electrical wire **(see illustration 7.4c)**. With the terminals connected, make sure the kill switch is in the RUN position, hold the + gearchange switch in and turn the ignition ON and observe the gear indicator. If there are stored fault codes, the indicator will flash "-". If there are no stored fault codes the indicator "-" will come on for 2 seconds at intervals of 3 seconds. Release the + gearchange switch.

4 The gear indicator gives long (1.2 second) and short (0.4 second) "-" flashes to give out the fault code. A long flash is used to indicate the first digit of a double digit fault code (i.e. 10 and above). If a single digit fault code is being displayed (i.e. 0 – 9), there will be a number of short flashes equivalent to the code being displayed. For example, eight short (0.4 sec) flashes indicates the fault code 8, two long (1.2 sec) flashes followed by three short (0.4 sec) flashes indicates the fault code number 23. If there is more than one fault code, there will be a gap before the other codes are revealed (the codes will be revealed in order, starting with the lowest and finishing with the highest). Once all codes have been revealed, the PCM will continuously run through the code(s) stored in its memory, revealing each one in turn with a short gap between them. The fault codes are shown in the table.

Fault code (No. of flashes)	Symptoms	Possible causes
1 (2018-on models)	DCT gearchange pedal (option) inoperative	Faulty gearchange pedal meachanism, faulty angle sensor or wiring
7 (2018-on models)	Difficult to start when cold	Faulty ECT sensor or wiring
8 (2016/17 models)	Gearchange inoperative	Faulty TP sensor or wiring
8 (2018-on models)	Road speed limited to 75 mph (120 km/h), HSTC inoperative	Faulty TP sensor or wiring
9	Gearchange works normally	Faulty clutch line EOP sensor or wiring
11	Gearchange inoperative	Faulty VS sensor or wiring
19	Engine does not run, gearchange inoperative	Faulty CKP sensor or wiring
21	Gearchange inoperative	Faulty gearchange angle sensor or wiring
22 and 23	Gearchange inoperative	Faulty gearchange mechanism or angle sensor
24	Gearchange inoperative	Faulty gearchange control motor or wiring
27	Gearchange inoperative	Faulty TR sensor or wiring, or gearchange mechanism
31	Gearchange inoperative	Faulty ignition hold relay in PCM, blown DCT 30A fuse, loose PCM connector
32	Gearchange inoperative	Faulty PCM power input, faulty fail-safe relay in PCM, blown DCT 30A fuse
37	Gearchange inoperative	Faulty ignition hold relay in PCM, blown DCT 7.5A fuse, faulty PCM power input
41	N-D switch inoperative	Faulty N-D switch or wiring
42	Gearchange switch inoperative	Faulty gearchange switch or wiring
44	Gearchange works normally	Faulty EOT sensor or wiring
47	Gearchange inoperative	Faulty No. 1 clutch EOP sensor or wiring
48	Gearchange inoperative	Faulty No. 2 clutch EOP sensor or wiring
49	Gearchange inoperative	Low oil pressure in clutch line, faulty clutch line EOP sensor or wiring
51	Gearchange inoperative	Faulty TR sensor or wiring
52	Gearchange works normally or inoperative (depending on exact fault)	Neutral switch stuck off or on, faulty neutral switch wiring
53	Gearchange inoperative	Faulty inner input shaft sensor or wiring
54	Gearchange inoperative	Faulty outer input shaft sensor or wiring
55	Gearchange inoperative	Faulty No. 1 linear solenoid valve or wiring
56	Gearchange inoperative	Faulty No. 2 linear solenoid valve or wiring
57	Gearchange inoperative	Faulty gearchange mechanism, faulty TR sensor or wiring
58	Engine does not run, gearchange inoperative	Faulty No. 1 clutch or oil circuit
59	Engine does not run, gearchange inoperative	Faulty No. 2 clutch or oil circuit
61	Gearchange inoperative	No. 1 clutch oil pressure low, faulty No. 1 EOP sensor or wiring, faulty No. 1 linear solenoid valve or wiring
62	Gearchange inoperative	No. 1 clutch oil pressure high, faulty No. 1 EOP sensor or wiring, faulty No. 1 linear solenoid valve or wiring
63	Gearchange inoperative	No. 2 clutch oil pressure low, faulty No. 2 EOP sensor or wiring, faulty No. 2 linear solenoid valve or wiring
64	Gearchange inoperative	No. 2 clutch oil pressure high, faulty No. 2 EOP sensor or wiring, faulty No. 2 linear solenoid valve or wiring
65	Gearchange inoperative	Faulty front or rear wheel speed sensor or wiring, faulty VS sensor or wiring, faulty ABS modulator
66	Gearchange inoperative	Faulty rear wheel speed sensor or wiring, faulty pulse ring, faulty ABS modulator
67	Gearchange inoperative	Faulty front wheel speed sensor or wiring, faulty pulse ring, faulty ABS modulator
68	Gearchange inoperative	Faulty No. 1 clutch, faulty VS sensor or wiring
69	Gearchange inoperative	Faulty No. 2 clutch, faulty VS sensor or wiring
71	Gearchange inoperative	Faulty VS sensor or wiring, faulty inner input shaft sensor or wiring
72	Gearchange inoperative	Faulty VS sensor or wiring, faulty outer input shaft sensor or wiring
84	Gearchange inoperative	Faulty CPU in PCM
91, 92, 93, 94, 103 (2018-on models)	see Section 7	see Section 7

5 Once all the codes have been revealed, switch off the ignition and (where necessary) remove the auxiliary wire or SCS connector from the data link connector. Identify the faulty component or circuit using the table above, then refer to the following check procedures.

6 First make sure that the relevant system wiring connector(s) is/are securely connected and free of corrosion – poor connections are the cause of the majority of problems. Also check the wiring itself for any obvious faults or breaks, and use a continuity tester to check the wiring between the component, its connectors and the PCM, and where present the green wire for continuity to earth, referring to the wiring diagram for your model at the end of Chapter 8. Next refer to Section 9 to see if there are any other specific checks that can be made on that particular component using home equipment.

7 Also make sure that any fault is not due to poor maintenance – i.e. check the engine oil level (see *Pre-ride checks*), and if necessary change the oil and filters (see Chapter 1), and carry out an oil pressure check (see Chapter 2). It is also worth removing the sensor(s)

9.4a Brake light switch wiring connectors (arrowed)

in question (Section 9) and checking that the sensing tip or head is clean and not obstructed by anything.

8 If this fails to reveal the cause of the problem, the motorcycle should be taken to a Honda dealer for testing. They will have the special tools that should locate the fault quickly and simply. If a system component or its circuit are not at fault the PCM could be the problem.

9 Once the fault has been identified and corrected, reset the system by removing the fault code from the ECM/PCM memory. To do this on 2016 models, check the ignition is switched OFF, then bridge the grey/blue and green/blue wire terminals of the data link connector (DLC) (see Step 3). Make sure the kill switch is in the RUN position, then hold the gearchange + switch in and turn the ignition switch ON. Release the + gearchange switch and press the – switch, then press the + switch. The gear indicator should start to flash "-" for 2 seconds at intervals of 3 seconds, indicating that all fault codes have been erased. Turn off the ignition then remove the auxiliary wire. Turn the ignition on again and check the warning light (in some cases it may be necessary to repeat the erasing procedure more than once). On 2017-on models refer to Step 10 in Section 7 to erase the fault code(s).

---

9 Engine management system (PGM-FI and DCT) sensors 🔧

Caution: Make sure the ignition is switched OFF before disconnecting/reconnecting any fuel injection system wiring connector. If a connector is disturbed with the ignition switched ON the ECM/PCM could be damaged.

PGM-FI sensors

Throttle position (TP) sensor

1 On 2016/17 models the TP sensor is an integral part of the throttle body and should not be removed from it. If the sensor is faulty fit a new throttle body (Section 4).

2 On 2018-on models the TP sensor is an integral part of the TBW unit on the throttle body, which itself is an integral part of the throttle body and should not be removed from it. If the sensor is faulty fit a new throttle body (Section 4).

Accelerator position sensor (APS) – 2018-on models

3 Remove the right-hand mirror, handlebar end-weight and hand guard (see Chapter 7).

4 Disconnect the wires from the brake light switch **(see illustration)**. Unscrew the two master cylinder assembly clamp bolts, noting how the lower bolt secures the wiring clip bracket, and position the assembly clear of the handlebar, making sure no strain is placed on the hydraulic hose **(see illustration)**. Keep the master cylinder reservoir upright to prevent possible fluid leakage.

5 Raise the fuel tank (see Chapter 4).

6 Release and disconnect the APS wiring connector, and on the Adventure Sports model disconnect the heated grip wiring connector **(see illustration)**. Feed the wiring up to the sensor, noting its routing and releasing it from the clips.

7 Undo the right-hand switch housing screws and detach the front half of the housing, then undo the four screws and detach the rear half of the housing from the APS **(see illustrations)**.

8 Undo the APS clamp screw and displace the clamp to clear the pin from the hole in the handlebar **(see illustration)**. Slide the twistgrip off the handlebar, noting how it engages the APS, then slide the APS off **(see illustration)**.

9.4b Master cylinder clamp bolts (arrowed)

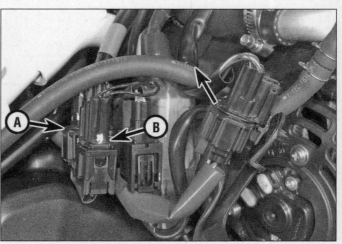

9.6 APS connector (A), heated grip connector (B)

9.7a Undo the two screws…

9.7b …and displace the front of the housing…

9.7c …then undo the four screws…

9 Installation is the reverse of removal. Make sure the twistgrip aligns and engages correctly with the APS **(see illustration 9.8b)**. Make sure the APS clamp pin locates in the hole in the handlebar **(see illustration)**. Fit the front brake master cylinder clamp with the UP mark facing up and with the clamp mating surfaces aligned with the mark on the top of the handlebar **(see illustration)**. Tighten the clamp bolts to 10 Nm, tightening the top bolt first, and not forgetting to secure the wiring clip bracket with the lower bolt **(see illustration)**.

Manifold absolute pressure (MAP) sensor

10 Remove the air filter housing (Section 3).
11 Disconnect the sensor wiring connector **(see illustration 4.21)**.
12 Undo the screw, displace the sensor and disconnect the hose from the underside **(see illustration)**.
13 Installation is the reverse of removal – check the hoses from the sensor to the throttle body are securely connected at each end and are in good condition **(see illustration 4.30)**.

Intake air temperature (IAT) sensor

14 Remove the air filter housing (Section 3) – the sensor is on the underside.

Check

15 Connect an ohmmeter to the wire terminals on the sensor and check the resistance. If it is not within the range given in the Specifications at the beginning of the Chapter the sensor

9.7d …and displace the rear half

9.8a Undo the clamp screw, noting how the clamp locates

9.8b Slide the twistgrip and APS off, noting how they seat together

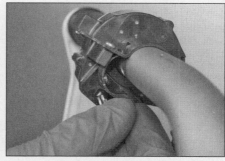

9.9a Make sure the bracket hooks in at the top and the pin locates in the hole

9.9b Align the master cylinder and fit the clamp. Alignment mark (arrowed)

9.9c Make sure the bracket is above the wiring and correctly located

9.12 MAP sensor screw (A) and hose (B)

9.22 Speed sensor wiring connector (A) and mounting bolt (B)

9.26a Release the wiring clip...

9.26b ...then disconnect the connector

could be faulty – note though that the reading given is for an air temperature of 40°C (104°F), which is quite high, so make allowances if the air is cool. Alternatively run the engine until it is warm, which will increase the temperature in the air filter housing, or remove the sensor and heat it gently with a hair dryer. The important thing is that the sensor does not show zero or infinite resistance.

Removal and installation

16 Undo the screws and remove the sensor.
17 Installation is the reverse of removal – make sure the O-ring is fitted.

Engine coolant temperature (ECT) sensor

18 See Chapter 3, Section 3.

Engine oil pressure (EOP) sensor

19 See Chapter 8, Section 16.

Vehicle speed sensor

20 To check the sensor circuit see Chapter 8, Section 15.
21 Remove the battery and the battery box (see Chapter 8).
22 Disconnect the wiring connector **(see illustration)**.
23 Unscrew the bolt and remove the sensor **(see illustration 9.22)**. Remove O-ring – a new one must be fitted. While the sensor is removed plug the orifice with clean rag.
24 Installation is the reverse of removal – fit a new O-ring and smear it with oil.

Oxygen sensor

Check

25 Apart from the wiring and connector checks that are outlined in Section 7, the

operation of the oxygen sensor itself cannot be checked – if the sensor circuit is good (have this checked by a dealer for confirmation) and the sensor is thought to be faulty, replace it with a new one.
26 To check the sensor heater release and disconnect the sensor wiring connector **(see illustrations)**. Connect an ohmmeter between the white wire terminals on models with standard transmission or the red/white and white wire terminals on models with DCT on the sensor side of the connector and check that the resistance is between 6.7 and 10.5 ohms. Also check that there is no continuity to earth (ground) in each white wire. If the resistance is not as specified or if there is continuity to earth, replace the sensor with a new one.

Removal and installation

Note: *The oxygen sensor is delicate and will not work if dropped or knocked, or if any cleaning materials are used on it. Make sure the exhaust system is cold. A special socket to accommodate the sensor wiring can be bought from Honda, part No. FRXM17, or from a good tool supplier, and it enables the sensor to be tightened to the correct torque on installation. Otherwise use an open-ended spanner.*
27 You can remove the sensor using a spanner after removing the outer cover and heat shields from the exhaust system (Section 17) and disconnecting the sensor wiring connector **(see illustrations 9.26a and b)**, but if you are using the socket mentioned above then remove the exhaust system (Section 17).
28 Unscrew the oxygen sensor and remove it

from the exhaust system **(see illustration)**
29 Installation is the reverse of removal. Tighten the sensor to 24.5 Nm.

Crankshaft position (CKP) sensor

Special tool: *To test the CKP sensor Honda specify to use a peak voltage adapter (Honda pt. no. 07HGJ-0020100 in Europe, or IgnitionMate MTP07-0286 in the US) plus an aftermarket digital multimeter having an impedance of 10 M-ohm/DCV minimum to test the CKP sensor. Have the sensor tested by a dealer if necessary.*
30 If a peak voltage adapter is available the sensor's peak voltage can be checked. Make sure the ignition is OFF. On models with standard transmission make sure it is in neutral. On models with DCT remove the starter relay (see Chapter 8) and connect between the green/red and green wire terminals on the loom side of the connector using a jumper wire. On 2016/17 models disconnect the 33-pin grey connector from the ECM/PCM, and on 2018-on models disconnect the 33-pin black connector from the ECM/PCM (see Section 10). Connect the peak voltage adaptor positive probe to the yellow wire terminal in the connector and the negative probe to the white/yellow terminal. Set the kill switch to RUN and turn the ignition ON. Crank the engine over on the starter motor and note the peak voltage registered on the meter – it should be above the minimum given in the Specifications at the beginning of this Chapter.
31 If the reading is not as specified check the wiring from the ECM/PCM connectors to the alternator/CKP sensor 6-pin connector, referring to Chapter 8, Section 29 to access the connector. You can also repeat the peak voltage test at the yellow and white/yellow wire terminals in the alternator/CKP sensor 6-pin connector if required, but first reconnect the ECM/PCM connector and the battery.
32 If the CKP sensor is faulty replace the alternator stator with a new one (see Chapter 8) – the sensor is an integral part of the stator and is not available separately.

Lean angle sensor

33 Remove the headlight (see Chapter 8).
34 Undo the nuts and remove the sensor **(see illustration)**.

9.28 Oxygen sensor

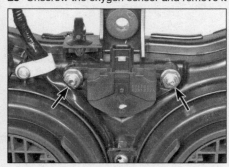

9.34 Lean angle sensor nuts (arrowed)

9.36 Allow the shock absorber to rest on the swingarm as shown

9.37 Inner input shaft sensor wiring connector (A) and mounting bolts (B)

9.41 Outer input shaft sensor wiring connector (A) and mounting bolt (B)

9.45 Gearchange control motor cover bolts

9.47 TR sensor wiring connector (arrowed)

9.48a Remove the cover...

35 Installation is the reverse of removal. Make sure the sensor is fitted with the UP arrow pointing up.

DCT sensors

Input shaft sensors

Inner shaft sensor

36 Displace the rear shock absorber (see Chapter 5) and rest it as shown **(see illustration)**- there is no need to remove the swingarm.

37 Release and disconnect the sensor wiring connector **(see illustration)**.

38 Unscrew the bolts and remove the sensor **(see illustration 9.37)**. Remove the O-ring – a new one must be fitted. While the sensor is removed plug the orifice with clean rag.

39 Installation is the reverse of removal – use a new O-ring and smear it with oil.

Outer shaft sensor

40 Remove the battery and the battery box (see Chapter 8).

41 Disconnect the sensor wiring connector **(see illustration)**.

42 Unscrew the bolt and remove the sensor **(see illustration 9.41)**. Remove the O-ring – a new one must be fitted. While the sensor is removed plug the orifice with clean rag.

43 Installation is the reverse of removal – fit a new O-ring and smear it with oil.

Transmission range (TR) sensor

44 Remove the front sprocket cover (see Chapter 6).

45 Remove the gearchange control motor cover **(see illustration)**.

46 Displace the rear shock absorber (see Chapter 5) and rest it as shown **(see illustration 9.36)**- there is no need to remove the swingarm.

47 Release and disconnect the sensor wiring connector **(see illustration)**.

48 Unscrew the bolt and remove the sensor cover, then remove the sensor **(see illustrations)**. Remove the O-ring **(see illustration)** – a new one must be fitted.

49 Installation is the reverse of removal. Fit a new O-ring smeared with oil **(see illustration 9.48c)**. Align the flats on the sensor and the selector drum shaft end **(see illustration)**. Fit the cover and tighten the sensor bolt to 12 Nm **(see illustration 9.48a)**. Make sure

9.48b ...then remove the sensor

9.48c Sensor O-ring (arrowed)

9.49a Align the flats when fitting the sensor

9.49b Make sure the wiring is correctly routed

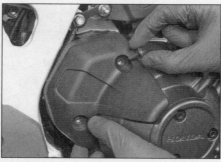

9.50a Undo the screws and remove the cover…

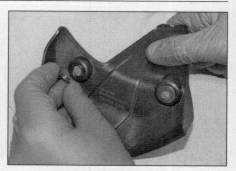

9.50b …noting the collars

9.52 Gearchange shaft angle sensor wiring connector (arrowed)

9.53 Unscrew the bolt

9.54 Fit a new O-ring (arrowed), and align the flats

9.56a Undo the screws and remove the cover…

the wiring is correctly routed when fitting the control motor cover (see illustration).

Gearchange shaft angle sensor

50 Remove the trim piece from the clutch cover (see illustrations).
51 Displace the rear shock absorber (see Chapter 5) and rest it as shown (see illustration 9.36)- there is no need to remove the swingarm.
52 Release and disconnect the sensor wiring connector (see illustration).
53 Unscrew the bolt and remove the sensor (see illustration). Remove the O-ring (see illustration 9.54) – a new one must be fitted.

54 Installation is the reverse of removal. Fit a new O-ring smeared with oil, align the flats on the sensor and the gearchange shaft end, and tighten the sensor bolt to 12 Nm (see illustration).

Clutch engine oil pressure (EOP) sensors

55 Drain the engine oil (see Chapter 1).
56 Remove the clutch EOP sensor cover (see illustrations).
57 There are three EOP sensors for the clutch oil, the clutch oil line sensor, the No. 1 clutch sensor and the No. 2 clutch sensor (see illustration). As required disconnect the

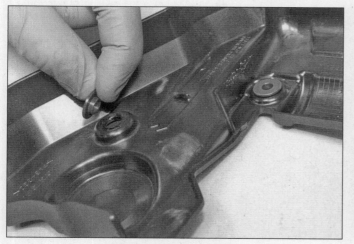

9.56b …noting the collars

9.57 Clutch line EOP sensor and connector (A), No. 1 clutch EOP sensor and connector (B), No. 2 clutch EOP sensor and connector (C)

clutch oil line EOP sensor wiring connector (3-pin grey), the No. 1 clutch EOP sensor wiring connector (3-pin grey), and/or the No. 2 clutch EOP sensor wiring connector (3-pin black).

58 Unscrew and remove the sensor(s) as required. Remove the O-ring – a new one must be fitted.

59 Installation is the reverse of removal. Fit a new O-ring smeared with oil. Tighten the sensor to 20 Nm.

Engine oil temperature (EOT) sensor

60 Drain the engine oil (see Chapter 1).

61 Release and disconnect the oxygen sensor wiring connector **(see illustrations 9.26a and b).**

62 Disconnect the EOT sensor wiring **(see illustration)**.

63 Unscrew and remove the sensor. Remove the sealing washer **(see illustration 9.64)** – a new one must be used.

64 Installation is the reverse of removal – use a new sealing washer, smear oil onto the sensor threads and seating surface, and tighten the sensor to 15 Nm **(see illustration)**.

---

10 Engine control module/ Powertrain control module (ECM/PCM)

1 Models with standard transmission have an ECM, models with DCT have a combined ECM and PCM

Check

2 The ECM/PCM itself cannot be checked, but a process of elimination of other possible faulty components can point to it being faulty. First check the FI system fuses (see Chapter 8) and relays (Section 11). Next disconnect the ECM/PCM wiring connectors (see below) and check for loose or broken terminal pins in the connector or socket, then check for continuity in each wire to/from the ECM/PCM and to its related component or connector, or to earth (ground) as appropriate, according to the wiring diagram for your model at the end of Chapter 8, and referring to the electrical system fault finding section at the beginning of it. If any wire does not show continuity check the connectors and terminals in the

9.62 EOT sensor wiring connector

circuit before assuming there is a break in the wire. Alternatively take the bike to a Honda dealer for checking on their diagnostic tester.

Removal

3 Make sure the ignition is OFF. Remove the fuel tank (Section 2).

4 On models without an EVAP system release the fuel tank breather hoses from their guides on the ECM/PCM cover.

5 On models with an EVAP system disconnect the throttle body hose from the 3-way joint **(see illustration 4.23)**, disconnect the purge control valve wiring connector and displace the valve, and release the fuel tank breather hose from its guides on the ECM/PCM cover **(see illustrations)**.

6 Unscrew the ECM/PCM cover bolt (2016/17 models) or release the twist clip (2018-on models) **(see illustration)**. Lift the ECM/PCM

10.5a Disconnect the purge control valve wiring connector and undo the screws (arrowed)…

9.64 Fit the sensor using a new sealing washer

and disconnect the wiring connectors **(see illustrations)**.

Installation

7 Installation is the reverse of removal. If a new ECM/PCM is being fitted on models with a HISS system, refer to Section 24 to register it. If a new ECM/PCM is being fitted carry out the clutch initialise learning procedure below.

Clutch initialise learning – models with DCT

8 If a new dual clutch or a new ECM/PCM has been fitted the clutch initialise learning procedure must be carried out. If a new ECM/PCM has been fitted, when the ignition is turned on for the first time the letters D and S will be displayed below the gear position indicator to confirm and remind this.

9 First make sure that there are no current

10.5b …release the hose from the clips and move the valve and hoses aside

10.6a Release the cover (2018 model shown)…

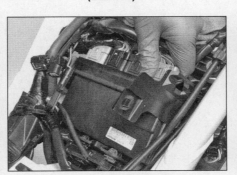

10.6b …lift the ECM/PCM…

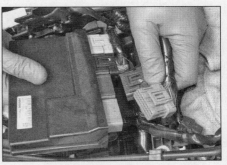

10.6c …and disconnect the wiring

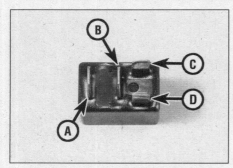

11.3 Relay test terminal identification

11.6a Fuel pump relay (arrowed) – 2018-on models

11.6b FI and engine stop relay holder (arrowed)

faults being displayed in either the PGM-FI or DCT systems.

10 Warm the engine up to normal working temperature, making sure the low or extremely low oil temperature warnings on the gear indicator are not showing, but it does not get hot enough for the cooling to come on (though if they do make sure they go off again), then stop it.

11 With the kill switch set to run, press and hold the D mode end of the N-D switch and turn the ignition on. The engine warning light should come on. Wait until the warning light goes off then release the N-D switch. If a new PCM has been fitted D and S will be displayed below the gear indicator, if a new dual clutch has been fitted D and S are not displayed.

12 Now operate the N-D switch as follows: press and release the D mode, then the D mode again, then the N mode, then the D mode, then the N mode. The PCM is ready to perform the 'clutch initialise learning' process when "-" is displayed on the gear indicator at 2 second intervals.

13 Start the engine and let it idle until the "-" stops flashing and the D and S letters are no longer shown. Stop the engine. If the procedure was unsuccessful the "-" will flash at 0.5 second intervals or the D and S do not go off, in which case start again.

14 Start the engine again, then press the D mode on the N-D switch and check that D is displayed below the gear indicator.

11 Engine management system relays

1 The following relays are fitted. On all models the relays are identical. Note that the starter circuit relay fitted on DCT models is not the same as the starter motor relay, which is fitted on all models and is covered in Chapter 8.

● On 2016/17 models with standard transmission there are two relays that control circuits in the engine management system, the FI relay and the fuel pump relay.

● On 2016/17 models with DCT there are three relays that control circuits in the

engine management system, the FI relay, the fuel pump relay and the starter circuit relay.

● On 2018-on models with standard transmission there are four relays that control circuits in the engine management system, the FI relay, the fuel pump relay, the engine stop relay and the TBW (throttle-by-wire) relay.

● On 2018-on models with DCT there are five relays that control circuits in the engine management system, the FI relay, the fuel pump relay, the starter circuit relay, the engine stop relay and the TBW relay.

Check

2 Remove the relay (see below).

3 Set a multimeter to the ohms x 1 scale and connect it across the relay's A and B terminals **(see illustration)**. There should be no continuity (infinite resistance). Using a fully-charged 12 volt battery and two insulated jumper wires, connect the positive (+) terminal of the battery to the D terminal on the relay, and the negative (–) terminal to the C terminal on the relay. At this point the relay should be heard to click and the multimeter read 0 ohms (continuity). If this is the case the relay is proved good. If the relay does not click when battery voltage is applied and still indicates no continuity (infinite resistance) across its terminals, it is faulty and must be replaced with a new one.

4 If the relay is good refer to the wiring diagram for your model at the end of Chapter 8 and to electrical system fault finding (see

Chapter 8 Section 2) and check the wiring and connectors in the circuit to and from the relay.

Removal and installation

5 To access the FI and fuel pump relays on 2016/17 models remove the right-hand side cover (see Chapter 7). Release the relay holder and remove the cover, then pull the relevant relay out of its socket.

6 To access the fuel pump relay on 2018-on models remove the ETC tray (see Chapter 7). To remove the fuel pump relay release the relay and remove the cover, then pull the relay out of its socket **(see illustration)**. To access the FI and engine stop relays refer to Chapter 6, Section 14 to access the ABS modulator, then disconnect the brake hoses from it. To remove the FI and engine stop relays release the relay holder and remove the cover, then pull the relevant relay out of its socket **(see illustration)**.

7 To access the starter circuit relay on models with DCT remove the right-hand side cover (see Chapter 7). Release the relay and remove the cover, then pull the relay out of its socket **(see illustration)**.

8 To access the TBW relay on 2018-on models remove the fuel tank (Section 2). Release the relay holder and remove the cover, then pull the relay out of its socket **(see illustration)**.

9 Installation is the reverse of removal. On 2018-on models, if the FI or engine stop relay has been removed, refer to Chapter 6, Section 14 for details on connecting the brake hoses to the modulator, and bleed the rear brake system afterwards.

11.7 Starter circuit relay (arrowed)

11.8 TBW relay (arrowed)

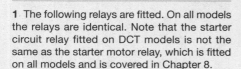

12.8 Release the connector tab and pull the connector off the valve

12.9a Remove the two screws to free the plate …

12.9b …then lift the valve out

12 Idle air control valve (2016/17 models)

Check

1 Idle speed is controlled automatically by a valve on the top of the throttle body that adjusts a flow of air that by-passes the throttle valves. The valve is actuated by the ECM/ PCM and adjusts according to information received from sensors on engine and air temperature and throttle position. When the ignition is switched ON the valve self-checks by turning through its range of movement, and you should be able to hear this with the fuel tank removed. If there is a fault, a code should be indicated by the warning light in the instrument cluster (see Section 7).

2 If the engine idle speed is not 1200±100 rpm, and there is no fault indicated, check the throttle cable freeplay, spark plugs, air filter and the valve clearances (see Chapter 1).

3 Next raise the fuel tank (Section 2). Inspect the intake ducts between the throttle bodies and the cylinder head for loose clamps or splits that could cause an air leak, causing a weak mixture.

4 If a fault code is given, remove the fuel tank (Section 2). Disconnect the control valve wiring connector. Check the connector wires and terminals are secure and clean. Using an ohmmeter check the resistance between the two outer terminals, and between the

two inner terminals, is within the range given in the Specifications at the beginning of the Chapter – if it isn't the IACV is faulty. Also check whether there is continuity between the two left-hand terminals, and between the two right-hand terminals – if there is the IACV is faulty.

5 If necessary remove and check the valve (see below), then reconnect the wiring turn the ignition ON and check the valve moves and beeps.

6 If the resistance readings for the valve are as specified but the valve does not work, check there is continuity in each wire between the connector and the ECM/PCM, and none of the wires show continuity to earth. If all is good the ECM could be faulty.

Removal

7 Remove the fuel tank (Section 2).

8 Disconnect the control valve wiring connector (see illustration).

9 Undo the control valve screws and remove the plate, then draw the valve out (see illustrations). Remove the O-ring – a new one must be used. Check the action of the valve by turning it.

10 To remove the control valve housing remove the fuel rail and injectors (Section 5). Undo the housing screws and remove the housing and its seal – a new seal must be used.

Installation

11 If removed fit the housing using a new

seal and tighten the screws. Install the fuel rail and injectors (Section 5).

12 Fit a new O-ring onto the valve and smear it with clean oil. Turn the valve clockwise until lightly seated (see illustration). Align the groove in the valve with the pin in its housing, turning the valve back if required, then insert the valve (see illustration). Fit the plate, seating the cut-out over the lug on the valve, and tighten the screws (see illustration).

13 Install the fuel tank (Section 2). Run the engine and check the fuel system is working correctly before taking the bike out on the road.

13 Fuel pressure check

⚠️ *Warning: Refer to the precautions given in Section 1 before starting work.*

Note: *A pressure gauge along with some adapters and hoses that are compatible with the quick-release fittings of the bike's fuel hose are required for this check. Honda can supply the various parts required, but it may be cheaper to get a dealer to perform the check, especially as hopefully you will not need the equipment more than once.*

1 Refer to Section 2 to raise the fuel tank,

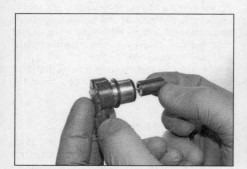

12.12a Carefully thread the valve in towards the head of the unit

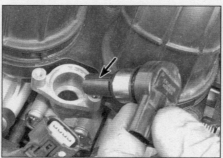

12.12b Groove in valve (arrowed) must align with pin in housing bore

12.12c Ensure the plate is fitted the correct way round

disconnect the fuel pump wiring connector, release any residual fuel pressure, and disconnect the fuel hose.

2 Connect the fuel gauge assembly between the fuel tank and the disconnected fuel hose.

3 Reconnect the fuel pump wiring connector. Start the engine and allow it to idle at the specified speed. Note the pressure present in the fuel system by reading the gauge, then turn the engine off. Compare the reading obtained to that given in the Specifications at the beginning of the Chapter.

4 If the fuel pressure is higher than specified, the pressure regulator in the fuel pump or the pump itself is faulty and the pump must be replaced with a new one (Section 14).

5 If the fuel pressure is lower than specified, first check for a leak, which should be obvious

from the smell of fuel. If there are no leaks check for a pinched or blocked tank breather/EVAP hose or fuel hose. Next remove the pump (Section 14), and check the strainer for a blockage (though this is unlikely), and replace the filter with a new one. If the pressure is still low with a new filter either the pressure regulator or the pump itself is faulty, and so the pump must be replaced with a new one.

6 On completion, disconnect the pump wiring connector and release the fuel pressure, then remove the fuel gauge assembly, being prepared to catch any residual fuel. Reconnect the bike's fuel hose and the pump wiring and lower the tank.

7 Start the engine and check that there is no sign of fuel leakage.

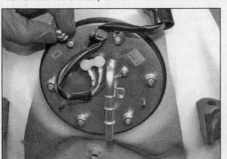
14.7a Unscrew the nuts…

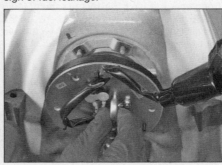
14.7b …and carefully draw the pump out

14.9a Undo the screw and release the earth wire…

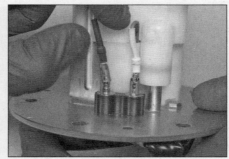
14.9b …and disconnect the supply wire

14.9c Release the tabs…

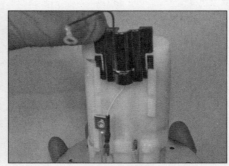
14.9d …and remove the sensor

14 Fuel pump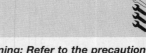

 Warning: Refer to the precautions in Section 1 before starting work.

Check

1 The fuel pump is located inside the fuel tank. The fuel pump should run for a few seconds when the ignition is switched ON to pressurise the fuel system, and then cut out until the engine is started. Check that it does this – you can hear it run. If it doesn't, first check the ENG STOP fuse (see Chapter 8).

2 If the fuse is good raise the fuel tank (see Section 2).

3 Make sure the ignition is switched OFF then disconnect the fuel pump wiring connector **(see illustration 2.6)**. Connect the positive (+) lead of a voltmeter to the yellow/red wire terminal on the loom side of the connector and the negative (–) lead to the black/white wire terminal. Switch the ignition ON whilst noting the reading obtained on the meter.

4 If battery voltage is present for a few seconds, the fuel pump circuit is operating correctly and the fuel pump itself is faulty and must be replaced with a new one.

5 If no reading is obtained, first check the pump relay (Section 11). Next check the fuel pump and pump relay circuit wiring for continuity and make sure all the connectors are free from corrosion and are securely connected. Repair/replace the wiring as necessary and clean the connectors using electrical contact cleaner. If this fails to reveal the fault, check all the components in the pump and relay circuit. If no fault can be found the ECM/PCM could be faulty.

Removal

6 Remove as much fuel as possible from the tank using a suction pump, then remove the tank (Section 2). Make sure the fuel cap is secure, then place the tank upside down on plenty of rag. Clean the base of the tank and the pump mounting plate.

7 Unscrew the fuel pump mounting plate nuts, noting the position of the domed nut **(see illustration)**. Carefully lift the pump assembly from the tank along with the mounting plate seal **(see illustration)**.

8 Remove the seal, noting how it fits **(see illustration 14.15a)** – a new one must be used.

Filter replacement

9 Disconnect the reserve sensor wiring **(see illustrations)**. Release the tabs and slide the sensor up off the pump **(see illustrations)**.

10 Disconnect the pump wiring, then remove the backing plate from each earth screw

14.10a Disconnect the pump earth wire and supply wire...

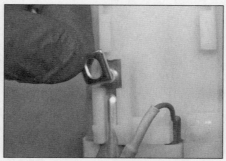

14.10b ...and remove the earth terminal backing plates

14.10c Release the clips...

14.10d ...and remove the filter/pump motor assembly

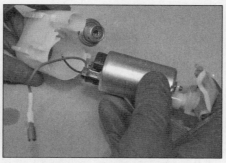

14.11a Remove the pump...

14.11b ...and the pressure regulator

terminal **(see illustrations)**. Release the clip on each side and carefully pull the filter/ pump motor assembly up off the base **(see illustrations)**.

11 Withdraw the pump motor from the filter, then pull the pressure regulator out **(see illustrations)**. Check the strainer for signs of dirt and clean it if necessary **(see illustration)** – note that the strainer is part of the fuel pump and is not available separately, so if the strainer is clogged and cannot be cleaned, or is damaged, a new pump assembly (which comes built-up with a new filter), must be fitted.

12 Remove the O-rings from the filter union on the pump base, from the pump motor, and from the pressure regulator **(see illustration)** – new O-rings are supplied with the new filter.

13 Fit the new O-rings and reassemble the pump in reverse order of disassembly – when fitting the filter assembly onto the pump base

14.11c Filter is part of pump assembly

make sure the terminals, clips and wiring all locate correctly **(see illustration)**.

Installation

14 Make sure the wiring terminal screws and connectors are tight.

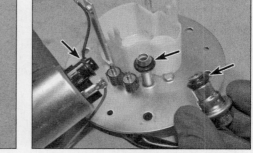

14.12 Remove the O-rings (arrowed)

15 Make sure the mounting plate and tank surfaces are clean and dry. Fit the new seal onto the plate with the projection aligned with the fuel pipe and carefully pull the rubber pegs through the holes in the plate so the ribs seat on the outer side **(see illustrations)**.

14.13 Make sure the pump supply wire is correctly routed

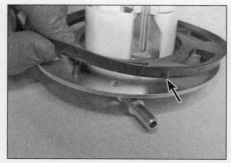

14.15a Align the projection (arrowed) with the pipe...

14.15b ...and pull the pegs through

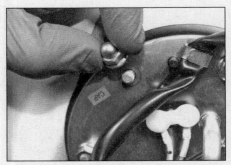

14.17 Make sure the domed nut is in its correct place

15.8 Fuel level sensor nuts (arrowed)

16 Carefully manoeuvre the pump assembly into the tank, making sure it is correctly positioned as shown, and seat the seal and plate over the studs (see illustration 14.7b).

17 Fit the nuts, making sure the domed nut is in its correct position, and tighten them finger-tight (see illustration). Now tighten them evenly and a little at a time in a criss-cross sequence to 12 Nm.

18 Install the fuel tank (Section 2).

15 Fuel level sensor and fuel reserve sensor

Check

1 The level sensor circuit consists of the level sensor and the reserve sensor in the fuel tank and the fuel gauge, which is part of the instrument cluster LCD display. Under normal circumstances with the tank full all segments of the gauge will show, and when there are only about 3.4 litres left the final segment will flash. The system performs its own self diagnosis when the ignition is turned ON: if an open or short circuit is detected in the wiring the display will operate as follows – the centre segment comes on, then the adjacent two segments also come on, followed by the outer segments so all are on, then the segments will go out in the same way starting from the centre until all are out, and this pattern will repeat until the fault is repaired.

Fuel level sensor

2 If a fault is indicated, raise the fuel tank and disconnect the fuel level sensor wiring connector (Section 2). Disconnect the instrument cluster wiring connector (see Chapter 8). Using a multi-meter check for continuity in the red/blue wire between the sensor connector and the instrument cluster connector, and in the green wire from the sensor connector to earth. If the wiring is good check the sensor as follows.

3 Remove the level sensor (see below). Check the float arm for damage and check for fuel inside the float, and check that the arm moves up and down smoothly and freely. Also check the wiring. Set the meter to measure resistance and connect it to the sensor wiring terminals, then manually move the float up and down to simulate movement between the full and empty positions, and compare the resistance readings to those given in the Specifications at the beginning of the Chapter. If they are not as specified replace the level sensor with a new one. If all is good the instrument cluster could be faulty (see Chapter 8).

Fuel reserve sensor

4 If a fault is indicated, raise the fuel tank and disconnect the fuel pump wiring connector (Section 2). Disconnect the instrument cluster wiring connector (see Chapter 8). Using a multi-meter check for continuity in the red/black wire between the pump connector and the instrument cluster connector, and in the green wire from the pump connector to earth. If the wiring is good test the sensor as follows.

5 The sensor is a thermo switch that reacts to the difference in temperature that occurs in the transition between being submerged in fuel and exposed to the air. The switch is open when submerged in fuel and closed when in the air.

6 Remove the fuel pump, then remove the sensor from it (Section 14). Check the wiring. Fill a jar big enough to hold the sensor with petrol (gasoline). Connect a multi-meter set to test continuity to the sensor wiring terminals. With the pump exposed to the air there should be continuity, and with the pump submerged in the fuel there should be no continuity. If not replace the fuel pump with a new one – the sensor is not available separately. If all is good the instrument cluster could be faulty (see Chapter 8).

Removal and installation

Fuel level sensor

7 Remove as much fuel as possible from the tank using a suction pump, then remove the tank (Section 2). Make sure the fuel cap is secure, then place the tank upside down on plenty of rag. Clean the base of the tank and the pump mounting plate.

8 Unscrew the sensor mounting plate nuts (see illustration). Carefully draw the sensor out of the tank, noting its orientation and taking care not to snag the float arm. Remove the O-ring – a new one must be used.

9 Fit a new O-ring smeared with oil into the groove. Manoeuvre the sensor into the tank, aligning the hole in the mounting plate with the pin, and tighten the nuts evenly and a little at a time in a criss-cross sequence. After installing the tank check there is no leakage from around the sensor.

Fuel reserve sensor

10 The sensor is an integral component of the fuel pump assembly and is not available separately – see Section 14.

16 Throttle cables (2016/17 models)

Removal

1 Remove the fuel tank (Section 2).

2 For best access remove the air filter housing (Section 3) to ensure the new cables are routed correctly and through the guides provided; the ends of the cable are easily accessible with the housing in situ.

3 Slacken the locknut holding the closing (rear) cable in the bracket on the throttle body then slip the cable out of the bracket (see illustration). Fully slacken the opening (front) cable locknut and back off the adjuster nut to get maximum freeplay then slip the cable out of the bracket (see illustration). Disengage each cable end from the throttle pulley (see illustrations 16.12a and b).

16.3a Slacken locknut and slip closing cable out...

16.3b ...followed by opening cable

16.5 Handguard moved down out of the way of the switch screws

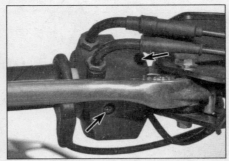

16.6a Two screws (arrowed) retain the switch/housing halves

16.6b Remove the closing...

4 Note the routing of the old cables as you withdraw them.

5 Remove the handguard screw and rotate the handguard down to give access to the right-hand handlebar switch screws **(see illustration)**. Also slacken the master cylinder clamp bolts and rotate the master cylinder/brake lever assembly slightly to improve access to the screws.

6 Undo the housing screws and separate the halves **(see illustration)**. Detach the cable ends from the pulley **(see illustrations)**.

7 Unscrew the closing cable elbow nut and withdraw the cable from the housing **(see illustration)**. Thread the opening cable elbow out of the housing.

Installation

8 Fit the throttle opening cable into the upper socket of the throttle pulley housing and thread the elbow in without it becoming tight on the bottom of the threads – the elbow must stay loose so that it aligns itself **(see illustration)**. Fit the closing cable into the lower socket **(see illustration)**. Thread the closing cable nut into the housing, leaving it loose.

9 Locate the housing on the handlebar so that the pin locate in the hole in the handlebar **(see illustration)**. Lubricate the cable ends with multi-purpose grease and locate them in the pulley **(see illustration)**.

10 Refit the switch unit, then fit the screws and tighten them **(see illustration)**.

16.6c ...and opening cable ends from the pulley

16.7 Unscrew the closing cable nut and then slacken the opening cable nut to thread the cable elbow out of the housing

16.8a Thread the opening cable into the housing

16.8b Fitting the closing cable into the housing

16.9a Pin in housing locates in hole in handlebar (arrowed)

16.9b Cable ends correctly located in the throttle twistgrip pulley

16.10 Make sure the switch unit fits fully against the housing before securing with the two screws

16.12a Fit the opening cable around the pulley channel and into the front socket

16.12b Fit the closing cable into the rear socket

16.12c Tightening the closing cable locknut

11 Feed the cables down to the throttle bodies, making sure they are routed as noted on removal.

12 Fit the opening cable end into the front socket in the pulley on the throttle body pulley **(see illustration)** and locate its adjuster

into the front of the bracket. Fit the closing cable into the rear socket in the pulley **(see illustration)** and its adjuster into the rear of the bracket. Make sure the retaining plate locates correctly over the inner edge of the bracket on each cable. Tighten the locknut to secure the

closing cable in the bracket **(see illustration)**. Use the adjuster nut on the opening cable to set the correct amount of cable freeplay at the grip flange, then tighten its locknut.

13 Tighten the cable elbow nuts on the throttle pulley housing. Check the throttle cable freeplay (see Chapter 1) and make further adjustment if necessary at the fine adjuster on the upper end of the cable. Check the throttle opens fully and smoothly, and closes when released. Turn the handlebars back-and-forth to make sure the cables don't cause the steering to bind.

14 Install the air filter housing if it was removed (Section 3). Install the fuel tank (Section 2). Refer to Chapter 6, Section 8, Step 15 for information on positioning the brake master cylinder. When fitting the hand guard engage its tab with the slot in the bracket.

15 Start the engine and check that the idle speed does not rise as the handlebars are turned. If it does, the throttle cables are routed incorrectly. Correct the problem before riding the motorcycle.

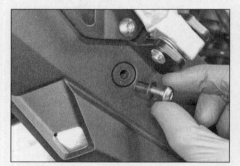

17.1a Undo the outer cover screw and remove the collar...

17.1b ...then slide the cover forwards off the rubbered tabs on the heat shield

17 Exhaust system

⚠ *Warning: If the engine has been running the exhaust system will be very hot. Allow the system to cool before carrying out any work.*

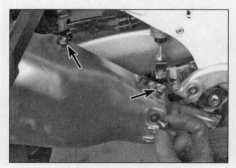

17.1c Undo the heat shield screws...

17.1d ...and remove the shield

HAYNES HINT *Exhaust system nuts and bolts tend to become corroded and seized. It is advisable to spray them with a penetrating fluid before attempting to slacken them.*

Removal

Silencer

1 Remove the outer cover and the heat shield **(see illustrations)**. Remove the rubbers from the tabs on the shield if required.

2 Slacken the clamp bolts **(see illustration)**.

3 Unscrew the silencer mounting bolt and remove the washers, and ease the silencer off the downpipe assembly **(see illustrations)**.

17.2 Silencer clamp bolts (arrowed)

17.3a Unscrew the bolt...

17.3b ...and draw the silencer off

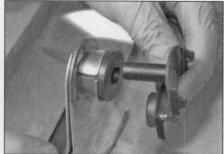

17.3c Remove the bracket from the bush

17.4 Fit a new sealing ring (arrowed) if necessary

Remove the bracket from the inner side of the mount **(see illustration)**.

4 Check the condition of the sealing ring and replace it with a new one if it is damaged or deformed or no longer sealing correctly **(see illustration)**. If you do need to fit a new one, remove the clamp first then dig the old one out. Before fitting the new one expand the tangs on the end of the pipe slightly, and ease the new one in carefully as they are easily damaged.

5 Remove the tail cap and cover from the silencer if required, noting the arrangement of the washers, collars and grommets.

6 Check the condition of all mounting components and replace them with new ones if necessary.

Downpipe assembly

7 Remove the silencer (see above).

8 On the Adventure Sports model remove the sump guard (see Chapter 7).

9 Release and disconnect the oxygen sensor wiring **(see illustrations 9.26a and b)**.

10 Unscrew the mounting bolt nut **(see illustration)**. Unscrew the nuts securing the downpipe flanges to the cylinder head and slide the flanges off **(see illustrations)**. Support the assembly, then withdraw the mounting bolt, draw the flanges off the studs and manoeuvre the downpipe assembly off **(see illustrations)**.

11 Remove the sealing ring from each port in the cylinder head **(see illustration)** – new ones must be used.

12 Note the collar in the mount and remove it for safekeeping if required **(see illustration)**.

17.10a Remove the nut from the inner end of the bolt but leave the bolt in place for now

17.10b Unscrew the downpipe nuts...

17.10c ...and displace the flanges

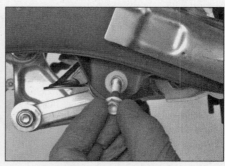

17.10d Withdraw the bolt...

17.10e ...and remove the system

17.11 Remove the sealing rings

17.12 Remove the collar

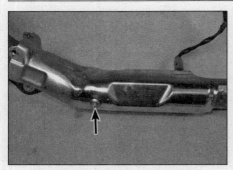

17.13a Undo the rear shield screw (arrowed), then slide the shield back off the tabs

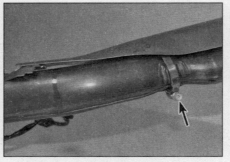

17.13b Release the front shield clamp (arrowed), then slide the shield forwards off the tab

17.14 Fit a new sealing ring into each port

Check the condition of the nuts and bolt, collar and mounting rubber and replace them with new ones if necessary.

13 If required remove the heat shields **(see illustrations).**

Installation

14 Installation is the reverse of removal, noting the following:

● Replace any damaged, deformed or deteriorated mounting rubbers with new ones. Replace any badly corroded clamp, collars, nuts, bolts and washers with new ones. Make sure the collars are fitted in the rubbers.

● Check that the amount of protrusion of each stud from the cylinder head is 22.5 to 23.5 mm.

● Use a new sealing ring in each cylinder head port, and dab them with grease to stick them in place **(see illustration).**

● Apply a smear of copper grease to all nuts and bolt to prevent them from seizing up. Fit and secure all mounts finger-tight before fully tightening them. On the downpipe assembly tighten the flange nuts before the mounting bolt, and tighten them to 20 Nm. Tighten the silencer clamp bolts to 17 Nm.

● Do not forget to reconnect the oxygen sensor wiring connector, and make sure the wiring is correctly routed and secured.

● Run the engine and check the system for leaks.

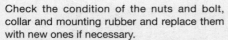

18 Pulse secondary air (PAIR) system

General information

1 To reduce the amount of unburned hydrocarbons released in the exhaust gases, a pulse secondary air (PAIR) system is fitted. The system consists of the control valve (mounted above the valve cover), the reed valves (fitted in the valve cover), the hose from the air filter housing to the inlet union on the control valve, and the hose from the outlet union on the control valve to the reed valve housing. The control valve is actuated electronically by the ECM/PCM.

2 Under normal operating conditions the valve is open allowing filtered air to be drawn from the air filter housing, through the control valve and the reed valves and cylinder head passages and into the exhaust ports. The air mixes with the exhaust gases, causing any unburned particles of the fuel in the mixture to be burnt in the exhaust port/pipes. This process changes a considerable amount of hydrocarbons and carbon monoxide into relatively harmless carbon dioxide and water. The reed valves in the valve cover are fitted to prevent the flow of exhaust gases back up the cylinder head passages and into the air filter housing.

Testing

3 Start the engine and warm it up to normal temperature, then stop it.

4 Remove the air filter housing (Section 3). Check that the PAIR hose from the air filter housing is clean – the presence of carbon deposits indicates a faulty system.

5 Displace the control valve (see below, but leave the hose connected to the outlet union on 2018-on models) and disconnect the wiring connector **(see illustration 18.10c).** Clean the end of the air filter housing hose. Manually check the operation of the system by blowing through the hose – air should flow through the control valve and reed valves. Using a pair of auxiliary wires apply battery voltage (12 volts) across the control valve terminals and repeat the check – no air should flow through the control valve. Disconnect the battery. If the valve does not behave as described check its resistance (Step 7).

6 Now suck on the air filter hose union; you should not be able to suck air back up the hose, indicating the reed valves are closing and sealing correctly. If you can suck air through, remove the valves (see below). Check the reed on each valve seats correctly all round, then carefully push it up off its seat to check that it is not stuck **(see illustrations).** Clean the base plates and valve housings. Fit the valves and test the system again. Replace the valves with new ones if necessary.

7 Check the resistance of the control valve solenoid by connecting an ohmmeter between its terminals and compare the reading obtained to that given in the Specifications at the beginning of this Chapter **(see illustration).** Replace the valve with a new one if faulty.

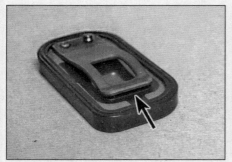

18.6a Check there is no gap between the reed and its seat...

18.6b ...then gently push up on the underside of the reed to check it is not stuck

18.7 Measuring the resistance of the control valve solenoid

18.10a Detach the air outlet hose...

18.10b ...then displace the valve...

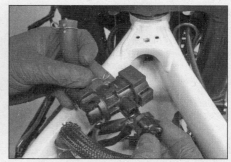

18.10c ...and disconnect the wiring

Component renewal

Control valve

8 Remove the air filter housing (Section 3).

9 On 2016/17 models unscrew the control valve bolts and remove the collars. Displace the valve and disconnect the wiring connector. Release the clamps, disconnect the hoses and remove the valve.

10 On 2018-on models release the clamp and detach the hose from the air outlet (left-hand) union on the valve **(see illustration)**. Displace the valve and disconnect the wiring **(see illustrations)**. If required disconnect the hose from the air inlet union **(see illustration)**.

11 Installation is the reverse of removal.

Reed valves

12 Remove the control valve (see above), then remove the ignition coil assembly (Section 22).

13 Release the clamp and detach the hose from the reed valve cover **(see illustration)**.

14 Unscrew the bolts and remove the cover **(see illustration)**. Remove the reed valves and the base plates, noting which way around they fit **(see illustrations)**.

15 Installation is the reverse of removal. Make sure the reed valve components and housings are clean and free of carbon deposits, and that the base plates and valves seat correctly. Clean the threads of the cover bolts and apply some fresh threadlock, and tighten the bolts to 12 Nm.

18.10d Detach the air inlet hose

18.13 Disconnect the hose (arrowed)

19 Catalytic converter

General information

1 There is a catalytic converter incorporated in the exhaust system to minimise the level of exhaust pollutants released into the atmosphere.

2 A catalytic converter consists of a canister containing a fine mesh impregnated with a catalyst material, over which the hot exhaust gases pass. The catalyst speeds up the oxidation of harmful carbon monoxide, unburned hydrocarbons and soot, effectively reducing the quantity of harmful products released into the atmosphere via the exhaust gases.

3 The catalytic converter is of the closed-loop type with exhaust gas oxygen content information being fed back to the ECM/PCM by the oxygen sensor.

4 The oxygen sensor contains a heating element which is controlled by the ECM/PCM. When the engine is cold, the ECM switches on the heating element which warms the exhaust gases as they pass over the sensor. This brings the catalytic converter quickly up to its normal operating temperature and decreases the level of exhaust pollutants emitted whilst the engine warms up. Once the engine is sufficiently warmed up, the ECM switches off the heating element.

5 Refer to Section 17 for exhaust system removal and installation, and Section 9 for oxygen sensor removal and installation information.

18.14a Remove the cover...

18.14b ...the reed valve...

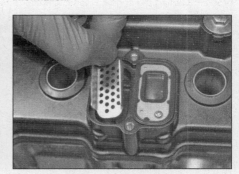

18.14c ...and its base plate

Precautions

6 A catalytic converter is a reliable and simple device which needs no maintenance in itself, but there are some facts of which an owner should be aware if the converter is to function properly for its full service life.

● DO NOT use leaded or lead replacement petrol (gasoline) – the additives will coat the precious metals, reducing their converting efficiency and will eventually destroy the catalytic converter.
● Always keep the ignition and fuel systems well-maintained in accordance with the manufacturer's schedule – if the fuel/air mixture is suspected of being incorrect have it checked on an exhaust gas analyser.
● If the engine develops a misfire, do not ride the bike at all (or at least as little as possible) until the fault is rectified.
● DO NOT use fuel or engine oil additives – these may contain substances harmful to the catalytic converter.
● DO NOT continue to use the bike if the engine burns oil to the extent of leaving a visible trail of blue smoke.
● Remember that the catalytic converter and oxygen sensor are FRAGILE – do not strike them with tools during servicing work.

20 Evaporative Emission Control (EVAP) system

General information

1 The evaporative emission control system (EVAP) is fitted on all California market and Euro 4 compliant models. The system minimises the escape of fuel vapour into the atmosphere. The fuel tank is sealed and a charcoal canister collects the fuel vapours generated when the motorcycle is parked and stores them until they can be cleared from the canister, via the purge control valve, into the throttle body to be burned by the engine during normal combustion. The purge control valve for the fuel tank vapour is opened and closed by the ECM/PCM.

2 The valve should be tested if there is a problem starting the engine when it is hot.

Testing

Purge control valve

3 Remove the fuel tank (Section 2).
4 Disconnect the valve wiring connector, then undo the two screws, displace the valve and disconnect the hoses from it **(see illustration 10.5a)**.
5 Check the operation of the control valve by blowing through the inlet (canister hose) union – air should not flow through the valve and out the outlet hose union. Connect battery voltage (12 volts) across the valve terminals, connecting the positive lead to the black/white wire terminal, and repeat the check

– air should flow through the valve if it is functioning correctly.
6 If an ohmmeter is available, check the resistance of the control valve windings and compare the reading obtained to that given in the Specifications. Replace the valve with a new one if the reading differs.

Charcoal canister

7 The canister cannot be tested and there is no reason for it to ever require attention.

21 Ignition system check

⚠️ **Warning: The energy levels in electronic systems can be very high. On no account should the ignition be switched on whilst the plugs or caps are being held. Shocks from the HT circuit can be most unpleasant. Secondly, it is vital that the engine is not turned over or run with any of the plug caps removed, and that the plugs are soundly earthed (grounded) when the system is checked for sparking. The ignition system components can be seriously damaged if the HT circuit becomes isolated.**

1 As no means of adjustment is available, any failure of the system can be traced to failure of a system component or a simple wiring fault. Of the two possibilities, the latter is by far the most likely. In the event of failure, check the system in a logical fashion, as described below.
2 Make sure the ignition is OFF. Referring to Chapter 1, Section 22 for access, pull the caps off the spark plugs. Connect the cap of the coil being tested to a spare spark plug (preferably use a new plug). Earth the plug against the cylinder head.

⚠️ **Warning: Do not remove the spark plugs from the engine to perform this check – atomised fuel being pumped out of the open spark plug hole could ignite, causing severe injury! Make sure the plug is securely held against the bolt head – if it is not earthed when the engine is turned over, the ECM/ PCM could be damaged.**

3 Having observed the above precautions, check that the kill switch is in the RUN position and the transmission is in neutral, then turn the ignition switch ON and turn the engine over on the starter motor. If the system is in good condition a regular, fat blue spark should be evident at the plug electrode. If the spark appears thin or yellowish, or is non-existent, further investigation is necessary. Turn the ignition OFF and repeat the check for the other coils if and as required.
4 The ignition system must be able to produce a spark that is capable of jumping at least a 6 mm gap. Simple ignition spark gap testing tools are commercially available – follow the manufacturer's instructions **(see illustration)**.

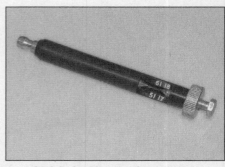

21.4 An ignition spark gap tester

5 If the test results are good the entire ignition system can be considered good. If the spark appears thin or yellowish, or is non-existent, further investigation is necessary.
6 First make sure that the battery is fully charged and that all fuses are in good condition (see Chapter 8).
7 The likely faults are listed below, starting with the most probable source of failure. Work through the list systematically, referring to the subsequent sections for full details of the necessary checks and tests.

● Loose, corroded or damaged wiring connections, broken or shorted wiring between any of the component parts of the ignition system.
● Loose spark plug cap or lead connection, faulty spark plug cap or HT lead, faulty spark plug, dirty, worn or corroded plug electrodes.
● Faulty neutral, clutch or sidestand switch (see Chapter 8).
● Faulty ignition coil(s) (Section 22).
● Faulty ignition switch or engine kill switch (see Chapter 8).
● Faulty crankshaft position (CKP) sensor (Section 9) or damaged triggers on alternator rotor (see Chapter 8).
● Faulty relay (Section 11).
● Faulty ECM/PCM (Section 10).

8 If the above checks don't reveal the cause of the problem, have the ignition system tested by a Honda dealer.

22 Ignition coils

Special tool: *For a definitive test of the coils Honda specify to use a peak voltage adapter (Honda pt. no. 07HGJ-0020100 in Europe, or IgnitionMate MTP07-0286 in the US) plus an aftermarket digital multimeter having an impedance of 10 M-ohm/DCV minimum (see Step 5). Have the coil(s) tested by a dealer if necessary.*

Check

1 Remove the ignition coil assembly (see below).

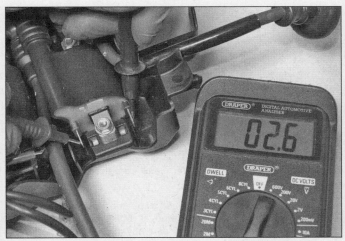

22.3 To test the coil primary resistance, connect the multimeter leads to the primary wiring terminals

22.4a To test the coil secondary resistance, connect the multimeter probes as shown

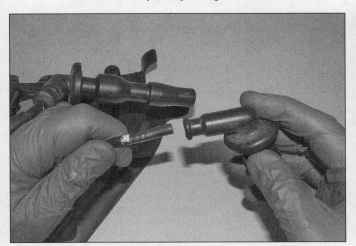

22.4b Unscrew the cap from the lead and test the coil again

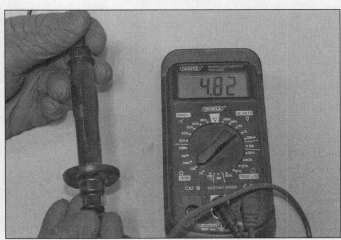

22.4c Checking a spark plug cap resistance

2 Check each coil visually for loose or damaged connectors and terminals, cracks and other damage.

3 To check the condition of the primary windings, disconnect the primary wiring connectors from the coil being tested – if necessary, remove the coil from the tray to do this (see below). Set a multimeter to the ohms x 1 scale. Connect the meter probes to the primary terminals on the coil and measure the resistance **(see illustration)**. If the reading obtained is not as given in the Specifications, it is likely that the coil is defective.

4 To check the resistance of the secondary windings, set the meter to the K-ohm scale. Connect one meter probe to the contact in the spark plug cap and the other to one of the primary terminals and measure the resistance **(see illustration)**. If the reading obtained is not as given in the Specifications (resistance with plug cap), unscrew the plug cap and test the coil again, this time inserting the probe into the end of the HT lead **(see**

illustration). If the reading obtained is not as given in the Specifications (resistance without plug cap) it is likely the coil is defective. If the reading is good check the resistance of the plug cap, and if that is not as specified replace the cap with a new one **(see illustration)**.

5 If a peak voltage adapter is available (see **Special tool** note) the coil's primary peak voltage can be checked. This must be done with the coil assembly in situ. Remove the air filter housing (Section 3). Disconnect all the spark plug caps, then fit a new spark plug into the cap of the coil being tested and earth it against the cylinder head or connect it to a good earth using a lead with crocodile clips. Connect the peak voltage adaptor positive probe to the blue/black (No. 1 primary (main) coil), blue/white (No. 1 secondary (sub) coil), blue/red (No. 2 primary (main) coil) or blue/ yellow (No. 2 secondary (sub) coil) wire terminal. Connect the negative probe to earth. On models with standard transmission make

sure it is in neutral. With the ignition ON and the kill switch set to RUN, battery voltage should be shown on the meter. Crank the engine over on the starter motor and note the peak voltage registered on the meter – it should be above the minimum given in the Specifications at the beginning of this Chapter.

> **HAYNES HINT** *Note if a fault exists in the ignition circuit for one cylinder you can swap the coils over to check if the fault then appears on the other cylinder. If so, the coil is confirmed faulty.*

Removal and installation

6 Remove the throttle body (Section 3). Remove the PAIR system control valve (Section 18).

7 Pull the caps off the spark plugs.

8 Release and disconnect the ignition switch,

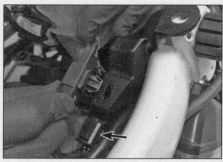

22.8 Release and disconnect the ignition switch connector, and where fitted the HISS connector (arrowed) – 2018 model shown

22.9a Release the wiring tie on the left side…

22.9b …and from the cross-piece

22.10 Disconnect the coil sub-loom connector

22.11a Release the pegs from the grommets…

assembly and all other components in reverse order of removal. Make sure the the plate nuts are all correctly in place. Make sure the pegs on the tray locate in the grommets **(see illustration 22.11a)**. Make sure the plug caps are pushed fully down onto the plugs, and make sure all wiring, cables and hoses are correctly routed and secured.

23 Ignition timing

General information

1 Since no provision exists for adjusting the ignition timing and since no component is subject to mechanical wear, there is no need for regular checks; only if investigating a fault such as a loss of power or a misfire should the ignition timing be checked.

2 The ignition timing is checked dynamically (engine running) using a stroboscopic lamp. The inexpensive neon lamps should be adequate in theory, but in practice may produce a pulse of such low intensity that the timing mark remains indistinct. If possible, one of the more precise xenon tube lamps should be used, powered by an external

and where fitted the HISS receiver, wiring connector(s) **(see illustration)**.
9 Release the wiring loom from the tie on the left-hand side, and on 2018-on models release the wiring tie from the frame cross-piece **(see illustrations)**.
10 Disconnect the coil assembly wiring connector **(see illustration)**.
11 Draw the coil assembly back to release the pegs from the grommets and manoeuvre it out **(see illustrations)**.
12 If you are removing a coil or coils from the tray, mark and note which fits where according

to the numbers marked on the leads and the tray, or by the length of lead and type of plug cap, and the routing of the leads and wiring **(see illustration)**. Disconnect the primary wiring connectors of the coil being removed, then unscrew the bolts and remove the coil (or do it the other way round if access to the connectors is restricted) – the coil mounted on the underside of the tray on 2016/17 models has conventional nuts on the ends of the bolt, while all other bolts thread into the plate nuts that locate in the tray.
13 Install the ignition coils and the coil

22.11b …and manoeuvre the coil assembly out, feeding the HT leads up and noting their positions

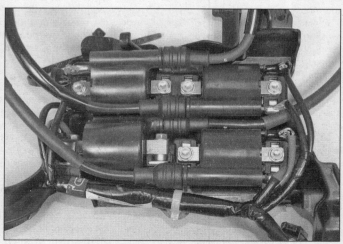

22.12 Coil arrangement on 2018 models

source of the appropriate voltage. Do not use the machine's own battery as an incorrect reading may result from stray impulses within the machine's electrical system.

Check

3 Warm the engine up to normal operating temperature then stop it.

4 Connect the timing light lead to the HT lead for the No. 1 (left-hand) cylinder secondary spark plug.

5 Unscrew the timing inspection cap from the alternator cover **(see illustration)**. Check the condition of its O-ring and get a new one if necessary.

6 The dynamic timing mark on the rotor which indicates the firing point at idle speed for the No. 1 cylinder is the line next to the F mark. The static timing mark with which this should align is the notch in the inspection hole rim.

 HAYNES HINT *The timing mark can be highlighted with white paint to make it more visible under the stroboscope light.*

7 Start the engine and aim the light at the static timing mark.

8 With the machine idling, the timing mark should align with the notch. Now increase engine speed above 3000 rpm. The dynamic timing mark should move clockwise in relation to the static mark. This confirms the ignition is advancing.

9 As already stated, there is no means of adjusting the ignition timing. If the ignition timing is incorrect, or suspected of being incorrect, one of the ignition system components is at fault, and the system must be tested as described in the preceding Sections of this Chapter.

10 When the check is complete, fit the timing inspection cap, using a new O-ring if necessary, and smear the O-ring with oil and the cap threads with grease **(see illustration 23.5)**. Tighten the cap to 6 Nm.

24 Immobiliser system

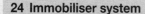

General information

1 An immobiliser system (known as HISS – Honda Ignition Security System) is fitted either as standard or as an option (depending on market) as an anti-theft device. The system will only allow the machine to be started if the correct registered key is used to turn the ignition ON. The system consists of a transponder in the ignition key, a receiver fitted around the ignition switch, and the ECM/PCM.

2 When the ignition is switched ON, the ECM/PCM sends power through the receiver to the transponder. The transponder sends a coded signal back through the receiver

23.5 Unscrew the timing inspection cap. Check the O-ring (arrowed)

to the ECM/PCM. If the signal sent by the transponder matches the signal stored in the unit's memory, the HISS immobiliser indicator light in the instrument cluster comes on for two seconds then goes out, and the ECM/PCM allows the engine to be started. If the key code signal is not recognised, or if there is a fault in the system, the indicator light stays on. If the light stays on, or if the light does not come on at all, refer to the fault diagnosis and troubleshooting Sections below.

3 The ECM/PCM can store the codes for up to four registered keys. These keys should be kept separately (i.e. not on the same key-ring) as the proximity of another key to the one being used in the switch can lead to the signal from it being jammed, and the bike will not start. The key has a built in transponder which can be damaged if the key is dropped or knocked, gets too hot, is too close to a magnetic object, or is submerged in water for too long. If all the keys are lost, the ECM/PCM must be replaced with a new one, so always make sure you have at least one spare key. If a new key is obtained, it must be registered into the system before the bike can be started with the key.

Key registration with the old ignition switch

Special tools: *The following procedures refer to the Honda special tools (part nos. 07XMZ-MBW0101 and 070MZ-MEC0101) – these are wiring loom adapters to connect a spare battery into the loom side of the HISS diagnostic wiring connector.*

4 Obtain a new key from a Honda dealer, and have it cut to match the original key. Get a spare 12V battery and make sure it is fully charged.

5 Remove the rider's seat (see Chapter 7). Release and disconnect the HISS wiring connector **(see illustration)**. Connect the special tools together at the connector, then connect the wiring connector end to the HISS connector, and connect the red clip of the tool to the battery positive (+) terminal and the black clip to the battery negative (–) terminal.

6 Set the kill switch to RUN then turn the ignition switch ON using your original key. The immobiliser indicator light should come on and stay on – if it starts to flash after ten seconds,

24.5 HISS diagnostic wiring connector (arrowed) – 2018 model shown

then there is a fault in the system, which will have gone into fault diagnosis, and the pattern of the flashes it emits should be matched with the fault code (see below). Now disconnect the red clip from the battery positive terminal and leave it disconnected for at least two seconds, then reconnect it. The indicator should now come on for two seconds, then begin to flash repeatedly four times. This indicates that the system is in registration mode. At this point the registrations of all keys except the one in the switch will have been cancelled, so if you have another spare apart from the new one you want to register, this will also have to be registered.

7 Turn the ignition OFF and remove the original key, placing it well away from the receiver.

8 Insert the new key into the switch and turn it ON. The indicator should now come on for two seconds, then begin to flash repeatedly four times. This indicates that the system has registered the new key. If the indicator starts to flash after ten seconds, then there is a fault in the system, which will have gone into fault diagnosis, and the pattern of the flashes it emits should be matched with the fault code (see below). Turn the ignition OFF and remove the key.

9 To register any other spare keys that will have been cancelled, repeat Step 8. Up to four keys can be registered.

10 On completion turn the ignition OFF, then remove the special tool and reconnect the HISS wiring connector. Now turn the ignition ON using any of the registered keys to return the system to normal mode.

11 Check that all registered keys can start the motorcycle.

Key registration with a new ignition switch

12 Obtain a new switch and two (or more) new keys.

13 Remove the faulty switch (see Chapter 8), but retain the HISS receiver to fit with the new switch.

14 Remove the rider's seat (see Chapter 7). Release and disconnect the HISS wiring connector **(see illustration 24.5)**. Connect the special tools together at the connector, then connect the wiring connector end to the HISS connector, and connect the red clip of the tool to the battery positive (+) terminal and the

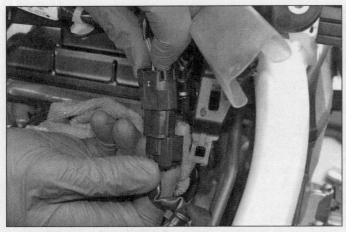

24.38a HISS receiver wiring connector – 2018 model shown

24.38b Undo the screw (arrowed) on each side

black clip to the battery negative (–) terminal.
15 Place one of the original registered keys for the faulty switch next to the receiver.
16 Connect the new ignition switch to its connector in the wiring loom, but keep it away from the receiver. Set the kill switch to run then turn the new switch ON with one of the new keys. The immobiliser indicator light should come on and stay on, which means the ECM/PCM recognises the old key that is next to the receiver – if it starts to flash after ten seconds, then there is a fault in the system, which will have gone into fault diagnosis, and the pattern of the flashes it emits should be matched with the fault code (see below). Now disconnect the red clip from the battery positive terminal and leave it disconnected for at least two seconds, then reconnect it. The indicator should now come on for two seconds, then begin to flash repeatedly four times. This indicates that the system is in registration mode. At this point the registrations of all keys except the one near the receiver will have been cancelled.
17 Turn the ignition OFF and remove the new key.
18 Install the new ignition switch, then fit the receiver onto it (see Chapter 8).
19 Insert the new key into the switch and turn it ON. The indicator should now come on for two seconds, then begin to flash repeatedly four times. This indicates that the system has registered the new key. If the indicator starts to flash after ten seconds, then there is a fault in the system, which will have gone into fault diagnosis, and the pattern of the flashes it emits should be matched with the fault code (see below). Turn the ignition OFF and disconnect the red clip of the special tool from the battery positive terminal.
20 Turn the ignition ON using the newly registered key. The indicator light should come on for two seconds, then go off.
21 Turn the ignition OFF and reconnect the red clip to the battery positive terminal.
22 Turn the ignition ON using the newly registered key. The indicator light should

come on and stay on – if it starts to flash after ten seconds, then there is a fault in the system, which will have gone into fault diagnosis, and the pattern of the flashes it emits should be matched with the fault code (see below). Now disconnect the red clip from the battery positive terminal and leave it disconnected for at least two seconds, then reconnect it. The indicator should now come on for two seconds, then begin to flash repeatedly four times. This indicates that the system is in registration mode. At this point the registrations of all old keys (for the faulty switch) are cancelled.
23 Turn the ignition OFF and remove the key, placing it well away from the receiver.
24 Insert the second new unregistered key and turn the ignition ON. The indicator should now come on for four seconds, then begin to flash repeatedly four times. This indicates that the system has registered the second new key. Turn the ignition OFF and remove the key.
25 To register any other new spare keys, repeat Step 24. Up to four keys can be registered.
26 On completion turn the ignition OFF, then remove the special tool and reconnect the HISS wiring connector. Now turn the ignition ON using any of the registered keys to return the system to normal mode.
27 Check that all newly registered keys can start the motorcycle.

Key registration with a new ECM/PCM (engine/powertrain control module)

28 Obtain a new ECM/PCM along with two new keys. Install the new ECM/PCM (Section 10). Have the keys cut to match the original key for your ignition switch.
29 Set the kill switch to run. Insert a new key into the switch and turn it ON. The indicator should now come on for two seconds, then begin to flash repeatedly four times. This indicates that the system has registered the new key. If the indicator stays on for ten seconds then starts to flash, then there is a

fault in the system, which will have gone into fault diagnosis, and the pattern of the flashes it emits should be matched with the fault code (see below).
30 Turn the ignition OFF and remove the key.
31 Insert the second new key and turn the ignition ON. The indicator should now come on for two seconds, then begin to flash repeatedly four times. This indicates that the system has registered the second new key.
32 Turn the ignition OFF and remove the key.
33 The new ECM will only register two new keys at this stage. If you have a third key to register, refer to Steps 4 to 10 to register it, noting that you will need the special tool mentioned therein.
34 Check that both newly registered keys can start the motorcycle.

Fault diagnosis

35 There are two fault diagnosis modes, one for faults that occur during normal use, and one for a fault that occurs when registering a new key. Make sure you refer to the correct table when matching the fault code pattern.
36 If the indicator light has come on and stayed on during normal use, remove the rider's seat (see Chapter 7). Release and disconnect the HISS wiring connector **(see illustration 24.5)**. Connect the special tools together at the connector, then connect the wiring connector end to the HISS connector, and connect the red clip of the tool to the battery positive (+) terminal and the black clip to the battery negative (–) terminal.
37 Set the kill switch to run then turn the ignition switch ON. The indicator light will come on for ten seconds, then start to flash. This means it has entered diagnostic mode, and the pattern of the flashes indicates the fault that has occurred. The pattern repeats continuously. Match the pattern with the fault codes below, making sure you refer to the relevant table. If the indicator stays on after ten seconds and does not flash, then there is no fault logged in the system.

If fault is indicated during normal use

Flash pattern	Fault	Solution
Two short, one long, one short	Faulty ECM/PCM	Install new ECM/PCM
Two short, two long	Faulty receiver or wiring	Check the wiring and connectors in the HISS circuit, referring to Section 2 in Chapter 8 and to the wiring diagram for your model. If the wiring is good fit a new receiver.
One long, three short	Signal jammed by other key	Place other key away (at least 50 mm) from the receiver
One long, two short, one long	Signal jammed by other key	Place other key away (at least 50 mm) from the receiver

If fault is indicated during key registration

Flash pattern	Fault	Solution
One short, one long, one short, one long	Key already registered	Use a new or cancelled key
Two short, two long	Faulty receiver or wiring	Check the wiring and connectors in the HISS circuit, referring to Section 2 in Chapter 8 and to the wiring diagram for your model. If the wiring is good fit a new receiver.
One short, one long, two short	Key already registered on old ECM/PCM	Use a new key

Replacement

38 To replace the receiver, remove the air filter housing (Section 3), then release and disconnect the receiver wiring connector **(see illustration)**. Feed the wiring back to the receiver, freeing it from any ties and noting its routing. Undo the screws and remove the receiver **(see illustration)**. How you access the screws will depend on the screwdrivers you have – a very long one can be inserted from below between the headlight and the yokes, or a very short one can be used from the top, or remove the fairing side panels, inner panel cover, inner panel, front cover, and headlight as required until you get the access you need.

39 To replace the ECM/PCM see Section 10.

Notes

Chapter 5
Frame and suspension

Contents

Section number

Footrests, brake pedal and gearchange lever 3
Fork oil change. 7
Fork overhaul 8
Fork removal and installation 6
Frame inspection and repair. 2
General Information 1
Handlebars and levers 5

Section number

Rear shock absorber 11
Rear suspension linkage 12
Sidestand 4
Steering head bearings 10
Steering stem 9
Suspension adjustment 14
Swingarm 13

Degrees of difficulty

Easy, suitable for novice with little experience	Fairly easy, suitable for beginner with some experience	Fairly difficult, suitable for competent DIY mechanic	Difficult, suitable for experienced DIY mechanic	Very difficult, suitable for expert DIY or professional

Specifications

Front forks

Fork oil type	10W fork oil (Pro-Honda suspension fluid SS8)
Fork oil capacity (per fork)	
Standard models	721 ± 2.5 cc
Adventure Sports models.	695 ± 2.5 cc
Fork oil level*	
Standard models	95 mm
Adventure Sports models.	110 mm
Fork spring free length (min)	
Standard models	
Standard.	433.7 mm
Service limit	425.0 mm
Adventure Sports models	
Standard.	465.7 mm
Service limit	456.4 mm

* Oil level is measured from the top of the tube with the fork spring removed and the leg fully compressed.

Steering head bearings

Bearing pre-load (see text).	9.8 to 14.7 N (1.0 to 1.5 kgf; 2.2 to 3.3 lbf)

Torque settings

Clutch lever/parking brake lever assembly clamp bolts	10 Nm
Fork damper cartridge bolt.	34 Nm
Fork clamp bolts	
Top yoke	22 Nm
Bottom yoke	25 Nm
Fork top bolt.	35 Nm
Front brake master cylinder clamp bolts	10 Nm

Torque settings (continued)

Handlebar clamp bolts	32 Nm
Handlebar holder nuts	39 Nm
Levers	
Pivot screw	1 Nm
Pivot screw locknut	6 Nm
Rear shock absorber bolts/nuts	
Upper	54 Nm
Lower	44 Nm
Sidestand pivot bolt	10 Nm
Sidestand pivot bolt nut	
2016/17 models	29 Nm
2018-on models	42 Nm
Sidestand switch bolt	10 Nm
Steering head bearing adjuster nut	15 Nm
Steering stem nut	100 Nm
Suspension linkage bolts/nuts	
Linkage rod-to-frame	45 Nm
Linkage arm-to-swingarm	74 Nm
Linkage arm-to shock absorber	44 Nm
Linkage rod-to-linkage arm	55 Nm
Swingarm pivot bolt nut	80 Nm

1 General Information

1 All models have a steel semi-double cradle frame.
2 Front suspension is by a pair of fully adjustable 45 mm oil-damped telescopic forks.
3 Rear suspension is by aluminium swingarm and a fully adjustable single shock absorber via a rising-rate linkage.
4 The swingarm pivots through the frame and the engine.

2 Frame inspection and repair

1 The frame should not require attention, except to touch up any places where the paint has fallen off, unless accident damage has occurred. In most cases, fitting a new frame is the only satisfactory remedy for accident damage. A few frame specialists have the jigs and other equipment necessary for straightening frames to the required standard of accuracy, but even then there is no simple way of assessing to what extent the frame may have been over stressed.
2 After a high mileage, the frame should be examined closely for signs of cracking or splitting at the welded joints. Loose engine mounting bolts can cause ovaling or fracturing of the mounting points. Minor damage can often be repaired by specialised welding, depending on the extent and nature of the damage.
3 Remember that a frame that is out of alignment will cause handling problems. If, as the result of an accident, misalignment is suspected, it will be necessary to strip the machine completely so the frame can be thoroughly checked.

3 Footrests, brake pedal and gearchange lever

Footrests

Removal

1 To remove the rider's footrests remove the split pin and washer from the bottom of the footrest pivot pin, then withdraw the pivot pin and remove the footrest (see illustration). Note the fitting of the return spring.
2 To remove the passenger footrests, remove the split pin from the bottom of the footrest pivot pin, withdraw the pin and remove the footrest along with the detent plate, ball and spring, noting how they locate (see illustrations). Take care not to lose the ball as it is under pressure from the spring.
3 You can replace the rider's footrest rubbers with new ones – unscrew the bolt on the

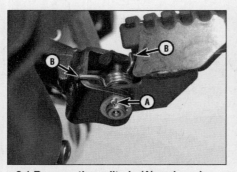

3.1 Remove the split pin (A) and washer, then draw the pivot pin out the top – note how the spring ends (B) locate

3.2a Remove the split pin (arrowed) and washer, then draw the pivot pin out the top...

3.2b ...and note the fitting of the detent plate, ball and spring (arrowed) as you remove the footrest

3.5 Note the alignment before sliding the pedal off

3.8a Straighten the ends…

3.8b …remove the split pin…

3.8c …then withdraw the clevis pin

3.9a Unhook the pedal spring…

3.9b …and the switch spring

3.10a Slacken the bolt (A), unscrew the bolt (B)…

3.10b …pivot the bracket down and remove the washer

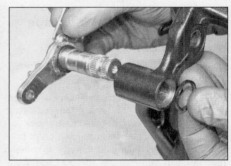

3.10c Remove the pivot and the dust seals

underside to release the rubber and its set plate, then remove the plate from the rubber.

Installation

4 Installation is the reverse of removal. Apply a small amount of grease to the pivot pin.

Brake pedal and pivot

Pedal removal

5 Note the alignment of the slit in the pedal clamp with the punch mark on the end of the shaft, then unscrew the clamp bolt and slide the pedal off **(see illustration)**.

Pedal pivot removal

6 Remove the pedal (Step 5).
7 Remove the exhaust system (see Chapter 4).
8 Straighten the ends of the split pin and withdraw it from the master cylinder pushrod clevis pin, then withdraw the clevis pin **(see illustrations)**. A new split pin must be used.
9 Unhook the brake pedal return spring from

the footrest bracket and then from the pivot arm **(see illustration)**. Unhook the brake light switch spring from the pivot arm **(see illustration)**.
10 Slacken the lower bolt securing the footrest bracket, then unscrew the upper one, pivot the bracket down and remove the washer from between it and the frame **(see illustrations)**. Withdraw the pivot and remove the dust seals **(see illustration)**.

Installation

11 Installation is the reverse of removal, noting the following:
● Clean any old grease off the pedal and pivot, then apply fresh grease. Fit the seals with the lipped side facing out of the pivot bore **(see illustration 3.10c)**.
● Make sure the spring ends are secure **(see illustrations 3.9b and a)**.
● Use a new split pin on the master cylinder pushrod clevis pin **(see illustration)**.

● Align the slit in the pedal clamp with the punch mark on the shaft **(see illustration 3.5)**.
● Check the operation of the rear brake light switch (see Chapter 1).

3.11 Use a new split pin and bend its ends round to lock it in place

3.12 Note the alignment before sliding the arm off

3.13a Unscrew the pivot bolt...

3.13b ...and remove the seals

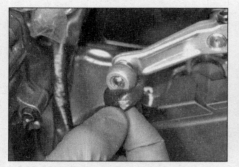

3.15a Check the boots and lubricate the joints

3.15b Linkage rod locknuts (arrowed)

● Align the slit in the linkage arm clamp with the punch mark on the gearchange shaft **(see illustration 3.12)**.
● Adjust the gear lever height as required by slackening the locknuts, turning the upper one clockwise as it has left-hand threads and screwing the linkage rod in or out of the lever and arm ball joints **(see illustration 3.15b)** – Honda specify that for the lever to be set at its standard height the length of the rod between the ball joints should be within the range 186.2 to 187.2 mm. Tighten the locknuts on completion.

4 Sidestand

Removal

1 Support the bike using an auxiliary stand.
2 Unscrew the sidestand switch bolt and displace the switch, noting how it locates **(see illustration)** – there is no need to disconnect its wiring connector or remove it completely, just let it hang from its wiring.
3 Unscrew the nut from the pivot bolt **(see illustration)**. Unscrew the pivot bolt, displace the stand and unhook the springs. Remove the pivot bolt sleeve.

Installation

4 Apply molybdenum disulphide grease to the pivot bolt and sleeve, and to the sliding surfaces on the stand. Hook the springs up and ease the stand onto the bracket **(see illustration)**. Use a screwdriver as a lever

Gearchange lever and linkage (models with standard transmission)

Removal

12 Note the alignment of the punch mark on the gearchange shaft with the slit in the linkage arm, then unscrew the linkage arm bolt and slide the arm off the shaft **(see illustration)**.
13 Unscrew the gearchange lever pivot bolt and remove the lever and linkage assembly **(see illustration)**. Remove the dust seal from each side of the lever pivot **(see illustration)**.
14 If you want to separate the lever and arm from the linkage rod measure the length of the rod between the lever and arm ball joints (including the locknuts) as this determines the height of the lever relative to the footrest. Slacken the linkage rod locknuts **(see illustration 3.15b)**, turning the upper one clockwise as it has left-hand threads, then unscrew the rod and separate it from the

lever and the arm – as the rod is reverse-threaded on the upper end it will simultaneously unscrew from both lever and arm when turned in the one direction.

Installation

15 Installation is the reverse of removal, noting the following:
● Check the condition of the rubber boots that sit over the ball joints and replace them with new ones if necessary **(see illustration 3.15a)**. Clean the ball joints and check for wear and play, and if necessary fit a new linkage arm and lever – the joints are not available separately. Pack some grease into the joints.
● Clean off all old grease from the pivot bolt and its bore in the lever and apply fresh grease. Check the condition of the seals and replace them with new ones if necessary. Fit the seals with the lipped side facing out **(see illustration 3.13b)**.

4.2 Unscrew the bolt (arrowed) and lift the switch off

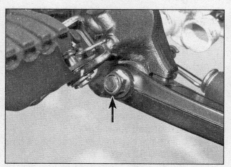

4.3 Unscrew the nut (arrowed)

4.4 Fit the springs as shown

to move the stand against spring tension to align the holes and fit the sleeve and pivot bolt. Tighten the bolt to 10 Nm. Fit the nut finger-tight, then counter-hold the bolt and tighten the nut to 29 Nm on 2016/17 models, and to 42 Nm on 2018-on models **(see illustration 4.3)**. Check the springs hold the stand securely up when not in use – an accident is almost certain to occur if the stand extends while the machine is in motion.

5 Fit the sidestand switch, locating the tab in the inner side of the switch in the hole in the stand, and on all models fitting the cut-out section in the body around the post **(see illustration 4.2)**. Clean the threads of the bolt and apply some threadlock, or use a new bolt, and tighten it to 10 Nm.

6 Check the operation of the stand and switch (see Chapter 1).

5 Handlebars and levers

Handlebar removal

Note: *The handlebars can be displaced from the top yoke without detaching any of the assemblies from them – follow Step 11 to*

unscrew the bolts and remove the clamps, then displace the assembly and rest it on some rag.

1 As a precaution, remove the fuel tank (see Chapter 4) – though not actually necessary, this will prevent the possibility of any damage in case a tool slips or you drop something.

2 Remove the mirrors (see Chapter 7).

3 Remove the handlebar weights and hand guards (see Chapter 7).

4 Disconnect the wires from the brake light switch **(see illustration)**. Unscrew the two master cylinder assembly clamp bolts, noting how the lower bolt secures the wiring clip bracket where fitted, and position the assembly clear of the handlebar, making sure no strain is placed on the hydraulic hose **(see illustration)**. Keep the master cylinder reservoir upright to prevent possible fluid leakage.

5 On models with standard transmission disconnect the wires from the clutch switch. Release the clutch cable from the clip **(see illustration 5.6b)**. Unscrew the two clutch lever assembly clamp bolts and position the assembly clear of the handlebar, making sure no strain is placed on the cable **(see illustration 5.6c)**.

6 On models with DCT disconnect the wires from the parking brake switch **(see illustration)**. Release the parking brake cable from the clip **(see illustration)**. Unscrew the

two parking brake lever assembly clamp bolts and position the assembly clear of the handlebar, making sure no strain is placed on the cable **(see illustration)**.

7 Undo the left-hand switch housing screws and detach the housing **(see illustration)**.

8 Slide the grip off the left-hand end of the handlebar – on standard models you may need to insert a suitable tool (that won't scratch the handlebar) between the grip and the top of the handlebar from the inner end, then squirt some lubricant (such as WD40) in the gap (shield your eyes from any sprayback) and allow it to work its way round by moving the tool around. If the grip has been glued on, you will probably have to slit it with a knife to remove it, which means replacing it with a new one. On the Adventure Sports model disconnect and release the heated grip wiring for more slack if necessary, and take care when removing the grip from the handlebar so as not to damage the element or the switch – do not use tools as described for the standard type grip.

9 On 2016/17 models unscrew the right-hand switch housing screws and detach the housing **(see illustration 16.6a in chapter 4)**.

10 On 2018-on models undo the right-hand switch housing screws and detach the front half of the housing, then undo the four screws and detach the rear half of the housing from

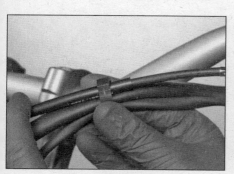

5.4a Brake light switch connectors (arrowed)

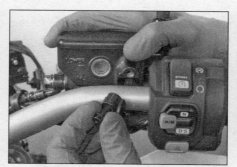

5.4b Displace the master cylinder

5.6a Parking brake switch connectors (arrowed)

5.6b Release the cable

5.6c Parking brake lever clamp bolts (arrowed)

5.7 Left-hand switch housing screws (arrowed)

5.10a Undo the two screws...

5.10b ...and detach the front of the housing...

5.10c ...then undo the four screws...

5.10d ...and detach the rear

5.10e Undo the clamp screw, noting how the clamp locates

the APS (accelerator position sensor) **(see illustrations)**. Undo the APS clamp screw **(see illustration)**.

11 Ease the blanking caps out of the handlebar clamp bolts **(see illustration)**. Unscrew the bolts, remove the clamps and slide the handlebar out of the throttle pulley, and on 2018-on models the APS **(see illustrations)**.

12 If required unscrew the handlebar holder nuts on the underside of the top yoke and remove the washers, then draw the holders up out of the yoke and remove the washers and rubbers **(see illustration)**.

Installation

13 Installation is the reverse of removal, noting the following.

● Check the condition of the handlebar holder rubbers and fit new ones if they are damaged or deformed. Leave the holder nuts finger-tight until the handlebars have been fitted to ensure correct alignment, then tighten the holder nuts to 39 Nm.

● On 2016/17 models slide the throttle twistgrip onto the handlebar before fitting the handlebar onto the yoke.

● On 2018-on models slide the APS and throttle twistgrip onto the handlebar before fitting the handlebar onto the yoke **(see illustration 5.11c)**. Make sure the APS clamp pin locates in the hole in the handlebar **(see illustration 5.10e)**.

● Align the marks on the back of the handlebar with the outer sides of the clamp/holder mating surfaces **(see illustration 5.13a)**. Tighten the handlebar

5.11a Remove the blanking caps

5.11b Handlebar clamp bolts (arrowed)

5.11c Slide the twistgrip and APS off, noting how they seat together

5.12 Handlebar holder nut (arrowed)

5.13a Align the clamp mating surfaces with the mark (arrowed)

5.13b Align the clamp mating surfaces with the mark (arrowed)

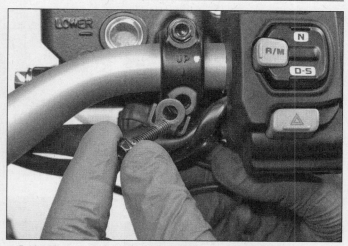

5.13c Make sure the bracket is above the wiring and correctly located

clamp bolts to 32 Nm, tightening the front bolts first, then the rear, so that the gap is at the back.

● To fit the grip onto the left handlebar on standard models, clean the handlebar and apply Honda Bond A or Pro Honda handgrip cement or equivalent to the handlebar and leave for 3 to 5 minutes, then slide the grip on and up against the handlebar switch housing and rotate it when in place to evenly distribute the glue. Allow the glue to dry for at least one hour before riding the bike.

● To fit the grip onto the left handlebar on the Adventure Sports model, clean the handlebar and apply Honda Bond A or Pro Honda handgrip cement or equivalent to the first 10 cm of the handlebar, then spray the handlebar and inside the grip with isopropyl alcohol. Align the bottom of the switch so it is 4 mm below the bottom of the dimmer switch and ease the grip on and up against the handlebar switch housing, taking care not to twist or crease

it, and avoiding putting pressure on the switch, and do not tap on its end – if it gets stuck spray some more isopropy alcohol on the exposed part of the handlebar. Allow the glue to dry for at least one hour before riding the bike, and do not use the heater higher than level 2 for one week.

● Fit the front brake master cylinder and clutch lever/parking brake lever assembly clamps with the UP mark facing up and with the clamp mating surfaces aligned with the mark on the top of the handlebar (see illustration 5.13b). Tighten the clamp bolts to 10 Nm, tightening the top bolt first, and where fitted not forgetting to secure the wiring clip bracket with the lower bolt for the brake master cylinder clamp (see illustration 5.13c).

● Locate the pin in the left-hand switch housing in its hole in the handlebar. Tighten the upper housing screw first, then the lower.

● On 2016/17 models locate the pin in the right-hand switch housing in its hole in the

handlebar and seat the housing correctly around the twistgrip. Tighten the upper housing screw first, then the lower.

● On 2018-on models make sure the twistgrip is correctly aligned and engaged with the APS before fitting the switch housing halves (see illustrations 5.10d, c, b and a). Tighten the upper screw in the front half of the housing first, then the lower.

● Do not forget to reconnect the front brake light switch and clutch/parking brake switch wiring connectors (see illustrations 5.4a and 5.6a).

● Check the operation of the throttle and clutch, and check and adjust cable freeplay as required according to model (see Chapter 1).

Levers

14 To remove the front brake lever, undo the lever pivot bolt locknut and remove the collar, noting how it locates in the hand guard bracket, then undo the pivot bolt and remove the lever (see illustrations).

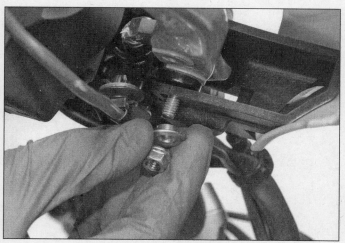

5.14a Unscrew the locknut on the underside and remove the collar...

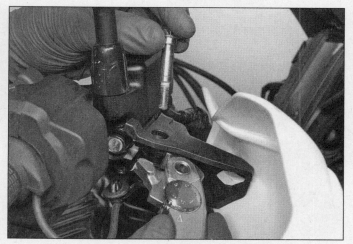

5.14b ...then unscrew the bolt and remove the lever

5.15a Loosen the lockring (arrowed) and thread the adjuster in

5.15b Fully slacken the nut (arrowed)…

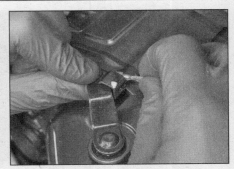

5.15c …then free the cable end

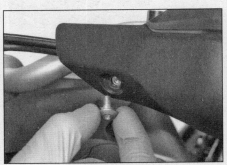

5.15d Undo the screw…

5.15e …and pivot the hand guard down

5.15f Unscrew the locknut on the underside and remove the collar…

15 On models with standard transmission, to remove the clutch lever you need maximum freeplay in the cable – loosen the cable adjuster lockring then thread the adjuster fully into the bracket, then fully slacken the front nut securing the cable in the bracket on the crankcase and detach the cable end from the release arm **(see illustrations)**. Undo the hand guard screw, release the guard from the bracket and pivot it down **(see illustrations)** – if it doesn't pivot easily slacken the end-weight bolt slightly. Undo the lever pivot bolt locknut and remove the collar, noting how it locates in the hand guard bracket, then undo the pivot bolt and remove the bracket, then remove the lever, detaching the cable end as you do **(see illustrations)**.

16 On models with DCT, to remove the parking brake lever you need freeplay in the cable – loosen the cable adjuster lockring then thread the adjuster fully into the bracket **(see illustration 5.15a)**, then remove the caliper cover, slacken the pushrod locknut

5.15g …then unscrew the bolt and remove the hand guard bracket…

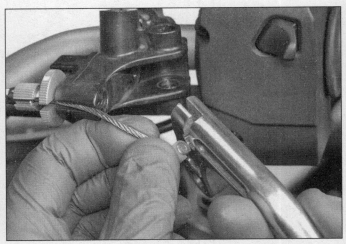

5.15h …displace the lever and release the cable from it

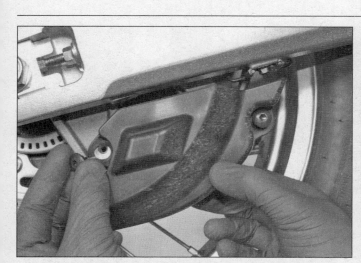

5.16a Undo the screws and remove the cover

5.16b Slacken the nut and turn the pushrod out

and turn the pushrod anti-clockwise **(see illustrations)**. Undo the hand guard screw, release the guard from the bracket and pivot it down **(see illustrations 5.15d and e)** – if it doesn't pivot easily slacken the end-weight bolt slightly. Release the cable from the adjuster in the lever bracket **(see illustration)**. Undo the lever pivot bolt locknut and remove the collar, noting how it locates in the hand

guard bracket, then undo the pivot bolt and remove the hand guard bracket and then the lever, detaching the cable end as you do **(see illustrations)**.

17 Installation is the reverse of removal. Apply silicone grease to the contact area between the front brake master cylinder pushrod tip and the brake lever and to the pivot screw shaft. Apply multi-purpose grease

to the clutch lever/parking brake lever pivot screw shaft, cable end, and the contact areas between the lever and its bracket. Tighten each pivot screw lightly, then hold it and tighten the locknut. Make sure the lug on the hand guard locates in its hole in the bracket **(see illustration)**. Adjust clutch/parking brake cable cable freeplay (see Chapter 1).

5.16c Align the slots and slip the cable out

5.16d Unscrew the locknut on the underside and remove the collar...

5.16e ...then unscrew the bolt and remove the hand guard bracket...

5.16f ...displace the lever...

5.16g ...and release the cable from it

5.17 Make sure the hand guard locates correctly

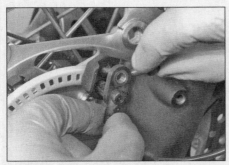

6.5 Displace the sensor from the fork

6.6 Fork clamp bolts (arrowed)

6.7 Slacken the top bolt

6.8a Slacken the bottom clamp bolts (arrowed)…

6.8b …and draw the fork down and out of the yokes

6.10 Set the top of the fork tube level with the top yoke

6 Fork removal and installation

Removal

1 For best access and to avoid the possibility of damage remove the fairing side panels (see Chapter 7).
2 Remove the front mudguard (see Chapter 7).
3 Remove the front wheel (see Chapter 6). Tie the front brake calipers back so they are out of the way.
4 Note the routing of all cables, hoses and wiring around the forks.
5 Unscrew the wheel speed sensor bolt and displace the sensor **(see illustration)**.
6 Slacken the fork clamp bolts in the top yoke **(see illustration)**.
7 If the fork oil is being changed, or if the fork is to be disassembled, stick a single layer of insulating or masking tape around the fork top bolt to protect its finish, then slacken the bolt **(see illustration)**.
8 Slacken the fork clamp bolts in the bottom yoke, and remove the fork by twisting it and pulling it downwards **(see illustrations)**.

> **HAYNES HINT** *If the fork legs are seized in the yokes, spray the area with penetrating oil and allow time for it to soak in before trying again.*

Installation

9 Remove all traces of corrosion from the fork tube and the yokes. As you fit each fork make sure all cables, hoses and wiring are routed on the correct side of the fork.
10 Slide the fork up through the bottom yoke and into the top yoke, and set it so the top of the tube (not the top bolt) is level with the upper surface of the yoke, then tighten the fork clamp bolts in the bottom yoke to 25 Nm **(see illustration)**.
11 If the fork oil was changed or if the fork has been dismantled, tighten the fork top bolt to 35 Nm **(see illustration 6.7)**.
12 Now tighten the fork clamp bolts in the top yoke to 22 Nm **(see illustration 6.6)**.
13 Fit the wheel speed sensor **(see illustration 6.5)**.
14 Install the front wheel (see Chapter 6) and the front mudguard (see Chapter 7).
15 Install the fairing side panels (see Chapter 7).
16 Check the operation of the front forks and brakes before taking the machine out on the road.

7 Fork oil change

Special tool: *Either the Honda stopper plate or a large disc washer with a slot cut in it is required for this procedure – see Step 5 for details.*

1 After a high mileage the fork oil will deteriorate and its damping and lubrication qualities will be impaired. Always change the oil in both fork legs.
2 Refer to Section 14 and set the spring pre-load and rebound damping to their minimum settings, counting the number of turns so they can be reset to the same setting later.
3 Remove the fork (Section 6) – make sure you loosen the top bolt while the leg is still clamped in the bottom yoke.
4 Unscrew the fork top bolt from the top of the outer tube **(see illustration)**. The bolt will remain on the damper rod, held by the locknut. Slide the outer tube down gently until it seats on the bottom.
5 Next you need either the Honda stopper plate (Pt. No. 070MF-MBZC130 in Europe or

7.4 Thread the top bolt out of the tube

7.5 Pull the spacer down and slip the washer under the nut

7.6a Hold the locknut and loosen the top bolt...

7.6b ...then unscrew the top bolt and draw the adjuster rod out...

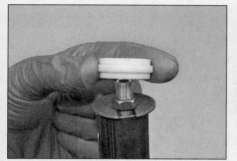

7.6c ...and remove the seat

7.7a Remove the slotted washer...

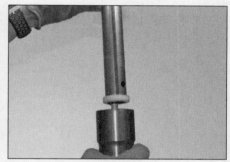

7.7b ...and the spacer

07AMB-KZ3A100 in the US), or an equivalent made from a large disc washer with a slot cut in it so it fits around the damper rod and seats on top of the spacer **(see illustration 7.7a)**. With the aid of an assistant, pull up on the fork top bolt and the spacer seat just below it, then pull the spacer down to compress the spring and expose the locknut on the damper rod – insert the stopper plate or slotted washer under the locknut and on top of the spacer, keeping the spacer seat above it **(see illustration)**. Carefully release the pressure on the spacer and allow the plate or slotted washer to rest against the underside of the locknut under spring pressure.

6 Counter-hold the locknut using one spanner and loosen the top bolt assembly using another spanner on the spring pre-load adjuster, then thread the top bolt off and draw the damping adjuster rod out **(see illustrations)**. Remove the spacer seat **(see illustration)**.

7 Push down on the spacer and remove the plate or slotted washer, then carefully allow the spring to relax **(see illustration)**. Remove the spacer **(see illustration)**.

8 Invert the fork leg over an oil drain tray and tip the oil out, collecting the spring as it slides out **(see illustration)**. Pump the fork and damper rod several times to expel as much fork oil as possible **(see illustration)**. Support the fork upside down in the container for a while to allow as much oil as possible to drain, then pump the fork and rod again. If the fork oil contains metal particles inspect the fork

7.8a Drain the oil and remove the spring

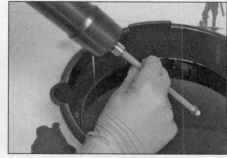

7.8b Pump the damper rod

bushes for wear (see Section 8). Wipe any excess oil off the spring and spacer.

9 Stand the fork upright. Slowly pour in the specified quantity of the specified grade of fork oil **(see illustration)**. Draw the outer tube

7.9a Add the oil slowly to prevent air bubbles

fully up, then cover the top with your hand and slowly push it down **(see illustration)**. Remove your hand and draw it up, and repeat two or three times. Now pump the damper rod slowly until oil comes out of the hole in the

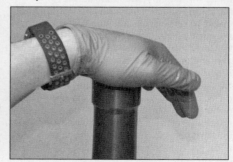

7.9b Bleed the air from the oil as described...

7.9c ...then pump the rod until oil comes out the hole

7.9d Measure the distance from the top of the tube to the oil

7.10a Set the locknut 10.5 mm from the top

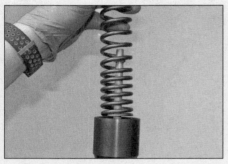

7.10b The end with the close wound coils goes in first

7.11 Fit the washer under the nut

7.13 Check and lubricate the O-ring (arrowed), then thread the top bolt into the tube

rod, noting that it may take quite a few pumps **(see illustration)**. Slide the inner tube down gently until it seats on the bottom, and leave to stand for five minutes. After this measure the oil level from the top of the tube **(see illustration)**. Add or subtract oil until it is at the level given in the Specifications at the beginning of the Chapter for your model.

10 Position the locknut so there is 10.5 mm of thread exposed above it **(see illustration)**. Fit the spring with the closer wound coils at the bottom **(see illustration)**. Pull the damper rod out as far as possible, then fit the spacer with the coloured rim seat at the bottom **(see illustration 7.7b)**.

11 Keeping the damper rod extended pull the spacer down to compress the spring, then insert the stopper plate or slotted washer under the locknut **(see illustration)**.

12 Fit the spacer seat **(see illustration 7.6c)**. Insert the damping adjuster rod and thread the top bolt onto the damper rod **(see illustration 7.6b)**. Counter-hold the locknut and tighten the top bolt assembly securely against it using a spanner on the pre-load adjuster as before **(see illustration 7.6a)**. Press down on the spacer to compress the spring and remove the plate or slotted washer, then carefully release the spring pressure **(see illustration 7.5)**. Check that the spacer seat is correctly located between the spacer and the top bolt.

13 Check the top bolt O-ring and fit a new one if it is damaged or deformed **(see**

illustration). Smear some fork oil onto the O-ring. Extend the outer tube and thread the top bolt into it, making sure it does not cross-thread, and tighten it as much as possible holding the inner tube by hand. Tighten the top bolt to the specified torque setting when the fork has been installed in the bike and is held in the bottom yoke, but before the top yoke clamp bolt is tightened.

14 Install the fork (see Section 6). Reset the spring pre-load and rebound damping adjusters as noted or required (see Section 14).

8 Fork overhaul

Disassembly

Special tool: *A fork seal driver is necessary for this procedure – see Step 20 for details.*

1 Refer to Section 14 and set the spring pre-load and rebound damping to their minimum settings, counting the number of turns so they can be reset to the same setting later.

2 Remove the fork (Section 6) – make sure you loosen the top bolt while the leg is still clamped in the bottom yoke.

3 Always dismantle the fork legs separately to avoid interchanging parts and thus causing an

accelerated rate of wear. Store all components in separate, clearly marked containers.

4 Lay the fork flat on the bench with the caliper mounting lugs to the left. Hold the fork down and slacken the damper cartridge bolt in the base of the fork **(see illustration)**. If the damper cartridge rotates inside the fork whilst attempting to unscrew the bolt, compress the fork so that the spring exerts pressure on the cartridge body whilst the bolt is unscrewed. Alternatively, if available use an air wrench.

5 Refer to Section 7, Steps 4 to 8 and drain the oil from the fork.

6 Remove the damper cartridge bolt and its sealing washer from the bottom of the fork **(see illustration 8.24c)**. A new sealing washer must be used on reassembly.

7 Withdraw the damper cartridge from inside the fork tube, then tip the cartridge seat out

8.4 Slacken the damper cartridge bolt

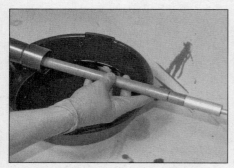

8.7a Withdraw the damper cartridge…

8.7b …and tip the seat out

8.8 Prise out the dust seal using a
flat-bladed screwdriver

(see illustrations). Pump the damper a few times over the oil drain tray to expel any residual oil.

8 Carefully prise out the dust seal from the bottom of the outer tube (see illustration).

9 Carefully prise out the oil seal retaining ring, taking care not to scratch the surface of the inner tube (see illustration).

10 To separate the inner and outer tubes it is necessary to displace the bottom bush and oil seal from the bottom of the outer tube. The top bush on the inner tube will not pass through the bottom bush, and this can be used to good effect. Grasp the inner tube in one hand and the outer tube in the other and compress them slightly, then pull them apart so that the top bush strikes the bottom bush (see illustration). Repeat this operation until the bottom bush and seal are tapped out (see illustration).

11 To remove the top bush carefully lever its ends apart using a screwdriver and slide it out of its recess (see illustration). Slide the bottom bush, the oil seal washer, the oil seal, the retaining ring and the dust seal off the inner tube, noting which way up they fit. A new oil seal and dust seal must be used, and it is good practice to also fit new bushes as they are not expensive. Note that Honda specify to fit a new top bush if it is removed from its recess.

Inspection

12 Clean all parts in solvent and blow them dry with compressed air, if available.

13 Check the fork inner tube for score marks, dents, pitting, scratches, flaking of its surface and excessive or abnormal wear. Fit a new tube if any are found. Check the inner tube for runout using V-blocks and a dial gauge.

If the inner tube is bent, it should not be straightened – fit a new one.

14 Check the fork outer tube for cracks. Check the fork seal seat and housing for nicks, gouges and scratches. If damage is evident, leaks will occur. Also check the oil seal washer for damage or distortion and fit a new one if necessary.

15 Check the spring for cracks and other damage. Measure the spring free length and compare the measurement to the figure given in the Specifications at the beginning of the Chapter (see illustration). If it has sagged below the service limit, fit new springs in both forks. Do not fit only one new spring.

16 Examine the working surfaces of the two bushes (i.e. the inner surface of the bottom bush and the outer surface of the top bush) (see illustration). If the grey Teflon outer surface has been worn away to reveal the copper inner surface over more than 75% of

8.9 Prise out the retaining ring using a
flat-bladed screwdriver

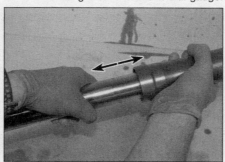

8.10a To separate the tubes pull them
apart firmly several times…

8.10b …the slide-hammer effect will
displace the oil seal, washer and top bush

8.11 Carefully lever the ends apart to
expand it over the rim of its recess, then
side the other components off

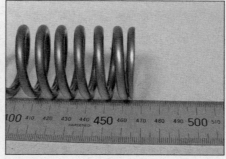

8.15 Measure the free length of the spring

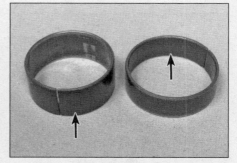

8.16 Check the working surface (arrowed)
of each bush for wear

8.18a Use insulating tape to cover sharp edges…

8.18b …then slide the components over it in the order given and with the seals the correct way round as shown

8.18c Fit the top bush into its recess

the surface area, or if the bushes are scored or badly scuffed, fit new ones. Note that it is a good idea to fit new bushes as a matter of course as part of a fork overhaul.

17 Check the damper cartridge and rod for damage and wear. Hold the body of the cartridge and pump the rod in and out. If any wear or damage is found, or if the rod does not move smoothly in the damper, fit a new one.

Reassembly

18 Wrap some thin insulating tape over the edges of the recess for the top bush in the inner tube to protect the seal lips **(see illustration)**. Smear some oil over the tape, and also over the oil seal lips and the surfaces of the bottom bush. Slide the new dust seal, retaining ring, new oil seal, oil seal washer and bottom bush onto the inner tube, making sure they are the correct way round **(see illustration)**. Remove the tape, then lubricate the surfaces of the new top bush and fit it into its recess in the top of the inner tube **(see illustration)**.

19 Slide the inner tube fully into the outer tube **(see illustration)**. Support the fork upside down, and have an assistant hold the inner tube and the components on it up. Slide the bottom bush into the bottom of the outer tube and push it into the top of its recess, then slide the washer onto the bush **(see illustration)**.

20 Using either the special service tool (part No. 07KMD-KZ30100) or after-market equivalent fork seal driver kit suitable for a 45 mm fork, start to drive the bottom bush into its recess, as far as it will go to the limit of the tool's reach **(see illustrations)**. Lift the washer to check the bush is going in square, then seat the washer back on the bush.

21 Slide the oil seal down and push it into the top of the outer tube, then drive it and the bush fully in using the seal driver until the retaining clip groove is visible **(see illustrations)**.

22 Fit the retaining ring, making sure it

8.19a Slide the inner tube into the outer tube

8.19b Slide the bush down and into the outer tube, and seat the washer on it

8.20a Fit the driver around the fork and onto the washer…

8.20b …then fit the slide hammer and drive the bush into its recess until the driver comes up against the rim of the outer tube

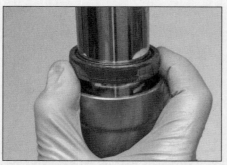

8.21a Slide the seal down and into the outer tube

8.21b Fit the tools and drive the seal and bush in until they seat…

8.21c …and the retaining ring groove (arrowed) is fully exposed

8.22 Fit the retaining ring in its groove...

8.23 ...then press the dust seal in

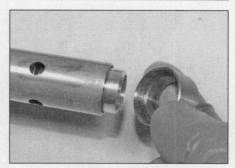

8.24a Fit the seat...

8.24b ...and insert the damper cartridge

8.24c Fit the bolt using a new sealing washer...

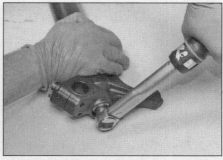

8.24d ...and tighten to the specified torque

is correctly located in its groove **(see illustration)**.

23 Press the dust seal into the top of the outer tube **(see illustration)**.

24 Lay the fork flat on the bench with the caliper mounting lugs to the right. Fit the seat onto the bottom of the damper cartridge **(see illustration)**. Slide the damper fully into the fork **(see illustration)**. Fit a new sealing washer onto the cartridge bolt, fit the bolt into the bottom of the fork and thread it into the cartridge, and tighten it to 34 Nm **(see illustrations)**. If the cartridge rotates inside the tube as you tighten the bolt, wait until the fork is fully reassembled and tighten it then (the pressure of the spring on the cartridge will prevent it from turning).

25 Refer to Section 7, Steps 9 to 13 and fill the fork with oil and finish reassembly.

26 If necessary now fully tighten the damper cartridge bolt to 34 Nm **(see illustration 8.24d)**.

27 Install the fork (see Section 6). Reset the spring pre-load and rebound damping adjusters as noted or required (see Section 14).

9 Steering stem

Special tool: *Either the Honda special tool (part No. 07916-KA50100), equivalent peg*

spanner, or a suitably sized C-spanner is necessary for this procedure.

Removal

1 Remove the fuel tank, and for best access the air filter housing (see Chapter 4). Remove the windshield, and for best access the front cover, the inner panel covers and the inner panels (see Chapter 7).

2 Release the front brake hose from its guide next to the ignition switch, and displace the brake hose guide from the bottom yoke **(see illustrations)**.

3 Remove the front forks (Section 6) – fully unscrew the right-hand fork clamp bolts in the top yoke to release the wiring guide bracket, rather than just slackening them **(see illustration)**.

9.2a Release the grommet on the hose from the guide...

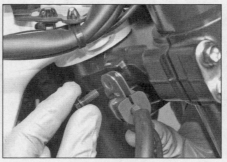

9.2b ...and displace the guide from the bottom yoke

9.3 Remove the right-hand fork clamp bolts to release the bracket

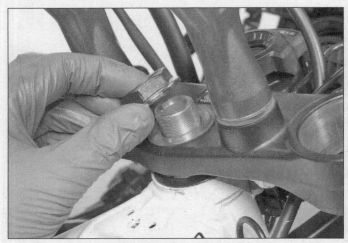

9.4a Unscrew the steering stem nut...

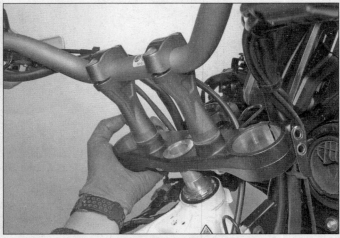

9.4b ...lift the top yoke assembly off...

9.4c ...and secure it clear as shown

4 Unscrew the steering stem nut **(see illustration)**. Lift the top yoke/handlebar assembly up off the steering stem and cable-tie it to the windshield bracket, using rag to protect the yoke and other components **(see illustrations)**.

5 If the peg spanner mentioned above is not available, make an alignment mark between the adjuster nut and the frame – this can serve as a rough guide for the tightness of the adjuster nut on installation. As you unscrew the nut count the number of turns.

6 Support the bottom yoke and unscrew the adjuster nut using the peg-spanner, or a C-spanner located in one of the notches **(see illustration)**. Gently lower the bottom yoke and steering stem out of the frame **(see illustration)**.

7 Remove the grease seal and the inner race and bearing from the top of the steering

9.6a Unscrewing the nut using a C-spanner

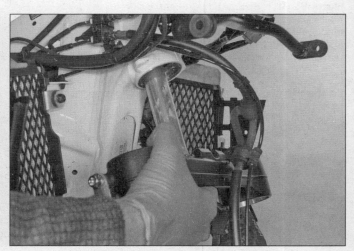

9.6b Remove the bottom yoke/steering stem

9.7a Remove the seal...

9.7b ...and the inner race and upper bearing from the head...

9.7c ...and the lower bearing from the stem

9.11a Hold the upper bearing components in place as you lift the stem up to prevent dislodging them

9.11b Thread the adjuster nut on and tighten it finger-tight

head **(see illustrations)**. Remove the bearing from the base of the steering stem **(see illustration)**.

8 Remove all traces of old grease from the bearings and races and check them for wear or damage as described in Section 10. Do not attempt to remove the races from the steering head or the steering stem unless they are to be replaced with new ones.

Installation

9 Smear a liberal quantity of Urea based multi-purpose grease with EP2 rating onto the bearing races, and work some grease well into both the upper and lower bearings. Also smear the grease seal lip, using a new seal if necessary, and the adjuster nut threads.

10 Fit the lower bearing onto the steering stem **(see illustration 9.7c)**. Fit the upper bearing and its inner race into the top of the steering head **(see illustration 9.7b)**. Fit the grease seal **(see illustration 9.7a)**.

11 Fit the steering stem/bottom yoke up into the head and support it then thread the adjuster nut on **(see illustrations)**.

12 If you have the Honda or equivalent peg spanner tighten the adjuster nut to 15 Nm, then turn the steering from lock-to-lock five

times, then reapply the same torque setting to the nut. Check that the steering stem moves smoothly (though it may feel a bit tight, but this is normal as the weight of the forks and wheel is not influencing the feel) from lock-to-lock – note that it is best to check and if necessary reset the bearing adjustment as described in Chapter 1 after the forks and front wheel and all other components have been installed.

13 If you are using a C-spanner, tighten the nut the number of turns recorded on removal using a C-spanner until the marks align **(see illustration)**. Turn the steering from lock-to-lock five times, then slacken the nut slightly, and tighten it again until the marks align. Check that the steering stem moves smoothly (though it may feel a bit tight, but this is normal as the weight of the forks and wheel is not influencing the feel) from lock-to-lock. Install the forks and wheel, then refer to the procedure in Chapter 1 and check the feel of the bearings as described, and adjust if necessary.
Caution: Take great care not to apply excessive pressure because this will cause premature failure of the bearings.
14 Fit the top yoke/handlebar assembly onto the steering stem **(see illustration 9.4b)**.

Fit the steering stem nut and tighten it nut finger-tight **(see illustration 9.4a)**. Temporarily install one of the forks to align the top and bottom yokes, and secure it by tightening the bottom yoke clamp bolts only. Now tighten the steering stem nut to 100 Nm.

15 Install the remaining components in a reverse of the removal procedure, referring to the relevant Sections or Chapters.

16 Carry out a final check of the steering head bearing freeplay as described in Chapter 1, and if necessary re-adjust.

9.13 Tightening the nut using a C-spanner

10 Steering head bearings

10.3a Check the outer races in the top...

10.3b ...and bottom of the steering head

Inspection

1 Remove the steering stem (Section 9).

2 Remove all traces of old grease from the bearings and races and check them for wear or damage.

3 The outer races in the top and bottom of the steering head should be polished and free from indentations **(see illustrations)**. Inspect the bearing balls for signs of wear, damage or discoloration, and examine the ball cage for signs of cracks or splits. If there are any signs of wear on any of the above components both upper and lower bearing assemblies must be replaced with a new set. Only remove the outer races in the steering head and the lower bearing inner race on the steering stem if they need to be replaced with new ones – do not re-use them once they have been removed.

Replacement

4 The outer races are an interference fit in the steering head, and to remove then you need an expanding knife-edge puller with a slide-hammer attachment: to remove the upper race insert the puller through the race from the top, then expand it so it seats against the underside of the race, then attach the slide-hammer and use it to knock the race out **(see illustrations)**; to remove the lower race insert the puller through the race from the underside, then expand it so it seats against the top of the race, then attach the slide-hammer and use it to knock the race out **(see illustrations)**.

5 Press the new outer races into the

10.4a Seat and lock the puller under the rim of the upper race...

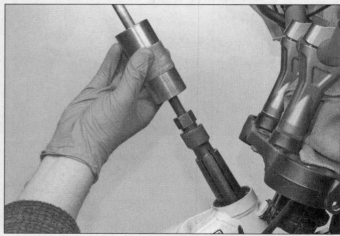

10.4b ...and use the slide-hammer to jar it out

10.4c Seat and lock the puller on top of the rim of the lower race...

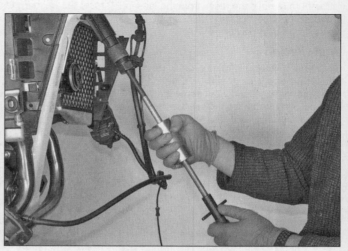

10.4d ...and use the slide-hammer to jar it out

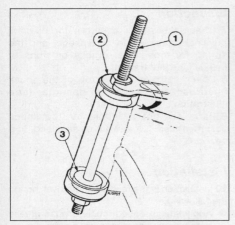

10.5 Drawbolt arrangement for fitting steering stem bearing races

1 Long bolt or threaded bar
2 Thick washer
3 Guide for lower race

head using a drawbolt arrangement **(see illustration)**, or drive them in using a large diameter tubular drift. Make sure the drawbolt washer or drift (as applicable) bears only on the outer edge of the race and does not contact the working surface.

HAYNES HiNT *Installation of new bearing outer races is made much easier if the races are left in the freezer for a while. This causes them to contract slightly making them a looser fit. Alternatively, use a freeze spray.*

6 Only remove the lower bearing inner race from the steering stem if a new one is being fitted. To remove the race, first thread the steering stem nut onto the top then position the yoke on its front for stability – the nut will protect the threads from the transmitted force of the impact of the chisel. Tap under the rim of the seal that sits under the race using a cold chisel or a punch, working around the rim so it is driven off square **(see illustration)**. Using a hot air gun with a narrow nozzle to expand the race should help it to release, but make

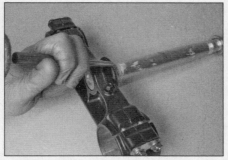

10.6a Remove the lower bearing race using a cold chisel or a punch...

sure you are not heating the stem as well. If the race is firmly in place it will be necessary to use a puller, or you can carefully cut it off using a Dremel or an angle grinder, but make sure you don't cut anything other than the race **(see illustration)**. Take the steering stem to a Honda dealer if required.

7 Remove the dust seal and replace it with a new one. Smear the new one with grease.

8 Fit the new seal and lower race onto the steering stem. Drive the new race into position using a length of tubing with an internal diameter slightly larger than the steering stem, but make sure it does not contact the working surface of the race **(see illustration)** – heating the race and cooling the steering stem will make installation easier, or use an hydraulic press if necessary.

9 Install the steering stem (Section 9).

11 Rear shock absorber

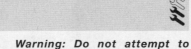

⚠️ *Warning: Do not attempt to disassemble the shock absorber in the home workshop. It is nitrogen-charged under high pressure. Improper disassembly could result in serious injury.*

Removal

1 Support the motorcycle on an auxiliary stand or stands so that no weight is transmitted through any part of the rear suspension (see

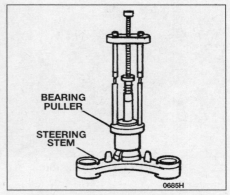

10.6b ...or using a puller if necessary

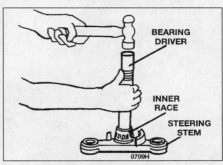

10.8 Drive the new inner race on using a suitable bearing driver or a length of pipe that bears only against the inner rim and not the bearing surface

illustration 12.1a)- both stands can be placed under the footrest brackets, unless you are removing the suspension linkage rods as well in which case place the stands as described in Section 12. Tie the front brake lever to the handlebar so the bike can't roll forward **(see illustration 12.1b)**.

2 Remove the regulator/rectifier (see Chapter 8).

3 Detach the linkage rod from the linkage arm and swing the rod down **(see illustrations)**.

4 Detach the bottom of the shock absorber from the linkage arm **(see illustration)**.

5 Remove the swingarm (Section 13) – you can leave the linkage arm connected to it.

6 Unscrew the nut from the upper mounting bolt, then support the shock absorber, withdraw the bolt and remove the shock **(see illustration)**.

11.3 Unscrew the nut, withdraw the bolt and swing the rod down

11.4 Unscrew the nut, withdraw the bolt and swing the arm clear of the shock

11.6 Unscrew the nut, withdraw the bolt and remove the shock absorber

11.7 Check for oil on the rod

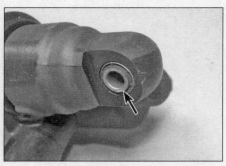

11.8 Check the bush (arrowed)

Inspection

7 Check the shock absorber for obvious physical damage and oil leakage, and the spring for looseness, cracks or signs of fatigue **(see illustration)**.

8 Check the bush in the top of the shock absorber for wear or damage **(see illustration)**.

9 Parts are not available for the shock absorber itself. If it is worn or damaged, fit a new one.

Installation

10 Installation is the reverse of removal, noting the following:

● Apply lithium-based multi-purpose grease to the shock absorber pivot points.
● Insert all bolts from the left.
● Tighten the shock absorber upper mounting bolt/nut to 54 Nm, the lower mounting bolt/nut to 44 Nm, and the linkage rod-to-arm bolt/nut to 55 Nm.

12 Rear suspension linkage

Removal

1 Support the motorcycle on an auxiliary stand or stands so that no weight is transmitted through any part of the rear suspension **(see illustration)**. To withdraw the linkage rods-to-frame bolt the left-hand footrest/sidestand assembly must be removed, so make sure any auxiliary stand is clear of the footrest/sidestand bracket. Tie the front brake lever to the handlebar so the bike can't roll forward **(see illustration)**.

2 Remove the left-hand footrest/sidestand assembly **(see illustration)**.

12.1a Axle stands are a good way of supporting the bike – the right-hand one can go under the footrest bracket but the left-hand one must be under the frame. Note the blocks of wood to prevent metal-to-metal contact

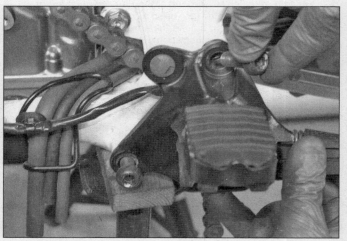

12.1b After-market tool for holding the front brake lever on

12.2 Unscrew the two bolts and remove the footrest/stand assembly

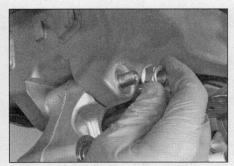

12.5a Unscrew the nut...

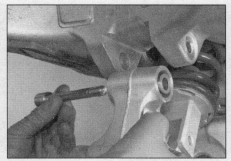

12.5b ...withdraw the bolt and remove the arm

12.6a Unscrew the nut...

12.6b ...withdraw the bolt and remove the rod

12.7a Withdraw the sleeves from the arm and rod...

12.7b ...noting which fits where according to length

3 Detach the linkage rod from the linkage arm and swing the rod down **(see illustration 11.3)**.

4 Detach the bottom of the shock absorber from the linkage arm **(see illustration 11.4)**.

5 Detach the linkage arm from the swingarm **(see illustrations)**.

6 Detach the linkage rod from the frame **(see illustrations)**.

Inspection

7 Withdraw the sleeves from the linkage arm and rod **(see illustrations)**.

8 Thoroughly clean all components, removing all traces of dirt, corrosion and grease.

9 Check the linkage arm and rod and their mounts on the swingarm, shock absorber and frame, looking for obvious signs of wear such as heavy scoring, or for damage such as cracks or distortion. Replace worn or damaged components with new ones as required.

10 Check the condition of the grease seals and bearings – note that in the linkage arm the grease seals for the shock absorber and swingarm mounts are the standard type, but for the linkage rod mount, and in the linkage rod, they are part of the bearing. Fit the sleeves back in and check for play between them and the bearings. Refer to *Tools and Workshop Tips* in the Reference section for more information on bearings. Inspect all components closely, looking for obvious signs of wear such as heavy scoring, or for damage such as cracks or distortion. Replace worn

or damaged components with new ones as required.

11 If required, lever out the grease seals from the shock absorber and swingarm mounts in the linkage arm using a seal hook or screwdriver **(see illustration)**. New ones must be used.

12 To remove the bearing from the shock absorber mount drive it out of the bore using a suitable driver or socket or draw it out using a drawbolt (one can be made up as described in *Tools and Workshop Tips* in the Reference section), or push it out using a hydraulic press. To remove the bearing from each side of the swingarm and linkage rod mounts in the linkage arm, and from the linkage rod, use an internal expanding puller with slide hammer attachment. Do not re-use the bearings after removing them.

13 The new bearings must be pressed or drawn into their bores, not driven in. When

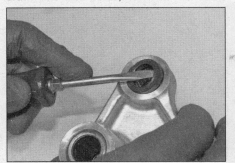

12.11 Lever the seals out

fitting the new bearings into the linkage rod mount in the linkage arm, and into the linkage rod, make sure the sealed end faces out and set them so they sit flush with the arm or rod. When fitting the new bearing into the shock absorber mount make sure it is as central as possible in the bore – the recess between each outer end and the rim of the bore must be 5.8 to 6.2 mm, otherwise one seal will be recessed and the other will sit proud. When fitting the new bearings into the swingarm mount the recess between each outer end and the rim of the bore must be 5.3 to 5.7 mm.

14 Lubricate the needle bearings, sleeves and seals with molybdenum disulphide grease.

15 Press the new seals squarely into place in the shock absorber and swingarm mounts in the linkage arm, with the marked flat side facing out **(see illustration)**. Fit the sleeves **(see illustrations 12.7b and a)**.

12.15 Press the new seals in using your fingers

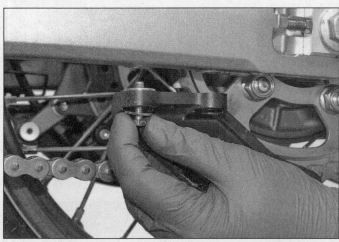

13.2 Unscrew the two bolts, noting the washers, and remove the guard

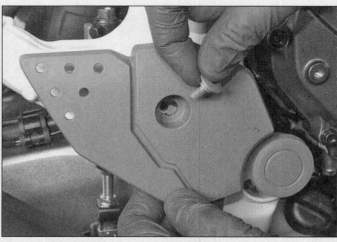

13.4 Undo the screw to release each guard

Installation

16 Installation is the reverse of removal, noting the following:

- Apply molybdenum disulphide grease to the pivot points.
- Fit the linkage rod with the UP mark side facing up (see illustration 12.6b).
- Insert all bolts from the left.
- Tighten the linkage rod-to-frame bolt/nut to 45 Nm, the linkage arm-to-swingarm bolt/nut to 74 Nm, the shock absorber lower mounting bolt/nut to 44 Nm, and the linkage rod-to-arm bolt/nut to 55 Nm.

13 Swingarm

Removal

1 Support the motorcycle on an auxiliary stand or stands so that no weight is transmitted through any part of the rear suspension (see illustration 12.1a)- both stands can be placed under the footrest brackets, unless you are removing the suspension linkage rods as well in which case place the stands as described in Section 12. Tie the front brake lever to the handlebar so the bike can't roll forward (see illustration 12.1b).

2 Remove the front sprocket cover (see Chapter 6). Remove the lower chain guard (see illustration).

3 Remove the rear wheel (see Chapter 6).

4 Remove the heel guard from each side of the frame (see illustration).

5 Unscrew the bolts and remove the chain guard (see illustration).

6 Release the brake hose and wheel speed sensor wiring, and the parking brake cable on models with DCT, from the swingarm (see illustrations). Displace the brake caliper assembly from the swingarm and tie it up out of the way.

7 Detach the suspension linkage arm from the swingarm (see illustrations 12.5a and b).

8 Unscrew the nut from the right-hand end of the swingarm pivot bolt nut, holding the pivot bolt head if it turns (see illustration).

9 Withdraw the swingarm pivot bolt and manoeuvre the swingarm back out of the frame (see illustration).

10 Remove the chain slider from the swingarm if necessary, noting the shaped washers (see illustration). If it is badly worn or damaged, fit a new one.

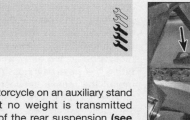

13.5 Chain guard bolts (arrowed)

13.6a Brake hose/sensor wiring guide screws (arrowed)...

13.6b ...and brake cable guide bolt (arrowed) on DCT models

13.8 Unscrew the nut

13.9 Withdraw the bolt and remove the swingarm

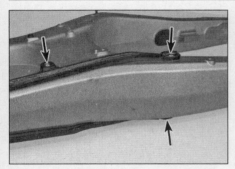

13.10 Chain slider is secured by three screws (arrowed)

13.11a Remove the sleeve…

13.11b …and the sleeve and spacer

Inspection

11 Remove the sleeve from the left-hand pivot and the sleeve and spacer from the right-hand one **(see illustrations)**.

12 Thoroughly clean all pivot components, removing all traces of dirt, corrosion and grease.

13 Check the swingarm closely, looking for obvious signs of wear such as heavy scoring, or for damage such as cracks or distortion.

14 Check the condition of the grease seals and bearings – there is a ball bearing and a needle bearing in the right-hand pivot and a needle bearing in the left. Check the ball bearings run smoothly. Fit the sleeve back in each needle bearing and check for play between them. Refer to *Tools and Workshop Tips* in the Reference section for more information on bearings. Inspect all components closely, looking for obvious signs of wear such as heavy scoring, or for damage such as cracks or distortion.

15 If new seals or bearings are required lever the seals out using a seal hook or screwdriver **(see illustrations)**.

16 Remove the circlip from the right-hand side **(see illustration)**. Remove the ball bearing using an internal expanding puller with slide-hammer attachment, or drive it out using a socket inserted through the needle bearing from the inner side of the pivot and located on the inner race. Remove the needle bearing from each pivot in the same way, or using a drawbolt arrangement as described in *Tools and Workshop Tips* in the Reference

13.15a Lever the grease seal out…

13.15b …from each side of each pivot

section. If necessary use a hydraulic press. Note that the bearings cannot be reused once they have been removed.

17 Press or draw the new needle bearings in with the marked side facing the outer side of the swingarm, and set the right-hand one so the outer end is recessed 4.5 to 5.0 mm below the rim of the bore, and the left-hand one so it is recessed 5.0 to 5.5 mm – do not drive the bearings in, you will ruin them. Smear molybdenum disulphide grease onto the bearings.

18 Press or drive the new ball bearing in with the marked side facing out until it seats, using a bearing driver or socket that contacts the outer race of the bearing, not the inner race. Secure it with a new circlip, making sure it locates in the groove **(see illustration 13.16)**. Pack the bearing with molybdenum disulphide grease.

19 Press the new seals squarely into place with the marked flat side facing out **(see illustration)**. Fit the sleeve into the left-hand pivot and the sleeve and spacer into the right-hand one **(see illustrations 13.11a and b)**.

Installation

20 If removed, fit the chain slider, making sure it locates correctly over the lug at the front, and the mounting bosses fit in the holes **(see illustration)**.

21 Clean the swingarm pivot bolt and smear it with grease.

22 Offer up the swingarm, making sure the drive chain is looped over the front, and slide the pivot bolt through from the left-hand side **(see illustration 13.9)**.

23 Lubricate the nut threads and seating face with engine oil then fit the nut and tighten it

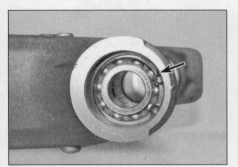

13.16 A circlip (arrowed) secures the ball bearing in the outside of the right-hand pivot

13.19 Press the new seals in using your fingers so they are flush

13.20 Fit the slot over the lug

to 80 Nm, counter-holding the bolt head **(see illustration 13.8)**. Check the swingarm moves up and down smoothly and freely.

24 Connect the linkage arm to the swingarm and tighten the bolt/nut to 74 Nm **(see illustrations 12.5b and a)**.

25 Install the remaining components in reverse order.

26 Check and adjust the drive chain slack (see Chapter 1). Check the operation of the rear suspension and brake before taking the machine on the road.

14 Suspension adjustment

Front forks

1 The front forks are adjustable for spring pre-load and both rebound and compression damping. Always make sure both forks are set equally.

2 Spring pre-load is adjusted using a socket or spanner on the adjuster flats **(see illustration)** – a spanner should be provided in the toolkit. Turn the adjuster clockwise to increase pre-load and anti-clockwise to decrease it. To set the standard position, turn the adjuster fully anti-clockwise until it stops, then turn it clockwise 5 full turns on models with standard transmission, and 8.5 full turns on models with DCT.

3 Rebound damping is adjusted using a screwdriver in the slot in the top of the damper rod protruding from the pre-load adjuster **(see illustration 14.2)**. Turn it clockwise to increase damping and anti-clockwise to decrease it. To set the standard position, turn the adjuster fully clockwise until it stops, then turn it anti-clockwise 2 1/4 turns so the punch mark on

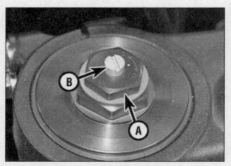

14.2 Spring pre-load adjuster (A); rebound damping adjuster (B)

the adjuster aligns with the index punch mark under the directional arrow on the pre-load adjuster.

4 Compression damping is adjusted using a screwdriver in the slot in the adjuster which is in the bottom of the fork **(see illustration)**. Turn it clockwise to increase damping and anti-clockwise to decrease it. To set the standard position, turn the adjuster fully clockwise until it stops, then turn it anti-clockwise 8 clicks on standard models and 4 clicks on the Adventure Sports model.

Rear shock absorber

5 The shock absorber is adjustable for spring pre-load and both rebound and compression damping.

6 Spring pre-load is adjusted by turning the knob on the left-hand side of the bike **(see illustration)**. Turn the adjuster clockwise to increase pre-load and anti-clockwise to decrease it. To set the standard position, turn the adjuster fully anti-clockwise until it stops, then turn it clockwise to the first click, which is the lowest setting, then turn it 7 clicks more.

7 Rebound damping adjustment is made

14.4 Compression damping adjuster (arrowed)

by turning the adjuster on the bottom of the shock absorber on the left-hand side using a flat-bladed screwdriver **(see illustration)**. To increase the damping, turn the adjuster clockwise. To decrease the damping, turn the adjuster anti-clockwise. To set the standard position, turn the adjuster clockwise until it stops, then turn it anti clockwise 11 clicks on 2016/17 standard models, 9 clicks on 2018-on standard models, and 13 clicks on the Adventure Sports model, so the punch mark on the adjuster aligns with the index punch mark on the shock absorber.

8 Compression damping adjustment is made by turning the adjuster on the right-hand side of the shock absorber reservoir using a flat-bladed screwdriver **(see illustration)**. To increase the damping, turn the adjuster clockwise. To decrease the damping, turn the adjuster anti-clockwise. To set the standard position, turn the adjuster clockwise until it stops, then turn it anti-clockwise 14 clicks on standard models and 19 clicks on the Adventure Sports model, so the punch mark on the adjuster aligns with the index punch mark on the reservoir body.

14.6 Spring pre-load adjuster (arrowed)

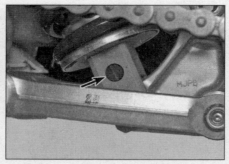

14.7 Rebound damping adjuster (arrowed)

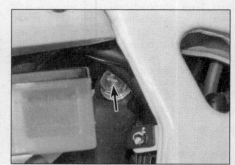

14.8 Compression damping adjuster (arrowed)

Chapter 6
Brakes, wheels and final drive

Contents

Section number

ABS components	14
ABS fault diagnosis	13
ABS operation	12
Brake hoses and fittings	10
Brake system bleeding and fluid change	11
Drive chain	21
Front brake calipers	3
Front brake discs	4
Front brake master cylinder	5
Front brake pads	2
Front wheel	17
General Information	1

Section number

Rear brake caliper	7
Rear brake disc	8
Rear brake master cylinder	9
Rear brake pads	6
Rear sprocket coupling/rubber dampers	23
Rear wheel	18
Sprockets	22
Tyres	20
Wheel alignment check	16
Wheel bearings	19
Wheel runout	15

Degrees of difficulty

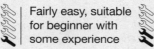

Easy, suitable for novice with little experience	Fairly easy, suitable for beginner with some experience	Fairly difficult, suitable for competent DIY mechanic	Difficult, suitable for experienced DIY mechanic	Very difficult, suitable for expert DIY or professional

Specifications

Brake fluid
Brake fluid type .... DOT 4

Brake discs
Disc thickness
  Front discs
    Standard .... 4.5 mm
    Service limit .... 3.5 mm
  Rear disc
    Standard .... 6.0 mm
    Service limit .... 5.0 mm
Disc maximum runout
  Front discs .... 0.2 mm
  Rear discs .... 0.3 mm

ABS system
Wheel speed sensor air gap
  Front .... 0.40 to 1.15 mm
  Rear .... 0.40 to 1.06 mm

Wheels
Maximum wheel runout (front and rear)
  Axial (side-to-side) .... 1.0 mm
  Radial (out-of-round) .... 1.0 mm
Maximum axle runout (front and rear) .... 0.2 mm

Tyres
Tyre pressures .... see Pre-ride checks
Tyre sizes*
  Front 90/90-21M/C (54H)
  Rear 150/70-R18M/C (70H)
*Refer to the owners handbook or the tyre information label for approved tyre brands.

Final drive

Drive chain slack and lubricant	see Chapter 1
Drive chain type	DID 525HV3-130ZB (124 links)
Sprocket sizes (No. of teeth)	
Front (engine) sprocket	16
Rear (wheel) sprocket	42

Torque settings

ABS pulse ring screws	7 Nm
ABS wheel speed sensor bolt	10 Nm
Brake caliper bleed valves	5.5 Nm
Brake hose banjo bolts	34 Nm
Brake pipe nuts	14 Nm
Front axle nut	60 Nm
Front axle clamp bolts	22 Nm
Front brake caliper mounting bolts	45 Nm
Front brake disc bolts	20 Nm
Front brake master cylinder clamp bolts	10 Nm
Front sprocket bolt	54 Nm
Parking brake caliper mounting bolts	31 Nm
Rear axle nut	100 Nm
Rear brake caliper rear slider pin bolt	22 Nm
Rear brake disc bolts	42 Nm
Rear brake pad retaining pin	17 Nm
Rear brake master cylinder mounting bolts	14 Nm
Rear sprocket nuts	100 Nm

1 General Information

1 All models are fitted with steel spoked wheels designed for tubed tyres only. Both front and rear brakes are hydraulically operated disc brakes. Models with DCT also have a cable operated parking brake on the rear disc.

2 All models have a pair of four piston calipers acting on 310 mm floating discs at the front, and a single piston sliding caliper acting on a 256 mm disc at the rear.

3 An anti-lock braking system (ABS) is fitted either as standard or as an option, depending on market and year. The system prevents the wheels from locking up under hard braking or on uneven road surfaces. A sensor on each wheel transmits information about the speed of rotation to the control unit in the ABS modulator – if the unit senses that a wheel is about to lock, it releases brake pressure to that wheel momentarily, preventing a skid.

Caution: Disc brake components rarely require disassembly. Do not disassemble components unless absolutely necessary. If an hydraulic brake hose is loosened or disconnected, the banjo union sealing washers must be replaced with new ones and the system must be bled upon reassembly. Do not use solvents on internal brake components. Solvents will cause the seals to swell and distort. Use only clean DOT 4 brake fluid for cleaning. Use care when working with brake fluid as it can injure your eyes and it will damage painted surfaces and plastic parts.

2 Front brake pads

Note: *Honda recommend using new caliper mounting bolts. This is because the bolts are pre-treated with a locking compound. If they are not available clean up the old bolts and fit them using a suitable non-permanent thread locking compound that is commercially available.*

Caution: Do not operate the front brake lever while the caliper is off the disc.

1 For best freedom of movement in the caliper remove the front mudguard cover **(see illustration)**.

2 Unscrew the caliper mounting bolts and slide the caliper off the disc **(see illustration)**.

3 Slide one pad towards the centre until the lug on each end is clear of its slot in the caliper and remove it, then repeat for the other pad **(see illustration)**. If there is not enough clearance to remove the first pad ease the pads apart to push the pistons back in to create more clearance.

4 Inspect the surface of each pad for contamination and check that the friction material has not worn to or beyond its service limit (see Chapter 1). If any pad is worn,

2.1 Undo the screw, release the clips and remove the mudguard cover

2.2 Unscrew the bolts and slide the caliper off

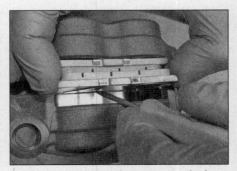

2.3 Move the pad to the centre so the lugs clear the slots then draw it out

2.6a Remove the pad spring if required

2.6b Push the pistons into the caliper using one of the methods described

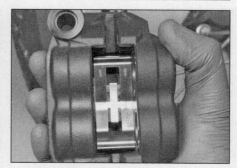

2.9a Make sure the spring is clean...

2.9b ...and correctly fitted

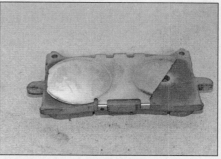

2.10 Make sure the shims are seated and secure

fouled with oil or grease, or heavily scored or damaged, fit a complete set of new pads. Also check that wear is even across each pad – uneven wear is indicative of a sticking or seized piston (see Steps 6 and 7). It is not possible to degrease the friction material; if the pads are contaminated in any way they must be replaced with new ones.

5 If the pads are in good condition clean them carefully, using a fine wire brush that is completely free of oil and grease to remove all traces of road dirt and corrosion. Using a pointed instrument, dig out any embedded particles of foreign matter. Spray with a dedicated brake cleaner.

6 Remove the pad spring from the caliper if required, noting which way round it fits **(see illustration)**. Clean around the exposed section of each piston to remove any dirt or debris that could cause the seals to be damaged. If new pads are being fitted, now push the pistons all the way back into the caliper to create room for them. If the old pads are still serviceable push the pistons in a little way. To push the pistons back use finger pressure or a piece of wood as leverage, or place the old pads back in the caliper and use a metal bar or a screwdriver inserted between them (but take care not to damage the friction surface if the pads are being re-used), or use grips and a piece of wood, with rag or card to protect the caliper body **(see illustration)**. Alternatively obtain a proper piston-pushing tool. It may be necessary to remove the master cylinder reservoir cover, plate and diaphragm and siphon out some fluid (Section 11). If the pistons are difficult to push back, remove the bleed valve cap, then attach a length of clear hose to the bleed valve and place the open end in a suitable container, then open the valve and try again (Section 11). Take great care not to draw any air into the system. If in doubt, bleed the brake afterwards.

7 If a piston appears seized, first block or hold the other pistons using wood or cable-ties, then apply the brake lever and check whether the piston in question moves at all. If it moves out but can't be pushed back in the chances are there is some hidden corrosion stopping it. If it doesn't move at all, or to fully clean

and inspect the pistons, overhaul the caliper (Section 3).

8 Check the condition of the brake disc (Section 4).

9 Clean the pad spring and fit it into the caliper if removed, making sure the arrows point in the direction of disc rotation and it locates correctly **(see illustrations)**.

10 Where fitted make sure the shim is correctly seated on the back of each pad **(see illustration)**.

11 Fit the pads into the caliper with the rounded edges of the lugs facing the top of the caliper and so the friction material on each pad faces the middle, and seat the pad lugs in the slots, pushing the pad against the spring to align them **(see illustrations)**.

12 Slide the caliper onto the disc making sure the pads locate correctly on each side **(see illustration 2.2)**. Either fit the new caliper mounting bolts, or clean the threads of the original bolts and apply fresh thread locking compound, then tighten them to 45 Nm.

13 Fit the mudguard cover, on 2018 models seating the hose for the left-hand caliper in the front cut-out in the cover, and making sure the cover clips locate correctly in the slots in the mudguard **(see illustration 2.1)**.

14 Operate the brake lever until the pads contact the disc. Check the level of fluid in the reservoir and top-up if necessary (see *Pre-ride checks*).

15 Test the brakes before riding the bike. Note that new pads will need to bed in.

2.11a Fit the pads with the rounded edges facing in...

2.11b ...so the flat edges are seated as shown

3.1a Unscrew the brake hose banjo bolt (arrowed)…

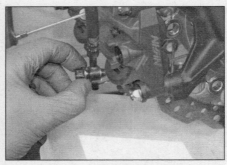

3.1b …and catch the fluid in the tray (there won't be much)

3.1c You can use a nut and bolt and the sealing washers to seal the brake hose…

3.1d …or a dedicated tool such as this sprung clamp with conical rubbers that seat in the eye of the banjo union

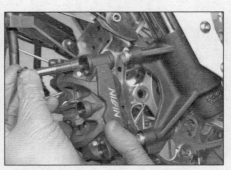

3.2a Unscrew the bolts and remove the caliper…

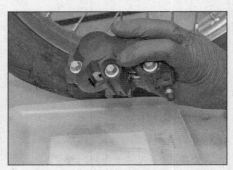

3.2b …and tip any residual fluid out

3 Front brake calipers

> **Warning: To prevent damage from spilled brake fluid, always cover paintwork when working on the braking system, and have plenty of absorbent rag handy to catch and mop up any spilled fluid, and a suitable container into which brake fluid can be tipped. Caliper overhaul must be done in a clean workspace to avoid the possibility of dirt entering the system. Do not use petroleum-based solvents to clean brake system components – use only clean DOT**

4 brake fluid, a dedicated brake cleaner, or denatured alcohol.

Removal

Note: *Honda recommend using new caliper mounting bolts. This is because the bolts are pre-treated with a locking compound. If they are not available clean up the old bolts and fit them using a suitable non-permanent thread locking compound that is commercially available. If you are overhauling the caliper you need and E12 type socket for the caliper assembly bolts.*

Note: *Do not operate the brake lever while the caliper is off the disc.*

1 Place a drain tray under the claiper, then unscrew the brake hose banjo bolt and detach the banjo union(s), noting the alignment **(see**

illustrations). Fit a hose clamp onto the hose(s), and/or seal the banjo union(s) using a nut and bolt and the sealing washers, or a dedicated tool or tools **(see illustrations)**, or wrap plastic foodwrap around it/them. New sealing washers must be fitted on reassembly.

2 Unscrew the caliper mounting bolts and slide the caliper off the disc **(see illustration)**. Tip the residual brake fluid into a container **(see illustration)**.

Overhaul

3 Fit the caliper back onto the disc with the assembly bolts facing out and lightly tighten the mounting bolts **(see illustration)**. Slacken the assembly bolts using an E12 type socket, then remove the caliper from the disc **(see illustration)**.

3.3a Fit the caliper the wrong way round…

3.3b …so you can slacken the assembly bolts

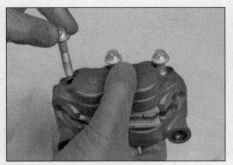

3.4a Remove the bolts...

3.4b ...and split the caliper...

3.4c ...then remove the pads...

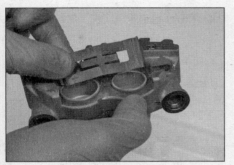

3.4d ...and the spring

3.5 Fluid passage seal (arrowed)

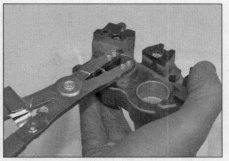

3.7 Using a dedicated tool to draw a piston out

4 Unscrew the assembly bolts and split the caliper body, then remove the brake pads and the pad spring, noting how it fits **(see illustrations)**.
5 Remove the fluid passage seal – a new one must be used **(see illustration)**.
6 Clean the caliper using brake system cleaner and an old toothbrush or similar. Mark the inside of each piston so it can be refitted into the bore it came from.
7 The pistons can usually be removed using a pair of external circlip pliers, or there are dedicated piston removal tools available – grip the inner wall of the piston then twist and pull the piston out, keeping it square to the bore wall until it is free **(see illustration)**.

Caution: Do not try to remove a piston by levering it out or by using grips that bear on the outer wall – leverage will damage the caliper and grips will damage the surface of the piston.
8 If the pistons are difficult to remove using a hand tool, use compressed air. Place some rag over the pistons and the caliper, then apply the compressed air gradually and progressively to the fluid passage and allow the pistons to ease most of the way out of their bores, controlling their movement so they are displaced evenly. When they are almost out remove them by hand.
9 If either piston sticks in its bore and cannot be removed, fit a new caliper.

10 Remove the dust seals and pistons seals from their grooves **(see illustration)**- if you use a metal tool take care not to scratch the bore or groove. New seals must be used.
11 Clean the grooves and bores with clean brake fluid, then cover the caliper in rag and blow through the fluid passages with compresssed air. Check the caliper body for cracks and the piston and bore walls for surface defects.
12 Clean the pistons and check their outer surface for defects. Replace the pistons with new ones if necessary.
13 Lubricate the new piston seals with new brake fluid, then carefully fit them into the lower grooves in the bores **(see illustration)**.

3.10 Extracting the old seals from their grooves

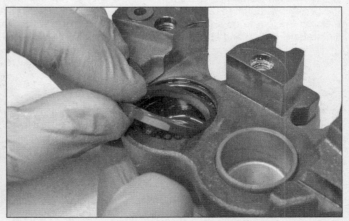

3.13 Make sure the new piston seal seats correctly in the lower groove

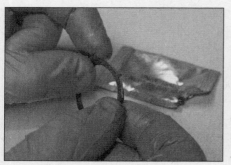

3.14a Lubricate the dust seals...

3.14b ...and fit them in the upper grooves

3.15a Fit the pistons into their original bores...

3.15b ...and push them all the way in

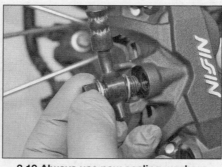

3.19 Always use new sealing washers

4 Front brake discs

Inspection

1 Inspect the surface of the disc for score marks and other damage. Light scratches are normal after use and won't affect brake operation, but deep grooves and heavy score marks will reduce braking efficiency and accelerate pad wear. If a disc is badly grooved it must be replaced with a new one.

2 The disc must not be allowed to wear down to a thickness less than the service limit given in the Specifications at the beginning of the Chapter and stamped on the disc **(see illustration)**. Check the thickness of the disc in the middle of the pad contact area using a micrometer **(see illustration)** – do not measure across the rim of the disc with a ruler. Replace the disc with a new one if necessary.

3 To check if the disc is warped, position the bike on an auxiliary stand with the front wheel raised off the ground. Mount a dial gauge to the fork leg, with the gauge plunger touching the surface of the disc about 10 mm from its outer edge **(see illustration)**. Rotate the wheel and watch the gauge needle, comparing the reading with the limit listed in the Specifications at the beginning of this Chapter. If the runout is greater than the service limit, check the wheel bearings for play (see Chapter 1). If the bearings are worn, fit new ones (Section 19) and repeat this check. If the disc runout is still excessive, remove the disc (Steps 4 and 5) and check for corrosion where it seats on the hub and clean it up if necessary. You can also try moving the disc around the wheel one bolt hole at a time and after each movement rechecking for runout. In most cases a new disc will have to be fitted.

Removal

Note: *Honda recommend using new disc mounting bolts. This is because the bolts are pre-treated with a locking compound. If they are not available clean up the old bolts and reinstall them using a suitable non-permanent thread locking compound that is commercially available.*

14 Lubricate the new dust seals with silicone grease and fit them into the upper grooves in the bores **(see illustrations)**.

15 Lubricate the exterior of the pistons with new brake fluid. Identify the pistons from the marks made on removal. Fit the closed end of the pistons squarely into the bores and push them all the way in using your fingers, making sure the seals do not dislodge **(see illustrations)**. Wipe off any excess fluid as it will attract dirt.

16 Fit a new fluid passage seal **(see illustration 3.5)**.

17 Fit the pad spring with the arrows pointing in the direction of disc rotation **(see illustrations 3.4d and 2.9a and b)**. Fit the pads, then join the caliper halves and tighten the assembly bolts to 27 Nm, mounting them on the fork to do so if necessary **(see illustrations 3.4c, b and a)**.

Installation

18 Slide the caliper onto the disc making sure the pads locate correctly on each side **(see illustration 3.2a)**. Either fit the new caliper mounting bolts, or clean the threads of the original bolts and apply fresh thread locking compound, then tighten them to 45 Nm.

19 Connect the brake hose to the caliper using new sealing washers on each side of the banjo union(s) – on 2016/17 models for the left-hand caliper that means three sealing washers, one on the outer side of each union and one between them **(see illustration)**. Align the hose as noted on removal and tighten the banjo bolt to 34 Nm **(see illustration 3.1a)**.

20 Top up the reservoir with DOT 4 brake fluid and bleed the system as described in Section 11. Check that there are no fluid leaks and test the brake before riding the bike.

4.2a The outer face of the disc is marked with the wear limit

4.2b Check the thickness using a micrometer

4 Remove the wheel (Section 17). Set the wheel on some wood blocks with disc being removed facing up. Before removing the left-hand disc remove the ABS pulse ring from it if required (Section 14).

5 If you are not fitting a new disc, mark the relationship of the disc to the wheel so it can be installed in the same position. Unscrew the disc bolts, loosening them evenly and a little at a time in a criss-cross pattern to avoid distorting the disc, then remove the disc (see illustration).

Installation

6 Before fitting the disc, make sure there is no dirt or corrosion where the disc seats on the hub, and on models with ABS where the pulse ring seats on the disc. If the disc does not sit flat when it is bolted down, it will appear to be warped when checked or when the front brake is used.

7 Fit the disc with its marked side facing out (see illustration 4.2a), aligning the previously applied matchmarks (if you're refitting the original disc).

8 Either fit the new bolts, or clean the threads of the original bolts and apply fresh thread locking compound, and tighten them evenly and a little at a time in a criss-cross pattern to 20 Nm. Clean the disc using acetone or brake system cleaner. If a new disc has been installed, remove any protective coating from its working surfaces and fit new brake pads.

9 On models with ABS fit the pulse ring onto the left-hand disc if removed (Section 14).

10 Install the wheel (Section 17).

11 Operate the brake lever until the pads contact the disc. On models with ABS check the wheel speed sensor air gap (Section 13).

12 Test the brakes before riding the bike.

5 Front brake master cylinder

Warning: To prevent damage from spilled brake fluid, always cover paintwork when working on the braking system, and have plenty of absorbent rag handy to catch and mop up any spilled fluid, and a

4.3 Checking disc runout with a dial gauge

suitable container into which brake fluid can be tipped. Overhaul must be done in a clean workspace to avoid the possibility of dirt entering the system. Do not use petroleum-based solvents to clean brake system components – use only clean DOT 4 brake fluid, a dedicated brake cleaner, or denatured alcohol.

Removal

1 Remove the hand guard and the mirror (see Chapter 7).

2 Remove the brake lever (see Chapter 5). Remove the hand guard bracket.

3 Remove the brake light switch (see Chapter 8).

4 Slacken the reservoir cover screws. Unscrew the brake hose banjo bolt and detach the banjo union, noting its alignment (see illustration). Seal the banjo union using

5.4 Brake hose banjo bolt (arrowed)

4.5 Brake disc bolts (arrowed) – on models with ABS the pulse ring sits on top of the left-hand disc

a nut and bolt and the two sealing washers or a dedicated tool (see illustration 3.1c or d), or wrap plastic foodwrap around it. New sealing washers must be fitted on reassembly.

5 Unscrew the two master cylinder assembly clamp bolts, noting how the lower bolt secures the wiring clip bracket where fitted, and remove the clamp, then lift the master cylinder away from the handlebar (see illustration).

6 Remove the reservoir cover, diaphragm plate and diaphragm and drain the fluid into a suitable container. Wipe any remaining fluid out of the reservoir with a clean rag.

Overhaul

7 Remove the rubber boot (see illustration).

8 The piston assembly is secured by a circlip – release it using internal circlip pliers and draw out the piston and spring (see illustrations).

5.5 Unscrew the bolts and remove the master cylinder

5.7 Ease the boot out

5.8a Release the circlip…

5.8b …and remove the piston and spring

5.11 Rebuild kit components

5.12a Make sure the seal is fitted as shown

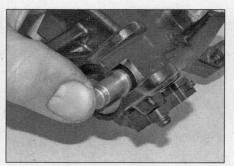

5.12b Fit the cup onto the spring

5.12c Slide the spring and piston into the bore

9 Clean inside the master cylinder with clean brake fluid. If filtered and un-lubricated compressed air is available blow it through the fluid passages.

10 Check the bore for surface defects and replace the master cylinder with a new one if any are evident.
11 All the internal components are supplied

in a rebuild kit – use all of the new parts regardless of the apparent condition of the old ones **(see illustration)**.
12 If not already in place fit the seal onto the piston with the wider side facing the inner end **(see illustration)**. Fit the cup onto the narrow end of the spring, locating the peg on its cupped side in the hole **(see illustration)**. Lubricate the cup with clean brake fluid then slide the wide end of the spring into the master cylinder. Lubricate the piston and seal with new brake fluid, then seat the piston against the cup and push the assembly into the master cylinder, making sure the lips of the cup and seal do not turn inside out **(see illustration)**.
13 Push the piston in and fit the new circlip into the groove, using a small screwdriver to square it up and seat it if necessary **(see illustrations)**. Release the piston and check the circlip is correctly seated.
14 Carefully push the wide end of the boot into the master cylinder and locate the narrow end in the groove in the end of the piston **(see illustrations)**.

Installation

15 Fit the master cylinder onto the handlebar, aligning the clamp joint with the mark on the top of the handlebar, then fit the clamp with the UP mark facing up **(see illustration)**. Tighten the upper bolt first, then the lower, to 10 Nm, where fitted not forgetting to secure the wiring clip bracket with the lower bolt.
16 Connect the brake hose to the master cylinder using new sealing washers on each

5.13a Push the piston in...

5.13b ...and fit the circlip...

5.13c ...using a small screwdriver to push it in if necessary

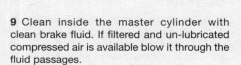

5.14a Fit the new rubber boot...

5.14b ... making sure it locates as shown

5.15 Align the clamp mating surfaces with the mark (arrowed)

side of the banjo union **(see illustration 3.19)**. Align the hose as noted on removal and tighten the banjo bolt to 34 Nm **(see illustration 5.4)**.

17 Install the brake light switch (see Chapter 8).

18 Install the hand guard holder and brake lever (see Chapter 5). Install the hand guard (see Chapter 7).

19 Fill the reservoir with DOT 4 brake fluid and bleed the system as described in Section 11.

20 Check that there are no fluid leaks and test the brake before riding the bike.

6 Rear brake pads

Hydraulic brake – all models

Note: *Honda recommend using new caliper slider pin bolts. This is because they are pre-treated with a locking compound. If they are not available clean up the old bolts and fit them using a suitable non-permanent thread locking compound that is commercially available.*

Caution: Do not operate the brake pedal while the caliper is off the disc.

1 Unscrew the pad retaining pin **(see illustration)**.

2 Unscrew the rear slider pin bolt, pivot the caliper up off the disc and remove the pads **(see illustrations)**.

3 Unscrew the front slider pin bolt and lift the caliper off the bracket **(see illustration)**.

4 Withdraw the sleeve from the rubber boot in the caliper **(see illustration)**. Clean off all traces of corrosion and hardened grease from the slider pin bolts, rubber boots and sleeve **(see illustration)**. Replace the boots with new ones if they are damaged, deformed or deteriorated.

5 Inspect the surface of each pad for contamination and check that the friction material has not worn to or beyond its service limit (see Chapter 1). If either pad is worn, fouled with oil or grease, or heavily scored or damaged, fit new pads. It is not possible to degrease the friction material; if the pads

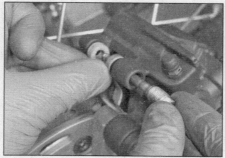

6.1 Unscrew and remove the pin

6.2a Unscrew the bolt...

6.2b ...raise the caliper and remove the pads

6.3 Unscrew the bolt and displace the caliper

are contaminated in any way they must be replaced with new ones.

6 If the pads are in good condition clean them carefully, using a fine wire brush that is completely free of oil and grease to remove all traces of road dirt and corrosion. Using a pointed instrument, dig out any embedded particles of foreign matter. Spray with a dedicated brake cleaner.

7 Remove the pad spring from the caliper if required, noting which way round it fits **(see illustration 6.11)**. Clean around the exposed section of the piston to remove any dirt or debris that could cause the seals to be damaged. If new pads are being fitted, now push the piston all the way back into the caliper to create room for them. If the old pads are still serviceable push the piston in a little way. To push the piston back use finger pressure or a piece of wood as leverage, or

place the old pads back in the caliper and use a metal bar or a screwdriver inserted between them (but take care not to damage the friction surface if the pads are being re-used), or use grips and a piece of wood, with rag or card to protect the caliper body **(see illustration)**. Alternatively obtain a proper piston-pushing tool. It may be necessary to remove the master cylinder reservoir cap, plate and diaphragm and siphon out some fluid (Section 11). If the piston is difficult to push back, remove the bleed valve cap, then attach a length of clear hose to the bleed valve and place the open end in a suitable container, then open the valve and try again (Section 11). Take great care not to draw any air into the system. If in doubt, bleed the brake afterwards.

8 If the piston appears seized apply the brake pedal and check whether the piston moves at all. If it moves out but can't be pushed

6.4a Withdraw the sleeve and check the caliper boot...

6.4b ...and the boot in the bracket

6.7 Press the piston in as described to make clearance for the new pads

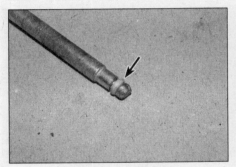

6.9 Stopper ring (arrowed)

6.11 Make sure the spring is clean and correctly fitted

6.13 Check the pads seat correctly against the guide

back in the chances are there is some hidden corrosion stopping it. If it doesn't move at all, or to fully clean and inspect the piston, disassemble and overhaul the caliper (Section 7).

9 Remove all traces of corrosion from the pad pin and check for wear and damage. Check the condition of the stopper ring on the pin and replace it with a new one if it is damaged or deformed **(see illustration)**.

10 Check the condition of the brake disc (Section 8).

11 Clean the pad spring and fit it into the caliper if removed, making sure it locates correctly **(see illustration)**. Clean the pad guide on the bracket and check it is correctly fitted **(see illustration 6.4b)**.

12 Smear the sliding sections of the pin bolts and inside the rubber boots with silicone grease, then fit the sleeve into the caliper boot **(see illustration 6.4a)**. Either obtain a new front slider pin bolt, or clean the threads

of the original bolt and apply fresh thread locking compound. Fit the caliper onto the bracket, fit the front slider pin bolt and tighten it finger-tight **(see illustration 6.3)**.

13 Fit the pads into the caliper so the friction material on each pad faces the disc **(see illustration 6.2b)**, and seat the pads against the guide on the bracket **(see illustration)**. Pivot the caliper down over the pads. Either fit a new rear slider pin bolt, or clean the threads of the original bolt and apply fresh thread locking compound, and tighten it finger-tight **(see illustration 6.2a)**.

14 Smear silicone grease around the pad pin stopper ring **(see illustration 6.9)**. Push the pads up against the spring to align the holes then insert the pad pin and tighten it finger-tight **(see illustration 6.1)**.

15 Tighten the slider pin bolts, tightening the rear one to 22 Nm (no specification is given for the front one), then tighten the pad pin to 17 Nm.

16 Operate the brake pedal until the pads contact the disc.

17 Check the level of fluid in the reservoir and top-up if necessary (see *Pre-ride checks*).

18 Test the brake before riding the bike.

Parking brake – models with DCT

Note: *Honda recommend using new caliper mounting bolts, slider pin bolt and pad pins. This is because they are pre-treated with a locking compound. If they are not available clean up the old bolts and fit them using a suitable non-permanent thread locking compound that is commercially available.*

19 Slacken the pad retaining pins **(see illustration)**.

20 Remove the caliper cover **(see illustration)**. Slacken the slider pin bolt, then unscrew the caliper mounting bolts and slide the caliper off the disc **(see illustrations)**. For best freedom of movement disconnect the cable from the caliper **(see illustrations)**.

6.19 Slacken the pins (arrowed)

6.20a Unscrew the bolts and remove the cover

6.20b Slacken the slider pin bolt (arrowed), unscrew the mounting bolts and displace the caliper

6.20c Pull the rubber boot off...

6.20d ...lift the cable out of the bracket...

6.20e ...and detach the end from the arm

6.21 Withdraw the pad pins and remove the pads

6.22a Unscrew the bolt…

6.22b …and slide the caliper and bracket apart

21 Unscrew and remove the pad pins, then remove the pads, noting how they locate (see illustration).

22 Unscrew the slider pin bolt and slide the caliper off the bracket (see illustrations).

23 Withdraw the sleeve from the rubber boot in the caliper (see illustration). Clean off all traces of corrosion and hardened grease from the slider pin bolts, rubber boots and sleeve (see illustration). Replace the boots with new ones if they are damaged, deformed or deteriorated.

24 Inspect the surface of each pad for contamination and check that the friction material has not worn to or beyond its service limit (see Chapter 1). If any pad is worn, fouled with oil or grease, or heavily scored or damaged, fit new pads. It is not possible to degrease the friction material; if the pads are contaminated in any way they must be replaced with new ones.

25 If the pads are in good condition clean

them carefully, using a fine wire brush that is completely free of oil and grease to remove all traces of road dirt and corrosion. Using a pointed instrument, dig out any embedded particles of foreign matter. Spray with a dedicated brake cleaner.

26 Remove the pad spring from the caliper if required, noting which way round it fits (see illustration 6.29). Clean around the exposed section of the piston to remove any dirt or debris that could cause the seal to be damaged. If new pads are being fitted, slacken the piston pushrod locknut and thread the piston all the way back into the caliper to create room for them (see illustration). If the old pads are still serviceable thread the piston in a little way.

27 Check the cable arm turns smoothly and freely. If not, or to fully clean and inspect the piston and worn drive, disassemble and overhaul the caliper (Section 7).

28 Remove all traces of corrosion from the pad pins and check for wear and damage.

29 Clean the pad spring and fit it into the caliper if removed, making sure it locates correctly (see illustration).

30 Smear the sliding sections of the pin bolts and inside the rubber boots with silicone grease, then fit the sleeve into the front boots (see illustration 6.23a), locating the outer lip of each boot in the groove (see illustration). Either obtain a new front slider pin bolt, or clean the threads of the original bolt and apply fresh thread locking compound. Fit the caliper onto the bracket, fit the front slider pin bolt and tighten it finger-tight (see illustrations 6.22b and a).

31 Fit the pads into the caliper so the friction material on each pad faces the other (see illustration). Either fit new pad pins, or clean the threads of the original pins and apply fresh thread locking compound. Push the

6.23a Withdraw the sleeve…

6.23b …and check the boots

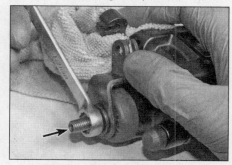

6.26 Slacken the locknut and turn the pushrod (arrowed) out to retract the piston

6.29 Make sure the spring is clean and correctly fitted

6.30 Make sure the boot lips locate correctly

6.31 Seat the pads in the caliper

pads up against the spring to align the holes then insert the pad pins and tighten them finger-tight **(see illustration 6.21)**.

32 Connect the cable to the caliper if disconnected **(see illustrations 6.20e, d and c)**.

33 Either fit new caliper mounting bolts, or clean the threads of the original bolts and apply fresh thread locking compound. Slide the caliper onto the disc and tighten the mounting bolts to 31 Nm **(see illustration 6.20b)**. Tighten the slider pin bolt to 22 Nm, then tighten the pad pins to 17 Nm **(see illustration 6.20a)**.

34 Adjust the cable freeplay (see Chapter 1). Test the brake.

35 Fit the caliper cover **(see illustration 6.19)**.

7 Rear brake caliper

Hydraulic brake caliper – all models

⚠️ **Warning: To prevent damage from spilled brake fluid, always cover paintwork when working on the braking system, and have plenty of absorbent rag handy to catch and mop up any spilled fluid, and a suitable container into which brake fluid can be tipped. Caliper overhaul must be done in a clean workspace to avoid the possibility of dirt entering the system. Do not use petroleum-based solvents to clean brake system components – use only clean DOT 4 brake fluid, a dedicated brake cleaner, or denatured alcohol.**

Removal

Note: *Do not operate the brake pedal while the caliper is off the disc.*

1 Unscrew the brake hose banjo bolt and detach the banjo union, noting its alignment. Seal the banjo union using a nut and bolt and two sealing washers or a dedicated tool **(see illustrations 3.1c and d)**, or wrap plastic foodwrap around it. New sealing washers must be used on reassembly.

2 Remove the brake pads and the caliper (Section 6, Steps 1 to 3).

Overhaul

3 Remove the pad spring, noting how it fits **(see illustration 6.11)**.

4 Clean the caliper using brake system cleaner and an old toothbrush or similar.

5 The piston can usually be removed using a pair of straight external circlip pliers. There are also dedicated piston removal tools available, but make sure you choose one that is suitable for this caliper. Grip the inner wall of the piston then twist and pull the piston out, keeping it square to the bore wall until it is free **(see illustration 3.7)**.

Caution: Do not try to remove the piston by levering it out or buy using grips that bear on the outer wall – leverage will damage the caliper and grips will damage the surface of the piston.

6 If the piston is difficult to remove using a hand tool, use compressed air. Place some rag between the piston and the caliper, then apply the compressed air gradually and progressively to the fluid inlet and allow the piston to ease most of the way out of the bore. When it is almost out remove it using circlip pliers or by hand.

7 If the piston sticks in its bore and cannot be removed, replace the caliper with a new one.

8 Remove the dust seal and piston seal from their grooves using a tool that will not scratch the bore or grooves **(see illustration 3.10)**. New seals must be used.

9 Clean the grooves and bore with clean brake fluid, then cover the caliper in rag and blow through the fluid passages with compresssed air. Check the caliper body for cracks and the piston and bore walls for surface defects, and replace the caliper with a new one if necessary.

10 Lubricate the new piston seal with new brake fluid, then carefully fit it into the inner groove in the bore **(see illustration 3.13)**.

11 Lubricate the new dust seal with silicone grease and fit it into the upper groove in the bore **(see illustrations 3.14a and b)**.

12 Lubricate the exterior of the piston with new brake fluid. Fit the closed end of the piston squarely into the bore and push it all the way in using your fingers, making sure the seals do not dislodge **(see illustrations 3.15a and b)**. Wipe off any excess grease or fluid as it will attract dirt.

13 Clean the pad spring and fit it into the caliper, making sure it locates correctly **(see illustration 6.11)**.

Installation

14 Install the brake pads and caliper as described in Section 6, Steps 12 to 15.

15 Connect the brake hose using new sealing washers on each side of the banjo union **(see illustration 3.19)**, and align it as noted on removal. Tighten the banjo bolt to 34 Nm.

16 Top up the fluid reservoir with DOT 4 brake fluid and bleed the system as described in Section 11.

17 Check that there are no fluid leaks and test the brake before riding the bike.

Parking brake caliper and cable – models with DCT

Caliper removal

18 Refer to Section 6, Steps 19 to 22.

Caliper overhaul

19 Remove the pad spring, noting how it fits **(see illustration 6.29)**.

20 Clean the caliper using brake system cleaner and an old toothbrush or similar.

21 Hold the cable arm, unscrew the locknut and remove the arm, noting its alignment **(see illustration)**. Remove the rubber boot **(see illustration)**.

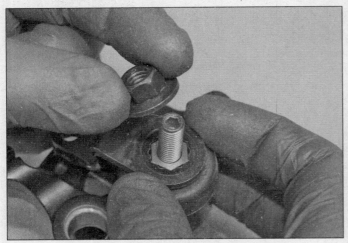

7.21a Unscrew the nut and remove the arm…

7.21b …and the boot

7.22a Thread the pushrod into the caliper…

7.22b …to remove the piston…

7.22c …then remove the worm drive

22 Turn the pushrod clockwise using a hex key in its end and withdraw the piston/pushrod from the worm drive when free **(see illustrations)**. Thread the worm drive out **(see illustration)**.

23 Remove the dust seal from its groove using a tool that will not scratch the bore or grooves **(see illustration)**. A new seal must be used.

24 Clean all components. Check the caliper body for cracks and the bore and piston walls for surface defects, and replace the caliper with a new one if necessary – a new caliper will come ready assembled with all components except the pads and mounting bolts.

25 Lubricate the new dust seal with silicone grease and fit it into the groove in the bore **(see illustration 7.23)**.

26 Lubricate the worm drive threads with a smear of silicone grease and thread it fully into the caliper so the punch mark is opposite (i.e on the other side to, not aligned with) the upper index line on the caliper **(see illustration 7.22c)**. Now turn the worm drive clockwise approximately 120° to align the punch mark with the lower index line.

27 Hold the worm drive and thread the piston/pushrod all the way into it **(see illustrations 7.22b and a)**.

28 Lubricate the rubber boot lip with silicone grease and fit it onto the caliper so the lip

7.23 The seal (arrowed) sits in a groove

7.28 Make sure the boot locates correctly

seats in the groove in the top of the worm drive **(see illustration)**.

29 Fit the cable arm onto the worm drive hex, aligning the punch marks **(see illustration)**. Secure the arm with the locknut **(see illustration 7.21a)**.

30 Clean the pad spring and fit it into the caliper, making sure it locates correctly **(see illustration 6.29)**.

Caliper installation

31 Install the brake pads and caliper as described in Section 6, Steps 23-on.

Parking brake cable

32 Remove the fuel tank, and for best access

the air filter housing (see Chapter 4). For best access at the lever remove the hand guard (see Chapter 7).

33 Create maximum freeplay in the cable (see Chapter 1).

34 Refer to Section 6 to remove the caliper cover and disconnect the cable from the caliper.

35 Draw the cable out to the front, releasing it from the guides on the swingarm and noting its routing **(see illustrations)**.

36 Align the slots in the adjuster and lockring at the handlebar end of the cable with that in the lever bracket, then pull the outer cable end from the socket in the adjuster and release

7.29 Fit the arm, aligning the punch marks

7.35a Release the cable from the guide on the underside of the swingarm…

7.35b …and from the guides on the top

7.36a Align the slots and free the cable from the adjuster…

7.36b …and from the lever

8.3 Rear brake disc bolts (arrowed)

the inner cable from the lever **(see illustrations)**.

37 Installation is the reverse of removal. Apply grease to the cable ends. Make sure the cable is correctly routed. Adjust the amount of brake lever freeplay (see Chapter 1).

8 Rear brake disc

Inspection

1 Refer to Section 4 of this Chapter, noting that the dial gauge should be attached to the swingarm.

Removal

Note: *Honda recommend using new disc mounting bolts. This is because the bolts are pre-treated with a locking compound.*

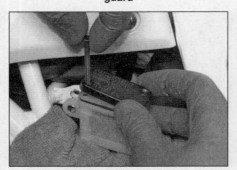

9.1 Undo the screw and remove the heel guard

9.2b …remove the cover, plate and diaphragm and drain the fluid

It is possible, however, to clean up the old bolts and reinstall them using a suitable non-permanent thread locking compound that is commercially available.

2 Remove the rear wheel (Section 18). Set the wheel on some wood blocks with the disc facing up.

3 If you are not replacing the disc with a new one, mark the relationship of the disc to the wheel so it can be installed in the same position. Unscrew the disc bolts, loosening them evenly and a little at a time in a criss-cross pattern to avoid distorting the disc, then remove the disc **(see illustration)**.

Installation

4 Before fitting the disc, make sure there is no dirt or corrosion where the disc seats on the hub. If the disc does not sit flat when it is bolted down, it will appear to be warped when checked or when the rear brake is used.

5 Fit the disc with its marked side facing out,

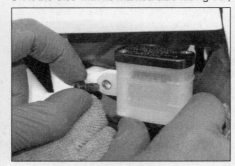

9.2a Displace the reservoir…

9.3 Unscrew the banjo bolt (arrowed)

aligning the previously applied matchmarks (if you're refitting the original disc).

6 Either fit the new bolts, or clean the threads of the original bolts and apply fresh thread locking compound. Tighten the bolts evenly and a little at a time in a criss-cross pattern to 42 Nm. Clean the disc using acetone or brake system cleaner. If a new disc has been installed, remove any protective coating from its working surfaces and fit new brake pads.

7 Install the wheel (Section 18).

8 Operate the brake pedal several times to bring the pads into contact with the disc.

9 Test the brake before riding the bike.

9 Rear brake master cylinder

⚠️ *Warning: To prevent damage from spilled brake fluid, always cover paintwork when working on the braking system. Overhaul must be done in a clean workspace to avoid the possibility of dirt entering the system. Do not use petroleum-based solvents to clean brake system components – use only clean DOT 4 brake fluid, a dedicated brake cleaner, or denatured alcohol.*

Removal

1 Remove the heel guard from the right-hand side of the frame **(see illustration)**.

2 Unscrew the bolt securing the fluid reservoir and draw it out, then undo the reservoir cover screws and remove the cover, diaphragm plate and diaphragm **(see illustrations)**. Pour the brake fluid into a suitable container. Wipe any remaining fluid out of the reservoir with a clean rag. Check the diaphragm for damage and deformation. Fit the reservoir back onto its mount. Release the clamp securing the reservoir hose to the master cylinder and detach the hose, and wrap it in some rag to catch the residual fluid.

3 Unscrew the brake hose banjo bolt and detach the banjo union, noting its alignment **(see illustration)**. Seal the banjo union using a nut and bolt and the two sealing washers or a dedicated tool **(see illustrations 3.1c and d)**,

9.4a Straighten the ends...

9.4b ...and remove the split pin...

9.4c ...then withdraw the clevis pin

or wrap plastic foodwrap around it. New sealing washers must be fitted on reassembly.

4 Straighten the ends of the split pin and withdraw it from the master cylinder pushrod clevis pin, then withdraw the clevis pin **(see illustrations)**. A new split pin must be used.

5 Unscrew the master cylinder bolts and remove the master cylinder **(see illustration)**. Tip any residual fluid into a container.

Overhaul

6 Inspect the reservoir hose for cracks or splits and replace it with a new one if necessary. If required, undo the screw securing the union and detach it from the master cylinder **(see illustration)**. A new O-ring must be used. Check the hose clamps for corrosion and deformation and replace them with new ones if necessary.

7 Slacken the locknut on the top of the clevis **(see illustration)**. Note how far the clevis is threaded up the pushrod (see Step 14), then thread it off, followed by the locknut **(see illustration)**.

8 Pull the rubber boot out of the master cylinder and off the pushrod **(see illustration)**. Release the circlip using internal circlip pliers, and draw out the pushrod, piston assembly and spring **(see illustrations)**.

9 Clean the inside of the master cylinder with fresh DOT 4 brake fluid. If compressed air is available blow it through the fluid passages.

Caution: NEVER use a petroleum-based solvent to clean brake system components.

9.5 Master cylinder bolts (arrowed)

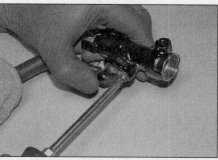

9.6 Remove the hose union if required

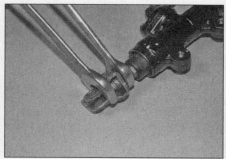

9.7a Slacken the locknut...

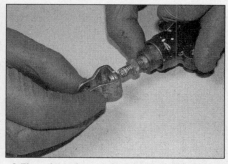

9.7b ...then thread the clevis and locknut off

9.8a Remove the boot...

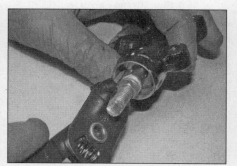

9.8b ...then release the circlip...

9.8c ...and remove the piston and spring

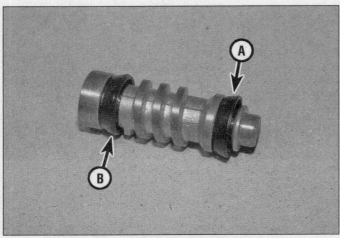

9.12a Make sure the cup (A) and seal (B) are fitted as shown

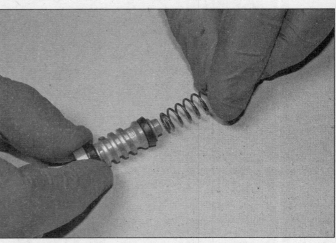

9.12b Fit the spring onto the piston

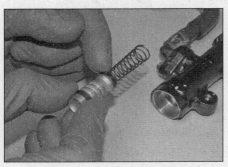

9.12c Lubricate the cup and seal

10 Check the master cylinder bore for surface defects and replace the cylinder with a new one if necessary.

11 All the internal components are supplied in the rebuild kit – use all of the new parts regardless of the apparent condition of the old ones.

12 If not already in place fit the cup and seal onto the piston with their wider sides facing the inner end **(see illustration)**. Fit the narrow end of the spring onto the inner end of the piston **(see illustration)**. Lubricate the piston, cup and seal with new brake fluid, then slide the assembly into the master cylinder, spring first, making sure the lips of the cup and seal do not turn inside out **(see illustration)**.

13 Fit the circlip onto the pushrod with its chamfered side up against the washer. Fit the rounded end of the pushrod against the end of the piston, push the piston in and seat the circlip in its groove in the master cylinder **(see** **illustrations)**. Release the pushrod and check the circlip is securely located. Fit the boot onto the pushrod and into the master cylinder **(see illustrations)**.

14 Thread the locknut and clevis onto the pushrod, position the clevis as noted on removal, and tighten the locknut against it **(see illustrations 9.7b and a)**. The position of the clevis affects brake pedal height. Honda specify an adjustment range for the position of the clevis on the pushrod of 83.0 to 85.0 mm as measured from the centre of the master cylinder's bottom mounting bolt hole to the centre of the clevis pin hole (where the clevis pin joins the pedal to the pushrod), measured parallel to the centreline of the master cylinder **(see illustration)**.

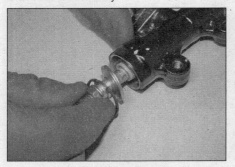

9.13a Push the piston in...

9.13b ...fit the circlip in...

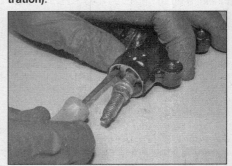

9.13c ...and push it into its groove

9.13d Fit the boot...

9.13e ...locating it as shown

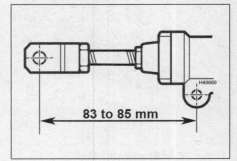

9.14 Clevis position adjustment range

83 to 85 mm

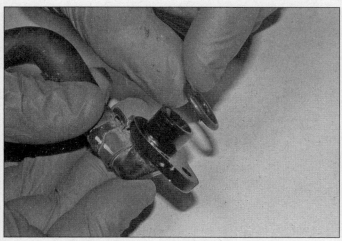

9.15a Fit the new O-ring onto the union…

9.15b …then fit the union

15 If the reservoir hose union was removed clean the threads of the screw and apply fresh threadlock. Fit a new O-ring smeared with brake fluid onto the union, then press the union into the master cylinder and secure it with the screw **(see illustrations)**.

Installation

16 Fit the master cylinder and tighten the bolts to 14 Nm **(see illustration 9.5)**.
17 Align the clevis with the brake pedal and insert the clevis pin **(see illustration 9.4c)**. Fit a new split pin and bend the ends of the pin round to lock it **(see illustration)**.
18 Connect the reservoir hose and secure it with the clamp.
19 Connect the brake hose using new sealing washers on each side of the banjo union **(see illustration 3.19)**, and align it as shown **(see illustration 9.3)**. Tighten the banjo bolt to 34 Nm.
20 Fit the heel guard **(see illustration 9.1)**.
21 Fill the reservoir with DOT 4 brake fluid and bleed the system as described in Section 11.
22 Check that there are no fluid leaks and test the brake before riding the bike.

10 Brake hoses and fittings

Inspection

1 To fully inspect all the brake hoses and pipes on models with ABS raise and support the fuel tank (see Chapter 4), then remove the ETC tray (see Chapter 7).
2 Check brake hose condition according to the brake system check interval in the service schedule (see Chapter 1). Twist and flex the hoses while looking for cracks, bulges and seeping hydraulic fluid. Check extra carefully around the areas where the hoses connect

with the banjo fittings, as these are common areas for hose failure.
3 On models with ABS also check the brake pipes, the hose and pipe joints, and the modulator, referring to the relevant Sections of this Chapter, for signs of fluid leakage and for any dents or cracks in the pipes.
4 Inspect the banjo fittings connected to the brake hoses and the pipe joints on ABS models. If the fittings are rusted, scratched or cracked, fit new hoses as required.

Removal and installation

5 Remove the air filter housing (see Chapter 4) and the ETC tray (see Chapter 7).
6 Drain all old brake fluid from the system (Section 11).
7 The brake hoses have banjo fittings on each end on models without ABS, and on the rear brake system on models with ABS. On the front brake system on models with ABS the hoses have banjo fittings onto the caliper and

master cylinder, and joints that the pipes to and from the modulator thread into with flare nuts **(see illustration)**. Cover the surrounding area with plenty of rags and unscrew the banjo bolt(s) or flare nut at each end of the hose, noting the alignment of the fitting with the master cylinder or brake caliper **(see illustrations 3.1a, 5.4 and 9.3)**. On models with ABS unscrew the pipe joint mounting bolt. Free the hose from any clips or guides and remove it, noting its routing. Discard the banjo union sealing washers. Do not operate the brake lever or pedal while a brake hose is disconnected.
8 Position the new hose, making sure it isn't twisted or otherwise strained, and ensure that it is correctly routed through any clips or guides and is clear of all moving components. On models with ABS fit the pipe joint mounting bolt.
9 Check that the fittings align correctly, then fit the banjo bolt(s), using new sealing

9.17 Use a new split pin

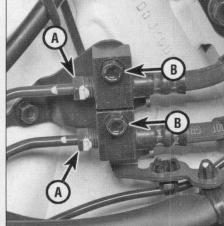

10.7 Flare nuts (A) secure the pipes at each end, and each hose-to-pipe joint is secured by a bolt (B)

11.3 Brake bleeding kit set-up

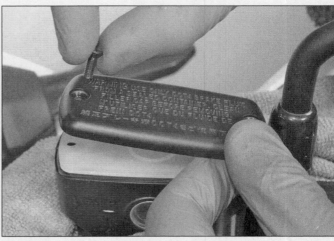

11.5 Remove the cover, plate and diaphragm from the reservoir

washers on both sides of the fitting(s) **(see illustration 3.19)**. Tighten the banjo bolt(s) to 34 Nm. Refer to the next step for the brake pipe flare nut on models with ABS.

10 On models with ABS make sure the new pipe is correctly positioned and fitted into the clips before tightening the nuts. If the correct tools are available tighten the nuts to 14 Nm.

11 Refill the system with new DOT 4 brake fluid and bleed the air from it (Section 11).

12 Check the operation of the brakes before riding the motorcycle.

11 Brake system bleeding and fluid change

Bleeding

1 Bleeding a brake is the process of removing aerated brake fluid from the system. Bleeding is necessary whenever a brake system hydraulic connection is loosened, after a component or hose is replaced with a new one, when a master cylinder or caliper is overhauled, or when there is a spongy feel to the lever and it travels all the way back to the handlebar, and where braking force is less than it should be, and it is not due to any mechanical fault in the system (i.e. a sticking piston in the caliper, or a pad that is not moving as it should due to corrosion, for example on the pad pin). Leaks in the system may also allow air to enter, but leaking brake fluid will reveal their presence and warn you of the need for repair.

2 Brake bleeding is considered by some as a bit of a black art – seasoned professionals sometimes have trouble getting a good firm feel in the brake lever, while a first timer may have no trouble at all. One of the problems, particularly with the front brakes, is that you are working against natural principles – science dictates that air bubbles in a liquid will rise to the top, but the process entails pumping the brake fluid and any air bubbles it contains down, from the master cylinder at the top to the bleed valve in the caliper at the bottom, so while the fluid is moving down the air bubbles will want to rise. Air bubbles can also get trapped, particularly where there are high points in its path, and when there are extra components and pipes such as on models with ABS.

3 To bleed the brakes using the conventional method, you will need some new DOT 4 brake fluid, a length of clear flexible hose, a small container partially filled with clean brake fluid, some rags, and a spanner to fit the brake caliper bleed valve. Bleeding kits that include the hose, a one-way valve and a container are available relatively cheaply from a good auto store, and simplify the task **(see illustration)**.

4 Cover painted components to prevent damage in the event that brake fluid is spilled. *Caution: Brake fluid attacks painted finishes and plastics – to prevent damage from spilled fluid, always cover paintwork when working on the braking system, and clean up any spills immediately using brake cleaner.*

Front brake system

5 Turn the handlebars so the reservoir is level. Undo the reservoir cover screws and remove the cover, diaphragm plate and diaphragm **(see illustration)**. Slowly pump the brake lever a few times to dislodge any air bubbles from the holes in the bottom of the reservoir.

6 Pull the dust cap off the bleed valve on the first caliper **(see illustration)** – both calipers must be bled, but it does not matter which is done first. If using a ring spanner (which is preferable to an open-ended one) fit it onto the valve **(see illustration)**. Attach one end of the bleeding hose to the bleed valve and, if not using a kit, submerge the other end in the clean brake fluid in the container.

7 Check the fluid level in the reservoir – keep it topped up and do not allow the level to drop below the bottom of the window during the procedure **(see illustration)**.

11.6a Pull the dust cap off

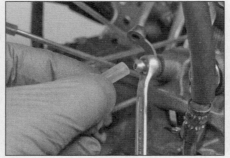

11.6b Fit a ring spanner onto the valve hex then connect the hose

11.7 Keep the reservoir topped up

11.8 Bleeding the front brake system

11.11a Pull the dust cap off the bleed valve

8 Slowly pump the brake lever three or four times, then hold it in and open the bleed valve a quarter turn **(see illustration)**. When the valve is opened, brake fluid will flow out into the clear tubing, and the lever will move toward the handlebar. If there is air in the system there will be air bubbles in the brake fluid coming out of the caliper.

9 When the fluid stops flowing tighten the bleed valve, then slowly release the brake lever. Repeat the process until no air bubbles are visible in the brake fluid leaving the caliper, and the lever is firm when applied, topping the reservoir up when necessary. On completion tighten the bleed valve. Repeat the procedure for the second caliper.

Rear brake system

10 Unscrew the reservoir bolt and displace the reservoir so the cover is clear **(see illustration 9.2a)**. Undo the cover screws and remove the cover, diaphragm plate and diaphragm **(see illustration 9.2b)**. Fit the

reservoir back onto its bracket, making sure it is level and correctly located. Slowly pump the brake pedal a few times to dislodge any air bubbles from the holes in the bottom of the reservoir.

11 Pull the dust cap off the bleed valve on the caliper **(see illustration)**. If using a ring spanner (which is preferable to an open-ended one) fit it onto the valve **(see illustration)**. Attach one end of the bleeding hose to the bleed valve and, if not using a kit, submerge the other end in the clean brake fluid in the container.

12 Check the fluid level in the reservoir – keep it topped up and do not allow the level to drop below the lower level line during the procedure **(see illustration)**.

13 Slowly pump the brake pedal three or four times, then hold it down and open the bleed valve a quarter turn **(see illustration)**. When the valve is opened, brake fluid will flow out into the clear tubing, and the pedal will move down. If there is air in the system there will be

11.11b Fit a ring spanner onto the valve hex then connect the hose

air bubbles in the brake fluid coming out of the caliper.

14 When the fluid stops flowing tighten the bleed valve, then slowly release the brake pedal. Repeat the process until no air bubbles are visible in the brake fluid leaving the caliper, and the pedal is firm when applied,

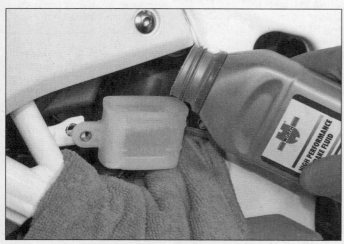

11.12 Keep the reservoir topped up

11.13 Bleeding the rear brake system

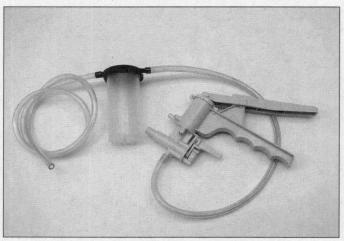

11.17 A vacuum-operated brake bleeding tool

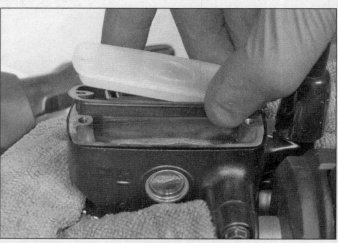

11.19 Make sure the diaphragm is fully seated all round before fitting the plate and cover

topping the reservoir up when necessary. On completion tighten the bleed valve.

Both systems

15 If it is not possible to produce a firm feel to the lever or pedal, remove body panels as required (see Chapter 7), and on models with ABS raise the fuel tank (see Chapter 4), and look for any high point in the system in which a pocket of air may become trapped. Displace and agitate the hose or pipe so the bubble can be dislodged (but take care not to bend a pipe on ABS models) – tapping it may help. If necessary displace the master cylinder and/or the caliper, and free the brake hose(s) from its guides and move the parts around to dislodge the air and encourage it towards a bleed valve – refer to the relevant Sections as required to displace components. On ABS models it is not practical to disturb the modulator as the pipes have to be detached, allowing more air to enter the system – if you cannot get the system to bleed correctly take the bike to a Honda dealer.

16 If you are still having trouble the fluid may be full of many tiny air bubbles rather than a few big ones. To remedy this apply some pressure to the system, for the front brake by tying the front brake lever lightly back to the handlebar, and for the rear by tying a weight to the brake pedal – do not apply too much pressure or the cup and seals in the master cylinder and caliper may fail. Let the fluid stabilise for a few hours, after which the tiny bubbles should either have risen to the top in the reservoir, or have formed into one or more big bubbles that can be more easily bled out by repeating the bleeding procedure.

17 If bleeding the system using the conventional tools and methods stated does not give satisfactory results, or if otherwise preferred, you can use a commercially available vacuum-type brake bleeding tool, such as the Mity-vac shown, following the manufacturer's instructions (see illustration). This type of tool literally sucks the fluid out

by creating a vacuum at the bleed valve. Users of such tools often get confused by the amount of air that appears to be in the brake fluid – more often than not this is caused by the vacuum sucking air past the bleed valve threads (air provides less resistance to the vacuum than the brake fluid) where it mixes with the fluid being drawn out. If this is the case the vacuum applied may be too great, or the bleed valve may have been loosened too much. One way to get round this is to remove the bleed valve and thread some PTFE tape around its threads, but note that doing so will be a bit messy, so have some rag to hand.

18 When the system has been successfully bled there should be a good and progressively firm feel as the lever or pedal is applied, and the lever or pedal should not be able to travel all the way back to the handlebar or down to its stop.

19 On completion remove the equipment used and make sure the bleed valve is tight (to 5.5 Nm if you have a suitable torque wrench), then fit the dust cap. Top-up the reservoir, then fit the diaphragm, diaphragm plate, and cover (see illustration). Fit the rear fluid reservoir onto its bracket, making sure it is level and correctly located. Check for spilled brake fluid and clean up as required. Check the entire system for fluid leaks.

20 Test the brakes before riding the bike.

Fluid change

21 Changing the brake fluid is a similar process to bleeding the brakes and requires the same materials plus a suitable tool (such as a syringe, or alternatively lots of absorbent rag or paper) for siphoning the fluid out of the reservoir.

22 Cover painted components and fit the equipment to the relevant caliper following the appropriate Steps in the bleeding procedure given above. Remove the reservoir cover, diaphragm plate and diaphragm and

siphon the old fluid out of the reservoir (see illustration 11.5 or 9.2a and b). Wipe the reservoir clean. Fill the reservoir with new brake fluid (see illustration 11.7 or 11.12). Pump the brake lever or pedal as described above then hold it in or down and open the bleed valve (see illustrations 11.8 or 11.13). When the valve is opened, brake fluid will flow into the clear tubing, and the lever will move toward the handlebar, or the pedal will move down.

23 When the fluid stops flowing tighten the bleed valve, then slowly release the brake lever or pedal. Keep the reservoir topped-up with new fluid at all times or air may enter the system and greatly increase the length of the task. Repeat the process until new fluid can be seen emerging from the caliper bleed valve.

HAYNES HiNT *Old brake fluid is invariably much darker in colour than new fluid, making it easy to see when all old fluid has been expelled from the system.*

24 On completion remove the equipment used and make sure the bleed valve is tight (to the torque setting specified at the beginning of the Chapter if you have a suitable torque wrench), then fit the dust cap. Top-up the reservoir, then fit the diaphragm, diaphragm plate, and cover. Check for spilled brake fluid and clean up as required. Check the entire system for fluid leaks.

25 Check the operation of the brakes before riding the motorcycle.

Draining the system for overhaul

26 Draining the brake fluid is again a similar process to bleeding the brakes. The quickest and easiest way is to use a commercially available vacuum-type brake bleeding tool (see Step 17) – follow the manufacturer's

instructions. Otherwise follow the procedure described above for changing the fluid, but quite simply do not put any new fluid into the reservoir – the system fills itself with air instead.

27 When it comes to refilling the system start by adding new fluid from a sealed container to the reservoir, then perform the bleeding procedure as described above until the fluid comes out of the bleed valve, and keep at it until you are certain there is no more air left in the system.

12 ABS operation

1 The anti-lock brake system (ABS) prevents the wheels from locking up under hard braking or on uneven road surfaces. A sensor on each wheel transmits information about the speed of rotation to the control unit in the ABS modulator; if the unit senses that a wheel is about to lock, it releases brake pressure to that wheel momentarily, preventing a skid.

2 The anti-lock system is self-checking and is activated when the ignition switch is turned on – the ABS indicator light in the instrument cluster will come on and will remain on until road speed increases above 6 mph (10 kmh) at which point, if the ABS is normal, the light will go off. If the ABS indicator light does not come on initially there is a fault in the system – see Section 13.

3 If the indicator light remains on or flashes, or starts flashing while the machine is being ridden, there is a fault in the system and the ABS function will be switched off – the brakes will still function but in normal mode. If you turn the ignition OFF while the light is flashing, the fault code will not be displayed again if the ignition is switched on again, but will be stored in the system's memory.

4 To retrieve any stored fault codes, remove the rider's seat (see Chapter 7). Locate the engine management system data link connector (DLC), which is a red blanked single-sided 4-pin connector under the front of the passenger seat **(see illustration)**. Remove the blanking cap from the connector **(see illustration)**. Either fit the Honda SCS service connector (Part No. 070PZ-ZY30100, available from your dealer), or its after-market equivalent, or bridge the grey/blue and green/blue wire terminals of the connector with a piece of electrical wire **(see illustration)**. With the terminals connected, make sure the kill switch is in the RUN position then turn the ignition ON and observe the ABS indicator light. If there are stored fault codes, the light will come on for 2 seconds, then go out for 3.6 seconds, then start to flash the fault code. If there are no stored fault codes the light will come on for 2 seconds, then go out for 3.6 seconds, then come on and stay on. Do not apply the brake lever or pedal during code retrieval.

5 The indicator light emits long (1.3 second) and short (0.3 second) flashes to give out the fault code. A long flash is used to indicate the first digit of the double-digit fault code. For example, two long (1.3 sec) flashes followed by three short (0.3 sec) flashes indicates the fault code number 23. If there is more than one fault code, there will be a 3.6 sec gap before the next code is revealed (the codes are revealed in ascending numerical order). Once all codes have been revealed, the display will continuously run through the code(s) stored in its memory, revealing each one in turn with a short gap between them.

6 Once all the codes have been revealed, switch off the ignition and (where necessary) remove the auxiliary wire or SCS connector from the data link connector. Identify the faulty component or circuit using the table in Section 13, then refer to the check procedures.

7 Once the fault has been corrected, erase the fault code(s) as follows. Follow Step 4 to connect the terminals in the DLC. Hold the front brake lever on and with the kill switch set to run turn the ignition switch on – the ABS light should come on for two seconds, then go out. When the light goes out immediately release the brake lever – the light should come on. When the light comes on, immediately apply the brake lever – the light should go out. When the light goes out, immediately release the brake lever. The code(s) should now be erased, in which case the light will flash twice, then come on and stay on.

8 Turn the ignition switch OFF and remove the auxiliary wire or SCS connector when the code or codes have been erased. Check that the ABS is operating normally (see Step 2).

9 If necessary, repeat the reset procedure.

Caution: The ABS indicator may diagnose a fault if tyre sizes other than those specified by Honda are fitted, if the tyre pressures are incorrect, if the machine has been run continuously over bumpy roads, if the front wheel comes off the ground whilst riding (wheelie) or if the machine is on an auxiliary stand with the engine running and the rear wheel turning.

12.4a Data link connector (arrowed)

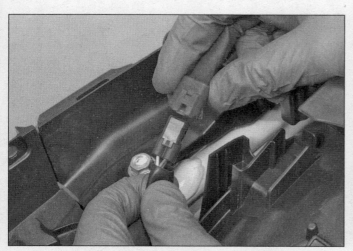

12.4b Displace the connector and remove the cap

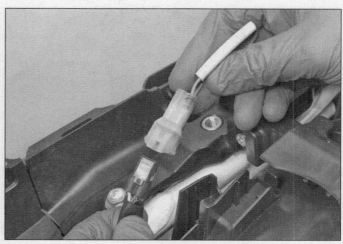

12.4c Honda SCS service connector

13 ABS fault diagnosis

ABS system checks

Note: *Before carrying out any specific checks, follow the procedure in Section 12 to erase the fault code, then activating the self-checking procedure. If the fault code is the result of unusual riding or conditions or a temporary glitch, the indicator light will go off. If the fault code reappears perform the following checks.*

1 If a fault is indicated in the ABS, first check that the battery is fully charged, then check the ABS fuses (see Chapter 8).

2 In the case of faults related to the wheel speed sensors and/or pulse rings, measure the air gap between the wheel speed sensor and the pulse ring with a feeler gauge **(see illustrations)**, then compare the result with the Specification given at the beginning of the Chapter. The gap is not adjustable – if it is outside the specification, check that the sensor and pulse ring fixings are tight. Also check that the components are not damaged and that there is no dirt or anything else on the sensor tip or between the slots in the pulse ring. If any of the components are damaged they must be replaced with new ones.

3 Refer to Chapter 8, Section 2 for general electrical fault finding procedures and equipment, and check the wiring and connectors in the circuit related to the fault code given, referring to Section 14 for access to the components and their wiring connectors. Carry out all checks with the ignition switch OFF.

4 If after a thorough check, the source of a fault has not been identified, have the system tested by a Honda dealer.

Fault code table

Fault codes	Faulty component or system	Possible causes
No code displayed	ABS light does not come on with ignition	Blown ABS fuse
	ABS light on all the time	Faulty wiring or wiring connector
		Faulty modulator
		Faulty ABS indicator light
11, 12, 15, 21	Front wheel speed sensor circuit	Faulty wiring or wiring connector
	Front wheel speed sensor	Faulty sensor
	Front wheel pulse ring	Damaged pulse ring
13, 14, 15, 23	Rear wheel speed sensor circuit	Faulty wiring or wiring connector
	Rear wheel speed sensor	Faulty sensor
	Rear wheel pulse ring	Damaged pulse ring
31, 32, 33, 34	Modulator solenoid valve	Faulty modulator
41 and 42	Front wheel lock – riding conditions	Faulty sensor
	Front wheel speed sensor circuit	Faulty wiring or wiring connector
	Front wheel speed sensor	Damaged pulse ring
	Front wheel pulse ring	
43	Rear wheel lock – riding conditions	Faulty wiring or wiring connector
	Rear wheel speed sensor circuit	Faulty sensor
	Rear wheel speed sensor	Damaged pulse ring
	Rear wheel pulse ring	
51, 52, 53	Modulator motor lock	Faulty modulator
		Faulty wiring
		Blown ABS 30A modulator fuse
54	Relay circuit	Blown ABS 30A modulator fuse
		Faulty relay circuit
		Faulty modulator
61	Power supply voltage low	ABS 7.5A or 10A fuse
		Faulty wiring or wiring connector
		Faulty modulator
62	Power supply voltage high	Faulty wiring or wiring connector
		Faulty modulator
71	Incorrect tyre size	Incorrect tyre
81	CPU in modulator control unit	Faulty modulator
82	Rear ABS OFF indicator does not work	Faulty indicator or wiring

13.2a Measuring the front sensor air gap

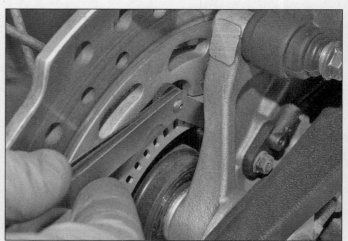

13.2b Measuring the rear sensor air gap

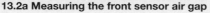

14.2a Front wheel sensor wiring connector (arrowed)

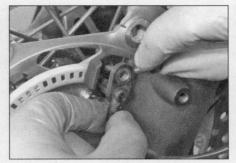

14.2b Unscrew the bolt and draw the sensor out

14.6 Pulse ring screws (arrowed)

14 ABS components

Front wheel sensor

1 Remove the air filter housing (see Chapter 4). Remove the front mudguard (see Chapter 7).

2 Release and disconnect the sensor wiring connector **(see illustration)**. Feed the connector down to the sensor, releasing the ties and guides, and noting its routing. Unscrew the sensor bolt and remove the sensor **(see illustration)**.

3 Make sure the tip of the sensor, its mounting surfaces, and the pulse ring are clean. Clean the threads of the bolt and apply fresh threadlock. Fit the sensor and tighten the bolt to 10 Nm. Feed the wiring up to the connector, routing and securing it as noted on removal.

4 Check the air gap (Section 13, Step 2). Install the air filter housing (see Chapter 4) and the front mudguard (see Chapter 7).

Front pulse ring

5 Remove the front wheel (Section 17).

6 Undo the three screws and remove the pulse ring **(see illustration)**.

7 Before fitting the pulse ring, make sure there is no dirt or corrosion where it seats on the disc. If the ring does not sit flat when it is screwed down, it may create a fault code.

8 Either fit the ring using new screws, or clean the threads of the original ones and apply fresh thread locking compound, and tighten them evenly and a little at a time in a criss-cross pattern to 7 Nm.

9 Install the wheel (Section 17).

10 Check the wheel speed sensor air gap (Section 13, Step 2).

Rear wheel sensor

11 Remove the rear wheel (Section 18). Remove the ETC tray (see Chapter 7).

12 Disconnect and release the sensor wiring connector **(see illustration)**. If access is too restricted by the brake hose to the modulator on 2016/17 models refer below and disconnect the hose.

13 Feed the connector down to the sensor, releasing it from its guides, and noting its routing **(see illustration 7.35b)**. Displace caliper bracket from the swingarm, unscrew the sensor bolt and remove the sensor **(see illustration)**.

14 Make sure the tip of the sensor, its mounting surfaces, and the pulse ring are clean. Fit the sensor and tighten the bolt to 10 Nm. Feed the wiring up to the connector, routing and securing it as noted on removal. If the brake hose was disconnected from the modulator refer below to connect it, then bleed the brake system (Section 11).

15 Install the wheel (Section 18). Check the air gap (Section 13, Step 2). Install the ETC tray (see Chapter 7).

Rear pulse ring

16 Remove the rear wheel (Section 18).

17 Undo the three screws and remove the pulse ring **(see illustration)**.

18 Before fitting the pulse ring, make sure there is no dirt or corrosion where it seats on the disc. If the ring does not sit flat when it is screwed down, it may create a fault code.

19 Either fit the ring using new screws, or clean the threads of the original ones and apply fresh thread locking compound, and tighten them evenly and a little at a time in a criss-cross pattern to 7 Nm.

20 Install the wheel (Section 18).

21 Check the wheel speed sensor air gap (Section 13, Step 2).

Modulator

Note: *Before removing the modulator it is best to drain all old brake fluid from the brake system, then fill with new fluid on installation (Section 11). The modulator cannot be dismantled for overhaul, and no component parts are available. If it fails, it must be replaced with a new one.*

2016/17 models

22 Remove the luggage rack (see Chapter 7).

23 Disconnect the rear turn signal and licence plate light wiring connectors. Undo the tail cover screws, one on each side with a collar, and two on the underside. Release the tabs and remove the tail cover by drawing it back.

24 Disconnect the seat lock cable.

25 Remove the regulator/rectifier (see Chapter 8).

26 On Europe models without ABS or DCT

14.12 Rear wheel sensor wiring connector (arrowed)

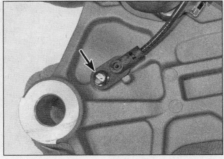

14.13 Rear wheel sensor bolt (arrowed)

14.17 Pulse ring screws (arrowed)

14.44 Displace the relays (arrowed)

14.45 Push the locking tab (A) rearward to release the connector (B)

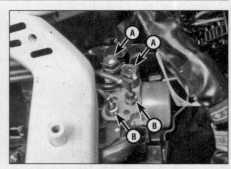

14.47 Brake hose banjo bolts (A), brake pipe nuts (B)

displace the turn signal relay, on Europe models with ABS or DCT disconnect the turn signal relay wiring, and on US models remove the turn signal relay (see Chapter 8, Section 10).

27 Remove the fuel tank and the exhaust system (see Chapter 4).

28 Release the wiring tie from the left-hand side.

29 On models with the EVAP system disconnect the hoses from the EVAP canister.

30 Release the wiring connectors and fan relay from the tray. Release the rear wheel speed sensor wiring from the guide on the right-hand side of the frame, above the rear brake master cylinder.

31 Release and disconnect the modulator wiring connector.

32 Unscrew the brake pipe joint bolts to give some freedom of movement in the pipes when disconnected from the modulator. Cover the area around the modulator with clean rag to prevent damage to paintwork in the event that brake fluid is spilled.

33 Unscrew the brake hose banjo bolts and detach the banjo unions, noting their alignment. Seal each banjo union using a nut and bolt and the two sealing washers or a dedicated tool **(see illustrations 3.1c and d)**, or wrap plastic foodwrap around it. New sealing washers must be fitted on reassembly.

34 Unscrew the brake pipe nuts and detach the pipes. Plug the ends of the pipes or wrap something tightly around them to minimise fluid loss if the system wasn't drained, and to prevent dirt entering the system.

35 Unscrew the two modulator mounting bolts.

36 Unscrew the bolt securing each side of the tray. Release the tray and drop it down.

37 Where fitted remove the EVAP canister.

38 Release the modulator bracket from the lug on the frame and remove the modulator, taking care not to snag the brake pipes.

39 If required unscrew the two bolts and remove the modulator from the bracket.

40 Note the collars in the rubber mounts – replace the rubbers with new ones if cracked or hardened.

41 Installation is the reverse of removal, noting the following:
● Smear the pipe nut threads with clean brake fluid. If the correct tools are available tighten them to 14 Nm.
● Use a new sealing washer on each side of the banjo unions. Align the hoses as shown and tighten the banjo bolts to 34 Nm.
● Make sure the wiring connector is secure.
● Follow the procedure in Section 11 to refill and bleed the brake system. Check that there are no fluid leaks and test the brakes before riding the bike.

Caution: Brake fluid attacks painted finishes and plastics – to prevent damage from spilled fluid, always cover paintwork when working on the braking system, and clean up any spills immediately using brake cleaner.

2018-on models

42 Remove the fuel tank (see Chapter 4).

43 Remove the ETC tray (see Chapter 7).

44 Release the rear wheel speed sensor wiring connector **(see illustration 14.12)** and release the relays from their mounts **(see illustration)**.

45 Release and disconnect the modulator wiring connector **(see illustration)**.

46 Unscrew the brake pipe joint bolts to give some freedom of movement in the pipes when disconnected from the modulator. Cover the area around the modulator with clean rag to prevent damage to paintwork in the event that brake fluid is spilled.

47 Unscrew the brake hose banjo bolts and detach the banjo unions, noting their alignment **(see illustration)**. Seal each banjo union using a nut and bolt and the two sealing washers or a dedicated tool **(see illustrations 3.1c and d)**, or wrap plastic foodwrap around it. New sealing washers must be fitted on reassembly.

48 Unscrew the brake pipe nuts and detach the pipes **(see illustration 14.47)**. Plug the ends of the pipes or wrap something tightly around them to minimise fluid loss if the system wasn't drained, and to prevent dirt entering the system.

49 Unscrew the two modulator mounting bolts **(see illustration)**.

50 Release the modulator bracket from the lug on the frame and remove the modulator, taking care not to snag the brake pipes **(see illustration)**.

51 If required unscrew the two bolts and remove the modulator from the bracket.

52 Note the collars in the rubber mounts – replace the rubbers with new ones if cracked or hardened.

53 Installation is the reverse of removal, noting the following:
● Smear the pipe nut threads with clean brake fluid. If the correct tools are available tighten them to 14 Nm.
● Use a new sealing washer on each side of the banjo unions. Align the hoses as shown and tighten the banjo bolts to 34 Nm.
● Make sure the wiring connector is secure.
● Follow the procedure in Section 11 to refill and bleed the brake system. Check that there are no fluid leaks and test the brakes before riding the bike.

Caution: Brake fluid attacks painted finishes and plastics – to prevent damage from spilled fluid, always cover paintwork when working on the braking system, and clean up any spills immediately using brake cleaner.

14.49 Modulator mounting bolts (arrowed)

14.50 Release the bracket from the lug (arrowed)

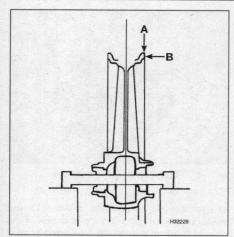

15.2 Check the wheel for radial (out-of-round) runout (A) and axial (side-to-side) runout (B)

15 Wheel runout

1 In order to carry out a proper inspection of the wheels, it is necessary to support the bike securely in an upright position so that the wheel being inspected is raised off the ground. Clean the wheels thoroughly to remove mud and dirt that may interfere with the inspection procedure or mask defects. Make a general check of the wheels (see Chapter 1) and tyres (see *Pre-ride checks*).

2 Attach a dial gauge to the fork or the swingarm and position its tip against the side of the wheel rim **(see illustration)**. Spin the wheel slowly and check the axial (side-to-side) runout at the rim.

3 In order to accurately check radial (out of round) runout with the dial gauge, remove the wheel from the machine, and the tyre from the wheel. With the axle clamped in a vice and the dial gauge positioned on the top of the rim, the wheel can be rotated to check the runout.

4 An easier, though slightly less accurate, method is to attach a stiff wire pointer to the fork or the swingarm and position the end a fraction of an inch from the edge of the wheel rim where the wheel and tyre join. If the wheel is true, the distance from the pointer to the rim will be constant as the wheel is rotated. If wheel runout is excessive, check the wheel bearings very carefully before renewing the wheel.

5 If wheel runout is excessive, first check the wheel bearings. If they are good, it should be possible to realign the wheel by adjusting the spokes, but to do this accurately takes knowledge and skill, and should be left to an experienced wheel builder.

16 Wheel alignment check

1 Misalignment of the wheels due to a bent frame or forks can cause strange and possibly serious handling problems. If the frame or forks are at fault, repair by a frame specialist or renewal are the only options.

2 To check wheel alignment you will need an assistant, a length of string or a perfectly straight piece of wood and a ruler. A plumb bob or spirit level for checking that the wheels are vertical will also be required.

3 Support the bike on an auxiliary stand. Measure the width of both tyres at their widest points. Subtract the smaller measurement from the larger measurement, then divide the difference by two. The result is the amount of offset that should exist between the front and rear tyres on both sides of the machine.

4 If the string method is used, have your assistant hold one end of it about halfway between the floor and the rear axle, with the string touching the back edge of the rear tyre sidewall.

5 Run the other end of the string forward and pull it tight so that it is roughly parallel to the floor **(see illustration)**. Slowly bring the string into contact with the front edge of the rear tyre sidewall, then turn the front wheel until it is parallel with the string. Measure the distance from the front tyre sidewall to the string.

6 Repeat the procedure on the other side of the motorcycle. The distance from the front tyre sidewall to the string should be equal on both sides.

7 As previously mentioned, a perfectly straight length of wood or metal bar may be substituted for the string **(see illustration)**.

8 If the distance between the string and tyre is greater on one side, or if the rear wheel appears to be out of alignment, and the chain adjustment markers are equally set (see Chapter 1), have your machine checked by a Honda dealer or frame specialist.

9 If the front-to-back alignment is correct, the wheels still may be out of alignment vertically.

10 Using a plumb bob or spirit level, check the rear wheel to make sure it is vertical. To do this, hold the string of the plumb bob against the tyre upper sidewall and allow the weight to settle just off the floor. If the string touches both the upper and lower tyre sidewalls and is perfectly straight, the wheel is vertical. If it is not, adjust the stand until it is.

11 Once the rear wheel is vertical, check the front wheel in the same manner. If both wheels are not perfectly vertical, the frame and/or major suspension components are bent.

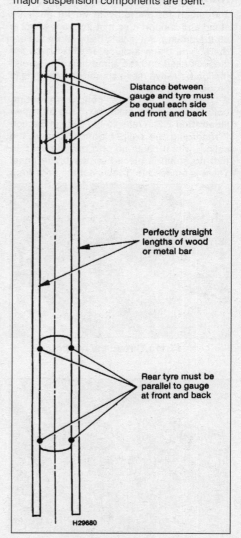

Distance between gauge and tyre must be equal each side and front and back

Perfectly straight lengths of wood or metal bar

Rear tyre must be parallel to gauge at front and back

16.7 Wheel alignment check using a straight-edge

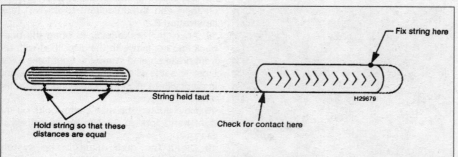

Fix string here

String held taut

Check for contact here

Hold string so that these distances are equal

16.5 Wheel alignment check using string

17.3 Axle nut with cap (A), axle clamp bolts (B)

17.5 Withdraw the axle and remove the wheel

17.6 Remove the spacers

17 Front wheel

Removal

1 Position the motorcycle on an auxiliary stand and support it so that the front wheel is off the ground. If a jack is being placed under the engine place a piece of wood between the jack head and the sump guard to spread the load. Always make sure the motorcycle is properly supported.

2 Unscrew the brake caliper mounting bolts and slide the calipers off the disc **(see illustration 2.2)** – refer to the Note in Section 2 regarding the caliper bolts. Support the caliper with a cable-tie or a bungee cord so that no strain is placed on the brake hose. There is no need to disconnect the hose from

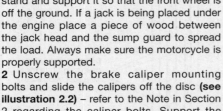

17.11a Thread the nut on

17.11b Multi-size axle hex bit available from good tool suppliers

the caliper. Do not operate the front brake lever with the caliper displaced.

3 Where fitted remove the cap from the left-hand end of the axle. Unscrew the axle nut **(see illustration)**.

4 Slacken the axle clamp bolts on the bottom of each fork **(see illustration 17.3)**.

5 Take the weight of the wheel, then knock the axle through from the left using a soft-faced mallet to prevent damage to the threads, then withdraw it from the right and remove the wheel **(see illustration)**.

6 Remove the spacer from each side of the wheel **(see illustration)**. Clean all old grease off the spacers, axle and seals.

Caution: Don't lay the wheel down on the disc.

7 Check the axle is straight by rolling it on a flat surface such as a piece of plate glass (first wipe off all old grease and remove any corrosion using steel wool). If the equipment

is available, place the axle in V-blocks and measure the runout using a dial gauge. If the axle is bent or the runout exceeds the limit specified, replace it with a new one.

8 Check the condition of the grease seals and wheel bearings (Section 19).

Installation

9 Apply a smear of grease to the inside of the wheel spacers and the seals, then fit the spacers into the seals **(see illustration 17.6)**.

10 Manoeuvre the wheel into position between the forks with the directional arrow on the tyre pointing in the direction of forward rotation. Apply a thin coat of grease to the axle.

11 Lift the wheel into place, making sure the spacers remain in position, then slide the axle all the way in from the right-hand side, setting its outer end flush with the fork **(see illustration 17.5)**. Thread the nut onto the left-hand end, then counter-hold the head of the axle using a 17 mm hex bit, or temporarily tighten the axle clamp bolts to 22 Nm if you don't have a bit, and tighten the axle nut to 60 Nm **(see illustrations)**. Where fitted press the cap into the end of the axle **(see illustration)**.

12 Loosen the axle clamp bolts on the right-hand fork, then tighten the clamp bolts on the left fork to 22 Nm – after tightening the second bolt, tighten the first one again as it may well have loosened a bit as the second closed the clamp on that side, and after doing that tighten the second one again, and so on until both are at 22 Nm.

13 Lower the front wheel to the ground. Slide the brake calipers onto the discs and tighten the bolts (using new ones, or the old ones cleaned and threadlocked) to 45 Nm **(see illustration 2.2)**.

14 Apply the brake lever to bring the pads back into contact with the disc, then with the front brake applied pump the front forks a few times to settle all components in position, and in particular to align the right-hand fork on the axle.

15 Now tighten the axle clamp bolts on the right-hand fork to 22 Nm as described in Step 12.

16 Clean the disc using brake system cleaner. On models with ABS check the wheel speed sensor air gap (Section 13, Step 2). Test the brake before riding the bike.

17.11c Tighten the nut to the specified torque

17.11d Fit the cap

18.1 After-market tool for holding the front brake lever on

18.2a Unscrew the axle nut and remove the washer...

18.2b ...and the adjustment marker

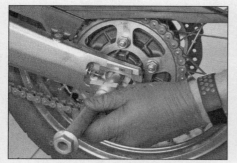

18.3 Withdraw the axle and lower the wheel

18.4a Slip the chain off the sprocket

18.4b Draw the wheel back and displace the caliper bracket when clear

18 Rear wheel

Removal

1 Support the bike on an auxiliary stand so that the rear wheel is off the ground. Always make sure the motorcycle is properly supported. On models with DCT make sure the parking brake is off. Fully slacken the chain (see Chapter 1). Tie the front brake on so the bike can't roll forward **(see illustration)**.

2 Unscrew the axle nut and remove the washer and the adjustment marker **(see illustrations)**.

3 Take the weight of the wheel, then withdraw the axle from the left-hand side, bringing the adjustment marker with it, and lower the wheel to the ground **(see illustration)**. If the axle is difficult to withdraw, drive it out using a soft-faced mallet to prevent damage to the threads.

4 Disengage the chain from the sprocket **(see illustration)**. Draw the wheel back until the caliper bracket is clear of its guide on the swingarm, then lift it out from between the swingarm and the wheel and support it clear **(see illustration)**. Remove the wheel. Fit the caliper bracket back onto the swingarm if required, and secure it using a cable-tie.

Note: *Don't lay the wheel down on the disc or sprocket – set the wheel on wood blocks or lean it against something with the tyre in*

contact. *Do not operate the brake pedal with the wheel removed.*

5 Remove the shouldered spacer from the left-hand side of the wheel and the plain spacer from the right-hand side **(see illustrations)**. Clean all old grease off the spacers, axle and seals.

6 Check the axle is straight by rolling it on a flat surface such as a piece of plate glass (if the axle is corroded, first remove the corrosion with steel wool). If the equipment is available, place the axle in V-blocks and check the runout using a dial gauge. If the axle is bent or the runout exceeds the limit specified at the beginning of the Chapter, replace it with a new one.

7 Check the condition of the grease seals and wheel bearings (Section 19).

Installation

8 Apply a smear of grease to the inside of the wheel spacers and the seals. Fit the

18.5a Remove the shouldered left-hand spacer...

shouldered spacer into the left-hand side of the wheel and the plain spacer into the right-hand side **(see illustrations 18.5a and b)**. Apply a thin coat of grease to the axle. If the caliper bracket is located on the swingarm displace it and support it clear.

9 Fit the adjustment marker onto the axle.

10 Manoeuvre the wheel into position between the ends of the swingarm. Slide the brake caliper bracket between the wheel and the swingarm and locate it on its guide **(see illustration 18.4b)**. Engage the drive chain with the sprocket **(see illustration 18.4a)**.

11 Lift the wheel into position, guiding the disc between the pads, and slide the axle in from the left **(see illustration 18.3)**, making sure the spacers and caliper bracket remain correctly installed. Locate the adjustment marker against the swingarm. Check that everything is correctly aligned. Fit the

18.5b ...and the plain right-hand spacer

adjustment marker onto the right-hand end of the axle, then fit the washer and the axle nut, but leave it loose at this stage **(see illustrations 18.2b and a)**.

12 Adjust the drive chain slack (see Chapter 1). On completion counter-hold the head of the axle and tighten the nut to 100 Nm **(see illustration)**.

13 Clean the brake disc using brake system cleaner. Operate the brake pedal several times to bring the pads into contact with the disc. On models with ABS check the wheel speed sensor air gap (Section 13, Step 2).

14 Test the brake before riding the bike.

19 Wheel bearings

Note: *Always replace the wheel bearings in sets, never individually. Avoid using a high pressure cleaner on the wheel bearing area.*

Front wheel bearings

1 Remove the wheel (Section 17). If required remove the discs to prevent them or the ABS pulse ring (where fitted) being damaged or distorted during bearing removal (Section 4). Support the wheel on wood blocks so that the wheel rim takes the weight of the wheel.

2 Inspect the seals and bearings – check that the bearing inner race turns smoothly and that the outer race is a tight fit in the hub (see *Tools and Workshop Tips* in the Reference Section). Do not remove the bearings unless they are going to be replaced with new ones.

19.3 Lever out the bearing seals

18.12 Tighten the axle nut to the specified torque

3 If new components are needed lever out the bearing seal from each side of the hub using a flat-bladed screwdriver or a seal hook **(see illustration)**. Take care not to damage the hub. Discard the seals as new ones must be fitted on reassembly.

4 Move the centre spacer to one side to expose the inner race of the bearing **(see illustration)**. Locate a drift on the exposed race of the lower bearing and drive the bearing out **(see illustration)**. If you can't get sufficient purchase, remove the upper bearing using an internal expanding puller with slide-hammer attachment, which can be obtained commercially – select the correct attachment and locate it between the inner race of the bearing and the spacer, then tighten the inner bolt to expand and lock the puller **(see illustration 19.14b)**. Attach the slide-hammer, hold the wheel firmly down and jar the bearing out **(see illustration 19.14c)**.

19.4a Push the spacer across

Having removed the first bearing remove the spacer that fits between the bearings.

5 Remove the other bearing using a suitable drift (such as a socket on an extension) inserted from the top and located on the inner race.

6 Thoroughly clean the hub area of the wheel with a suitable solvent and inspect the bearing housing for scoring and wear.

7 Drive the new bearings into the hub using a bearing driver or suitable socket that bears on the outer race only, not the inner race **(see illustration)**. Fit the left-hand bearing first, with its marked side facing outwards. Drive the bearing in squarely and all the way onto its seat.

8 Turn the wheel over and fit the bearing spacer. Fit the right-hand bearing in the same way as the first.

9 Fit the new seals into the hub using finger pressure, then level them with the rim using a small block of wood **(see illustration)**. Smear the seal lips with grease.

10 Install the brake disc, and on ABS models the pulse ring, if removed (Section 4). Clean the disc using brake system cleaner, then install the wheel (Section 17).

Rear wheel bearings

11 Remove the wheel (Section 18). If required remove the disc (Section 8), and on ABS models the pulse ring (Section 14), to prevent it/them being damaged or distorted during bearing removal. Support the wheel on wood blocks so that the wheel rim takes the weight of the wheel. Lift the sprocket coupling out of the hub **(see illustration)**.

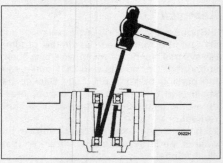

19.4b Drive the bearing out using a drift located as shown

19.7 Using a socket to drive the bearing in

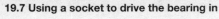

19.9 Fit the seal, setting it flush with the rim

19.11 Lift the sprocket coupling off the wheel

19.13 Lever out the bearing seal

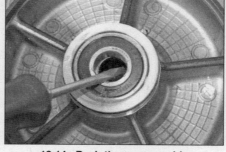

19.14a Push the spacer aside

19.14b Locate the puller under the bearing and tighten it...

12 Inspect the seal and the bearings in both sides of the hub – check that the bearing inner race turns smoothly and that the outer race is a tight fit in the hub (see *Tools and Workshop Tips* in the Reference section). Do not remove the bearings unless they are going to be replaced with new ones.

13 If new components are needed lever out the bearing seal from the right-hand side of the hub using a flat-bladed screwdriver or a seal hook **(see illustration)**. Take care not to damage the hub. Discard the seal as a new one should be fitted on reassembly.

14 Move the centre spacer to one side to expose the inner race of the bearing **(see illustration)**. Locate a drift on the exposed race of the lower bearing and drive the bearing out **(see illustration 19.4b)**. If you can't get sufficient purchase, remove the upper bearing using an internal expanding puller with slide-hammer attachment, which can be obtained commercially – select the correct attachment and locate it behind the inner race of the bearing, then tighten the inner bolt to expand and lock the puller **(see illustration)**. Attach the slide-hammer, hold the wheel firmly down and jar the bearing out **(see illustration)**. Having removed the first bearing remove the spacer that fits between the bearings.

15 Remove the other bearing using a suitable drift (such as a socket on an extension) inserted from the top and located on the inner race.

16 Thoroughly clean the hub area of the wheel with a suitable solvent and inspect the bearing housing for scoring and wear.

19.14c ...then fit the slide-hammer and jar the bearing out

17 Drive the new bearings into the hub using a bearing driver or suitable socket that bears on the outer race only, not the inner race **(see illustration)**. Fit the right-hand bearing first, with its marked side facing outwards. Drive the bearing in squarely and all the way onto its seat.

18 Turn the wheel over and fit the bearing spacer. Fit the second bearing in the same way as the first.

19 Fit the new seal into the right-hand side of the hub using finger pressure, then level it with the rim using a small block of wood **(see illustration)**. Smear the seal lips with grease.

20 Check the sprocket coupling/rubber dampers (Section 23). Check the condition of the hub O-ring and clean it or replace it with a new one if necessary **(see illustration)**. Smear the O-ring with oil. Fit the sprocket coupling into the wheel **(see illustration 19.11)**. Clean

19.17 Using a socket to drive the bearing in

the brake disc using acetone or brake system cleaner. Install the wheel (Section 18).

Sprocket coupling bearing

21 Remove the wheel (Section 18). Lift the sprocket coupling out of the hub **(see illustration 19.11)**.

22 Inspect the seal and bearing – check that the bearing inner races turn smoothly and that the outer race is a tight fit in the coupling (see *Tools and Workshop Tips* in the Reference Section). Do not remove the bearing unless it is being replaced with a new one.

23 If new components are needed lever out the bearing seal using a flat-bladed screwdriver or a seal hook **(see illustration)**. Take care not to damage the rim of the coupling. Discard the seal – a new one must be fitted.

24 Remove the bearing spacer from inside

19.19 Fit the seal, setting it flush with the rim

19.20 Fit a new O-ring (arrowed) if necessary

19.23 Lever out the bearing seal

19.24 Drive the spacer out of the bearing from the outside

19.25 Drive the bearing out from the inside

27 Drive the new bearing into the hub using a bearing driver or suitable socket that bears on the outer race only, not the inner race **(see illustration)**. Fit the bearing with its marked side facing outwards. Drive the bearing in squarely and all the way onto its seat.

28 Turn the coupling over and seat the inner race of the bearing on a socket, then fit the spacer into the bearing and tap it in until it seats **(see illustrations)**.

29 Fit the new seal into the coupling using finger pressure, then level it with the rim using a small block of wood **(see illustration)**. Smear the seal lip with grease.

30 Check the sprocket coupling/rubber dampers (Section 23). Check the condition of the hub O-ring and clean it or replace it with a new one if necessary **(see illustration 19.20)**. Smear the O-ring with oil. Fit the sprocket coupling into the wheel. Install the wheel (Section 18).

the coupling – if it is tight place the coupling on the work surface, sprocket side up, and drive it out using a 15 mm socket **(see illustration)**.

25 Support the coupling on blocks of wood, sprocket side down, and drive the bearing out from the inside using a bearing driver or socket located on the inner race **(see illustration)**.

26 Thoroughly clean the coupling with a suitable solvent and inspect the bearing housing for scoring and wear.

19.27 Using a socket to drive the bearing in

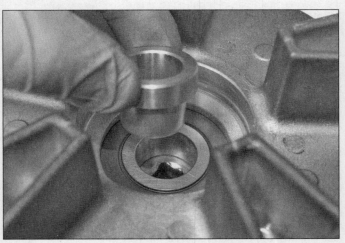

19.28a Support the inner race of the bearing and fit the spacer...

19.28b ...and tap it fully in

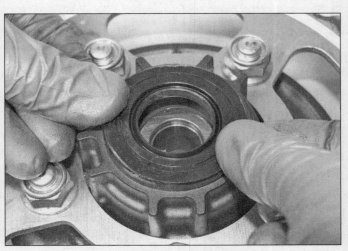

19.29 Press the new seal into the hub

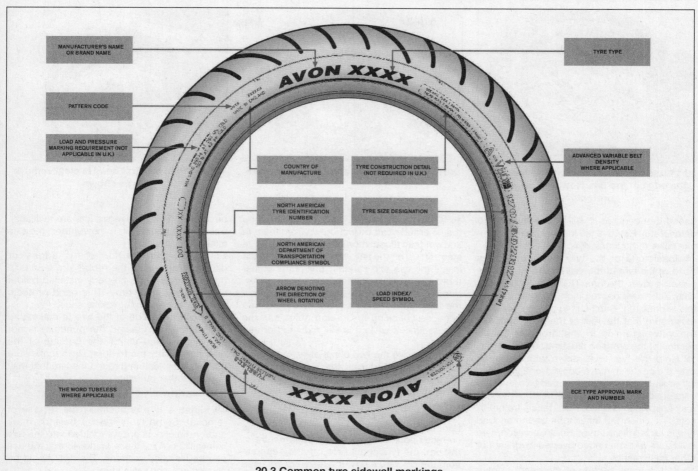

20.3 Common tyre sidewall markings

Labels in figure:

MANUFACTURER'S NAME OR BRAND NAME

PATTERN CODE

LOAD AND PRESSURE MARKING REQUIREMENT (NOT APPLICABLE IN U.K.)

THE WORD TUBELESS WHERE APPLICABLE

TYRE TYPE

ADVANCED VARIABLE BELT DENSITY WHERE APPLICABLE

ECE TYPE APPROVAL MARK AND NUMBER

COUNTRY OF MANUFACTURE

TYRE CONSTRUCTION DETAIL (NOT REQUIRED IN U.K.)

NORTH AMERICAN TYRE IDENTIFICATION NUMBER

TYRE SIZE DESIGNATION

NORTH AMERICAN DEPARTMENT OF TRANSPORTATION COMPLIANCE SYMBOL

ARROW DENOTING THE DIRECTION OF WHEEL ROTATION

LOAD INDEX/ SPEED SYMBOL

20 Tyres

General information

1 The wheels are designed to take tubed tyres only. Tyre sizes are given in the Specifications at the beginning of this chapter.
2 Refer to the *Pre-ride checks* at the beginning of this manual for tyre maintenance.
3 When selecting new tyres, refer to the tyre information in the Owner's Handbook or ask a dealer. Make sure that front and rear tyre types are compatible, the correct size and correct speed rating **(see illustration)**.
4 It is recommended that tyres are fitted by a motorcycle tyre specialist rather than attempted in the home workshop. A specialist will be able to balance the wheels after tyre fitting.

Changing tubed tyres

5 Tyre changing is a specialist task. If you attempt it at home you'll need at least two motorcycle tyre levers and some rim protectors. The rim protectors will prevent damage to the rims by the tyre levers. Following tyre renewal, the wheel should be balanced by a tyre specialist. The following procedure is illustrated with a generic cast alloy wheel.

Removal

6 Begin by removing the wheel from the motorcycle. If the tyre is going to be re-used, mark it next to the valve stem with chalk.
7 Deflate the tyre by removing the valve stem core. When it is fully deflated, push the bead of the tyre away from the rim on both sides. In some extreme cases, this can only be accomplished with a bead breaking tool, but most often it can be carried out with tyre levers **(see illustration)**. Riding on a deflated tyre to break the bead is not recommended, as damage to the rim and tyre will occur.
8 Dismounting a tyre is easier when the tyre is warm, so an indoor tyre change is recommended in cold climates. The rubber gets very stiff and is difficult to manipulate when cold.
9 Place the wheel on a thick pad or old blanket. This will help keep the wheel and tyre from slipping around. Take care to protect the disc/sprocket from damage – if necessary, remove it.
10 Once the bead is completely free of the rim, lubricate the inside edge of the rim and the tyre bead with soap and water or rubber lubricant (do not use any type of petroleum-

20.7 Deflate the tyre. After pushing the tyre beads away from rim flanges push the tyre bead into the well of the rim at the point opposite the valve. Insert a tyre lever adjacent to the valve and work the bead over the edge of the rim

20.11 Use two levers to work the bead over the edge of the rim. Note the use of rim protectors

20.14 Remove the inner tube from the tyre

20.15 When the first bead is clear remove tyre as shown

based lubricant, as it will cause the tyre to deteriorate). Remove the locknut and push the tyre valve through the rim.

11 Insert one of the tyre levers under the bead of the tyre at the valve stem and lift the bead up over the rim. This should be fairly easy. Take care not to pinch the inner tube as this is done. If it is difficult to pry the bead up, make sure that the rest of the bead opposite the valve stem is in the dropped centre section of the rim **(see illustration)**.

12 Hold the tyre lever down with the bead over the rim, then move about 1 or 2 inches to either side and insert the second tyre lever. Be careful not to cut or slice the bead or the tyre may split when inflated. Also, take care not to catch or pinch the inner tube as the second tyre lever is levered over. For this reason, tyre levers are recommended over screwdrivers or other implements.

13 With a small section of the bead up over the rim, one of the levers can be removed and reinserted 1 or 2 inches farther around the rim until about 1/4 of the tyre bead is above the rim edge. Make sure that the rest of the bead is in the dropped centre of the rim. At this point, the bead can usually be pulled up over the rim by hand.

14 Once all of the first bead is over the rim, the inner tube can be withdrawn from the tyre and rim **(see illustration)**. Push in on the valve stem, lift up on the tyre next to the stem, reach inside the tyre and carefully pull out the inner tube. It is usually not necessary to completely remove the tyre from the rim to fit a new the inner tube, however it is recommended because checking for foreign objects in the tyre is difficult while it is still mounted on the rim.

15 To remove the tyre completely, make sure the bead is broken all the way around on the remaining edge, then stand the tyre and wheel up on the tread and grab the wheel with one hand. Push the tyre down over the same edge of the rim while pulling the rim away from the tyre **(see illustration)**. If the bead is correctly positioned in the dropped centre of the rim, the tyre should roll off and separate from the rim very easily. If tyre levers are used to work this last bead over the rim, the outer edge of the rim may be marred. If a tyre lever is necessary, be sure to protect the rim as described earlier.

Inspection

16 Fit a new inner tube when fitting a new tyre and also if the existing inner tube is

punctured. Puncture repair kits are available, but the expense of a new inner tube is minimal.

17 Check the rim for sharp edges or damage. Make sure the rubber rim tape is in good condition and properly installed before inserting the inner tube. This band protects the inner tube from the spoke ends.

18 Check the inside of the tyre to make sure the object that caused the puncture is not still inside. Also check the outside of the tyre, particularly the tread area, to make sure nothing is projecting through the tyre that may cause another puncture.

Installation

19 Fitting a tyre is basically the reverse of removal. Some tyres have a balance mark and/or directional arrows molded into the tyre sidewall. Look for these marks so that the tyre can be installed properly. The dot should be aligned with the valve stem.

20 If the tyre was not removed completely to fit the inner tube, the inner tube should be inflated just enough to make it round **(see illustrations)**. Sprinkle it with talcum powder, which acts as a dry lubricant, then carefully lift up the tyre edge and install the new inner tube with the valve stem next to the hole in the rim.

20.20a Partially inflate the inner tube and insert it in the tyre

20.20b Work the first bead over rim and feed the valve through the hole in the rim. Partially screw on the retaining ring to hold the valve in place

20.21a Check the inner tube is correctly positioned and work the second bead over the rim, starting at a point opposite the valve

20.21b Work the final bead over rim while pushing valve inwards to ensure the inner tube is not trapped

Once the inner tube is in place, push the valve stem through the rim and start the locknut on the stem.

21 Lubricate the tyre bead, then push it over the rim edge and into the dropped centre section opposite the inner tube valve stem. Work around each side of the rim, carefully pushing the bead over the rim **(see illustrations)**. The last section may have to be levered on with tyre levers. If so, take care not to pinch the inner tube as this is done.

22 Once the bead is over the rim edge, check to see that the inner tube valve stem is pointing to the centre of the hub. If it's angled slightly in either direction, rotate the tyre on the rim to straighten it out. Thread the locknut the rest of the way onto the stem but don't tighten it completely.

23 Inflate the inner tube to approximately 40 psi (2.7 Bar) and check to make sure the guidelines on the tyre sidewalls are the same distance from the rim around the circumference of the tyre.

 Warning: Do not overinflate the inner tube or the tube may burst.

24 After the tyre bead is correctly seated on the rim, adjust the tyre pressure to the correct amount (see *Pre-ride checks* at the beginning of the manual), then tighten the valve stem locknut securely and tighten the cap.

25 It is recommended that a motorcycle tyre specialist balances the wheel.

21 Drive chain

Note: *If a new chain is being fitted you should also fit new sprockets (Section 22) – running a new chain on old sprockets will rapidly increase chain wear. Refer to Chapter 1 for details of routine chain maintenance and checks.*

Special tool: *The chain can be removed after removal of the swingarm (see Chapter 5), or split using a chain breaking/riveting tool. Use either the Honda service tool, Pt. No. 07HMH-MR10103 in Europe or MR1010C in the US, or one of several commercially-available chain tools (but the cheap ones are best avoided). If the chain has a soft link it can be recognised by the staked ends of the link's two pins which look as if they have been deeply centre-punched, instead of peened over as with all the other pins.*

Removal

1 Support the motorcycle on an auxiliary stand so that the rear wheel is off the ground. Locate the soft link in a suitable position to work on by rotating the back wheel **(see illustration)**. Slacken the drive chain (see Chapter 1). It is possible that an endless chain (having no soft link) may be fitted, in which case the pin ends of one link will have to be ground off in order to use the chain tool successfully.

2 Remove the chain guard from the swingarm **(see illustration)**.

3 Remove the front sprocket cover (Section 22). If you are fitting new sprockets slacken the front sprocket bolt now, shifting the gearbox into a high gear and holding the rear brake on to prevent the sprocket turning.

4 Separate the chain at the soft link using the chain tool, following carefully the manufacturer's operating instructions (see also *Tools and Workshop Tips* in the Reference Section). Remove the chain from the bike, noting its routing around the swingarm.

5 If you are fitting new sprockets do so now (Section 22).

Installation

Warning: NEVER fit a drive chain that uses a clip-type master (split) link. Use ONLY the correct service tools to secure the staked-type of soft link – if you do not have access to such tools, have the chain replaced by a Honda dealer.

Note: *The specifications referred to in Steps 9 and 10 only apply to the DID drive chain fitted as original equipment (see Specifications). Make sure the chain you are fitting has the correct number of links, which is 124. If necessary remove any excess links using the tool before fitting the chain.*

6 Thoroughly clean all old chain lube and dirt from the chainguards, swingarm, rear wheel hub area and front sprocket area of the engine.

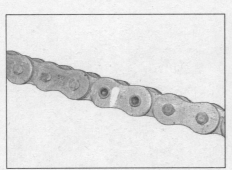

21.1 If the chain has a soft link it can be easily identified by its different pin ends

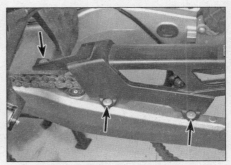

21.2 Unscrew the bolts (arrowed) and remove the chain guard

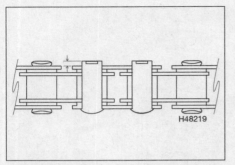

21.8 Measure the pin projection from the sideplate

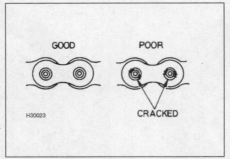

21.9a Check staking for any signs of cracking

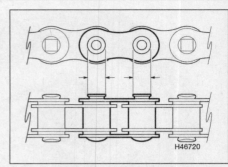

21.9b Check the diameter of the staked pin ends

Use a degreaser or chain cleaner aerosol and old toothbrush to remove stubborn deposits.

7 Route the new drive chain around the sprockets leaving the two ends mid-way between the sprockets along the bottom run.

8 Referring to *Tools and Workshop Tips* in the Reference Section, fit the new soft link from the inside using new O-rings. Fit the new sideplate using new O-rings and with its identification marks facing out and press it into position using the tool. Measure the amount that the soft link pins project from the sideplate – it must be 1.3 to 1.5 mm **(see illustration)**. Stake the new link using the chain tool, following carefully the instructions of both the chain manufacturer and the tool manufacturer. DO NOT re-use old soft link components.

9 After staking, check the pin ends for any signs of cracking **(see illustration)**. If there is any evidence of cracking, the soft link, O-rings

and sideplate must be removed and replaced with a new set. Measure the diameter of the staked pin ends in two directions and check they are evenly staked to 5.5 to 5.8 mm wide **(see illustration)**. Check that the link pivots freely.

10 If necessary tighten the front sprocket bolt now, preventing the sprocket turning as done on removal. Install the sprocket cover (Section 22).

11 Install the chainguard.

12 Adjust and lubricate the chain (see Chapter 1).

22 Sprockets

Note: *If new sprockets are being fitted you should also fit a new drive chain (Section 21)*

– *running an old chain on new sprockets will rapidly increase sprocket wear. Refer to Chapter 1 for routine sprocket wear checks.*

Front sprocket cover

1 On models with standard transmission note the alignment of the punch mark on the gearchange shaft with the slit in the linkage arm, then uscrew the linkage arm bolt and slide the arm off the shaft, and pivot the linkage clear of the sprocket cover **(see illustration)**.

2 Release the sidestand switch wiring clip from the cover, and note its routing in the guides **(see illustration)**.

3 Unscrew the bolts and remove the cover, releasing the wiring from the channel in the front of the cover **(see illustrations)**. Note the guide plate fitted in the cover and remove it if required **(see illustration)**.

4 Fit the guide plate onto the cover if removed **(see illustration 22.3c)**. Fit the cover, fitting the wiring into the channel, and tighten its bolts **(see illustrations 22.3b and a)**.

5 Secure the sidestand switch wiring **(see illustration 22.2)**.

6 On models with standard transmission slide the gearchange linkage arm onto the shaft, aligning the slit in the clamp with the punch mark, then tighten the pinch bolt **(see illustrations 22.1)**.

Sprockets

Front sprocket

7 Remove the front sprocket cover (see Steps 1 to 3).

8 On standard transmission models shift

22.1 Note the alignment before sliding the arm off

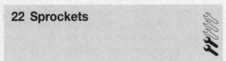

22.2 Release the clip and free the wiring from the guides

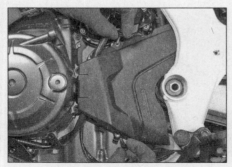

22.3a Unscrew the bolts

22.3b Release the wiring and note its routing as you remove the cover

22.3c Remove the guide if required

22.8 Unscrew the bolt and remove the washer

22.10 Draw the sprocket off the shaft and disengage the chain

the gearbox into a high gear, then have an assistant apply the rear brake whilst you unscrew the sprocket bolt and remove the washer **(see illustration)**. On DCT models apply the parking brake and have an assistant apply the rear brake whilst you unscrew the sprocket bolt and remove the washer.

9 Fully slacken the drive chain (see Chapter 1). If a new chain is being fitted split and remove the old one now (Section 21). If the rear sprocket is being removed as well, remove the rear wheel now to give full slack (Section 18). Otherwise disengage the chain from the rear sprocket if required to provide more slack.

10 Slide the sprocket off the shaft, then slip the sprocket out of the chain (unless it had been removed) **(see illustration)**.

11 Engage the new sprocket with the chain (if in place), making sure the marked side is facing out, and slide it on the shaft **(see illustration 22.10)**.

12 If removed, fit the rear sprocket now (see below), and install the wheel (Section 18). If a new chain is being fitted do so now (Section 21). If the chain was merely disengaged, fit it back onto the rear sprocket. Take up the slack in the chain.

13 Fit the sprocket bolt with its washer **(see illustration 22.8)**. Hold the rear brake on and tighten the bolt to 54 Nm.

14 Fit the sprocket cover (see Steps 4 to 6). Adjust and if necessary lubricate the chain (see Chapter 1).

Rear sprocket

15 Remove the rear wheel (Section 18). Rest it sprocket side up on some blocks of wood.

16 Unscrew the sprocket nuts and lift the sprocket off the studs, noting which way round it fits **(see illustration)**.

17 Fit the new sprocket over the studs and onto the hub with the marked side facing out. Fit the nuts and tighten them evenly and in a criss-cross sequence to 100 Nm.

18 Install the rear wheel (Section 18).

---

23 Rear sprocket coupling/ rubber dampers

1 Remove the rear wheel (Section 18). Lay the wheel on some blocks of wood with the sprocket facing up. Check for rotational play between the sprocket coupling and the wheel

hub by trying to turn the sprocket in both directions. Any play indicates worn rubber damper segments.

Caution: Do not lay the wheel down on the disc.

2 Lift the sprocket coupling off the wheel leaving the rubber dampers in position **(see illustration 19.11)**. Note the spacer in the inner side of the bearing – it should be a tight fit. Check the coupling for cracks or any obvious signs of damage.

3 Lift the rubber damper segments from the wheel and check them for cracks, hardening and general deterioration **(see illustration)**. Replace them with a new set if necessary.

4 Check the condition of the hub O-ring and clean it or replace it with a new one if necessary **(see illustration 19.20)**. Smear the O-ring with oil.

5 Checking and replacement procedures for the sprocket coupling bearing are in Section 19.

6 Installation is the reverse of removal. Make sure the spacer is correctly fitted in the bearing. Align the coupling correctly with the rubber dampers and press it fully into the hub.

7 Install the wheel (Section 18).

22.16 Rear sprocket nuts (arrowed)

23.3 Check the rubber dampers as described

Chapter 7
Bodywork

Contents

Section number

ETC tray 12
Fairing side panels 7
Front mudguard 16
Fuel tank covers.. 11
General Information 1
Handlebar weights and hand guards 15
Headlight cover 8
Inner panel covers 9
Inner panels 10

Section number

Luggage rack 4
Mirrors 13
Seats and seat bracket 3
Side covers.. 5
Sump guard 17
Tail light cover (2018-on models) 6
Trim clips 2
Windshield 14

Degrees of difficulty

Easy, suitable for novice with little experience	Fairly easy, suitable for beginner with some experience	Fairly difficult, suitable for competent DIY mechanic	Difficult, suitable for experienced DIY mechanic	Very difficult, suitable for expert DIY or professional

1 General Information

1 In the case of damage to the bodywork, it is usually necessary to remove the broken component and replace it with a new (or used) one. Note that there are however some companies that specialise in 'plastic welding' and there are a number of bodywork repair kits now available for motorcycles.

2 When attempting to remove any body panel, first study it closely, noting any fasteners and associated fittings, to be sure of returning everything to its correct place on installation. Refer to Section 2 for more information on the types of trim clip used and how to release and refit them. In some cases the aid of an assistant will be required when removing panels, to help avoid the risk of damage to paintwork. Once the evident fasteners have been removed, try to withdraw the panel as described but DO NOT FORCE IT – if it will not release, check that all fasteners have been removed and try again.

3 When installing a body panel, first study it closely, noting any fasteners and associated fittings removed with it, to be sure of returning everything to its correct place. Check that all fasteners are in good condition, including the trim clips and damping/rubber mounts; replace any faulty fasteners with new ones before the panel is reassembled. Check also that all mounting brackets are straight and repair them or replace them with new ones if necessary before attempting to install the panel.

4 Tighten the fasteners securely, but be careful not to overtighten any of them or the panel may break (not always immediately) due to the uneven stress.

2 Trim clips

1 Three types of plastic trim clip may be used, so carefully note which fits where when removing the body panels.

2 The first and most widely used type has a centre pin that you push into the body of the clip to allow the clip to be drawn out of the panel (see illustrations). To install the clip, first expand the pawls of the clip body and push the centre pin back out (see illustration). Now fit the clip body into its

2.2a Push the centre pin (arrowed)...

2.2b ...into the body to release the clip

2.2c Push the centre pin out before installing the clip, then push it in when installed to lock it

2.3 Pull the centre pin (arrowed) out to release the clip, and push it back in to lock it

2.4a Undo the centre screw then pull the clip out

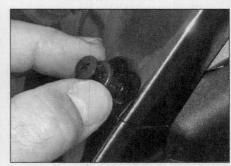

2.4b Fit the clip in the hole then push the centre in to lock it

hole, then push the centre pin in so that it is flush with the clip head. The clip should now be locked in place.

3 The second type has a protruding centre pin that you pull out of the body of the clip to allow the clip to be drawn out of the panel **(see illustration)**. To install the clip, fit the clip body into its hole, then push the centre pin in. The clip should now be locked in place.

4 The third type of trim clip has a Phillips screw head in the centre that you unscrew, then pull the body of the clip out of the panel **(see illustration)**. When installing them, insert it in the panel then push the centre fully into the body **(see illustration)**. As they are made of plastic, the threads easily become worn in which case the centres may not unscrew. If

this happens, lever the centre out of the body using a small screwdriver and replace the trim clip with a new one.

3 Seats and seat bracket

Rider's seat

1 Unlock the seat using the ignition key, turning it clockwise, then draw the seat up and forward to remove it **(see illustration)**.
2 Installation is the reverse of removal – make sure the seat locates correctly, with the upper

or lower hook locating in the bracket on the tank according to the seat height required **(see illustration)**. Push down on the back of the seat to engage the latch.

Seat bracket

3 Remove the rider's seat.
4 Remove the fuel tank rear cover (Section 11).
5 Unscrew the two bolts, lift the bracket and disconnect the seat lock cable **(see illustrations)**.
6 On 2018-on models remove the seat lock cover **(see illustration)**.
7 Installation is the reverse of removal.

3.1 Unlock the seat and lift it up

3.2 Locate the required hook in the bracket

3.5a Seat bracket bolts (arrowed)

3.5b Lift the bracket...

3.5c ...and disconnect the cable

3.6 Remove the cover

3.9 Two bolts retain the passenger seat

3.10 Locate the tabs under the hooks

4.4a Unscrew the bolt on each side at the back…

Passenger seat

8 Remove the rider's seat.
9 Unscrew the two bolts, noting the collars, then draw the seat forwards, noting how the tabs locate **(see illustration)**.
10 Installation is the reverse of removal – make sure the tabs locate correctly under the hooks **(see illustration)**.

4.4b …the two bolts (arrowed) on each side on the top…

4.4c …and the two bolts with collars at the back…

4 Luggage rack

1 Remove the seats (Section 3).
2 On standard models remove the side covers (Section 5).
3 On 2016/17 models unscrew the bolt on each side and the six bolts on top, noting the collars with the rear ones and the washers with the other four, and remove the rack.
4 On 2018-on standard models unscrew the bolts at the back and the six bolts on top, noting the collars with the rear ones and the washers with the other four, and remove the rack **(see illustrations)**.
5 On the Adventure Sports model unscrew the four bolts and remove the rack releasing the two rubber pads from the side covers **(see illustrations)**.
6 Installation is the reverse of removal.

4.4d …then lift the rack off, noting how the pegs locate in the grommets

4.5a Unscrew the bolts (arrowed)…

5 Side covers

Standard models

1 Remove the seats (Section 3).
2 Unscrew the bolt and remove it with its collar **(see illustration)**.
3 Carefully release the tabs along the top and the bottom, then ease the snap-fit clip

4.5b …and release the rubbers as you remove the rack

5.2 Remove the bolt and collar

5.3a Release the tabs...

5.3b ...along the top...

5.3c ...and the bottom...

5.3d ...then release the clip

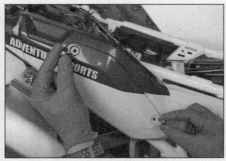

5.7a Undo the screws...

5.7b ...and remove the cover

out of its socket and remove the cover **(see illustrations)**.

4 Installation is the reverse of removal.

Adventure Sports model

5 Remove the seats (Section 3).

6 Remove the luggage rack (Section 4).

7 When removing the right-hand panel undo the two screws and remove the storage cover **(see illustrations)**.

8 Unscrew the two bolts on the outside of the cover **(see illustration)**.

9 Undo the three screws along the top of the inner side **(see illustration)**.

10 Carefully release the tabs along the top and the bottom, then ease the snap-fit clip out of its socket and remove the cover **(see illustrations)**.

11 Installation is the reverse of removal.

5.8 Remove the bolts...

5.9 ...and the screws

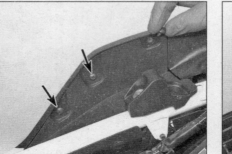

5.10a Release the tabs...

5.10b ...along the top...

5.10c ...and the bottom...

5.10d ...then release the clip

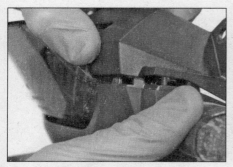

6.2a Release the rear tabs...

6.2b ...and the side tabs

6.3a Undo the screws...

6.3b ...then release the side tabs...

6.3c ...and the rear tabs

6 Tail light cover (2018-on models)

1 Remove the luggage rack (Section 4).
2 On standard models release the tabs along the back and the sides and remove the cover (see illustrations).
3 On the Adventure Sports model undo the two screws (see illustration). Release the tabs along the sides and the back and remove the cover (see illustrations).
4 Installation is the reverse of removal.

7 Fairing side panels

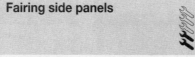

Note: For information on releasing trim clips refer to Section 2.

Standard models

1 Remove the fuel tank side cover(s) (Section 11).
2 Undo the two screws along the top (see illustration).
3 Release and remove the four trim clips at the front (see illustration).
4 Release the tabs from the fan shroud and the fuel tank front cover and the headlight cover, then ease the rear and

7.2 Undo the screws...

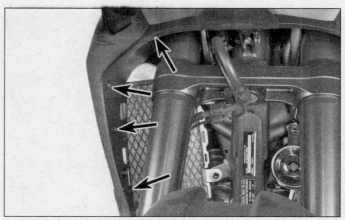

7.3 ...and release the trim clips (arrowed)

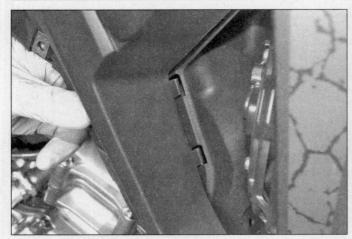

7.4a Release the tabs from the shroud...

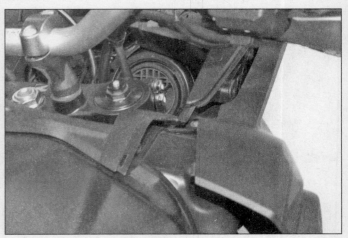

7.4b ...the tank cover...

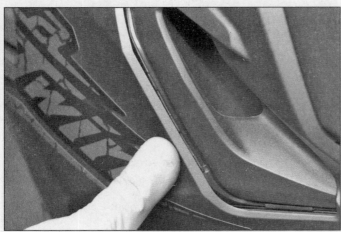

7.4c ...and the headlight cover...

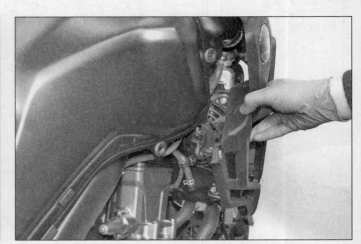

7.4d ...then release the rear and side pegs...

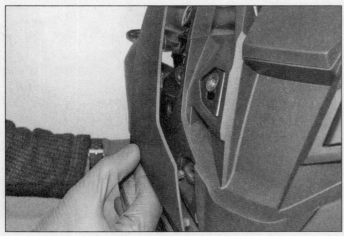

7.5a ...the front pegs...

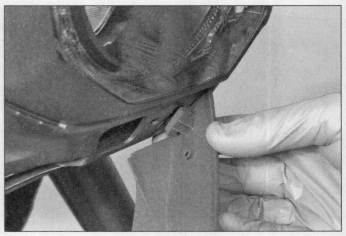

7.5b ...and the tabs

7.8a Unscrew the bottom bolt on each side and remove the washer

7.8b Support the bars, unscrew the top bolt on each side and remove the washer...

7.8c ...then remove the bars

7.8d Remove the collars for the bottom mounts...

7.8e ...and the top mounts

side pegs out of the grommets (see illustrations).

5 Ease the front pegs out of the grommets and release the front tabs from the headlight cover (see illustrations).

6 If required disassemble the panel sections by undoing the screws that join them.

7 Installation is the reverse of removal. Make sure the grommets are in good condition and correctly seated. Smear them with oil to make the fitting and subsequent removal of the cover easier.

Adventure Sports model

8 Remove the protection bars (see illustrations).

9 Undo the two screws along the top, and the two screws at the front with the plastic and rubber washers (see illustrations).

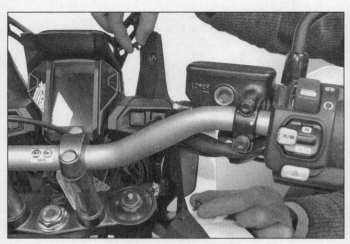

7.9a Undo the top screws...

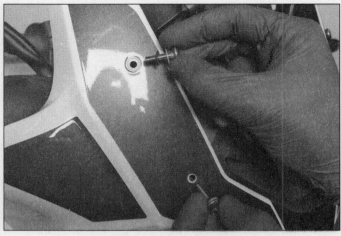

7.9b ...and the front screws, noting the washers

7.10 Release the trim clips (arrowed)

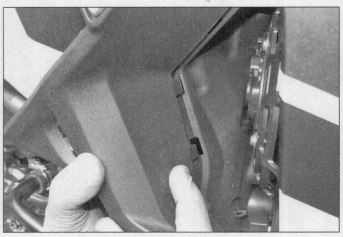

7.11a Release the tabs from the shroud…

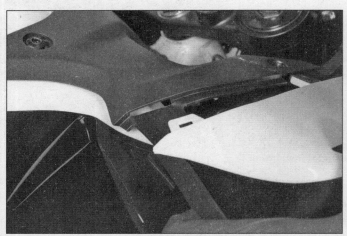

7.11b …the tank cover…

7.11c …and the headlight cover…

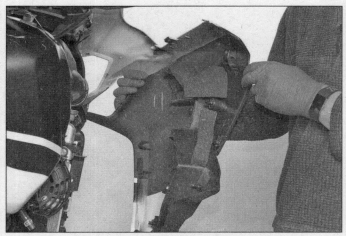

7.11d …then release the pegs…

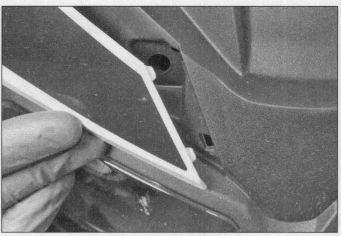

7.11e …the upper front tabs…

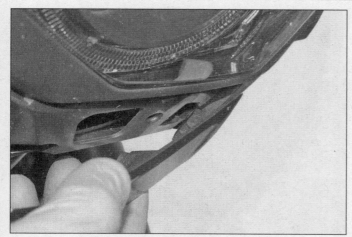

7.11f ...and the lower front tabs

7.12 The screws are on the inner side of the panel

10 Release and remove the four trim clips at the front **(see illustration)**.

11 Release the tabs from the fan shroud and the fuel tank front cover and the headlight cover, then ease the pegs out of the grommets and release the front tabs from the headlight cover **(see illustrations)**.

12 If required disassemble the panel sections by undoing the screws that join them **(see illustration)**.

13 Installation is the reverse of removal. Make sure the grommets are in good condition and correctly seated. Smear them with liquid soap to make the fitting and subsequent removal of the cover easier.

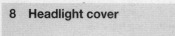

8   Headlight cover

Note: *For information on releasing trim clips refer to Section 2.*

1 Remove the windshield (Section 14).
2 Remove the fairing side panels (Section 7).
3 Release the two trim clips and remove the bottom section of the cover **(see illustrations)**.
4 On 2016/17 models undo the screws and release the trim clip on each side.

8.3a Release the trim clip (arrowed) on each side...

Release the front cover from the inner panel cover and draw it forwards, noting how it locates.

5 On 2018-on models release the twist clip and the trim clip on each side **(see illustrations)**. Undo the two screws on each side, then release the tabs and draw the cover

8.3b ...and remove the bottom section

8.5a Release the twist clips...

8.5b ...and the trim clips...

8.5c ...then undo the screws...

8.5d ...release the tabs...

8.5e ...and remove the cover...

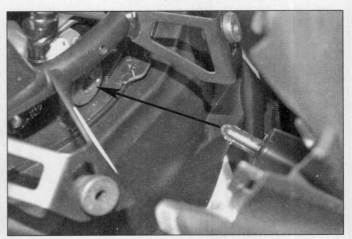

8.5f ...noting how the peg locates

forwards, noting how the peg locates in the grommet **(see illustrations)**.
6 Installation is the reverse of removal.

9 Inner panel covers

Note: *For information on releasing trim clips refer to Section 2.*

Right-hand side

1 Remove the headlight cover (Section 8).
2 Disconnect the turn signal wiring connector **(see illustration)**.
3 Undo the screw and release the trim clips, displace the panel and where fitted disconnect the rear ABS switch or rear ABS and G switch wiring connector, according to model **(see illustrations)**.

4 If required remove the turn signal and/or switch(es) (see Chapter 8).
5 Installation is the reverse of removal.

Left-hand side

6 Remove the headlight cover (Section 8).
7 Disconnect the turn signal wiring connector **(see illustration)**.
8 Where fitted, release the auxiliary socket wiring, displace the two front sub-loom wiring

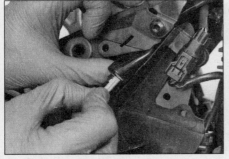

9.2 Disconnect the turn signal wiring

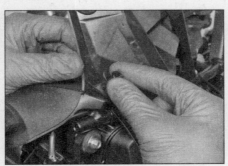

9.3a Undo the screw...

9.3b ...and release the trim clips...

9.3c ...then displace the panel and disconnect the switch wiring

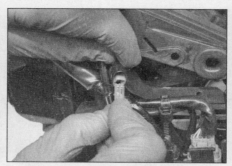

9.7 Disconnect the turn signal wiring

9.8a Release the wiring tie

connectors from the air filter housing, then disconnect the auxiliary socket wiring **(see illustrations)**.

9 Undo the screw and release the trim clips, and remove the panel **(see illustrations)**.

10 If required remove the turn signal and/or auxiliary socket (see Chapter 8).

11 Installation is the reverse of removal.

10 Inner panels

Note: *For information on releasing trim clips refer to Section 2.*

1 Remove the inner panel cover (Section 9).

2 Release the wiring connector clip from the panel **(see illustration)**.

3 Release the front of the air intake duct from the panel **(see illustration)**.

4 Release the trim clip at the front **(see illustration)**.

5 Release the panel from the radiator shroud

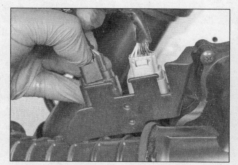

9.8b Displace the front loom connectors...

9.8c ...then disconnect the socket connector

9.9a Undo the screw...

9.9b ...and release the trim clips

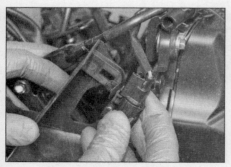

10.2 Release the connector...

10.3 ...the air duct...

10.4 ...and the trim clip

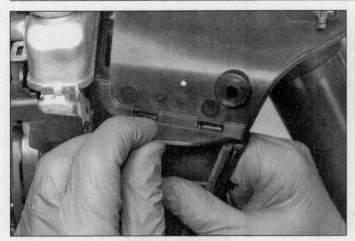

10.5a Release the tabs...

10.5b ...and remove the panel

11.2 Undo the screws

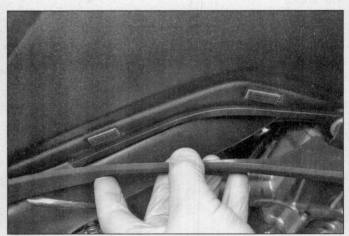

11.3a Release the Velcro...

then draw it forwards and remove it **(see illustrations)**.

6 Installation is the reverse of removal. Make sure the wiring connectors are securely connected.

11 Fuel tank covers

Note: *For information on releasing trim clips refer to Section 2.*

Side covers (standard models)

1 Remove the rider's seat (Section 3).
2 Undo the two screws **(see illustration)**.
3 Carefully pull the cover away to release the two Velcro patches, then draw it forwards to release the tabs at the rear **(see illustrations)**.
4 Installation is the reverse of removal.

Front cover

5 Remove the fairing side panels (Section 7).
6 Undo the screw on each side and remove the cover **(see illustration)**.

7 Installation is the reverse of removal.

Rear cover

8 On standard models remove the tank side covers (see above).

11.3b ...and the tabs

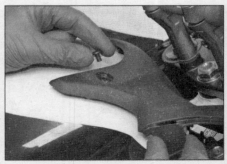

11.6 Undo the screw on each side

11.9 Release the trim clips then lift the cover out

12.3a Displace the fuse boxes...

12.3b ...release the trim clip...

9 Release the trim clip on each side and remove the cover, noting how it locates **(see illustration)**.
10 Installation is the reverse of removal.

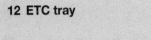

12 ETC tray

Note: *For information on releasing trim clips refer to Section 2.*
1 Remove the rider's seat and seat bracket (Section 3).
2 On 2016/17 models release the fuse boxes, connector and wiring from the tray. Release the four trim clips and remove the tray.
3 On 2018-on models release the fuse boxes from the tray, then release the trim clip and remove the tray, noting how the peg locates in the grommet **(see illustrations)**.
4 Installation is the reverse of removal.

13 Mirrors

1 Pull the rubber boot up off the base of the mirror stem **(see illustration)**.

12.3c ...and pull the peg from the grommet

2 To remove the complete mirror unscrew it using the base bolt **(see illustration 13.1)**.
3 To remove the mirror stem from the base bolt, slacken the top nut by turning it clockwise, then unscrew the mirror from the base bolt, again turning it clockwise **(see illustration 13.1)**. If required unscrew the base bolt.
4 Installation is the reverse of removal.
5 To adjust the position of the mirror stem slacken the locknut clockwise, adjust the mirror, then tighten the locknut anti-clockwise.

13.1 Mirror top nut (A) and base bolt (B)

14 Windshield

1 Undo the screws, noting the plastic and rubber washers, and remove the windshield **(see illustration)**.
2 Remove the rubber well-nuts and the end covers from the bracket if required **(see illustration)**.
3 Installation is the reverse of removal.

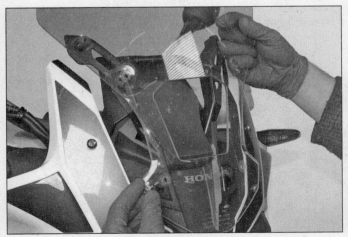

14.1 Note the washers with the screws

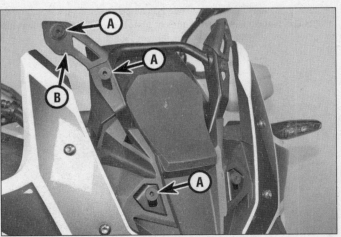

14.2 Remove the well-nuts (A) and end cover (B) from each side

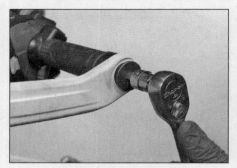

15.1a Undo the screw…

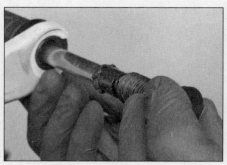

15.1b …draw the inner weight out…

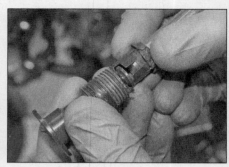

15.1c …and disengage the screw from it

15.1d Remove the outer weight

15.2a Undo the screw

15 Handlebar weights and hand guards

1 Undo the handlebar end-weight screw and draw the inner weight out, noting how the inner end of the screw locates in it **(see illustrations)**. Remove the outer weight from end of the handlebar, noting how the hand guard locates around its outer rim **(see illustration)**.
2 Undo the screw and remove the hand guard, noting how it locates in the bracket **(see illustrations)**. To remove the bracket remove the relevant lever (see Chapter 5).
3 Check the inner weight rubbers and O-ring and replace them with new ones if damaged or deformed **(see illustration)**.
4 Installation is the reverse of removal.

16 Front mudguard

1 Remove the cover from each side, noting how it locates and the routing of the brake hose **(see illustrations)**.
2 Release the front wheel speed sensor wiring from the left-hand side of the mudguard **(see illustration)**.

15.2b The tab on the guard seats in a slot in the bracket

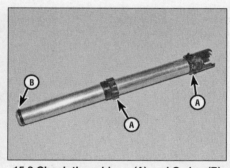

15.3 Check the rubbers (A) and O-ring (B)

16.1a Undo the screw…

16.1b …release the tabs and remove the cover

16.2 Release the sensor wiring

16.3 Unscrew the brake hose joint bolt

16.4a Undo the screws on each side…

16.4b …and remove the mudguard

3 Release the brake hose joint from the top of the mudguard **(see illustration)**.

4 Undo the two screws on each side and draw the mudguard forwards **(see illustrations)**.

5 Note the collars fitted into the inner side of each mounts **(see illustration)**.

6 Installation is the reverse of removal. When fitting the mudguard make sure the rear sections are on the outside of the mounts **(see illustration)**. When fitting the left-hand cover on 2018-on models route the brake hose in the front cut-out **(see illustration)**.

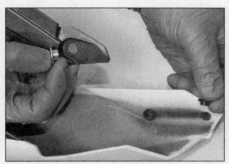

16.5 Remove the collars if required

16.6a Seat the rear section on the outside

17 Sump guard

1 On standard models undo the two screws at the front, and the screw on the left-hand side, noting the washer and sleeve, then draw the guard to the left to release the right-hand rear mounting grommet from the lug on the frame **(see illustrations)**.

2 On the Adventure Sports model undo the two screws at the front, noting the washers, and the two bolts on each side, noting the washers with the upper bolts and the washer and sleeve with the left-rear bolt, then draw the guard to the left to release the mounting

16.6b On 2018-on models route the hose in the front cut-out

17.1a Undo the front screws…

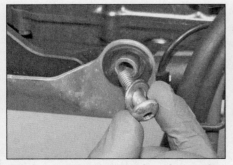

17.1b …and the screw and washer on the left…

17.1c …noting the sleeve

17.1d Release the grommet from the lug

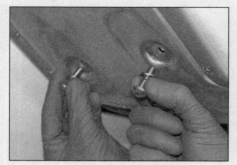

17.2a Undo the front screws...

17.2b ...and the upper bolt on each side, noting the washers

17.2c The right rear bolt is shouldered...

17.2d ...the left rear bolt has a washer and sleeve

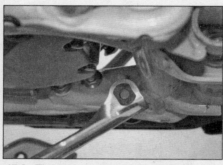

17.2e The grommet at the back locates on a lug on the frame

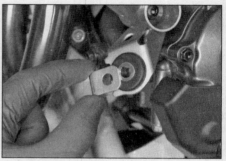

17.2f Remove the clip nuts if required

grommet at the back from the lug on the frame **(see illustrations)**. Note the clip-nut for each upper side bolt on the protection bar

and remove it for safekeeping if required, and note the sleeve in the grommet in the mount **(see illustration)**.

3 Installation is the reverse of removal. Make sure all grommets, washers and sleeves are fitted.

Chapter 8
Electrical system

Contents

Section number

Alternator 29
Battery and battery box removal and installation................ 3
Battery maintenance and charging 4
Brake light and parking brake warning light switches 13
Charging system testing.................................... 28
Clutch switch 22
Diode block (models with standard transmission) 23
Electrical system fault finding............................... 2
Fuses 5
Gear position switch, gear position sensor, neutral switch,
   gearchange shaft switch 20
General Information 1
Handlebar switches, and ABS and G switches 18
Headlight 7
Heated grips and grip controller (Adventure Sports model)....... 19
Horn 24

Section number

Ignition switch 17
Instrument (combination meter) check and replacement.......... 15
Instrument (combination meter) removal and installation 14
Licence plate light bulb 9
Lighting system check 6
Oil pressure switch or sensor............................... 16
Regulator/rectifier... 30
Sidestand switch 21
Starter motor overhaul 27
Starter motor relay 25
Starter motor removal and installation........................ 26
Tail light... 8
Turn signal assemblies..................................... 12
Turn signal bulbs (models without LED turn signals) 11
Turn signal/hazard/emergency stop circuit 10
Wiring diagrams 31

Degrees of difficulty

Easy, suitable for novice with little experience	Fairly easy, suitable for beginner with some experience	Fairly difficult, suitable for competent DIY mechanic	Difficult, suitable for experienced DIY mechanic	Very difficult, suitable for expert DIY or professional

Specifications

Battery

2016/17 models

Type	YTZ14S
Capacity	12 V, 11.2 Ah
Voltage	
Fully-charged.............................	13.0 to 13.2 V
Discharged	below 12.3 V
Charging rate	
Normal	1.1 A for 5 to 10 hrs
Quick	5.5 A for 1 hr
Current leakage	0.66 mA (max.)

2018-on models

Type	ELIIY HY110 (lithium-ion)
Capacity	12 V, 6.0 Ah
Voltage	
Fully-charged.............................	13.5 to 14.0 V
Discharged	below 10.8 V
Charging	see Section 4
Current leakage	0.66 mA (max.)

Charging system

Alternator stator coil resistance	0.1 to 1.0 ohm
Output (capacity)	490 W @ 5000 rpm
Regulated voltage	15.5 V @ 5000 rpm

Lighting

Headlight . . . . LED
Sidelight . . . . LED
Brake/tail light . . . . LED
Licence plate light . . . . 5W capless bulb
Turn signal lights
  2016/17 models
    Europe . . . . 21 W x 4 amber bulbs or LED
    US . . . . 21/5 W x 2 (front) 21 W x 2 (rear) amber bulbs, or LED
  2018-on models . . . . LED
Instrument and warning lights . . . . LED

Torque settings

Alternator cover bolts. . . . . 12 Nm
Alternator rotor bolt . . . . 137 Nm
Alternator stator bolts. . . . . 12 Nm
CKP sensor bolts . . . . 12 Nm
Fork clamp bolts (top yoke) . . . . 22 Nm
Gearchange shaft switch . . . . 12 Nm
Gear position sensor bolt. . . . . 12 Nm
Gear position switch bolt . . . . 10 Nm
Ignition switch bolts . . . . 26 Nm
Neutral switch. . . . . 12 Nm
Oil pressure sensor (models with DCT) . . . . 22 Nm
Oil pressure switch (models with standard transmission) . . . . 12 Nm
Sidestand switch bolt. . . . . 10 Nm
Steering stem nut. . . . . 100 Nm

1 General Information

1 All models have a 12 volt electrical system charged by a three-phase alternator with a separate regulator/rectifier.

2 The regulator maintains the charging system output within the specified range to prevent overcharging, and the rectifier converts the ac (alternating current) output of the alternator to dc (direct current) to power the lights and other components and to charge the battery. The alternator rotor is mounted on the left-hand end of the crankshaft.

3 The starter motor is mounted on the top of the crankcase behind the cylinders. The starting system includes the motor, the battery, the relay and the various wires and switches. Some of the switches are part of a starter interlock system.

Note: *Keep in mind that electrical parts, once purchased, often cannot be returned. To avoid unnecessary expense, make very sure the faulty component has been positively identified before buying a replacement part.*

2 Electrical system fault finding

1 A typical electrical circuit consists of an electrical component, the switches, relays, etc, related to that component and the wiring and connectors that link the component to the battery and the frame.

2 Before tackling any troublesome electrical circuit, first study the wiring diagram thoroughly to get a complete picture of what makes up that individual circuit. Trouble spots, for instance, can often be narrowed down by noting if other components related to that circuit are operating properly or not. If several components or circuits fail at one time, chances are the fault lies either in the fuse or in a common earth (ground) connection, as several circuits are often routed through the same fuse and earth (ground) connections.

3 Electrical problems often stem from simple causes, such as loose or corroded connections or a blown fuse. Prior to any electrical fault finding, always visually check the condition of the fuse, wires and connections in the problem circuit. Intermittent failures can be especially frustrating, since you can't always duplicate the failure when it's convenient to test. In such situations, a good practice is to clean all connections in the affected circuit, whether or not they appear to be good – where possible use a dedicated electrical cleaning spray along with sandpaper, wire wool or other abrasive material to remove corrosion, and a dedicated electrical protection spray to prevent further problems. All of the connections and wires should also be wiggled to check for looseness which can cause intermittent failure.

4 If you don't have a multimeter it is highly advisable to obtain one – they are not expensive and will enable a full range of electrical tests to be made **(see illustration)**. Go for a modern digital one with LCD display as they are easier to use. A continuity tester and/or test light are useful for certain electrical checks as an alternative, though are limited in their usefulness compared to a multimeter **(see illustrations)**. Note that needle tipped probes will be needed to access most of the connector pins due to their small size.

2.2 Multi-circuit earth point

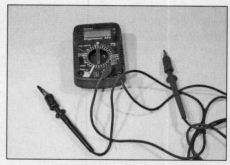

2.4a A digital multimeter can be used for all electrical tests

Continuity checks

5 The term continuity describes the uninterrupted flow of electricity through an electrical circuit. Continuity can be checked with a multimeter set either to its continuity function (a beep is emitted when continuity is found), or to the resistance (ohms / Ω) function, or with a dedicated continuity tester. Both instruments are powered by an internal battery, therefore the checks are made with the ignition OFF. As a safety precaution, always disconnect the battery negative (-) lead before making continuity checks, particularly if ignition switch checks are being made.

6 If using a multimeter, select the continuity function if it has one, or the resistance (ohms) function. Touch the meter probes together and check that a beep is emitted or the meter reads zero, which indicates continuity. If there is no continuity there will be no beep or the meter will show infinite resistance. After using the meter, always switch it OFF to conserve its battery.

7 A continuity tester can be used in the same way – its light should come on or it should beep to indicate continuity in the switch ON position, but should be off or silent in the OFF position.

8 Note that the polarity of the test probes doesn't matter for continuity checks, although care should be taken to follow specific test procedures if a diode or solid-state component is being checked.

Switch continuity checks

9 If a switch is at fault, trace its wiring to the wiring connectors. Separate the connectors and inspect them for security and condition. A build-up of dirt or corrosion here will most likely be the cause of the problem – clean up and apply a water dispersant such as WD40, or alternatively use a dedicated contact cleaner and protection spray.

10 If using a multimeter, select the continuity function if it has one, or the resistance (ohms) function, and connect its probes to the terminals in the connector **(see illustration)**. Simple ON/OFF type switches, such as brake light switches, only have two wires whereas combination switches, like the handlebar

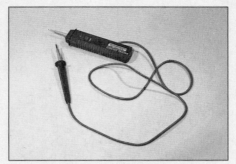

2.4b A battery-powered continuity tester

switches, have many wires. Study the wiring diagram to ensure that you are connecting to the correct pair of wires. Continuity should be indicated with the switch ON and no continuity with it OFF.

Wiring continuity checks

11 Many electrical faults are caused by damaged wiring, often due to incorrect routing or chaffing on frame components. Loose, wet or corroded wire connectors can also be the cause of electrical problems.

12 A continuity check can be made on a single length of wire by disconnecting it at each end and connecting the meter or continuity tester probes to each end of the wire **(see illustration)**. Continuity (low or no resistance – 0 ohms) should be indicated if the wire is good. If no continuity (high resistance) is shown, suspect a broken wire.

13 To check for continuity to earth in any earth wire connect one probe of your meter or tester to the earth wire terminal in the connector and the other to the frame, engine, or battery earth (-) terminal. Continuity (low or no resistance – 0 ohms) should be indicated if the wire is good. If no continuity (high resistance) is shown, suspect a broken wire or corroded or loose earth point (see below).

Voltage checks

14 A voltage check can determine whether power is reaching a component. Use a multimeter set to the dc voltage scale, or

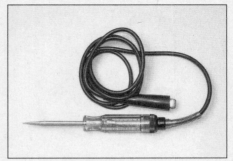

2.4c A simple test light is useful for voltage tests

a test light. The test light is the cheaper component, but the meter has the advantage of being able to give a voltage reading.

15 Connect the meter or test light in parallel, i.e. across the load **(see illustration)**.

16 First identify the relevant wiring circuit by referring to the wiring diagram at the end of this manual. If other electrical components share the same power supply (i.e. are fed from the same fuse), take note whether they are working correctly – this is useful information in deciding where to start checking the circuit.

17 If using a meter, check first that the meter leads are plugged into the correct terminals on the meter (red to positive (+), black to negative (-). Set the meter to the dc volts function, where necessary at a range suitable for the battery voltage – 0 to 20 vdc. Connect the meter red probe (+) to the power supply wire and the black probe to a good metal earth (ground) on the bike's frame or directly to the battery negative terminal. Battery voltage should be shown on the meter with the ignition switch, and if necessary any other relevant switch, ON.

18 If using a test light, connect its positive (+) probe to the power supply terminal and its negative (-) probe to a good earth (ground) on the bike's frame. With the switch, and if necessary any other relevant switch, ON, the test light should illuminate.

19 If no voltage is indicated, work back towards the fuse continuing to check for voltage. When you reach a point where there

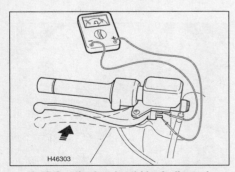

2.10 Continuity should be indicated across switch terminals when the lever is operated

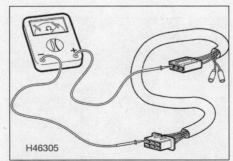

2.12 Wiring continuity check. Connect the meter probes across each end of the same wire

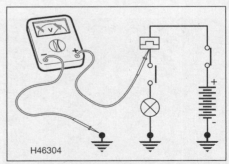

2.15 Voltage check. Connect the meter positive probe to the component and the negative probe to earth

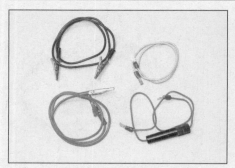

2.23 A selection of insulated jumper wires

3.2a Toolbox is retained by bracket on 2016/17 models

3.2b Tool box screws on 2018-on models

is voltage, you know the problem lies between that point and your last check point.

Earth (ground) checks

20 Earth connections are made either directly to the engine or frame via the mounting of the component, or by a separate wire into the earth circuit of the wiring harness. Alternatively a short earth wire is sometimes run from the component directly to the bike's frame.

21 Corrosion is a common cause of a poor earth connection, as is a loose earth terminal fastener.

22 If total or multiple component failure is experienced, check the security of the main

earth lead from the negative (-) terminal of the battery and the main earth point on the frame **(see illustration 2.2)**. If corroded, dismantle the connection and clean all surfaces back to bare metal. Remake the connection and prevent further corrosion from forming by smearing battery terminal grease over the connection.

23 To check the earth of a component, use an insulated jumper wire to temporarily bypass its earth connection **(see illustration)** – connect one end of the jumper wire to the earth terminal or metal body of the component and the other end to the bike's frame. If the circuit works with the jumper wire installed, the earth circuit is faulty.

24 To check an earth wire first check for corroded or loose connections, then check the wiring for continuity (Step 12) between each connector in the circuit in turn, and then to its earth point, to locate the break.

3   Battery and battery box removal and installation

Battery

1 Make sure the ignition is switched OFF.
2 Remove the tool box **(see illustrations)**.
3 On 2016/17 models open the battery box lid **(see illustration)**. Unscrew the negative (–) lead bolt first and disconnect the lead from the earth point **(see illustration)**. Pull the battery tray out slightly to access the positive lead bolt. Unscrew the bolt and disconnect the positive lead from the battery **(see illustration)**. Slide the battery tray out of the box and remove the battery in its tray. Disconnect the negative lead from the battery, then remove the battery from the tray.
4 On 2018-on models release the trim clip and remove the retainer **(see illustration)**.

3.3a Unclip the battery box lid at the bottom edge

3.3b Disconnect the negative lead from the earth point

3.3c Ease the battery out, then disconnect the positive lead

3.3d Slide the battery and its tray out of the box

3.4a Remove the retainer

3.4b Disconnect the negative lead first…

3.4c …then the positive…

3.4d …and remove the battery

Unscrew the negative (–) terminal bolt first and disconnect the lead from the battery **(see illustration)**. Lift up the red insulating cover to access the positive (+) terminal, then unscrew the bolt and disconnect the lead **(see illustration)**. Draw the battery out of the box **(see illustration)**.

5 Installation is the reverse of removal. Clean the battery terminals and lead ends with a wire brush, emery paper or steel wool. Reconnect the leads, connecting the positive (+) terminal first.

Battery box

6 Remove the battery (see above).
7 Remove the cover from the right-hand side of the battery box **(see illustrations)**.
8 Remove the ECM/PCM, and the throttle body and intake ducts (see Chapter 4).
9 Release the wiring and wiring connectors from the top of the box **(see illustrations)**. On 2016/17 models with ABS unscrew the brake pipe/hose joint bolt and release the pipes from the clips to give some movement in the pipes.
10 Release the fuse boxes, starter relay and the wiring connector from the right-hand side of the box as required according to model, and disconnect the wiring connector **(see illustrations)**.
11 Unscrew the battery box bolts and lift the box out, noting how it locates on the engine

3.7a Undo the screw…

3.7b …and remove the cover, noting how it hooks onto the engine mounting spacer

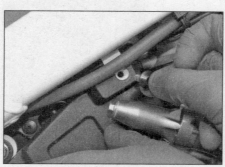

3.9a Release the wiring tie…

3.9b …and clip…

3.9c …and the connector clips (2018 model shown)

3.10a Release all the electrical components from the box…

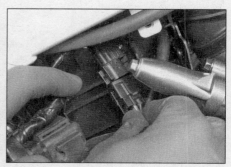

3.10b …and disconnect the connector

mount spacer on each side, and releasing the battery lead where necessary **(see illustrations)**.

12 Installation is the reverse of removal.

4 Battery maintenance and charging

3.11a Unscrew the bolts...

3.11b ...and remove the box...

Maintenance-free gel battery – 2016/17 models

Caution: Even though the battery is sealed, be extremely careful when handling or working around the battery. The electrolyte is very caustic and an explosive gas (hydrogen) is given off when the battery is charging.

Check

1 The battery fitted as standard to 2016/17 models is of the maintenance free (sealed) lead-acid gel type, therefore requiring no regular maintenance. However, the following checks should still be performed.

2 Check the state of charge by measuring the voltage at the battery terminals, referring to Section 3 for access. Connect the voltmeter positive (+) probe to the battery positive (+) terminal, and the negative (–) probe to the battery negative (–) terminal **(see illustration)**. When fully-charged there should be 13.0 to 13.2 volts. If the voltage falls below 12.3 volts, remove the battery and recharge it as described below.

3 Check the battery terminals and leads are tight and free of corrosion. If corrosion is evident, clean the terminals as described above, then protect them from further corrosion by applying petroleum jelly or battery terminal grease after the leads have been reconnected.

4 Keep the battery case clean to prevent current leakage, which can discharge the battery over a period of time (especially when it sits unused).

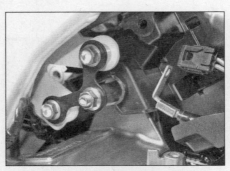

3.11c ...noting how it hooks onto the engine mounting spacer...

3.11d ...and release the lead

5 If the motorcycle sits unused for long periods of time, check and if necessary charge the battery once every month to six weeks.

Charging

6 Remove the battery (Section 3).

7 Connect the charger to the battery, making sure that the positive (+) lead on the charger is connected to the positive (+) terminal on the battery, and the negative (–) lead is connected to the negative (–) terminal **(see illustration)**.

8 Honda recommends that the battery is charged at the normal rate given in the

Specifications at the beginning of the Chapter. A higher 'quick charge' rate that can be used if absolutely necessary is also specified, but note that exceeding this could cause the battery to overheat, buckling the plates and rendering it useless. If a normal domestic charger is used check that after a possible initial peak, the charge rate falls to a safe level. If the battery becomes hot during charging **stop**. Further charging will cause damage. Note that there are many bike-specific chargers available from good suppliers that are designed for the maintenance and recovery of motorcycle batteries, in

4.2 Check battery voltage

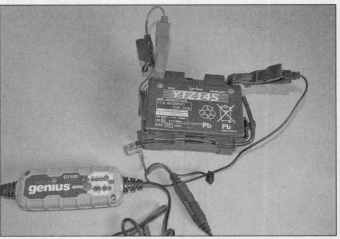

4.7 Battery connected to a charger

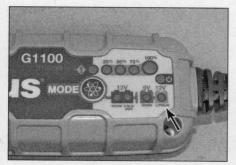

4.13 Make sure the charger is suitable for lithium-ion batteries

5.2a Draw the relay out...

5.2b ...and remove the cover...

particular catering for the requirements of heavily discharged MF batteries. They are not expensive, and are a worthwhile investment, especially if the bike is not used over winter. Follow the manufacturer's instructions.

9 If the battery discharges rapidly or does not charge correctly fit a new battery.

10 Install the battery (Section 3).

Lithium-ion battery – 2018-on models

Check

11 The battery fitted as standard to 2018-on models is of the lithium-ion type and requires no regular maintenance.

12 Check the state of charge by measuring the voltage at the battery terminals, referring to Section 3 for access. Connect the voltmeter positive (+) probe to the battery positive (+) terminal, and the negative (–) probe to the battery negative (–) terminal. When fully-charged there should be 13.5 to 14.0 volts. If the voltage falls below 10.8 volts, remove the battery and recharge it as described below.

Charging

Caution: A charger marked as suitable for lithium-ion batteries must be used – do not use a standard battery charger designed for lead-acid batteries. Never trickle charge a lithium-ion battery..

13 Connect the charger to the battery, making sure that the positive (+) lead on the charger is connected to the positive (+) terminal on the

5.2c ...to access the fuses on the starter relay...

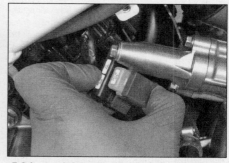

5.2d ...and those in separate fuse holders

battery, and the negative (–) lead is connected to the negative (–) terminal **(see illustration)**. Observe the charge instructions on the battery case – do not exceed 15V charge voltage and charge in a low ambient temperature, i.e. avoid the battery overheating.

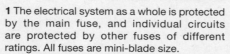

5 Fuses

1 The electrical system as a whole is protected by the main fuse, and individual circuits are protected by other fuses of different ratings. All fuses are mini-blade size.

2 The main fuse is integral with the starter relay – to access it remove the cover from the right-hand side of the battery box **(see**

illustrations 3.7a and b). Displace the relay and remove the cover – the fuse is under it, and its location is marked on the top of the cover **(see illustrations)**. A spare main fuse is housed in the bottom of the relay holder. On 2016/17 models the FI fuse is also housed in the relay, and on 2018-on models the ABS M fuse is in the relay. On 2016/17 models the ABS main 30A fuse, and on 2016/17 models with DCT the DCT M fuse, and on 2018-on models the ABS FSR and FI fuses, and on models with DCT the DCT M fuse, are housed in boxes clipped to the battery box next to the relay **(see illustrations)**. Unclip the lid(s) to access the fuse(s) **(see illustration)**.

3 All other fuses are housed in the fuseboxes, located under the rider's seat **(see illustration)**. Remove the seat for access (see

5.2e Fuse identities and ratings are marked on the lids

5.2f Open the lids to access the fuses

5.3a Fuseboxes (arrowed)

5.3b Unclip the lids to access the fuses

5.5a Pull the fuse out

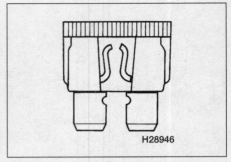

5.5b A blown fuse can be identified by a break in its element

Chapter 7). The location, identity and rating of each fuse is marked on the box lid. Unclip the lid to access the fuses **(see illustration)**. Fuse values are listed in the wiring diagrams at the end of this Chapter.

4 A spare fuse of each rating is provided in the fusebox.

5 The fuses can be removed and checked visually – use the tool provided in the toolkit, your fingers, or a suitable pair of pliers **(see illustration)**. A blown fuse is easily identified by a break in the element **(see illustration)**, but if there is any doubt check the fuse for continuity (Section 2). Each fuse is clearly marked with its rating and must only be replaced by a fuse of the correct rating. If a spare fuse is used, always replace it with a new one so that a spare of each rating is carried on the bike at all times.

⚠️ *Warning: Never put in a fuse of a higher rating or bridge the terminals with any other substitute, however temporary it may be. Serious damage may be done to the circuit, or a fire may start.*

6 If the new fuse blows immediately check the wiring circuit very carefully for evidence of a short-circuit. Look for bare wires and chafed, melted or burned insulation.

7 Occasionally a fuse will blow or cause an open-circuit for no obvious reason. Corrosion of the fuse ends and fusebox terminals may occur and cause poor fuse contact. If this happens, remove the corrosion with a wire brush or emery paper, then spray the fuse end and terminals with electrical contact cleaner.

6.3a Headlight relay (arrowed)

<table>
<tr><td>**6**</td><td>**Lighting system check**</td></tr>
</table>

Note: *Refer to electrical system fault finding in Section 2 and to the wiring diagram for your model at the end of this Chapter.*

Headlight

1 The headlight comprises a number of LEDs. If the headlight does not work, check the main fuse, the headlight (HI and LO) fuse(s) and the ILLUMI STOP HORN fuse (Section 5). If the headlight fuse blows repeatedly check the headlight circuit wiring for a short. Next check the headlight and left-hand switch housing wiring connectors are securely connected and in good condition, then check the dimmer switch and passing switch in the housing (see Sections 7and 18). Next check the relay (Step 3). If they are good, the problem lies in the wiring or connectors – check all the wiring in the headlight and headlight relay circuit, and make sure there is continuity to earth in the green wire, referring to Section 2 and to the Wiring diagram for your model. If no fault can be found fit a new headlight.

2 If an individual LED within the headlight has failed all the other LEDs will work but the overall brightness of the headlight will be affected. The only solution is to fit a new headlight.

3 On 2016/17 models remove the right-hand side cover, and on 2018-on models remove the ETC tray (see Chapter 7). Release the relay and remove the cover, then pull the relay out of its

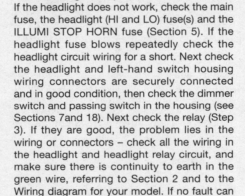

6.3b Relay test set-up

socket. Test it as follows **(see illustrations)** : set a multimeter to the ohms x 1 scale and connect it across the relay's A and B terminals. There should be no continuity (infinite resistance). Using a fully-charged 12 volt battery and two insulated jumper wires, connect the positive (+) terminal of the battery to the D terminal on the relay, and the negative (–) terminal to the C terminal. At this point the relay should be heard to click and the meter read 0 ohms (continuity). If this is the case the relay is good. If the relay does not click when battery voltage is applied and indicates no continuity (infinite resistance) across its terminals, it is faulty and must be replaced with a new one.

Tail and brake light

4 The tail/brake light comprises a number of LEDs. If the light does not work at all, check the ILLUMI STOP HORN fuse (Section 5). Next check the tail light wiring connector is securely connected and in good condition. If they are good, the problem lies in the wiring or connectors – check all the wiring in the tail light circuit, and make sure there is continuity to earth in the green wire, referring to Section 2 and to the Wiring diagram for your model. If no fault can be found fit a new tail light.

5 If an individual LED within the light has failed all the other LEDs will work but the overall brightness of the headlight will be affected. The only solution is to fit a new tail light.

6 If the tail light LEDs work but the brake light LEDs don't check there is battery voltage at the green/yellow wire terminal in the bulbholder with the ignition ON, and first with the front brake lever on, then with the rear brake pedal on. If voltage is present with one brake on but not the other, then the switch or its wiring is faulty. If voltage is present in both cases, check there is continuity to earth (ground) in the green wire from the bulbholder. If no voltage is indicated, check the wiring and connectors between the brake light and the brake light switches, then check the switches themselves. Refer to Section 13 for the switch testing procedures.

Licence plate light

7 If the light fails to work, check the bulb (Section 9). If the bulb is good, check there is battery voltage at the brown wire terminal in the bulbholder with the ignition switch ON. If voltage is present, check there is continuity to earth (ground) in the green wire from the bulbholder. If no voltage is indicated, check the wiring and connectors between the light and the fusebox.

7 Headlight

Removal

1 Remove the headlight cover (see Chapter 7).
2 Disconnect the open air temperature sensor wiring connector **(see illustration)**.
3 Unscrew the headlight mounting bolts, noting the washers **(see illustration)**.
4 Disconnect the instrument wiring connector **(see illustration)**.
5 Release the wiring from its tie then disconnect the lean angle sensor and headlight wiring connectors **(see illustrations)**.
6 Lift the headlight off its bottom locating lugs and remove it **(see illustration)**.
7 If required remove the lean angle sensor (see Chapter 4) and the open air temperature sensor (Section 15) from the headlight.

Installation

8 Installation is the reverse of removal. Make sure the collars are fitted in the mounting grommets **(see illustration)**. Check the operation of the headlight and sidelight. Check the headlight aim (see Chapter 1).

8 Tail light

Removal

1 On 2016/17 models remove the luggage rack (see Chapter 7). Disconnect the rear turn signal and licence plate light wiring

7.2 Disconnect the sensor wiring

7.3 Unscrew the two bolts on each side

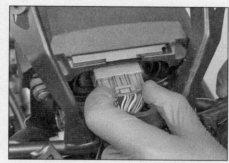

7.4 Disconnect the instrument wiring

7.5a Release the wiring tie

7.5b Disconnect the lean angle sensor connector…

7.5c …and the headlight connectors

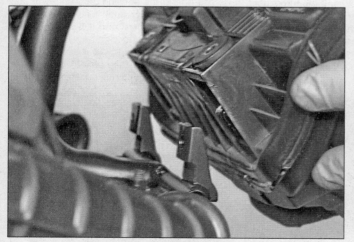

7.6 Lift the headlight off the bracket

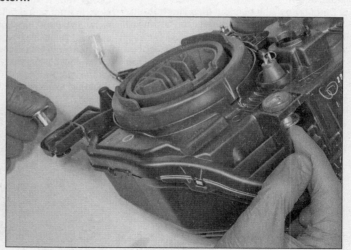

7.8 Each mount has a collar in a grommet – make sure the collars are fitted in the correct way, which is in the opposite direction to which the bolts fit

8.3 Disconnect the wiring

8.4 Tail light nuts (arrowed)

9.1 Undo the screws and remove the lens

connectors. Undo the tail cover screws, one on each side with a collar, and two on the underside. Release the tabs and remove the tail cover by drawing it back.

2 On 2018-on models remove the tail light cover (see Chapter 7).

3 Disconnect the tail light wiring connector **(see illustration)**.

4 Unscrew the nuts and remove the tail light, noting how the peg locates in the grommet **(see illustration)**. Note the collars for the nuts in the side mounting grommets.

Installation

5 Installation is the reverse of removal. Make sure the collars are fitted in the side mounting grommets. Check the operation of the tail and brake lights.

9 Licence plate light bulb

Note: *It is a good idea to use a paper towel or dry cloth when handling bulbs to prevent injury if it breaks, and to increase bulb life.*

1 Undo the screws and remove the lens **(see illustration)**.

2 Carefully pull the bulb out **(see illustration)**.

3 Check the socket terminals for corrosion and clean them if necessary.

4 Push the new bulb in. Check the rubber seal is correctly seated, then fit the lens **(see illustration)** – do not overtighten the screws as the lens and threads are easily damaged.

10 Turn signal/hazard/emergency stop circuit

1 If an individual turn signal fails on models with a standard filament bulb, first check the bulb and its socket (Section 11). If the bulb is good, and on models fitted with LED turn signals, check the turn signal wiring connector, referring to Section 12 for access.

2 On models with LED turn signals, if an individual LED within the turn signal has failed all the other LEDs will work but the overall brightness of the light will be affected. The only solution is to fit a new turn signal.

3 If all the turn signals fail to work, check the ILLUMI STOP HORN fuse and the CLOCK TURN fuse (Section 5). If they are good, the problem lies in the wiring or connectors, or the switch. Refer to Section 2 and to the wiring diagram for your model and check the wiring and connectors in the turn signal circuit. Refer to Section 18 for the switch testing procedures.

4 2016/17 Europe market models without ABS or DCT and 2018-on US models have a diode block in the turn signal/hazard warning circuit that is housed under the passenger seat, in front of the tail light. If the turn signal/hazard warning function is faulty and the turn signals, relay and wiring are good, remove the passenger seat (see Chapter 7), remove the diode block and test it in the same way as the starter interlock circuit diode block as described in Section 23.

5 If no fault can be found, fit a new turn signal relay as follows:

6 On European models without ABS or DCT remove the ETC tray (see Chapter 7) – the relay is under the back of the fuel tank mount. Displace the relay, remove the cover and disconnect the wiring.

7 On all other European models remove the ABS modulator (see Chapter 6). On 2016/17 models remove the relay. On 2018-on models disconnect the wiring then remove the relay **(see illustration)**. The turn signal relay on 2018-on Europe models features an emergency stop system. Under hard braking the rear turn signals will flash.

8 On US models remove the fuel tank (see Chapter 4). Release the relay and disconnect the wiring.

11 Turn signal bulbs (models without LED turn signals)

Note: *It is a good idea to use a paper towel or dry cloth when handling bulbs to prevent injury if the bulb should break and to increase bulb life.*

1 Undo the screw securing the lens and detach it from the housing, noting how it fits. Remove the rubber seal if it is loose, and replace it with a new one if it is damaged, deformed or deteriorated.

2 Push the bulb in and twist it anti-clockwise to release it. Check the socket terminals for corrosion and clean them if necessary.

9.2 Pull the bulb out

9.4 Check the seal is correctly located

10.7 Turn signal relay wiring connector (arrowed)

12.2 Turn signal nut (arrowed)

12.5 Right-hand turn signal connector (A), left-hand turn signal connector (B)

12.6 Turn signal nut (arrowed)

3 Line up the pins of the new bulb with the slots in the socket, then push the bulb in and turn it clockwise until it locks into place. Note that the pin slots in the bulbholder are off-set to allow only the fitting of an amber bulb.
4 Fit a new rubber seal if required, and make sure it is properly seated and does not get pinched. Fit the lens onto the housing, locating the tab in the cut-out in the housing, and fit the screw – do not overtighten it as it is easy to strip the threads or crack the lens.

12 Turn signal assemblies

Front turn signals

1 Remove the inner panel cover (see Chapter 7).
2 Undo the nut and remove the turn signal, taking care as you draw the wire through **(see illustration)**. Remove the mounting plate from the rubber base and the rubber base from the cover if necessary, noting how they locate.
3 Installation is the reverse of removal. Check the operation of the turn signal.

Rear turn signals

4 On 2016/17 models remove the luggage rack, and on 2018-on models remove the tail light cover (see Chapter 7).
5 Disconnect the turn signal wiring connector **(see illustration)**.
6 Undo the nut and remove the turn signal,

taking care as you draw the wire through **(see illustration)**. Remove the mounting plate from the rubber base and the rubber base from the panel if necessary, noting how they locate.
7 Installation is the reverse of removal. Check the operation of the turn signal.

13 Brake light and parking brake warning light switches

Circuit check

Note: *Refer to electrical system fault finding in Section 2 and to the wiring diagram for your model at the end of this Chapter.*

Brake light switches

1 Before checking the switches, and if not already done, check the brake light circuit (Section 6).
2 The front brake light switch is mounted on the underside of the brake master cylinder. Disconnect the wiring connectors from the switch **(see illustration)**. Using a continuity tester, connect the probes to the terminals of the switch. With the brake lever at rest, there should be no continuity. With the brake lever applied, there should be continuity. If the switch does not behave as described, replace it with a new one.
3 The rear brake light switch is mounted on the inner side of the frame above the brake pedal **(see illustration 13.9)**. To access the wiring connector remove the battery box (Section 3). Disconnect the wiring connector

(see illustration). Using a continuity tester, connect the probes to the terminals on the switch side of the wiring connector. With the brake pedal at rest, there should be no continuity. With the brake pedal applied, there should be continuity. If the switch does not behave as described, replace it with a new one, although check first that the spring has not become detached or broken, and the switch is adjusted correctly (see Chapter 1).
4 If the switches are good, check for voltage at the black/red wire connector with the ignition switch ON – there should be battery voltage. If there's no voltage present, check the wiring between the connector and the fusebox (see the wiring diagrams at the end of this Chapter). If voltage is present, check the other wire for continuity to the brake light, referring to the relevant wiring diagram. Repair or renew the wiring as necessary.

Parking brake warning light switch (models with DCT)

5 The parking brake light switch is mounted on the underside of the parking brake lever bracket. Disconnect the wiring connectors from the switch **(see illustration)**. Bridge the connectors using an auxiliary wire and turn the ignition on. If the light in the instruments comes on the switch is faulty. Test the switch using a continuity tester, connecting the probes to the terminals of the switch. With the brake lever at rest, there should be no continuity. With the brake lever applied, there should be continuity. If the switch does not behave as described, replace it with a new one.

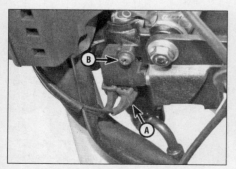

13.2 Front brake light switch wiring connectors (A) and screw (B)

13.3 Rear brake switch wiring connector (arrowed)

13.5 Parking brake switch wiring connectors (arrowed)

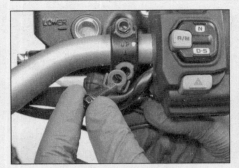

13.7 Unscrew the bottom master cylinder clamp bolt to release the wiring clip bracket

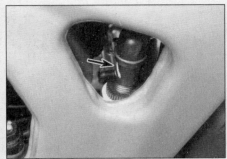

13.9 Rear brake light switch (arrowed)

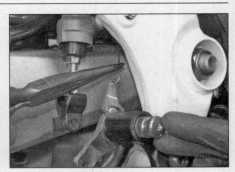

13.10 Unhook the spring

6 If the switch is good and the instrument light does not come on check the wiring and connectors in the circuit. If the wiring is good the fault could be in the instruments.

Switch replacement

Front brake light switch

7 The switch is mounted on the underside of the brake master cylinder. Disconnect the wiring connectors from the switch **(see illustration 13.2)**. Where fitted you will have to displace the wiring clip bracket from the brake master cylinder clamp **(see illustration)**. Undo the single screw securing the switch to the master cylinder **(see illustration 13.2)**.

8 Installation is the reverse of removal. Make sure the switch is correctly located before tightening the screw. The switch isn't adjustable.

Rear brake light switch

9 The switch is mounted on the inside of the frame on the right-hand side **(see illustration)**. To access the wiring connector remove the battery box (Section 3). Disconnect the switch wiring connector and feed it down to the switch noting its routing **(see illustration 13.3)**.

10 Detach the end of the switch spring from the brake pedal pivot arm **(see illustration)**. Lift the switch out of its bracket.

11 Installation is the reverse of removal. Make sure the brake light comes on just before the rear brake pedal takes effect. If adjustment is necessary, refer to Chapter 1, Section 6.

Parking brake warning light switch (models with DCT)

12 The switch is mounted on the underside of the parking brake lever bracket. Disconnect the wiring connectors from the switch **(see illustration 13.5)**. Undo the single screw securing the switch to the bracket **(see illustration)**.

13 Installation is the reverse of removal. Make sure the switch is correctly located before tightening the screw. The switch isn't adjustable.

14 Instrument (combination meter) removal and installation

Removal

1 Remove the inner panel covers (see Chapter 7).

2 Remove the headlight (Section 7).

3 Pull back the dust cover and unplug the instrument wiring connector **(see illustration)**.

4 Undo the screws, noting the washers, and remove the instrument cluster **(see illustrations)**.

Installation

5 Installation is the reverse of removal. Check the rubber grommets and replace them with new ones if necessary. Make sure the washers are fitted with the screws.

15 Instrument (combination meter) check and replacement

Check

Note: *Refer to electrical system fault finding in Section 2 and to the wiring diagram for your model at the end of this Chapter.*

13.12 Parking brake switch screw (arrowed)

14.3 Release the wiring connector

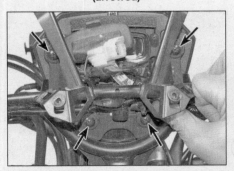

14.4a Instrument cluster screws (arrowed) – 2016/17

14.4b Instrument cluster screws (arrowed) – 2018-on

14.4c Lift the instrument cluster off and remove the cover – 2018-on

Instrument cluster power check

1 When the ignition is turned on all instrument displays and functions should come on for a few seconds.

2 If they don't, remove the headlight cover (see Chapter 7). Disconnect the instrument wiring connector and check for loose or broken connections **(see illustration 7.4)**.

3 To check the power input wire to the instruments, check for battery voltage between the black/red wire terminal in the instrument connector and a good earth (ground) with the ignition switch ON. There should be battery voltage. If there is no voltage, first check the ILLUMI STOP fuse (Section 5), and if that is good refer to the wiring diagrams and check the wire between the instrument cluster and the fusebox for loose or broken connections or a damaged wire.

4 To check the back-up power input wire to the instruments, check for battery voltage between the red/white wire terminal in the instrument connector and a good earth (ground) with the ignition switch OFF. There should be battery voltage. If there is no voltage, first check the CLOCK TURN fuse (Section 5), and if that is good refer to the wiring diagrams and check the wire between the instrument cluster and the fusebox for loose or broken connections or a damaged wire.

5 If there is voltage, and to check the earth (ground) wire, check for continuity between the green wire terminal and earth (ground). If there is no continuity, check the circuit for loose or broken connections or a damaged wire and repair as necessary.

6 On 2016/17 models, if there is a problem in the TXD (serial communication) line between the instruments the ECM the engine management, oil pressure, and coolant temperature and torque control warning lights stay on, the torque control OFF and S/D/G indicators won't work, the mileage function display shows "---", remaining fuel shows "--", the gear position is blinking and the torque control level and engine temperature displays are blinking. To check the serial communication line, disconnect the ECM 33-pin black wiring connector (see Chapter 4). Check there is continuity in the black wire from the instrument wiring connector to the B16 terminal in the ECM wiring connector, and check there is no continuity to earth. If not trace the fault, and repair as necessary.

7 If the power input, earth and TXD wires are good, but there is no display or instrument function, then the instrument printed circuit board (PCB) is faulty. Disassemble the instrument cluster and replace the instrument/ PCB with a new one (see below).

Speedometer and vehicle speed sensor

8 Refer to Step 2 to access the instrument wiring connector and check it for loose or broken connections.

9 Remove the battery box (Section 3). Disconnect the speed sensor wiring connector **(see illustration)**. Check the connector for loose terminals. With the ignition switch ON, check for battery voltage between the black/ red or black (according to model) (+) and green (-) wire terminals on the wiring loom side of the connector. If there is no voltage refer to the wiring diagrams and check the wires for continuity to the fusebox and earth respectively and repair any loose or broken connection or damaged wire. If all is good check there is continuity in the pink wire to the instrument wiring connector.

10 If all is good so far replace the speed sensor with a new one (see below). If this fails to cure the problem replace the instrument PCB with a new one (see below).

Tachometer

11 If the tachometer does not work, first check the TXD line (Step 6), then check the CKP sensor (see Chapter 4).

12 If they are good have the system checked by a Honda dealer.

All other functions

13 If none of the functions are working, check the instrument cluster power input, earth and TXD (serial communication) wires (see above). If all is good, disassemble the instrument cluster (see below) and check for any obvious internal fault. If none is apparent replace the instrument/PCB with a new one.

14 If an individual function is not working, refer to the relevant Chapter or Section in

15.9 Speed sensor wiring connector (arrowed)

this chapter and check the component and its circuit. If the component and its circuit are good the instrument is faulty. See below for the open air temperature display sensor.

Instrument and warning lights

15 All instrument and warning lights are LEDs, which are part of the instrument cluster printed circuit board and are not available individually. If one of the LEDs fails disassemble the instrument cluster and replace the instrument/PCB with a new one (see below).

Instrument disassembly and replacement

16 Remove the instrument cluster (Section 14).

17 Undo the screws on the back and remove the rear cover, then remove the instrument/ PCB from the front cover **(see illustrations)**.

18 Installation is the reverse of removal. Do not over-tighten the screws.

Vehicle speed sensor

19 See Chapter 4, Section 9.

Open air temperature sensor

20 The open air temperature sensor is mounted on the back of the headlight on the right-hand side. To access it remove the headlight cover (see Chapter 7).

21 Disconnect the wiring connector **(see illustration 7.2)**.

22 Undo the screw and remove the sensor **(see illustration)**.

23 Installation is the reverse of removal.

15.17a Instrument cluster screws on the rear cover – 2016/17...

15.17b ... and 2018-on models

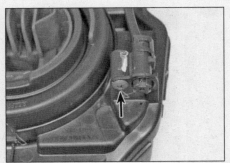

15.22 Open air temperature sensor screw (arrowed)

16.5a Undo the screws...

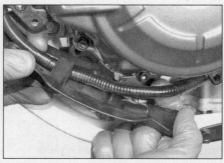

16.5b ...displace the cover and release the wiring from it

16.5c Disconnect the wiring

16 Oil pressure switch or sensor

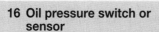

1 The oil pressure warning light should come on when the ignition switch is turned ON and go out a few seconds after the engine is started. If the oil pressure warning light does not go out or comes on whilst the engine is running, stop the engine immediately and carry out an oil level check (see *Pre-ride checks*), and if the level is correct, an oil pressure check (see Chapter 2).

Check

Note: *Refer to electrical system fault finding in Section 2 and to the wiring diagram for your model at the end of this Chapter.*

Models with standard transmission

2 If the oil pressure warning light does not come on when the ignition is turned ON, but all other instrument functions work, remove the sump guard (see Chapter 7). Remove the alternator wiring cover **(see illustrations 16.5a and b)**. Pull the rubber cover off the oil pressure switch, and undo the screw securing the wiring connector. With the ignition switched ON, earth (ground) the wire on the crankcase and check that the warning light comes on. If the light comes on, the switch is faulty.

3 If the light still does not come on, check there is continuity in the wire between the switch and the instrument wiring connector (Section 15). Repair the wiring if necessary. If

all the wiring is good and the switch is good the instrument could be faulty.

4 If the warning light does not go out when the engine is started or comes on whilst the engine is running, yet the oil pressure is satisfactory, detach the wire from the oil pressure switch (see above). With the wire detached and the ignition switched ON the light should be out. If it is illuminated, the wire between the ECM/PCM and the switch is earthed (grounded) at some point. If the wiring is good, the switch must be assumed faulty and replaced with a new one.

Models with DCT

5 If the oil pressure warning light does not come on when the ignition is turned ON, but all other instrument functions work, remove the sump guard (see Chapter 7). Remove the alternator wiring cover **(see illustrations)**. Disconnect the sensor wiring connector **(see illustration)**. Check the wiring and connectors in the sensor circuit, referring to Section 2 and to the Wiring Diagram for your model.

6 If the wiring is good either the sensor or the instrument is faulty. First fit a new sensor (see below). If that does not solve the problem it is best to have the system tested by a Honda dealer.

Removal and installation

Models with standard transmission

7 The oil pressure switch is screwed into the left-hand side of the crankcase. Drain the engine oil (see Chapter 1).

8 Remove the wiring cover **(see illustrations 16.5a and b)**. Pull the rubber cover

off the switch, then undo the screw securing the wiring connector.

9 Unscrew and remove the switch – be prepared to catch any residual oil with a rag.

10 To refit apply a suitable sealant to the upper portion of the switch threads near the switch body, leaving the bottom 3 to 4 mm of thread clean. Thread the switch into the crankcase and tighten to 12 Nm.

11 Attach the wiring connector and secure it with the screw, then fit the rubber cover. Fit the wiring cover **(see illustrations 16.5b and a)**.

12 Fill the engine with the correct type and quantity of oil (see Chapter 1).

13 Run the engine and check that the switch operates correctly and without oil leakage.

Models with DCT

14 The oil pressure sensor is screwed into the left-hand side of the crankcase. Drain the engine oil (see Chapter 1).

15 Remove the wiring cover **(see illustrations 16.5a and b)**. Disconnect the wiring connector **(see illustration 16.5c)**.

16 Unscrew and remove the sensor and its O-ring **(see illustrations)** – be prepared to catch any residual oil with a rag.

17 Fit the sensor using a new O-ring smeared with oil **(see illustration 16.16b)**. Thread the sensor into the crankcase and tighten to 22 Nm **(see illustration 16.6a)**.

18 Connect the wiring connector **(see illustration 16.5c)**. Fit the wiring cover **(see illustrations 16.5b and a)**.

19 Fill the engine with the correct type and quantity of oil (see Chapter 1).

20 Run the engine and check that the switch operates correctly and without oil leakage.

17 Ignition switch

> ⚠ **Warning: To prevent the risk of short circuits, disconnect the battery negative (–) lead before making any ignition switch checks.**

Check

Note: *Refer to electrical system fault finding in Section 2 and to the wiring diagram for your model at the end of this Chapter.*

16.16a Unscrew the sensor...

16.16b ...and remove the O-ring

1 The switch can be checked for continuity using an ohmmeter or a continuity test light. Always disconnect the battery negative (–) lead, which will prevent the possibility of a short circuit, before making the checks (Section 3).

2 Remove the fuel tank (see Chapter 4). Release and disconnect the ignition switch brown 2-pin connector **(see illustration 17.7a)**. Check for loose or broken connections.

3 Using an ohmmeter or a continuity tester, check the continuity between the terminals in the switch side of the connector – continuity should exist when the switch is in the ON position. If not check the wiring between the connector and the switch, and if that is good remove the contact plate from the bottom of the switch (see below), clean the contacts and check them for wear and damage. If required fit a new contact plate – it is available separately. If the switch barrel is faulty replace the complete switch with a new one – the barrel only comes with a contact plate fitted.

4 If the switch is good, reconnect the battery. Check there is battery voltage at the red wire terminal in the loom side of the connector. If not, there is a break in the wire between the connector and the battery. If there is voltage

check the red/black wire for continuity to the fusebox.

Removal

5 Disconnect the battery negative (–) lead (Section 3).

6 Remove the air filter housing (see Chapter 4).

7 Disconnect the ignition switch wiring connector, and on models with a HISS system the receiver wiring connector **(see illustrations)**. Feed the wiring back to the switch, freeing it from all clips and ties and noting the routing.

8 Release the wiring, cable(s) and hose from the top yoke as required according to model. Check that everything is free from the top yoke.

9 Displace the handlebars from the top yoke (see Chapter 5).

10 Slacken the left-hand fork clamp bolts in the top yoke and unscrew the right-hand ones **(see illustration)**. Unscrew the steering stem nut **(see illustration)**. Lift the top yoke up off the steering stem and forks and remove it.

11 Undo the contact plate screws and remove the plate from the bottom of the switch **(see illustration)**. On models with a HISS system undo the receiver screws and displace it from the top of the switch.

12 One-way security bolts, which can be done up but not undone using conventional tools, are fitted – to remove them you have to drill the heads off or drive them around until loose using a cold chisel. To do this make sure the yoke is adequately supported or secured in a vice and protected by rag, and remove the handlebar holders if necessary.

Installation

13 Installation is the reverse of removal. Use new ignition switch bolts and tighten them to 26 Nm. Tighten the steering stem nut to 100 Nm, then tighten the fork clamp bolts to 22 Nm. Make sure the wiring, cable(s) and hose are correctly routed and secured. Refer to Chapter 5 to install the handlebar holders and handlebars.

18 Handlebar switches, and ABS and G switches

1 Generally speaking, the switches are reliable and trouble-free. Most troubles, when they do occur, are caused by dirty or corroded contacts, but wear and breakage of internal parts is a possibility that should not be

17.7a Release and disconnect the ignition switch wiring connector…

17.7b …and where fitted the HISS wiring connector – 2018 model shown

17.10a Fully unscrew the right-hand clamp bolts to release the wiring clip bracket

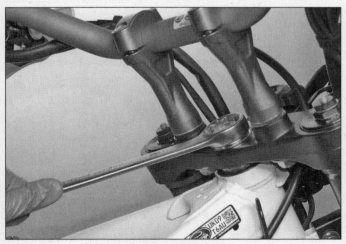

17.10b Unscrew the nut

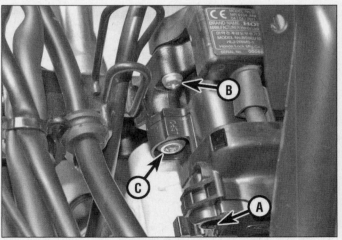

17.11 Contact plate screws (A), HISS receiver screws (B), ignition switch bolts (C)

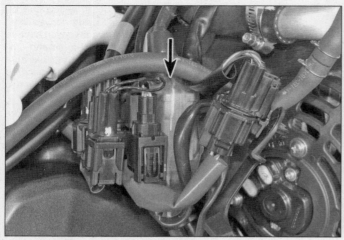

18.3a Right-hand switch connector(s) (arrowed)

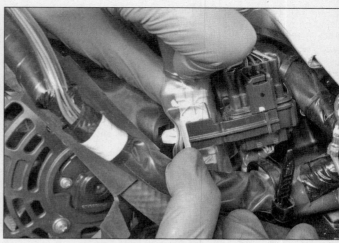

18.3b Left-hand switch connectors

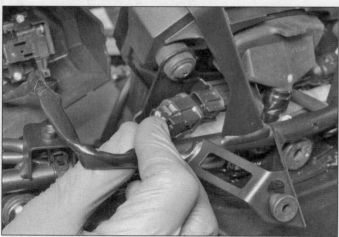

18.3c ABS/G switch connector

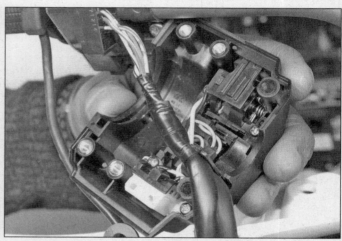

18.5 Clean and check all internal connections and contacts

overlooked. If breakage does occur, the entire switch and related wiring harness will have to be replaced with a new one, as individual parts are not available.

Check

Note: *Refer to electrical system fault finding in Section 2 and to the wiring diagram for your model at the end of this Chapter.*

2 The switches can be checked for continuity using an ohmmeter or a continuity test light. Always disconnect the battery negative (–) lead, which will prevent the possibility of a short circuit, before making the checks (Section 3).

3 To access the handlebar switch connectors, remove the relevant fairing side panel (see Chapter 7) – the connector(s) for the right-hand switch housing is/are behind the right-hand panel, and the connectors for the left-hand switch are behind the left-hand panel. To access the ABS/G switch connector displace the inner panel cover (see Chapter 7). Release and disconnect the connector(s) as required **(see illustrations)**. Check for loose or broken connections.

4 Check for continuity between the terminals of the switch connector with the switch in the various positions (i.e. switch off – no continuity, switch on – continuity) – see the wiring diagram for your model at the end of this Chapter. Continuity should exist between the terminals connected by a solid line on the diagram when the switch is in the indicated position.

5 If the continuity check indicates a problem exists, displace the handlebar switch housing (see below), and spray the switch contacts with electrical contact cleaner (there is no need to remove the switch completely) **(see illustration)**. If switch components are damaged or broken it should be obvious.

Removal and installation

Handlebar switches

6 Refer to Step 3 and disconnect the switch wiring connector(s). Feed the wiring back to the switch, freeing it from any clips and ties and noting the routing.

7 When removing the right-hand switch disconnect the wires from the brake light

switch **(see illustration 13.2)**. When removing the left-hand switch disconnect the wires from the clutch switch on models with standard transmission **(see illustration 22.2)**, or from the parking brake light switch on models with DCT **(see illustration 13.5)**.

8 To remove the left-hand switch housing undo the screws and free the switch from the handlebar by separating the halves **(see illustration)**.

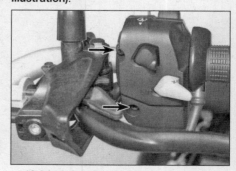

18.8 Left-hand switch housing screws (arrowed)

18.10a Displace the master cylinder

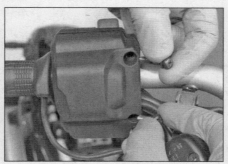

18.10b Undo the two screws...

18.10c ...and displace the front of the housing...

9 To remove the right-hand switch housing on 2016/17 models refer to Chapter 4 and detach the throttle cables.

10 To remove the right-hand switch housing on 2018-on models unscrew the two master cylinder assembly clamp bolts, noting how the lower bolt secures the wiring clip bracket, and position the assembly clear of the handlebar, making sure no strain is placed on the hydraulic hose **(see illustration)**. Keep the master cylinder reservoir upright to prevent possible fluid leakage. Undo the right-hand switch housing screws and detach the front half of the housing, then undo the four screws and detach the rear half of the housing from the APS (accelerator position sensor) **(see illustrations)**.

11 Installation is the reverse of removal. Make sure the pin in the left-hand switch housing, and in the right-hand housing on 2016/17 models, locates in the hole in the handlebar. On 2018-on models fit the front brake master cylinder clamp with the UP mark facing up and with the clamp mating surfaces aligned with the mark on the top of the handlebar **(see illustration)**. Tighten the clamp bolts to 10 Nm, tightening the top bolt first, and not forgetting to secure the wiring clip bracket with the lower bolt **(see illustration)**.

ABS and G switches

12 Remove the right-hand inner panel cover (see Chapter 7).

18.10d ...then undo the four screws...

18.10e ...and displace the rear

13 Undo the screws and remove the switch(es) **(see illustration)**.

14 Installation is the reverse of removal.

---

19 Heated grips and grip controller (Adventure Sports model)

System check

1 If the heated grips do not work first check the OP fuse (Section 5 and the wiring diagram at the end of this Chapter).

2 If a fault is detected in the heated grip system the heat level indicator in the instrument will blink E1, E2 or E3, and the LED in the switch on the left grip will simultaneously blink once, twice or three times accordingly.

3 E1 indicates a low voltage to the heater, so first check the battery (Section 4).

4 E2 indicates a short circuit somewhere in the heated grip circuit.

5 E3 indicates a faulty grip heater switch or heater matrix, or a fault somewhere in the circuit.

6 To check the system remove the fairing side panels and the left-hand side cover for access to the grip wiring connectors and the controller (see Chapter 7). Refer to Section 2 and to the wiring diagram for your model, and check the wiring and connectors

18.11a Align the master cylinder and fit the clamp

18.11b Make sure the bracket is above the wiring and correctly located

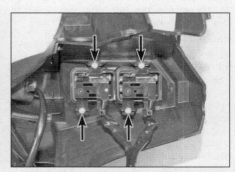

18.13 ABS/G switch screws (arrowed)

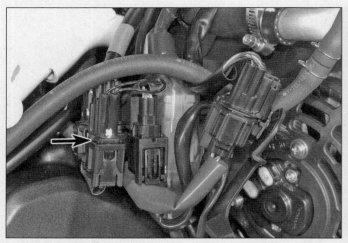

19.6a Right-hand grip wiring connector (arrowed)

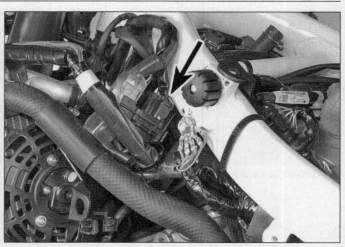

19.6b Left-hand grip wiring connectors (arrowed)

(see illustrations). Also check the resistance of each grip heater matrix by connecting the meter to the terminals in the grip side of the 2-pin connector – there should be 7.4 to 9 ohms resistance.

7 If no specific fault can be found in any of the wiring, in the switch or either of the grips themselves, then it is likely there is a fault in the controller.

Heated grips

Removal

8 Remove the handlebar weight and handguard, and the fairing side panel (see Chapter 7).

9 Disconnect the grip wiring connector(s) **(see illustration 19.6a or b)**. Feed the wiring up to the grip, releasing it from its ties and guides and noting its routing.

10 To remove the right-hand grip, which is integral with the throttle twistgrip, refer to Chapter 4, Section 9 and follow the procedure to remove the APS (accelerator position switch) to the point where the twistgrip is slid off the handlebar, noting that there is no need to raise the fuel tank and disconnect the APS wiring connector or to remove the APS itself.

11 To remove the left-hand grip refer to Chapter 5, Section 5.

Installation

12 Installation is the reverse of removal.

13 To fit the grip onto the left handlebar, clean the handlebar and apply Honda Bond A or Pro Honda handgrip cement or equivalent to the first 10 cm of the handlebar, then spray the handlebar and inside the grip with isopropyl alcohol. Align the bottom of the switch so it is 4 mm below the bottom of the dimmer switch and ease the grip on and up against the handlebar switch housing, taking care not to twist or crease it, and avoiding putting pressure on the switch, and do not

tap on its end – if it gets stuck spray some more isopropy alcohol on the exposed part of the handlebar. Allow the glue to dry for at least one hour before riding the bike, and do not use the heater higher than level 2 for one week.

Heated grip controller

14 Remove the left-hand side cover (see Chapter 7).

15 Release the controller and disconnect the wiring connector.

16 Installation is the reverse of removal.

---

20 Gear position switch, gear position sensor, neutral switch, gearchange shaft switch

---

1 2016/17 models with standard transmission have a gear position switch. 2018-on models with standard transmission have a gear position sensor, a neutral switch and a gearchange shaft switch. Models with DCT have a neutral switch and a transmission range (TR) sensor (TR sensor covered in Chapter 4).

Gear position switch

2 The gear position sensor is behind the front sprocket cover. Check the transmission is in neutral.

3 Remove the front sprocket cover (see Chapter 6, Section 22).

4 Displace the rear shock absorber (see Chapter 5) and rest it as shown so you can access the switch wiring connector on the back of the engine **(see illustration)**- there is no need to remove the swingarm.

5 Trace the wiring from the switch and disconnect the connector.

6 Clean the area around the switch, then unscrew the bolt and remove the switch.

Remove the O-ring – a new one should be used.

7 Fit the switch using a new O-ring smeared with oil. Align the pin on the switch with the hole in the selector drum, fit the switch and tighten the bolt to 10 Nm.

8 Connect the wiring and check the operation of the switch.

9 Install the shock absorber and sprocket cover.

Gear position sensor

10 The gear position sensor is behind the front sprocket cover. Check the transmission is in neutral.

11 Remove the front sprocket cover (see Chapter 6, Section 22).

12 Displace the rear shock absorber (see Chapter 5) and rest it as shown so you can access the switch wiring connector on the back of the engine **(see illustration 20.4)**- there is no need to remove the swingarm.

13 Trace the wiring from the switch and disconnect the connector.

14 Clean the area around the switch, then unscrew the bolt and remove the cover and

20.4 Displace and rest the shock as shown

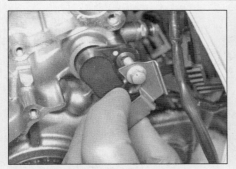

20.14a Remove the cover...

20.14b ...then remove the switch

20.14c Switch O-ring (arrowed)

the switch **(see illustrations)**. Remove the O-ring **(see illustration)** – a new one should be used.

15 Fit the switch using a O-ring smeared with oil. Align the flats on the switch and the selector drum, fit the switch and cover and tighten the bolt to 12 Nm **(see illustration)**.

16 Connect the wiring and check the operation of the switch.

17 Install the shock absorber and sprocket cover.

Neutral switch

18 The switch is on the back of the engine on the left-hand side **(see illustration)**. Pull the rubber terminal cover off the switch, unscrew the nut and disconnect the wire from the switch.

19 Clean the area around the switch, then unscrew it from the crankcase. Remove the sealing washer – a new one should be used.

20 Smear the switch threads and seating surface with oil, fit a new sealing washer and tighten the switch to 12 Nm.

21 Connect the wiring and check the operation of the neutral light **(see illustration 20.18)**.

Gearchange shaft switch (shift spindle switch)

22 The switch is on the back of the engine in the middle.

23 Displace the rear shock absorber (see Chapter 5) and rest it as shown so you can access the switch, which is on the back of the engine in the middle **(see illustration 20.4)** - there is no need to remove the swingarm.

20.15 Align the flats when fitting the sensor

24 Pull the rubber terminal cover off the switch, unscrew the nut and disconnect the wire from the switch.

25 Clean the area around the switch, then unscrew it from the crankcase. Remove the sealing washer – a new one should be used.

26 Smear the switch threads and seating surface with oil, fit a new sealing washer and tighten the switch to 12 Nm.

27 Connect the wiring.

21 Sidestand switch

1 The sidestand switch is mounted on the stand pivot.

Check

Note: *Refer to electrical system fault finding in*

20.18 Neutral switch (arrowed)

Section 2 and to the wiring diagram for your model at the end of this Chapter.

2 Remove the battery box (Section 3). Disconnect the sidestand switch 2-pin black wiring connector **(see illustration)**.

3 Check the operation of the switch using an ohmmeter or continuity test light. Connect the meter between the terminals on the switch side of the connector. With the sidestand up there should be continuity (zero resistance) between the terminals, and with the stand down there should be no continuity (infinite resistance).

4 If the switch does not perform as described, it is faulty.

Removal

5 Remove the front sprocket cover (see Chapter 6, Section 22). On models with DCT remove the gearchange control motor cover.

6 Remove the battery box (Section 3). Disconnect the switch 2-pin black wiring connector **(see illustration 21.2)**. Feed the wiring down to the switch, noting the routing.

7 Unscrew the switch bolt and remove the switch from the stand, noting how it fits **(see illustration)**. Honda specify that the switch bolt be replaced with a new one every time it is disturbed – the new bolt has a locking compound already applied to its threads. However there is nothing to stop you cleaning up the threads on the old bolt and applying a suitable non-permanent thread locking compound on installation.

21.2 Sidestand switch wiring connector (arrowed)

21.7 Unscrew the bolt and lift the switch off, noting how it locates

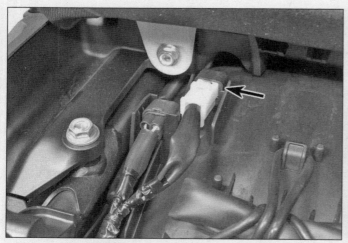

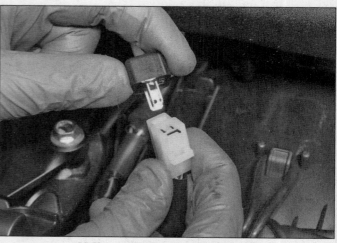

23.3a Release the diode block (arrowed)...

23.3b ...and pull it out of the socket

Installation

8 Fit the new switch onto the sidestand, making sure the tab locates in the hole, and the lug on the stand bracket locates into the cut-out in the switch body **(see illustration 21.7)**. Secure the switch with a new or cleaned and threadlocked bolt and tighten to 10 Nm.
9 Feed the wiring up to its connector, making sure it is correctly routed, and reconnect it.
10 Refer to Chapter 1 and check the operation of the sidestand switch/starter interlock circuit. Fit the front sprocket cover (see Chapter 6), on models with DCT the control motor cover, and the battery box (Section 3).

22 Clutch switch

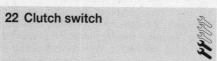

1 The clutch switch is mounted in the clutch lever bracket.

Check

Note: *Refer to electrical system fault finding in Section 2 and to the wiring diagram for your model at the end of this Chapter.*
2 To check the switch, disconnect the wiring connectors. Connect the probes of an ohmmeter or a continuity tester to the

two switch terminals. With the clutch lever pulled in there should be continuity. With the clutch lever out, there should be no continuity (infinite resistance).
3 If the switch is good, check the other components (sidestand switch, gear position/ neutral switch, diode block) in the starter safety circuit, and check the wiring between them for continuity, and the connectors for loose or broken connections.

Removal and installation

4 The clutch switch is mounted in the lever bracket.
5 Pull the boot off the switch and disconnect the wiring connectors.
6 Undo the screw and remove the switch, noting how it locates.
7 Installation is the reverse of removal. Refer to Chapter 1 and check the operation of the sidestand switch/starter interlock circuit.

23 Diode block (models with standard transmission)

Note: *Refer to electrical system fault finding in Section 2 and to the wiring diagram for your model at the end of this Chapter.*
1 The starter interlock safety circuit diode block

plugs into a connector in the large fusebox on 2016/17 models, and into the wiring loom on 2018-on models. Remove the rider's seat for access (see Chapter 7). The diode block contains two diodes, which are part of the starter interlock safety circuit (see Chapter 1).
2 On 2016/17 models refer to Section 5, open the large fusebox lid and pull the diode block out of its socket.
3 On 2018-on models release the diode block from its holder and pull it out of the socket **(see illustrations)**.
4 On 2016/17 models, using an ohmmeter or continuity tester, connect the positive (+) probe to one of the outer terminals of the diode block and the negative (–) probe to the middle terminal of the block **(see illustration)**. The diode being tested should show continuity. Now reverse the probes. The diode should show no continuity. Repeat the tests between the other outer terminal and the middle terminal. The same results should be achieved. If it doesn't behave as stated, replace the diode block with a new one.
5 On 2018-on models, using an ohmmeter or continuity tester, connect the positive (+) probe to terminal A of the diode block and the negative (–) probe to terminal B of the block **(see illustration)**. The diode being tested should show continuity. Now reverse the probes. The diode should show no continuity. Repeat the tests between the A and C terminals. The same results should be achieved. If it doesn't behave as stated, replace the diode block with a new one.

24 Horn

Check

Note: *Refer to electrical system fault finding in Section 2 and to the wiring diagram for your model at the end of this Chapter.*
1 The horn is mounted in front of the left-hand

23.4 Test the diode as described

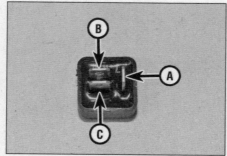

23.5 Test the diode as described

radiator on the left-hand side. If it doesn't work first check the fuse (Section 5).

2 Disconnect the wiring connectors from the horn **(see illustration)**. Check them for loose wires. Using two jumper wires, apply voltage from a fully-charged 12V battery directly to the terminals on the horn. If the horn doesn't sound, fit a new one.

3 If the horn sounds, check there is voltage at the black wire connector with the ignition ON and the horn switch (button) pressed.

4 If no voltage was present, check the wire for continuity between the horn and the switch in the left-hand switch housing. Next, with the ignition switch ON, check that there is voltage at the black/red wire to the horn switch. If there is, check the switch contacts in the switch housing (Section 18).

5 If there isn't voltage at the black/red wire, check the wire from the switch to the fusebox.

24.2 Pull the connectors off the terminals

24.7 Removing the horn

Replacement

6 The horn is mounted in front of the left-hand radiator.

7 Disconnect the wiring connectors from the horn **(see illustration 24.2)**. Unscrew the bolt and remove the horn **(see illustration)**.

8 Fit the horn and check that it works.

25 Starter motor relay

Check

Note: *Refer to electrical system fault finding in Section 2 and to the wiring diagram for your model at the end of this Chapter.*

1 If the starter circuit is faulty, first check the fuses (Section 5).

2 To access the relay (and if not already done) remove the cover from the right-hand side of the battery box **(see illustrations 3.7a and b)**.

3 Displace the relay and remove the cover **(see illustrations 5.2a and b)**.

4 Unscrew the bolt securing the starter motor lead, identified by the letter M marked on the relay (the other lead, marked B, is the battery lead), and position the lead away from the relay **(see illustration)**.

5 With the ignition switch ON, the engine kill switch in the RUN position, the sidestand down and the transmission in neutral, press the starter switch. The relay should be heard to click.

6 If the relay doesn't click, switch off the ignition and remove the relay as described below; test it as follows:

7 Set a multimeter to the ohms x 1 scale and connect it across the relay's starter motor (M) and battery (B) lead terminals. There should be no continuity. Using a fully-charged 12 volt battery and two insulated jumper wires, connect the positive (+) terminal of the battery to terminal C on the relay, and the negative (–) terminal to the terminal D on the relay **(see illustration)**. At this point the relay should be heard to click and the multimeter read 0 ohms (continuity). If this is the case the relay is proved good. If the relay does not click when battery voltage is applied and indicates no continuity (infinite resistance) across its terminals, it is faulty.

8 If the relay is good, check for continuity in the main lead from the battery to the relay. Also check that the terminals and connectors at each end of the lead are tight and corrosion-free.

9 Next check for battery voltage at the white

wire terminal in the connector with the ignition ON, the kill switch in the RUN position and the starter button pressed. If there is no voltage, check the wiring between the relay wiring connector and the starter button.

10 If voltage is present, on models with standard transmission check that there is continuity to earth in the green/red wire with the transmission in neutral (note that there will be a very slight resistance due to the diodes in the starter interlock circuit). If there is no continuity check the wiring and connectors between the relay, and the neutral switch, then if that is good check the switch itself and the diode block. On models with DCT check there is continuity in the green/red wire to the starter circuit relay, and if there is check the relay itself (see Chapter 4). If there is no continuity check the wiring and connectors in the relay circuit.

Replacement

11 Disconnect the battery, then remove the cover from the right-hand side of the battery box **(see illustrations 3.7a and b)**.

12 Displace the relay and remove the cover **(see illustrations 5.2a and b)**.

13 Disconnect the relay wiring connector **(see illustration)**. Unscrew the bolts securing

25.4 Starter motor lead (A), battery lead (B)

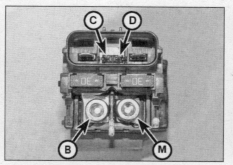

25.7 Starter relay terminal identification

25.13 Disconnect the wiring connector

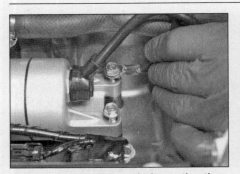

26.2a Unscrew the two bolts, noting the earth lead…

26.2b …and remove the starter motor

26.4 Fit a new O-ring (arrowed) and lubricate it

the starter motor and battery leads to the relay and detach the leads **(see illustration 25.4)**. If the relay is being replaced with a new one, remove the fuses and fit them into the new relay. If you are fitting a new rubber sleeve remove the spare main fuse from its pocket and fit it into the new sleeve.

14 Installation is the reverse of removal. Connect the lead from the starter motor to the terminal marked M and the lead from the battery to the terminal marked B, and make sure the terminal bolts are securely tightened **(see illustration 25.4)**. Do not forget to fit the fuses into the relay and the spare into the rubber sleeve, if removed – on 2016/17 models make sure you fit the 15A fuse next to the red/white wire terminal and the 30A fuse next to the red wire terminal. Connect the negative (–) lead last when reconnecting the battery.

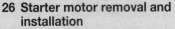

26 Starter motor removal and installation

Removal

1 The starter motor is mounted on the crankcase behind the cylinders. Remove the battery box (Section 3).

2 Unscrew the two bolts securing the starter motor to the crankcase, noting the earth lead on 2018-on models **(see illustration)**. Slide the starter motor out, using a screwdriver as leverage if required **(see illustration)**.

3 Remove the O-ring on the end of the starter motor – a new one must be used **(see illustration 26.4)**.

Installation

4 Fit a new O-ring onto the end of the starter motor, making sure it is seated in its groove **(see illustration)**. Apply a smear of engine oil to the O-ring.

5 Manoeuvre the motor into position and slide it into the crankcase, meshing the starter motor teeth with those of the starter idle/reduction gear **(see illustration 26.2b)**. Fit the mounting bolts, on 2018-on models securing the earth lead with the front bolt, and tighten them **(see illustration 26.2a)**.

6 Install the battery box (Section 3).

27 Starter motor overhaul

Check

1 Remove the starter motor (Section 26). Cover the body in some rag and clamp the motor mounting lugs in a soft-jawed vice – do not overtighten it.

2 Detach the lead from the motor **(see illustration)**.

3 Using a fully-charged 12 volt battery and two insulated jumper wires, connect the positive (+) terminal of the battery to the protruding terminal on the starter motor, and the negative (–) terminal to one of the motor's mounting lugs. At this point the starter motor should spin. If this is the case the motor is proved good, though it is worth disassembling it and checking it if you suspect it of not working properly under load. If the motor does not spin, disassemble it for inspection.

Disassembly

4 Remove the starter motor (Section 26).

5 Detach the lead from the motor **(see illustration 27.2)**.

6 Note the alignment marks between the main housing and the front and rear covers, or make your own if they aren't clear **(see illustration)**.

7 Unscrew the two long bolts, noting the O-rings, and remove the front cover from the motor **(see illustrations)**.

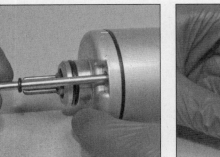

27.2 Pull back the terminal cover then unscrew the nut and detach the lead

27.6 Note the alignment marks between the housing and the covers

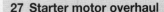

27.7a Unscrew the bolts…

27.7b …and remove the front cover…

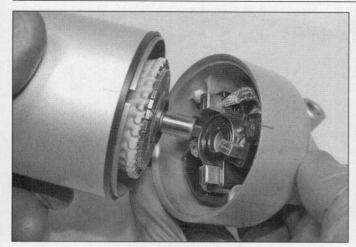

27.8 …and the rear cover

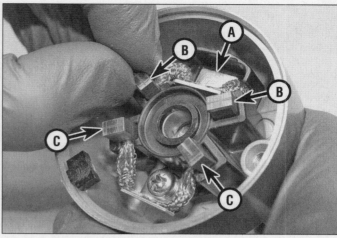

27.10 Terminal bolt (A) and positive brushes (B), negative brushes (C)

8 Remove the rear cover **(see illustration)**.

9 Withdraw the armature from the main housing **(see illustration 27.28)** – it is held in by the attraction of the magnets, so take care not to lose your grip on the armature before the magnets lose theirs.

10 At this stage check for continuity between the terminal bolt and the positive brushes **(see illustration)** – there should be continuity (zero resistance). Check for continuity between the terminal bolt and the cover – there should be no continuity (infinite resistance). Also check for continuity between the negative and positive brushes – there should be no continuity (infinite resistance). If there is no continuity when there should be or *viceversa*, identify the faulty component and replace it with a new one.

11 Displace the brushes and remove the springs **(see illustrations)**.

12 Noting the correct fitted location of each component, unscrew the nut from the terminal bolt and remove the plain washer, the insulator and the terminal shield **(see illustrations)**. Remove the O-ring from the terminal bolt and remove the positive brushes and terminal bolt **(see illustrations)**.

13 Undo the screw and remove the negative

27.11a Lift the brushes out…

27.11b …and remove the springs

27.12a Undo the nut…

27.12b …remove the plain washer and the insulator…

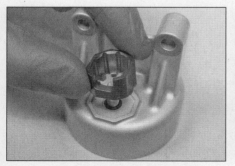

27.12c… and the shield

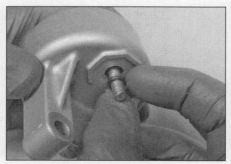

27.12d Remove the O-ring…

27.12e …then remove the positive brush/ terminal bolt assembly

27.13a Undo the screw...

27.13b ...remove the negative brushes...

27.13c ...the brush holder...

brushes, then remove the brush holder **(see illustrations)**.

14 Remove the housing locating tab from the rear cover for safekeeping **(see illustration)**.

Inspection

15 The parts of the starter motor that are most likely to require attention are the brushes. No specification is given for the minimum brush length, but when new they are 12 mm long, so if they get down to about 6 mm or if they are cracked fit new brushes **(see illustration)**.

16 Inspect the commutator bars on the armature for scoring, scratches and discoloration. The commutator can be cleaned and polished with crocus cloth, but do not use sandpaper or emery paper. After cleaning, wipe away any residue with a

cloth soaked in electrical system cleaner or denatured alcohol.

17 Using an ohmmeter or a continuity test light, check for continuity between the commutator bars **(see illustration)**. Continuity should exist between each bar and all of the others. Also, check for continuity between the commutator bars and the armature shaft **(see illustration)**. There should be no continuity (infinite resistance) between the commutator and the shaft. If the checks indicate otherwise, the armature is defective and a new starter motor must be fitted – the armature is not available separately.

18 Check the front end of the armature shaft for worn, cracked, chipped and broken teeth.

19 Inspect the front and rear covers for signs of cracks or wear. Check the oil seal and the needle bearing in the front cover and the

bush in the rear cover for wear and damage **(see illustration)** – the seal, bearing, bush and covers are not listed as being available separately so if necessary a new starter motor must be fitted.

20 Inspect the magnets in the main housing and the housing itself for cracks.

21 Inspect the terminal bolt shield **(see illustration 27.12c)**, insulator **(see illustration 27.12b)**, and O-ring **(see illustration 27.12d)**, and the sealing rings on the housing **(see illustration)**, for signs of damage, deformation and deterioration and fit new ones if necessary.

Reassembly

22 Fit the housing locating tab into the rear cover with the protruding tab facing the rim **(see illustration 27.14)**.

27.14 ...and the locating tab

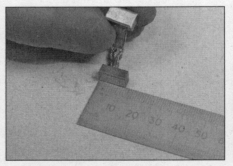

27.15 Measure the length of each brush

27.17a There should be continuity between the bars...

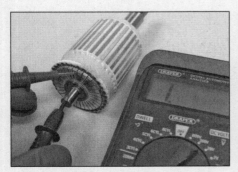

27.17b ...and no continuity between the bars and the shaft

27.19 Check the front cover seal and bearing and the rear cover bush

27.21 Housing sealing rings (arrowed)

23 Fit the brush holder into the rear cover **(see illustration 27.13c)**. Fit the negative brushes and secure them with the screw **(see illustrations 27.13b and a)**.

24 Fit the terminal bolt and positive brushes into the brush holder, then fit the O-ring **(see illustrations 27.12e and d)** – feed the O-ring all way down onto the base of the bolt so it insulates the bolt from the rear cover **(see illustration)**. Fit the terminal shield with the cut-out for the lead at the top, then fit the insulator and the washer and secure them with the nut **(see illustrations 27.12c, b and a)**.

25 Fit the brush springs into their housings, then seat the brushes on them, with the wires in the slots **(see illustrations 27.11b and a)**.

26 To check for correct installation do the continuity checks described in Step 10.

27 If removed fit the sealing rings onto each end of the main housing **(see illustration 27.21)**.

28 Grasp the housing and carefully allow the armature to be drawn in, making sure the cut-out in the housing is at the same end as the commutator bars **(see illustration)**.

29 Apply a smear of grease to the short end of the shaft. Fit the rear cover, aligning the tab so it locates in the cut-out in the housing rim, and making sure the brushes remain square and seat against the commutator **(see illustration 27.8)**.

30 Apply a smear of grease to the front cover oil seal lip. Slide the front cover on, aligning the marks **(see illustration 27.7b)**.

31 Check the alignment marks are correctly aligned **(see illustration 27.6)**, then fit the long bolts with their O-rings and tighten them **(see illustration 27.7a)**.

32 Connect the starter lead to the motor and secure it with the nut **(see illustration 27.2)**. Fit the rubber cover over the terminal.

33 Install the starter motor (Section 26).

28 Charging system testing

1 If the performance of the charging system is suspect, the system as a whole should be checked first, followed by testing of the individual components.Before beginning the checks, make sure the battery is fully charged and that all system connections are clean and tight (Section 3 and Section 4).

2 Checking the output of the charging system and the performance of the various components within the charging system requires the use of a multimeter (with voltage, current, resistance checking facilities).

3 When making the checks, follow the procedures carefully to prevent incorrect connections or short circuits resulting in irreparable damage to electrical system components.

Output test

4 Refer to Section 3 to access the battery. Start the engine and warm it up.

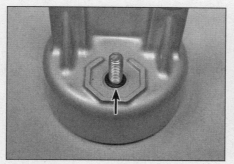

27.24 Seat the O-ring (arrowed) between the bolt and the cover as shown

5 To check the regulated (DC) voltage output, allow the engine to idle with the headlight main beam (HI) turned ON. Connect a multimeter set to the 0-20 volts DC scale to the leads or terminals of the battery with the positive (+) meter probe to positive (+) lead or terminal and the negative (-) meter probe to battery negative (-) lead or terminal **(see illustration)**.

6 Slowly increase the engine speed to 5000 rpm and note the reading obtained. Compare the result with that given in the Specifications at the beginning of this Chapter. If the regulated voltage output is outside the specification, check the alternator and the regulator/rectifier (Section 29and Section 30).

Leakage test

Caution: Always connect an ammeter in series, never in parallel with the battery, otherwise it will be damaged. Do not turn the ignition ON or operate the starter motor when the ammeter is connected – a sudden surge in current will blow the meter's fuse.

| *Clues to a faulty regulator are constantly blowing bulbs, with brightness varying considerably with engine speed, and battery overheating.* |

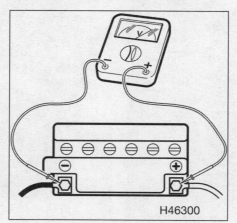

28.5 Checking the charging rate – connect the meter as shown

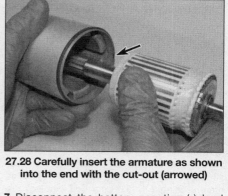

27.28 Carefully insert the armature as shown into the end with the cut-out (arrowed)

7 Disconnect the battery negative (-) lead (Section 3).

8 Set the multimeter to the Amps function, selecting a high amp range initially, and then bring it down to the mA (milli Amp) range when doing the test. If there is a high current flow in the circuit it may blow the meter's fuse if a low range is initially selelcted.

9 On 2016/17 models connect the meter negative (-) probe to the battery negative (-) lead, and the positive (+) probe to the earth point the disconnected negative (-) lead bolts to.

10 On 2018-on models connect the meter negative (-) probe to the battery negative (-) terminal, and the positive (+) probe to the disconnected negative (-) lead **(see illustration)**.

11 Battery current leakage should not exceed the maximum limit (see Specifications). If a higher leakage rate is shown there is a short circuit in the wiring, although if an after-market alarm is fitted, its current draw should be taken into account. Disconnect the meter and reconnect the battery negative (-) lead.

12 If leakage is indicated, refer to Wiring Diagrams at the end of this Chapter to systematically disconnect individual electrical components and repeat the test until the source is identified.

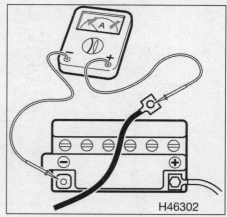

28.10 Checking the charging system leakage rate – connect the meter as shown

29 Alternator

Check

1 Disconnect the light grey wiring connector with the three yellow wires from the regulator/rectifier **(see illustrations 30.1)**. Check the connector terminals for corrosion and security.
2 Using a multimeter set to the ohms x 1 (ohmmeter) scale measure the resistance between each pair of yellow wires on the alternator side of the connector, thereby taking three readings. If the stator coil windings are in good condition the reading should be as given in the Specifications at the beginning of the Chapter. If not, check the wiring between the connector and the stator is in good condition, and check there is no continuity to earth in any of the wires. If the wiring is good and there is continuity the alternator stator coil assembly is faulty.

Removal

3 Drain the engine oil (see Chapter 1). Do not fit the dipstick back into the cover.
4 Remove the front sprocket cover (see Chapter 6, Section 22).
5 Remove the alternator wiring cover **(see illustrations 16.5a and b)**.
6 Remove the battery box (Section 3).
7 On models with standard transmission remove the gearchange shaft cover **(see illustrations)**. Disconnect the wire from the oil pressure switch. Disconnect the speed sensor wiring connector (3-pin black) **(see illustration 15.9)**.
8 On models with DCT remove the gearchange control motor cover **(see illustration)**. Disconnect the EOP sensor wiring connector **(see illustration 16.5c)**.

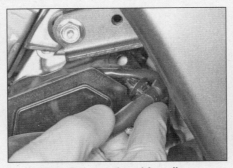

29.7a Release the wiring clip...

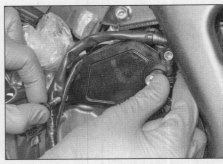

29.7b ...then unscrew the bolts and remove the cover

29.8 Gearchange control motor cover

29.9 Alternator loom 6-pin connector (arrowed)

9 Disconnect the alternator assembly 6-pin black wiring connector **(see illustration)**. Disconnect the light grey wiring connector with the three yellow wires from the regulator/rectifier **(see illustration 30.1)**. Feed the wiring down to the alternator cover, releasing its clips and noting its routing.
10 Working in a criss-cross pattern, evenly slacken the alternator cover bolts, noting the positions of the two longer bolts that secure

the wiring cover brackets, and the position of the wiring clip bracket **(see illustration)**. Draw the cover off the engine, noting that it will be restrained by the force of the rotor magnets, and be prepared to catch any residual oil **(see illustration)**. Remove the dowels from either the cover or the crankcase if they are loose **(see illustration 29.22d)**. Remove the oil jet if required, noting which way round it fits **(see illustration 29.22c)**.
11 Withdraw the starter idle/reduction

29.10a Unscrew the bolts (arrowed)...

29.10b ...and remove the cover

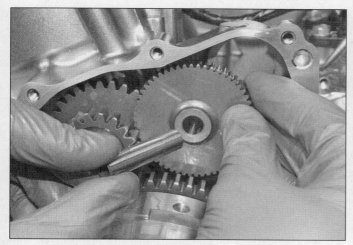

29.11a Remove the rear idle/reduction gear first…

29.11b …then the front one

29.12 Using a rotor strap to hold the rotor while unscrewing the bolt

29.13a Thread the puller into the rotor…

gear shafts and remove the gears **(see illustrations)**.

12 To remove the rotor bolt it is necessary to stop the rotor from turning using either a commercially available rotor strap, or by counter-holding the flats on the rotor boss using a large, preferably offset, spanner **(see illustration)**. Unscrew the bolt and remove the washer.

13 To remove the rotor from the shaft it is necessary to use a rotor puller – use either

the Honda tool (Pt No. 07733-0020001 in Europe, or 07933-3950000 in the US) or a commercially available equivalent designed for this bike. Thread the rotor puller into the centre of the rotor and turn it until the rotor is displaced from the shaft, holding the rotor as before to prevent the engine turning **(see illustrations)**. If the rotor doesn't come off easily tap the end of the tool when it is tight. If the starter driven gear does not come

away with the rotor slide it off the end of the crankshaft. Remove the woodruff key from its slot if loose **(see illustration)**.

14 To remove the stator/CKP sensor assembly from the cover, unscrew their bolts, free the wiring grommet and remove the assembly **(see illustration)**.

15 If required remove the needle bearing, starter driven gear and starter clutch from the back of the rotor (see Chapter 2).

29.13b …then hold the rotor and turn the puller

29.13c Woodruff key (arrowed)

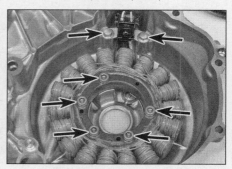

29.14 Stator and CKP sensor bolts (arrowed)

29.16 Smear some sealant around the cut-out

29.19 Slide the rotor onto the shaft

29.20a Lubricate and fit the bolt and its washer...

29.20b ...and tighten it to the specified torque

29.22a Apply the sealant...

Installation

16 Fit the stator into the cover, aligning the rubber wiring grommet with the groove **(see illustration 29.14)**. Clean the threads of the stator and CKP sensor bolts and apply fresh threadlock. Fit the bolts and tighten them to 12 Nm. Apply a sealant (such as Threebond 1207B or equivalent) to the wiring grommet cut-out in the cover, then press the grommet into the cut-out **(see illustration)**.

17 If removed fit the starter clutch onto the rotor and the starter driven gear into the starter clutch and the needle bearing into the driven gear hub (see Chapter 2).

18 Clean all old sealant off the cover and crankcase mating surfaces and wipe them with a suitable solvent. Clean the tapered end of the crankshaft and the corresponding mating surface on the inside of the rotor with a suitable solvent. Make sure the Woodruff key is in its slot **(see illustration 29.13c)**.

19 Make sure that no metal objects have attached themselves to the magnet on the inside of the rotor. Align the slot in the rotor with the Woodruff key and slide the rotor onto the shaft **(see illustration)**.

20 Apply some clean oil to the rotor bolt threads, the underside of the head, and the washer **(see illustration)**. Fit the bolt with its washer and tighten it to 137 Nm, holding the rotor as on removal **(see illustration)**.

21 Lubricate the idle/reduction gear shafts with molybdenum disulphide oil (50/50 molybdenum disulphide grease and engine oil). Position the front gear, making sure the related gear teeth engage correctly and insert the shaft, making sure it locates in its bore in the crankcase, then repeat for the rear gear **(see illustration 29.11b and a)**.

22 Apply a smear of sealant (such as Threebond 1207B or equivalent) to the alternator cover mating surface on the crankcase **(see illustration)**. If removed fit the dowels into the crankcase **(see illustration)**. If removed fit the oil jet into the cover with the wider hole facing out **(see illustration)**. Fit the cover, noting that the rotor magnets will forcibly draw the cover/stator on, making sure the dowels locate **(see illustration 29.10b)**. Fit the cover bolts, securing the wiring cover brackets with the longer bolts and not forgetting the wiring clip bracket, and tighten

29.22b ...and fit the dowels (arrowed)...

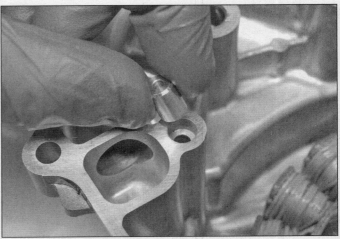

29.22c ...and fit the oil jet if removed

29.22d Fit the wiring cover brackets and clip bracket as shown, and secure the cover brackets with the longer bolts

29.23 On models with DCT make sure the wiring is correctly routed when fitting the gearchange control motor cover

them evenly in a criss-cross sequence to 12 Nm **(see illustration)**.
23 Reconnect the wiring and fit the battery box and covers in reverse order of removal according to model, making sure the wiring is correctly routed and secured **(see illustration)**.
24 Fill the engine with the correct type and quantity of oil (see Chapter 1). Install all remaining parts.

30 Regulator/rectifier

Check

1 Disconnect the regulator/rectifier wiring connectors **(see illustration)**. Check the connector terminals for corrosion and security.
2 Set the multimeter to the 0 to 20 dc volts setting. Connect the meter positive (+) probe to the red wire terminal in the black connector and the negative (–) probe to a suitable ground (earth) and check for voltage. Full battery voltage should be present at all times.
3 Switch the multimeter to the resistance (ohms) scale. Check for continuity between

30.1 Disconnect the wiring connectors

the green wire terminal in the black connector and ground (earth). There should be continuity to earth.
4 If the above checks do not provide the expected results check the wiring and connectors for shorts, breaks, and loose or corroded terminals (see the Wiring Diagrams).
5 If the wiring is good, check the alternator stator coil (Section 29). If that is good the regulator/rectifier unit is probably faulty. Honda provide no test data for the unit itself. Take it to a Honda dealer for confirmation of its condition before replacing it with a new one.

 Clues to a faulty regulator are constantly blowing bulbs, with brightness varying considerably with engine speed, and battery overheating.

Removal and installation

6 Disconnect the regulator/rectifier wiring connectors **(see illustration 30.1)**.
7 Unscrew the two bolts and remove the regulator/rectifier **(see illustration)**.
8 Installation is the reverse of removal.

30.7 Regulator/rectifier bolts (arrowed)

31 Wiring diagrams

1 Complete wiring diagrams follow, most spread over four pages. Use the numbers connecting the wires at the page break to link them.
2 The following is a key to component names given in abbreviated detail:
A/M switch – AT (automatic) and MT (manual) switch (DCT)
APS – accelerator position sensor
CKP – crankshaft position sensor
DLC – data link connector
ECM/PCM – engine control module/power control module
ECT – engine coolant temperature sensor
EOP – engine oil pressure sensor
EVAP – evaporative emission control system
FI relay – fuel injection relay
G switch – traction control (DCT)
HSTC – Honda selectable torque control
IAT – intake air temperature sensor
IACV – idle air control valve (2016/17)
MAP – manifold absolute pressure sensor
N-D switch – neutral (DCT)
PAIR – pulse secondary air system
TCS – torque control switch
TBW – throttle by wire
TP – throttle position sensor
TR – transmission range sensor (DCT)
VS – vehicle speed sensor
3 On 2018-on models a CAN-BUS (controlled area networking) links the instruments and ECM/PCM. On the wiring diagrams CANL (low) is represented by the black wire and CANH (high) by the black/red wire.

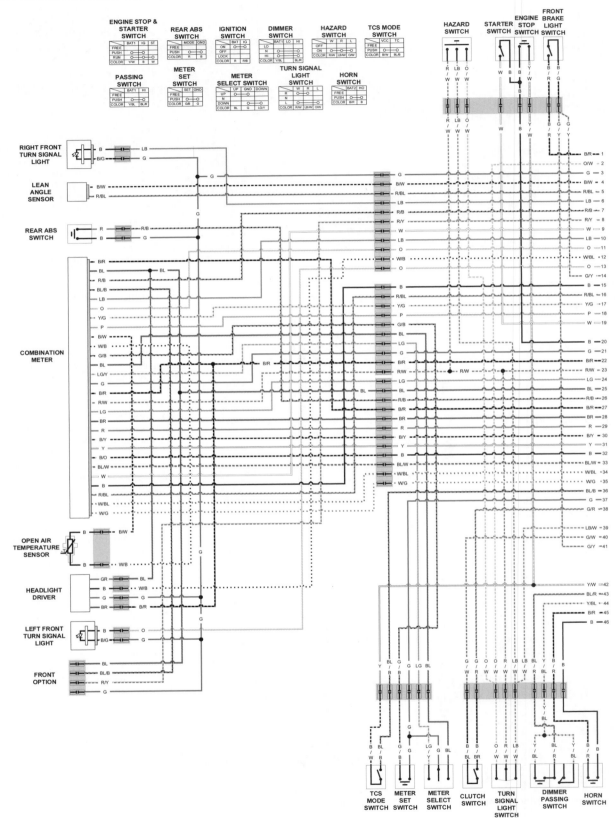

UK/EUROPE CRF1000A 2016-2017 (1 / 4)

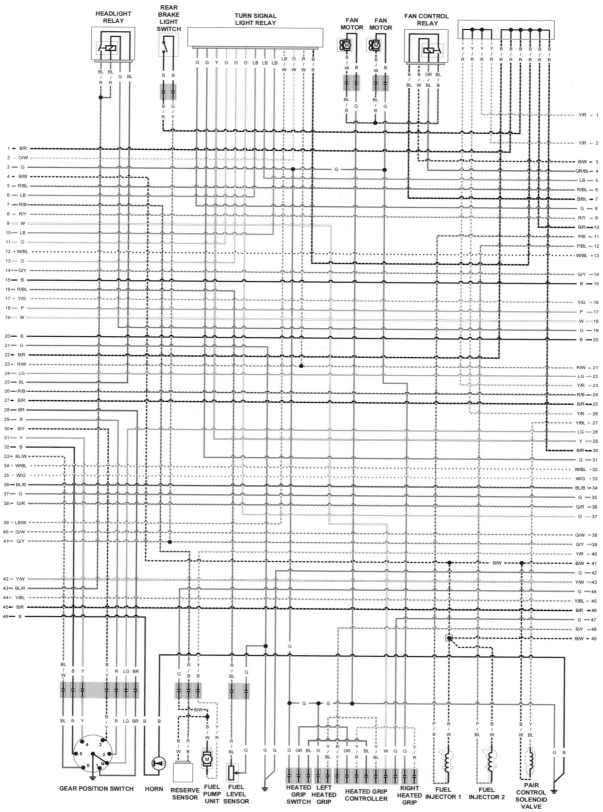

UK/EUROPE CRF1000A 2016-2017 (2 / 4)

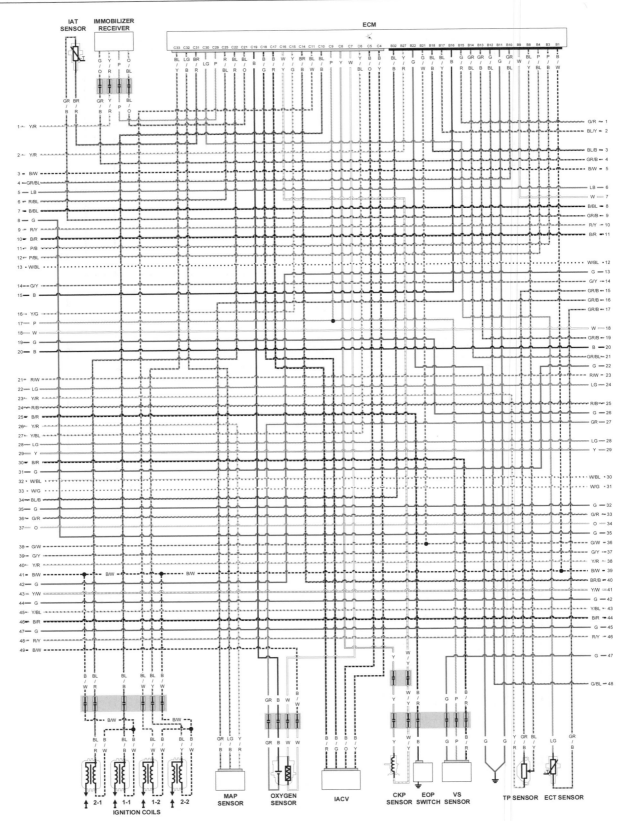

UK/EUROPE CRF1000A 2016-2017 (3 / 4)

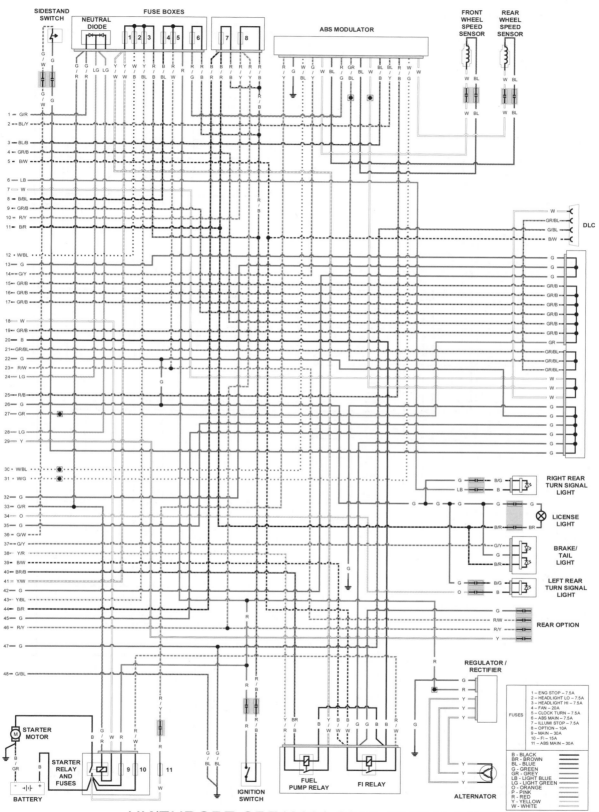

UK/EUROPE CRF1000A 2016-2017 (4 / 4)

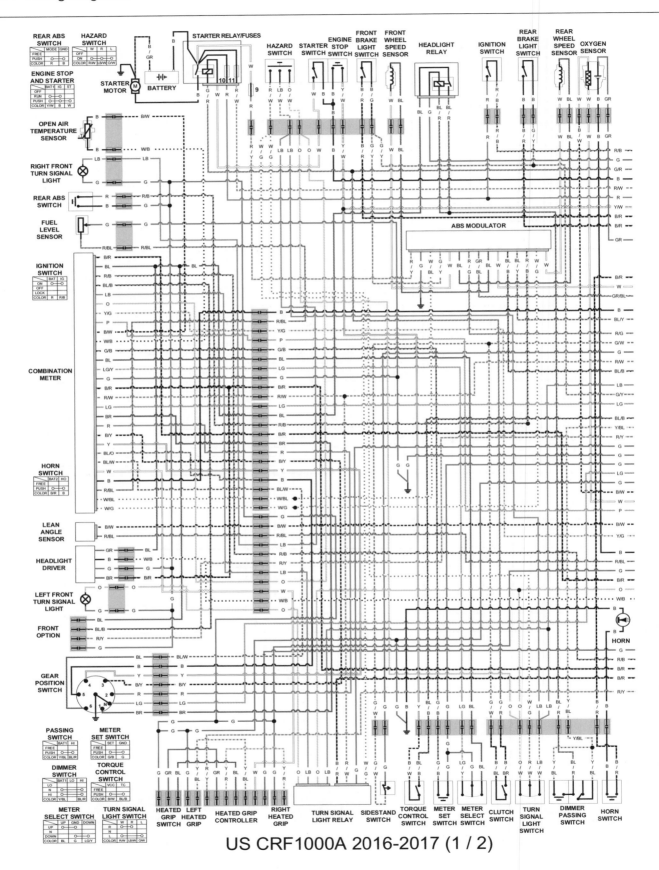

US CRF1000A 2016-2017 (1 / 2)

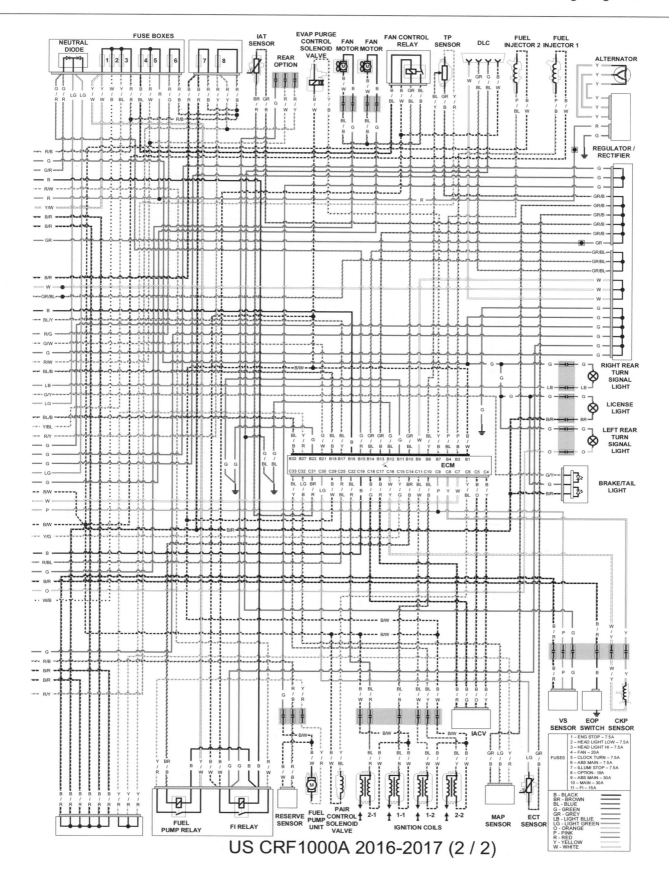

US CRF1000A 2016-2017 (2 / 2)

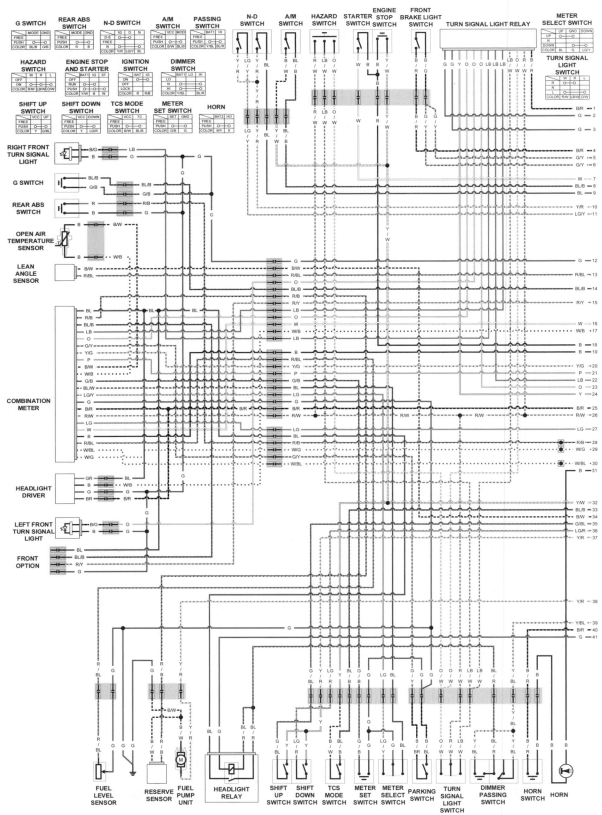

UK/EUROPE CRF1000 D 2016-2017 (1 / 4)

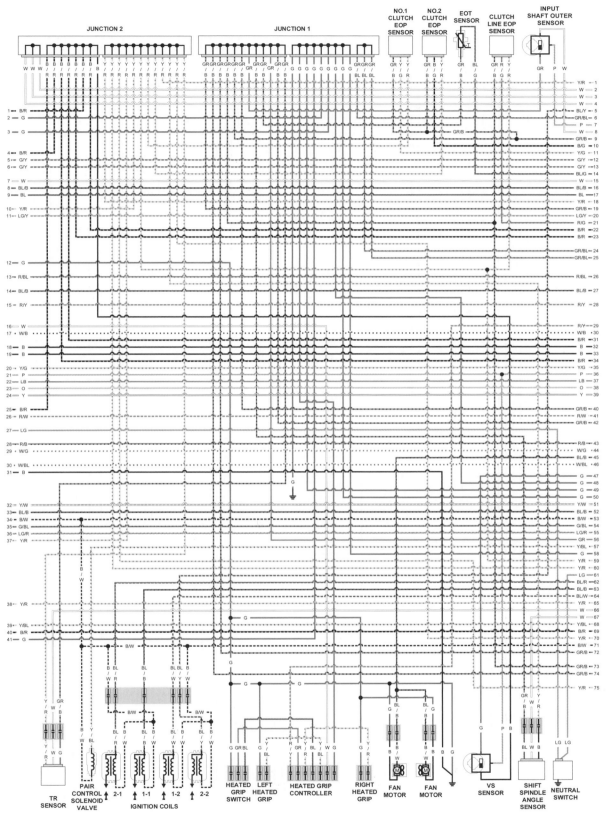

UK/EUROPE CRF1000 D 2016-2017 (2 / 4)

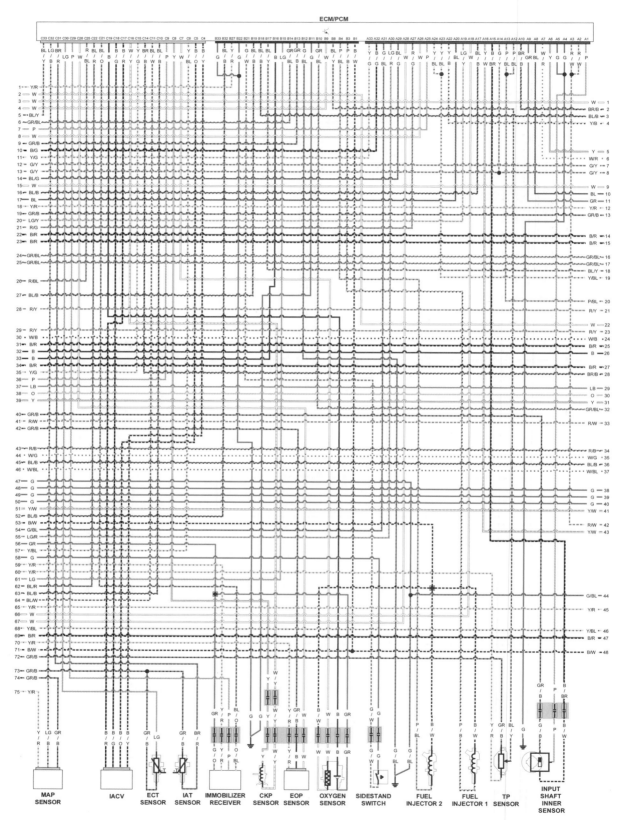

UK/EUROPE CRF1000 D 2016-2017 (3 / 4)

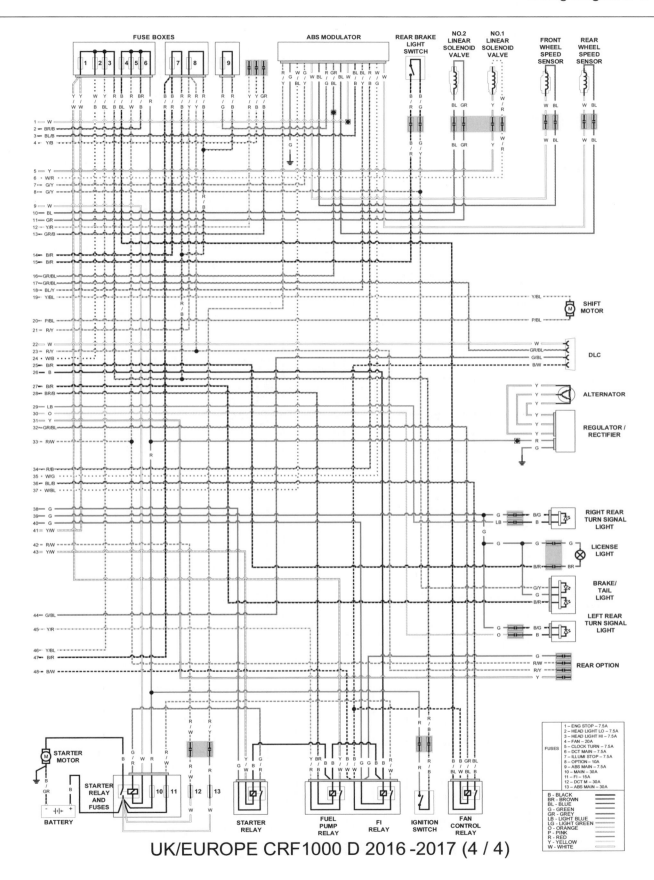

UK/EUROPE CRF1000 D 2016 -2017 (4 / 4)

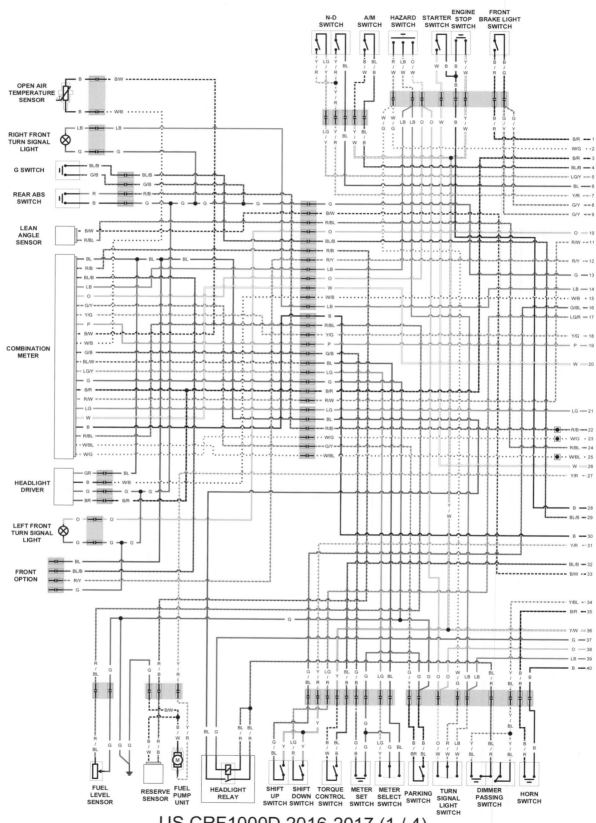

US CRF1000D 2016-2017 (1 / 4)

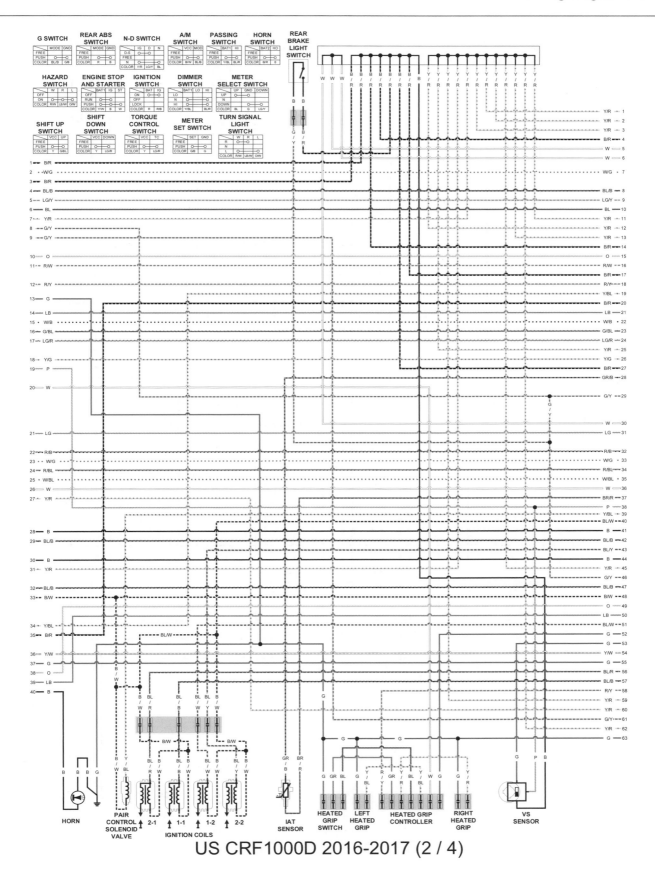

US CRF1000D 2016-2017 (2 / 4)

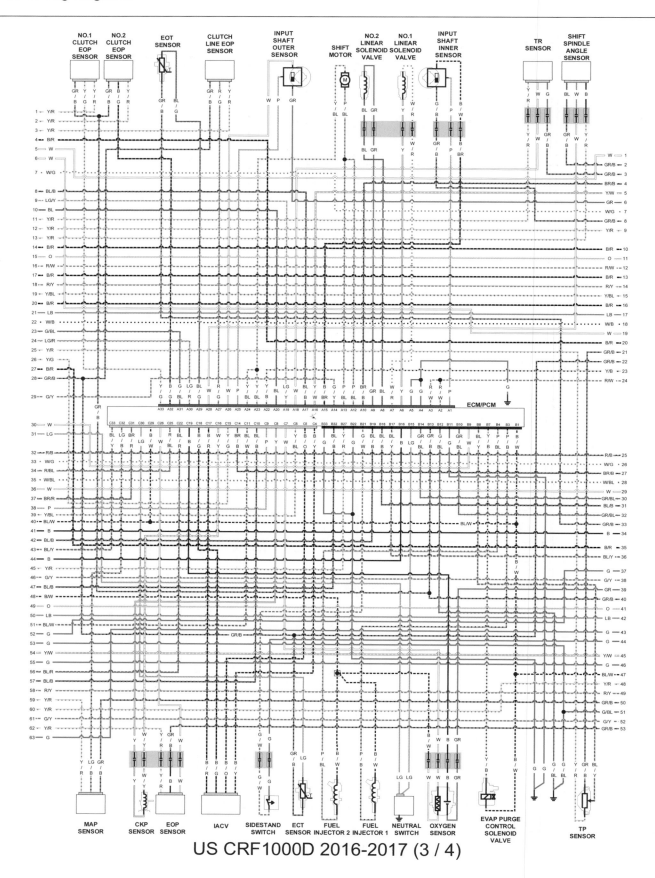

US CRF1000D 2016-2017 (3 / 4)

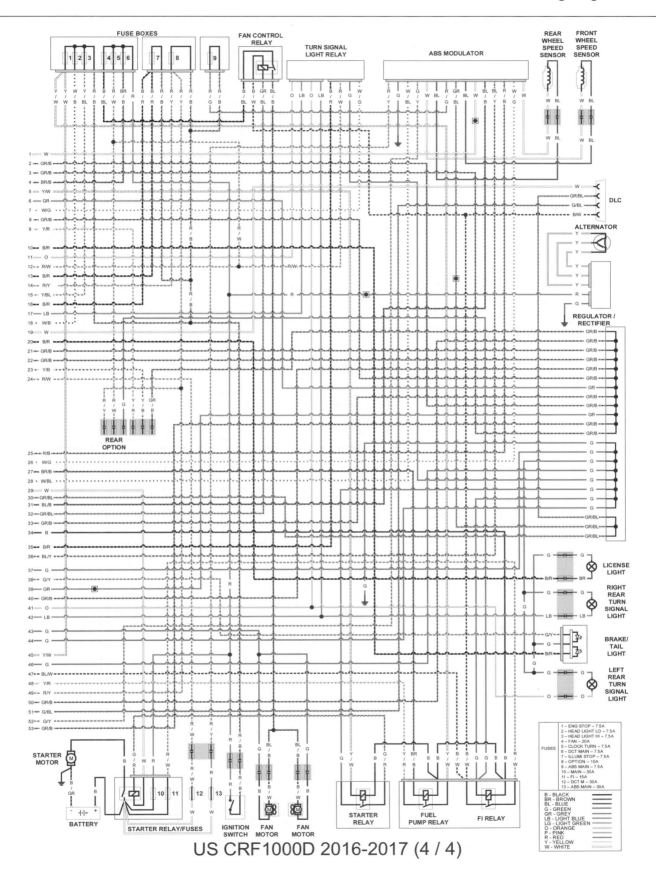

US CRF1000D 2016-2017 (4 / 4)

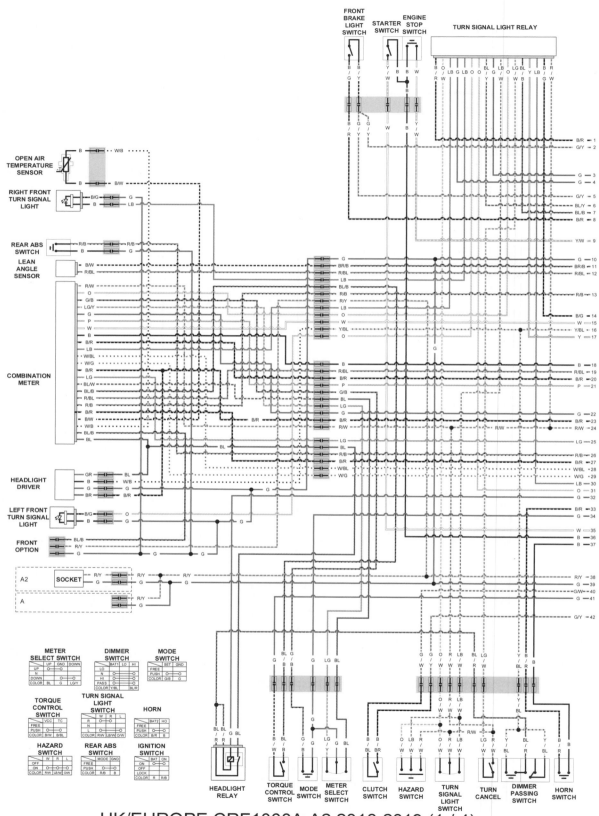

UK/EUROPE CRF1000A,A2 2018-2019 (1 / 4)

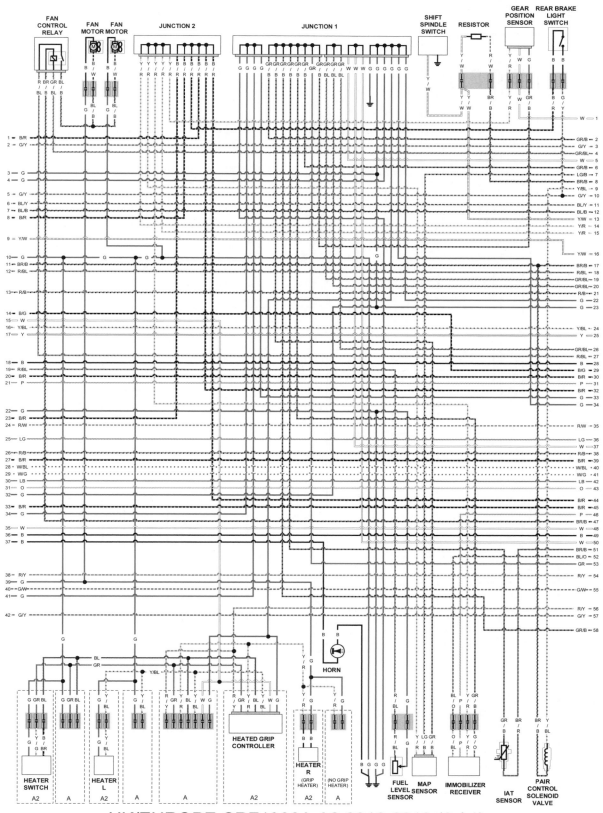

UK/EUROPE CRF1000A,A2 2018-2019 (2 / 4)

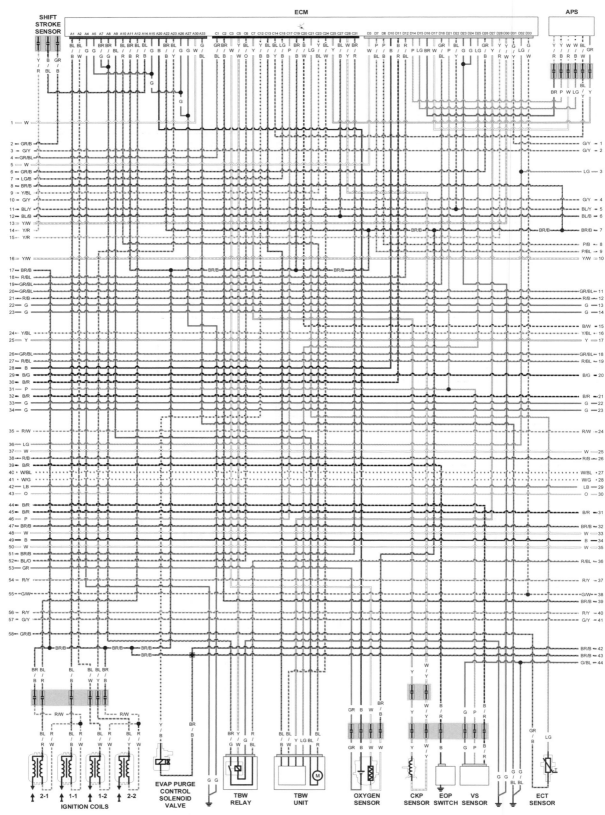

UK/EUROPE CRF1000A,A2 2018-2019 (3 / 4)

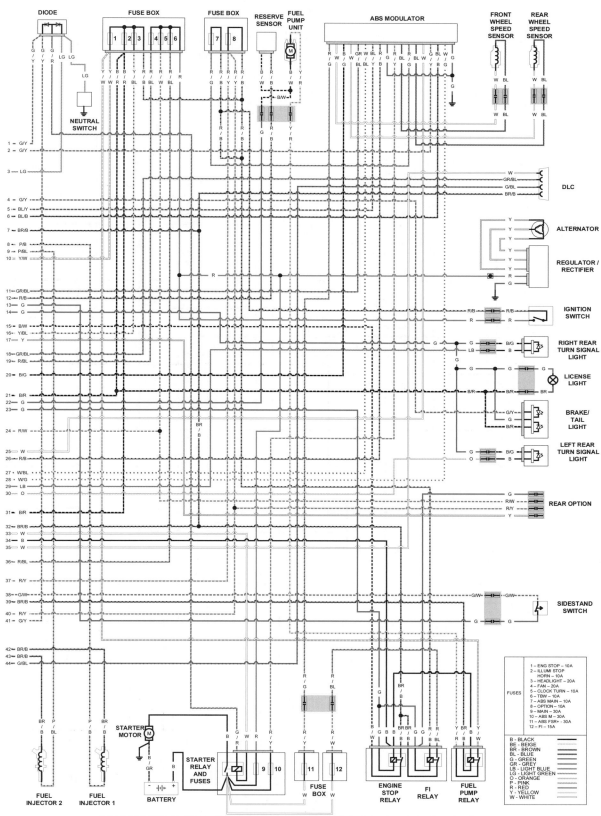

UK/EUROPE CRF1000A,A2 2018-2019 (4 / 4)

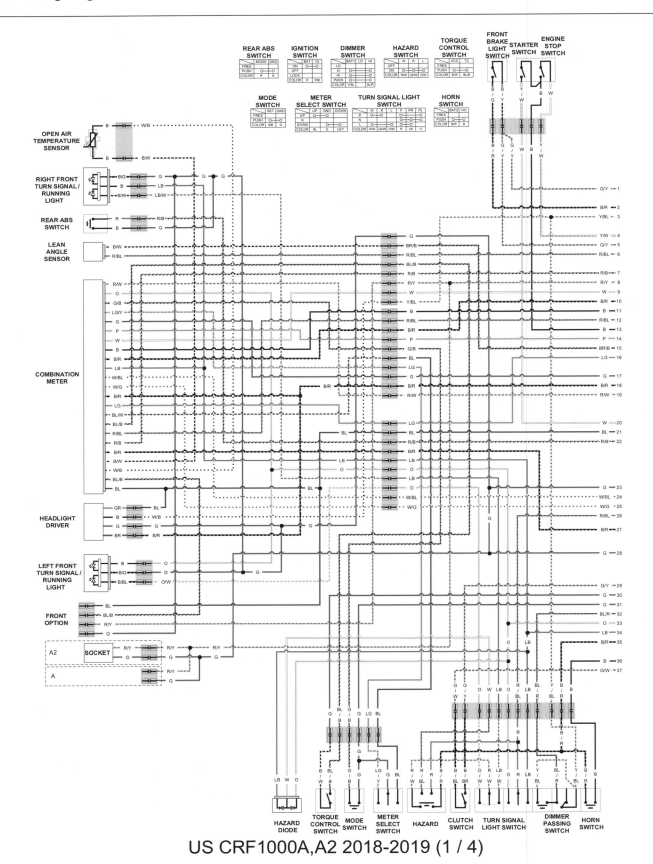

US CRF1000A,A2 2018-2019 (1 / 4)

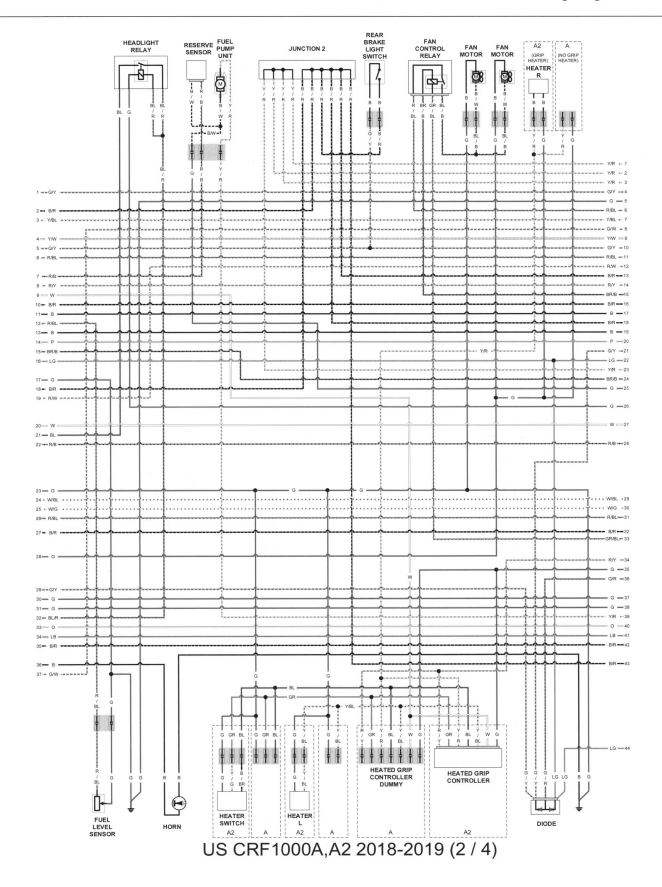

US CRF1000A,A2 2018-2019 (2 / 4)

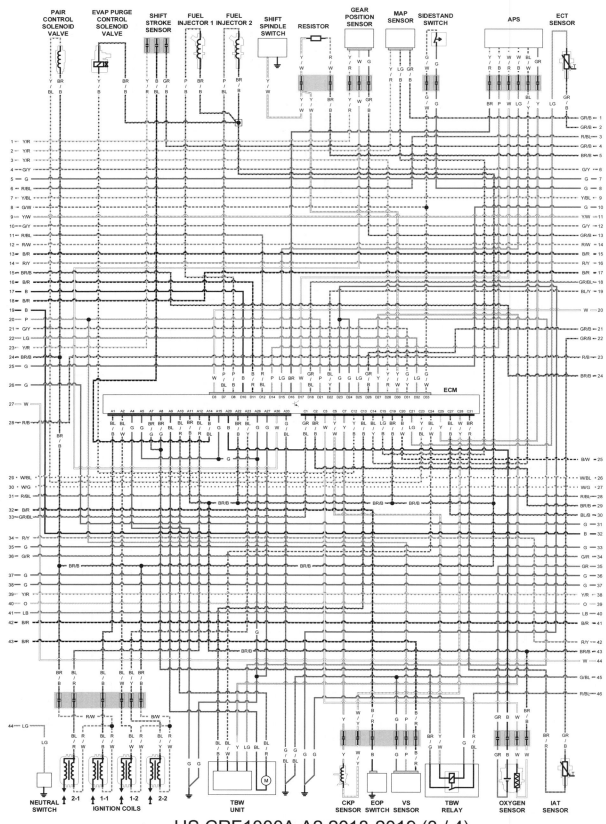

US CRF1000A,A2 2018-2019 (3 / 4)

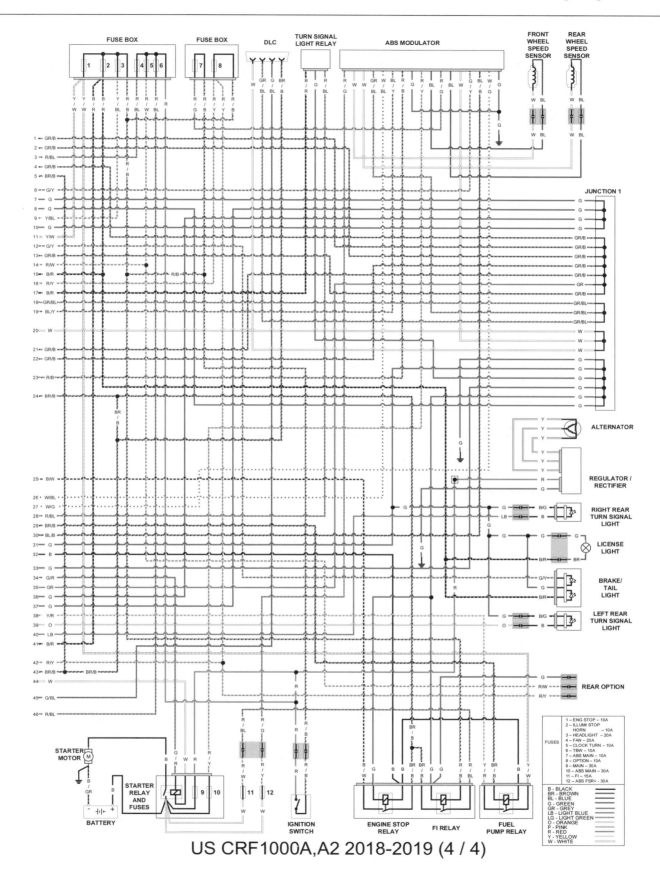

US CRF1000A,A2 2018-2019 (4 / 4)

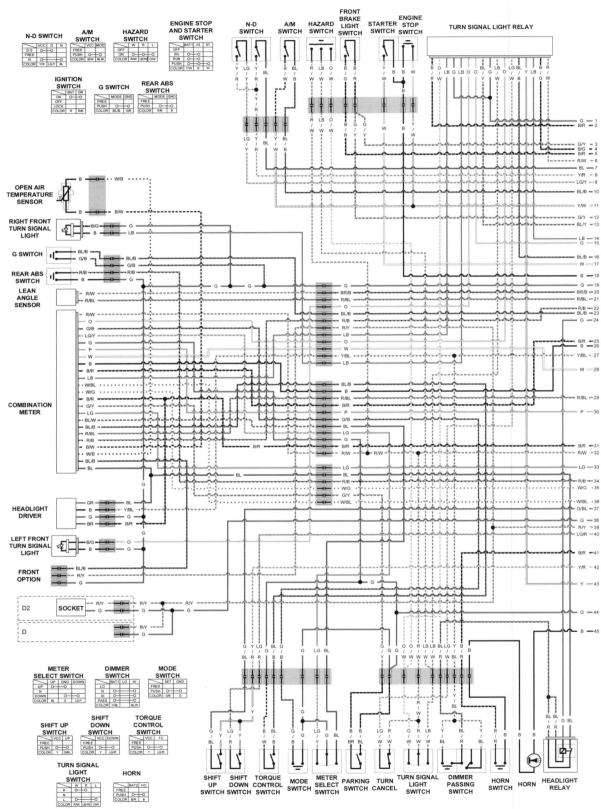

UK/EUROPE CRF1000D,D2 2018-2019 (1 / 4)

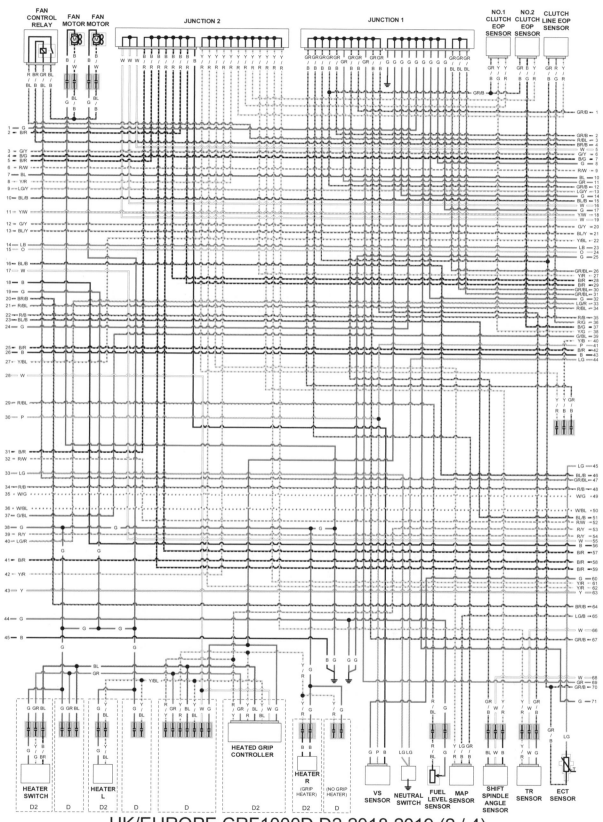

UK/EUROPE CRF1000D,D2 2018-2019 (2 / 4)

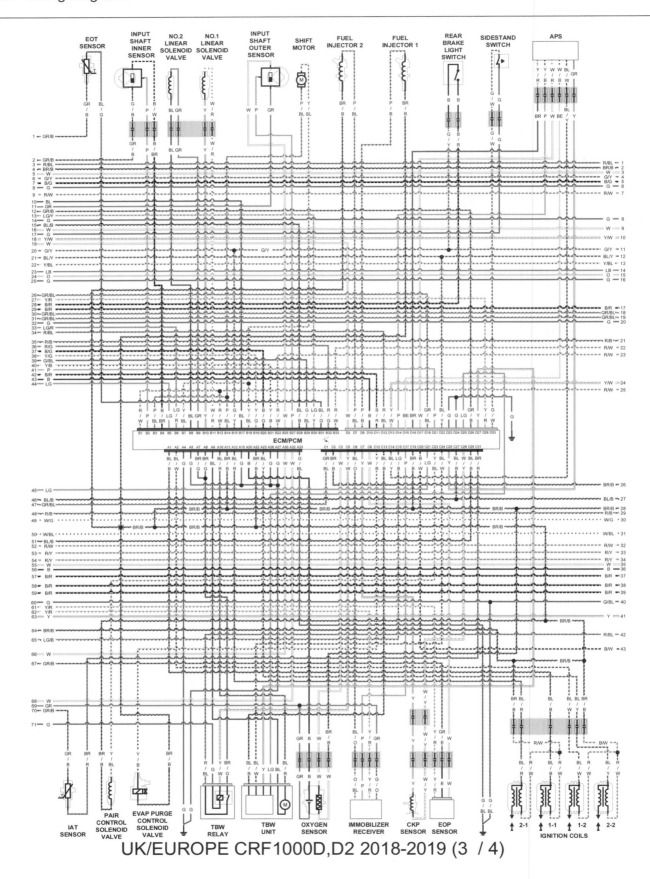

UK/EUROPE CRF1000D,D2 2018-2019 (3 / 4)

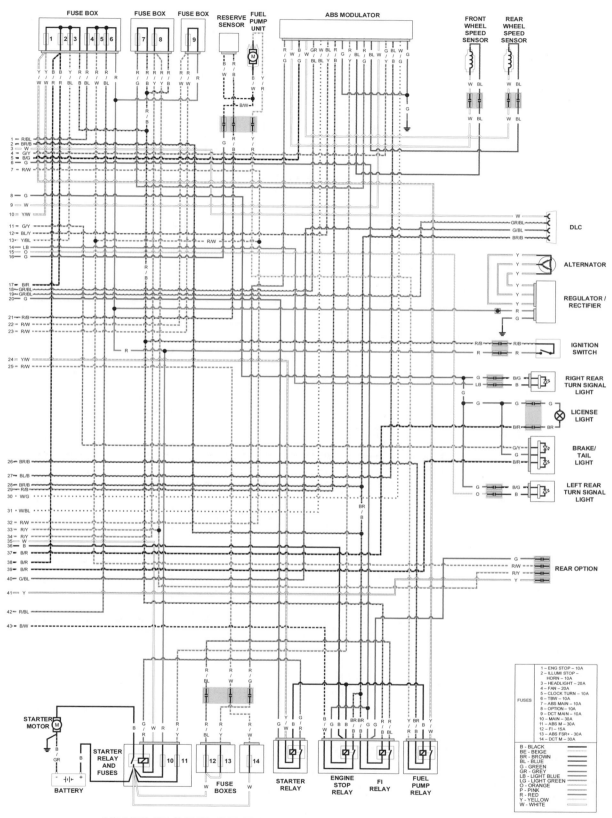

UK/EUROPE CRF1000D,D2 2018-2019 (4 / 4)

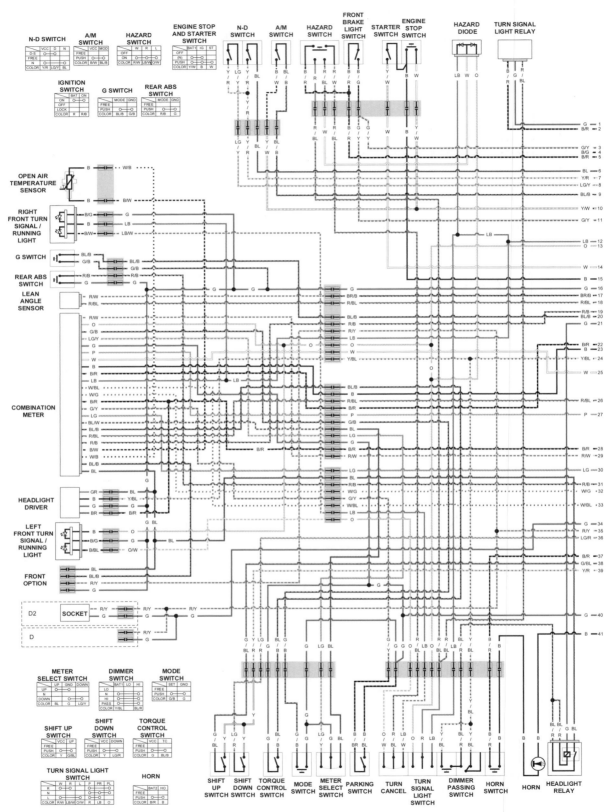

US CRF1000D,D2 2018-2019 (1 / 4)

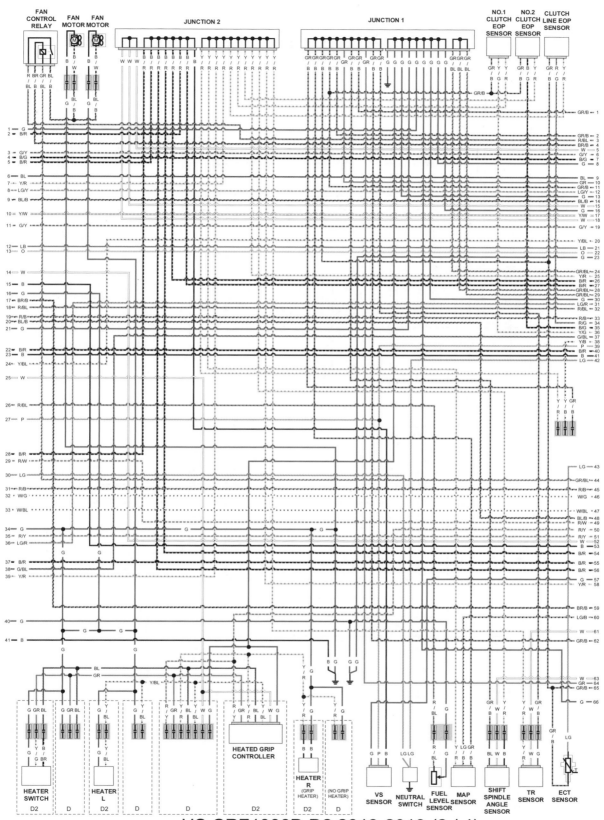

US CRF1000D,D2 2018-2019 (2 / 4)

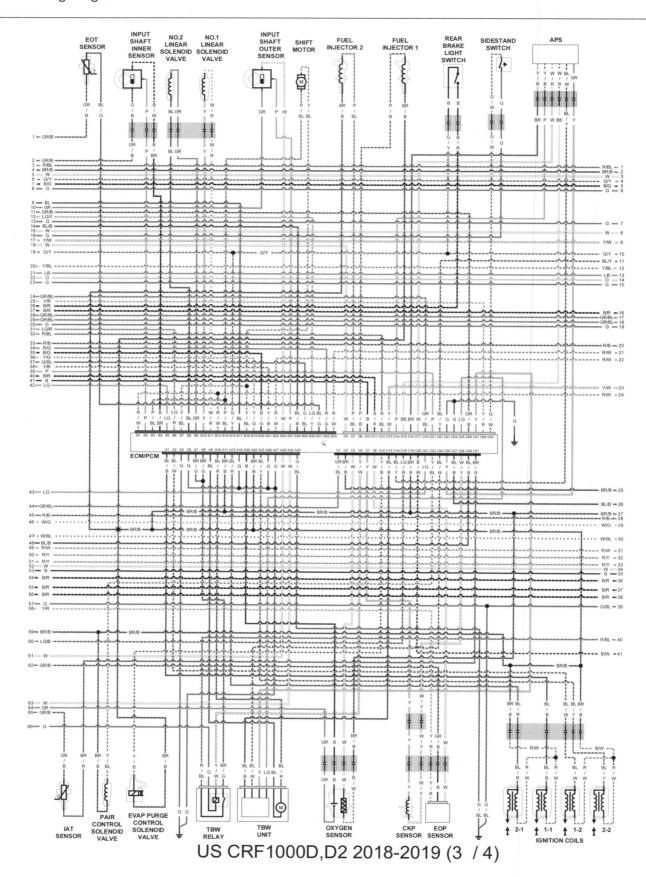

US CRF1000D,D2 2018-2019 (3 / 4)

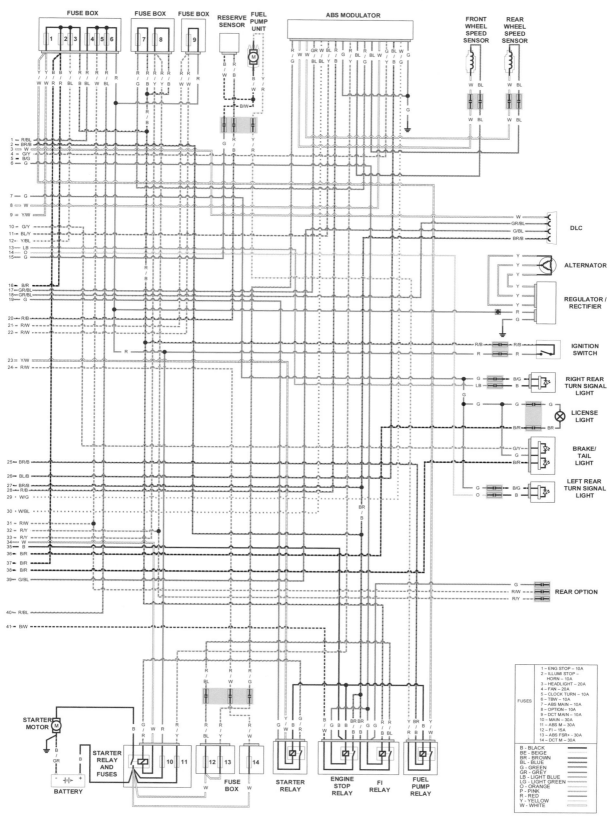

US CRF1000D,D2 2018-2019 (4 / 4)

Notes

Reference

Tools and Workshop Tips

REF•2

● Building up a tool kit and equipping your workshop ● Using tools ● Understanding bearing, seal, fastener and chain sizes and markings ● Repair techniques

Security

REF•20

● Locks and chains ● U-locks ● Disc locks ● Alarms and immobilisers ● Security marking systems ● Tips on how to prevent bike theft

Lubricants and fluids

REF•23

● Engine oils ● Transmission (gear) oils ● Coolant/anti-freeze ● Fork oils and suspension fluids ● Brake/clutch fluids ● Spray lubes, degreasers and solvents

MOT Test Checks

REF•26

● A guide to the UK MOT test ● Which items are tested ● How to prepare your motorcycle for the test and perform a pre-test check

Storage

REF•31

● How to prepare your motorcycle for going into storage and protect essential systems ● How to get the motorcycle back on the road

Conversion Factors

REF•34

34 Nm × 0.738 = 25 lbf ft

● Formulae for conversion of the metric (SI) units used throughout the manual into Imperial measures

Fault Finding

REF•35

● Common faults and their likely causes ● Links to main chapters for testing and repair procedures

Index

REF•44

Buying tools

A toolkit is a fundamental requirement for servicing and repairing a motorcycle. Although there will be an initial expense in building up enough tools for servicing, this will soon be offset by the savings made by doing the job yourself. As experience and confidence grow, additional tools can be added to enable the repair and overhaul of the motorcycle. Many of the specialist tools are expensive and not often used so it may be preferable to hire them, or for a group of friends or motorcycle club to join in the purchase.

As a rule, it is better to buy more expensive, good quality tools. Cheaper tools are likely to wear out faster and need to be renewed more often, nullifying the original saving.

> ⚠️ **Warning: To avoid the risk of a poor quality tool breaking in use, causing injury or damage to the component being worked on, always aim to purchase tools which meet the relevant national safety standards.**

The following lists of tools do not represent the manufacturer's service tools, but serve as a guide to help the owner decide which tools are needed for this level of work. In addition, items such as an electric drill, hacksaw, files, soldering iron and a workbench equipped with a vice, may be needed. Although not classed as tools, a selection of bolts, screws, nuts, washers and pieces of tubing always come in useful.

For more information about tools, refer to the Haynes *Motorcycle Workshop Practice Techbook* (Bk. No. 3470).

Manufacturer's service tools

Inevitably certain tasks require the use of a service tool. Where possible an alternative tool or method of approach is recommended, but sometimes there is no option if personal injury or damage to the component is to be avoided. Where required, service tools are referred to in the relevant procedure.

Service tools can usually only be purchased from a motorcycle dealer and are identified by a part number. Some of the commonly-used tools, such as rotor pullers, are available in aftermarket form from mail-order motorcycle tool and accessory suppliers.

Maintenance and minor repair tools

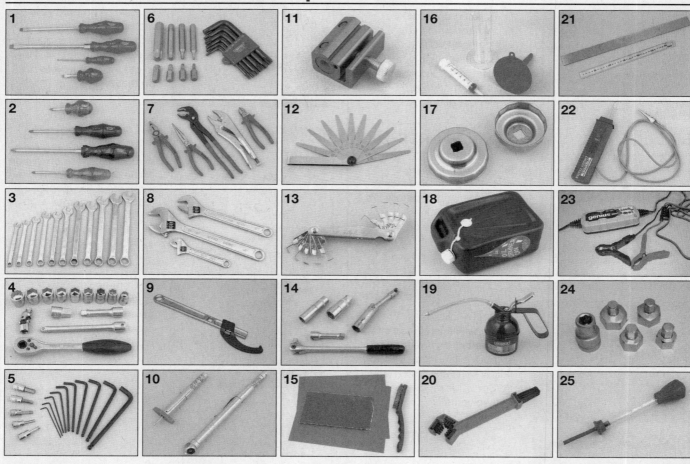

1 Set of flat-bladed screwdrivers
2 Set of cross-head screwdrivers (JIS type)
3 Combination open-end and ring spanners
4 Socket set (3/8 inch or 1/2 inch drive)
5 Set of Allen keys or bits
6 Set of Torx keys or bits
7 Pliers, cutters and self-locking grips (Mole grips)
8 Adjustable spanners
9 C-spanner
10 Tread depth gauge and tyre pressure gauge
11 Cable oiler clamp
12 Feeler gauges
13 Spark plug gap measuring tool
14 Spark plug spanner or deep plug sockets
15 Wire brush and emery paper
16 Calibrated syringe, measuring vessel and funnel
17 Oil filter adapters
18 Oil drainer can or tray
19 Pump type oil can
20 Chain cleaning brush
21 Straight-edge and steel rule
22 Continuity tester
23 Battery charger
24 Hex bit set for wheel axle bolt
25 Anti-freeze tester

Repair and overhaul tools

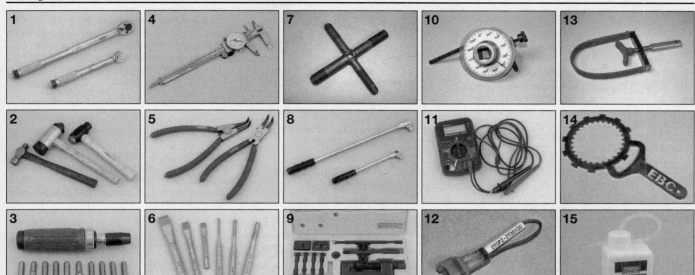

1 Torque wrench
(small and mid-ranges)
2 Conventional, plastic or
soft-faced hammers
3 Impact driver set

4 Vernier gauge
5 Circlip pliers (internal and
external, or combination)
6 Set of cold chisels
and punches

7 Alternator rotor extractor
8 Breaker bars
9 Chain breaking/
riveting tool set

10 Angle tightening gauge
11 Multimeter (measures
amps, volts and ohms)
12 Honda SCS service
connector

13 Strap wrench
14 Clutch holder
15 One-man brake
bleeder kit

Specialist tools

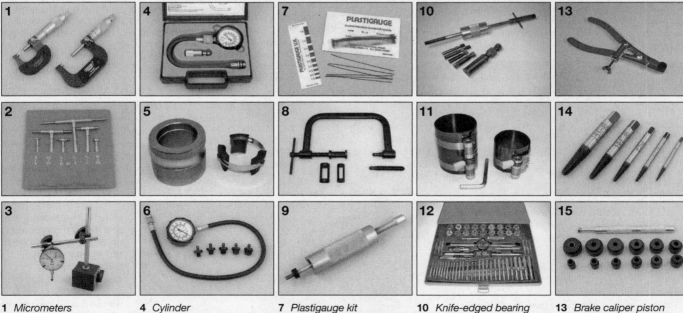

1 Micrometers
(external type)
2 Telescoping gauges
3 Dial gauge

4 Cylinder
compression gauge
5 Fork seal driver
6 Oil pressure gauge

7 Plastigauge kit
8 Valve spring compressor
9 Piston pin drawbolt tool

10 Knife-edged bearing
pullers and slide
hammers
11 Piston ring clamp
12 Tap and die set

13 Brake caliper piston
extractor
14 Screw extractor set
15 Bearing driver set

1 Workshop equipment and facilities

The workbench

● Work is made much easier by raising the bike up on a ramp - components are much more accessible if raised to waist level. The hydraulic or pneumatic types seen in the dealer's workshop are a sound investment if you undertake a lot of repairs or overhauls **(see illustration 1.1)**.

1.1 Hydraulic motorcycle ramp

● If raised off ground level, the bike must be supported on the ramp to avoid it falling. Most ramps incorporate a front wheel locating clamp which can be adjusted to suit different diameter wheels. When tightening the clamp, take care not to mark the wheel rim or damage the tyre - use wood blocks on each side to prevent this.
● Secure the bike to the ramp using tie-downs **(see illustration 1.2)**. If the bike has only a sidestand, and hence leans at a dangerous angle when raised, support the bike on an auxiliary stand.

1.2 Tie-downs are used around the passenger footrests to secure the bike

● Auxiliary (paddock) stands are widely available from mail order companies or motorcycle dealers and attach either to the wheel axle or swingarm pivot **(see illustration 1.3)**. If the motorcycle has a centrestand, you can support it under the crankcase to prevent it toppling whilst either wheel is removed **(see illustration 1.4)**.

1.3 This auxiliary stand attaches to the swingarm pivot

1.4 Always use a block of wood between the engine and jack head when supporting the engine in this way

Fumes and fire

● Refer to the Safety first! page at the beginning of the manual for full details. Make sure your workshop is equipped with a fire extinguisher suitable for fuel-related fires (Class B fire - flammable liquids) - it is not sufficient to have a water-filled extinguisher.
● Always ensure adequate ventilation is available. Unless an exhaust gas extraction system is available for use, ensure that the engine is run outside of the workshop.
● If working on the fuel system, make sure the workshop is ventilated to avoid a build-up of fumes. This applies equally to fume build-up when charging a battery. Do not smoke or allow anyone else to smoke in the workshop.

Fluids

● If you need to drain fuel from the tank, store it in an approved container marked as suitable for the storage of petrol (gasoline) **(see illustration 1.5)**. Do not store fuel in glass jars or bottles.

1.5 Use an approved can only for storing petrol (gasoline)

● Use proprietary engine degreasers or solvents which have a high flash-point, such as paraffin (kerosene), for cleaning off oil, grease and dirt - never use petrol (gasoline) for cleaning. Wear rubber gloves when handling solvent and engine degreaser. The fumes from certain solvents can be dangerous - always work in a well-ventilated area.

Dust, eye and hand protection

● Protect your lungs from inhalation of dust particles by wearing a filtering mask over the nose and mouth. Many frictional materials still contain asbestos which is dangerous to your health. Protect your eyes from spouts of liquid and sprung components by wearing a pair of protective goggles **(see illustration 1.6)**.

1.6 A fire extinguisher, goggles, mask and protective gloves should be at hand in the workshop

● Protect your hands from contact with solvents, fuel and oils by wearing rubber gloves. Alternatively apply a barrier cream to your hands before starting work. If handling hot components or fluids, wear suitable gloves to protect your hands from scalding and burns.

What to do with old fluids

● Old cleaning solvent, fuel, coolant and oils should not be poured down domestic drains or onto the ground. Package the fluid up in old oil containers, label it accordingly, and take it to a garage or disposal facility. Contact your local authority for location of such sites or ring the oil care hotline.

OIL CARE

Note: It is antisocial and illegal to dump oil down the drain. To find the location of your local oil recycling bank in the UK, call 03708 506 506 or visit www.oilbankline.org.uk

In the USA, note that any oil supplier must accept used oil for recycling.

2 Fasteners - screws, bolts and nuts

Fastener types and applications

Bolts and screws

● Fastener head types are either of hexagonal, Torx or splined design, with internal and external versions of each type (see illustrations 2.1 and 2.2); splined head fasteners are not in common use on motorcycles. The conventional slotted or Phillips head design is used for certain screws. Bolt or screw length is always measured from the underside of the head to the end of the item (see illustration 2.11).

2.1 Internal hexagon/Allen (A), Torx (B) and splined (C) fasteners, with corresponding bits

2.2 External Torx (A), splined (B) and hexagon (C) fasteners, with corresponding sockets

● Certain fasteners on the motorcycle have a tensile marking on their heads, the higher the marking the stronger the fastener. High tensile fasteners generally carry a 10 or higher marking. Never replace a high tensile fastener with one of a lower tensile strength.

Washers (see illustration 2.3)

● Plain washers are used between a fastener head and a component to prevent damage to the component or to spread the load when torque is applied. Plain washers can also be used as spacers or shims in certain assemblies. Copper or aluminium plain washers are often used as sealing washers on drain plugs.

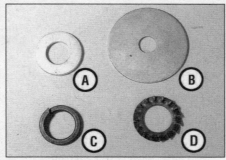

2.3 Plain washer (A), penny washer (B), spring washer (C) and serrated washer (D)

● The split-ring spring washer works by applying axial tension between the fastener head and component. If flattened, it is fatigued and must be renewed. If a plain (flat) washer is used on the fastener, position the spring washer between the fastener and the plain washer.
● Serrated star type washers dig into the fastener and component faces, preventing loosening. They are often used on electrical earth (ground) connections to the frame.
● Cone type washers (sometimes called Belleville) are conical and when tightened apply axial tension between the fastener head and component. They must be installed with the dished side against the component and often carry an OUTSIDE marking on their outer face. If flattened, they are fatigued and must be renewed.
● Tab washers are used to lock plain nuts or bolts on a shaft. A portion of the tab washer is bent up hard against one flat of the nut or bolt to prevent it loosening. Due to the tab washer being deformed in use, a new tab washer should be used every time it is disturbed.
● Wave washers are used to take up endfloat on a shaft. They provide light springing and prevent excessive side-to-side play of a component. Can be found on rocker arm shafts.

Nuts and split pins

● Conventional plain nuts are usually six-sided (see illustration 2.4). They are sized by thread diameter and pitch. High tensile nuts carry a number on one end to denote their tensile strength.

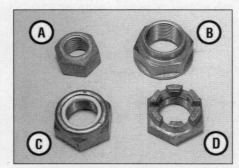

2.4 Plain nut (A), shouldered locknut (B), nylon insert nut (C) and castellated nut (D)

● Self-locking nuts either have a nylon insert, or two spring metal tabs, or a shoulder which is staked into a groove in the shaft - their advantage over conventional plain nuts is a resistance to loosening due to vibration. The nylon insert type can be used a number of times, but must be renewed when the friction of the nylon insert is reduced, ie when the nut spins freely on the shaft. The spring tab type can be reused unless the tabs are damaged. The shouldered type must be renewed every time it is disturbed.
● Split pins (cotter pins) are used to lock a castellated nut to a shaft or to prevent slackening of a plain nut. Common applications are wheel axles and brake torque arms. Because the split pin arms are deformed to lock around the nut a new split pin must always be used on installation - always fit the correct size split pin which will fit snugly in the shaft hole. Make sure the split pin arms are correctly located around the nut (see illustrations 2.5 and 2.6).

2.5 Bend split pin (cotter pin) arms as shown (arrows) to secure a castellated nut

2.6 Bend split pin (cotter pin) arms as shown to secure a plain nut

> *Caution: If the castellated nut slots do not align with the shaft hole after tightening to the torque setting, tighten the nut until the next slot aligns with the hole - never slacken the nut to align its slot.*

● R-pins (shaped like the letter R), or slip pins as they are sometimes called, are sprung and can be reused if they are otherwise in good condition. Always install R-pins with their closed end facing forwards (see illustration 2.7).

2.7 **Correct fitting of R-pin. Arrow indicates forward direction**

Circlips (see illustration 2.8)

● Circlips (sometimes called snap-rings) are used to retain components on a shaft or in a housing and have corresponding external or internal ears to permit removal. Parallel-sided (machined) circlips can be installed either way round in their groove, whereas stamped circlips (which have a chamfered edge on one face) must be installed with the chamfer facing away from the direction of thrust load **(see illustration 2.9)**.

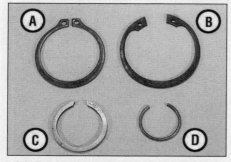

2.8 **External stamped circlip (A), internal stamped circlip (B), machined circlip (C) and wire circlip (D)**

● Always use circlip pliers to remove and install circlips; expand or compress them just enough to remove them. After installation, rotate the circlip in its groove to ensure it is securely seated. If installing a circlip on a splined shaft, always align its opening with a shaft channel to ensure the circlip ends are well supported and unlikely to catch **(see illustration 2.10)**.

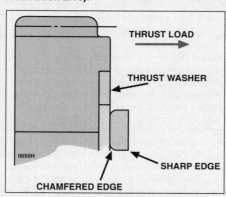

2.9 **Correct fitting of a stamped circlip**

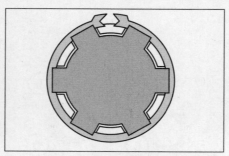

2.10 **Align circlip opening with shaft channel**

● Circlips can wear due to the thrust of components and become loose in their grooves, with the subsequent danger of becoming dislodged in operation. For this reason, renewal is advised every time a circlip is disturbed.
● Wire circlips are commonly used as piston pin retaining clips. If a removal tang is provided, long-nosed pliers can be used to dislodge them, otherwise careful use of a small flat-bladed screwdriver is necessary. Wire circlips should be renewed every time they are disturbed.

Thread diameter and pitch

● Diameter of a male thread (screw, bolt or stud) is the outside diameter of the threaded portion **(see illustration 2.11)**. Most motorcycle manufacturers use the ISO (International Standards Organisation) metric system expressed in millimetres, eg M6 refers to a 6 mm diameter thread. Sizing is the same for nuts, except that the thread diameter is measured across the valleys of the nut.
● Pitch is the distance between the peaks of the thread **(see illustration 2.11)**. It is expressed in millimetres, thus a common bolt size may be expressed as 6.0 x 1.0 mm (6 mm thread diameter and 1 mm pitch). Generally pitch increases in proportion to thread diameter, although there are always exceptions.
● Thread diameter and pitch are related for conventional fastener applications and the accompanying table can be used as a guide. Additionally, the AF (Across Flats), spanner or socket size dimension of the bolt or nut **(see illustration 2.11)** is linked to thread and pitch specification. Thread pitch can be measured with a thread gauge **(see illustration 2.12)**.

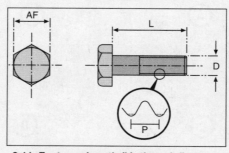

2.11 **Fastener length (L), thread diameter (D), thread pitch (P) and head size (AF)**

2.12 **Using a thread gauge to measure pitch**

AF size	Thread diameter x pitch (mm)
8 mm	M5 x 0.8
8 mm	M6 x 1.0
10 mm	M6 x 1.0
12 mm	M8 x 1.25
14 mm	M10 x 1.25
17 mm	M12 x 1.25

● The threads of most fasteners are of the right-hand type, ie they are turned clockwise to tighten and anti-clockwise to loosen. The reverse situation applies to left-hand thread fasteners, which are turned anti-clockwise to tighten and clockwise to loosen. Left-hand threads are used where rotation of a component might loosen a conventional right-hand thread fastener.

Seized fasteners

● Corrosion of external fasteners due to water or reaction between two dissimilar metals can occur over a period of time. It will build up sooner in wet conditions or in countries where salt is used on the roads during the winter. If a fastener is severely corroded it is likely that normal methods of removal will fail and result in its head being ruined. When you attempt removal, the fastener thread should be heard to crack free and unscrew easily - if it doesn't, stop there before damaging something.
● A smart tap on the head of the fastener will often succeed in breaking free corrosion which has occurred in the threads **(see illustration 2.13)**.
● An aerosol penetrating fluid (such as WD-40) applied the night beforehand may work its way down into the thread and ease removal. Depending on the location, you may be able to make up a Plasticine well around the fastener head and fill it with penetrating fluid.

2.13 **A sharp tap on the head of a fastener will often break free a corroded thread**

● If you are working on an engine internal component, corrosion will most likely not be a problem due to the well lubricated environment. However, components can be very tight and an impact driver is a useful tool in freeing them (see illustration 2.14).

2.14 Using an impact driver to free a fastener

● Where corrosion has occurred between dissimilar metals (eg steel and aluminium alloy), the application of heat to the fastener head will create a disproportionate expansion rate between the two metals and break the seizure caused by the corrosion. Whether heat can be applied depends on the location of the fastener - any surrounding components likely to be damaged must first be removed (see illustration 2.15). Heat can be applied using a paint stripper heat gun or clothes iron, or by immersing the component in boiling water - wear protective gloves to prevent scalding or burns to the hands.

2.15 Using heat to free a seized fastener

● As a last resort, it is possible to use a hammer and cold chisel to work the fastener head unscrewed (see illustration 2.16). This will damage the fastener, but more importantly extreme care must be taken not to damage the surrounding component.

Caution: Remember that the component being secured is generally of more value than the bolt, nut or screw - when the fastener is freed, do not unscrew it with force, instead work the fastener back and forth when resistance is felt to prevent thread damage.

2.16 Using a hammer and chisel to free a seized fastener

Broken fasteners and damaged heads

● If the shank of a broken bolt or screw is accessible you can grip it with self-locking grips. The knurled wheel type stud extractor tool or self-gripping stud puller tool is particularly useful for removing the long studs which screw into the cylinder mouth surface of the crankcase or bolts and screws from which the head has broken off (see illustration 2.17). Studs can also be removed by locking two nuts together on the threaded end of the stud and using a spanner on the lower nut (see illustration 2.18).

2.17 Using a stud extractor tool to remove a broken crankcase stud

2.18 Two nuts can be locked together to unscrew a stud from a component

● A bolt or screw which has broken off below or level with the casing must be extracted using a screw extractor set. Centre punch the fastener to centralise the drill bit, then drill a hole in the fastener (see illustration 2.19). Select a drill bit which is approximately half to three-quarters the diameter of the fastener

2.19 When using a screw extractor, first drill a hole in the fastener . . .

and drill to a depth which will accommodate the extractor. Use the largest size extractor possible, but avoid leaving too small a wall thickness otherwise the extractor will merely force the fastener walls outwards wedging it in the casing thread.

● If a spiral type extractor is used, thread it anti-clockwise into the fastener. As it is screwed in, it will grip the fastener and unscrew it from the casing (see illustration 2.20).

2.20 . . . then thread the extractor anti-clockwise into the fastener

● If a taper type extractor is used, tap it into the fastener so that it is firmly wedged in place. Unscrew the extractor (anti-clockwise) to draw the fastener out.

> ⚠ *Warning: Stud extractors are very hard and may break off in the fastener if care is not taken - ask an engineer about spark erosion if this happens.*

● Alternatively, the broken bolt/screw can be drilled out and the hole retapped for an oversize bolt/screw or a diamond-section thread insert. It is essential that the drilling is carried out squarely and to the correct depth, otherwise the casing may be ruined - if in doubt, entrust the work to an engineer.

● Bolts and nuts with rounded corners cause the correct size spanner or socket to slip when force is applied. Of the types of spanner/socket available always use a six-point type rather than an eight or twelve-point type - better grip

2.21 Comparison of surface drive ring spanner (left) with 12-point type (right)

is obtained. Surface drive spanners grip the middle of the hex flats, rather than the corners, and are thus good in cases of damaged heads **(see illustration 2.21)**.

● Slotted-head or Phillips-head screws are often damaged by the use of the wrong size screwdriver. Allen-head and Torx-head screws are much less likely to sustain damage. If enough of the screw head is exposed you can use a hacksaw to cut a slot in its head and then use a conventional flat-bladed screwdriver to remove it. Alternatively use a hammer and cold chisel to tap the head of the fastener around to slacken it. Always replace damaged fasteners with new ones, preferably Torx or Allen-head type.

A dab of valve grinding compound between the screw head and screwdriver tip will often give a good grip.

Thread repair

● Threads (particularly those in aluminium alloy components) can be damaged by overtightening, being assembled with dirt in the threads, or from a component working loose and vibrating. Eventually the thread will fail completely, and it will be impossible to tighten the fastener.

● If a thread is damaged or clogged with old locking compound it can be renovated with a thread repair tool (thread chaser) **(see illustrations 2.22 and 2.23)**; special thread

2.22 A thread repair tool being used to correct an internal thread

2.23 A thread repair tool being used to correct an external thread

chasers are available for spark plug hole threads. The tool will not cut a new thread, but clean and true the original thread. Make sure that you use the correct diameter and pitch tool. Similarly, external threads can be cleaned up with a die or a thread restorer file **(see illustration 2.24)**.

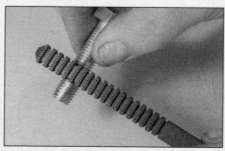

2.24 Using a thread restorer file

● It is possible to drill out the old thread and retap the component to the next thread size. This will work where there is enough surrounding material and a new bolt or screw can be obtained. Sometimes, however, this is not possible - such as where the bolt/screw passes through another component which must also be suitably modified, also in cases where a spark plug or oil drain plug cannot be obtained in a larger diameter thread size.

● The diamond-section thread insert (often known by its popular trade name of Heli-Coil) is a simple and effective method of renewing the thread and retaining the original size. A kit can be purchased which contains the tap, insert and installing tool **(see illustration 2.25)**. Drill out the damaged thread with the size drill specified **(see illustration 2.26)**. Carefully retap the thread **(see illustration 2.27)**. Install the

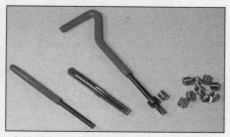

2.25 Obtain a thread insert kit to suit the thread diameter and pitch required

2.26 To install a thread insert, first drill out the original thread . . .

2.27 . . . tap a new thread . . .

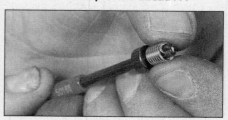

2.28 . . . fit insert on the installing tool . . .

2.29 . . . and thread into the component . . .

2.30 . . . break off the tang when complete

insert on the installing tool and thread it slowly into place using a light downward pressure **(see illustrations 2.28 and 2.29)**. When positioned between a 1/4 and 1/2 turn below the surface withdraw the installing tool and use the break-off tool to press down on the tang, breaking it off **(see illustration 2.30)**.

● There are epoxy thread repair kits on the market which can rebuild stripped internal threads, although this repair should not be used on high load-bearing components.

Thread locking and sealing compounds

● Locking compounds are used in locations where the fastener is prone to loosening due to vibration or on important safety-related items which might cause loss of control of the motorcycle if they fail. It is also used where important fasteners cannot be secured by other means such as lockwashers or split pins.

● Before applying locking compound, make sure that the threads (internal and external) are clean and dry with all old compound removed. Select a compound to suit the component being secured - a non-permanent general locking and sealing type is suitable for most applications, but a high strength type is needed for permanent fixing of studs in castings. Apply a drop or two of the compound to the first few threads of the fastener, then thread it into place and tighten to the specified torque. Do not apply excessive thread locking compound otherwise the thread may be damaged on subsequent removal.

● Certain fasteners are impregnated with a dry film type coating of locking compound on their threads. Always renew this type of fastener if disturbed.

● Anti-seize compounds, such as copper-based greases, can be applied to protect threads from seizure due to extreme heat and corrosion. A common instance is spark plug threads and exhaust system fasteners.

3 Measuring tools and gauges

Feeler gauges

● Feeler gauges (or blades) are used for measuring small gaps and clearances **(see illustration 3.1)**. They can also be used to measure endfloat (sideplay) of a component on a shaft where access is not possible with a dial gauge.

● Feeler gauge sets should be treated with care and not bent or damaged. They are etched with their size on one face. Keep them clean and very lightly oiled to prevent corrosion build-up.

3.1 Feeler gauges are used for measuring small gaps and clearances - thickness is marked on one face of gauge

● When measuring a clearance, select a gauge which is a light sliding fit between the two components. You may need to use two gauges together to measure the clearance accurately.

Micrometers

● A micrometer is a precision tool capable of measuring to 0.01 or 0.001 of a millimetre. It should always be stored in its case and not in the general toolbox. It must be kept clean and never dropped, otherwise its frame or measuring anvils could be distorted resulting in inaccurate readings.

● External micrometers are used for measuring outside diameters of components and have many more applications than internal micrometers. Micrometers are available in different size ranges, eg 0 to 25 mm, 25 to 50 mm, and upwards in 25 mm steps; some large micrometers have interchangeable anvils to allow a range of measurements to be taken. Generally the largest precision measurement you are likely to take on a motorcycle is the piston diameter.

● Internal micrometers (or bore micrometers) are used for measuring inside diameters, such as valve guides and cylinder bores. Telescoping gauges and small hole gauges are used in conjunction with an external micrometer, whereas the more expensive internal micrometers have their own measuring device.

External micrometer

Note: *The conventional analogue type instrument is described. Although much easier to read, digital micrometers are considerably more expensive.*

● Always check the calibration of the micrometer before use. With the anvils closed (0 to 25 mm type) or set over a test gauge

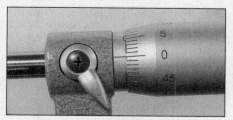

3.2 Check micrometer calibration before use

(for the larger types) the scale should read zero **(see illustration 3.2)**; make sure that the anvils (and test piece) are clean first. Any discrepancy can be adjusted by referring to the instructions supplied with the tool. Remember that the micrometer is a precision measuring tool - don't force the anvils closed, use the ratchet (4) on the end of the micrometer to close it. In this way, a measured force is always applied.

● To use, first make sure that the item being measured is clean. Place the anvil of the micrometer (1) against the item and use the thimble (2) to bring the spindle (3) lightly into contact with the other side of the item **(see illustration 3.3)**. Don't tighten the thimble down because this will damage the micrometer - instead use the ratchet (4) on the end of the micrometer. The ratchet mechanism applies a measured force preventing damage to the instrument.

● The micrometer is read by referring to the linear scale on the sleeve and the annular scale on the thimble. Read off the sleeve first to obtain the base measurement, then add the fine measurement from the thimble to obtain the overall reading. The linear scale on the sleeve represents the measuring range of the micrometer (eg 0 to 25 mm). The annular scale

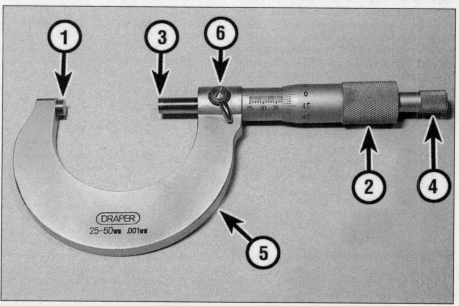

3.3 Micrometer component parts

1 *Anvil*	3 *Spindle*	5 *Frame*
2 *Thimble*	4 *Ratchet*	6 *Locking lever*

on the thimble will be in graduations of 0.01 mm (or as marked on the frame) - one full revolution of the thimble will move 0.5 mm on the linear scale. Take the reading where the datum line on the sleeve intersects the thimble's scale. Always position the eye directly above the scale otherwise an inaccurate reading will result.

In the example shown the item measures 2.95 mm (**see illustration 3.4**):

Linear scale	2.00 mm
Linear scale	0.50 mm
Annular scale	0.45 mm
Total figure	2.95 mm

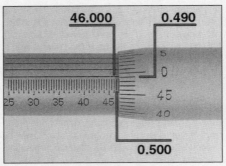

3.5 Micrometer reading of 46.99 mm on linear and annular scales . . .

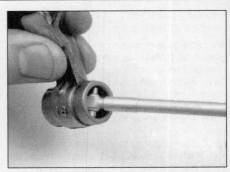

3.7 Expand the telescoping gauge in the bore, lock its position . . .

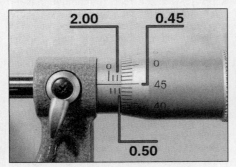

3.4 Micrometer reading of 2.95 mm

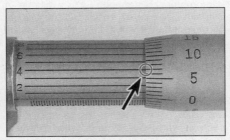

3.6 . . . and 0.004 mm on vernier scale

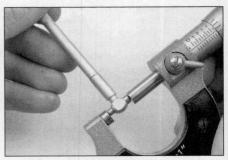

3.8 . . . then measure the gauge with a micrometer

Most micrometers have a locking lever (6) on the frame to hold the setting in place, allowing the item to be removed from the micrometer.
● Some micrometers have a vernier scale on their sleeve, providing an even finer measurement to be taken, in 0.001 increments of a millimetre. Take the sleeve and thimble measurement as described above, then check which graduation on the vernier scale aligns with that of the annular scale on the thimble **Note:** *The eye must be perpendicular to the scale when taking the vernier reading - if necessary rotate the body of the micrometer to ensure this.* Multiply the vernier scale figure by 0.001 and add it to the base and fine measurement figures.

In the example shown the item measures 46.994 mm (**see illustrations 3.5 and 3.6**):

Linear scale (base)	46.000 mm
Linear scale (base)	00.500 mm
Annular scale (fine)	00.490 mm
Vernier scale	00.004 mm
Total figure	46.994 mm

Internal micrometer

● Internal micrometers are available for measuring bore diameters, but are expensive and unlikely to be available for home use. It is suggested that a set of telescoping gauges and small hole gauges, both of which must be used with an external micrometer, will suffice for taking internal measurements on a motorcycle.
● Telescoping gauges can be used to

measure internal diameters of components. Select a gauge with the correct size range, make sure its ends are clean and insert it into the bore. Expand the gauge, then lock its position and withdraw it from the bore (**see illustration 3.7**). Measure across the gauge ends with a micrometer (**see illustration 3.8**).
● Very small diameter bores (such as valve guides) are measured with a small hole gauge. Once adjusted to a slip-fit inside the component, its position is locked and the gauge withdrawn for measurement with a micrometer (**see illustrations 3.9 and 3.10**).

Vernier caliper

Note: *The conventional linear and dial gauge type instruments are described. Digital types are easier to read, but are far more expensive.*
● The vernier caliper does not provide the precision of a micrometer, but is versatile in being able to measure internal and external diameters. Some types also incorporate a depth gauge. It is ideal for measuring clutch plate friction material and spring free lengths.
● To use the conventional linear scale vernier, slacken off the vernier clamp screws (1) and set its jaws over (2), or inside (3), the item to be measured (**see illustration 3.11**). Slide the jaw into contact, using the thumbwheel (4) for fine movement of the sliding scale (5) then tighten the clamp screws (1). Read off the main scale (6) where the zero on the sliding scale (5) intersects it, taking the whole number to the left of the zero; this provides the base measurement. View along the sliding scale and select the division which

3.9 Expand the small hole gauge in the bore, lock its position . . .

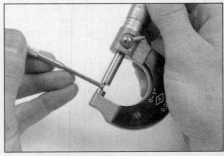

3.10 . . . then measure the gauge with a micrometer

lines up exactly with any of the divisions on the main scale, noting that the divisions usually represents 0.02 of a millimetre. Add this fine measurement to the base measurement to obtain the total reading.

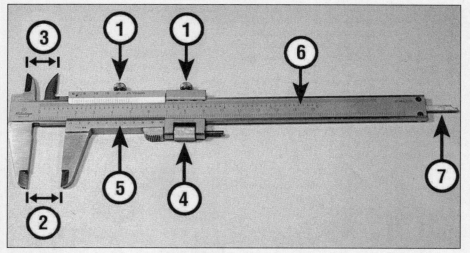

3.11 Vernier component parts (linear gauge)

1 Clamp screws	3 Internal jaws	5 Sliding scale	7 Depth gauge
2 External jaws	4 Thumbwheel	6 Main scale	

In the example shown the item measures 55.92 mm **(see illustration 3.12)**:

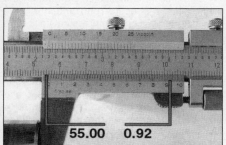

3.12 Vernier gauge reading of 55.92 mm

Base measurement	55.00 mm
Fine measurement	00.92 mm
Total figure	55.92 mm

● Some vernier calipers are equipped with a dial gauge for fine measurement. Before use, check that the jaws are clean, then close them fully and check that the dial gauge reads zero. If necessary adjust the gauge ring accordingly. Slacken the vernier clamp screw (1) and set its jaws over (2), or inside (3), the item to be measured **(see illustration 3.13)**. Slide the jaws into contact, using the thumbwheel (4) for fine movement. Read off the main scale (5) where the edge of the sliding scale (6) intersects it, taking the whole number to the left of the zero; this provides the base measurement. Read off the needle position on the dial gauge (7) scale to provide the fine measurement; each division represents 0.05 of a millimetre. Add this fine measurement to the base measurement to obtain the total reading.

In the example shown the item measures 55.95 mm **(see illustration 3.14)**:

Base measurement	55.00 mm
Fine measurement	00.95 mm
Total figure	55.95 mm

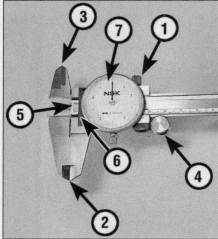

3.13 Vernier component parts (dial gauge)

1 Clamp screw	5 Main scale
2 External jaws	6 Sliding scale
3 Internal jaws	7 Dial gauge
4 Thumbwheel	

3.14 Vernier gauge reading of 55.95 mm

Plastigauge

● Plastigauge is a plastic material which can be compressed between two surfaces to measure the oil clearance between them. The width of the compressed Plastigauge is measured against a calibrated scale to determine the clearance.

● Common uses of Plastigauge are for measuring the clearance between crankshaft journal and main bearing inserts, between crankshaft journal and big-end bearing inserts, and between camshaft and bearing surfaces. The following example describes big-end oil clearance measurement.

● Handle the Plastigauge material carefully to prevent distortion. Using a sharp knife, cut a length which corresponds with the width of the bearing being measured and place it carefully across the journal so that it is parallel with the shaft **(see illustration 3.15)**. Carefully install both bearing shells and the connecting rod. Without rotating the rod on the journal tighten its bolts or nuts (as applicable) to the specified torque. The connecting rod and bearings are then disassembled and the crushed Plastigauge examined.

3.15 Plastigauge placed across shaft journal

● Using the scale provided in the Plastigauge kit, measure the width of the material to determine the oil clearance **(see illustration 3.16)**. Always remove all traces of Plastigauge after use using your fingernails.

Caution: Arriving at the correct clearance demands that the assembly is torqued correctly, according to the settings and sequence (where applicable) provided by the motorcycle manufacturer.

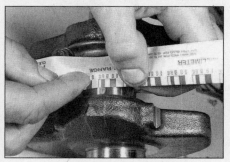

3.16 Measuring the width of the crushed Plastigauge

Dial gauge or DTI (Dial Test Indicator)

● A dial gauge can be used to accurately measure small amounts of movement. Typical uses are measuring shaft runout or shaft endfloat (sideplay) and setting piston position for ignition timing on two-strokes. A dial gauge set usually comes with a range of different probes and adapters and mounting equipment.

● The gauge needle must point to zero when at rest. Rotate the ring around its periphery to zero the gauge.

● Check that the gauge is capable of reading the extent of movement in the work. Most gauges have a small dial set in the face which records whole millimetres of movement as well as the fine scale around the face periphery which is calibrated in 0.01 mm divisions. Read off the small dial first to obtain the base measurement, then add the measurement from the fine scale to obtain the total reading.

In the example shown the gauge reads 1.48 mm **(see illustration 3.17)**:

Base measurement	1.00 mm
Fine measurement	0.48 mm
Total figure	1.48 mm

3.17 Dial gauge reading of 1.48 mm

● If measuring shaft runout, the shaft must be supported in vee-blocks and the gauge mounted on a stand perpendicular to the shaft. Rest the tip of the gauge against the centre of the shaft and rotate the shaft slowly whilst watching the gauge reading **(see illustration 3.18)**. Take several measurements along the length of the shaft and record the

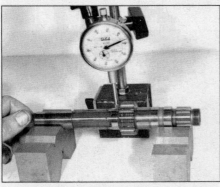

3.18 Using a dial gauge to measure shaft runout

maximum gauge reading as the amount of runout in the shaft. **Note:** *The reading obtained will be total runout at that point - some manufacturers specify that the runout figure is halved to compare with their specified runout limit.*

● Endfloat (sideplay) measurement requires that the gauge is mounted securely to the surrounding component with its probe touching the end of the shaft. Using hand pressure, push and pull on the shaft noting the maximum endfloat recorded on the gauge **(see illustration 3.19)**.

3.19 Using a dial gauge to measure shaft endfloat

● A dial gauge with suitable adapters can be used to determine piston position BTDC on two-stroke engines for the purposes of ignition timing. The gauge, adapter and suitable length probe are installed in the place of the spark plug and the gauge zeroed at TDC. If the piston position is specified as 1.14 mm BTDC, rotate the engine back to 2.00 mm BTDC, then slowly forwards to 1.14 mm BTDC.

Cylinder compression gauges

● A compression gauge is used for measuring cylinder compression. Either the rubber-cone type or the threaded adapter type can be used. The latter is preferred to ensure a perfect seal against the cylinder head. A 0 to 300 psi (0 to 20 Bar) type gauge (for petrol/gasoline engines) will be suitable for motorcycles.

● The spark plug is removed and the gauge either held hard against the cylinder head (cone type) or the gauge adapter screwed into the cylinder head (threaded type) **(see illustration 3.20)**. Cylinder compression is measured with the engine turning over, but not running. The

3.20 Using a rubber-cone type cylinder compression gauge

gauge will hold the reading until manually released.

Oil pressure gauge

● An oil pressure gauge is used for measuring engine oil pressure. Most gauges come with a set of adapters to fit the thread of the take-off point **(see illustration 3.21)**. If the take-off point specified by the motorcycle manufacturer is an external oil pipe union, make sure that the specified replacement union is used to prevent oil starvation.

3.21 Oil pressure gauge and take-off point adapter (arrow)

● Oil pressure is measured with the engine running (at a specific rpm) and often the manufacturer will specify pressure limits for a cold and hot engine.

Straight-edge and surface plate

● If checking the gasket face of a component for warpage, place a steel rule or precision straight-edge across the gasket face and measure any gap between the straight-edge and component with feeler gauges **(see illustration 3.22)**. Check diagonally across the component and between mounting holes **(see illustration 3.23)**.

3.22 Use a straight-edge and feeler gauges to check for warpage

3.23 Check for warpage in these directions

● Checking individual components for warpage, such as clutch plain (metal) plates, requires a perfectly flat plate or piece or plate glass and feeler gauges.

4 Torque and leverage

What is torque?

● Torque describes the twisting force about a shaft. The amount of torque applied is determined by the distance from the centre of the shaft to the end of the lever and the amount of force being applied to the end of the lever; distance multiplied by force equals torque.

● The manufacturer applies a measured torque to a bolt or nut to ensure that it will not slacken in use and to hold two components securely together without movement in the joint. The actual torque setting depends on the thread size, bolt or nut material and the composition of the components being held.

● Too little torque may cause the fastener to loosen due to vibration, whereas too much torque will distort the joint faces of the component or cause the fastener to shear off. Always stick to the specified torque setting.

Using a torque wrench

● Check the calibration of the torque wrench and make sure it has a suitable range for the job. Torque wrenches are available in Nm (Newton-metres), kgf m (kilograms-force metre), lbf ft (pounds-feet), lbf in (inch-pounds). Do not confuse lbf ft with lbf in.

● Adjust the tool to the desired torque on the scale (see illustration 4.1). If your torque wrench is not calibrated in the units specified, carefully convert the figure (see Conversion Factors). A manufacturer sometimes gives a torque setting as a range (8 to 10 Nm) rather than a single figure - in this case set the tool midway between the two settings. The same torque may be expressed as 9 Nm ± 1 Nm. Some torque wrenches have a method of locking the setting so that it isn't inadvertently altered during use.

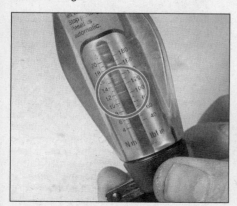

4.1 Set the torque wrench index mark to the setting required, in this case 12 Nm

● Install the bolts/nuts in their correct location and secure them lightly. Their threads must be clean and free of any old locking compound. Unless specified the threads and flange should be dry - oiled threads are necessary in certain circumstances and the manufacturer will take this into account in the specified torque figure. Similarly, the manufacturer may also specify the application of thread-locking compound.

● Tighten the fasteners in the specified sequence until the torque wrench clicks, indicating that the torque setting has been reached. Apply the torque again to double-check the setting. Where different thread diameter fasteners secure the component, as a rule tighten the larger diameter ones first.

● When the torque wrench has been finished with, release the lock (where applicable) and fully back off its setting to zero - do not leave the torque wrench tensioned. Also, do not use a torque wrench for slackening a fastener.

Angle-tightening

● Manufacturers often specify a figure in degrees for final tightening of a fastener. This usually follows tightening to a specific torque setting.

● A degree disc can be set and attached to the socket (see illustration 4.2) or a protractor can be used to mark the angle of movement on the bolt/nut head and the surrounding casting (see illustration 4.3).

4.2 Angle tightening can be accomplished with a torque-angle gauge . . .

4.3 . . . or by marking the angle on the surrounding component

Loosening sequences

● Where more than one bolt/nut secures a component, loosen each fastener evenly a little at a time. In this way, not all the stress of the joint is held by one fastener and the components are not likely to distort.

● If a tightening sequence is provided, work in the REVERSE of this, but if not, work from the outside in, in a criss-cross sequence (see illustration 4.4).

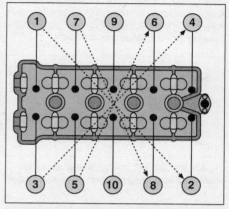

4.4 When slackening, work from the outside inwards

Tightening sequences

● If a component is held by more than one fastener it is important that the retaining bolts/nuts are tightened evenly to prevent uneven stress build-up and distortion of sealing faces. This is especially important on high-compression joints such as the cylinder head.

● A sequence is usually provided by the manufacturer, either in a diagram or actually marked in the casting. If not, always start in the centre and work outwards in a criss-cross pattern (see illustration 4.5). Start off by securing all bolts/nuts finger-tight, then set the torque wrench and tighten each fastener by a small amount in sequence until the final torque is reached. By following this practice,

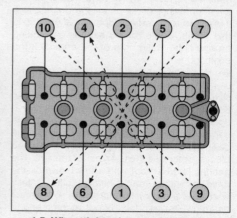

4.5 When tightening, work from the inside outwards

the joint will be held evenly and will not be distorted. Important joints, such as the cylinder head and big-end fasteners often have two- or three-stage torque settings.

Applying leverage

● Use tools at the correct angle. Position a socket wrench or spanner on the bolt/nut so that you pull it towards you when loosening. If this can't be done, push the spanner without curling your fingers around it **(see illustration 4.6)** - the spanner may slip or the fastener loosen suddenly, resulting in your fingers being crushed against a component.

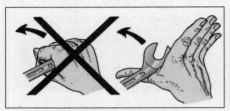

4.6 If you can't pull on the spanner to loosen a fastener, push with your hand open

● Additional leverage is gained by extending the length of the lever. The best way to do this is to use a breaker bar instead of the regular length tool, or to slip a length of tubing over the end of the spanner or socket wrench.
● If additional leverage will not work, the fastener head is either damaged or firmly corroded in place (see Fasteners).

5 Bearings

Bearing removal and installation

Drivers and sockets

● Before removing a bearing, always inspect the casing to see which way it must be driven out - some casings will have retaining plates or a cast step. Also check for any identifying markings on the bearing and if installed to a certain depth, measure this at this stage. Some roller bearings are sealed on one side - take note of the original fitted position.
● Bearings can be driven out of a casing using a bearing driver tool (with the correct size head) or a socket of the correct diameter. Select the driver head or socket so that it contacts the outer race of the bearing, not the balls/rollers or inner race. Always support the casing around the bearing housing with wood blocks, otherwise there is a risk of fracture. The bearing is driven out with a few blows on the driver or socket from a heavy mallet. Unless access is severely restricted (as with wheel bearings), a pin-punch is not recommended unless it is moved around the bearing to keep it square in its housing.

● The same equipment can be used to install bearings. Make sure the bearing housing is supported on wood blocks and line up the bearing in its housing. Fit the bearing as noted on removal - generally they are installed with their marked side facing outwards. Tap the bearing squarely into its housing using a driver or socket which bears only on the bearing's outer race - contact with the bearing balls/rollers or inner race will destroy it **(see illustrations 5.1 and 5.2)**.
● Check that the bearing inner race and balls/rollers rotate freely.

5.1 Using a bearing driver against the bearing's outer race

5.2 Using a large socket against the bearing's outer race

Pullers and slide-hammers

● Where a bearing is pressed on a shaft a puller will be required to extract it **(see illustration 5.3)**. Make sure that the puller clamp or legs fit securely behind the bearing and are unlikely to slip out. If pulling a bearing

5.3 This bearing puller clamps behind the bearing and pressure is applied to the shaft end to draw the bearing off

off a gear shaft for example, you may have to locate the puller behind a gear pinion if there is no access to the race and draw the gear pinion off the shaft as well **(see illustration 5.4)**.

> **Caution: Ensure that the puller's centre bolt locates securely against the end of the shaft and will not slip when pressure is applied. Also ensure that puller does not damage the shaft end.**

5.4 Where no access is available to the rear of the bearing, it is sometimes possible to draw off the adjacent component

● Operate the puller so that its centre bolt exerts pressure on the shaft end and draws the bearing off the shaft.
● When installing the bearing on the shaft, tap only on the bearing's inner race - contact with the balls/rollers or outer race with destroy the bearing. Use a socket or length of tubing as a drift which fits over the shaft end **(see illustration 5.5)**.

5.5 When installing a bearing on a shaft use a piece of tubing which bears only on the bearing's inner race

● Where a bearing locates in a blind hole in a casing, it cannot be driven or pulled out as described above. A slide-hammer with knife-edged bearing puller attachment will be required. The puller attachment passes through the bearing and when tightened expands to fit firmly behind the bearing **(see illustration 5.6)**. By operating the slide-hammer part of the tool the bearing is jarred out of its housing **(see illustration 5.7)**.
● It is possible, if the bearing is of reasonable weight, for it to drop out of its housing if the casing is heated as described opposite.

5.6 Expand the bearing puller so that it locks behind the bearing . . .

5.7 . . . attach the slide hammer to the bearing puller

If this method is attempted, first prepare a work surface which will enable the casing to be tapped face down to help dislodge the bearing - a wood surface is ideal since it will not damage the casing's gasket surface. Wearing protective gloves, tap the heated casing several times against the work surface to dislodge the bearing under its own weight **(see illustration 5.8)**.

5.8 Tapping a casing face down on wood blocks can often dislodge a bearing

● Bearings can be installed in blind holes using the driver or socket method described above.

Drawbolts

● Where a bearing or bush is set in the eye of a component, such as a suspension linkage arm or connecting rod small-end, removal by drift may damage the component. Furthermore, a rubber bushing in a shock absorber eye cannot successfully be driven out of position. If access is available to a engineering press, the task is straightforward. If not, a drawbolt can be fabricated to extract the bearing or bush.

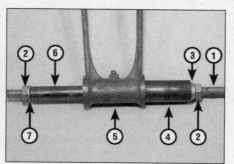

5.9 Drawbolt component parts assembled on a suspension arm

1 Bolt or length of threaded bar
2 Nuts
3 Washer (external diameter greater than tubing internal diameter)
4 Tubing (internal diameter sufficient to accommodate bearing)
5 Suspension arm with bearing
6 Tubing (external diameter slightly smaller than bearing)
7 Washer (external diameter slightly smaller than bearing)

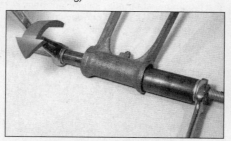

5.10 Drawing the bearing out of the suspension arm

● To extract the bearing/bush you will need a long bolt with nut (or piece of threaded bar with two nuts), a piece of tubing which has an internal diameter larger than the bearing/bush, another piece of tubing which has an external diameter slightly smaller than the bearing/bush, and a selection of washers **(see illustrations 5.9 and 5.10)**. Note that the pieces of tubing must be of the same length, or longer, than the bearing/bush.

● The same kit (without the pieces of tubing) can be used to draw the new bearing/bush back into place **(see illustration 5.11)**.

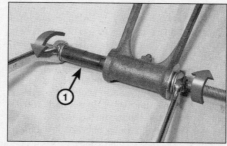

5.11 Installing a new bearing (1) in the suspension arm

Temperature change

● If the bearing's outer race is a tight fit in the casing, the aluminium casing can be heated to release its grip on the bearing. Aluminium will expand at a greater rate than the steel bearing outer race. There are several ways to do this, but avoid any localised extreme heat (such as a blow torch) - aluminium alloy has a low melting point.

● Approved methods of heating a casing are using a domestic oven (heated to 100°C) or immersing the casing in boiling water **(see illustration 5.12)**. Low temperature range localised heat sources such as a paint stripper heat gun or clothes iron can also be used **(see illustration 5.13)**. Alternatively, soak a rag in boiling water, wring it out and wrap it around the bearing housing.

> ⚠ **Warning: All of these methods require care in use to prevent scalding and burns to the hands. Wear protective gloves when handling hot components.**

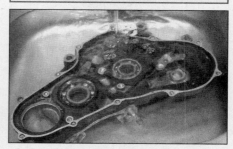

5.12 A casing can be immersed in a sink of boiling water to aid bearing removal

5.13 Using a localised heat source to aid bearing removal

● If heating the whole casing note that plastic components, such as the neutral switch, may suffer - remove them beforehand.

● After heating, remove the bearing as described above. You may find that the expansion is sufficient for the bearing to fall out of the casing under its own weight or with a light tap on the driver or socket.

● If necessary, the casing can be heated to aid bearing installation, and this is sometimes the recommended procedure if the motorcycle manufacturer has designed the housing and bearing fit with this intention.

● Installation of bearings can be eased by placing them in a freezer the night before installation. The steel bearing will contract slightly, allowing easy insertion in its housing. This is often useful when installing steering head outer races in the frame.

Bearing types and markings

● Plain shell bearings, ball bearings, needle roller bearings and tapered roller bearings will all be found on motorcycles **(see illustrations 5.14 and 5.15)**. The ball and roller types are usually caged between an inner and outer race, but uncaged variations may be found.

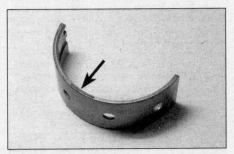

5.14 Shell bearings are either plain or grooved. They are usually identified by colour code (arrow)

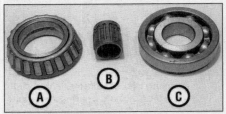

5.15 Tapered roller bearing (A), needle roller bearing (B) and ball journal bearing (C)

● Shell bearings (often called inserts) are usually found at the crankshaft main and connecting rod big-end where they are good at coping with high loads. They are made of a phosphor-bronze material and are impregnated with self-lubricating properties.

● Ball bearings and needle roller bearings consist of a steel inner and outer race with the balls or rollers between the races. They require constant lubrication by oil or grease and are good at coping with axial loads. Taper roller bearings consist of rollers set in a tapered cage set on the inner race; the outer race is separate. They are good at coping with axial loads and prevent movement along the shaft - a typical application is in the steering head.

● Bearing manufacturers produce bearings to ISO size standards and stamp one face of the bearing to indicate its internal and external diameter, load capacity and type **(see illustration 5.16)**.

● Metal bushes are usually of phosphor-bronze material. Rubber bushes are used in suspension mounting eyes. Fibre bushes have also been used in suspension pivots.

5.16 Typical bearing marking

Bearing fault finding

● If a bearing outer race has spun in its housing, the housing material will be damaged. You can use a bearing locking compound to bond the outer race in place if damage is not too severe.

● Shell bearings will fail due to damage of their working surface, as a result of lack of lubrication, corrosion or abrasive particles in the oil **(see illustration 5.17)**. Small particles of dirt in the oil may embed in the bearing material whereas larger particles will score the bearing and shaft journal. If a number of short journeys are made, insufficient heat will be generated to drive off condensation which has built up on the bearings.

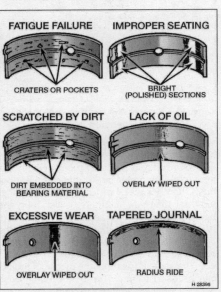

5.17 Typical bearing failures

● Ball and roller bearings will fail due to lack of lubrication or damage to the balls or rollers. Tapered-roller bearings can be damaged by overloading them. Unless the bearing is sealed on both sides, wash it in paraffin (kerosene) to remove all old grease then allow it to dry. Make a visual inspection looking to dented balls or rollers, damaged cages and worn or pitted races **(see illustration 5.18)**.

● A ball bearing can be checked for wear by listening to it when spun. Apply a film of light oil to the bearing and hold it close to the ear - hold the outer race with one hand and spin the

5.18 Example of ball journal bearing with damaged balls and cages

5.19 Hold outer race and listen to inner race when spun

inner race with the other hand **(see illustration 5.19)**. The bearing should be almost silent when spun; if it grates or rattles it is worn.

6   Oil seals

Oil seal removal and installation

● Oil seals should be renewed every time a component is dismantled. This is because the seal lips will become set to the sealing surface and will not necessarily reseal.

● Oil seals can be prised out of position using a large flat-bladed screwdriver **(see illustration 6.1)**. In the case of crankcase seals, check first that the seal is not lipped on the inside, preventing its removal with the crankcases joined.

6.1 Prise out oil seals with a large flat-bladed screwdriver

● New seals are usually installed with their marked face (containing the seal reference code) outwards and the spring side towards the fluid being retained. In certain cases, such as a two-stroke engine crankshaft seal, a double lipped seal may be used due to there being fluid or gas on each side of the joint.

● Use a bearing driver or socket which bears only on the outer hard edge of the seal to install it in the casing - tapping on the inner edge will damage the sealing lip.

Oil seal types and markings

● Oil seals are usually of the single-lipped type. Double-lipped seals are found where a liquid or gas is on both sides of the joint.
● Oil seals can harden and lose their sealing ability if the motorcycle has been in storage for a long period - renewal is the only solution.
● Oil seal manufacturers also conform to the ISO markings for seal size - these are moulded into the outer face of the seal (see illustration 6.2).

6.2 These oil seal markings indicate inside diameter, outside diameter and seal thickness

7 Gaskets and sealants

Types of gasket and sealant

● Gaskets are used to seal the mating surfaces between components and keep lubricants, fluids, vacuum or pressure contained within the assembly. Aluminium gaskets are sometimes found at the cylinder joints, but most gaskets are paper-based. If the mating surfaces of the components being joined are undamaged the gasket can be installed dry, although a dab of sealant or grease will be useful to hold it in place during assembly.
● RTV (Room Temperature Vulcanising) silicone rubber sealants cure when exposed to moisture in the atmosphere. These sealants are good at filling pits or irregular gasket faces, but will tend to be forced out of the joint under very high torque. They can be used to replace a paper gasket, but first make sure that the width of the paper gasket is not essential to the shimming of internal components. RTV sealants should not be used on components containing petrol (gasoline).
● Non-hardening, semi-hardening and hard setting liquid gasket compounds can be used with a gasket or between a metal-to-metal joint. Select the sealant to suit the application: universal non-hardening sealant can be used on virtually all joints; semi-hardening on joint faces which are rough or damaged; hard setting sealant on joints which require a permanent bond and are subjected to high temperature and pressure. **Note:** *Check first if the paper gasket has a bead of sealant*

impregnated in its surface before applying additional sealant.
● When choosing a sealant, make sure it is suitable for the application, particularly if being applied in a high-temperature area or in the vicinity of fuel. Certain manufacturers produce sealants in either clear, silver or black colours to match the finish of the engine. This has a particular application on motorcycles where much of the engine is exposed.
● Do not over-apply sealant. That which is squeezed out on the outside of the joint can be wiped off, whereas an excess of sealant on the inside can break off and clog oilways.

Breaking a sealed joint

● Age, heat, pressure and the use of hard setting sealant can cause two components to stick together so tightly that they are difficult to separate using finger pressure alone. Do not resort to using levers unless there is a pry point provided for this purpose (see illustration 7.1) or else the gasket surfaces will be damaged.
● Use a soft-faced hammer (see illustration 7.2) or a wood block and conventional hammer to strike the component near the mating surface. Avoid hammering against cast extremities since they may break off. If this method fails, try using a wood wedge between the two components.

> **Caution: If the joint will not separate, double-check that you have removed all the fasteners.**

7.1 If a pry point is provided, apply gently pressure with a flat-bladed screwdriver

7.2 Tap around the joint with a soft-faced mallet if necessary - don't strike cooling fins

Removal of old gasket and sealant

● Paper gaskets will most likely come away complete, leaving only a few traces stuck

Most components have one or two hollow locating dowels between the two gasket faces. If a dowel cannot be removed, do not resort to gripping it with pliers - it will almost certainly be distorted. Install a close-fitting socket or Phillips screwdriver into the dowel and then grip the outer edge of the dowel to free it.

on the sealing faces of the components. It is imperative that all traces are removed to ensure correct sealing of the new gasket.
● Very carefully scrape all traces of gasket away making sure that the sealing surfaces are not gouged or scored by the scraper (see illustrations 7.3, 7.4 and 7.5). Stubborn deposits can be removed by spraying with an aerosol gasket remover. Final preparation of

7.3 Paper gaskets can be scraped off with a gasket scraper tool . . .

7.4 . . . a knife blade . . .

7.5 . . . or a household scraper

7.6 Fine abrasive paper is wrapped around a flat file to clean up the gasket face

7.7 A kitchen scourer can be used on stubborn deposits

the gasket surface can be made with very fine abrasive paper or a plastic kitchen scourer **(see illustrations 7.6 and 7.7)**.
● Old sealant can be scraped or peeled off components, depending on the type originally used. Note that gasket removal compounds are available to avoid scraping the components clean; make sure the gasket remover suits the type of sealant used.

8 Chains

Breaking and joining final drive chains

● Drive chains for all but small bikes are continuous and do not have a clip-type connecting link. The chain must be broken using a chain breaker tool and the new chain securely riveted together using a new soft rivet-type link. Never use a clip-type connecting link instead of a rivet-type link, except in an emergency. Various chain breaking and riveting tools are available, either as separate tools or combined as illustrated in the accompanying photographs - read the instructions supplied with the tool carefully.

> ⚠ **Warning: The need to rivet the new link pins correctly cannot be overstressed - loss of control of the motorcycle is very likely to result if the chain breaks in use.**

● Rotate the chain and look for the soft link. The soft link pins look like they have been

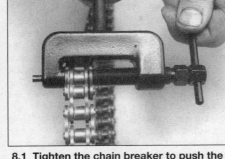

8.1 Tighten the chain breaker to push the pin out of the link . . .

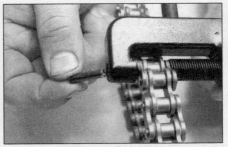

8.2 . . . withdraw the pin, remove the tool . . .

8.3 . . . and separate the chain link

deeply centre-punched instead of peened over like all the other pins **(see illustration 8.9)** and its sideplate may be a different colour. Position the soft link midway between the sprockets and assemble the chain breaker tool over one of the soft link pins **(see illustration 8.1)**. Operate the tool to push the pin out through the chain **(see illustration 8.2)**. On an O-ring chain, remove the O-rings **(see illustration 8.3)**. Carry out the same procedure on the other soft link pin.

> *Caution: Certain soft link pins (particularly on the larger chains) may require their ends to be filed or ground off before they can be pressed out using the tool.*

● Check that you have the correct size and strength (standard or heavy duty) new soft link - do not reuse the old link. Look for the size marking on the chain sideplates **(see illustration 8.10)**.
● Position the chain ends so that they are engaged over the rear sprocket. On an O-ring

8.4 Insert the new soft link, with O-rings, through the chain ends . . .

8.5 . . . install the O-rings over the pin ends . . .

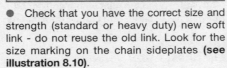

8.6 . . . followed by the sideplate

chain, install a new O-ring over each pin of the link and insert the link through the two chain ends **(see illustration 8.4)**. Install a new O-ring over the end of each pin, followed by the sideplate (with the chain manufacturer's marking facing outwards) **(see illustrations 8.5 and 8.6)**. On an unsealed chain, insert the link through the two chain ends, then install the sideplate with the chain manufacturer's marking facing outwards.
● Note that it may not be possible to install the sideplate using finger pressure alone. If using a joining tool, assemble it so that the plates of the tool clamp the link and press the sideplate over the pins **(see illustration 8.7)**. Otherwise, use two small sockets placed over

8.7 Push the sideplate into position using a clamp

8.8 Assemble the chain riveting tool over one pin at a time and tighten it fully

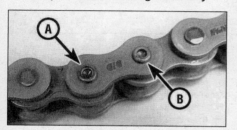

8.9 Pin end correctly riveted (A), pin end unriveted (B)

the rivet ends and two pieces of the wood between a G-clamp. Operate the clamp to press the sideplate over the pins.

● Assemble the joining tool over one pin (following the maker's instructions) and tighten the tool down to spread the pin end securely **(see illustrations 8.8 and 8.9)**. Do the same on the other pin.

> ⚠ **Warning: Check that the pin ends are secure and that there is no danger of the sideplate coming loose. If the pin ends are cracked the soft link must be renewed.**

Final drive chain sizing

● Chains are sized using a three digit number, followed by a suffix to denote the chain type **(see illustration 8.10)**. Chain type is either standard or heavy duty (thicker sideplates), and also unsealed or O-ring/X-ring type.

● The first digit of the number relates to the pitch of the chain, ie the distance from the centre of one pin to the centre of the next pin **(see illustration 8.11)**. Pitch is expressed in eighths of an inch, as follows:

8.10 Typical chain size and type marking

8.11 Chain dimensions

| Sizes commencing with a 4 (eg 428) have a pitch of 1/2 inch (12.7 mm) |
| Sizes commencing with a 5 (eg 520) have a pitch of 5/8 inch (15.9 mm) |
| Sizes commencing with a 6 (eg 630) have a pitch of 3/4 inch (19.1 mm) |

● The second and third digits of the chain size relate to the width of the rollers, again in imperial units, eg the 525 shown has 5/16 inch (7.94 mm) rollers **(see illustration 8.11)**.

9 Hoses

Clamping to prevent flow

● Small-bore flexible hoses can be clamped to prevent fluid flow whilst a component is worked on. Whichever method is used, ensure that the hose material is not permanently distorted or damaged by the clamp.

a) A brake hose clamp available from auto accessory shops **(see illustration 9.1)**.
b) A wingnut type hose clamp **(see illustration 9.2)**.

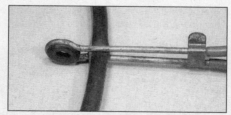

9.1 Hoses can be clamped with an automotive brake hose clamp . . .

9.2 . . . a wingnut type hose clamp . . .

c) Two sockets placed each side of the hose and held with straight-jawed self-locking grips **(see illustration 9.3)**.
d) Thick card each side of the hose held between straight-jawed self-locking grips **(see illustration 9.4)**.

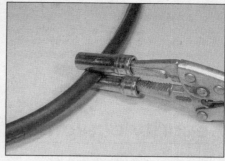

9.3 . . . two sockets and a pair of self-locking grips . . .

9.4 . . . or thick card and self-locking grips

Freeing and fitting hoses

● Always make sure the hose clamp is moved well clear of the hose end. Grip the hose with your hand and rotate it whilst pulling it off the union. If the hose has hardened due to age and will not move, slit it with a sharp knife and peel its ends off the union **(see illustration 9.5)**.

● Resist the temptation to use grease or soap on the unions to aid installation; although it helps the hose slip over the union it will equally aid the escape of fluid from the joint. It is preferable to soften the hose ends in hot water and wet the inside surface of the hose with water or a fluid which will evaporate.

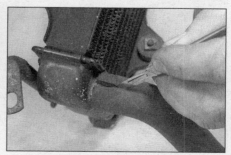

9.5 Cutting a coolant hose free with a sharp knife

Introduction

In less time than it takes to read this introduction, a thief could steal your motorcycle. Returning only to find your bike has gone is one of the worst feelings in the world. Even if the motorcycle is insured against theft, once you've got over the initial shock, you will have the inconvenience of dealing with the police and your insurance company.

The motorcycle is an easy target for the professional thief and the joyrider alike and the official figures on motorcycle theft make for depressing reading; on average a motor-cycle is stolen every 16 minutes in the UK!

Motorcycle thefts fall into two categories, those stolen 'to order' and those taken by opportunists. The thief stealing to order will be on the look out for a specific make and model and will go to extraordinary lengths to obtain that motorcycle. The opportunist thief on the other hand will look for easy targets which can be stolen with the minimum of effort and risk.

Whilst it is never going to be possible to make your machine 100% secure, it is estimated that around half of all stolen motorcycles are taken by opportunist thieves. Remember that the opportunist thief is always on the look out for the easy option: if there are two similar motorcycles parked side-by-side, they will target the one with the lowest level of security. By taking a few precautions, you can reduce the chances of your motorcycle being stolen.

Security equipment

There are many specialised motorcycle security devices available and the following text summarises their applications and their good and bad points.

Once you have decided on the type of security equipment which best suits your needs, we recommended that you read one of the many equipment tests regularly carried out by the motorcycle press. These tests

Ensure the lock and chain you buy is of good quality and long enough to shackle your bike to a solid object

compare the products from all the major manufacturers and give impartial ratings on their effectiveness, value-for-money and ease of use.

No one item of security equipment can provide complete protection. It is highly recommended that two or more of the items described below are combined to increase the security of your motorcycle (a lock and chain plus an alarm system is just about ideal). The more security measures fitted to the bike, the less likely it is to be stolen.

Lock and chain

Pros: *Very flexible to use; can be used to secure the motorcycle to almost any immovable object. On some locks and chains, the lock can be used on its own as a disc lock (see below).*

Cons: *Can be very heavy and awkward to carry on the motorcycle, although some types*

will be supplied with a carry bag which can be strapped to the pillion seat.

● Heavy-duty chains and locks are an excellent security measure **(see illustration 1).** Whenever the motorcycle is parked, use the lock and chain to secure the machine to a solid, immovable object such as a post or railings. This will prevent the machine from being ridden away or being lifted into the back of a van.

● When fitting the chain, always ensure the chain is routed around the motorcycle frame or swingarm **(see illustrations 2 and 3).** Never merely pass the chain around one of the wheel rims; a thief may unbolt the wheel and lift the rest of the machine into a van, leaving you with just the wheel! Try to avoid having excess chain free, thus making it difficult to use cutting tools, and keep the chain and lock off the ground to prevent thieves attacking it with a cold chisel. Position the lock so that its lock barrel is facing downwards; this will make it harder for the thief to attack the lock mechanism.

Pass the chain through the bike's frame, rather than just through a wheel . . .

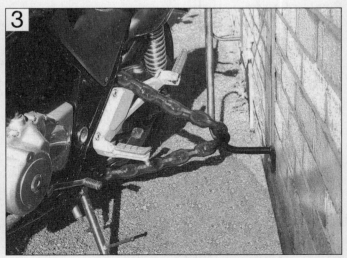

. . . and loop it around a solid object

U-locks

Pros: *Highly effective deterrent which can be used to secure the bike to a post or railings. Most U-locks come with a carrier which allows the lock to be easily carried on the bike.*

Cons: *Not as flexible to use as a lock and chain.*

● These are solid locks which are similar in use to a lock and chain. U-locks are lighter than a lock and chain but not so flexible to use. The length and shape of the lock shackle limit the objects to which the bike can be secured **(see illustration 4)**.

Disc locks

Pros: *Small, light and very easy to carry; most can be stored underneath the seat.*

Cons: *Does not prevent the motorcycle being lifted into a van. Can be very embarrassing if*

U-locks can be used to secure the bike to a solid object – ensure you purchase one which is long enough

A typical disc lock attached through one of the holes in the disc

you forget to remove the lock before attempting to ride off!

● Disc locks are designed to be attached to the front brake disc. The lock passes through one of the holes in the disc and prevents the wheel rotating by jamming against the fork/brake caliper **(see illustration 5)**. Some are equipped with an alarm siren which sounds if the disc lock is moved; this not only acts as a theft deterrent but also as a handy reminder if you try to move the bike with the lock still fitted.

● Combining the disc lock with a length of cable which can be looped around a post or railings provides an additional measure of security **(see illustration 6)**.

Alarms and immobilisers

Pros: *Once installed it is completely hassle-free to use. If the system is 'Thatcham' or 'Sold Secure-approved', insurance companies may give you a discount.*

Cons: *Can be expensive to buy and complex to install. No system will prevent the motorcycle from being lifted into a van and taken away.*

● Electronic alarms and immobilisers are available to suit a variety of budgets. There are three different types of system available: pure alarms, pure immobilisers, and the more expensive systems which are combined alarm/immobilisers **(see illustration 7)**.

● An alarm system is designed to emit an audible warning if the motorcycle is being tampered with.

● An immobiliser prevents the motorcycle being started and ridden away by disabling its electrical systems.

● When purchasing an alarm/immobiliser system, check the cost of installing the system unless you are able to do it yourself. If the motorcycle is not used regularly, another consideration is the current drain of the system. All alarm/immobiliser systems are powered by the motorcycle's battery; purchasing a system with a very low current drain could prevent the battery losing its charge whilst the motorcycle is not being used.

A disc lock combined with a security cable provides additional protection

A typical alarm/immobiliser system

Indelible markings can be applied to most areas of the bike – always apply the manufacturer's sticker to warn off thieves

Chemically-etched code numbers can be applied to main body panels . . .

. . . again, always ensure that the kit manufacturer's sticker is applied in a prominent position

Security marking kits

Pros: *Very cheap and effective deterrent. Many insurance companies will give you a discount on your insurance premium if a recognised security marking kit is used on your motorcycle.*

Cons: *Does not prevent the motorcycle being stolen by joyriders.*

● There are many different types of security marking kits available. The idea is to mark as many parts of the motorcycle as possible with a unique security number **(see illustrations 8, 9 and 10)**. A form will be included with the kit to register your personal details and those of the motorcycle with the kit manufacturer. This register is made available to the police to help them trace the rightful owner of any motorcycle or components which they recover should all other forms of identification have been removed. Always apply the warning stickers provided with the kit to deter thieves.

Ground anchors, wheel clamps and security posts

Pros: *An excellent form of security which will deter all but the most determined of thieves.*

Cons: *Awkward to install and can be expensive.*

● Whilst the motorcycle is at home, it is a good idea to attach it securely to the floor or a solid wall, even if it is kept in a securely locked garage. Various types of ground anchors, security posts and wheel clamps are available for this purpose **(see illustration 11)**. These security devices are either bolted to a solid concrete or brick structure or can be cemented into the ground.

Permanent ground anchors provide an excellent level of security when the bike is at home

Security at home

A high percentage of motorcycle thefts are from the owner's home. Here are some things to consider whenever your motorcycle is at home:
● Where possible, always keep the motorcycle in a securely locked garage. Never rely solely on the standard lock on the garage door, these are usual hopelessly inadequate. Fit an additional locking mechanism to the door and consider having the garage alarmed. A security light, activated by a movement sensor, is also a good investment.

● Always secure the motorcycle to the ground or a wall, even if it is inside a securely locked garage.
● Do not regularly leave the motorcycle outside your home, try to keep it out of sight wherever possible. If a garage is not available, fit a motorcycle cover over the bike to disguise its true identity.
● It is not uncommon for thieves to follow a motorcyclist home to find out where the bike is kept. They will then return at a later date. Be aware of this whenever you are returning

home on your motorcycle. If you suspect you are being followed, do not return home, instead ride to a garage or shop and stop as a precaution.
● When selling a motorcycle, do not provide your home address or the location where the bike is normally kept. Arrange to meet the buyer at a location away from your home. Thieves have been known to pose as potential buyers to find out where motorcycles are kept and then return later to steal them.

Security away from the home

As well as fitting security equipment to your motorcycle here are a few general rules to follow whenever you park your motorcycle.
● Park in a busy, public place.
● Use car parks which incorporate security features, such as CCTV.

● At night, park in a well-lit area, preferably directly underneath a street light.
● Engage the steering lock.
● Secure the motorcycle to a solid, immovable object such as a post or railings with an additional lock. If this is not possible,

secure the bike to a friend's motorcycle. Some public parking places provide security loops for motorcycles.
● Never leave your helmet or luggage attached to the motorcycle. Take them with you at all times.

Lubricants and fluids

A wide range of lubricants, fluids and cleaning agents is available for motor-cycles. This is a guide as to what is available, its applications and properties.

Four-stroke engine oil

● Engine oil is without doubt the most important component of any four-stroke engine. Modern motorcycle engines place a lot of demands on their oil and choosing the right type is essential. Using an unsuitable oil will lead to an increased rate of engine wear and could result in serious engine damage. Before purchasing oil, always check the recommended oil specification given by the manufacturer. The manufacturer will state a recommended 'type or classification' and also a specific 'viscosity' range for engine oil.

● The oil 'type or classification' is identified by its API (American Petroleum Institute) rating. The API rating will be in the form of two letters, e.g. SG. The S identifies the oil as being suitable for use in a petrol (gasoline) engine (S stands for spark ignition) and the second letter, ranging from A to J, identifies the oil's performance rating. The later this letter, the higher the specification of the oil; for example API SG oil exceeds the requirements of API SF oil. **Note:** *On some oils there may also be a second rating consisting of another two letters, the first letter being C, e.g. API SF/CD. This rating indicates the oil is also suitable for use in a diesel engines (the C stands for compression ignition) and is thus of no relevance for motorcycle use.*

● The 'viscosity' of the oil is identified by its SAE (Society of Automotive Engineers) rating. All modern engines require multigrade oils and the SAE rating will consist of two numbers, the first followed by a W, e.g. 10W/40. The first number indicates the viscosity rating of the oil at low temperatures (W stands for winter – tested at –20ºC) and the second number represents the viscosity of the oil at high temperatures (tested at 100ºC). The lower the number, the thinner the oil. For example an oil with an SAE 10W/40 rating will give better cold starting and running than an SAE 15W/40 oil.

● As well as ensuring the 'type' and 'viscosity' of the oil match the recommendations, another consideration to make when buying engine oil is whether to purchase a standard mineral-based oil, a semi-synthetic oil (also known as a synthetic blend or synthetic-based oil) or a fully-synthetic oil. Although all oils will have a similar rating and viscosity, their cost will vary considerably; mineral-based oils are the cheapest, the fully-synthetic oils the most expensive with the semi-synthetic oils falling somewhere in-between. This decision is very much up to the owner, but it should be noted that modern synthetic oils have far better lubricating and cleaning qualities than traditional mineral-based oils and tend to retain these properties for far longer. Bearing in mind the operating conditions inside a modern, high-revving motorcycle engine it is highly recommended that a fully synthetic oil is used. The extra expense at each service could save you money in the long term by preventing premature engine wear.

● As a final note always ensure that the oil is specifically designed for use in motorcycle engines. Engine oils designed primarily for use in car engines sometimes contain additives or friction modifiers which could cause clutch slip on a motorcycle fitted with a wet-clutch.

Two-stroke engine oil

● Modern two-stroke engines, with their high power outputs, place high demands on their oil. If engine seizure is to be avoided it is essential that a high-quality oil is used. Two-stroke oils differ hugely from four-stroke oils. The oil lubricates only the crankshaft and piston(s) (the transmission has its own lubricating oil) and is used on a total-loss basis where it is burnt completely during the combustion process.

● The Japanese have recently introduced a classification system for two-stroke oils, the JASO rating. This rating is in the form of two letters, either FA, FB or FC – FA is the lowest classification and FC the highest. Ensure the oil being used meets or exceeds the recommended rating specified by the manufacturer.

● As well as ensuring the oil rating matches the recommendation, another consideration to make when buying engine oil is whether to purchase a standard mineral-based oil, a semi-synthetic oil (also known as a synthetic blend or synthetic-based oil) or a fully-synthetic oil. The cost of each type of oil varies considerably; mineral-based oils are the cheapest, the fully-synthetic oils the most expensive with the semi-synthetic oils falling somewhere in-between. This decision is very much up to the owner, but it should be noted that modern synthetic oils have far better lubricating properties and burn cleaner than traditional mineral-based oils. It is therefore recommended that a fully synthetic oil is used. The extra expense could save you money in the long term by preventing premature engine wear, engine performance will be improved, carbon deposits and exhaust smoke will be reduced.

● Always ensure that the oil is specifically designed for use in an injector system. Many high quality two-stroke oils are designed for competition use and need to be pre-mixed with fuel. These oils are of a much higher viscosity and are not designed to flow through the injector pumps used on road-going two-stroke motorcycles.

Transmission (gear) oil

● On a two-stroke engine, the transmission and clutch are lubricated by their own separate oil bath which must be changed in accordance with the Maintenance Schedule.
● Although the engine and transmission units of most four-strokes use a common lubrication supply, there are some exceptions where the engine and gearbox have separate oil reservoirs and a dry clutch is used.
● Motorcycle manufacturers will either recommend a monograde transmission oil or a four-stroke multigrade engine oil to lubricate the transmission.
● Transmission oils, or gear oils as they are often called, are designed specifically for use in transmission systems. The viscosity of these oils is represented by an SAE number, but the scale of measurement applied is different to that used to grade engine oils. As a rough guide a SAE90 gear oil will be of the same viscosity as an SAE50 engine oil.

Shaft drive oil

● On models equipped with shaft final drive, the shaft drive gears are will have their own oil supply. The manufacturer will state a recommended 'type or classification' and also a specific 'viscosity' range in the same manner as for four-stroke engine oil.
● Gear oil classification is given by the number which follows the API GL (GL standing for gear lubricant) rating, the higher the number, the higher the specification of the oil, e.g. API GL5 oil is a higher specification than API GL4 oil. Ensure the oil meets or

exceeds the classification specified and is of the correct viscosity. The viscosity of gear oils is also represented by an SAE number but the scale of measurement used is different to that used to grade engine oils. As a rough guide an SAE90 gear oil will be of the same viscosity as an SAE50 engine oil.
● If the use of an EP (Extreme Pressure) gear oil is specified, ensure the oil purchased is suitable.

Fork oil and suspension fluid

● Conventional telescopic front forks are hydraulic and require fork oil to work. To ensure the forks function correctly, the fork oil must be changed in accordance with the Maintenance Schedule.
● Fork oil is available in a variety of viscosities, identified by their SAE rating; fork oil ratings vary from light (SAE 5) to heavy (SAE 30). When purchasing fork oil, ensure the viscosity rating matches that specified by the manufacturer.
● Some lubricant manufacturers also produce a range of high-quality suspension fluids which are very similar to fork oil but are designed mainly for competition use. These fluids may have a different viscosity rating system which is not to be confused with the SAE rating of normal fork oil. Refer to the manufacturer's instructions if in any doubt.

Brake and clutch fluid

● All disc brake systems and some clutch systems are hydraulically operated. To ensure correct operation, the hydraulic fluid must be changed in accordance with the Maintenance Schedule.
● Brake and clutch fluid is classified by its DOT rating with most motorcycle manufacturers specifying DOT 3 or 4 fluid. Both fluid types are glycol-based and can be mixed together without adverse effect; DOT 4 fluid exceeds the requirements of DOT 3

fluid. Although it is safe to use DOT 4 fluid in a system designed for use with DOT 3 fluid, never use DOT 3 fluid in a system which specifies the use of DOT 4 as this will adversely affect the system's performance. The type required for the system will be marked on the fluid reservoir cap.
● Some manufacturers also produce a DOT 5 hydraulic fluid. DOT 5 hydraulic fluid is silicone-based and is not compatible with the glycol-based DOT 3 and 4 fluids. Never mix DOT 5 fluid with DOT 3 or 4 fluid as this will seriously affect the performance of the hydraulic system.

Coolant/antifreeze

● When purchasing coolant/antifreeze, always ensure it is suitable for use in an aluminium engine and contains corrosion inhibitors to prevent possible blockages of the internal coolant passages of the system. As a general rule, most coolants are designed to be used neat and should not be diluted whereas antifreeze can be mixed with distilled water to provide a coolant solution of the required strength. Refer to the manufacturer's instructions on the bottle.
● Ensure the coolant is changed in accordance with the Maintenance Schedule.

Chain lube

● Chain lube is an aerosol-type spray lubricant specifically designed for use on motorcycle final drive chains. Chain lube has two functions, to minimise friction between the final drive chain and sprockets and to prevent corrosion of the chain. Regular use of a good-quality chain lube will extend the life of the drive chain and sprockets and thus maximise the power being transmitted from the transmission to the rear wheel.
● When using chain lube, always allow some time for the solvents in the lube to evaporate before riding the motorcycle. This will minimise the amount of lube which will

'fling' off from the chain when the motorcycle is used. If the motorcycle is equipped with an 'O-ring' chain, ensure the chain lube is labelled as being suitable for use on 'O-ring' chains.

Degreasers and solvents

● There are many different types of solvents and degreasers available to remove the grime and grease which accumulate around the motorcycle during normal use. Degreasers and solvents are usually available as an aerosol-type spray or as a liquid which you apply with a brush. Always closely follow the manufacturer's instructions and wear eye protection during use. Be aware that many solvents are flammable and may give off noxious fumes; take adequate precautions when using them (see Safety First!).

● For general cleaning, use one of the many solvents or degreasers available from most motorcycle accessory shops. These solvents are usually applied then left for a certain time before being washed off with water.

Brake cleaner is a solvent specifically designed to remove all traces of oil, grease and dust from braking system components. Brake cleaner is designed to evaporate quickly and leaves behind no residue.

Carburettor cleaner is an aerosol-type solvent specifically designed to clear carburettor blockages and break down the hard deposits and gum often found inside carburettors during overhaul.

Contact cleaner is an aerosol-type solvent designed for cleaning electrical components. The cleaner will remove all traces of oil and dirt from components such as switch contacts or fouled spark plugs and then dry, leaving behind no residue.

Gasket remover is an aerosol-type solvent designed for removing stubborn gaskets from engine components during overhaul. Gasket remover will minimise the amount of scraping required to remove the gasket and therefore reduce the risk of damage to the mating surface.

Spray lubricants

● Aerosol-based spray lubricants are widely available and are excellent for lubricating lever pivots and exposed cables and switches. Try to use a lubricant which is of the dry-film type as the fluid evaporates, leaving behind a dry-film of lubricant. Lubricants which leave behind an oily residue will attract dust and dirt which will increase the rate of wear of the cable/lever.

● Most lubricants also act as a moisture dispersant and a penetrating fluid. This means they can also be used to 'dry out' electrical components such as wiring connectors or switches as well as helping to free seized fasteners.

Greases

● Grease is used to lubricate many of the pivot-points. A good-quality multi-purpose grease is suitable for most applications but some manufacturers will specify the use of specialist greases for use on components such as swingarm and suspension linkage bushes. These specialist greases can be purchased from most motorcycle (or car) accessory shops; commonly specified types include molybdenum disulphide grease, lithium-based grease, graphite-based grease, silicone-based grease and high-temperature copper-based grease.

Gasket sealing compounds

● Gasket sealing compounds can be used in conjunction with gaskets, to improve their sealing capabilities, or on their own to seal metal-to-metal joints. Depending on their type, sealing compounds either set hard or stay relatively soft and pliable.

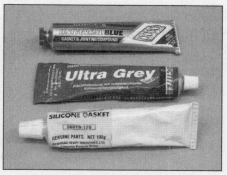

● When purchasing a gasket sealing compound, ensure that it is designed specifically for use on an internal combustion engine. General multi-purpose sealants available from DIY stores may appear visibly similar but they are not designed to withstand the extreme heat or contact with fuel and oil encountered when used on an engine (see 'Tools and Workshop Tips' for further information).

Thread locking compound

● Thread locking compounds are used to secure certain threaded fasteners in position to prevent them from loosening due to vibration. Thread locking compounds can be purchased from most motorcycle (and car) accessory shops. Ensure the threads of the both components are completely clean and dry before sparingly applying the locking compound (see 'Tools and Workshop Tips' for further information).

Fuel additives

● Fuel additives which protect and clean the fuel system components are widely available. These additives are designed to remove all traces of deposits that build up on the carburettors/injectors and prevent wear, helping the fuel system to operate more efficiently. If a fuel additive is being used, check that it is suitable for use with your motorcycle, especially if your motorcycle is equipped with a catalytic converter.

● Octane boosters are also available. These additives are designed to improve the performance of highly-tuned engines being run on normal pump-fuel and are of no real use on standard motorcycles.

About the MOT Test

In the UK, all vehicles more than three years old are subject to an annual test to ensure that they meet minimum safety requirements. A current test certificate must be issued before a machine can be used on public roads, and is required before a road fund licence can be issued. Riding without a current test certificate will also invalidate your insurance.

For most owners, the MOT test is an annual cause for anxiety, and this is largely due to owners not being sure what needs to be checked prior to submitting the motorcycle for testing. The simple answer is that a fully roadworthy motorcycle will have no difficulty in passing the test.

This is a guide to getting your motorcycle through the MOT test. Obviously it will not be possible to examine the motorcycle to the same standard as the professional MOT tester, particularly in view of the equipment required for some of the checks. However, working through the following procedures will enable you to identify any problem areas before submitting the motorcycle for the test.

It has only been possible to summarise the test requirements here, based on the regulations in force at the time of printing. Test standards are becoming increasingly stringent, although there are some exemptions for older vehicles. More information about the test and defect categories can be obtained from the MOT Inspection Manual for Motor Bicycle and Side Car testing at www.gov.uk.

Many of the checks require that one of the wheels is raised off the ground. If the motorcycle doesn't have a centre stand, note that an auxiliary stand will be required. Additionally, the help of an assistant may prove useful.

Check that the frame number is clearly visible.

Electrical System

Lights, turn signals, horn and reflector

● With the ignition on, check the operation of the following electrical components.
  a) *Headlight and tail light. Check that both illuminate in the low and high beam switch positions.*
  b) *Side lights. Check that the front sidelight or position light and tail light illuminate in this switch position.*
  c) *Turn signals. Check that all flash at the correct rate, and that the warning light(s) function correctly. Check that the turn signal switch works correctly.*
  d) *Hazard warning system (where fitted). Check that all four turn signals flash in this switch position.*
  e) *Brake stop light. Check that the light comes on when the front and rear brakes are independently applied.*
  f) *Horn. Check that the sound is continuous and of reasonable volume.*
● Check that there is a red reflector on the rear of the machine, either mounted separately or as part of the tail light lens.
● Check the condition of the headlight, tail light and turn signal lenses.

Headlight beam height

● The MOT tester will perform a headlight beam height check using specialised beam setting equipment **(see illustration 1)**.

This equipment will not be available to the home mechanic, but if you suspect that the headlight is incorrectly set or may have been maladjusted in the past, you can perform a rough test as follows.
● Position the bike in a straight line facing a brick wall. The bike must be off its stand, upright and with a rider seated. Measure the height from the ground to the centre of the headlight and mark a horizontal line on the wall at this height. Position the motorcycle 3.8 metres from the wall and draw a vertical line up the wall central to the centreline of the motorcycle. Switch to dipped beam and check that the beam pattern falls slightly lower than the horizontal line and to the left of the vertical line **(see illustration 2)**.

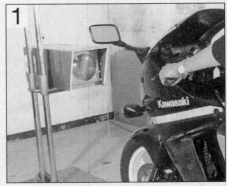

Headlight beam height checking equipment

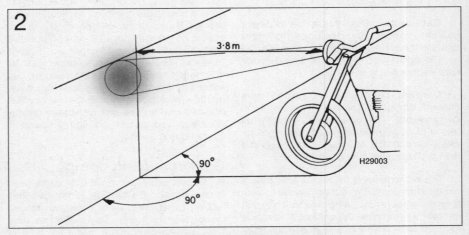

Home workshop beam alignment check

Exhaust System and Final Drive

Exhaust

● Check that the exhaust mountings are secure and that the system does not foul any of the rear suspension components.

● Start the motorcycle. When the revs are increased, check that the exhaust is neither holed nor leaking from any of its joints. On a linked system, check that the collector box is not leaking due to corrosion.

● Note that the exhaust decibel level ("loudness" of the exhaust) is assessed at the discretion of the tester. If the motorcycle was first used on or after 1st January 1985 the silencer must carry the BSAU 193 stamp, or a marking relating to its make and model, or be of OE (original equipment) manufacture. If the silencer is marked NOT FOR ROAD USE, RACING USE ONLY or similar, it will fail the MOT.

Final drive

● Check that the chain is in good condition and does not have excessive slack. Also check that the sprocket is securely mounted on the rear wheel hub. Check that the chain guard is in place.

Steering and Suspension

Steering

● With the front wheel raised off the ground, rotate the steering from lock to lock. The handlebar or switches must not contact the fuel tank or be close enough to trap the rider's hand. Problems can be caused by damaged lock stops on the lower yoke and frame, or by the fitting of non-standard handlebars.

● When performing the lock-to-lock check, also ensure that the steering moves freely without drag or notchiness. Steering movement can be impaired by poorly routed cables, or by overtight head bearings or worn bearings. The tester will perform a check of the steering head bearing lower race by mounting the front wheel on a surface plate, then performing a lock to lock check with the weight of the machine on the lower bearing (see illustration 3).

● Grasp the fork lowers and attempt to push and pull on the forks (see illustration 4).

Front wheel mounted on a surface plate for steering head bearing lower race check

Any play in the steering head bearings will be felt. Note that in extreme cases, wear of the front fork bushes can be misinterpreted for head bearing play.

● Check that the handlebars are securely mounted.

● Check that the handlebar grip rubbers are secure. They should by bonded to the bar left end and to the throttle cable pulley on the right end.

Front suspension

● With the motorcycle off the stand, hold the front brake on and pump the front forks up and down (see illustration 5). Check that they are adequately damped.

Checking the steering head bearings for freeplay

Hold the front brake on and pump the front forks up and down to check operation

Inspect the area around the fork dust seal for oil leakage (arrow)

Bounce the rear of the motorcycle to check rear suspension operation

Checking for rear suspension linkage play

● Inspect the area above and around the front fork oil seals **(see illustration 6)**. There should be no sign of oil leaking down the fork.

Rear suspension

● With the motorcycle off the stand and an assistant supporting the motorcycle by its handlebars, bounce the rear suspension **(see illustration 7)**. Check that the suspension components do not foul on any of the cycle parts and check that the shock absorber(s) provide adequate damping.

● Visually inspect the rear shock absorber and check that there is no sign of oil leakage from its damper.
● With the rear wheel raised off the ground, grasp the wheel at the highest point and attempt to pull it up **(see illustration 8)**. Any play in the swingarm pivot or suspension linkage bearings will be felt as movement **(see illustration 9)**.
● With the rear wheel raised off the ground, grasp the swingarm ends and attempt to move the swingarm from side to side and forwards and backwards – any play indicates wear of the swingarm pivot bearings **(see illustration 10)**.

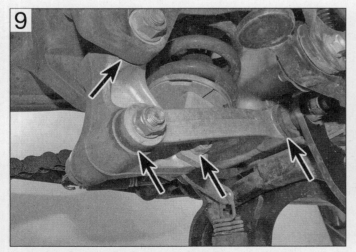

Worn suspension linkage pivots (arrows) are usually the cause of play in the rear suspension

Grasp the swingarm at the ends to check for play in its pivot bearings

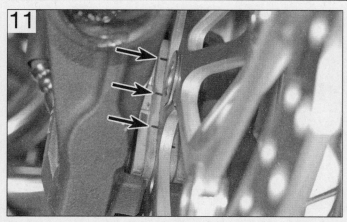

Brake pad wear can be viewed without removing the caliper. Most pads have wear indicator grooves (arrowed).

Check for wheel bearing play by trying to move the wheel about the axle (spindle)

Brakes, Wheels and Tyres

Brakes

● With the wheel raised off the ground, apply the brake then free it off, and check that the wheel is about to revolve freely without brake drag.

● Examine the discs. Check they are securely mounted and not cracked.

● View the pad material through the caliper mouth and check that the pads are not worn down beyond the limit **(see illustration 11)**.

● Examine the flexible hoses from top to bottom. Have an assistant hold the brake on so that the fluid in the hose is under pressure, and check that there is no sign of fluid leakage, bulges or cracking. If there are any metal brake pipes or unions, check that these are free from corrosion and damage.

● On models with ABS, check that the self-check warning light in the instrument panel works.

● The MOT tester will perform a test of the motorcycle's braking efficiency based on a calculation of rider and motorcycle weight. Although this cannot be carried out at home, you can at least ensure that the braking systems are properly maintained. Check the fluid level, lever/pedal feel (bleed of air if its spongy) and pad material.

Wheels and tyres

● Check the wheel condition. Spoked wheels should be checked for broken, corroded, loose or bent spokes.

● With the wheel raised off the ground, spin the wheel and visually check that the tyre and wheel run true. Check that the tyre does not foul the suspension or mudguards.

● With the wheel raised off the ground, grasp the wheel and attempt to move it about the axle (spindle) **(see illustration 12)**. Any play felt here indicates wheel bearing failure.

● Check the tyre tread depth, tread condition and sidewall condition **(see illustration 13)**.

● Check the tyre type. Front and rear tyre types must be compatible and be suitable for road use. Tyres marked NOT FOR ROAD USE, COMPETITION USE ONLY or similar, will fail the MOT.

● If the tyre sidewall carries a direction of rotation arrow, this must be pointing in the direction of normal wheel rotation **(see illustration 14)**.

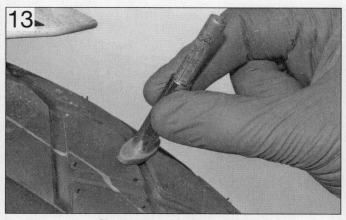

Checking the tyre tread depth

Tyre direction of rotation arrow can be found on tyre sidewall

Wheel axle nut (A) and clamp bolts (B)

Two straightedges are used to check wheel alignment

● Check that the wheel axle (spindle) nuts are properly secured (see illustration 15).
● Wheel alignment is checked with the motorcycle off the stand and a rider seated.

With the front wheel pointing straight ahead, two perfectly straight lengths of metal or wood and placed against the sidewalls of both tyres (see illustration 16). The gap each side of the front

tyre must be equidistant on both sides. Incorrect wheel alignment may be due to a cocked rear wheel (often as the result of poor chain adjustment) or in extreme cases, a bent frame.

General checks and condition

● Check the security of all major fasteners, bodypanels, seat, fairings (where fitted) and mudguards.

● Check that the rider and pillion footrests, handlebar levers, brake pedal and stand are securely mounted.
● Check that the fuel filler cap is secure.
● Check that there are no fluids leaking from

the motorcycle, i.e. fuel, engine oil, coolant and brake fluid.
● Check for corrosion on the frame or any load-bearing components. If severe, this may affect the structure, particularly under stress.

Sidecars

● A motorcycle fitted with a sidecar requires additional checks relating to the stability of the machine and security of attachment and

swivel joints, plus specific wheel alignment (toe-in) requirements. Additionally, tyre and lighting requirements differ from conventional

motorcycle use. Owners are advised to check MOT test requirements with an official test centre.

Preparing for storage

Before you start

If repairs or an overhaul is needed, see that this is carried out now rather than left until you want to ride the bike again.

Give the bike a good wash and scrub all dirt from its underside. Make sure the bike dries completely before preparing for storage.

Engine

● Remove the spark plug(s) and lubricate the cylinder bores with approximately a teaspoon of motor oil using a spout-type oil can **(see illustration 1)**. Reinstall the spark plug(s). Crank the engine over a couple of times to coat the piston rings and bores with oil. If the bike has a kickstart, use this to turn the engine over. If not, flick the kill switch to the OFF position and crank the engine over on the starter **(see illustration 2)**. If the nature on the ignition system prevents the starter operating with the kill switch in the OFF position, remove the spark plugs and fit them back in their caps; ensure that the plugs are earthed (grounded) against the cylinder head when the starter is operated **(see illustration 3)**.

 Warning: It is important that the plugs are earthed (grounded) away from the spark plug holes otherwise there is a risk of atomised fuel from the cylinders igniting.

 HAYNES HiNT *On a single cylinder four-stroke engine, you can seal the combustion chamber completely by positioning the piston at TDC on the compression stroke.*

● Drain the carburettor(s) otherwise there is a risk of jets becoming blocked by gum deposits from the fuel **(see illustration 4)**.

● If the bike is going into long-term storage, consider adding a fuel stabiliser to the fuel in the tank. If the tank is drained completely, corrosion of its internal surfaces may occur if left unprotected for a long period. The tank can be treated with a rust preventative especially for this purpose. Alternatively, remove the tank and pour half a litre of motor oil into it, install the filler cap and shake the tank to coat its internals with oil before draining off the excess. The same effect can also be achieved by spraying WD40 or a similar water-dispersant around the inside of the tank via its flexible nozzle.

● Make sure the cooling system contains the correct mix of antifreeze. Antifreeze also contains important corrosion inhibitors.

● The air intakes and exhaust can be sealed off by covering or plugging the openings. Ensure that you do not seal in any condensation; run the engine until it is hot,

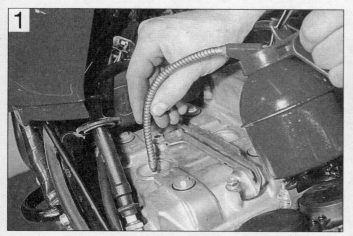

Squirt a drop of motor oil into each cylinder

Flick the kill switch to OFF . . .

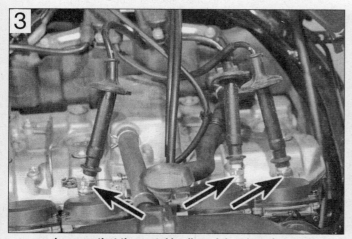

. . . and ensure that the metal bodies of the plugs (arrows) are earthed against the cylinder head

Connect a hose to the carburettor float chamber drain stub (arrow) and unscrew the drain screw

Exhausts can be sealed off with a plastic bag

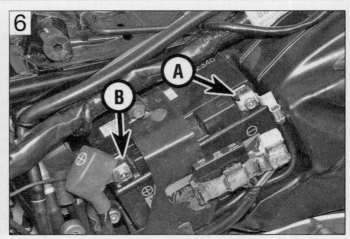
Disconnect the negative lead (A) first, followed by the positive lead (B)

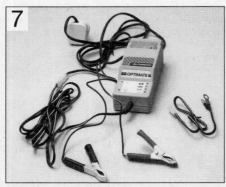
Use a suitable battery charger - this kit also assess battery condition

then switch off and allow to cool. Tape a piece of thick plastic over the silencer end(s) **(see illustration 5)**. Note that some advocate pouring a tablespoon of motor oil into the silencer(s) before sealing them off.

Battery – lead-acid type

● Remove it from the bike - in extreme cases of cold the battery may freeze and crack its case **(see illustration 6)**.

● Check the electrolyte level and top up if necessary (conventional refillable batteries). Clean the terminals.
● Store the battery off the motorcycle and away from any sources of fire. Position a wooden block under the battery if it is to sit on the ground.
● Give the battery a trickle charge for a few hours every month **(see illustration 7)**.

Tyres

● Place the bike on its centrestand or an auxiliary stand which will support the motorcycle in an upright position. Position wood blocks under the tyres to keep them off the ground and to provide insulation from damp. If the bike is being put into long-term storage, ideally both tyres should be off the ground; not only will this protect the tyres, but will also ensure that no load is placed on the steering head or wheel bearings.
● Deflate each tyre by 5 to 10 psi, no more or the beads may unseat from the rim, making subsequent inflation difficult on tubeless tyres.

Pivots and controls

● Lubricate all lever, pedal, stand and footrest

pivot points. If grease nipples are fitted to the rear suspension components, apply lubricant to the pivots.
● Lubricate all control cables.

Cycle components

● Apply a wax protectant to all painted and plastic components. Wipe off any excess, but don't polish to a shine. Where fitted, clean the screen with soap and water.
● Coat metal parts with Vaseline (petroleum jelly). When applying this to the fork tubes, do not compress the forks otherwise the seals will rot from contact with the Vaseline.
● Apply a vinyl cleaner to the seat.

Storage conditions

● Aim to store the bike in a shed or garage which does not leak and is free from damp.
● Drape an old blanket or bedspread over the bike to protect it from dust and direct contact with sunlight (which will fade paint). This also hides the bike from prying eyes. Beware of tight-fitting plastic covers which may allow condensation to form and settle on the bike.

Getting back on the road

Engine and transmission

● Change the oil and replace the oil filter. If this was done prior to storage, check that the oil hasn't emulsified - a thick whitish substance which occurs through condensation.
● Remove the spark plugs. Using a spout-type oil can, squirt a few drops of oil into the cylinder(s). This will provide initial lubrication as the piston rings and bores comes back into contact. Service the spark plugs, or fit new ones, and install them in the engine.

● Check that the clutch isn't stuck on. The plates can stick together if left standing for some time, preventing clutch operation. Engage a gear and try rocking the bike back and forth with the clutch lever held against the handlebar. If this doesn't work on cable-operated clutches, hold the clutch lever back against the handlebar with a strong elastic band or cable tie for a couple of hours **(see illustration 8)**.
● If the air intakes or silencer end(s) were blocked off, remove the bung or cover used.
● If the fuel tank was coated with a rust

Hold clutch lever back against the handlebar with elastic bands or a cable tie

preventative, oil or a stabiliser added to the fuel, drain and flush the tank and dispose of the fuel sensibly. If no action was taken with the fuel tank prior to storage, it is advised that the old fuel is disposed of since it will go off over a period of time. Refill the fuel tank with fresh fuel.

Frame and running gear

● Oil all pivot points and cables.
● Check the tyre pressures. They will definitely need inflating if pressures were reduced for storage.
● Lubricate the final drive chain (where applicable).
● Remove any protective coating applied to the fork tubes (stanchions) since this may well destroy the fork seals. If the fork tubes weren't protected and have picked up rust spots, remove them with very fine abrasive paper and refinish with metal polish.
● Check that both brakes operate correctly. Apply each brake hard and check that it's not possible to move the motorcycle forwards, then check that the brake frees off again once released. Brake caliper pistons can stick due to corrosion around the piston head, or on the sliding caliper types, due to corrosion of the slider pins. If the brake doesn't free after repeated operation, take the caliper off for examination. Similarly drum brakes can stick

due to a seized operating cam, cable or rod linkage.
● If the motorcycle has been in long-term storage, renew the brake fluid and clutch fluid (where applicable).
● Depending on where the bike has been stored, the wiring, cables and hoses may have been nibbled by rodents. Make a visual check and investigate disturbed wiring loom tape.

Battery

● If the battery has been previously removal and given top up charges it can simply be reconnected. Remember to connect the positive cable first and the negative cable last.
● On conventional refillable batteries, if the battery has not received any attention, remove it from the motorcycle and check its electrolyte level. Top up if necessary then charge the battery. If the battery fails to hold a charge and a visual checks show heavy white sulphation of the plates, the battery is probably defective and must be renewed. This is particularly likely if the battery is old. Confirm battery condition with a specific gravity check.
● On sealed (MF) batteries, if the battery has not received any attention, remove it from the motorcycle and charge it according to the information on the battery case - if the battery fails to hold a charge it must be renewed.

Starting procedure

● If a kickstart is fitted, turn the engine over a couple of times with the ignition OFF to distribute oil around the engine. If no kickstart is fitted, flick the engine kill switch OFF and the ignition ON and crank the engine over a couple of times to work oil around the upper cylinder components. If the nature of the ignition system is such that the starter won't work with the kill switch OFF, remove the spark plugs, fit them back into their caps and earth (ground) their bodies on the cylinder head. Reinstall the spark plugs afterwards.
● Switch the kill switch to RUN, operate the choke and start the engine. If the engine won't start don't continue cranking the engine - not only will this flatten the battery, but the starter motor will overheat. Switch the ignition off and try again later. If the engine refuses to start, go through the fault finding procedures in this manual. **Note:** *If the bike has been in storage for a long time, old fuel or a carburettor blockage may be the problem. Gum deposits in carburettors can block jets - if a carburettor cleaner doesn't prove successful the carburettors must be dismantled for cleaning.*

● Once the engine has started, check that the lights, turn signals and horn work properly.

● Treat the bike gently for the first ride and check all fluid levels on completion. Settle the bike back into the maintenance schedule.

Conversion factors

Length (distance)

Inches (in)	x 25.4	= Millimetres (mm)	x 0.0394	= Inches (in)
Feet (ft)	x 0.305	= Metres (m)	x 3.281	= Feet (ft)
Miles	x 1.609	= Kilometres (km)	x 0.621	= Miles

Volume (capacity)

Cubic inches (cu in; in³)	x 16.387	= Cubic centimetres (cc; cm³)	x 0.061	= Cubic inches (cu in; in³)
Imperial pints (Imp pt)	x 0.568	= Litres (l)	x 1.76	= Imperial pints (Imp pt)
Imperial quarts (Imp qt)	x 1.137	= Litres (l)	x 0.88	= Imperial quarts (Imp qt)
Imperial quarts (Imp qt)	x 1.201	= US quarts (US qt)	x 0.833	= Imperial quarts (Imp qt)
US quarts (US qt)	x 0.946	= Litres (l)	x 1.057	= US quarts (US qt)
Imperial gallons (Imp gal)	x 4.546	= Litres (l)	x 0.22	= Imperial gallons (Imp gal)
Imperial gallons (Imp gal)	x 1.201	= US gallons (US gal)	x 0.833	= Imperial gallons (Imp gal)
US gallons (US gal)	x 3.785	= Litres (l)	x 0.264	= US gallons (US gal)

Mass (weight)

Ounces (oz)	x 28.35	= Grams (g)	x 0.035	= Ounces (oz)
Pounds (lb)	x 0.454	= Kilograms (kg)	x 2.205	= Pounds (lb)

Force

Ounces-force (ozf; oz)	x 0.278	= Newtons (N)	x 3.6	= Ounces-force (ozf; oz)
Pounds-force (lbf; lb)	x 4.448	= Newtons (N)	x 0.225	= Pounds-force (lbf; lb)
Newtons (N)	x 0.1	= Kilograms-force (kgf; kg)	x 9.81	= Newtons (N)

Pressure

Pounds-force per square inch (psi; lbf/in²; lb/in²)	x 0.070	= Kilograms-force per square centimetre (kgf/cm²; kg/cm²)	x 14.223	= Pounds-force per square inch (psi; lbf/in²; lb/in²)
Pounds-force per square inch (psi; lbf/in²; lb/in²)	x 0.068	= Atmospheres (atm)	x 14.696	= Pounds-force per square inch (psi; lbf/in²; lb/in²)
Pounds-force per square inch (psi; lbf/in²; lb/in²)	x 0.069	= Bars	x 14.5	= Pounds-force per square inch (psi; lbf/in²; lb/in²)
Pounds-force per square inch (psi; lbf/in²; lb/in²)	x 6.895	= Kilopascals (kPa)	x 0.145	= Pounds-force per square inch (psi; lbf/in²; lb/in²)
Kilopascals (kPa)	x 0.01	= Kilograms-force per square centimetre (kgf/cm²; kg/cm²)	x 98.1	= Kilopascals (kPa)
Millibar (mbar)	x 100	= Pascals (Pa)	x 0.01	= Millibar (mbar)
Millibar (mbar)	x 0.0145	= Pounds-force per square inch (psi; lbf/in²; lb/in²)	x 68.947	= Millibar (mbar)
Millibar (mbar)	x 0.75	= Millimetres of mercury (mmHg)	x 1.333	= Millibar (mbar)
Millibar (mbar)	x 0.401	= Inches of water (inH₂O)	x 2.491	= Millibar (mbar)
Millimetres of mercury (mmHg)	x 0.535	= Inches of water (inH₂O)	x 1.868	= Millimetres of mercury (mmHg)
Inches of water (inH₂O)	x 0.036	= Pounds-force per square inch (psi; lbf/in²; lb/in²)	x 27.68	= Inches of water (inH₂O)

Torque (moment of force)

Pounds-force inches (lbf in; lb in)	x 1.152	= Kilograms-force centimetre (kgf cm; kg cm)	x 0.868	= Pounds-force inches (lbf in; lb in)
Pounds-force inches (lbf in; lb in)	x 0.113	= Newton metres (Nm)	x 8.85	= Pounds-force inches (lbf in; lb in)
Pounds-force inches (lbf in; lb in)	x 0.083	= Pounds-force feet (lbf ft; lb ft)	x 12	= Pounds-force inches (lbf in; lb in)
Pounds-force feet (lbf ft; lb ft)	x 0.138	= Kilograms-force metres (kgf m; kg m)	x 7.233	= Pounds-force feet (lbf ft; lb ft)
Pounds-force feet (lbf ft; lb ft)	x 1.356	= Newton metres (Nm)	x 0.738	= Pounds-force feet (lbf ft; lb ft)
Newton metres (Nm)	x 0.102	= Kilograms-force metres (kgf m; kg m)	x 9.804	= Newton metres (Nm)

Power

Horsepower (hp)	x 745.7	= Watts (W)	x 0.0013	= Horsepower (hp)

Velocity (speed)

Miles per hour (miles/hr; mph)	x 1.609	= Kilometres per hour (km/hr; kph)	x 0.621	= Miles per hour (miles/hr; mph)

Fuel consumption*

Miles per gallon, Imperial (mpg)	x 0.354	= Kilometres per litre (km/l)	x 2.825	= Miles per gallon, Imperial (mpg)
Miles per gallon, US (mpg)	x 0.425	= Kilometres per litre (km/l)	x 2.352	= Miles per gallon, US (mpg)

Temperature

Degrees Fahrenheit = (°C x 1.8) + 32   Degrees Celsius (Degrees Centigrade; °C) = (°F - 32) x 0.56

* It is common practice to convert from miles per gallon (mpg) to litres/100 kilometres (l/100km), where mpg x l/100 km = 282

This Section provides an easy reference-guide to the more common faults that are likely to afflict your machine. Obviously, the opportunities are almost limitless for faults to occur as a result of obscure failures, and to try and cover all eventualities would require a book. Indeed, a number have been written on the subject.

Successful troubleshooting is not a mysterious 'black art' but the application of a bit of knowledge combined with a systematic and logical approach to the problem. Approach any troubleshooting by first accurately identifying the symptom and then checking through the list of possible causes, starting with the simplest or most obvious and progressing in stages to the most complex.

Take nothing for granted, but above all apply liberal quantities of common sense.

The main symptom of a fault is given in the text as a major heading below which are listed the various systems or areas which may contain the fault. Details of each possible cause for a fault and the remedial action to be taken are given, in brief, in the paragraphs below each heading. Further information should be sought in the relevant Chapter.

Engine doesn't start or is difficult to start

☐ Starter motor doesn't rotate
☐ Starter motor rotates but engine does not turn over
☐ Starter works but engine won't turn over (seized)
☐ No fuel flow
☐ Engine flooded
☐ No spark or weak spark
☐ Compression low
☐ Stalls after starting or rough idle

Poor running at low speeds

☐ Spark weak
☐ Fuel/air mixture incorrect
☐ Compression low
☐ Poor acceleration

Poor running or no power at high speed

☐ Firing incorrect
☐ Fuel/air mixture incorrect
☐ Compression low
☐ Knocking or pinking
☐ Miscellaneous causes

Overheating

☐ Engine overheats
☐ Firing incorrect
☐ Fuel/air mixture incorrect
☐ Compression too high
☐ Engine load excessive
☐ Lubrication inadequate
☐ Miscellaneous causes

Clutch problems

☐ Clutch slipping
☐ Clutch not disengaging completely

Gearchanging problems

☐ Doesn't go into gear, or on models with standard transmission lever doesn't return
☐ Jumps out of gear
☐ Overselects

Abnormal engine noise

☐ Knocking or pinking
☐ Piston slap or rattling
☐ Valve noise
☐ Other noise

Abnormal driveline noise

☐ Clutch noise
☐ Transmission noise
☐ Final drive noise

Abnormal frame and suspension noise

☐ Front end noise
☐ Shock absorber noise
☐ Brake noise

Oil pressure warning light comes on

☐ Engine lubrication system
☐ Electrical system

Excessive exhaust smoke

☐ White smoke
☐ Black smoke
☐ Brown smoke

Poor handling or stability

☐ Handlebar hard to turn
☐ Handlebar shakes or vibrates excessively
☐ Machine pulls to one side
☐ Poor shock absorbing qualities

Braking problems

☐ Brakes are spongy, don't hold
☐ Brake lever or pedal pulsates
☐ Brakes drag

Electrical problems

☐ Battery dead or weak
☐ Battery overcharged

Engine doesn't start or is difficult to start

Starter motor doesn't rotate

☐ Engine kill switch OFF.
☐ Fuse blown. Check the main fuse and the FI and engine stop fuses (see Chapter 8).
☐ Battery voltage low. Check and recharge battery (see Chapter 8).
☐ Starter motor defective. Make sure the wiring to the starter is secure. Make sure the starter relay clicks when the start button is pushed. If the relay clicks, then the fault is in the wiring or motor (see Chapter 8).
☐ Starter switch not contacting. The contacts could be wet, corroded or dirty. Disassemble and clean the switch (see Chapter 8).
☐ Wiring open or shorted. Check all wiring connections and harnesses to make sure that they are dry, tight and not corroded. Also check for broken or frayed wires that can cause a short to earth (ground) (see Chapter 8).
☐ Ignition switch defective. Check the switch and replace with a new one if it is defective (see Chapter 8).
☐ Engine kill switch defective. Check for wet, dirty or corroded contacts. Clean or replace the switch with a new one as necessary (see Chapter 8).
☐ Faulty neutral switch, sidestand switch or clutch switch. Check the wiring to each switch and the switch itself (see Chapter 8).
☐ Faulty diode (see Chapter 8).
☐ Fuel injection system shutdown due to system fault (see Chapter 4).

Starter motor rotates but engine does not turn over

☐ Starter clutch defective. Inspect and repair or replace with a new one (see Chapter 2).
☐ Damaged idler or starter gears. Inspect and replace the damaged parts (see Chapter 2).

Starter works but engine won't turn over (seized)

☐ Seized engine caused by one or more internally damaged components. Failure due to wear, abuse or lack of lubrication. Damage can include seized valves, camshafts, pistons, crankshaft, connecting rod bearings, or transmission gears or bearings.

No fuel flow

☐ No fuel in tank.
☐ Fuel tank breather/EVAP hose obstructed (see Chapter 4).
☐ Faulty fuel pump relay. Check the relay (see Chapter 4).
☐ Fuel pump faulty or blocked (see Chapter 4).
☐ Fuel hose clogged. Remove the fuel hose and carefully blow through it (see Chapter 4).
☐ Fuel rail or injector clogged. For both of the injectors to be clogged, either a very bad batch of fuel has been used, or some other foreign material has entered the tank. In some cases, if a machine has been unused for several months, the fuel turns to a varnish-like liquid that can cause an injector needle to stick to its seat. Use an injection system cleaner fuel additive, following the manufacturer's instructions – it is best to first drain the tank and fuel system and add the recommended amount of fresh fuel. If necessary remove the fuel rail and injectors and have the injectors cleaned (see Chapter 4).

Engine flooded

☐ Injector needle valve worn or stuck open causing excess fuel to be admitted to the throttle body. In this case, the injector should be replaced with a new one (see Chapter 4).
☐ Starting technique incorrect. Under normal circumstances (i.e. if all the components of the fuel injection system are good) the machine should start with the throttle closed.

No spark or weak spark

☐ Ignition switch OFF.
☐ Engine kill switch turned to the OFF position.
☐ Ignition or kill switch shorted. This is usually caused by water, corrosion, damage or excessive wear. The switches can be disassembled and cleaned with electrical contact cleaner (see Chapter 8). If cleaning does not help, replace the switches.
☐ Battery voltage low. Check and recharge the battery as necessary (see Chapter 8).
☐ Spark plug caps not making good contact. Make sure that the caps fit snugly over the plug ends (see Chapter 1).
☐ Spark plugs dirty, defective or worn out. Locate reason for fouled plugs using spark plug condition pictures and follow the plug maintenance procedures (see Chapter 1).
☐ Incorrect spark plugs. Wrong type or heat range. Check and install correct plugs (see Chapter 1).
☐ Ignition coil or spark plug cap defective. Test and renew if necessary (see Chapter 4).
☐ Fuel injection system shutdown due to system fault (see Chapter 4).
☐ Crankshaft position (CKP) sensor defective (see Chapter 4).
☐ Faulty engine stop relay or lean angle sensor (see Chapter 4).
☐ Engine/powertrain control module (ECM/PCM) defective (see Chapter 4).
☐ Wiring shorted or broken between:
Ignition switch and engine kill switch (or blown fuse)
ECM and engine kill switch
ECM and ignition coils
ECM and CKP sensor
☐ Make sure that all wiring connections are clean, dry and tight. Look for chafed and broken wires.

Compression low

☐ Spark plugs loose. Remove the plugs and inspect their threads (see Chapter 1). Reinstall and tighten correctly.
☐ Cylinder head not sufficiently tightened down. If the cylinder head is suspected of being loose, then there's a chance that the gasket or head is damaged if the problem has persisted for any length of time. The head bolts should be tightened to the proper torque and in the correct sequence (see Chapter 2).
☐ Improper valve clearance. This means that the valve is not closing completely and compression pressure is leaking past the valve. Check and adjust the valve clearances (see Chapter 1).
☐ Cylinder and/or piston worn. Excessive wear will cause compression pressure to leak past the rings. This is usually accompanied by worn rings as well. A top-end overhaul is necessary (see Chapter 2).
☐ Piston rings worn, weak, broken, or sticking. Broken or sticking piston rings usually indicate a lubrication or fuelling problem that causes excess carbon deposits to form on the pistons and rings. Top-end overhaul is necessary (see Chapter 2).
☐ Piston ring-to-groove clearance excessive. This is caused by excessive wear of the piston ring lands. Fit new piston(s) (see Chapter 2).
☐ Cylinder head gasket damaged. If a head is allowed to become loose, or if excessive carbon build-up on the piston crown and combustion chamber causes extremely high compression, the head gasket may leak. Retorquing the head is not always sufficient to restore the seal, so a new gasket is necessary (see Chapter 2).
☐ Cylinder head warped. This is caused by overheating or improperly tightened head bolts. Machine shop resurfacing or a new head is necessary (see Chapter 2).
☐ Valve spring broken or weak. Caused by component failure or wear. The springs must be replaced with new ones (see Chapter 2).
☐ Valve not seating properly. This is caused by a bent valve (from over-revving or improper valve adjustment), burned valve or seat (improper fuelling) or an accumulation of carbon deposits on the seat. The valves must be cleaned and/or renewed and the seats serviced (see Chapter 2).

Engine doesn't start or is difficult to start (continued

Stalls after starting or rough idle

- [ ] Engine idle speed incorrect. Faulty idle speed control system (see Chapter 1).
- [ ] Ignition malfunction (see Chapter 4).
- [ ] Fuel injection system malfunction (see Chapter 4).
- [ ] Fuel contaminated. The fuel can be contaminated with either

dirt or water, or can change chemically if the machine has been unused for several months. Drain the tank and fuel system (see Chapter 4).
- [ ] Intake air leak. Check for loose throttle body-to-intake duct connections or a loose or damaged PAIR vacuum hose (see Chapter 4).
- [ ] Air filter clogged. Fit new air filters (see Chapter 1).

Poor running at low speeds

Spark weak

- [ ] Battery voltage low. Check and recharge battery (see Chapter 8).
- [ ] Spark plug caps not making good contact. Make sure that the caps fit snugly over the plug ends (see Chapter 1).
- [ ] Spark plugs dirty, defective or worn out. Locate reason for fouled plugs using spark plug condition pictures and follow the plug maintenance procedures (see Chapter 1).
- [ ] Incorrect spark plugs. Wrong type or heat range. Check and install correct plugs (see Chapter 1).
- [ ] Ignition coil or spark plug cap defective. Test and replace with a new one if necessary (see Chapter 4).

Fuel/air mixture incorrect

- [ ] Fuel tank breather/EVAP hose obstructed (see Chapter 4).
- [ ] Fuel pump faulty or blocked (see Chapter 4).
- [ ] Fuel hose clogged. Remove the fuel hose and carefully blow through it (see Chapter 4).
- [ ] Fuel rail or injector clogged. For both of the injectors to be clogged, either a very bad batch of fuel has been used, or some other foreign material has entered the tank. In some cases, if a machine has been unused for several months, the fuel turns to a varnish-like liquid that can cause an injector needle to stick to its seat. Use an injection system cleaner fuel additive, following the manufacturer's instructions – it is best to first drain the tank and fuel system and add the recommended amount of fresh fuel. If necessary remove the fuel rail and injectors and have the injectors cleaned (see Chapter 4).
- [ ] Intake air leak. Check for loose throttle body-to-intake duct connections, or loose or damaged vacuum hoses (see Chapter 4).
- [ ] Air filter clogged. Fit new air filters (see Chapter 1).

Compression low

- [ ] Spark plugs loose. Remove the plugs and inspect their threads (see Chapter 1). Reinstall and tighten correctly.
- [ ] Cylinder head not sufficiently tightened down. If the cylinder head is suspected of being loose, then there's a chance that the gasket or head is damaged if the problem has persisted for any length of time. The head bolts should be tightened to the proper torque and in the correct sequence (see Chapter 2).
- [ ] Improper valve clearance. This means that the valve is not closing

completely and compression pressure is leaking past the valve. Check and adjust the valve clearances (see Chapter 1).
- [ ] Cylinder and/or piston worn. Excessive wear will cause compression pressure to leak past the rings. This is usually accompanied by worn rings as well. A top-end overhaul is necessary (see Chapter 2).
- [ ] Piston rings worn, weak, broken, or sticking. Broken or sticking piston rings usually indicate a lubrication or fuelling problem that causes excess carbon deposits to form on the pistons and rings. Top-end overhaul is necessary (see Chapter 2).
- [ ] Piston ring-to-groove clearance excessive. This is caused by excessive wear of the piston ring lands. Piston renewal is necessary (see Chapter 2).
- [ ] Cylinder head gasket damaged. If the head is allowed to become loose, or if excessive carbon build-up on the piston crown and combustion chamber causes extremely high compression, the head gasket may leak. Retorquing the head is not always sufficient to restore the seal, so a new gasket is necessary (see Chapter 2).
- [ ] Cylinder head warped. This is caused by overheating or improperly tightened head bolts. Machine shop resurfacing or head renewal is necessary (see Chapter 2).
- [ ] Valve spring broken or weak. Caused by component failure or wear. The springs must be replaced with new ones (see Chapter 2).
- [ ] Valve not seating properly. This is caused by a bent valve (from over-revving or improper valve adjustment), burned valve or seat (improper fuelling) or an accumulation of carbon deposits on the seat (from fuelling or lubrication problems).
- [ ] The valves must be cleaned and/or renewed (see Chapter 2).

Poor acceleration

- [ ] Timing not advancing. The crankshaft position sensor (CKP) or the engine/powertrain control module (ECM/PCM) may be defective (see Chapter 4).
- [ ] Engine oil viscosity too high. Using a heavier oil than that recommended can damage the oil pump or lubrication system and cause drag on the engine. Drain the oil and fill with the recommended grade and quantity (see Chapter 1).
- [ ] Brakes dragging. Usually caused by debris which has entered the brake caliper piston seals, or from a warped disc or bent axle (see Chapter 6).

Poor running or no power at high speed

Firing incorrect

☐ Spark plug caps not making good contact. Make sure that the caps fit snugly over the plug ends and that the wiring is secure (see Chapter 1).

☐ Spark plugs dirty, defective or worn out. Locate reason for fouled plugs using spark plug condition pictures and follow the plug maintenance procedures (see Chapter 1).

☐ Incorrect spark plugs. Wrong type or heat range. Check and install correct plugs (see Chapter 1).

☐ Ignition coil or spark plug cap defective. Test and renew if necessary (see Chapter 4).

☐ Faulty ECM/PCM (engine/powertrain control module) (see Chapter 4).

Fuel/air mixture incorrect

☐ Fuel tank breather/EVAP hose obstructed (see Chapter 4).

☐ Fuel pump faulty or blocked (see Chapter 4).

☐ Fuel hose clogged. Remove the fuel hose and carefully blow through it (see Chapter 4).

☐ Fuel rail or injector clogged. For both of the injectors to be clogged, either a very bad batch of fuel has been used, or some other foreign material has entered the tank. In some cases, if a machine has been unused for several months, the fuel turns to a varnish-like liquid that can cause an injector needle to stick to its seat. Use an injection system cleaner fuel additive, following the manufacturer's instructions – it is best to first drain the tank and fuel system and add the recommended amount of fresh fuel. If necessary remove the fuel rail and injectors and have the injectors cleaned (see Chapter 4).

☐ Intake air leak. Check for loose throttle body-to-intake duct connections (see Chapter 4).

☐ Air filter clogged. Fit new air filters (see Chapter 1).

Compression low

☐ Spark plugs loose. Remove the plugs and inspect their threads. Reinstall and tighten correctly (see Chapter 2).

☐ Cylinder head not sufficiently tightened down. If the cylinder head is suspected of being loose, then there's a chance that the gasket or head is damaged if the problem has persisted for any length of time. The head bolts should be tightened to the proper torque and in the correct sequence (see Chapter 2).

☐ Improper valve clearance. This means that the valve is not closing completely and compression pressure is leaking past the valve. Check and adjust the valve clearances (see Chapter 1).

☐ Cylinder and/or piston worn. Excessive wear will cause compression pressure to leak past the rings. This is usually accompanied by worn rings as well. A top-end overhaul is necessary (see Chapter 2).

☐ Piston rings worn, weak, broken, or sticking. Broken or sticking piston rings usually indicate a lubrication or fuelling problem that causes excess carbon deposits to form on the pistons and rings. Top-end overhaul is necessary (see Chapter 1).

☐ Piston ring-to-groove clearance excessive. This is caused by excessive wear of the piston ring lands. Piston renewal is necessary (see Chapter 1).

☐ Cylinder head gasket damaged. If a head is allowed to become loose, or if excessive carbon build-up on the piston crown and combustion chamber causes extremely high compression, the head gasket may leak. Retorquing the head is not always sufficient to restore the seal, so a new gasket is necessary (see Chapter 1).

☐ Cylinder head warped. This is caused by overheating or improperly tightened head bolts. Machine shop resurfacing or head renewal is necessary (see Chapter 1).

☐ Valve spring broken or weak. Caused by component failure or wear. The springs must be replaced with new ones (see Chapter 2).

☐ Valve not seating properly. This is caused by a bent valve (from over-revving or improper valve adjustment), burned valve or seat (improper fuelling) or an accumulation of carbon deposits on the seat (from fuelling or lubrication problems). The valves must be cleaned and/or renewed (see Chapter 2).

Knocking or pinking

☐ Carbon build-up in combustion chamber. Use of a fuel additive that will dissolve the adhesive bonding the carbon particles to the piston crown and chamber is the easiest way to remove the build-up. Otherwise, the cylinder head will have to be removed and decarbonised (see Chapter 2).

☐ Incorrect or poor quality fuel. Old or improper grades of fuel can cause detonation. This causes the pistons to rattle, thus the knocking or pinking sound. Drain old fuel and always use the recommended fuel grade (see Chapter 4).

☐ Spark plug heat range incorrect. Uncontrolled detonation indicates the plug heat range is too hot. The plug in effect becomes a glow plug, raising cylinder temperatures. Install the proper heat range plug (see Chapter 1).

☐ Improper air/fuel mixture. This will cause the cylinders to run hot, which leads to detonation. A blockage in the fuel system or an air leak can cause this imbalance (see Chapter 4).

Miscellaneous causes

☐ Throttle valve doesn't open fully. On 2016/17 models check the throttle cables and twistgrip freeplay (see Chapter 1). On 2018-on models check for a fault code related to the TBW system (see Chapter 4).

☐ Clutch slipping due loose or worn clutch components (see Chapter 2).

☐ Timing not advancing. The crankshaft position sensor (CKP) or the engine/powertrain control module (ECM/PCM) may be defective. If so, they must be replaced with new ones (see Chapter 4).

☐ Engine oil viscosity too high. Using a heavier oil than the one recommended can damage the oil pump or lubrication system and cause drag on the engine. Drain the oil and fill with the specified grade and quantity (see Chapter 1).

☐ Brakes dragging. Usually caused by debris which has entered the brake caliper piston seals, or from a warped disc or bent axle (see Chapter 1).

Overheating

Engine overheats

☐ Coolant level low. Check the level and add coolant (see *pre-ride checks*).

☐ Leak in cooling system. Check cooling system hoses and radiator for leaks and other damage (see Chapter 1). Repair or renew parts as necessary.

☐ Faulty thermostat (see Chapter 3).

☐ Faulty radiator cap. Remove the cap and have it pressure tested, or just fit a new one as they are not expensive (see Chapter 1).

☐ Coolant passages clogged. Drained, flush and refill the system with fresh coolant (see Chapter 1).

☐ Water pump defective. Remove and check the pump (see Chapter 1).

☐ Clogged or damaged radiator fins (see Chapter 1).

☐ Faulty cooling fan, relay or ECT sensor (see Chapter 3).

Firing incorrect

☐ Wrongly connected ignition coil wiring or plug leads (see Chapter 4).

☐ Spark plugs dirty, defective or worn out. Locate reason for fouled plugs using spark plug condition pictures and follow the plug maintenance procedures (see Chapter 1).

☐ Incorrect spark plugs. Wrong type or heat range. Check and install correct plugs (see Chapter 1).

☐ Ignition coil or spark plug cap defective. Test and replace with a new one if necessary (see Chapter 4).

☐ Faulty ECM/PCM (engine/powertrain control module).

Fuel/air mixture incorrect

☐ Fuel tank breather/EVAP hose obstructed (see Chapter 4).

☐ Fuel pump faulty or blocked (see Chapter 4).

☐ Fuel hose clogged. Remove the fuel hose and carefully blow through it (see Chapter 4).

☐ Fuel rail or injector clogged. For both of the injectors to be clogged, either a very bad batch of fuel has been used, or some other foreign material has entered the tank. In some cases, if a machine has been unused for several months, the fuel turns to a varnish-like liquid that can cause an injector needle to stick to its seat. Use an injection system cleaner fuel additive, following the manufacturer's instructions – it is best to first drain the tank and fuel system and add the recommended amount of fresh fuel. If necessary remove the fuel rail and injectors and have the injectors cleaned (see Chapter 4).

☐ Intake air leak. Check for loose throttle body-to-intake duct connections (see Chapter 4).

☐ Air filter clogged. Fit new air filter elements (see Chapter 1).

Compression too high

☐ Carbon build-up in combustion chamber. Use of a fuel additive that will dissolve the adhesive bonding the carbon particles to the piston crown and chamber is the easiest way to remove the build-up. Otherwise, the cylinder head will have to be removed and decarbonised (see Chapter 2).

☐ Improperly machined head surface or installation of incorrect gasket during engine assembly (see Chapter 2).

Engine load excessive

☐ Clutch slipping due to loose or worn clutch components (see Chapter 2).

☐ Engine oil level too high. Too much oil will cause pressurisation of the crankcase and inefficient engine operation. Check Specifications and drain to proper level (see Chapter 1).

☐ Engine oil viscosity too high. Using a heavier oil than the one recommended can damage the oil pump or lubrication system as well as cause drag on the engine.

☐ Brakes dragging. Usually caused by debris which has entered the brake caliper piston seals, or from a warped disc or bent axle (see Chapter 6).

Lubrication inadequate

☐ Engine oil level too low. Friction caused by intermittent lack of lubrication or from oil that is overworked can cause overheating. The oil provides a definite cooling function in the engine. Check the oil level (see *Pre-ride checks*).

☐ Low engine oil pressure. Check the pressure (see Chapter 2).

☐ Blocked oil filter. Fit a new one (see Chapter 1).

☐ Poor quality engine oil or incorrect viscosity or type. Oil is rated not only according to viscosity but also according to type. Some oils are not rated high enough for use in this engine. Check the Specifications section and change to the correct oil (see Chapter 1).

Miscellaneous causes

☐ Modification to exhaust system. Most aftermarket exhaust systems cause the engine to run leaner, which make them run hotter. When installing an accessory exhaust system, always check with the manufacturer/supplier as to whether the ECM/PCM requires re-mapping.

Clutch problems

Clutch slipping

☐ Insufficient clutch cable freeplay (models with standard transmission). Check and adjust (see Chapter 1).

☐ Clutch plates worn or warped. Overhaul the clutch (see Chapter 2).

☐ Clutch springs broken or weak (models with standard transmission) (see Chapter 2).

☐ Faulty clutch release mechanism (models with standard transmission). Replace any defective parts with new ones (see Chapter 2).

☐ Clutch centre or housing unevenly worn. This causes improper engagement of the plates. Replace the damaged or worn parts.

☐ Faulty DCT system (models with DCT) (see Chapters 2 and 4).

Clutch not disengaging completely

☐ Excessive clutch cable freeplay (models with standard transmission). Check and adjust (see Chapter 1).

☐ Faulty clutch release mechanism (models with standard transmission). Replace any defective parts with new ones (see Chapter 2).

☐ Clutch plates warped or damaged. This will cause clutch drag, which in turn will cause the machine to creep. Overhaul the clutch assembly (see Chapter 2).

☐ Clutch springs fatigued or broken (models with standard transmission) (see Chapter 2).

☐ Engine oil deteriorated. Old, thin oil will not provide proper lubrication for the plates, causing the clutch to drag. Change the oil and filter (see Chapter 1).

☐ Engine oil viscosity too high. Using a heavier oil than recommended can cause the plates to stick together. Change to the correct weight oil (see Chapter 1).

☐ Clutch housing guide seized on the transmission input shaft (models with standard transmission). Lack of lubrication, severe wear or damage can cause the bearing to seize. Overhaul of the clutch, and perhaps transmission, may be necessary to repair the damage (see Chapter 2).

☐ Loose clutch centre nut (models with standard transmission). Causes housing and centre misalignment putting a drag on the engine. Engagement adjustment continually varies. Overhaul the clutch (see Chapter 2).

☐ Faulty DCT system (models with DCT) (see Chapters 2 and 4).

Gearchanging problems

Doesn't go into gear, or on models with standard transmission lever doesn't return

☐ Clutch not disengaging (above).

☐ Gearchange mechanism stopper arm spring weak or broken, or arm roller broken or worn. Replace the spring or arm with a new one (see Chapter 2).

☐ Selector fork(s) bent, worn or seized. Overhaul the transmission (see Chapter 2).

☐ Gear(s) stuck on shaft. Most often caused by a lack of lubrication or excessive wear in transmission bearings and bushes. Overhaul the transmission (see Chapter 2).

☐ Selector drum binding. Caused by lubrication failure or excessive wear. Fit a new drum and/or its bearing(s) (see Chapter 2).

☐ Gearchange mechanism return spring weak or broken (see Chapter 2).

☐ Gearchange linkage arm broken. Splines stripped out of arm or shaft, caused by a loose linkage arm pinch bolt or from dropping the machine (see Chapter 2).

☐ Faulty DCT system (see Chapters 2 and 4).

Jumps out of gear

☐ Selector fork(s) worn (see Chapter 2).

☐ Selector fork groove(s) in selector drum worn (see Chapter 2).

☐ Gear pinion dogs or dog slots worn or damaged. The gear pinions should be inspected and renewed (see Chapter 2). No attempt should be made to repair the worn parts.

☐ Faulty DCT system (see Chapters 2 and 4).

Overselects

☐ Gearchange mechanism stopper arm spring weak or broken, or arm roller broken or worn. Renew the spring or arm (see Chapter 2).

☐ Gearchange mechanism return spring weak or broken (see Chapter 2).

☐ Faulty DCT system (see Chapters 2 and 4)

Abnormal engine noise

Knocking or pinking

☐ Carbon build-up in combustion chamber. Use of a fuel additive that will dissolve the adhesive bonding the carbon particles to the piston crown and chamber is the easiest way to remove the build-up. Otherwise, the cylinder head will have to be removed and decarbonised (see Chapter 2).

☐ Incorrect or poor quality fuel. Old or improper grades of fuel can cause detonation. This causes the pistons to rattle, thus the knocking or pinking sound. Drain old fuel and always use the recommended fuel grade (see Chapter 4).

☐ Spark plug heat range incorrect. Uncontrolled detonation indicates the plug heat range is too hot. The plug in effect becomes a glow plug, raising cylinder temperatures. Install the proper heat range plugs (see Chapter 1).

☐ Improper air/fuel mixture. This will cause the cylinders to run hot, which leads to detonation. A blockage in the fuel system or an air leak can cause this imbalance (see Chapter 4).

Piston slap or rattling

☐ Cylinder-to-piston clearance excessive. Cylinder and/or piston worn, usually accompanied by worn rings as well. A top-end overhaul is necessary (see Chapter 2).

☐ Piston ring(s) worn, broken or sticking. Overhaul the top-end (see Chapter 2).

☐ Piston pin, piston pin bore or connecting rod small-end worn from high mileage or seized due to lack of lubrication (see Chapter 2).

☐ Piston seizure damage. Usually from lack of lubrication or overheating. Replace the pistons and upper crankcase, as necessary, or rebore the cylinders (see Chapter 2).

☐ Connecting rod big-end clearance excessive. Caused by excessive wear or lack of lubrication. Replace worn parts (see Chapter 2).

☐ Connecting rod bent. Caused by over-revving, trying to start a badly flooded engine or from ingesting a foreign object into the combustion chamber. Replace the damaged parts (see Chapter 2).

Valve noise

☐ Incorrect valve clearances – check and adjust (see Chapter 1).

☐ Valve spring broken or weak. Check and replace weak valve springs with new ones (see Chapter 2).

☐ Camshaft or camshaft journals in the cylinder head worn or damaged. Lubrication failure at high rpm is usually the cause of damage due to insufficient oil or failure to change the oil at the recommended intervals. Since there are no replaceable bearings in the head, the head itself will have to be replaced with a new one (see Chapter 2).

Other noise

☐ Cylinder head gasket leaking. Check around the joint for blowing with the engine running. Fit a new gasket (see Chapter 2).

☐ Exhaust pipe leaking at cylinder head connection. Caused by incorrect fit of pipe(s), loose exhaust flange or damaged gasket. All exhaust system fasteners should be tightened evenly and carefully to avoid leaks. Fit new gaskets if necessary (see Chapter 4).

☐ Crankshaft runout excessive (see Chapter 2). Caused by a bent crankshaft (from over-revving) or damage from an upper cylinder component failure. Can also be attributed to dropping the machine on either of the crankshaft ends.

☐ Engine mounting bolts loose – ensure all the bolts are tightened to the specified torque settings (see Chapter 2).

☐ Crankshaft bearings worn (see Chapter 2).

☐ Cam chain rattle, due to worn chain or defective tensioner. Also worn chain tensioner/guide blades (see Chapter 2).

Abnormal driveline noise

Clutch noise

☐ Clutch housing/friction plate clearance excessive (see Chapter 2).
☐ Wear between the clutch centre splines and input shaft splines (see Chapter 2).
☐ Worn clutch housing needle bearing(s) or guide (see Chapter 2).

Transmission noise

☐ Bearings worn. Also includes the possibility that the shafts are worn. Overhaul the transmission (see Chapter 2).
☐ Gears worn or chipped (see Chapter 2).
☐ Metal chips jammed in gear teeth. Probably pieces from a broken clutch, gear or selector mechanism that were picked up by the gears. This will cause early bearing failure (see Chapter 2).

☐ Engine oil level too low (see *Pre-ride checks*). Causes a howl from transmission. Also affects engine power and clutch operation.

Final drive noise

☐ Chain not adjusted properly (see Chapter 1).
☐ Front or rear sprocket loose (see Chapter 6).
☐ Sprockets and/or chain worn. Fit new sprockets and chain (see Chapter 6).
☐ Rear sprocket warped. Fit a new sprocket (see Chapter 6).
☐ Rubber dampers worn in sprocket coupling (see Chapter 6).

Abnormal frame and suspension noise

Front end noise

☐ Low fluid level or improper viscosity oil in forks (see Chapter 5). This can sound like spurting and is usually accompanied by irregular fork action.
☐ Spring weak or broken. Makes a clicking or scraping sound. Fork oil, when drained, will have a lot of metal particles in it (see Chapter 5).
☐ Steering head bearings loose or damaged. Clicks when braking. Check and adjust or replace with new ones as necessary (see Chapter 1).
☐ Fork yoke clamp bolts loose – make sure all the bolts are tightened to the specified torque (see Chapter 5).
☐ Forks bent. Good possibility if machine has been dropped. Replace the inner and outer tubes with new ones as required (see Chapter 5).
☐ Front axle or axle clamp bolt(s) loose. Tighten them to the specified torque (see Chapter 6).
☐ Loose or worn wheel bearings. Check and replace with new ones as needed (see Chapter 6).

Shock absorber noise

☐ Fluid level incorrect. Indicates a leak caused by defective seal. Shock will be covered with oil. Replace shock with a new one or seek advice on repair from a suspension specialist (see Chapter 5).

☐ Defective shock absorber with internal damage. This is in the body of the shock and can't be remedied. The shock must be replaced with a new one (see Chapter 5).
☐ Bent or damaged shock body. Replace the shock with a new one (see Chapter 5).

Brake noise

☐ Squeal caused by dust on brake pads. Usually found in combination with glazed pads. Clean using brake cleaning solvent or fit new pads (see Chapter 6).
☐ Pads glazed. Caused by excessive heat from prolonged hard use or from contamination. DO NOT use sandpaper, emery cloth, carborundum cloth or any other abrasive to roughen the pad surfaces as abrasives will stay in the pad material and damage the disc. A very fine flat file can be used, but new pads is the best remedy (see Chapter 6).
☐ Contamination of brake pads. Oil or brake fluid can cause the brake pads to chatter or squeal, or just not work. Fit new pads (see Chapter 6). Identify the cause of the contamination, especially check the fork seals and caliper piston seals for leaking fluid (see Chapter 1). Clean disc thoroughly with brake system cleaner.
☐ Disc warped. Can cause a chattering, clicking or intermittent squeal. Usually accompanied by a pulsating lever and uneven braking. Replace the disc with new one (see Chapter 6).
☐ Loose or worn wheel bearings. Check and replace with new ones as needed (see Chapter 6).

Oil pressure warning light comes on

Engine lubrication system

☐ Engine oil level low. Inspect for leak or other problem causing low oil level and add recommended oil (see *Pre-ride checks*).
☐ Engine oil pump defective, blocked oil strainer gauze or failed pressure relief valve. Carry out an oil pressure check (see Chapter 2).
☐ Engine oil viscosity too low. Very old, thin oil or an improper weight of oil used in the engine. Change to correct oil (see Chapter 1).
☐ Camshaft or crankshaft journals worn (see Chapter 2). Excessive

wear causing drop in oil pressure. Abnormal wear could be caused by oil starvation at high rpm from low oil level or improper weight or type of oil.

Electrical system

☐ Oil pressure switch or sensor defective. Check the switch/sensor and replace it with a new one it if it is defective (see Chapter 8).
☐ Oil pressure warning LED or circuit defective. Check for pinched, shorted, disconnected or damaged wiring (see Chapter 8).

Excessive exhaust smoke

White smoke

- ☐ Piston rings worn or broken, causing oil from the crankcase to be pulled past the piston into the combustion chamber. Replace the rings with new ones (see Chapter 2).
- ☐ Cylinders worn or scored. Caused by overheating or oil starvation. Rebore cylinders and fit oversize pistons and rings (see Chapter 2).
- ☐ Valve stem oil seal damaged or worn. Replace the oil seals with new ones (see Chapter 2).
- ☐ Valve guide worn. Perform a complete valve job (see Chapter 2).
- ☐ Engine oil level too high, which causes the oil to be forced past the rings. Drain oil to the proper level (see Chapter 1).

- ☐ Head gasket broken between oil return and cylinder. Causes oil to be pulled into the combustion chamber. Replace the head gasket with a new ones and check the head for warpage (see Chapter 2).
- ☐ Abnormal crankcase pressurisation which forces oil past the rings, usually caused by a clogged breather (see Chapter 1).

Black smoke

- ☐ Air filter clogged. Fit new air filters (see Chapter 1).
- ☐ Fuel injection system malfunction (see Chapter 4).

Brown smoke

- ☐ Air filter poorly sealed or not installed (see Chapter 1).
- ☐ Fuel injection system malfunction (see Chapter 4).

Poor handling or stability

Handlebar hard to turn

- ☐ Steering head bearing adjuster nut too tight. Check adjustment (see Chapter 1).
- ☐ Bearings damaged. Roughness can be felt as the bars are turned from side-to-side. Replace the bearings with new ones (see Chapter 5).
- ☐ Races dented or worn. Denting results from wear in only one position (e.g., straight ahead), from a collision or hitting a pothole or from dropping the machine. Replace the bearings with new ones (see Chapter 5).
- ☐ Steering stem lubrication inadequate. Causes are grease getting hard from age or being washed out by high pressure car washes. Disassemble steering head and repack bearings, fit new bearings if necessary (see Chapter 5).
- ☐ Steering stem bent. Caused by a collision, hitting a pothole or by dropping the machine. Replace damaged part. Don't try to straighten the steering stem (see Chapter 5).
- ☐ Front tyre air pressure too low (see Pre-ride checks).

Handlebar shakes or vibrates excessively

- ☐ Tyres worn or out of balance (see Chapter 6).
- ☐ Swingarm bearings worn. Replace the bearings with new ones (see Chapter 5).
- ☐ Wheel rim(s) warped or damaged. Check wheels for runout (see Chapter 6).
- ☐ Wheel bearings worn (see Chapter 6). Worn front or rear wheel bearings can cause poor tracking. Worn front bearings will cause wobble.
- ☐ Fork yoke clamp bolts or handlebar clamp bolts loose. Tighten them to the specified torque (see Chapter 5).
- ☐ Engine mounting bolts loose. Will cause excessive vibration with increased engine rpm – make sure all the bolts are tightened to the specified torque settings (see Chapter 2).

Machine pulls to one side

- ☐ Frame bent. Definitely suspect this if the machine has been dropped. May or may not be accompanied by cracking near the steering head, swingarm mountings or engine mountings. Replace the frame with a new one.
- ☐ Wheels out of alignment (see Chapter 6). Caused by poor chain adjustment, improper location of axle spacers or from bent steering stem or frame.
- ☐ Forks bent. Disassemble the forks and replace the damaged parts (see Chapter 5).
- ☐ Swingarm bent or twisted. Replace the arm with a new one (see Chapter 5).
- ☐ Fork oil level uneven. Check and add or drain as necessary (see Chapter 5).

Poor shock absorbing qualities

- ☐ Too hard:
  Fork oil level excessive (see Chapter 5).
  Fork oil viscosity too high. Use the specified oil (see Chapter 5).
  Fork tube bent. Causes a harsh, sticking feeling (see Chapter 5).
  Fork internal damage (see Chapter 5).
  Shock shaft or body bent or damaged (see Chapter 5).
  Shock internal damage (see Chapter 5).
  Tyre pressure too high (see Pre-ride checks).
- ☐ Too soft:
  Fork oil level too low (see Chapter 5).
  Fork oil viscosity too light (see Chapter 5).
  Fork springs weak or broken (see Chapter 5).
  Fork or shock oil leaking (see Chapter 1).
  Shock internal damage (see Chapter 5).

Braking problems

Brakes are spongy, don't hold

☐ Low brake fluid level (see *Pre-ride checks*).
☐ Air in hydraulic system. Caused by inattention to master cylinder fluid level or by leakage. Locate problem and bleed brakes (see Chapter 6).
☐ Pads or disc worn (see Chapter 6).
☐ Contaminated pads. Caused by contamination with oil, grease, brake fluid, etc. Fit new pads (see Chapter 6). Identify the cause of the contamination, especially check the fork seals and caliper piston seals for leaking fluid. Clean disc thoroughly with brake system cleaner.
☐ Brake fluid deteriorated. Fluid is old or contaminated. Drain system, replenish with new fluid and bleed the system (see Chapter 6).
☐ Master cylinder internal seals worn or damaged causing fluid to bypass (see Chapter 6).
☐ Master cylinder bore scratched by foreign material or broken spring. Fit a new master cylinder (see Chapter 6).
☐ Disc warped. Replace disc and pads (see Chapter 6).
☐ ABS system faulty (where fitted) (see Chapter 6).

Brake lever or pedal pulsates

☐ Disc warped. Replace disc with new one (see Chapter 6).
☐ Axle bent. Replace axle with new one (see Chapter 6).
☐ Brake caliper bolts loose – tighten the bolts to the specified torque (see Chapter 6).
☐ Wheel warped or otherwise damaged (see Chapter 6).
☐ Wheel bearings damaged or worn (see Chapter 6).
☐ ABS system faulty (where fitted) (see Chapter 6).

Brakes drag

☐ Master cylinder piston seized. Caused by wear or damage to piston or cylinder bore (see Chapter 6).
☐ Lever or pedal balky or stuck. Check pivot and lubricate (see Chapter 5).
☐ Brake caliper piston seized in bore. Caused by corrosion or ingestion of dirt past deteriorated seal (see Chapter 6).
☐ Rear brake caliper binds. Caused by inadequate lubrication of caliper slider pins (see Chapter 6).
☐ Brake pad damaged. Pad material separated from backing plate. Usually caused by faulty manufacturing process or from contact with chemicals. Fit new pads (see Chapter 6).
☐ Pads improperly installed (see Chapter 6).
☐ Brake caliper incorrectly installed (see Chapter 6).
☐ ABS system faulty (where fitted) (see Chapter 6).

Electrical problems

Battery dead or weak

☐ Battery faulty. Confirm with battery condition check (see Chapter 8).
☐ Broken battery terminal making only occasional contact (see Chapter 8).
☐ Battery leads making poor contact (see Chapter 8).
☐ Load excessive. Caused by addition of high wattage lights or other electrical accessories.
☐ Ignition switch defective. Switch either earths (grounds) internally or fails to shut off system. Renew the switch (see Chapter 8).
☐ Regulator/rectifier defective (see Chapter 8).
☐ Alternator stator coil open or shorted (see Chapter 8).

☐ Charging system fault. Check for excessive current leakage (see Chapter 8).
☐ Wiring faulty. Wiring grounded (earthed) or connections loose in ignition, charging or lighting circuits (see Chapter 8).

Battery overcharged

☐ Regulator/rectifier defective. Overcharging is noticed when battery gets excessively warm (see Chapter 8).
☐ Battery faulty. Confirm with battery condition check (see Chapter 8)
☐ Battery amperage too low, wrong type or size of battery. Install manufacturer's specified amp-hour battery to handle charging load (see Chapter 8).

Note: *References throughout this index are in the form - "Chapter number" • "Page number"*

A

ABS – 6•1, 6•21, 6•22, 6•23
  switch – 8•15
Accelerator position sensor (APS) – 4•14
Air filter housing – 4•5
Air filters – 1•36
Alternator – 8•26

B

Balancer shafts – 2•50
Battery – 8•4
  maintenance and charging – 1•37, 8•6
  specification – 8•1
Bodywork – 7•1 *et seq*
Brake
  bleeding and fluid change – 6•18
  caliper – 6•4, 6•12
  disc – 6•6, 6•14
  fluid change – 1•14,
  fluid level check and top-up – 0•14
  fluid type – 1•8, 6•1
  hoses and fittings – 6•17
  master cylinder – 6•7, 6•14
  pad wear check – 1•12
  pad change – 6•2, 6•9
  rear pedal – 5•3
  rear pedal height – 1•13
  parking brake – 1•13, 6•10, 6•12
  specifications – 0•11, 6•1
  system check – 1•12
Brake lever – 5•7
  span adjuster – 1•13
Brake light circuit check – 8•8
Brake light switches – 8•11
  adjustment (rear) – 1•13

C

Cable
  clutch – 1•14, 2•34
  parking brake – 6•12
  seat lock – 7•2
  throttle – 1•16, 4•24
Caliper (brake) – 6•4, 6•12
Cam chain, sprockets and blades – 2•19
Cam chain tensioner – 2•13
Camshaft – 2•2, 2•14
Catalytic converter – 4•29
Chain (drive) – 6•33, REF•8
  check and adjustment – 1•9
  cleaning and lubrication – 1•10
  size – 6•2
  slack and lubricant – 1•8
Charging system – 8•1, 8•25
Clutch (DCT transmission) – 2•35
  initialise learning – 4•19
  sensors – 4•18
  specifications – 2•3
Clutch (standard manual
  transmission) – 2•26
  specifications – 2•2
Clutch cable – 2•34
  adjustment – 1•14
  freeplay – 1•8
Clutch lever – 5•8
Clutch switch – 8•20
Colour code label – 0•12
Combination meter – 8•12
Compression ratio – 2•1
Compression test – 2•5
Conversion factors – REF•34
Coolant
  change – 1•22
  hoses and unions – 3•7
  level check and top-up – 0•14

pressure cap – 1•22
reservoir – 3•7
type and system capacity – 1•8
Cooling system – 3•1 *et seq*
  check – 1•21
  ECT sensor – 3•3
  fans and relay – 3•2
  radiators – 3•4
  thermostat – 3•3
  water pump – 3•6
Connecting rods and bearings – 2•3, 2•65
Crankcase breather – 1•11
Crankcases – 2•59, 2•61
Crankshaft and main bearings – 2•3, 2•62
Crankshaft position sensor – 4•1, 4•16
Cush drive – 6•35
  check – 1•29
Cylinder bores – 2•3, 2•62
Cylinder head – 2•2, 2•20, 2•22

D

Data link connector (DLC) – 4•10
Diode block – 8•20
Dimensions – 0•11
Disc (brake) – 6•6, 6•14
Drive chain – 6•33, REF•8
  check and adjustment – 1•9
  cleaning and lubrication – 1•10
  size – 6•2
  slack and lubricant – 1•8
Dual clutch transmission (DCT)
  clutches – 2•35
  fault diagnosis/codes – 4•12
  gearshafts – 2•77
  PCM – 4•19
  sensors – 4•17

Note: *References throughout this index are in the form - "Chapter number" • "Page number"*

E

ECM – 4•19
ECT sensor – 3•1, 3•3, 4•1
Electrical system – 8•1 *et seq*
  wiring diagrams – 8•29
Emergency stop circuit (rear turn signals) – 8•10
Engine
  balancer shafts – 2•50
  bearings – 2•62
  cam chain, sprockets and blades – 2•19
  cam chain tensioner – 2•13
  compression test – 2•5
  connecting rods and bearings – 2•65
  crankcases – 2•59, 2•61
  crankshaft and main bearings – 2•62
  cylinder bores – 2•62
  cylinder head – 2•20, 2•22
  front sprocket and cover – 6•34
  oil and filter change – 1•17
  oil level and top-up – 0•13
  oil pressure check – 2•6
  oil pressure switch/sensor – 8•14
  oil pump – 2•3, 2•56
  oil sump and strainer – 2•54
  oil type and capacity – 1•8
  pistons and rings – 2•67
  primary drive gear – 2•49
  removal and installation – 2•6
  rocker arms and camshaft – 2•14
  running-in – 2•86
  specifications – 0•11, 1•8, 2•1
  starter clutch and gears – 2•25
  valve clearance adjustment – 1•29
  valve cover – 2•12
  valves – 2•22
Engine management – 4•9
  fault diagnosis/codes – 4•10, 4•12
  relays – 4•20
  sensors – 4•14
Engine number – 0•12
Engine stop relay – 4•20

Engine oil pressure (EOP) sensor – 8•14
Engine oil temperature sensor – 4•19
ETC tray – 7•13
EVAP (evaporative emission control) system – 1•25, 4•1, 4•30
Exhaust system – 4•26

F

Fairing side panels – 7•5
Fan relay – 3•3
Fans – 3•2
Fault diagnosis – REF•35
Fault diagnosis/codes
  ABS – 6•22
  DCT system – 4•12
  electrical system – 8•2
  immobiliser (HISS) – 4•34
  PGM-FI system – 4•10
Filter
  air – 1•36
  fuel – 4•22
  oil – 1•17
Footrests – 5•2
Frame – 5•2
Frame number – 0•12
Front brake
  bleeding – 6•18
  calipers – 6•4
  discs – 6•6
  fluid level – 0•14
  lever – 5•7
  light switch – 8•11
  master cylinder – 6•7
  pads – 6•2
Front forks
  checks – 1•26
  oil – 1•8, 1•27, 5•1
  oil change – 5•10
  overhaul – 5•12
  removal and installation – 5•10
Front mudguard – 7•14
Front sprocket and cover – 6•34

Front wheel – 6•26
  bearings – 6•28
Front wheel sensor and pulse ring – 6•23
Fuel – 4•1
Fuel filter – 1•16, 4•22
Fuel delivery system – 4•1 *et seq*
  checks – 1•15
  level/reserve sensor – 4•24
  pump – 4•22
  specifications – 4•1
  tank – 4•3
Fuel injection
  data – 4•1
  rail and injectors – 4•8
  relay – 4•20
  throttle body – 4•6
Fuel pressure – 4•1, 4•21
Fuel pump – 4•22
  relay – 4•20
Fuel tank – 4•3
  capacity – 0•11
Fuel tank covers – 7•12
Fuses – 8•7

G

G switch – 8•15
Gearbox
  shaft overhaul – DCT – 2•77
  shaft overhaul – standard transmission – 2•72
  shaft removal and installation – 2•70
Gear position switch/sensor – 8•18
Gear ratios – 2•4
Gearchange lever and linkage – 5•4
Gearchange mechanism
  DCT – 2•44
  standard transmission – 2•42
Gearchange shaft angle sensor – 4•18
Gearchange shaft switch – 8•19
Greases – 1•8, REF•25
Ground clearance – 0•11

Note: *References throughout this index are in the form - "Chapter number" • "Page number"*

H

Handlebar switches – 8•15
Handlebar weights and hand guards – 7•14
Handlebars – 5•5
Hazard light circuit – 8•10
Headlight – 8•9
    aim (beam height) – 1•25, REF•26
    check and relay – 8•8
Headlight cover – 7•9
Heated grips – 8•17
Height – 0•11
HISS (Honda Ignition Security
    System) – 4•33
Horn – 8•21

I

IACV (idle air control valve) – 1•16, 4•1,
    4•21
ID numbers – 0•12
Idle speed – 1•8, 1•16
Ignition coils – 4•2, 4•30
Ignition system – 4•2
    check – 4•30
Ignition switch – 8•14
Ignition timing – 4•2, 4•32
Immobiliser – 4•33
Injectors (fuel) – 4•1, 4•8
Inner panel covers – 7•10
Inner panels – 7•11
Input shaft sensors – 4•17
Instruments – 8•12
Intake air temperature sensor – 4•1, 4•15

L

Lean angle sensor – 4•16
Legal checks – 0•15
Length – 0•11
Level/reserve sensor (fuel) – 4•1, 4•22

Levers

Levers
    clutch – 5•8
    handlebar – 5•7
    parking brake – 5•8
Licence plate light
    bulb – 8•10
    circuit check – 8•8
Lighting – 8•2, 8•8
Linear solenoid valve (DCT) – 2•40
Lubricants – 1•8
    general – REF•23
Lubrication (general) – 1•29
Luggage rack – 7•3

M

Maintenance schedule – 1•2
Manifold absolute pressure (MAP)
    sensor – 4•15
Master cylinder
    front brake – 6•7
    rear brake – 6•14
Mirrors – 7•13
Model development – 0•10
Modulator (ABS) – 6•23
MOT test checks – REF•26
Mudguard (front) – 7•14

N

Neutral switch – 8•19

O

Oil (engine) – 1•8
    level check and top-up – 0•13
    oil and filter change – 1•17
Oil (front forks) – 1•27,
Oil pressure check – 2•6
Oil pressure relief valve – 2•56
Oil pressure switch/sensor – 8•14

Oil pump – 2•3, 2•56
Oil sump and strainer – 2•54
Open air temperature sensor – 8•13
Oxygen sensor – 4•1, 4•16

P

Pads (brake) – 6•2, 6•7
PAIR (pulse secondary air) system –
    1•24, 4•1, 4•28
Parking brake
    caliper and cable – 6•12
    check and adjustment – 1•13
    lever – 5•8
    light switch – 8•11
    pads – 6•10
PCM – 4•19
PGM-FI system – 4•10
Pistons and rings – 2•3, 2•67
Pre-ride checks – 0•13 et seq
Pressure relief valve – 2•56
Primary drive gear – 2•49
Pump
    fuel – 4•22
    oil – 2•56
    water – 3•6

R

Radiators – 3•4
    pressure cap – 3•1
Rear brake
    ABS – 6•21
    bleeding – 6•19
    caliper – 6•12
    disc – 6•14
    fluid level – 0•15
    light switch – 8•11
    master cylinder – 6•14
    pads – 6•9, 6•9
    pedal – 5•3
    pedal height – 1•13

Note: *References throughout this index are in the form - "Chapter number" • "Page number"*

Rear sprocket – 6•35
Rear suspension
   checks – 1•26
   linkage – 5•20
   shock absorber – 5•19
Rear wheel – 6•27
   bearings – 6•28
   cush drive – 1•29, 6•35
Rear wheel sensor and pulse
   ring – 6•23
Regulator/rectifier – 8•29
Relay
   engine stop – 4•20
   fan – 3•3
   FI – 4•20
   fuel pump – 4•20
   headlight – 8•8
   starter circuit – 4•20
   starter motor – 8•21
   TBW – 4•20
   turn signal – 8•10
Rocker arms – 2•2, 2•14
Routine maintenance – 1•1 *et seq*
Running-in – 2•86

S

Safety – 0•9, 0•15
SCS service connector – 4•10
Seat height – 0•11
Security – REF•20
Seats – 7•2
Selector drum and forks – 2•4, 2•83
Shock absorber – 5•19
Side covers – 7•3
Sidestand – 1•25, 5•4
Sidestand switch – 8•19
Spare parts – 0•12
Spark arrester – 1•37
Spark plugs – 1•8, 1•34
Specifications/data – 0•11, 1•8, 2•1, 3•1,
   4•1, 5•1, 6•1, 8•1

Sprockets – 6•34
   check – 1•11
   size – 6•2
Sprocket coupling – 6•35
   bearing – 6•29
Starter clutch – 2•2, 2•25
Starter interlock circuit – 1•25
   relay – 4•20
Starter motor – 8•22
Starter motor relay – 8•21
Steering head bearings – 5•18
   check and adjustment – 1•27
   pre-load – 1•8, 5•1
Steering stem – 5•15
Storage – REF•31
Sump guard – 7•15
Suspension
   checks – 1•26
   front forks – 5•10, 5•12
   travel – 0•11
   rear shock absorber – 5•19
   rear linkage – 5•20
Swingarm – 5•22

T

Tail light – 8•9
   check – 8•8
Tail light cover – 7•5
Tank (coolant) – 3•7
Tank (fuel) – 4•3
TBW (throttle by wire)
   APS (accelerator position sensor) – 4•14
   relay – 4•20
Temperature warning light – 3•3
Thermostat – 3•1, 3•3
Throttle body – 4•6
Throttle cables – 4•24
   freeplay – 1•8, 1•16
Throttle position (TP) sensor – 4•14
Throttle twistgrip – 1•17, 4•25, 5•5
Tools and workshop tips – REF•2 *et seq*

Torque settings – 1•8, 2•4, 3•1, 4•2, 5•1,
   6•2, 8•2
Transmission
   ratios – 2•4
   shaft overhaul – DCT – 2•77
   shaft overhaul – standard
     transmission – 2•72
   shaft removal and installation – 2•70
Transmission range sensor – 4•17
Trim clips – 7•1
Turn signals – 8•11
   bulbs – 8•10
   circuit and relay – 8•10
Tyres – 6•31
   pressures and tread depth – 0•16
   size – 0•11, 6•1

V

Valve clearances – 1•8, 1•29
Valve cover – 2•12
Valves – 2•2, 2•22
Vehicle speed sensor – 4•16, 8•13
VIN – 0•12

W

Water pump – 3•6
Weights – 0•11
Width – 0•11
Windshield – 7•13
Wheelbase – 0•11
Wheels
   alignment – 6•25
   front – 6•26
   rear – 6•27
   runout – 6•1, 6•25
   spoke checks – 1•28
   size – 0•11
Wheel bearings – 6•28
   checks – 1•29
Wiring diagrams – 8•29

Preserving Our Motoring Heritage

< The Model J Duesenberg Derham Tourster. Only eight of these magnificent cars were ever built – this is the only example to be found outside the United States of America

Almost every car you've ever loved, loathed or desired is gathered under one roof at the Haynes Motor Museum. Over 300 immaculately presented cars and motorbikes represent every aspect of our motoring heritage, from elegant reminders of bygone days, such as the superb Model J Duesenberg to curiosities like the bug-eyed BMW Isetta. There are also many old friends and flames. Perhaps you remember the 1959 Ford Popular that you did your courting in? The magnificent 'Red Collection' is a spectacle of classic sports cars including AC, Alfa Romeo, Austin Healey, Ferrari, Lamborghini, Maserati, MG, Riley, Porsche and Triumph.

A Perfect Day Out

Each and every vehicle at the Haynes Motor Museum has played its part in the history and culture of Motoring. Today, they make a wonderful spectacle and a great day out for all the family. Bring the kids, bring Mum and Dad, but above all bring your camera to capture those golden memories for ever. You will also find an impressive array of motoring memorabilia, a comfortable 70 seat video cinema and one of the most extensive transport book shops in Britain. The Pit Stop Cafe serves everything from a cup of tea to wholesome, home-made meals or, if you prefer, you can enjoy the large picnic area nestled in the beautiful rural surroundings of Somerset.

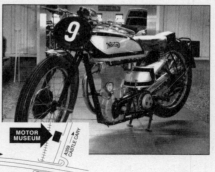

> John Haynes O.B.E., Founder and Chairman of the museum at the wheel of a Haynes Light 12.

< The 1936 490cc sohc-engined International Norton – well known for its racing success

The Museum is situated on the A359 Yeovil to Frome road at Sparkford, just off the A303 in Somerset. It is about 40 miles south of Bristol, and 25 minutes drive from the M5 intersection at Taunton.

Open 9.30am - 5.30pm (10.00am - 4.00pm Winter) 7 days a week, *except Christmas Day, Boxing Day and New Years Day*

Special rates available for schools, coach parties and outings Charitable Trust No. 292048